Europe
Lodging Guide

FIRST EDITION

2

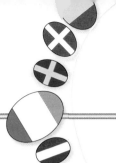

Credits

AAA
President and CEO: Robert Darbelnet
Executive Vice President, Publishing and Administration: Rick Rinner
Managing Director, Publishing: Alan Borne
Managing Director, GIS/Cartography and Administrations: Bob Hopkins

Director, Product Development: Bill Wood
Director, Publishing Operations: Susan Sears
Managing Editor: Margaret Cavanaugh
Development Editor: Greg Weekes
Cover Design: Mike McCrary
Cover Photo Research: Diane Norden, Patricia Nasser

Manager, Design: Mike McCrary
Manager, Pre-Press: Tim Johnson
Manager, Product Support: Linda Indolfi
Manager, Publishing Communications and Marketing: Josette Constantino
Manager, National Publications Sales: Robert Foley
Manager, Retail Sales – Travel Store: Sharon Edwards

Published by AAA Publishing, 1000 AAA Drive, Heathrow, Florida 32746

Text © AAA Publishing 2001

All rights reserved

Maps © Automobile Association Developments Ltd 2001

No part of the book may be reproduced in any form or by any electronic or mechanical means, including information storage and retrieval devices or systems, without prior written permission from the publisher, except that brief passages may be quoted for reviews.

The contents of this book are believed to be correct at the time of printing. The publishers are not responsible for any errors or omissions or for changes that occur after publication, or for the consequences of any reliance on the information provided by the same.

The *AAA Europe Lodging Guide* was created and produced for AAA Publishing by AA Publishing, Basingstoke, England.

Managing Editor: Jo Sturges. Contributors: Nia Williams, Steve Harbert, Pam Stagg
Design by Nautilus Design (UK) Ltd
Page make-up by Anton Graphics, Andover, England

Main cover photo: Pately Bridge, Yorkshire (R. Cord/H. Armstrong Roberts)
Inset cover photo: Sheep farmer (Mark Joseph/Stone)
Spine: Devon, England (A. Tovy/ H. Armstrong Roberts)

ISBN 1-56251-447-4

Cataloging-in Publication Data is on file with the Library of Congress.
Color separations by Anton Graphics, Andover, England
Printed and bound in Italy by Rotolito Lombarda SpA

Acknowledgements

The publishers would like to thank the following for their cooperation.
Ediciones El Pais S.A./Grupo Santillana de Edicions S.A. Madrid, Spain
The Danish Tourist Board
Dansk Kroferie, Horsens, Denmark
Swedish Travel & Tourism Council, London, England
Countryside Hotels, Åre, Sweden
Snillriket AB, Lidingë, Sweden
Lannoo, Tielt, The Netherlands
Mosaik Verlag GmbH, Verlagsgruppe Bertlsmann, München, Germany
The Norwegian Tourist Board

© Automobile Association Developments Limited 2001.

Ordnance Survey This product includes mapping data licensed from Ordnance Survey® with the permission of the Controller of Her Majesty's Stationery Office. © Crown copyright 2001. All rights reserved. License number 399221.

Northern Ireland mapping reproduced by permission of the Director and Chief Executive, Ordnance Survey of Northern Ireland, acting on behalf of the Controller of Her Majesty's Stationery Office © Crown copyright 2001. Permit No. 1674.

Republic of Ireland mapping based on Ordnance Survey Ireland by permission of the Government. Permit No. MP012301 © Government of Ireland.

Mapping produced by the Cartographic Department of The Automobile Association.

Contents

Map of Europe

How To Use This Guide

AAA commissioned this publication to fill a void in the travel market and to serve as a companion guide to the AAA *Europe TravelBook: The Guide to Premier Destinations*. The book is divided alphabetically by country, then by main destinations. If the hotel or B&B is not in the listed town but in a smaller town or village within a reasonable distance, it is listed under that name as well. We have used county or region names only in addresses.

The index at the back of this guide lists all towns and villages alphabetically. The country is also indicated.

Map References

Beside each location is a map reference that refers only to the map of the country at the beginning of each section. The maps introducing each country are very general, but they do show main destinations. In some areas, our specially selected hotels may be some distance from the nearest main town because of mountainous roads or sparse population. It is a good idea to confirm the distance/time from the locating town.

Price

The price range ($) for rooms is shown beside the hotel name.

$ = up to $80
$$ = $81–$144
$$$ = $145 and over

These ranges represent the average price of a double room for two people for one night including breakfast, unless stated otherwise. Prices may vary for different rooms and at different times of the year. Do check exactly what is included in the price when reserving your room.

Contacting Accommodations

Where possible the telephone, fax number, e-mail and web address are listed for ease of contact. For local telephone/fax numbers the international code will have to be added (and the first 0 deleted) if phoning from abroad (see pages 8–9).

Description

The description of the hotel tries to convey a flavor of the accommodations and the facilities available. However, hoteliers make frequent changes to their establishments. Although every effort has been to ensure accuracy, the publishers cannot be held responsible for any variations. We suggest you ensure any particular requirements are confirmed before reserving.

Rooms

Listed hotels offer private baths or showers and toilets in the rooms. We have not differentiated between those with baths or showers. Please check when reserving if you have a preference.

Symbols

	Number of rooms
	Swimming pool
Closed Dec. 24-25	Times closed
	American Express
	Diners Club
	Eurocard
	MasterCard
	Visa

Selection Criteria

The hotels in this guide have been carefully chosen to ensure that they provide a good standard throughout, including en suite facilities, pleasant surroundings and traditional food. No grading system is used as each establishment is of a reasonable standard, individual and not part of a chain. Most are character hotels and many are family-run.

Ratings

Unlike the widely recognized diamonds awarded by AAA to lodgings inspected in the United States, Canada, Mexico and the Caribbean, there is no universal system of rating accommodations in Europe. Even within individual countries, there can be several different systems of selection, operated by independent associations, the state or by self-regulating groups of hotels. If possible, look for the national tourist office star rating, or follow that of a reputable body such as the Automobile Association (AA) in Britain or the Swiss Hotel Association (SHA) in Switzerland. Most tourist offices apply star ratings ranging from one, given to good, clean establishments with limited facilities, to five, indicating deluxe standards with all the facilities. Star ratings do not determine hotel rates, which are based on market conditions. Rates charged for accommodations also vary from country to country.

Some Guidance

You may be able to obtain full details of the criteria applied to star-rated hotels from the national tourist office. For instance, the German National Tourist Office publishes a catalog setting out its classification criteria and the exact requirements for:
• Tourist hotels (including reception, breakfast, bath/shower and toilet on the same floor, and a fax service).
• Standard hotels (70 percent of rooms with private toilets and shower or bath, color television and beverages).
• Comfort (all rooms with shower or bath and toilet, plus color television and beverages).
• First Class (room service, mini-bar, laundry services, restaurant and bar).
• Luxury hotels (suites, 24-hour room service or concierge, restaurant, bar and a host of other special services).

Other tourist offices may not be able to provide you with such a specific list of criteria, but most will follow the same pattern of classification. Some also will list hotels not yet classified because they are new or undergoing refurbishment.

In Ireland, hotels and guest houses which have opted out of the classification system are marked "U" for unclassified, but in Switzerland the "U" classification indicates that the hotel is unique and does not fall into any category. In The Netherlands and Belgium the Benelux Hotel Classification is shared.

Brochures

Different types of accommodations, such as apartments, motels, hostels and pensions, are often rated according to separate systems, using a more limited star rating (one to three or four) or a distinct system of their own. Tourist offices generally have details of categories and lists of establishments with their ratings. There will often be special symbols or classifications for hotels in particularly impressive or unusual buildings or settings, such as converted castles, monasteries, ships or manor houses. Ask at the tourist office whether there is a list of such highly recommended accommodations.

How To Reserve Accommodations

Reserving accommodations in Europe is easier than it ever has been before, and there are several ways to go about it. The most traditional means of reserving a room is by letter (see page 13 for suggested wording). There are also suggested confirmation letters and slightly different versions for e-mails. Pages 12 - 15 have translations in French, German, Italian and Spanish.

International and higher star-rated hotels in most countries will be happy to deal with correspondence in English; smaller and more rural establishments may pose a language problem. Writing is a relatively slow process, of course, and any queries that arise on either side will add to the time and potential for confusion. Do not send a stamped, addressed envelope with your letter, as U.S. stamps will be invalid in European countries.

Fax or E-mail

Faxes and e-mails provide a quicker alternative. A growing number of hotels all over Europe have e-mail addresses, and more have fax numbers – but

again, the more isolated and smaller the establishment, the fewer facilities there are likely to be. We have provided both e-mail addresses and fax numbers for hotels wherever possible.

Beatenberg, Switzerland

If you do communicate with a hotel by letter, fax or e-mail, be sure to specify your requirements clearly: how many are in your party, what kind of room you want (double, single, twin, family), and for which nights; and whether you require breakfast, evening meal, easy access or a particular view. State your name and return address, and do not send money in advance.

Country Codes		To Call the Operator Within the Country
From the U.S. to:		
Austria	011 43	1611
Belgium	011 32	1307 (French) 1207 (Flemish)
Britain	011 44	100
Denmark	011 45	110 long distance operator 114
France	011 33	13
Germany	011 49	01188
Ireland	011 353	1190
(for calls made to and from Northern Ireland use Britain codes)		
Italy	011 39	10
The Netherlands	011 31	118
Portugal	011 351	099
Spain	011 34	1003
Sweden	011 46	07975
Switzerland	011 41	111

Bamburg, Germany

By Telephone

If you make a reservation by phone, the same language issues may occur, although hotel chains, larger hotels and city establishments will almost always be able to take your reservation in English. Telephone numbers are given only with the local code. Use the number as shown if phoning within the country.

To phone from the United States or Canada, omit the first zero from the local number and prefix with the appropriate country code. For example, the British number 01234 5555 becomes 011 44 1234 5555. The country codes are listed in the box on page 8.

To phone the United States or Canada from Europe, prefix the area code with 001.

Travel Agencies

Travel agencies are a popular way of making reservations, particularly for pre-packaged or independent tours (some tour operators only accept reservations made through agencies). Check out the relationship between agency and tour operator, as you may be offered biased advice by agencies that are on a commission. It's worth making careful inquiries about the agent's familiarity with accommodations and locations in your destination country, and make sure details of the hotel's size, location and services are readily available before you commit yourself. AAA Travel Agencies provide numerous services to help simplify the logistics of international travel planning, especially for the first-time visitor.

Specialty agents are a particularly good option for travelers seeking vacations with particular themes or activities, such as Renaissance art, medieval castles, walking, etc.

If you're traveling with a tour operator, make sure it is well-established and reputable: This is a volatile business, and operators have been known to go out of business leaving travelers out of pocket. Some operators have consumer protection programs, and those belonging to the National Tour Association and United States Tour Operators Association have to keep a reserve fund to cover the cost of making travel arrangements should the company get into trouble.

How To Reserve Accommodations

The Internet

The Internet provides another option for reserving airline tickets, rooms and rental cars. Some websites ask you to register before reserving, which means giving your name, address, phone number and e-mail address, and choosing a log-in name and password. You can use your credit card to reserve online. Electronic tickets, or e-tickets, are issued for airline flights, but you can request a "real" ticket to be sent through the mail. There is often an extra charge for this service.

Most European national tourist offices have their own websites, which offer practical advice, accommodations and sightseeing details; many give direct access to hotels, which you can often reserve online.

In Britain, the U.K. Automobile Association has an extensive online booking service, which you can access at www.theAA.com.

Venice, Italy

The following national tourism websites give information on individual countries:

Austria	www.anto.com
Belgium	www.visitbelgium.com
Britain	www.visitbritain.com
Denmark	www.visitdenmark.com
France	www.francetourism.com
Germany	www.deutschland-tourismus.de
Ireland	www.ireland.travel.ie
Italy	www.piuitalia2000.it
The Netherlands	www.nbt.nl
Portugal	www.portugal.org/tourism
Spain	www.okspain.org
Sweden	www.gosweden.org
Switzerland	www.switzerlandtourism.com

Sample Correspondence

Be sure to make it clear that you would like your private bathroom connected to your room. In some hotels, there may be a mixture of rooms with connected (or "en suite") bathrooms, and those with a bathroom across the hall.

 ENGLISH   **Confirmation of Reservation**

Your address in full with zip code

Establishment address in full with postal code and country

Date

Dear Sir or Madam,

I am writing to ask for information about rooms at your hotel. I hope to stay in (*Location*) on the nights of (*Dates*).

I would like to reserve a (single/double) room with private bath/shower and WC en suite, with breakfast included. I will be traveling alone/with (number of adults/children). We would require a cot in the parents' room.

I would be grateful if you would send me, by return mail, details of your prices and of any discounts available, and let me know whether you have any rooms available at that time.

Will you require a deposit? Can this be made by credit card? I enclose an International Reply Coupon.

Thank you for your help.

Sincerely,

Your Name

Your address in full with zip code

Establishment address in full with postal code and country

Date

Dear xxxx xxxx,

Thank you for the information about your hotel. I would like to confirm a reservation for the nights of (*Dates*) for a/number (single/double) room(s) with private bath/shower and WC en suite, with breakfast included. We will require a cot in the parents' room.

I look forward to meeting you on the (*date of first night*).

Sincerely,

Your Name

E-mail:

Dear Sir or Madam,

Please send me information about rooms at your hotel. I hope to stay in (*Location*) on the nights of (*Dates*).

I would like to reserve a (single/double) room with private bath/shower and WC en suite, with breakfast included. I will be traveling alone/with (number of adults/children). We would require a cot in the parents' room.

Please let me know details of your prices and of any discounts available, and whether you have any rooms available at that time.

Will you require a deposit? Can this be made by credit card?

Thank you for your help.

Your name
Your address in full with zip code
Your telephone number
Your e-mail address

E-mail:

Dear xxxx xxxx,

Thank you for the information about your hotel. I would like to confirm a reservation for the night of (*Dates*) for a/number (single/double) room(s) with a private bath/shower and WC en suite, with breakfast included.

I look forward to meeting you on the (date of first night).

Sincerely,

Your name
Your address in full with zip code
Your telephone number
Your e-mail address

Sample Correspondence

In French, if the person writing the letter is female an "e" needs to be added to certain words (see * below).

 FRENCH **Confirmation of Reservation**

Your address
in full
with zip code

Establishment address
in full
with postal code
and country

Date

Monsieur/Madame,

Je vous écris pour demander des renseignements sur les chambres dans votre hôtel. J'ai l'intention de séjourner à (*hotel name*) du …(*1st date*) jusqu'au … (*2nd date*).

Je voudrais retenir une (*or number of rooms*) chambre (pour une personne/avec un grand lit) avec bain/douche et toilette attenantes et le petit déjeuner compris. Je voyagerais seul(e)*/Nous sommes … adulte(s) et … enfant(s). Nous aurions besoin d'un lit d'enfant dans la chambre des parents.

Je vous serais reconnaissant(e)* de bien vouloir me communiquer, par retour du courrier, vos tarifs, vos promotions et la disponibilité de vos chambres pendant la période ci-dessus.

Faut-il verser des arrhes? Peut-on payer par carte de crédit?

Veuillez trouver ci-joint un coupon-réponse international.

Je vous remercie de votre aide.

Je vous prie d'agréer, Monsieur/Madame, l'expression de mes sentiments distingués.

Your address
in full
with zip code

Establishment address
in full
with postal code
and country

Date

Monsieur/Madame,

Je vous remercie des renseignements sur votre hôtel. Je confirme ainsi ma réservation du …(*1st date*) au … (*2nd date*) pour une/….. chambre(s) (pour une personne/avec un grand lit) avec bain/douche et toilette attenantes et le petit déjeuner compris. Nous aurons besoin d'un lit d'enfant dans la chambre des parents.

En attendant le plaisir de faire votre connaissance le …(*1st date*).

Je vous prie d'agréer, Monsieur/Madame, l'expression de mes sentiments distingués.

E-mail:

Monsieur/Madame,

Je vous serais reconnaissant(e)* de m'envoyer des renseignements sur les chambres dans votre hôtel. J'ai l'intention de séjourner à (*hotel name*) du …(*1st date*) jusqu'au … (*2nd date*).

Je voudrais retenir une chambre (or number of rooms) (pour une personne/avec un grand lit) avec bain/douche et toilette attenantes et le petit déjeuner. Je voyagerais seul(e)* /Nous sommes … adulte(s) et … enfant(s). Nous aurions besoin d'un lit d'enfant dans la chambre des parents.

Veuillez me communiquer vos tarifs, vos promotions et la disponibilité des chambres pendant la période ci-dessus.

Faut-il verser des arrhes? Peut-on payer par carte de crédit?

Je vous remercie de votre aide.

Your name
Your address in full with zip code
Your telephone number
Your e-mail address

E-mail:

Monsieur/Madame,

Je vous remercie des renseignements sur votre hôtel. Je confirme ainsi ma réservation du …(*1st date*) au … (*2nd date*) pour une/….. chambre(s) (pour une personne/avec un grand lit) avec bain/douche et toilette attenantes et le petit déjeuner compris. Nous aurons besoin d'un lit d'enfant dans la chambre des parents.

En attendant le plaisir de faire votre connaissance le …(*1st date*).

Cordialement

Your name
Your address in full with zip code
Your telephone number
Your e-mail address

Sample Correspondence

GERMAN — Confirmation of Reservation

*Your address
in full
with zip code*

*Establishment address
in full
with postal code
and country*

Date

Sehr geehrte Damen/Herren,

Ich wende mich heute an Sie weil ich gern Informationen über einen Aufenthalt in Ihrem Hotel hätte. Ich werde in der Zeit vom…(*1st date*) bis… (*2nd date*) in … (*hotel name*) zu sein.

Ich möchte gern ein (*or number of rooms*) Einzelzimmer/Doppelzimmer mit Bad/Dusche und Toilette, einschliesslich Frühstück, reservieren. Ich komme allein/mit … Erwachsenen (*adults*) und … Kind/Kindern (*children*). Wir würden ein Bett für ein Kleinkind im Elternzimmer benötigen.

Ich wäre Ihnen dankbar, wenn Sie mir postwendend Einzelheiten über Ihre Preise und mögliche Ermässigungen senden würden und mir mitteilen, ob Sie zu oben gennanter Zeit Zimmer frei haben.

Verlangen Sie eine Anzahlung? Wenn ja, kann diese mit Kreditkarte bezahlt werden?

Ich lege Ihnen einen internationalen Antwortschein bei und danke Ihnen im voraus für Ihre hilfe.

Mit freundlichen Grüssen,

*Your address
in full
with zip code*

*Establishment address
in full
with postal code
and country*

Date

Sehr geehrter/geehrte …,

Vielen Dank für die Askünfte über Ihr Hotel. Ich möchte hiermit meine Reservierung von einem(*or number of rooms*) Einzelzimmer/Doppelzimmer mit Bad/Dusche unde Toilette, einschliesslich Frühstück für die Nächte …(*1st date*) bis… (*2nd date*) bestätigen. Wir werden ein Kinderbett für ein Kleinkind im Zimmer benötigen.

Ich freue mich auf den Aufenthalt bei Ihnen.

Mit freundlichen Grüssen,

E-mail:

Sehr geehrte Damen/Herren,

Bitte senden Sie mir Informationen über Unterkunft in Ihrem Hotel. Ich hoffe, für die Nächte vom…(*1st date*) bis… (*2nd date*) in … (*hotel name*) sein.

Ich möchte gern ein Einzelzimmer/Doppelzimmer mit Bad/Dusche und Toilette, einschliesslich Frühstück, reservieren. Ich komme allein/mit … Erwachsenen (*adults*) und … Kind/Kindern (*children*). Wir würden ein Bett für ein Kleinkind im Elternzimmer benötigen.

Bitte informieren Sie mich über Ihre Preise und möglichen Ermässigungen und ob Sie zu den genannten Zeitpunkt Zimmer frei haben.

Ist eine Anzahlung erforderlich? Wenn ja, kann diese mit Kreditkarte bezahlt werden?

Vielen Dank für Ihre hilfe.

*Your name
Your address in full with zip code
Your telephone number
Your e-mail address*

E-mail:

Sehr geehrter/geehrte …

Vielen Dank für die Askünfte über Ihr Hotel. Ich möchte hiermit meine Reservierung von einem(*or number of rooms*) Einzelzimmer/Doppelzimmer mit Bad/Dusche unde Toilette, einschliesslich Frühstück für die Nächte …(*1st date*) bis… (*2nd date*) bestätigen. Wir werden ein Kinderbett für ein Kleinkind im Zimmer benötigen.

Ich freue mich auf den Aufenthalt bei Ihnen.

Mit freundlichen Grüssen,

*Your name
Your address in full with zip code
Your telephone number
Your e-mail address*

Sample Correspondence

Sample Correspondence

 ITALIAN **Confirmation of Reservation**

*Your address
in full
with zip code*

*Establishment address
in full
with postal code
and country*

Date

Caro Signore/Cara Signora,

Scrivo per domandarle delle informazioni relative alle camere del suo albergo. Vorrei risiedere a … (*hotel name*) dalla notte di … (*1st date*) alla … (*2nd date*).

Desidererei prenotare una (*or number of rooms*) camera singola/doppia con bagno/doccia ed il gabinetto privato, inclusa la prima colazione. Viaggerei da solo/con … adulti/…bambini. Avrei bisogno di una culla per il neonato da mettere in camera.

Le sarei grato se mi inviasse per giro posta, i dettagli delle sue tariffe e delle eventuali offerte speciali, facendomi sapere se avesse disponibilità di camere in questo momento.

Mi faccia sapere se avete bisogno di una caparra e se accetta il pagamento con carta di credito.

Le accludo a questa mia un tagliando internazionale da inviarmi per la risposta.

RingraziandoLa per la sua assistenza, invio cordiali saluti.

*Your address
in full
with zip code*

*Establishment address
in full
with post code
and country*

Date

Caro/a xxxx xxxxxxxxx,

RingraziandoLa per le informazioni ricevute relative al suo albergo. Vorrei confermarLe la prenotazione dalla notte di … (*1st date*) alla … (*2nd date*) per una (*or number of rooms*) camera/e singola/doppia con bagno/doccia ed il gabinetto privato, e con la prima colazione inclusa. Avrei bisogno di una culla per il neonato da mettere in camera.

In attesa di incontrarLa personalmente in data … (*1st date*), invio i miei più cordiali saluti.

E-mail:

Caro Signore/Cara Signora,

La prego di inviarmi alcune informazioni relative all' eventuale disponibilità di camere presso il suo albergo. Vorrei risiedere a … (*hotel name*) dalla notte di … (*1st date*) alla … (*2nd date*).

Vorrei prenotare una (*or number of rooms*) camera singola/doppia con bagno/doccia ed il gabinetto privato, e con la prima colazione inclusa. Viaggerei da solo/con … adulti/…bambini. Avrei bisogno di una culla per il neonato da mettere in camera.

La prego di farmi conoscere i dettagli delle sue tariffe, di eventuali offerte speciali e se avete camere libere in questo momento.

Mi faccia sapere se ha bisogno di una caparra e se accetta il pagamento con carta di credito.

RingraziandoLa in anticipo, invio distinti saluti.

Your name
Your address in full with zip code
Your telephone number
Your e-mail address

E-mail:

Caro/a xxxx xxxxxxxxx,

RingraziandoLa delle informazioni ricevute relative al suo albergo. Vorremmo confermarLe la seguente prenotazione dalla notte di … (*1st date*) alla … (*2nd date*) per una [*or number of rooms*] camera/e [singola/doppia] con bagno/doccia ed il gabinetto privato, e con la prima colazione inclusa. Avremmo bisogno di una culla per il neonato da mettere in camera.

In attesa di incontrarLa personalmente, inviamo cordiali saluti.

Your name
Your address in full with zip code
Your telephone number
Your e-mail address

In Spanish some word endings change with the sex of the writer. Use "a" instead of "o" if the writer is female.

═══ SPANISH ═══ | **Confirmation of Reservation**

Your address in full with zip code   *Establishment address in full with post code and country*

Date

Estimado/a Senor/a,

Me gustaría solicitar información sobre la reserva de habitaciones en su hotel. Estoy pensando hospedarme en …(*hotel name*), durante …(*1st date*) por … (*number of nights*) noches.

Quisiera reservar una (*or number of rooms*) habitación individual/doble con baño/ducha privado y desayuno incluído. Viajaré solo/a (*alone*) / con …adulto/s y … niño/s.Necesitaremos una cuna en la habitación de los padres.

Le estaría muy agradecido/a si por favor me enviara por escrito precios y descuentos disponibles, y hacerme saber si tiene habitaciones para esos días.

Podría por favor decirme si hace falta dejar depósito? Si es así, puedo pagar con tarjeta de crédito?

Le adjunto un Cupón de Respuesta Internacional.

Agradeciéndole su ayuda de antemano.

Le saluda atentamente

Your address in full with zip code   *Establishment address in full with post code and country*

Date

Estimado/a …

Muchas gracias por la información sobre su hotel. Me gustaría reservar una (*or number of rooms*) habitación individual/doble, con baño/ducha privados y desayuno incluído, para los días … (*dates*). Necesitaremos una cuna en la habitación de los padres.

Estaré encantado/a de conocerle/a el día … (*date of first night*)

Le saluda atentamente

E-mail:

Estimado/a Senor/a,

Podría por favor enviarme información sobre la reserva de habitaciones en su hotel? Me gustaría hospedarme en … (*hotel name*) durante … (*1st date*) por … (*number of nights*) noches.

Necesitaría reservar una(*or number of rooms*) habitación individual/doble con baño/ducha privados y desayuno incluído. Viajaré solo/a (*alone*) / con …adulto/s y … niño/s.Necesitaremos una cuna en la habitación de los padres.

Por favor envíeme los precios y descuentos disponibles y si tienen habitaciones para esta fecha.

Hace falta pagar un depósito por adelantado? Si es así, puedo pagar con tarjeta de crédito?

Muchas gracias por su ayuda

Your name
Your address in full with zip code
Your telephone number
Your e-mail address

E-mail:

Estimado/a ….

Muchas gracias por la información sobre su hotel. Me gustaría hacer la reserva de una (*or number of rooms*) habitación individual/doble, con baño/ducha privados y desayuno incluído, para los días … (*dates*). Necesitaremos una cuna en la habitación de los padres.

Estaré encantado/a de conocerle/a el día … (*date of first night*)

Atentamente

Practical Information

Passports and Visas

Passport application forms can be obtained by contacting any federal or state court or post office authorized to accept passport applications. U.S. passport agencies have offices in major cities. Passport information and application forms also are available on the U.S. State Department website at www.travel.state.gov or the National Passport Information center at (888) 362-8668. (There is a credit card charge for contacting the center by phone.)

Before departure, make sure your passport is valid at least six months prior to the expiration date; some European countries require this. You'll need your passport whenever you board an international flight. In some countries, you will be required to leave your passport with the hotel when you check in, for registering all foreign visitors with local police authorities. In addition, you must show your passport whenever you cash a traveler's check. Passports must also be shown whenever national borders are crossed, although in practice, border controls have been relaxed between many European Union member countries.

Photocopy the identification page; leave one copy with a relative or friend in case of emergency, and carry one with you in case your passport is lost or stolen. If this occurs, inform local police immediately and contact the nearest U.S. embassy or consulate. The U.S. State Department has a 24-hour traveler's hotline; phone (202) 647-5225.

Travel visas are not necessary to visit any of the countries in this book, but if you'll be traveling to other nations, check their entry requirements before you leave home.

Travel and Health Insurance

Make sure you are covered by insurance that will reimburse travel expenses if you need to cancel or cut short your trip due to unforeseen circumstances. You'll also need coverage for property loss or theft, emergency medical and dental treatment, and emergency evacuation if necessary. Before taking out additional insurance, check to see whether your current homeowners or medical coverage already covers you for travel abroad.

If you make a claim, your insurance company will need proof of the incident or expenditure. Keep copies of any police report and related documents, or doctor or hospital bills or statements, to submit with your insurance claim.

What to Pack

Travel as lightly as possible. Take layers of clothing and an umbrella to cope with the unpredictable weather of the European continent, which ranges from snow in the mountains to the mild, wet weather of the northern coasts to the baking heat of the Mediterranean.

Electrical appliances require an adapter and an electrical voltage converter to accommodate the 240-volt European current. It is a good idea to bring written prescriptions for any regular medication you may take or for glasses in case of an accident.

Green Card

If you drive a car in Europe, you will need a Green Card (sometimes called an International Insurance Certificate) to prove that you have liability insurance. Car rental agencies will provide this with the vehicle. A Green Card is advised for motorists taking their own vehicle overseas: AAA Travel Agencies can arrange this.

International Driving Permit

Although not specifically required, an International Driving Permit is a useful document containing your photograph and confirming that you hold a valid driver's license in your own country. It is available from AAA Travel Agencies.

Getting Around

Central public transportation information centers and tourist information offices can provide city transportation maps, and may sell travel tickets for public transportation, including those valid for multiple rides or more than one day.

Subway trains operate in several big cities. Buses generally have extensive routes in city centers and out to the provinces, and express services, or coaches, generally cover long-distance journeys. Some cities are served by trams (running on rails) or trolley buses (running on tires but powered by overhead cables).

Most countries operate trains across national borders. Local trains are often slow, but inter-city services are generally fast and efficient. It may be worth obtaining a Eurail pass from your travel agent: passes are valid for periods from a few days to three months.

Ferries operate regularly in the Scandinavian archipelago and along the Norwegian fjords; among the Scottish islands; between Britain and Ireland, Scandinavia, Germany, France, and Spain; and throughout the islands and coastal ports of the Mediterranean countries and islands.

Driving in Europe

The American Automobile Association maintains reciprocal agreements with motoring clubs throughout Europe.

Presentation of your valid AAA membership card at participating clubs usually allows you to receive services they give to their own members. The "Offices to Serve You Abroad" leaflet, available from your local AAA club, explains in detail the services you can expect.

Car Rental

To rent a car, you will need a valid U.S. driver's license and preferably an International Driving Permit (IDP), and you will probably be asked to show your passport. Depending on which rental company you use, you may be required to produce an additional credit card or further proof of identity for renting either premium or luxury cars. Most car rental companies in Europe will not rent to an individual under the age of 21.

If you intend to drive across national boundaries, tell the rental company, as this will affect both the rate and the type of insurance required. British and Irish rental agencies may require several days' notice to supply a car available for travel to continental Europe.

European cars are generally small and have manual transmissions. Rental cars rarely have air-conditioning. Reciprocal arrangements with European motoring clubs may not apply to rental cars.

Inquire about local taxes, and check exactly what insurance coverage is included in your package. You will need a Collision Damage Waiver (this may be covered by your personal automobile insurance policy or credit card company). A CDW may not cover certain types of damage; check the details.

AAA Travel Agencies can reserve a rental car before you leave and provide prepayment arrangements; contact your local agency for details.

EUROPEAN DISTANCE CHART

Road distances, in kilometers (km), are calculated by the shortest or quickest routes
(highways, main roads) from center to center and do not take into account
seasonal weather conditions.

Miles	Km
1	1.6
10	16
20	32
30	48
40	64
50	80
100	160
200	320
300	480
400	640
500	800
1000	1600

Cities (diagonal labels):

- Amsterdam (NL)
- Barcelona (E)
- Berlin (D)
- Bruges (B)
- Brussels (B)
- The Hague (NL)
- Dublin (IRL)
- Edinburgh (GB)
- Florence (I)
- Geneva (CH)
- Ghent (B)
- Innsbruck (A)
- Cologne (D)
- Copenhagen (DK)
- Lisbon (P)
- London (GB)
- Lyon (F)
- Madrid (E)
- Munich (D)
- Naples (I)
- Nice (F)
- Odense (DK)
- Oxford (GB)
- Paris (F)
- Porto (P)
- Rome (I)
- Salzburg (A)

Distance matrix (km):

```
1600
653 1889
269 1372 832
210 1403 773 101
64 1574 697 211 180
959 1958 1522 704 791 930
1092 2091 1655 837 924 1063 538
1387 1103 1228 1331 1219 1406 2001 2134
1004 809 1119 769 724 896 1355 1488 606
221 1367 783 52 56 191 742 875 1286 764
1001 1381 750 1061 956 1021 1751 1884 483 574 1011
262 1419 569 315 210 282 1005 1138 1132 749 265 747
926 2313 397 1132 1073 970 1822 1955 1899 1543 1084 1421 886
2370 1258 2908 2161 2168 2341 2747 2880 2359 2065 2156 2637 2345 3225
482 1481 1045 227 314 453 463 665 1524 878 526 1274 528 1345 2270
932 652 1233 779 734 906 1365 1498 693 153 774 727 751 1656 1908 888
1809 630 2347 1600 1607 1779 2186 2319 1700 1406 1595 1978 1784 2663 625 1709 1249
834 1396 583 894 789 854 1584 1717 641 587 844 163 580 1254 2677 1107 740 1993
1859 1577 1700 1803 1691 1878 2473 2606 474 1080 1758 955 1604 2371 2833 1996 1167 2174 1113
1396 681 1347 1268 1223 1394 1853 1986 421 541 1263 700 1142 1935 1937 1376 472 1278 858 895
765 2151 599 971 911 809 1660 1793 1737 1381 922 1260 724 165 3063 1183 1495 2502 1093 2209 1774
589 1588 1152 334 421 560 396 598 1631 985 372 1381 635 1452 2377 90 995 1816 1214 2103 1483 1290
509 1067 1047 300 307 480 888 1021 1141 542 295 953 484 1364 1856 411 466 1295 831 1614 954 1202 518
2170 1213 2708 1961 1968 2141 2547 2680 2159 1865 1956 2437 2145 3025 318 2070 1708 564 2477 2632 1737 2863 2177 1656
1663 1381 1504 1607 1495 1683 2277 2410 278 885 1562 759 1409 2175 2637 1800 971 1978 917 219 700 2014 1907 1419 2437
977 1535 726 1037 932 997 1727 1860 658 725 987 180 723 1397 2791 1250 879 2132 139 1129 875 1236 1347 987 2591 934
2078 1166 2616 1869 1876 2049 2454 2587 2067 1773 1864 2345 2053 2933 549 1977 1616 646 2385 2540 1645 2771 2084 1564 231 2345 2499
2354 1041 2892 2145 2152 2325 2733 2866 2111 1817 2140 2389 2329 3209 408 2256 1660 543 2404 2584 1689 3047 2363 1840 679 2389 2543
1542 2929 1013 1748 1689 1586 2438 2571 2515 2159 1700 2037 1502 620 3841 1961 2273 3279 1870 2986 2551 781 2068 1982 3641 2791 2013
628 1147 753 543 431 602 1213 1346 784 401 498 471 354 1177 2335 736 491 1744 360 1256 794 1015 843 489 2135 1060 516
1345 1256 1126 1289 1177 1364 1959 2092 256 584 1244 381 1090 1797 2512 1482 701 1853 539 728 574 1636 1589 1119 2312 532 436
1157 1843 637 1217 1112 1176 1907 2040 843 1020 1167 475 902 1577 3084 1430 1174 2440 434 1315 1161 1415 1537 1238 2884 1119 297
805 1804 1368 550 637 776 322 311 1847 1201 588 1597 851 1668 2593 339 1211 2032 1430 2319 1699 1506 295 734 2393 2123 1573
831 1095 844 775 663 851 1446 1579 591 285 730 284 577 1370 2351 969 306 1062 600 1209 1076 664 2151 867 445
```

	Santiago de Campostela (E)	Seville (E)	Stockholm (S)	Strasbourg (F)	Venice (I)	Vienna (A)	York (GB)	Zürich (CH)
	910							
	3548	3827						
	2042	2157	1739					
	2219	2266	2413	742				
	2791	2853	2193	807	605			
	2300	2579	2284	1059	1805	1735		
	2058	2105	1986	229	548	740	1292	

Austria

Austria is a small country, hemmed in by eight neighbors, but it packs an astounding variety of traditions and cultures, and has had a profound influence on the political life of Europe across the centuries. Its past glories are still part of the everyday scenery, in the form of baroque buildings and the continuing celebration of a golden age of music and culture. Even the most grandiose architecture is humbled, though, by the natural majesty of Austria's mountains.

Mountains and Valleys

Massive mountain chains cover nearly three-quarters of the land. Their sheer rock is split by plunging valleys, softened on the lower slopes by deep forests that eventually open out into fertile Alpine meadows, sparkling with colorful wildflowers and dotted with villages huddling around a picturesque church. Hikers and skiers often head for the lovely Tyrol region in the west, where Austria shares the Alps with Italy and Switzerland. Most Austrians live in flatter country, around the Danube (Donau) river, where grain, fruit and vineyards flourish in the Vienna basin.

The Viennese Effect

Vienna is a living monument to the days when Austria dominated European politics. For 600 years, until 1918, the Habsburg Empire wielded immense power, extending its influence from Spain and Hungary and infiltrating many other European royal families. Imperial splendor is stamped all over Vienna, with its vast monuments, public buildings and open squares. It could all be rather intimidating, but the saving grace is the elegance, ease and essential warmth of the people, which translates into a lively café society, busy *Bierkellen* (taverns) and relaxed, strolling crowds in the streets.

The Austrian Character

The Viennese are still considered a race apart by those outside the city. There are nine provinces in Austria, each one with its own particular characteristics. In fact, every valley community in this country of only 8 million people treasures its own dialect, traditions, costume and lifestyle over and above any broad national characteristics. It's quite common to see people sauntering through villages or towns wearing their regional versions of the national dress – the *lederhosen* (leather pants) or *dirndl* (bodiced dress) - and regional food, music and festivals are proudly celebrated.

When comparing themselves with other nations, Austrians like to say that they are generally lighthearted, friendly and hospitable. There's certainly a cordial politeness in everyday encounters – in the way children will open a door to let you through, or give up a seat on a bus, or in the way strangers are greeted with a *Grüss Gott* ("God's greeting"), still a common term in this deeply Catholic society.

Accommodations

There's a bewildering range of accommodations available to visitors to Austria. In addition to the standard range of one- to five-star hotels, a variety of guesthouses, inns and pensions all have confusingly similar names but separate classifications and categories. Be assured, though, that standards of comfort and service are universally high.

Standard bedrooms in Austria have twin beds, but usually as part of one large frame, containing two mattresses and two sets of bedding. It's not possible to pull the beds apart, and you will sleep in close proximity to your partner. Bedding consists of large, puffy feather quilts in cotton covers – renowned as some of the most comfortable quilts in the world! They are folded on the bed, to be opened up at bedtime. Televisions are less commonly found than in other countries, but private bathrooms are usually available. (All restrooms in Austria, public or private, are free, numerous and spotless.) Rooms in mountain areas often have small balconies so you can soak in the views.

Breakfasts are often served buffet-style, with a range of breads, cheeses, cooked meats, jam and honey. Some hotels offer the option of a boiled egg, cooked either in the kitchen or by you (with a mini water-boiler). Evening hotel meals generally include a main meat dish of either pork or veal. Many hotels charge for water from a faucet.

Food and Drink

Meals follow a more American than European schedule here, with lunch around noon and dinner any time after 6 p.m. Austrians eat and drink with gusto; an evening meal can be a noisy and spirited affair, but drunkenness is considered uncouth. You'll find waiters genuinely concerned that you enjoy your meal and downcast if you can't manage the vast portions.

Each region in Austria has its own specialties, but there are staples that appear everywhere. Heavy soups, meat, *knödel* (dumplings) and noodles are always on the menu, as is cream – which

is applied liberally to sauces, soups, coffees and desserts, often topped with Alpine whipped spirals. Main courses are often accompanied by sauerkraut (pickled cabbage), piles of potatoes, and salads – covered, naturally, in creamy dressings. Beer comes in many varieties, and there are excellent local wines. Schnapps, a strong fruit or herb-based liqueur, is drunk as a digestive aid.

Between meals, Austrians are passionate café-goers, indulging in coffee (the national drink, often in as many as 20-plus varieties), cakes, *apfelstrudel* (apple strudel) and *sachertorte*, a frosted chocolate cake with apricot jam. If you exhaust the possibilities of coffee, try a hot chocolate – rich, thick and heaped with the inevitable cap of cream. Austrian

AUSTRIA

Dress Tips

The climate is, of course, heavily affected by the mountains – which means being prepared for any eventuality. If you're climbing, take plenty of layers of warm clothing, to account for the dramatic drops in temperature as you gain altitude. Wherever you are, go equipped for sudden rainfall, as passing clouds are snagged against the mountain peaks.

Austria is still a very formal country. For evenings at the theater or opera, men should wear jacket and tie, and women a dress, suit or fashionable pants. When entering churches, whether for services or to look around, women should cover their shoulders and upper arms.

café society may not live up to its late 19th-century heyday, when the great writers and thinkers gathered to exchange or ponder ideas, but there's still a relaxed feel to the traditional coffeehouses, where it's quite appropriate for customers to spend an hour or so chatting and lingering over a couple of drinks and a gooey cake.

Note that all cafés, bars and restaurants provide coat hooks and umbrella stands. It's considered more respectful to leave your belongings there, rather than on the chair.

AUSTRIA

BRAUNAU　　C3
Schärding

Forstinger's Wirtshaus　**$$**
Schärding 4780, Unterer
Stadtplatz 3
☎ (0 77 12) 23 02
🖹 (0 77 12) 2 30 23
Located in a 400-year-old
building – a member of the
Romantic Group – this
establishment has created a
harmonious mix of traditional
character and modern comfort.

The rooms are particularly
charming, and there is an
attractive café terrace. Fly fishing
is available on the hotel's own
stretch of river.

 22

P

 🞐 ⓓ Ⓔ ▦

BREGENZ　　A2
Bregenz

Deuring Schlössle　**$$-$$$**
Bregenz 6900, Ehre-Guta
Platz 4
☎ (0 55 74) 4 78 00
🖹 (0 55 74) 4 78 00 80
ⓔ deuring@schloessle.vol.at
The remains of the Roman wall
and the Gothic façade reflect the
eventful history of this hotel. In

the 17th century the former
town defenses were converted
into a castle, and the atmosphere
of a private residence lives on in
the stylish old furniture and
valuable antiques. It provides
individually furnished rooms, a
fine terrace, and prestigious
facilities for parties and
conferences.

 9

P 🞐 ⓓ Ⓔ ▦

Eichenberg

Schönblick　**$-$$**
Eichenberg 6911, Dorf 6
☎ (0 55 74) 4 59 65
🖹 (0 55 74) 4 59 65
www.schoenblick.at
The hotel, high above Lake
Constance and built in the alpine
style, offers comfortable rooms,
conference facilities and a
terrace. Other attractions include
the indoor pool, sauna,

whirlpool, steam bath, solarium
and tennis court. The restaurant,
serving regional cuisine, has its
own wine and cheese cellar.

 13

P ⛱

Ⓔ ▦

DÜRNSTEIN　　D3
Spitz

Weinberghof　**$**
Spitz 3620, Am Hinterweg 17
☎ (0 27 13) 29 39
🖹 (0 27 13) 2 51 64
tiscover.com/weinberghof
The hotel, surrounded by
vineyards, offers Wachau-style
hospitality and tasteful
accommodation in attractive
rooms. Relax in the sauna,
solarium or lobby, with its quiet

corners for reading. Visit the old
wine cellar, play table tennis or
sit on the terrace.

13

P

🞐 ⓓ Ⓔ ▦

Weissenkirchen

Raffelsbergerhof　**$-$$**
Weissenkirchen 3610, Nr. 54
☎ (0 27 15) 22 01
🖹 (0 27 15) 22 01 27
The town of Weissenkirchen,
in the heart of Wachau, is
dedicated to wine. It has the
college of wine, a vineyard
museum and walks through the
vineyard slopes. The hotel is

located in a Renaissance building
dating from 1574, distinguished
by its archways and vaulted
ceilings. Guests will appreciate
the stylish rooms and the
copious breakfast buffet.

14

P

ⓓ Ⓔ ▦

Key to Symbols: 🖹 Fax ⓔ Email 🛏 Rooms P Parking ⛱ Swimming
🞐 American Express ⓓ Diners Club Ⓔ Eurocard ⬤ MasterCard ▦ Visa

FELDKIRCH A2
Feldkirch

Alpenrose $$
Feldkirch 6800, Rosengasse 4-6
☎ (0 55 22) 7 21 75
🖹 (0 55 22)72 17 55
www.tiscover.com/hotel-alpenrose
This Best Western hotel in the pedestrianized area is a former town house with a long history dating from the 16th century. It is furnished with antiques and offers comfortable rooms, a conference room, terrace and stylish restaurant. The menu ranges through classic, regional and international cuisine.

🛏 25
🅿

FREISTADT D3
Freistadt

Zum Goldenen Hirschen $
Freistadt 4240,
Böhmergasse 8-10
☎ (0 79 42) 72 25 80
🖹 (0 79 42) 7 22 58 40
The hotel, situated in a historic building thought to date from the 13th century, abuts the Böhmer Gate and has a splendid façade decorated with flowers. It offers all modern comforts, with tastefully furnished and well-equipped rooms and cozy restaurants serving sophisticated regional cuisine. Relax in the winter garden or romantic lawned garden overlooking the town moat.

🛏 31
🅿

GMUNDEN C2
Gmunden

Schlosshot. Freisitz Roith $$
Gmunden 4810,
Traunsteinstrasse 87
☎ (0 76 12) 6 49 05
🖹 (0 76 12) 6 49 05 17
www.tiscover.com/schlosshotel
Resembling a fairytale castle high above Lake Traun, the hotel is one of the oldest buildings in the area, dating from the 16th century. Guests are assured of wonderful views and comfortable accommodation in spacious and tastefully furnished rooms (some with balconies) or the magnificent suites. The restaurant serves an extensive menu and excellent wines from Austria's finest vineyards.

🛏 19
🅿

Grünau

Almtalhof $$
Grünau 4645
☎ (0 76 16) 82 04
🖹 (0 76 16) 82 04 66
🅴 almtal@magnet.at
It would be hard to imagine a more attractive "Romantic Hotel" than the Almtalhof, which has been offering hospitality since imperial times. The comfortable modern rooms are bathed in sunlight, decorated in warm colors, and afford fine views of Grünau and its surroundings. The elegant restaurant serves organic produce in regional dishes, and there are excellent health, fitness and leisure facilities.

🛏 24

🅿 ⊠ 🅴

GRAZ D2
Frohnleiten

Frohnleitnerhof $
Frohnleiten 8130,
Hauptplatz 14
☎ (0 31 26) 41 50
🖹 (0 31 26) 4 15 05 55
www.frohnleitnerhof.at
A charming hotel with a splendid view of the promenade, providing comfortable rooms with large balconies. Unwind, perhaps after a day's work in the modern conference facilities, in the exquisitely decorated sauna (choice of steam bath, herb sauna or dry sauna). Relax on the terrace or in the rustic brew room with a glass of Fronleitner Bräu.

🛏 28

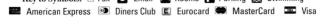
Key to Symbols: 🖹 Fax 🅴 Email 🛏 Rooms 🅿 Parking ⊠ Swimming
American Express ⓓ Diners Club 🅴 Eurocard 💳 MasterCard Visa

Sebersdorf

Schlosshotel Obermayerhofen
$$-$$$
Sebersdorf 8272, Neustift 1-3
☎ (0 33 33) 25 03
🗎 (0 33 33) 25 03 50
This imposing building on a
steep slope was converted into a
castle residence during the 18th
century. It is now a fine hotel
providing spacious rooms,
individually furnished with
faïence stoves and valuable
Oriental carpets. There are
modern conference facilities.
Other attractions are the copious
breakfast buffet, splendid terrace,
tea room and bar.

🛏 10

GROBMING   C2
Gröbming

Landhaus St. Georg $$
Gröbming 8962, Kulmweg 555
☎ (0 36 85) 2 27 40
🗎 (0 36 85) 2 27 40 60
www.st-georg.at
Idyllically located establishment
in the winter resort of
Gröbming, offering wood-
paneled public rooms,
comfortable bedrooms, a terrace
and superb fitness facilities,
including a sauna, solarium,
massage and an indoor pool.
Regional cuisine is the specialty
of the restaurant.

🛏 6

INNSBRUCK   B2
Innsbruck

Schwarzer Adler $$-$$$
Innsbruck 6020,
Kaiserjägerstrasse 2
☎ (05 12) 58 71 09
🗎 (05 12) 56 16 97
📧 romantikhotel-
innsbruck@netway.at
A "Romantic Hotel" in the heart
of the city, first licensed in 1624
and now offering light airy
rooms and suites with wood as a
dominant feature. The
Schwarzer Adler also is ideal for
conferences and parties, and
there is an extensive menu in the
cozy restaurant, the terrace or
the 16th-century vaulted cellar.

🛏 32

Seefeld

Sir Richard $$
Seefeld 6100, Innsbrucker
Strasse 162
☎ (0 52 12) 20 93
🗎 (0 52 12) 2 09 34
The Sir Richard is not only a
superb restaurant, but the
adjacent guesthouse offers
comfortable accommodation. In
the morning a fine breakfast is
served in the restaurant or in the
winter garden, which has a sun
terrace.

🛏 4
P

Tux

Lanersbacher Hof $$
Tux 6293, Lanersbach 388
☎ (0 52 87) 8 72 56
🗎 (0 52 87) 8 74 53
The Lanersbacher Hof, under
the expert management of the
Kraxner family, is a real gem.
The use of wood in the rooms
and luxury suites generates a
feeling of warmth and well-
being. Start the day with the
breakfast buffet, walk through
the Tirolean mountains, visit the
pool complex and relax in the
wine bar or bar.

🛏 33

Key to Symbols: 🗎 Fax   📧 Email   🛏 Rooms   P Parking   🏊 Swimming
American Express   Diners Club   Eurocard   MasterCard   Visa

KITZBÜHEL B2
Ellmau
Kaiserhof $$-$$$
Ellmau 6352, Harmstätt 8
☎ (0 53 58) 20 22
🖹 (0 53 58) 2 02 26 00
www.khof.at

The Kaiserhof stands high above Ellmau, with splendid views of the Wilde Kaiser Mountain. Rooms, suites and apartments are furnished in an elegant country style, and the hotel offers an excellent conference room and a restaurant with panoramic views. Relax in the cozy Tirolean Kaminstüberl, the winter garden, bar or terrace. The fitness suite provides a sauna, steam baths, pool and beauty salon.

🛏 10
P 🏊 ⬛ ◍ 🅴 💳

St. Johann
Gruber $-$$
St. Johann 6380, Gasteiger Strasse 18
☎ (0 53 52) 6 14 61
🖹 (0 53 52) 6 14 61 33

A Tirolean-style building quietly located in the spa park. With its abundant use of wood, it has a warm, cozy atmosphere and comfortable rooms. For relaxation, head for the sauna, solarium, steam bath and fitness room.

🛏 12
P
🅴 💳

KUFSTEIN B2
Ebbs
Unterwirt $
Ebbs 6341, Wildbichlerstrasse 38
☎ (0 53 73) 4 22 88
🖹 (0 53 73) 4 22 53

Behind the attractive façade of this historic building are a modern hotel with comfortable rooms and a cozy restaurant offering a sophisticated menu. Relax in the attractive garden, bar or terrace, perhaps after a visit to the sauna/solarium. The restaurant serves classic and regional cuisine.

🛏 25
P
⬛

Kufstein

Alpenrose $$
Kufstein 6330, Weissachstrasse 47
☎ (0 53 72) 6 21 22
🖹 (0 53 72) 62 12 27
www.bestwestern.ce.com/alpenrosekufstein

Quietly located hotel on the edge of Kufstein, offering comfortable rooms and a stylish restaurant serving international and regional cuisine. Unwind in the sauna, solarium and fitness room, or relax in the Ofenstube, the rustic bar.

🛏 22
P
⬛ ◍ 🅴 💳

LINZ D3
Linz
Drei Mohren $$
Linz 4020, Promenade 17
☎ (07 32) 7 72 62 60
🖹 (07 32) 7 72 62 66
www.austria-classic-hotels.at

The hotel, dating from 1565, is located in Landhaus Park in the Old Town. It is an "Austria Classic" establishment with exquisitely furnished accommodations and an elegant breakfast room. The Gelbe Salon is available for conferences, and in the evening guests meet in the spacious Kaminzimmer or for a drink in the bar. There also is an attractive terrace for summer use.

🛏 20
P ⬛ ◍ 🅴 💳

Key to Symbols: 🖹 Fax 🅴 Email 🛏 Rooms P Parking 🏊 Swimming ⬛ American Express ◍ Diners Club 🅴 Eurocard ⬛ MasterCard 💳 Visa

MELK   **D3**

Mühldorf

Burg Oberranna   **$$**
Mühldorf 3622, Oberranna 1
☎ (0 27 13) 82 21
▤ (0 27 13) 83 66
The castle, situated in the heart of Wachau and first documented in 1070, has been converted into an exquisite hotel with individually furnished apartments and rooms, a comfortable restaurant and breakfast room, and for relaxation, a sauna/solarium. The restaurant serves regional cuisine and good homestyle fare.

 5

RADSTADT   **C2**

Filzmoos

Hubertus   **$-$$**
Filzmoos 5532, Am Dorfplatz 1
☎ (0 64 53) 82 04
▤ (0 64 53) 8 20 66
A connoisseur's hotel in the center of Filzmoos, with a cozy atmosphere and tastefully furnished rooms in country-house style - ideal for a relaxing stay. Apartments also are available in a separate building. Facilities include a coffeehouse serving homemade bread and pastries, the Alm Bar and a terrace.

 16

Kleines Hotel Kärnten   **$$$**
Filzmoos 9580, Egger Seepromenade 8
☎ (0 42 54) 23 75
▤ (0 42 54) 23 75 23
e kkk@net4you.co.at
The hotel has an idyllic lakeside location in the midst of a large park, with the Karawanken Mountains as a backdrop. Fine materials, modern art and splendid floral displays distinguish the individually furnished rooms and apartments. The stylish restaurant offers a sophisticated menu and first-class wine list, and in the afternoon cakes straight from the oven are served on the terrace.

 12

SALZBURG   **C2**

Anif

Schlosswirt   **$$**
Anif 5081, Halleiner Bundesstrasse 22
☎ (0 62 46) 7 21 75
▤ (0 62 46)72 17 58
www.schlosswirt-anif.com
This 600-year-old inn is located close to the famous Anif water castle. Now a gem of a hotel, it has a range of comfortable rooms and two suites. Other features include a garden with chestnut trees, a café terrace, winter garden and bar. Regional and international cuisine is served in the restaurant, and stylish facilities are available for conferences and parties.

 26

Salzburg

Altstadthotel Wolf-Dietrich **$$**
Salzburg 5020, Wolf-Dietrich-Strasse 7
☎ (06 62) 87 12 75
▤ (06 62) 88 23 20
www.salzburg-hotel.at
This hotel is credited with having the first organic restaurant in Austria, which is located in a former wine cellar. In addition it offers individually furnished rooms, a splendid terrace, and leisure facilities including an indoor pool, sauna and solarium.

 29

Maria Plain $$
Salzburg 5101,
Plainbergweg 41
☎ (06 62) 4 50 70 10
🖹 (06 62) 45 07 01 19
📧 info@mariaplain.com
The Maria Plain, with its cosy rooms and romantic garden, dispenses genuine hospitality. The Mosshammer family offers an imaginative menu, with local

delicacies and products from their own butcher shop. It's worth visiting just for the homemade cakes.

 22

WIEN (VIENNA)   E3

Wien

Altwienerhof $-$$
Wien 1150, Herklotzgasse 6
☎ (01) 8 92 60 00
🖹 (01) 26 00 08
www.altwienerhof.at
This hotel is located away from the city center on the road to Schönbrunn. Under the expert management of the Kellner

family, it offers comfortable, individually furnished rooms. Other attractions include the copious breakfast buffet, attractive terrace and winter garden. A theater and concert ticket service is available.

 17

ZELL AM SEE   C2

Zell am See

St. Georg $$
Zell am See 5700,
Schillerstrasse 32
☎ (0 65 42) 7 68
🖹 (0 65 42) 76 83 00
www.tiscover.com/st.georg.
zellamsee
Quietly located hotel on the edge of the Old Town, offering comfortable accommodations, a superb conference room, a stylish

bar and a wine shop with tasting sessions. Leisure facilities comprise a pool, sauna and solarium, and the room price includes dinner and a breakfast buffet.

 25

ZELL AM ZILLER   B2

Wald im Pinzgau

Jagdschloss Graf Recke $-$$
Wald im Pinzgau 5742,
Rosenthal 62
☎ (0 65 65) 64 17
🖹 (0 65 65) 69 20
This hunting manor, constructed in 1926 from one of the last remaining castles in Oberpinzgau, is now a stylish

hotel under the personal management of Count and Countess von der Recke. Facilities include a heated swimming pool, terrace, and a restaurant serving nouvelle and regional cuisine.

 18

ZWETTL   D3

Zwettl

Schwarz-Alm $$
Zwettl 3910, Gschwendt 43
☎ (0 28 22) 5 31 73
🖹 (0 28 22) 5 42 73 11
www.zwettler.co.at/zwettler/bier
hotel
Beautifully located in a forest clearing near Zwettl, this hotel offers comfortable rooms, superb conference facilities and a restaurant renowned for its

cuisine, including Waldviertel dumplings and dishes made from beer brewed in the Zwettl brewery. Relax on the sun terrace after a game of tennis or a session in the fitness room or pool complex.

 25

Belgium

*T*his tiny nation is a survivor, born of civil and international conflict and harboring acute differences of language, politics and territory. Sitting on the neck of the English Channel, Belgium has a semicircle of inland neighbors – The Netherlands, Germany, Luxembourg and France – who have each played a part in the country's development, through peace and war. Belgium's north-south divide of language and culture still reflects the influence of the Dutch and the French; and its role as the battlefield of Europe during World War I has left a legacy of graves and monuments, as well as the vivid images that resonate through towns such as Mons and Ieper. In the postwar era, Belgium has become the administrative focus of the European Union.

Town and Country

But Belgium is more than a melting-pot of other national identities: it has a very powerful identity of its own. The medieval streets and public buildings of Bruges and Brussels; the palpable sense of the past in Ghent and Antwerp, or in the regional cities of Louvain and Mechelen; the castles of Haspengouw, west of Brussels, and the dazzling works of art by Flemish Masters – all speak of a specific and valued history. Beyond the main cities is a landscape of farms, meadows and waterways. Even on the very edge of Brussels, you can find tranquility among the beech trees of the Forêt de Soignes. Along the short coastline are popular beach resorts and deserted dunes; lively towns such as Oostende and stylish ones such as De Haan. The hills of the Ardennes reach into the southern provinces of Namur and Liège, with their low-key charms of woods, rivers and moors.

The People

While the northern provinces that became The Netherlands rebelled against their Habsburg masters and took up the Protestant cause, the southern provinces that became Belgium stayed loyal and Catholic. This is still a conservative, Roman Catholic country, whose people are courteous but reserved. They may not approach visitors in spontaneous shows of friendship, but requests for advice or information will be answered politely.

The Language Issue

There is still a certain rivalry between the Flemings and the Walloons, who guard their linguistic and cultural traditions with passion. French is spoken in Brussels and Wallonia, Flemish in Ghent, Bruges and the north – attempting either language in the wrong place will not go down well. English is spoken to some extent all over Belgium. In Brussels, street signs are in Flemish and French; in most cases proper names look fairly similar in both languages. For instance, Bruges in French is Brugge in Flemish; Louvain in French is Leuven in Flemish. There are exceptions, though. Ghent, for example, is Gand in French, Gent in Flemish; Mechelen is Malines in French and Mechelen in Flemish. The best bet is to check with an English speaker.

Brussels' Grand Place and the annual Ommegang historical pageant which takes place in July

Accommodations

Good quality hotels are not hard to find in Belgium. Many privately run establishments offer comfortable accommodations and excellent service, and hotels approved by the national tourist authority display a shield at the door; there's also a reliable star-rating system. High standards are reflected in the prices, though – and accommodations are generally much more expensive here than in neighboring France.

Away from the smart but anonymous international business hotels of Brussels, bedrooms are often modestly furnished with either twin beds or one double. Single bedrooms do exist, but may have an inferior view or location within the hotel. Televisions and telephones are standard, and items such as hair dryers and complimentary toiletries are very common. Cheaper rooms may share bathrooms, but private facilities are the norm. Advertised prices are usually per room (rather than per person), unless they refer to a dinner, bed and breakfast package.

Breakfast is typically included in the cost of your room. At its most basic, it consists of bread and jam served with coffee, tea and perhaps orange juice. Larger hotels may add smoked meats, fish and cheeses.

Food and Drink

Belgians proudly proclaim themselves the inventors of the French fry, or *frites*, which form a frequent accompaniment to meals – especially the favorite *mosselen* (Belgian mussels cooked in a variety of tangy sauces). Traditional Belgian food focuses on beef and pork, with seafood specialties in the west, game figuring prominently in the Ardennes and wine-based sauces in Wallonian cuisine.

Popular lunchtime and dinnertime dishes include *maatjes*, raw herring swallowed whole, but not quite the raw experience it seems; *waterzooi*, a traditional, filling Flemish stew of fresh vegetables with rabbit or fish; *paling in 't groen*, freshwater eels in green herb sauce, or, in the Ardennes, pâté and smoked ham.

An early summer specialty is asparagus in a butter-based sauce, chopped boiled egg and chopped ham – often served with one of the excellent Belgian beers (*bière*), which tend to be

rich, mellow and smooth. Brewing is a prized art in Belgium: there are hundreds of different brews, some of which are as fine as wine. In Flemish areas the favored drink is *jenever*, a grain spirit.

Restaurant menus usually give you the dish of the day; you can see a wider selection of dishes by asking for the *kaart* (Flemish) or *carte* (French). In

Fast Food

Ignore the ubiquitous hamburgers and French fries and try *broodjes*, baguettes with delicious fillings, or the seasoned and smoked sausages sold on the street, especially in northern areas. For dessert, buy fresh *gaufres*, vanilla-flavored waffles spread with jam; or take the more expensive option and visit one of the famous chocolatiers, where individually made pralines, filled with liqueur or cream, and truffles are guaranteed to make your mouth water.

some areas of Brussels – particularly the rue des Bouchers – reasonably priced menus can be replaced with versions displaying more expensive house specialties as soon as you take your seat. If this happens (and you don't decide to take the pricier meal), leave and go somewhere else.

BELGIUM

BELGIUM

BELGIUM

ANTWERPEN C4

Antwerpen

Firean $$
Karel Oomsstraat 6, 2018
Antwerp, prov. Antwerpen
☎ 03-237 02 60
📄 03-238 11 68
📧 hotel.firean@skynet.be

Known as one of the most charming establishments in Belgium, this stylish building dates back to 1929 and was entirely renovated in 1986. The bedrooms are spacious and decorated with classic furniture. The original features of the building have been preserved, such as the art-deco architecture and the Tiffany-glass windows. A delicious breakfast is served in the morning. A friendly welcome and personal attention contribute to a relaxed atmosphere.
🛏 15

Marijke Vandepitte $
Britselei 49 bus 6, 2000
Antwerp, prov. Antwerpen
☎ 03-288 66 95
📄 03-288 66 95

Far away from the hustle and bustle of the city center, Marijke VandePitte has furnished two pretty rooms and a beautiful penthouse. Both rooms are attractively furnished, with exceptionally luxurious bathrooms, and there also is a roof apartment with a spacious lounge and a very modern bathroom, as well as a sunny terrace with fantastic views of the city. A comprehensive breakfast is served in the morning.
🛏 3

**Stevens Greta &
Franky De Jonge** $
Molenstraat 35, 2018 Antwerp,
prov. Antwerpen
☎ 03-259 15 90
📄 03-259 15 99
www.home.worldonline.be/~frd
ejong
📧 dj.greta@wol.be

Greta Stevens is the chairperson of the Antwerp Guild of guesthouses, and for years she has been a dedicated host to people who come to her house. The rooms have a very modern feel and offer excellent accommodation. As well as the standard breakfast, a more extensive one also is available. There are plans to open a breakfast restaurant in 2001.

🛏 3

t'Sandt $$
Zand 17-19, 2000 Antwerp,
prov. Antwerpen
☎ 03-232 93 90
📄 03-232 56 13

This building dates back to the 15th century, when it was used as the first toll house. The original style has been preserved as much as possible. The beautiful rococo facade and the listed staircase date back to 1850. Every suite is furnished in contemporary English style. The "pièce de résistance" is a luxurious suite with a view of the spire of Antwerpen's famous cathedral. This charming hotel has a rooftop terrace, an Italianate garden and a tranquil lounge.
🛏 17

BORGLOON D3

Boorgloon

Kasteel van Rullingen $$
Rullingen 1, 3840 Borgloon,
prov. Limburg
☎ 012-74 31 46
📄 012-74 54 86
www.ping.be/rullingen
📧 rullingen@ping.be

The Kasteel van Rullingen is situated in the midst of vast landscaped gardens, which include a moat and ponds. The castle was renovated in 1924 in 17th-century country style. This elegant hotel has murals and tapestries, impressive chandeliers and beautiful oak doors, and is well known for its refined cuisine. Each of the bedrooms has its own distinctive style, with simple, contemporary furnishings.

🛏 11

Key to Symbols: 📄 Fax Email 🛏 Rooms 🅿 Parking 🏊 Swimming

BROECHEM C4

Ranst (Broechem)

Bossenstein $$
Moor 16, 2520 Ranst
(Broechem), prov. Antwerpen
☎ 03-485 64 46
🗎 03-485 78 41

The lounge, bar and breakfast room of this hotel have views of the golf course and an impressive 15th-century castle. A friendly, lively atmosphere prevails, with a cozy restaurant, spacious lobby, wide corridors and generous bedrooms.

🛏 16

BRUGES A4

Bruges

Casa dell'angolo $$
Boeveriestraat 32, 8000 Bruges, prov. West-Vlaanderen
☎ 050-49 02 12
🗎 050-49 02 21
www.casa-dell-angolo.be
🅴 info@casa-dell-angolo.be

The Casa dell' Angelo is the beautifully renovated property of Frank and Annie Desmet. Downstairs, the cozy lounge looks out on the small inner garden. Upstairs are the bedrooms, furnished to the highest specification and equipped with the latest gadgets. The African wood floors, Indian tables and bedlinen from Senegal give the rooms an exotic atmosphere. The bathrooms are elegantly equipped. The loft bedroom offers view of Bruges' city center.

🛏 3

Hotel Prinsenhof $$
Ontvangerstraat 9, 8000 Bruges, prov. West-Vlaanderen
☎ 050-34 26 90
🗎 050-34 23 21
www.prinsenhof.be
🅴 info@prinsenhof.be

The modest façade of this hotel conceals the elegant interior within. The air-conditioned rooms are individually styled and equipped with every modern amenity. The elegant Flemish-style fireplace and ornate ceiling in the lounge takes you back to the time when Bruges was an important town. The reception here is warm and welcoming.

🛏 16

Romantik Pandhotel $$
Pandreitje 16, 8000 Brugge, prov. West-Vlaanderen
☎ 050-34 06 66
🗎 050-34 05 56
www.pandhotel.com
🅴 info@pandhotel.be

Hidden behind sturdy plantain trees, the Romantik hotel is a short distance from the landing stage of the Rozenhoed dock. This 18th-century residence is now a charming hotel where every room is decorated to a high standard. Each room is stylishly and individually equipped with every modern amenity. The library, elegant lounges and cozy bar create the atmosphere of a stylish English residence. A generous breakfast is served in the country-style breakfast room.

🛏 23

t' Boergoensche Cruyce $$
Wollestraat 41-43, 8000 Bruges, prov. West-Vlaanderen
☎ 050-33 79 26
🗎 050-34 19 68
🅴 The wooden façade of the hotel is one of the most photographed sights in Bruges. From the dock, with small boats coming and going, the tall outline of the Belfort in the background is delightful. The views from the hotel are especially attractive in the evening, when the fronts of the houses opposite are illuminated. The hotel is well known in Bruges for its excellent cuisine. The interior is in Flemish style, and the bedrooms are spacious and comfortable.

🛏 8

Key to Symbols: 🗎 Fax 🅴 Email 🛏 Rooms 🅿 Parking 🏊 Swimming

BRUSSELS — C3

Brussels

Les Bluets $
Berckmansstraat 124, 1060
Brussels, Brussel
☎ 02-534 39 83
▤ 02-543 09 70
e bluets@endora.com

An impressive, well-preserved house in beautiful belle-époque style that dates back to 1864, Les Bluets features ornate ceilings and original wooden paneling. The bedrooms are decorated with antique furniture in various styles. The many plants, rugs and paintings add up to give the whole interior an exotic atmosphere. Breakfast is served at the communal breakfast table.

 10

Manos Stephanie $$
Charleroise Steenweg 28, 1060
Brussels, Brussel
☎ 02-539 02 50
▤ 02-537 57 29
www.manoshotel.com
e manos@manoshotel.com

A beautiful building, situated on a busy road, with an elegant, exclusive atmosphere. The imposing hall is very spacious, with a marble floor and gold-framed mirrors and furniture. The charming en-suite bedrooms have been recently refurbished. There is a bar, and a cozy breakfast room in the style of a Roman courtyard. Weather permitting, guests can also enjoy their breakfast on the outdoor terrace.

 55

Noga $
Begijnhofstraat 38, 1000
Brussels, Brussel
☎ 02-218 67 63
▤ 02-218 16 03
www.hotelnoga.com

The homey atmosphere and cozy interior of this small hotel make guests forget the bustle of the city center. The bedrooms are warm and inviting, each with a bathroom fitted with a shower and separate toilet. After a peaceful night, a generous breakfast buffet is served with a choice of hot and cold dishes. The host makes sure that everything runs smoothly and offers useful information about the capital.

 19

COUVIN — C2

Couvin (Boussu-en-Fagne)

Le Manoir de la Motte $
Rue de la Motte 21, 5660
Couvin (Boussu-en-Fagne),
prov. Namen
☎ 060-34 40 13
▤ 060-34 67 17
e A small, beautiful castle surrounded by fens. From the 13th century onward it remained unchanged, until in 1689 a new owner filled in the moats and removed the drawbridge. The building can be reached via a small paved square and immediately enchants the visitor with its historic charm. A beautiful oak staircase leads to attractive, airy bedrooms with private bathrooms.

▭ 7

DIKSMUIDE — A3

Lo-Reninge

't Convent $$
Halve Reningen straat 1, 8647
Lo- Reninge, prov. West-
Vlaanderen
☎ 057-40 07 71
▤ 057-40 11 27
e couvent@itenera.be

The culinary skills of Chef Rudy Devolder are well known throughout the region, and together with his wife he has changed this former artist's property into an excellent hotel and restaurant. Especially popular are the truffle dishes. He also has his own vineyard and well-cared for kitchen garden. The bedrooms vary in style - charming luxury rooms, and spacious suites with furnishings in rustic Flemish and Venetian style.

▭ 15

DURBUY D2
Durbuy
Au Vieux Durbuy **$$**
Rue Jean de Boheme 6,
Durbury, prov.Luxemburg
☎ 086-21 32 62
🗎 086-21 24 65
e reservation@sanglier-d-ardennes.be
This exclusive hotel dates back to the 18th century and is situated in a small, pedestrianized street in the old town of Durbuy. Terracotta walls and divans placed around the open fireplace, an old wooden staircase and rustic furnishings create a charming atmosphere. Pastel-colored bedrooms have carefully selected ornaments as well as spacious bathrooms. The breakfast and the excellent dishes at dinner are served in the "Sanglier des Ardennes."

🛏 12

GESVES D2
Gesves

L'Aubergesves **$$**
Le Pourrain 4, 5340 Gesves,
prov. Namen
☎ 083-67 74 17
🗎 083-67 81 57
In the peaceful valley of the Samson, this quality hotel with old-fashioned service was formerly a farmhouse. Mr. Germay creates tasty dishes, while his wife looks after guests at mealtimes. All the rooms, which have kept their original character, blue stone floors and vaulted ceilings, can be reached via the public lounge.

🛏 6

GHENT B3
Ghent

Cours St. Georges -
St. Jorishof **$$**
Botermarkt 2, 9000 Ghend,
prov. Oost-Vlaanderen
☎ 09-224 24 24
🗎 09-224 26 40
www.hotelbel.com/cour-st-georges.htm
e courstgeorges@skynet.be
St. Jorishof, known as Cour St. Georges, has a fascinating past dating back to 1228. This is the oldest guest quarters in Europe, and the emperor Charlemagne often stayed here with his courtiers. The building boasts an imposing gothic hall with a magnificent fireplace. Most of the rooms are situated in two patrician houses on the other side of the street.

🛏 28

Ghent

La maison de Claudine **$**
Pussemierstraat 20, 9000
Ghend, prov. Oost-Vlaanderen
☎ 09-225 75 08
🗎 09-225 75 08
e maison.claudine@newmail.net
This 17th-century building lies tucked away in a small alleyway. The main building can be reached via the coach house. Books, magazines and sleeping cats create a homey atmosphere. On the first floor, the bedroom has views of the garden. The loft apartment is spacious and looks over the church spires of the city. The coach house has a separate entrance, with a lounge and bedroom on the first floor.

🛏 3

LICHTAART C4
Kasterlee
De Watermolen **$$**
Houtum 61, 2460 Kasterlee,
prov. Antwerpen
☎ 014-85 23 74
🗎 014-85 23 70
www.watermolen.be
e hotel.watermolen@club.innet.be
This water mill dates back to the 13th century, situated in beautiful, unspoiled surroundings on a small island, and has been carefully converted to a top-of-the-line restaurant and hotel. Special features of the restaurant are the painted beams and unique tiled floor. In the summer, guests can dine on the terrace in peaceful surroundings with a view of the river. The bedrooms are comfortable and have modern facilities.

🛏 18

Key to Symbols: 🗎 Fax Email Rooms Parking Swimming

Hostelerie Keravic　$$
Herentalssteenweg 72, Kasterlee
(Lichtaart), prov. Antwerpen
☎ 014-55 78 01
🖨 014-55 78 16
Half hidden between the pine forests of the Noorderkempen, the Hostellerie Keravic is situated on the edge of the woods. The lounge and restaurant have rustic furniture in a typical Flemish style with oak-beamed ceilings and terracotta tiles on the floors. The modestly furnished bedrooms are immaculate with spacious bathrooms equipped with both shower and bath. Guests are welcomed with flowers, chocolates and a complimentary fruit basket.

 9

MARCHE-EN-FAMENNE D2

Hotton (Hampteau)
Château d'Héblon　$$
Rue d'Heblon 1, 6990 Hotton (Hampteau), prov.Luxemburg
☎ 084-46 65 73
🖨 084-46 76 04
www.widehorest.be
The Château d'Héblon enjoys an excellent reputation throughout the region for its cuisine. This beautiful limestone building dates back to 1850 and was built against the backdrop of a rock wall. The bedrooms are spacious and decorated in 19th-century style. The chapel is a relic from the time it was owned by the former mayor of Bruges. The small restaurant, lounge and bar on the ground floor are furnished in keeping with the building.

🛏 9

Marche-en-Famenne

Château d'Hassonville　$$
Rue d'Hassonville 105, 6900 Marche-en-Famenne (Aye),
☎ 084-31 10 25
🖨 084-31 60 27
A combination of stone and human ingenuity resulted in the construction of the Château Hassonville, a hunting lodge built in 1687 under commission from the Sun King (Louis XIV, 1638-1715). There is a large park with the Grand Pavilion – a fairytale in glass and metal – which houses the restaurant. The quality of the dishes is exceptionally high, and the dining experience can be extended by a visit to the wine cellar. The guestrooms are furnished to a high standard.

🛏 20

MOL　**D4**

Mol-Wesel
Manoir Hippocampus　$$
Sint Jozeflaan 79, 2400 Mol-Wezel, prov. Antwerpen
☎ 014-81 08 08
🖨 014-81 45 90
The Manoir Hippocampus is situated in a peaceful village surrounded by lush, green countryside. This beautiful villa dates back to 1900 and is now a cozy hotel, where guests can enjoy the excellent culinary skills of the host and chef, Francis Scheyvaerts. The furnishings are in an English modern-classic style. Bedrooms are very attractive, spacious and stylish as well as equipped with every modern amenity.

🛏 3

NEERIJSE　**C3**

Huldenburg (Neerijse)
Kasteel van Neerijse　$$
Lindenhoflaan 1, 3040 Huidenberg (Neerijse), prov. Vlaams-Brabant
☎ 016-47 28 50
🖨 016-47 23 80
Once this castle had a water mill and a brewery, and later on it was used as a children's home and hospital. In 1983 it became Kasteel van Neerijse, an impressive hotel and restaurant. From the entrance gates a beautiful drive leads to the castle. The restaurant is well known for its excellent cuisine. This quietly situated hotel has a choice of comfortable bedrooms with views of the park.

🛏 26

Key to Symbols: 🖨 Fax Email 🛏 Rooms 🅿 Parking Swimming

NEUFCHATEAU D1

Bertrix (Biourges)

Château Les Tourelles $
Route de Neufchateau 36, 6880

Bertrix (Biourges),
prov. Luxemburg
☎ 061-41 19 09
▤ 061-41 45 32
www.dreamit.be/castles
e chat.lestourelles@skynet.be
The rustic interior of the
Château Les Tourelles is
magnificent and original. The
various objets d'art, antique
furniture and originally
decorated bedrooms, together
with a relaxed and sophisticated
atmosphere, will impress. The
cuisine is light, with a choice of
international dishes. The rooms
vary from Spanish-style furniture
to a four-poster bed to Oriental
style furnishings. A variety of
packages are offered.

🛏 9

SPA E2

Spa

La Villa de Fleurs, $
Rue Albin Body 31, 4900 Spa,
prov. Luik
☎ 087-79 50 50
▤ 087-79 50 60
www.users.skynet.be/hvdf
e hotel.vdf@skynet.be
Tastefully and sympathetically
renovated, the original style and
glamor of the 1880s have been
preserved where possible, which
gives this property an atmosphere
of elegance and serenity. The
bedrooms have modern
amenities and are equipped with
marble bathrooms. Beautiful
paintings and elegant furniture
accentuate ornate ceilings and
pastel walls. The dining rooms
overlook the garden and offer
guests the opportunity to enjoy a
meal in intimate surroundings.

🛏 12

STAVELOT E2

Stavelot (Ster-Francorchamps)

**Hostellerie Le Relais
du Crouly** $
Ster 306 A, 4970 Stavelot (Ster-
Francorchamps), prov. Luik
☎ 080-27 53 29
▤ 087-27 55 39
This beautiful house dates back
to 1870 and has vaulted ceilings,
wooden floors and oak panelling.
The restaurant's stone walls have
a country atmosphere, while the
tables are set with fine china and
cutlery and equipped with Louis
XVI-style chairs. The bedrooms
are in country style with
matching furnishings. During the
hunting festivals in October,
excellent dishes prepared with
local Belgian produce are served
by candlelight.

🛏 10

VERVIERS E3

Pépinster

Hostellerie Lafarque $$
Chemin des Douys 20, 4860
Pepinster, prov. Luik
☎ 087-460 651
▤ 087-469 728
e lafarque@relaischateaux.fr
With accolades from Michelin
and Relais de Chateaux, this
hotel has an excellent reputation.
The stylish interior comprises a
dining room decorated in pastel
colors. The elegant bedrooms are
situated on two floors and offer
comfortable accommodation.
This hotel also boasts superb
cuisine; the proprietor is
responsible for the inventive,
classic dishes prepared with only
the best possible ingredients.

🛏 6

VIEUXVILLE D2

Vieuxville

Le Château de Pologne $$
Route de Palogne 3, 4190
Vieuxville prov. Luik/Liege
☎ 086-21 38 74
▤ 086-21 38 76
www.johansens.com
e This century-old building is
situated amid mature trees and a
fishing stream, and was
constructed in the romantic style
of the late 1800s. The charming,
intimate character has been
preserved. The lounge has 19th-
century, English-style furniture.
Next to the lounge is the
breakfast area, where a large
breakfast is served in the
morning. The pleasant bedrooms
combine modern comfort with
classic elegance and have private
bathrooms equipped with a
shower or Jacuzzi.

🛏 6

Key to Symbols: Fax Email Rooms   Parking Swimming

Britain

*O*n an island barely 700 miles from tip to toe and less than 350 miles at its widest, several nations live cheek by jowl, each with its own distinct history and culture, each accommodating differences of region, dialect and tradition within its boundaries. England, Scotland and Wales, the nations of mainland Britain, share a variety of characteristics – landscapes ranging from fens to craggy peaks, and hamlets to brash industrial cities. The past is part of the scenery, whether it's a grouping of prehistoric standing stones, a Roman road, or a venerable church or cathedral.

Life beyond London

Devolving political power has emphasized the individual identities of the British nations, but the main focus of life continues to be London. The capital's attractions are well known: the historic monuments, squares and palaces, and the modern landmarks of city skyscrapers and the London Eye. But only a few miles outside the city limits you can find England at its rural best – village greens where cricket is played on summer weekends, country pubs where you can drink your warm beer by a roaring fire. The English coastline sweeps around from Cornwall's coves and rocky shoreline to the majestic white cliffs of Sussex, past the East Anglian marshes and toward the deserted northeastern coast. Inland, the cities provide architectural showplaces: Georgian elegance in Bath; the ancient university colleges of Oxford and Cambridge; half-timbered Tudor buildings in Stratford-upon-Avon; medieval York. In Manchester, Leeds, Birmingham and Liverpool, industrial growth has left a legacy of grand civic buildings and vibrant city life. Beyond the urban sprawl lie the Derbyshire peaks, the Yorkshire dales, the Lake District and the Northumbrian heights.

Wales

Some of the most striking landmarks in Wales are reminders of its conquest and rule by England: Conwy Castle, centerpiece of a preserved medieval walled town; Harlech Castle, aloof on its high hill; Caernarfon, watching over the yachts in the bay. Some have been restored in exuberant style, such as Cardiff Castle, right in the middle of the busy Welsh capital. The Welsh countryside can take the breath away, from the Snowdonia mountains of the north, to the sweeping coastline and the empty highlands of mid-Wales.

Scotland

Beyond the border country, where Robert the Bruce and Bonnie Prince Charlie fought their cause against English domination, the Scottish capital, Edinburgh, provides the nation's political and cultural focus, its planned Georgian New Town lying alongside the medieval muddle of the Old Town, and the castle presiding over everything. Less refined and proud of it, Glasgow is an exciting, robust city, full of Victorian architecture and the home of Charles Rennie Mackintosh's famous designs. Britain's most dramatic landscapes are found in the Highlands, with their mountain plateaus, deep glens and lochs, and great wilderness areas. To the far west and north is yet more spectacular mountain country, and out to sea lie the Isle of Skye and the mystical islands of the Hebrides.

Castle Combe

Britain

Accommodations

Accommodations in Britain range from the simple guest house – a room in a private house, sometimes with shared bathroom and a small breakfast room – to expensive hotels. Bed and breakfasts (B&Bs) are popular: rates usually include a breakfast of fried bacon, eggs, tomatoes and maybe sausages and baked beans, followed by toast, served with fruit juice and coffee or tea. Most hotels also offer cooked breakfasts – known as a "full" or "English" breakfast – but there may be alternatives, such as the continental breakfast (toast or croissants with butter and preserves), cereals or oatmeal. Many places provide hot and cold buffet arrangements. Some B&Bs offer an evening meal, but the menu may be limited. Many establishments, especially those in rural areas, also have self-catering accommodations available. These are often cottages or converted farm buildings with kitchens, enabling guests to cook for themselves.

Food and Drink

British food has become less stodgy and more healthy in recent years, although fish and chips are still a national favorite. Specialties include haggis (meat cooked in a sheep's stomach – tastier than it sounds), neeps and tatties (turnip and potatoes), local salmon and, of course, whisky in Scotland; Welsh lamb, leeks, cawl (a thick broth with meat, potatoes and vegetables), bara brith (a sweet, moist currant loaf best eaten with butter) and Welsh cakes (biscuit-like drop-scones, ideally served hot with sugar or butter) in Wales; and English regional items such as black pudding (blood sausage) in the north, savory or sweet Cornish pasties, and delicious tea-time treats such as Dorset apple cake, Bakewell tart or Devonshire cream teas – hot scones piled high with clotted (extra heavy) cream and jam.

C

D

E

F

ENGLAND

ALNMOUTH D4
Alnmouth

BARNSTAPLE C1
Bratton Fleming

Bracken House $$
EX31 4TG, Devon
☎ 01598 710320
🖹 01598 710115
www.brackenhousehotel.com
e holidays@brackenhouse
hotel.com
Dating back to 1840, this former
rectory has been lovingly restored

by Laurie and Prue Scott. Set in
eight acres of gardens and
grounds, Bracken House benefits
from splendid views over the
North Devon countryside. The
comfortable, well-equipped
bedrooms vary in size, and ground
floor rooms are available for the
less mobile. Interesting, home-
cooked dinners are served in the
elegant dining room, and a self-

catering cottage also is available.

🛏 8   Closed Nov.-Mar.
P 💳 💳

Croyde

Croyde Bay House $$
EX33 1PA, Devon
☎ 01271 890270
Croyde Bay House is a
charming, family-run hotel,
enjoying fine sea views from its
commanding position
overlooking Croyde Bay. The
bedrooms are thoughtfully
furnished and tastefully

decorated, with attractive decor
and pretty co-ordinating fabrics.
Public areas include a
comfortably appointed lounge, a
small bar and a sun lounge.

🛏 7
Closed mid-Nov. to Feb. 28
P 💳 💳

BATH D1
Bath

Apsley House Hotel $$
Newbridge Hill, BA1 3PT,
Somerset
☎ 01225 336966
🖹 01225 425462
www.apsley-house.co.uk
e info@apsley-house.co.uk
Located about a mile west of the
city center, this elegant Georgian
house was built for the Duke of
Wellington. The individual

bedrooms are beautifully
maintained and offer a high level
of comfort. The public areas are
spacious, elegantly furnished and
delightfully decorated. An
interesting range of breakfast
dishes is available.

🛏 9   Closed week of Dec. 25
P 💳 💳 💳

Haydon House $$
9 Bloomfield Park, BA2 2BY,
Somerset
☎ 01225 444919
🖹 01225 444919
www.bath.org/hotel/haydon.htm
e haydon.bath@btinternet.com
The spacious bedrooms are
individually and tastefully
appointed, soft color schemes
have been chosen and there are

many extra thoughtful touches.
The sumptuous living room
features some fine period
furniture and comfortable
seating. An extensive breakfast
menu is offered and includes
such delights as Scottish whisky
or rum porridge!

🛏 5
💳 💳 💳

High Buston Hall $$
High Buston, NE66 3QH,
Northumberland
☎ 01655 830606
🖹 01665 830707
www.members.aol.com/
highbuston
e highbuston@aol.com
This charming Georgian country
house offers views toward
Alnmouth and the

Northumberland coastline.
Bedrooms are well-proportioned
and adorned with period pieces.
Breakfast is taken around one
large table in the dining room,
and dinner is served by
appointment on Saturday only.
The owner, Therese Atherton, is
friendly, and this is a very
welcoming family home.

🛏 3 P

Kennard Hotel $$
11 Henrietta Street, BA2 6LL,
Somerset
☎ 01225 310472
📄 01225 460054
www.kennard.co.uk
📧 kennard@dircon.co.uk
This delightful town house is
ideally located within easy
walking distance of the city
center. Some bedrooms benefit
from splendid views of the city.
All rooms are comfortably
equipped with modern facilities.
A choice of English or
Continental breakfast is offered
in an attractive, stylish dining
room. Service is both friendly
and professional.

🛏 13 Closed Dec. 25-Jan. 1

Leighton House $$
139 Wells Road, BA2 3AL,
Somerset
☎ 01225 314769
📄 01225 443079
www.leighton-house.co.uk
📧 welcome@leighton-
house.co.uk
Built in the 1870s, Leighton
House is a wonderful example of
Victorian splendor close to the
city center. Bedrooms are
thoughtfully equipped and
individually decorated, and two
are located at ground floor level.
Breakfast is served in the
attractive dining room, which
overlooks the neatly tended
gardens.

🛏 8

Paradise House Hotel $$
Holloway, BA2 4PX, Somerset
☎ 01225 317723
📄 01225 482005
www.paradise-house.co.uk
📧 info@paradise-house.co.uk
This Georgian house was built
in 1720 from Bath stone. Many
bedrooms have fine views, and
all are decorated in opulent style.
Furnishings are elegant and
facilities modern. The lounge is
comfortable and relaxing, and
breakfast is served in the
attractive dining room.
Hospitality and service here are
friendly and professional.

🛏 10
Closed 3 days Xmas

Villa Magdala Hotel $$
Henrietta Road, BA2 6LX,
Somerset
☎ 01225 466329
📄 01225 483207
www.VillaMagdala.co.uk
📧 office@VillaMagdala.co.uk
A gracious and stylish Victorian
town house, Villa Magdala is a
short walk from the many and
varied city sights. Pleasant views
can be enjoyed from the
attractively furnished and
spacious bedrooms, all of which
are equipped to meet the
demands of any visitor. The
charming lounge and dining
room overlook one of Bath's
delightful parks.

🛏 17

Box

Cheney Cottage $
Ditteridge, SN13 8QF,
Wiltshire
☎ 01225 742346
📄 01225 742346
www.visitus.co.uk/bath/hotel/
cheney.htm
📧 cheneycottage@btinternet.com
Warm hospitality awaits guests
at this charming thatched house,
set in extensive well-tended
gardens with beautiful views of
the Box Valley. The rooms are all
attractively decorated and
equipped with such thoughtful
extras as shoe-cleaning kits,
cookies and fresh flowers. In the
old stable block, there are three
well-furnished en suite rooms.

🛏 6 Closed Dec.-Jan.

Key to Symbols: 📄 Fax 📧 Email 🛏 Rooms 🅿 Parking 🏊 Swimming
American Express Diners Club MasterCard Visa

Bradford-on-Avon

Burghope Manor $$
Winsley, BA15 2LA, Wiltshire
☎ 01225 723557
🖹 01225 723113
www.burghopemanor.co.uk
🅴 burghope.manor@virgin.net
Burghope Manor is a beautiful
13th-century manor house where
the day rooms have a very
pleasing atmosphere and still
reflect their full historic

character. Bedrooms, some in the
Dower House in the garden, are
all equipped with modern
facilities and comforts. Enjoyable
English breakfasts are served in
the spacious dining room.

🛏 6
Closed Dec. 25-Jan. 1
🅿 ▪️ 💳 💳

Norton St. Philip

The Plaine $$
Bell Hill, BA3 6LT, Somerset
☎ 01373 834723
🖹 01373 834101
www.theplaine.com
🅴 theplaine@easynet.co.uk
Dating from the 16th century,
this charming family home is
located in a peaceful village not
far from Bath. The tastefully
decorated and well-equipped

bedrooms all have four-poster
beds. Breakfast is served around
a large table family-style, and
although dinner is not available,
there are a number of good inns
nearby.

🛏 3
Closed Dec. 24-26
🅿 💳 💳

BOSTON E3

Holbeach

Pipwell Manor $
Washway Road, Saracens Head,
PE12 8AL, Lincolnshire
☎ 01406 423119
🖹 01406 423119
This period farmhouse sits in
beautiful grounds that feature a
miniature railroad with original
steam engines that runs around

the garden. The tastefully
furnished public rooms include
an attractive dining room and a
comfortable lounge with books
and TV. The bedrooms are
individually decorated and
delightfully furnished with well-
chosen pieces.

🛏 4 🅿

Lincoln

Minster Lodge Hotel $$
3 Church Lane, LN2 1QJ,
Lincolnshire
☎ 01522 513220
🖹 01522 513220
www.minsterlodge.com
🅴 minsterlodge@compuserve.
com
Expect a warm welcome at this
privately owned hotel just a short

walk from the city center.
Bedrooms are individually
decorated and furnished with
handmade pine furniture.
Breakfast is served at separate
tables in the attractive dining
room, and guests also have the
use of a comfortable lounge.

🛏 6

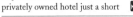

🅿 ▪️ 💳 💳

BOURNEMOUTH D1

Ringwood

Little Forest Lodge $
Poulner Hill, BH24 3HS,
Hampshire
☎ 01425 478848
🖹 01425 473564
This charming Edwardian
house, set in two acres of gardens
and woodland, offers high
standards of hospitality and
comfort. Bedrooms are
pleasantly decorated and

equipped with thoughtful extras.
Enjoyable home-cooked food is
served in the attractive wood-
paneled dining room. There is a
light and airy lounge with a
small bar and a wood-burning
fire.

🛏 6
🅿 💳 💳

BRIDLINGTON E3
Wold Newton

The Wold Cottage $
YO25 3HL, East Riding of
Yorkshire
☎ 01262 470696
▤ 01262 470696
e woldcott@wold-
newton.freeserve.co.uk
Set in open Wold countryside
with extensive views, this
Georgian house has been
skillfully restored and furnished.
Bedrooms are very comfortable
and spacious; one has a four-
poster bed and spa bath. Good
home-cooked evening meals (by
arrangement) are served in the
charming dining-room and full
use is made of local free-range
produce. A monument marks the
spot where a meteorite landed in
1795.

BRIGHTON E1
Arundel

Bonham's Country House $$
Barnham Road, Yapton,
BN18 0DX, West Sussex
☎ 01243 551301
▤ 01243 551301
Built in 1746, this delightful
house is run by Rodney and
Judith Dodd. Spacious bedrooms
are attractively decorated and
thoughtfully equipped. Guests
can relax in the comfortable
lounge and enjoy good home
cooking in the oak-paneled
dining room. A good range of
leisure facilities is available, and
sailing on a yacht can also be
arranged.

 3

BRISTOL D2
Bristol

Westbury Park Hotel $
37 Westbury Road, Westbury-
on-Trym, BS9 3AU, Bristol
☎ 0117 962 0465
▤ 0117 962 8607
Situated by the famous
Durdham Downs, this attractive
Victorian property offers
pleasantly decorated
accommodations with all-
modern comforts. Drinks are
served from a small bar in the
lounge, and at breakfast there is a
choice of cooked dishes served in
a stylishly furnished dining
room.

BUDE C1
Boscastle

**Tolcarne House Hotel &
Restaurant** $
Tintagel Road, PL35 0AS,
Cornwall
☎ 01840 250654
▤ 01840 250654
www.milford.co.uk/go/tolcarne.
html
e crown@tolhouse.eclipse.co.uk
Guests are assured of a warm
welcome from Margaret and
Graham Crown at their
charming Victorian residence.
The well-equipped bedrooms are
stylishly decorated. On cooler
evenings, an open fire burns in
the lounge; in addition, there is a
separate bar/lounge. A choice of
menus is offered in the elegant
dining room.

Crackington Haven

Manor Farm $$
Crackington Haven, EX23 0JW,
Cornwall
☎ 01840 230304
Set in beautiful gardens and
grounds, this charming manor
house enjoys splendid views over
the surrounding countryside.
Each bedroom is individually
furnished and elegantly
decorated. Delicious dinners (by
prior arrangement) are served
"dinner party style" around one
large table, and make use of fresh
local produce, prepared and
presented with great skill and
care. A self-service bar is
available in one of the cozy
lounges.

Trevigue Farm $
EX23 0LQ, Cornwall
☎ 01840 230418
🖹 01840 230418
Dating back to the 16th century, this National Trust farmhouse has been personally run by the Crocker family for many years. The well-furnished bedrooms retain many original features. The cozy lounges have Oriental rugs scattered over the flagstone floors, and log fires. Interesting meals are served in the converted barn or the farmhouse dining room; breakfast boasts home-produced bacon and many other items.

🛏 6
Closed 3 days around Dec. 25
P 🏧 VISA

Holsworthy

Clawford Vineyard $
Clawton, EX22 6PN, Devon
☎ 01409 254177
🖹 01409 254177
www.clawford.demon.co.uk
🅴 john.ray@clawford.co.uk
Situated in the peaceful Claw Valley, Clawford is a working vineyard and cider orchard. The spacious bedrooms are very well furnished and equipped, with the majority overlooking lakes and orchards. Public areas, including a comfortable lounge, spacious bar and gameroom benefit from similar views. Extensive fishing is available.

🛏 11
P 🏧 VISA

Tintagel

Polkerr Guest House $
PL34 0BY, Cornwall
☎ 01840 770382
Lavished with care from owners Robert and June Fry, Polkerr is a substantial stone house within easy walking distance of the center of Tintagel. The attractively decorated bedrooms are comfortable and thoughtfully furnished. Similarly, the groundfloor public areas, which include an elegant dining room and a sunny conservatory, are well presented and comfortable.

🛏 7
Closed Dec. 25
P

BURY ST. EDMUNDS E2

Beyton
Manorhouse $
The Green, IP30 9A, Suffolk
☎ 01359 270960
www.beyton.com
🅴 manorhouse@beyton.com
Quietly located in beautifully landscaped gardens overlooking the village green, this 16th-century former farmhouse retains such original features as exposed beams and open fireplaces. Bedrooms are tastefully decorated and individually furnished with period furniture. Memorable breakfasts are served in the elegant dining room, and guests also can enjoy the inviting hall lounge with its wood-burning stove.

🛏 4 P

Bury St. Edmunds
Twelve Angel Hill $$
12 Angel Hill, IP33 1UZ, Suffolk
☎ 01284 704088
🖹 01284 725549
Guests can expect a warm, friendly welcome at this elegant Georgian town house, situated close to the cathedral and within easy walking distance of the town center. The individual bedrooms are tastefully furnished with period pieces and have extra facilities such as pants presses, books and mineral water. There is a Tudor-style bar, a cozy lounge and an elegant breakfast room where guests can choose from an extensive menu.

🛏 6   Closed Jan.

P 💳 🄳 🏧 VISA

Key to Symbols: 🖹 Fax 🅴 Email 🛏 Rooms P Parking 🏊 Swimming
💳 American Express 🄳 Diners Club 🏧 MasterCard VISA Visa

BUXTON D3

Buxton

Grendon Guest House $
Bishops Lane, SK17 6UN,
Derbyshire
☎ 01298 79257
🖹 01298 79257
www.b-bbuxton.com
e freeserve@grendon
guesthouse.freeserve.co.uk
Grendon is a large Edwardian house standing in an acre of well-tended grounds, overlooking beautiful countryside. The bedrooms are particularly spacious and well-equipped, and include one room with a four-poster bed. Public rooms are comfortable and relaxing, and good home cooking is provided. The breakfast menu offers a wide variety. Friendly and personal service from the resident owners is guaranteed.

🛏 3 P 💳 💳

CARLISLE D4

Longtown

Bessiestown Farm Country Guest House $
Catlowdy, CA6 5QP, Cumbria
☎ 01228 577219
🖹 01228 577219
e bestbt2000@cs.com
John and Margaret Sisson have been welcoming guests to their delightful farmhouse for nearly 30 years. Comfortable bedrooms have many thoughtful touches, and there are several lounges in which guests can relax. A more recent addition is the luxury "Dove Cote" suite, furnished to the highest standards, with a king-sized four-poster bed, lounge area and spa bath.

🛏 5 P 🏊 💳 💳

CHELTENHAM D2

Blockley

Lower Brook House $$
Lower Street, GL56 9DS,
Gloucestershire
☎ 01386 700286
🖹 01386 700286
e lowerbrookhouse@cs.com
Located in pretty gardens at the edge of the village, Lower Brook House dates from the 17th century and retains much of its original charm, including polished flagstone floors, inglenook fireplaces and exposed beams. Imaginative dinners and comprehensive English breakfasts are eaten in the cozy but elegant dining room. Bedrooms are equipped with lots of thoughtful extras.

🛏 6
P 💳 💳

Cheltenham

Cleeve Hill Hotel $$
Cleeve Hill, GL52 3PR,
Gloucestershire
☎ 01242 672052
🖹 01242 679969
www.smoothhound.co.uk/hotels
/cleeve.html
e gbtoncleevehill@aol.com
This elegant hotel stands in a commanding position overlooking the Malvern Hills and Cotswold countryside. Bedrooms are well-equipped, with lots of thoughtful extras and excellent facilities. Spacious public rooms include a conservatory dining area, where guests can enjoy breakfast.

🛏 9
P 💳 💳

Georgian House $$
77 Montpellier Terrace,
GL50 1XA, Gloucestershire
☎ 01242 515577
🖹 01242 545929
www.smoothhound.co.uk/
hotels/geohse.html
e georgian_house@yahoo.com
Rich colors and fabrics have been used to create luxurious and comfortable accommodations at this beautiful Georgian town house. A complimentary glass of wine or beer welcomes guests to the house, and a very good choice of dishes is available at breakfast.

🛏 3
Closed Dec. 25-Jan. 1

💳 💳 💳 💳

Key to Symbols: 🖹 Fax e Email 🛏 Rooms P Parking 🏊 Swimming
💳 American Express 💳 Diners Club 💳 MasterCard 💳 Visa

Lypiatt House $$
Lypiatt Road, GL50 2QW,
Gloucestershire
☎ 01242 224994
🖷 01242 224996
Set in the Tivoli area, close to
fashionable Montpellier, this
early Victorian house offers
quality accommodation.
Bedrooms are spacious, and all
have a modern en suite bath or
shower room. Public areas retain
many original features, and the
living room has an extension
with a self-service bar.

🛏 10
🅿 ▦ ● ▦

Chipping Campden

The Malt House $$
Broad Campden, GL55 6UU,
Gloucestershire
☎ 01386 840295
🖷 01386 841334
www.malt-house.co.uk
🅴 nick@the-malt-
house.freeserve.co.uk
This elegant 17th-century house
and restaurant retains many of its
original features, including
exposed beams, leaded windows,
open fireplaces and wooden
paneling, providing excellent
accommodation together with
award-winning cuisine.
Bedrooms are comfortable, well-
equipped and furnished to reflect
the style of the house.

🛏 8   Closed Dec. 25-26

🅿 ▦ ◉ ● ▦

Guiting Power

Guiting Guest House $$
GL54 5TZ, Gloucestershire
☎ 01451 850470
🖷 01451 850034
freespace.virgin.net/guiting.
guest_house/
🅴 guiting.guest_house@virgin.
net
Dating back to the 16th century
and set in the unspoiled village of
Guiting Power, this beautiful
farmhouse retains many original
features, including oak beams,
inglenook fireplaces and polished
wooden floors. Bedrooms are
spacious, comfortable and
attractively decorated, all with a
wealth of extra touches. Breakfast
and dinner demonstrate flair and
imagination.

🛏 4   ● ▦

Winchcombe

Wesley House $$
High Street, GL54 5LJ,
Gloucestershire
☎ 01242 602366
🖷 01242 602405
www.wesleyhouse.co.uk
A popular restaurant is the focal
point of Wesley House, a 15th-
century, half-timbered building,
on the main street of this quaint
town. Menus offer an interesting
selection of award-winning
cuisine at dinner. Rooms, varying
in size, are individually
decorated, furnished and
equipped to a high standard. A
lounge/bar area, complete with
exposed stone walls and painted
beams, is the place for pre-dinner
drinks and afternoon tea.

🛏 5   Closed Jan. 14-Feb. 10

▦ ● ▦

Chester

Redland Private Hotel $$
64 Hough Green, CH4 8JY,
Cheshire
☎ 01244 671024
🖷 01244 681309
This delightful hotel has been
carefully and tastefully restored
to its former Victorian splendor.
Rooms are individually styled,
many with antique four-poster
and half-tester beds. Bathrooms
are spacious and appointed to a
high standard. Public areas
include a self-service bar and a
spacious drawing room, as well
as a sauna, solarium and laundry
room.

🛏 13
🅿 ▦ ● ▦

CIRENCESTER D2

Burford

Burford House **$$**
99 High Street, OX18 4QA,
Oxfordshire
☎ 01993 823151
🖷 01993 823240
www.burford-house.co.uk
🄴 stage@burfordhouse.co.uk
In the heart of this famous
Cotswold town, Burford House,
with its half-timbered and
mellow stone exterior, is a haven
for travelers. Bedrooms are
charming and include
thoughtful, homey extras. Two
comfortable lounges with roaring
log fires create a welcoming
feeling, and superb breakfasts
and light meals are served in the
dining room. The Hentys are
caring and attentive hosts who
ensure that a visit to their home
is a happy and memorable one.

🛏 7   American Express MasterCard Visa

Tetbury

Tavern House **$$**
Willesley, GL8 8QU,
Gloucestershire
☎ 01666 880444
🖷 01666 880254
www.ukbusiness.com/
tavernhousehotel
🄴 tavernhousehotel@
ukbusiness.com
This former inn, dating back to
the 17th century, has been
sympathetically restored to
provide accommodations of the
highest standard. Bedrooms are
individually decorated, well-
equipped and very comfortable.
The house retains all of its
original features including a fine
open fireplace, oak beams and an
idyllic walled garden providing a
perfect retreat.

🛏 4   P MasterCard Visa

COLCHESTER E2

Manningtree

Aldhams **$**
Bromley Road, Lawford,
CO11 2NE, Essex
☎ 01206 393210
🖷 01206 393210
🄴 coral.mcewen3@which.net
Located a short distance from
the village, this impressive
Lutyens-style house is set in
three acres of well-kept gardens
and surrounded by open
countryside. Bedrooms are
tastefully furnished and
decorated, and offer a number of
thoughtful extras. Guests can
also relax in the lovely, spacious
lounge with fireplace. Breakfast
is served in an attractive dining
room overlooking the gardens
beyond.

🛏 3   Closed Dec. 24-Jan. 2   P

Wix

Dairy House Farm **$$**
Bradfield Road, CO11 2SR,
Essex
☎ 01255 870322
🖷 01255 870186
Surrounded by 700 acres of
farmland, this sympathetically
converted Victorian farmhouse
offers all the peace of the
countryside, yet is within easy
reach of the port of Harwich and
the historic town of Colchester.
Bedrooms are tastefully furnished
and decorated, spacious and have
a good range of facilities.
Breakfast is served in the
attractive dining room, which
features an impressive mahogany
table, and there also is a
comfortable lounge with facilities
for making tea and coffee.

🛏 3   P

CRAWLEY E1

Horley

Vulcan Lodge Guest House **$**
27 Massetts Road, RH6 7DQ,
Surrey
☎ 01293 771522
🖷 01293 786206
www.vulcan-lodge.com
🄴 reservations@vulcan-
lodge.co.uk
This charming period house set
back from the main road is
convenient to Gatwick Airport.
Colin and Karen Moon, your
hosts, are friendly and ensure a
warm welcome. Bedrooms are all
individually decorated, well-
equipped and feature many
thoughtful extras. There is a
comfortable lounge, and
breakfast is served in a delightful
dining room.

🛏 4   P American Express MasterCard Visa

Key to Symbols: 🖷 Fax 🄴 Email 🛏 Rooms P Parking 🏊 Swimming
American Express Diners Club MasterCard Visa

DARLINGTON   D4

Darlington

Belper

Dannah Farm Country Guest House   **$$**
Bowmans Lane, Shottle,
DE56 2DR, Derbyshire
☎ 01773 550273
▤ 01773 550590
e reservations@dannah.
demon.co.uk
This 18th-century farmhouse is

DERBY   D3

Doveridge

Ilkeston

The Redhouse   **$$**
Wharncliffe Road, DE7 5GF,
Derbyshire
☎ 0115932 2965
▤ 0115 932 1253
www.ilkeston.u-net/redhouse
e info@theredhouse.net
Located on a leafy avenue close
to the historic market square,
this impressive red brick late

Matlock

Clow Beck House   **$$**
Monk End Farm, Croft on Tees,
DL2 2SW, County Durham
☎ 01325 721075
▤ 01325 720419
www.clowbeckhouse.co.uk
e heather@clowbeckhouse.co.uk
This impressive house stands in
attractive, well-tended gardens
and forms part of a working
farm. Most bedrooms are

still a working farm. Bedrooms
are comfortably furnished and
attractive, with good use of
colorful, soft furnishings and
decor. In addition to the lounge
bar there are two comfortable
lounges, one with a self-service
bar. Breakfasts are delicious,
using free-range eggs, organic
sausages and fresh homemade
bread.

Beeches Farmhouse   **$$**
Waldley, DE6 5LR, Derbyshire
☎ 01889 832602
▤ 01889 590559
e beechesfa@aol.com
This 18th-century farmhouse
offers a genuine taste of the
country not only in its location,
but also in the food that is
served. Barbara Tunnicliffe
spends much time researching

Victorian house retains many
original features which are
enhanced by quality decor.
Bedrooms have an individual
artist's theme and all are very
well-equipped. Breakfast is
served in the spacious lower
ground floor dining room; there
also is a very well stocked lounge
bar.

Robertswood Guest House   **$**
Farley Hill, DE4 3LL,
Derbyshire
☎ 01629 55642
▤ 01629 55642
e robertswood@supanet.com
Located north of town, this large
Victorian house stands in an
elevated position enjoying superb
views across the Derwent Valley.
There is a spacious lounge, and

contained in separate buildings.
All rooms are superbly decorated
and furnished, and are equipped
with a host of thoughtful extras.
A luxurious lounge is provided in
the house, and imaginative meals
are served in the stylish,
traditional dining room.

🛏 14
P ▦ 💳 💳

🛏 8   Closed Dec. 25-26
P 💳 💳 💳

old country recipes to make the
most of the fresh produce
available. Bedrooms are
comfortable and attractively
furnished, with many extras
including fruit, flowers and
delicious homemade cookies.

🛏 10
Closed Dec. 24-26
P ▦ 💳 💳

🛏 7   **P** 💳 💳

breakfast is served in the elegant,
attractively furnished dining
room.

🛏 8
P 💳 💳

Winster

The Dower House $
Main Street, DE4 2DH,
Derbyshire
☎ 01629 650931
🗎 01629 650932
www.smoothhound.co.uk/
hotels/dowerhou
📧 dowerhousederby@aol.com
This charming 16th-century
country house is set in a south-
facing walled garden. The

tastefully appointed, comfortable
and spacious bedrooms and the
beamed living room reflect the
character of the house. The
dining room has oak tables
where a hearty breakfast and, on
some evenings, delectable
dinners are served.

🛏 3 🅿

DORCHESTER   D1

Bettiscombe

Marshwood Manor $
DT6 5NS, Dorset
☎ 01308 868442
Friendly resident proprietors
warmly welcome guests to this,
their home and fine Victorian
manor house, built in 1853 and
set in 10 acres of gardens. With
the croquet lawn and putting
green, there is plenty to do in
addition to exploring the Dorset

countryside. Bedrooms are
prettily decorated and furnished
and both the lounge and dining
room are spacious and
comfortable. Good home-
cooked meals are served, with
traditional puddings a specialty.

🛏 6
Closed Dec-Jan
🅿

Dorchester

The Casterbridge Hotel $$
49 High East Street, DT1 1HU,
Dorset
☎ 01305 264043
🗎 01305 260884
www.casterbridgehotel.co.uk
📧 reception@casterbridgehotel.
co.uk
The hotel dates from the
Georgian period and is a short

walk from the town center.
Bedrooms, some of which are
situated off a concealed
courtyard annex, are well-
maintained and comfortable.
Public rooms consist of a
bar/library, a gracious living
room, and a dining room and
conservatory where a particularly
good breakfast is provided.
🛏 14 Closed Dec. 25-26

🔲 🔘 🔲 🔲

**Yalbury Cottage Hotel &
Restaurant** $$
Lower Bockhampton,
DT2 8PZ, Dorset
☎ 01305 262382
🗎 01305 266412
www.smoothhound.co.uk/
hotels/yalbury
📧 yalbury.cottage@virgin.net
Originally the home of the local
shepherd and keeper of the water

meadows, Yalbury Cottage is a
period thatched property in the
beautiful, rural hamlet of Lower
Bockhampton. The oak beamed
ceilings, inglenook fireplaces and
stone walls are features in both
the lounge and restaurant - the
ideal venue in which to enjoy the
hotel's award-winning cuisine.
Bedrooms overlook the colorful
gardens or adjacent fields.

🛏 8 Closed Dec. 28-Feb. 1
🅿 🔲 🔲

Weymouth

Bay Lodge Hotel $$
27 Greenhill,
DT4 7SW, Dorset
☎ 01305 782419
🗎 01305 782828
www.baylodge.co.uk
📧 barbara@baylodge.co.uk
Bay Lodge is situated in a quiet
location on the edge of town.
The dining room and lounge bar
have panoramic sea views, with

log fires burning during cooler
months. Bedrooms, in the main
house and adjacent annex, are
well-equipped, and are
appointed with attractive co-
ordinated fabrics. Some jacuzzi
bathrooms are available.

🛏 12
🅿 🔲 🔘 🔲 🔲

Key to Symbols: 🗎 Fax 📧 Email 🛏 Rooms 🅿 Parking 🏊 Swimming
🔲 American Express 🔘 Diners Club 🔲 MasterCard 🔲 Visa

Weymouth

Esplanade Hotel $$
141 The Esplanade, DT4 7NJ, Dorset
☎ 01305 783129

Owners Kathy and Len Paul provide caring hospitality at their attractive Georgian property located on the oceanfront. Most of the bedrooms enjoy ocean views, and although the rooms vary in size, they are particularly well furnished and attractively decorated, and include many thoughtful extras. There is a first-floor lounge overlooking the bay.

🛏 11
Closed Nov.-Mar.
🅿

DURHAM D4
Fir Tree
Greenhead Country House Hotel $$
DL15 8BL, County Durham
☎ 01388 763143
🖹 01388 763143

This smart and stylish house at the foot of the Weardale Valley is set in well-tended gardens. Bedrooms are spacious and modern, and all have been carefully equipped and comfortably furnished. Public rooms include a 50-foot-long beamed and stone-arched lounge. There is also a well-stocked bar.

🅿 🟦 ⓓ 💳 🔲

EASTBOURNE E1
Arlington

Bates Green $$
BN26 6SH, East Sussex
☎ 01323 482039
🖹 01323 482039

This restored 18th-century gamekeeper's cottage has individually furnished bedrooms, decorated in cottage style and equipped with extras such as mineral water and flowers. Guests can use the gardens and comfortable lounge, which has a log fire in winter. An extensive choice of breakfast items is provided in the cozy dining room.

🛏 3
Closed Dec. 22-27
🅿

Wilmington

Crossways Hotel $$
Lewes Road, BN26 5SG, East Sussex
☎ 01323 482455
🖹 01323 487811
✉ crosways@fastnet.co.uk

Under the perpetual scrutiny of the Neolithic "Long Man of Wilmington" this country hotel prides itself on the quality of its cuisine. Bedrooms, individually furnished and decorated to a high standard, feature an excellent range of facilities. Resident proprietors, David Stott and Clive James are well known for their superb hospitality.

🛏 7 Closed Dec. 24-Jan. 23
🅿 🟦 💳 🔲

ELY E2
Ely
Hill House Farm $
9 Main Street, Coveney, CB6 2DJ, Cambridgeshire
☎ 01353 778369

This charming Victorian farmhouse is situated in the delightful village of Coveney. The bedrooms are part of the main house. Each room has its own separate entrance, a bright appearance, and is thoughtfully equipped with useful extras. The public rooms feature a comfortably furnished living room and a separate dining room.

🛏 3
Closed Dec. 25

🅿 💳 🔲

Key to Symbols: 🖹 Fax ✉ Email 🛏 Rooms 🅿 Parking 🌊 Swimming
🟦 American Express ⓓ Diners Club 💳 MasterCard 🔲 Visa

EXETER C1

Exeter

The Edwardian $
30/32 Heavitree Road,
EX1 2LQ, Devon
☎ 01392 276102
🖷 01392 253393
e edwardex@globalnet.co.uk

Within walking distance of the city center, this attractive Edwardian terraced property offers stylish bedrooms – well-equipped, tastefully decorated and furnished in "period" style, some with four-posters. Books and local tourist information are provided in the comfortable lounge, where many personal touches and ornaments also are displayed.

🛏 12
Closed Dec. 25
P

Moretonhampstead

Blackaller Hotel & Restaurant $$
North Bovey, TQ13 8QY, Devon
☎ 01647 440322
🖷 01647 441131
httpc//ourworks.cs.com/ukblac
kaller

Enjoying the most tranquil of settings, Blackaller, a 17th-century woollen mill, is named after the black alder trees which grow along the nearby riverbanks. Bedrooms are spacious and comfortably furnished. The attractive dining room has an inglenook fireplace and exposed granite walls. The daily-changing menu features local produce; don't miss the honey, yogurt and muesli.

🛏 6   Closed Jan. & Feb. P

Whimple

Woodhayes Country House and Cottage $$
EX5 2TD, Devon
☎ 01404 822237
🖷 01404 822337
www.woodhayes-hotel.co.uk
e info@woodhayes-hotel.co.uk

Tucked away in the country, Woodhayes is a charming Georgian house. There are two tastefully decorated drawing rooms with open fires, in addition to an attractive farmhouse-style bar. Interesting and freshly prepared homecooking is served. The bedrooms are comfortable and spacious.

🛏 6
P

GUERNSEY E5

St. Peter Port

Midhurst House $
Candie Road, GY1 1OP,
Guernsey
☎ 01481 724391
🖷 01481 729451
freespace.virgin.net/midhurst.
house
e midhurst.house@virgin.net

This elegant Regency house is a 5-minute walk from the harbor and town center. The bedrooms are all individual in style, with many thoughtful touches such as fresh flowers and mineral water. Day rooms include a comfortable lounge lit by an unusual octagonal skylight. Pre-dinner drinks can be enjoyed in the walled garden before sampling the delicious homecooking.

🛏 6   Closed mid-Oct. to Easter

HASTINGS E1

Hastings & St. Leonards

Bryn-y-Mor $
12 Godwin Road, TN35 5JR,
East Sussex
☎ 01424 722744
🖷 01424 445933

This was built as a Victorian gentleman's residence and restored in keeping with the period. Original light fixtures and stained-glass windows are complemented by paintings and ornaments. Guests can enjoy a drink from the self-service bar while taking in the rooftop views of Old Hastings and the sea beyond. The lounge, which doubles as the breakfast room, leads to the terraced gardens. Bedrooms combine antique furniture and four-poster beds with modern amenities and smart facilities.

🛏 4

Key to Symbols: 🖷 Fax e Email 🛏 Rooms P Parking ⛱ Swimming American Express ◎ Diners Club MasterCard Visa

Herstmonceux

Wartling Place $$

Wartling Place, Wartling,
BN27 1RY, East Sussex
☎ 01323 832590
🖹 01323 831558
www.countryhouseaccomodation.
co.uk
e accom@wartlingplace.
prestel.co.uk

A superb, Grade II listed country home, set in two acres of mature, secluded gardens. Beautifully restored, with period furnishings, this guest house offers luxurious, individually decorated bedrooms and four-poster beds. Each room offers a range of extra facilities. This is an ideal base for exploring the castles, gardens and National Trust houses of Sussex and Kent.

🛏 3 🅿 ▦ 💳 💳

Rye

Cadborough $

Udimore Road, TN31 6AA,
East Sussex
☎ 01797 225426
🖹 01797 224097
www.marcomm.co.uk/
cadborough/
e apperly@marcomm.demon.
co.uk

Cadborough Farm was rebuilt in 1952 on the foundations of a 17th-century farmhouse. In an excellent location on the outskirts of Rye, it enjoys magnificent views across the Brede Valley toward the sea. Bedrooms are spacious and comfortable, and come with thoughtful extras such as fresh flowers, candies, home-made cookies, books and magazines.

🛏 3 Closed Dec. 24-26, Dec. 31-Jan. 1
🅿 💳 💳

Jeake's House $$

Mermaid Street, TN31 7ET,
East Sussex
☎ 01797 222828
🖹 01797 222623
www.rye-tourism.co.uk/jeakes/
e jeakeshouse@btinternet.com

Originally a wool store and later a Baptist school, the house stands on an ancient cobbled street. Bedrooms combine traditional elegance and comfort with modern amenities and thoughtful extras. Public rooms offer a high standard of comfort, and include an oak-beamed lounge and book-lined bar. Breakfast is served in the elegant galleried former chapel.

🛏 12
🅿 💳 💳

King Charles II Guest House $

4 High Street, TN31 7JE,
East Sussex
☎ 01797 224954

Known locally as the Black Boy (due to its association with King Charles II, a frequent visitor) this medieval building dates back to 1420 and in the 1930s was home to novelist Radclyffe Hall. The public rooms boast old black beams and ancient brick fireplaces made homey by fresh flowers and plants, and the bedrooms combine character and charm with modern convenience. There also is a tiny, flower-filled walled garden patio. Dinner is not available, but the owners are happy to recommend local restaurants, as well as advise on local history and places of interest. There is restricted on-street parking opposite the house.

🛏 3

Manor Farm Oast $

Workhouse Lane, TN36 4AJ,
East Sussex
☎ 01424 813787
🖹 01424 813787
e manor.farm.oast@lineone.
net

Surrounded by orchards, this mid-19th century house is set in a peaceful, rural location. Bedrooms are attractively decorated and have been tastefully converted to preserve the original features of the building. There are lots of thoughtful extras such as bathrobes, homemade cookies, bottled water and fresh flowers. Owner Kate Mylrea offers a very warm welcome and guests can enjoy tea and homemade cake in one of the two lounges.

🛏 3 Closed Dec. 28-Jan. 31
🅿 💳 💳

Key to Symbols: 🖹 Fax   **e** Email   🛏 Rooms   🅿 Parking   🏊 Swimming
💳 American Express   💳 Diners Club   💳 MasterCard   💳 Visa

Rye

The Old Vicarage Guest House $
66 Church Square, TN31 7HF, East Sussex
☎ 01797 222119
🖹 01797 227466
homepages.tesco.net/~oldvicaragerye/html
📧 oldvicaragerye@tesco.net

Ask any local where the "Pink House on the Square" is and it will be evident that you are seeking the Old Vicarage Guest House. Personally run by Julia and Paul Masters, guests can be assured of a warm and friendly stay. Each bedroom is individually designed and decorated with Laura Ashley fabrics and prints. Breakfast offers a great start to the day with homemade preserves, bread, local produce and Paul's renowned scones.

🛏 5   Closed Dec. 24-26   🅿

HEREFORD   D2

Fownhope

The Bowens Country House $
HR1 4PS, Herefordshire
☎ 01432 860430
🖹 01432 860430

Situated on two acres of grounds, that include a putting green and tennis court, this former 17th-century farmhouse retains many original features. Bedrooms are comfortable, well-equipped and homey and all have the benefit of modern en suite facilities, some including showers. Public areas include a living room with self-service bar (you keep track of what you've had and owe) and a cozy dining room.

🛏 10
🅿 💳 💳

Leominster

Hills Farm $
Leysters, HR6 0HP, Herefordshire
☎ 01568 750205
🖹 01568 750306
📧 conolly@bigwig.net

Situated in an idyllic, elevated location, parts of this property date from the 16th century, and many original features are retained. Bedrooms, in the main house and converted barns, are spacious yet homey. Dinner and English breakfasts are served in the dining room and conservatory. Adjacent is a comfortable living room with a woodburning stove.

🛏 5
Closed Nov.-Feb.
🅿 💳 💳

Ross-On-Wye

Lumleys $
Kern Bridge, Bishopswood, HR9 5QT, Herefordshire

☎ 01600 890040
🖹 0870 7062378
www.lumleys.force9.co.uk/
📧 helen@lumleys.force9.co.uk

Lumleys is a former Victorian roadside hostelry which has been transformed into a guest house while retaining much of its original character. Bedrooms are comfortable, well-equipped, tastefully decorated and filled with lots of extra personal touches to make guests feel at home. A room with a four-poster bed and its own patio area is available. Public areas are spacious and have some fine period pieces and ornaments. Separate tables are provided in the dining room.

🛏 3   🅿

HEXHAM   D3

Falstone

Pheasant Inn $$
Stannersburn, NE48 1DD, Northumberland
☎ 01434 240382
🖹 01434 240382
📧 thepheasantinn@kielderwater.demon.co.uk

This charming inn retains the character of a country pub while providing comfortable, modern accommodations, all contained around an adjoining courtyard. Originally a farmhouse, it features stone walls and low beamed ceilings in the bars. Delicious home-cooked meals are served there, or in pretty pine-furnished dining room.

🛏 11   Closed Dec. 25-26   🅿 💳 💳

Key to Symbols: 🖹 Fax 📧 Email 🛏 Rooms 🅿 Parking 🏊 Swimming
💳 American Express 💳 Diners Club 💳 MasterCard 💳 Visa

Hexham

Dene House $
Juniper, NE46 1SJ,
Northumberland
☎ 01434 673413
🖨 01434 673413
www.smoothhound.co.uk/hotels
/denehse.html
🄴 margaret@dene-
house.freeserve.co.uk
Set in the village of Juniper, this former farmhouse is backed by gardens and nine acres of meadow. The lounge has an old beamed ceiling and an open fire, but during warmer weather a sun lounge offers the perfect place to relax. Breakfast is served in the farmhouse kitchen. Bedrooms are well proportioned, furnished in pine and charmingly decorated.

🛏 3   🅿

HIGH WYCOMBE   D2

Bledlow

Cross Lanes $
Cross Lanes Cottage,
HP27 9PF, Buckinghamshire
☎ 01844 345339
🖨 01844 274165
This delightful cottage, parts of which date back to the 16th century, has an idyllic location in this conservation village. Bedrooms offer high levels of comfort, with quality furnishings and fabrics, as well as such extra amenities as fresh flowers and bottled water. The small dining room has low beamed ceilings and views over the pretty and well-kept garden. Guests also have a lounge in which to relax.

🛏 3   🅿

IPSWICH   E2

Lavenham

Lavenham Priory $$-$$$
Water Street, CO10 9RW,
Suffolk
☎ 01787 247404
🖨 01787 248472
www.lavenhampriory.co.uk
🄴 mail@lavenhampriory.co.uk
Benedictine monks originally owned this house that dates back to the 13th century. Today it has been restored to appear as it would have during the Elizabethan period. All rooms are furnished and equipped with great style and taste. Guests also have use of the Great Hall, with an inglenook fireplace and an adjoining lounge. Breakfast is served in the stunning Merchants Room or, in summer, in the courtyard herb garden.

🛏 5 Closed Dec. 21-Jan. 2
🅿   💳 💳

The Great House $$
Market Place, CO10 9QZ,
Suffolk
☎ 01787 247431
🖨 01787 248007
www.greathouse.co.uk
🄴 info@greathouse.co.uk
Overlooking the marketplace of this historic wool town, the restaurant is a major strength here and offers high quality rural French cuisine at lunch and dinner. The bedrooms tend to be very spacious and most have a separate living area; all offer a high level of comfort and boast a good range of extra facilities. Many of the original wooden beams have been retained, and one of the chimney breasts is thought to be part of the oldest standing structure in town.

🛏 5   Closed last 3 weeks in Jan.
💳 💳 💳

Stoke-By-Nayland

The Angel Inn $$
Polstead Street, CO6 4SA ,
Suffolk
☎ 01206 263245
🖨 01206 263373
After four centuries of providing hospitality to travelers, the inn continues to offer a high degree of comfort with a wealth of character. Many of the original features have been retained, including exposed brickwork and wooden beams. The restaurant has high beamed ceilings, and both the bar and restaurant serve excellent food.

🛏 6
Closed Dec. 25-26

🅿   💳 💳 💳 💳

Key to Symbols: 🖨 Fax 🄴 Email 🛏 Rooms 🅿 Parking 🏊 Swimming
💳 American Express 💳 Diners Club 💳 MasterCard 💳 Visa

JERSEY · E5

St. Aubin

The Panorama $
La Rue du Crocquet, JE3 8BZ, Jersey
☎ 01534 742429
🖨 01534 745940
www.jerseyisland.com/staubin/panorama

e Great views can be enjoyed from front-facing rooms and the terrace garden, where homebaked cream teas are served in the summer. Bedrooms, furnished to high standards, are well-equipped. Public areas are noteworthy for their antique fireplaces and also the huge collection of teapots on display.

🛏 17
Closed early Nov.-mid Mar.

St. Saviour

Champ Colin $
Rue du Champ Colin, JE2 7UN, Jersey
☎ 01534 851877
🖨 01534 854902

Enjoying a delightful location in the island's interior, this fine old stone house dates back to 1815. The charming bedrooms are furnished with antiques. The well-appointed breakfast room features an impressive granite fireplace.

🛏 3
Closed Dec. 18-Jan. 5

KENDAL · D4

Ambleside

Grey Friar Lodge Country House Hotel $
Clappersgate, LA22 9NE, Cumbria
☎ 015394 33158
🖨 015394 33158
www.cumbria-hotels.co.uk
e greyfriar@veen.freeserve.co.uk

This delightful former Victorian vicarage is a short distance from the town center, with views over the Brathay River and beyond. Most of the comfortable and individual bedrooms have beautiful antique furniture, and retain the elegance and character of the house. Some have four-poster beds.

🛏 8
Closed Dec. 11-Feb. 9

Riverside Lodge Country House $
Rothay Bridge, LA22 0EH, Cumbria
☎ 015394 34208
🖨 015394 31884
www.riversidelodge.co.uk
e alanrhone@riversidelodge.co.uk

In a delightful riverside setting, this fine period property is surprisingly secluded, yet within easy walking distance of the town center. Full of charm and character, the cozy lounge and pretty dining room having low beamed ceilings. Bedrooms vary in size and style, with most overlooking the peaceful river.

🛏 5

Rowanfield Country House $$
Kirkstone Road, LA22 9ET, Cumbria
☎ 015394 33686
🖨 015394 31569
www.rowanfield.com
e email@rowanfield.com

This Lakeland country house lies secluded in lovely gardens high above the town with delightful views across the valley and towards Windermere. Every bedroom is memorable; some are cozy and others, like the stunning attic room, more spacious. The dining room has a country cottage feel, with huge flagstones and a door leading to the garden.

🛏 7 Closed mid-Nov. to mid-Mar. (except Dec. 25 & Jan. 1)

Key to Symbols: 🖨 Fax e Email 🛏 Rooms P Parking 🏊 Swimming
■ American Express Ⓓ Diners Club ● MasterCard ▪ Visa

Coniston

Arrowfield Country Guest House $
Little Arrow, Torver, LA21 8AU, Cumbria
☎ 015394 41741

This Victorian house, set in an idyllic spot between Coniston and Torver has well equipped brightly co-ordinated bedrooms. The lounge is elegant, with deep, comfortable sofas. A substantial breakfast can be enjoyed in the light dining room. Guests can sample home-made preserves and honey, which also are available to buy and take home.

🛏 5
Closed Dec-Feb
🅿

Wheelgate Country Guest House $
Little Arrow, LA21 8AU, Cumbria
☎ 015394 41418
🖹 015394 41114
www.wheelgate.co.uk
✉ wheelgate@conistoncottages.co.uk

Joan and Roger Lupton offer guests a friendly and enthusiastic welcome to their home. Dating from 1640, the house provides attractive bedrooms, one with a four-poster bed. Lounges are comfortable, with deep sofas and antique furniture, and there is a cozy bar set aside for smokers. A hearty breakfast can be taken in the light dining room, preparing Lakeland walkers for their daily adventures.

🛏 5   Closed Dec.-Feb.
🅿 💳 💳

Crosthwaite

Crosthwaite House $
LA8 8BP, Cumbria
☎ 01539 568264
🖹 01539 568264
✉ crosthwaite.house@kencomp.net

This idyllic Georgian house is situated at the northern end of the Lyth Valley. Bedrooms are spacious and comfortably furnished, with a host of thoughtful extras. The reception rooms offer views over the valley and include a light, airy dining room and a lounge. Freshly prepared, imaginative meals are served in the dining room.

🛏 6
Closed mid-Nov. to Dec. 31
🅿

Hawkshead

Rough Close Country House $$
LA22 0QF, Cumbria
☎ 015394 36370
🖹 015394 36002

This delightful country house lies close to Esthwaite Water. The five-course evening meals are superb, as are the substantial breakfasts. A cozy lounge is available for guests to relax in, and there is a compact but well-stocked bar. Bedrooms are comfortably furnished, and many boast country garden views.

🛏 5
Closed Nov.-Feb.
🅿 💳 💳

Kendal

Low Jock Scar $
Selside, LA8 9LE, Cumbria
☎ 01539 823259
🖹 01539 823259
✉ philip@low-jock-scar.freeserve.co.uk

Far from the crowds but only a 10-minute drive to Kendal, this charming country guest house enjoys an idyllic riverside setting amid lovely woodland gardens. The conservatory dining room looks out on the gardens, and the interesting lounge is comfortable and relaxing. Bedrooms are individual in style and comfortably furnished; one has its own outside entrance.

🛏 5
Closed Nov.-Feb.
🅿 💳 💳

Key to Symbols: 🖹 Fax   ✉ Email   🛏 Rooms   🅿 Parking   🏊 Swimming
💳 American Express   💳 Diners Club   💳 MasterCard   💳 Visa

Near Sawrey
Ees Wyke Country House $$$
LA22 0JZ, Cumbria
☎ 015394 36393
🖹 015394 36393
John and Margaret Williams
create a friendly, relaxed
atmosphere at this fine Georgian
country house, once a holiday
home to Beatrix Potter. There
are comfortable lounges and a

spacious dining room where
delightful five-course dinners are
served. Breakfast dishes use local
produce.

🛏 8
Closed Jan.-Feb.
🅿

**Sawrey House Country Hotel
& Restaurant $$**
LA22 0LF, Cumbria
☎ 015394 36387
🖹 015394 36010
www.sawrey-house.com
✉ enquiries@sawrey-house.com
Close to Beatrix Potter's former
home, this hotel provides
comfortable, well-equipped
bedrooms with delightful views

of Esthwaite Water and the
surrounding fells. Charming
lounges offer deep sofas to relax
in and a roaring fire welcomes
guests in the cooler months.
There are wonderful views from
the restaurant where an
imaginative five-course dinner is
served in spacious surroundings.
Breakfasts are substantial and
might include roasted field

mushrooms with thyme and
brioche.

🛏 11   Closed Jan.
🅿 💳💳💳

Windermere

Dene House $-$$
Kendal Road, LA23 3EW,
Cumbria
☎ 015394 48236
🖹 015394 48236
✉ jdene@globalnet.co.uk
This smart Victorian house is
conveniently situated close
enough to the town to be handy,
but far enough away to escape
the busy crowds during the

summer. The bedrooms are well
proportioned, with modern
facilities.

🛏 7
🅿 💳

Howbeck $
New Road, LA23 2LA, Cumbria
☎ 015394 44739
🖹 015394 44739
www.howbeck.com
✉ enquiries@howbeck.com
Howbeck is conveniently
situated for Windermere town
and lake. Bedrooms are spacious,
comfortable and smartly
furnished. There is a dining

room with a small bar and a cozy
lounge at the front of the house.
Meals are freshly prepared using
local produce whenever possible.

🛏 10
🅿 💳💳

The Beaumont $$
Holly Rd, LA23 2AF, Cumbria
☎ 015394 47075
🖹 015394 47075
www.lakesbeaumont.co.uk
✉ thebeaumonthotel@
btinternet.com
Located just a short walk from
the town center, this well-kept
Victorian house offers
attractively furnished bedrooms,

with some four-poster rooms
also available. A freshly prepared
and substantial breakfast is
served in the light and airy
dining room. The comfortable
lounge is an inviting area for
guests to relax in.

🛏 10
Closed mid-Dec.-mid-Jan.
🅿 💳💳

Key to Symbols: 🖹 Fax ✉ Email 🛏 Rooms 🅿 Parking 🏊 Swimming
American Express Diners Club MasterCard Visa

KESWICK C4

Borrowdale

Greenbank $$
CA12 5UY, Cumbria
☎ 01768 777215

In the heart of Borrowdale, this delightful Victorian house enjoys breathtaking views across the valley to Derwentwater and north to Skiddaw. Bedrooms are comfortable and thoughtfully equipped, and the lounges, one with a self-service bar, offer panoramic views. A substantial Cumbrian breakfast is served in the dining room.

🛏 10
Closed Jan

Caldbeck

Swaledale Watch Farm House $
Whelpo, CA7 8HQ, Cumbria
☎ 01697 478409
🖷 01697 478409
🅴 nan.savage@talk21.com

Recently converted, this attractive former farmhouse stands next to a stream and looks out on the fells. Two of the spacious bedrooms are in a converted farm building and have their own living room. Food, prepared by the owners, is of high quality, and the evening meal should not be missed.

🛏 4
Closed Dec. 25
🅿

Keswick

Dalegarth House Country Hotel $$
Portinscale, CA12 5RQ, Cumbria
☎ 17687 72817
🖷 017687 72817
🅴 john@dalegarthhousehotel.freeserve.co.uk

This delightful house is peacefully situated in the lakeside village of Portinscale, just north of Keswick. Bedrooms come in a range of styles, and all are furnished to a high standard. Public rooms include two spacious lounges, one of which doubles as a bar, and an elegant restaurant where imaginative dinners are presented.

🛏 10
🅿

Derwent Cottage $
Portinscale, CA12 5RF, Cumbria
☎ 01768 774838
🅴 Dercott@btinternet.com

Derwent Cottage sits back from the main road and is surrounded by gardens. Enthusiastically run by the Newmans, it is comfortably furnished and offers attractive, cozy lounges and a small bar. The dining room is the venue for freshly prepared, home-cooked meals and hearty Cumbrian breakfasts. Bedrooms are spacious, well-furnished and include lots of personal touches.

🛏 6
Closed Nov.-Feb.
🅿

The Grange Country House $$
Manor Brow, Ambleside Road, CA12 4BA, Cumbria
☎ 01768 772500
🖷 01768 772500
🅴 sagem02458@talk21.com

This stylish Victorian residence is set in its own gardens just a short stroll from the town center. Spacious bedrooms are well-equipped, some featuring bare beams and delightful views across the town to the distant mountains. Imaginative meals are served in the stylish dining room. There also is a lounge and a bar.

🛏 10
🅿

Lorton

Winder Hall Country House $$
CA13 9UP, Cumbria
☎ 01900 85107
🖹 01900 85107
www.winderhall.co.uk
📧 winderhall@lowlorton.
freeserve.co.uk
Winder Hall is an impressive
house dating back to the 14th
century and features stone
mullions, leaded windows and
antiques. The lounge is
luxuriously furnished and the
elegant, spacious dining room is
the ideal venue for skillfully
prepared meals. Bedrooms range
from one with a massive four-
poster bed to cozier rooms, all
furnished with fine antiques or
pine.

LONDON E2

London Nw3

Sandringham Hotel $$$
3 Holford Road, Hampstead,
NW3 1AD, London
☎ 020 7435 1569
🖹 020 7431 5932
📧 sandrigham.hotel@virgin.net
Located on a quiet residential
street just a short walk from
Hampstead village and close to a
subway station. Bedrooms are
individual in style, all have TV,
telephone and thoughtful extras
such as mineral water and a
decanter of sherry. Breakfast is
not to be missed, with choices
such as French toast, eggs
Benedict, and smoked salmon
and scrambled eggs.

London Sw7

Five Sumner Place Hotel $$$
5 Sumner Place, South
Kensington, SW7 3EE, London
☎ 020 7584 7586
🖹 020 7823 9962
www.sumnerplace.com
📧 reservations@
summerplace.com
In the heart of South
Kensington, this elegant
Victorian terraced house has
been completely refurbished. All
the bedrooms are individually
designed and tastefully
decorated. Guests are able to
have breakfast among the shrubs
and flowers in the bright
Victorian-style conservatory, and
complimentary newspapers and
magazines are available.

Gallery Hotel $$$
8-10 Queensberry Place, South
Kensington, SW7 2EA, London
☎ 020 7915 0000
🖹 020 7915 4400
www.eeh.co.uk
📧 gallery@eeh.co.uk
This quiet location, so close to
Kensington and Knightsbridge is
popular with visitors from far
and wide. Bedrooms are
individually designed with fine
fabrics and fittings. Some rooms
have air conditioning. Public
rooms include the mahogany
paneled lounge with bar, where
daily newspapers are available.
At breakfast guests have the
option of an English buffet or
continental breakfast; 24-hour
room service is available.

LUDLOW D2

Ludlow

Number Twenty Eight $$
28 Lower Broad Street,
SY8 1PQ, Shropshire
☎ 01584 876996
🖹 01584 876860
www.numbertwentyeight.co.uk
📧 rossno28@btinternet.com
Situated in the Georgian/early
Victorian area of this historic
town, Number 28 is a
combination of three separate
houses, all retaining original
features and enhanced by quality
period furnishings. Each house
has a comfortable living room,
well-equipped bedrooms and
pretty gardens. Breakfast is
served in the cozy dining room
in the main house.

Key to Symbols: 🖹 Fax 📧 Email 🛏 Rooms 🅿 Parking 🏊 Swimming
🟦 American Express 🔷 Diners Club 💳 MasterCard 💳 Visa

LYME REGIS D1
Charmouth

Thatch Lodge Hotel & Restaurant $$-$$$
The Street, DT6 6PQ, Dorset
☎ 01297 560407
🖹 01297 560407
www.thatchlodgehotel.com
e thatchlodgehotel@cs.com
Dating back over 600 years, this charming property has been lovingly restored by its owners, and enjoys an air of peace and tranquility. Each of the well-equipped bedrooms has a character of its own, benefiting from many thoughtful extras; one room is located on the ground floor. A new feature is a garden view suite.

🛏 6
Closed mid-Jan. to mid-Mar.

MAIDSTONE E1
Biddenden

Bishopsdale Oast $-$$
TN27 8DR, Kent
☎ 01580 291027
🖹 01580 292321
www.bishopsdaleoast.co.uk
e bishopsdale@pavilion.co.uk
Guests receive a truly warm welcome at this red brick oast house (oast houses were used for drying hops for brewing). Dinners are a must, with fresh vegetables from the garden a highlight. The bedrooms are exceptionally well-equipped and have been decorated with taste and style.

🛏 4

Canterbury

Magnolia House $$
CT2 8AX, Kent
☎ 01227 765121
🖹 01227 765121
www.smoothhound.co.uk/hotels/magnoli.html
e magnolia_house_canterbury@yahoo.com
Magnolia House is personally run and offers guests a warm welcome. The attractive bedrooms have well co-ordinated furnishings and are provided with many extra touches. There is a pleasant lounge looking out over the front garden. Evening meals are a delight, but are served only by prior arrangement between November and February.

🛏 7 P

Thanington Hotel $$
140 Wincheap, CT1 3RY, Kent
☎ 01227 453227
🖹 01227 453225
www.thanington-hotel.co.uk
e thanington@lineone.net
This personally run hotel, close to the town center and the cathedral, consists of a fine Georgian building and an attractive modern extension housing some of the well-equipped bedrooms, each of which has a pants press and a safe. Three of the four rooms in the main house have four-poster beds. There is a small guest lounge and a well-appointed dining room.

🛏 15
Closed Dec. 25-26 & 31

Dover

Beulah House $
94 Crabble Hill, London Road, CT17 0SA, Kent
☎ 01304 824615
🖹 01304 828850
e owen@beaulahhouse94.freeserve.co.uk
Located a few minutes' drive from the town center, this impressive red brick Victorian house retains many original features, which are enhanced by the decor and furnishing styles within the public areas. Bedrooms and spacious and comfortable, with the majority having en suite or private facilities. Comprehensive breakfasts are eaten in the elegant dining room, and a comfortable living room also is available. Guests are welcome to view the fine mature gardens.

🛏 6 P

The Old Vicarage $$
Chilverton Elms, Hougham,
CT15 7AS, Kent
☎ 01304 210668
🖹 01304 225118
🄴 vicarage@csi.com
Outside Dover in the rolling Kent countryside, this delightful house, ably run by proprietors Mr. and Mrs. Evison, thoroughly deserves its excellent reputation.

The rooms are spacious and decorated with great taste and style, and guests are provided with a wealth of extra facilities. Breakfasts are served in the elegant dining room, with its polished wooden table and gleaming silver.

🛏 3
P 💳 💳

Maidstone

Ringlestone Inn & Farmhouse Hotel $$
Ringlestone Hamlet,
Harrietsham, ME17 1NX, Kent
☎ 01622 859900
🖹 01622 859966
www.ringlestone.com
🄴 bookings@ringlestone.com
This 16th-century inn, originally a hospice for monks, has delightful gardens, open grounds and features an inglenook fireplace, oak beams and brick and flint walls. Smart, modern bedrooms are housed in a nearby converted farmhouse and furnished with plenty of individual touches.

🛏 4
Closed Dec. 25

P 💳 💳 💳 💳

Sittingbourne

Hempstead House Country Hotel $$
London Road, Bapchild,
ME9 9PP, Kent
☎ 01795 428020
🖹 01795 436362
www.hempsteadhouse.co.uk
🄴 info@hempsteadhouse.co.uk
Hempstead House is set in three acres of mature gardens. Bedrooms are decorated with luxurious fabrics and designer tiles. The dining room leads onto a terrace where drinks or dinner, made using fresh local produce, can be enjoyed in the summer.

🛏 14
P 🏊
💳 💳 💳 💳

MANCHESTER D3
Knutsford

The Old Vicarage $$
Moss Lane, Over Tabley,
WA16 0PL, Cheshire
☎ 01565 652221
🖹 01565 755918
The Old Vicarage is a charming 19th-century house occupying two acres of landscaped grounds and gardens, convenient for access to the M6 highway. Bedrooms are attractively furnished and thoughtfully equipped.

🛏 4
Closed Jan. 2-18
P 💳 💳

MARLBOROUGH D1
Calne

Chilvester Hill House $
SN11 0LP, , Wiltshire
☎ 01249 813981
🖹 01249 814217
🄴 gill.dilley@talk21.com
This elegant Victorian house stands in well-kept grounds and a genuinely friendly welcome is assured. Bedrooms are spacious, comfortable and well-equipped, with many thoughtful extras such as bottled mineral water, magazines and cookies. A set dinner is available (by arrangement), served around one large table in the dining room. Dishes are freshly prepared from the best local produce, and many of the fruit and vegetables used are home-grown.

🛏 3
P 💳 💳 💳 💳

Key to Symbols: 🖹 Fax 🄴 Email 🛏 Rooms P Parking 🏊 Swimming 💳 American Express 💳 Diners Club 💳 MasterCard 💳 Visa

Lacock

At the Sign of the Angel **$$$**
6 Church Street, SN15 2LB,
Wiltshire
☎ 01249 730230
🖷 01249 730527
www.lacock.co.uk
Guests cannot fail to be
impressed by the historic
character of this former 15th-
century wool merchant's house
in the famous National Trust

village of Lacock. Bedrooms vary
in size, and all are individually
designed. Excellent meals are
served in the beamed dining
rooms, warmed, as is the inviting
lounge, by open fires.

🛏 10
Closed Dec. 23-30

Lydford

Moor View House **$$**
Vale Down, EX20 4BB, Devon
☎ 01822 820220
🖷 01822 820220
Built around 1870, this charming
house has elegant, beautifully
decorated rooms; the bedrooms
in particular are furnished with
an interesting and eclectic
collection of pieces revealing
many personal touches. Breakfast

and dinner are served
communally at a large oak
dining table.

🛏 4
🅿

Lynton

Victoria Lodge **$**
Lee Road, EX35 6BS, Devon
☎ 01598 753203
🖷 01598 753203
www.victorialodge.co.uk
🇪 info@victorialodge.co.uk
This Victorian house has been
decorated with quality fabrics
and furniture, and nothing has
been overlooked to ensure that

guests are offered every comfort.
Imaginative menus use the finest
local ingredients wherever
possible. A four-course dinner is
served on some evenings, usually
from Thursday through Sunday.

🛏 9
Closed Nov-Jan

Minehead

Glendower Hotel **$**
32 Tregonwell Rd, TA24 5DU,
Somerset
☎ 01643 707144
🖷 01643 708719
Conveniently located for both
the oceanfront and the town, this
well-run, friendly hotel stands on
an attractive terrace. Furnished
in keeping with the period of the
property, the public areas include

a spacious bar/lounge and a well-
appointed dining room. The
comfortable bedrooms are
attractively decorated and
equipped with modern comforts.

🛏 14

Simonsbath

Barkham **$**
Sandyway, EX36 3LU, Somerset
☎ 01643 831370
🖷 01643 831370
www.exmoor-vacations.co.uk
🇪 adie.exmoor@btinternet.com
Hidden away in a secret, wooded
valley, this beautifully restored
Georgian farmhouse is set in 12
acres of pasture with streams and

waterfalls. Delicious dinners are
available in the oak-paneled
dining room, where a traditional
breakfast also is served. The
attractively furnished and
decorated bedrooms are
comfortable. There is a spacious
drawing room as well.

🛏 3 🅿

NEWQUAY C1

Newquay

Degembris Farmhouse $
St Newlyn East, TR8 5HY,
Cornwall
☎ 01872 510555
🖹 01872 510230
📧 kathy@tally-connect.co.uk

Retaining much of its original character, this 18th-century farmhouse overlooks a wooded valley and offers tastefully decorated, pine-furnished bedrooms, the majority benefiting from the southerly views. A four-course meal is served in the beamed dining room. In addition, there is a comfortable lounge with a TV, and a selection of books and games. Guests also can enjoy the well-tended garden and walk along the farm trail.

🛏 5   Closed Dec. 25
P 💳 💳

Padstow

Cross House Hotel $$-$$$
Church Street, PL28 8BG,
Cornwall
☎ 01841 532391
🖹 01841 533633
www.crosshouse.co.uk
📧 info@crosshouse.co.uk

A charming Georgian property within easy walking distance of the harbor. The bedrooms are individually designed, and well furnished with modern facilities and many pleasing extras. Each room has its own VCR. Two very comfortable lounges are provided, and the premises are licensed. A choice of full English or continental breakfast is served in the cozy dining room.

🛏 9   P   💳 💳

NORWICH E2

Norwich

Catton Old Hall $$
Lodge Lane, Old Catton,
NR6 7HG, Norfolk
☎ 01603 419379
🖹 01603 400339
catton-hall.co.uk
📧 enquiries@catton-hall.co.uk

Expect a warm, friendly welcome at this charming Jacobean house. The building is full of original features such as flint, oak timbers and reclaimed Caen stone. Bold interior design along with a wealth of personal touches complement the well-chosen antique furnishings. Restful public rooms and relaxing bedrooms all have the stamp of the enthusiastic proprietors.

🛏 7   Closed Dec. 15-Jan. 5
P 💳 💳 💳 💳

OKEHAMPTON C1

Bridestowe

Week Farm $
EX20 4HZ, Devon
☎ 01837 861221
🖹 01837 861221
📧 weekfarm@biscuits.win-uknet

A complimentary cream tea is offered to welcome you to this 17th-century farmhouse. Bedrooms are furnished in traditional style, providing comfort and character. In cool weather log fires burn in the lounge, while the dining room is the setting for hearty English breakfasts and dinner by prior arrangement. There are self-catering cottages available in converted barns. Three fishing lakes connected by woodland walkways are being developed.

🛏 5   Closed Dec. 25
P 🏊 💳 💳

Chillaton

Tor Cottage $$
Chillaton, PL16 0JE, Devon
☎ 01822 860248
🖹 01822 860126
www.torcottage.demon.co.uk
📧 info@torcottage.demon.co.uk

This charming home is hidden in its own valley with 18 acres of grounds. The cottage-wing bedroom is beautifully appointed and has the benefit of a separate living room. The garden rooms, with open fires, are a few steps from the cottage and have been lovingly restored from former barns. The interesting gardens are a feature. Breakfast can be taken in the dining room or on the terrace (weather permitting), with an imaginative range of dishes available.

🛏 4   Closed Dec. 6-Jan.
P 🏊 💳 💳

Key to Symbols: 🖹 Fax 📧 Email 🛏 Rooms P Parking 🏊 Swimming
💳 American Express 💳 Diners Club 💳 MasterCard 💳 Visa

Jacobstowe

Higher Cadham Farm $
EX20 3RB, Devon
☎ 01837 851647
🖷 01837 851410
www.internetsouthwest.co.uk/
highercadham
📧 Jenny@highercadham.
freeserve.co.uk
For over 25 years, John and
Jenny King have been welcoming
guests to their charming
farmhouse located on the Tarka
Trail. Bedrooms are neatly
decorated and furnished in
modern pine. The locally popular
restaurant is open to the public
for morning coffee, lunch and
cream teas, so reserving is usually
essential. Children will enjoy the
animals as well as the large play
area.

🛏 9 Closed Dec. 🅿

Virginstow

**Percy's Country Hotel &
Restaurant** $
EX21 5EA, Devon
☎ 01409 211236
🖷 01409 211275
www.percys.co.uk
📧 info@percys.co.uk
Renowned for its contemporary,
country cuisine cooked by Tina
Bricknell-Webb, Percy's offers
relaxed and friendly service.
Imaginative meals are served in
the 16th-century Devon Long
House. With wonderful country
views, this comfortable, spacious
accommodation is exceptionally
well-equipped.

🛏 8 🅿

OXFORD   D2

Abingdon

Dinckley Court $$
Burcot, OX14 3DP, Oxfordshire
☎ 01865 407763
🖷 01865 407010
www.dinckleycourt.co.uk
📧 annette@dinckleycourt.co.uk
This former farmhouse is set in
extensive mature grounds by the
River Thames. The well-
equipped and homey bedrooms
all have quality modern facilities.
Hostess Annette Godfrey
prepares imaginative dinners
which are eaten at one family
table in the cozy kitchen. A
spacious, comfortable lounge also
is available.

🛏 5
🅿

Oxford

Burlington House $$
374 Banbury Road,
Summertown, OX2 7PP,
Oxfordshire
☎ 01865 513513
🖷 01865 311785
www.burlington-house.co.uk
📧 stay@burlington-house.co.uk
This impressive Victorian house
is situated in Summertown, one
of Oxford's premier residential
areas. It is just five minutes by
bus or taxi to the city center, and
there also are some good
restaurants within walking
distance. Bedrooms are stylishly
decorated and well co-ordinated.
The daily-changing breakfast
menu, cooked to order using the
freshest ingredients, always
includes a traditional breakfast as
well as alternatives.

🛏 11 Closed
Dec. 23-Jan. 3
🅿

**Fallowfields Country House
Hotel & Restaurant** $$$

Kingston Bagpuize,
Southmoor, OX13 5BH,
Oxfordshire
☎ 01865 820416
🖷 01865 821275
www.fallowfields.com
📧 stay@fallowfields.com
A warm and friendly welcome
can be expected from hosts Peta
and Anthony Lloyd. Each well-
equipped bedroom is full of
character. Richly co-ordinated
fabrics and furnishings reflect
the colorful history of this house,
once home to the Begum Aga
Khan. The kitchen garden
provides many ingredients for
the wide range of interesting
dishes on the dinner menu.

🛏 10
🅿

Thame

Upper Green Farm $
Manor Road, Towersey,
OX9 3QR, Oxfordshire
☎ 01844 212496
🖹 01844 260399
www.ugfarm.free-online.co.uk
e bandb@ugfarm.
free-online.co.uk
Upper Green Farm is
conveniently located for exploring the Cotswolds. The bedrooms are tastefully furnished, each with its own theme, and are all well-equipped with a number of thoughtful extras. Two rooms are in the main house, and the others, (including several ground floor rooms) are in a separate barn, which also offers a lounge.

🛏 10   Closed Dec. 25 and Jan. 1
P

Brough

Augill Castle $$
CA17 4DE, Cumbria
☎ 017683 41937
🖹 017683 41936
www.augillcastle.co.uk
e augill@aol.com
This carefully restored Victorian neo-Gothic castle is set in open farmland and conveniently located near the A66. Bedrooms have stylish period furniture, and some feature converted turret walk-in closets. There are opulent lounges, and dinner is served around a huge oak dining table. Excellent use is made of local produce on the set menu, and there is a selection of wines.

🛏 6 P 💳 💳

Kirkby Thore

Bridge End Farm $
CA10 1UZ, Cumbria
☎ 01768 361362
A charming 18th-century farmhouse situated on a pedigree Holstein dairy farm. Guests are assured of a warm welcome from Yvonne Dent, whose substantial homemade evening meals and breakfasts are delicious. The spacious and comfortable bedrooms are furnished with antiques and feature handmade patchwork quilts, as well as extras like fresh fruit, cookies and reading material. There also is a very restful guest lounge.

🛏 3
Closed Dec. 25
P

Penzance

Ennys $$
Trewhella Lane, St Hilary,
TR20 9BZ, Cornwall
☎ 01736 740262
🖹 01736 740055
www.ipl.co.uk/ennys.html
e ennys@zetnet.co.uk
A peaceful and tranquil hideaway, Ennys is the perfect place to escape and unwind. This beautiful 17th-century manor house comes complete with attractive gardens, grass tennis court and heated outdoor pool. Style abounds throughout, with carefully chosen artwork and interesting wall hangings, while bedrooms offer comfort. Self-catering apartments also are available.

🛏 5   Closed Nov. 1-Feb. 13
P 🏊 💳 💳

St Ives

Kynance Guest House $
The Warren, TR26 2EA,
Cornwall
☎ 01736 796636
Situated within walking distance of the picturesque harbor and Porthminster beach, the Kynance is a charming old property in the heart of town. The bedrooms are attractively decorated and well- equipped and some have stunning views. Guests can enjoy a varied choice at breakfast, including a vegetarian option. Dawn and Simon Norris are welcoming hosts, always on hand to advise guests on attractions and restaurants for evening dining. This is a no-smoking establishment.

🛏 6   Closed mid-Nov. to mid-Mar.
P 💳 💳

Key to Symbols: 🖹 Fax e Email 🛏 Rooms P Parking 🏊 Swimming
💳 American Express 💳 Diners Club 💳 MasterCard 💳 Visa

PLYMOUTH C1
Looe

Polperro
Landaviddy Manor $
Landaviddy Lane, PL13 2RT,
Cornwall
☎ 01503 272210
This former magistrate's house,
built in 1785, stands in two acres
of well-tended gardens just
outside Polperro. Bedrooms vary
in size and quality: Larger rooms
are furnished with wonderful

Trenderway Farm $$
Pelynt, PL13 2LY, Cornwall
☎ 01503 272214
🖷 01503 272991
📧 trenderwayfarm@hotmail.com
Genuine hospitality will be
found at this 16th-century
farmhouse, set in 400 acres of
beautiful countryside. The
bedrooms (two in the farmhouse
and two in the adjacent barn) are

Saltash

PORTSMOUTH D1
Bosham

St Aubyn's Guest House $
Marine Drive, Hannafore, West
Looe, PL13 2DH, Cornwall
☎ 01503 264351
🖷 01503 263670
www.staubyns.co.uk
📧 welcome@staubyns.co.uk
Standing in attractive gardens,
this impressive Victorian house
has uninterrupted sea views.
Bedrooms are spacious,

antique pieces; and a number
also benefit from lovely views
with distant glimpses of the sea.
There is a cozy bar, spacious
dining room and a comfortable
lounge.

 7
Closed late Sep.-mid-Mar.
P 💳 VISA

furnished with style and
equipped to a very high
standard. Hearty breakfasts, with
free-range eggs from the farm,
are served in the bright, airy
conservatory, and guests can
relax by the open fire in the
comfortable living room. Self-
catering accommodation also is
available in the Meadow Barn.

Crooked Inn $$
Stoketon Cross, PL12 4RZ,
Cornwall
☎ 01752 848177
🖷 01752 843203
www.crookedinn.co.uk
📧 crooked.inn@virgin.net
There is a warm welcome at this
well-run inn. Bedrooms,
furnished to a high standard,
have all the expected modern

Kenwood
Off A259, PO18 8PH,
West Sussex
☎ 01243 572727
🖷 01243 572738
Kenwood is a fine Victorian
house set in several acres of
gardens with views over the
harbor. A generous breakfast is
served in the bright conservatory,
which also contains a refrigerator

comfortable and well-equipped,
and some have access to
balconies. There is an elegantly
furnished lounge adjacent to the
breakfast room.

🛏 8
Closed Nov. 1-Easter
P 💳 VISA

🛏 4 Closed Dec. 25
P 💳 VISA

facilities and are in converted
buildings around the courtyard,
which is home to some friendly
farm animals. The inn restaurant
offers an extensive menu of
interesting, freshly cooked food.

🛏 18
P 🏊
💳 VISA

and microwave for guests who
wish to cater for themselves in
the evening. A lounge also is
available.

🛏 3
P 🏊

Rogate

Mizzards Farm $$
GU31 5HS, West Sussex
☎ 01730 821656
▤ 01730 821655
📧 julian.francis@hemscott.net

Mizzards Farm is a charming 16th-century house surrounded by delightful landscaped gardens. The peaceful and extensive grounds are part of a an area of outstanding natural beauty. There is a split-level drawing room with a grand piano, and the largest of the three antique-furnished bedrooms has a canopied bed set on a dais, with a marble bathroom.

 3
Closed Dec. 25

 P 🏊

Sutton

The White Horse Inn $$
RH20 1PS, West Sussex
☎ 01798 869221
▤ 01798 869291

Located in the heart of this pretty rural village, the White Horse is a fine Georgian building that has been sympathetically renovated to provide comfortable, well-furnished bedrooms and bright, attractive public rooms. Imaginative food is served.

🛏 5
P [American Express] [MasterCard] [Visa]

PRESTON D3
Whitewell

The Inn at Whitewell $$
BB7 3AT, Lancashire
☎ 01200 448222
▤ 01200 448298

This famous old inn is located deep in the beautiful Forest of Bowland, alongside the Hodder River. A wide range of food is available in the relaxed bar and also in the elegant restaurant. Bedrooms are particularly well-equipped, and furniture includes many fine antique and period pieces. Four excellent new Coach House suites have been added.

🛏 17
P [MasterCard] [Diners Club] [American Express] [Visa]

RAMSEY C4
Ramsey

The River House $$
IM8 3DA, Isle of Man
☎ 01624 816412
▤ 01624 816412

This beautiful Georgian house stands among extensive gardens beside the Sulby River. Accommodations are comfortable and spacious, with luxurious facilities. Cordon Bleu dinners are served from Sunday to Thursday in the elegant dining room. There is a separate breakfast room overlooking the river.

🛏 3
P

READING D2
Henley-on-Thames

Lenwade $
3 Western Road, RG9 1JL,
Oxfordshire
☎ 01491 573468
▤ 01491 573468
www.w3b-ink.com/lenwade
📧 lenwadeuk@compuserve.com

This popular hotel is in a quiet location, close to the center of Henley. The attractively furnished bedrooms are well-equipped and include many thoughtful extras. Breakfast is served around one large table in the dining room, and there is a comfortable lounge with satellite TV and an open fire. Children are welcome, and dogs are accepted by prior arrangement.

🛏 3 P

RICHMOND   D4

Leyburn

Park Gate House $$
Constable Burton,
DL8 2RG, North Yorkshire
☎ 01677 450466

This is a smartly presented house with a beautiful garden. Both the lounge and dining room are furnished in a traditional style, and the bedrooms come in a variety of sizes. Guests also can relax in the superb walled cottage garden in the summer. Fresh fruit compotes made from home-grown fruit and berries are part of the excellent breakfasts.

 4

P

Richmond

Whashton Springs Farm $
DL11 7JS, North Yorkshire
☎ 01748 822884
🖨 01748 826285

Warm hospitality, hearty breakfasts and excellent service are provided within this delightful Georgian farmhouse set in rolling countryside north of Richmond. The house is beautifully furnished, and all bedrooms have been thoughtfully equipped with home comforts. The garden rooms are contemporary in style, while those in the main house are more traditional.

🛏 8
Closed late Dec.-Jan. 31

 P

RIPON   D3

Bedale

Elmfield Country House $
Arrathorne, DL8 1NE,
North Yorkshire
☎ 01677 450558
🖨 01677 450557
www.s-h-systems.co.uk/hotels/
elmfield.html
e stay@elmfieldhouse.
freeserve.co.uk

This former gamekeeper's cottage enjoys a peaceful location. Bedrooms are spacious and comfortable, and one room boasts a four-poster bed. The lounge, with a small corner bar, leads to the dining room where a home-cooked dinner is offered. There also is a conservatory and a game room.

🛏 9
P

Knaresborough

Newton House Hotel $
5-7 York Place, HG5 0AD,
North Yorkshire
☎ 01423 863539
🖨 01423 869748
www.newtonhousehotel.com
e newtonhouse@
btinternet.com

This delightful 17th-century coaching inn is located only two minutes from the river, castle and market square. The hotel is entered through its own archway into a courtyard. The attractively decorated and well-equipped bedrooms include some four-posters and king-sized doubles. Guests can enjoy a lounge with small bar, and meals are served from a set menu in the dining room.

🛏 12   Closed Feb.
P

Masham

Bank Villa Guest House $
HG4 4DB, North Yorkshire
☎ 01765 689605
🖨 01765 689605

Old beams and antique furniture are attractive features of the bedrooms in this charming Georgian house. There are two comfortable lounges, and good home-cooked meals are served in a delightful dining room.

🛏 6
P

Ripon

Bay Tree Farm $
Aldfield, HG4 3BE,
North Yorkshire
☎ 01765 620394
🖹 01765 620394
Set in tranquil countryside, this delightful farmhouse is close to Fountains Abbey and offers a high standard of hospitality. Accommodation is provided in a converted barn and includes both family and ground floor rooms. Wholesome home-cooked food is served, and a comfortable lounge is provided for guests.

 6

Thirsk

Spital Hill $$
York Road, YO7 3AE,
North Yorkshire
☎ 01845 522273
🖹 01845 524970
www.wolsey-lodges.co.uk
🅴 wolsey@wolseylo.demon.co.uk
Robin and Ann Clough welcome guests to their fine Victorian house, set amid gardens and parkland and surrounded by open countryside. The atmosphere is very much that of a relaxed country house, with a lovely lounge and meals eaten communally at the one table in the dining room. Bedrooms are stylishly furnished and thoughtfully equipped with many extras.

5 P

SALISBURY D1
Barford St. Martin

Briden House $
West Street, Barford St. Martin, SP3 4AH, Wiltshire
☎ 01722 743471
🖹 01722 743471
www.smoothhound.co.uk/hotels/bridenho.html
🅴 bridenhouse@barford25.freeserve.co.uk
This charming property, situated not far from Salisbury, has been restored to its former glory. Bedrooms are pleasantly furnished and well-equipped. A home-cooked breakfast is served in the delightful beamed dining room.

4 P

Salisbury

Clovelly Hotel $
17-19 Mill Road, SP2 7RT, Wiltshire
☎ 01722 322055
🖹 01722 327677
www.clovellyhotel.co.uk
🅴 clovelly.hotel@virgin.net
Close to the railroad station, the Clovelly offers good standards of comfort and quality service. The proprietor also offers personalized driving tours around Wessex. The bedrooms are attractively-decorated and have well co-ordinated furnishings. Public areas include a lounge and breakfast room.

14 P

Cricket Field House Hotel $
Skew Bridge, Wilton Road, SP2 9NS, Wiltshire
☎ 01722 322595
🖹 01722 322595
www.cricketfieldhousehotel.com
🅴 information@cricketfieldhousehotel.com
This popular guest house is just one mile from the town center and adjacent to the South Wiltshire Cricket Ground. The cricket theme is conveyed subtly throughout. The majority of the bedrooms, including one designed for the less mobile, are in an annex behind the main house and overlook a pleasant courtyard. All are quiet, smart and spacious, with excellent facilities.

14 P

Websters $
11 Hartington Road, SP2 7LG, Wiltshire
☎ 01722 339779
🖹 01722 339779
📧 websters.salis@eclipse.co.uk
Situated on a quiet cul-de-sac close to Salisbury center, this welcoming home offers comfortable accommodations, with each room individually furnished. There is one ground-floor room suitable for guests with disabilities. The generous breakfasts, attractively served, make a perfect start to the day.

🛏 5 🅿 💳 💳

Thruxton

May Cottage $
SP11 8LZ, Hampshire
☎ 01264 771241
🖹 01264 771770
Built in 1740, and partly thatched, May Cottage enjoys a tranquil village setting. Guests will feel right at home, whether having tea with homemade cake in the pretty garden by the stream or relaxing in the private guest lounge. Bedrooms are comfortable and thoughtfully furnished in a traditional style, with quality furnishings.

🛏 3
Closed Dec. 25
🅿

Whiteparish

Newton Farmhouse $
Southampton Road, SP5 2QL, Wiltshire
☎ 01794 884416
🖹 01794 884416
www.newtonfarmhouse.co.uk
📧 reservations@ newtonfarmhouse.co.uk
Newton Farmhouse dates from the 16th century, originally gifted to Lord Nelson's family as part of the Trafalgar estate. It is conveniently located close to Salisbury and on the edge of the New Forest. The house has been thoughtfully restored, providing modern amenities yet retaining many of the original features. Bedrooms, most with period four-poster beds, are tastefully furnished and decorated.

🛏 8 🅿 🏊

SCARBOROUGH   E3

Helmsley

Plumpton Court $
High Street, Nawton,
YO62 7TT, North Yorkshire
☎ 01439 771223
🖹 01439 771223
www.swiftlink.pnc-uk.net/gh/1020.html
📧 plumptoncourt@ ukgateway.net

Plumpton Court is an attractive 17th-century stone house offering modern and well-equipped bedrooms. There is a cozy lounge bar with a real fire, and good home cooking is served in the pleasant dining room. There is a well-tended garden to the rear, as well as off-street parking.

🛏 7 🅿

Pickering

The Old Manse $
19 Middleton Road,
YO18 8AL, North Yorkshire
☎ 01751 476484
🖹 01751 477124
Formerly a Methodist minister's home, The Old Manse is now a comfortable and very well-furnished guest house. It is within easy walking distance of the town and steam railroad, and offers comfortable bedrooms and a cozy lounge. Good hospitality is provided by the resident owners.

🛏 8
🅿

SHEFFIELD D3

Hathersage

Old Barn $
Sheffield Road, S32 1DA,
Derbyshire
☎ 01433 650667
🖺 01433 650667
In an elevated location, backed
by Millstone Edge, this property
enjoys fine views across the valley
to the hills beyond. The original 16th-century barn was recently
converted into a comfortable,
modern guest accommodation,
and retains many original
features. Bedrooms are
attractively furnished and
comfortable. There is a large and
comfortable lounge with a variety
of board games.

🛏 3   Closed Nov.-Mar.   🅿 💳 💳

SHREWSBURY D2

Ironbridge

The Library House $$
11 Severn Bank, TF8 7AN,
Shropshire
☎ 01952 432299
🖺 01952 433967
www.libhouse.enta.net
📧 libhouse@enta.net
This delightful little 18th-
century guest house, located
almost directly opposite the
famous Iron Bridge, was once the village library. The house has
been modernized to provide
comfortable accommodations.
One bedroom has its own private
terrace with direct access to the
garden. Other facilities include a
comfortable lounge and an
attractive breakfast room.

🛏 4   Closed Dec. 25
🅿

Shrewsbury

The Day House $
Nobold, SY5 8NL, Shropshire
☎ 01743 860212
🖺 01734 860212
Dating from the 18th century
and extended in early Victorian
times, this impressive brick
house is situated in beautiful
gardens teeming with wildlife.
The public areas retain many of
the building's original features and are enhanced by fine period
furniture and ornaments.
Bedrooms are spacious and
comfortable, and all have the
benefit of en suite or private
bathrooms.

🛏 3
Closed Jan. 1 and Dec. 25
🅿

Wem

Soulton Hall $$
Soulton, SY4 5RS, Shropshire
☎ 01939 232786
🖺 01939 234097
www.soultonhall.
fsbusiness.co.uk
📧 j.a.ashton@farmline.com
This impressive hall has many
reminders of the antiquity of the
building, most notably the
sloping floors. The comfortable entrance lounge leads to bar on
one side and a restaurant on the
other. Bedrooms have mullioned
windows with many exposed
timbers, and one room is wood
paneled. There also are rooms in
the converted coach house across
the garden.

🛏 6
🅿 💳 💳 💳

SKIPTON D3

Grassington

Ashfield House Hotel $$
Summers Fold, BD23 5AE,
North Yorkshire
☎ 01756 752584
🖺 01756 752584
www.yorkshirenet.co.uk/stayat/a
shfieldhouse
📧 keilin@talk21.com
Linda and Keith Harrison offer friendly hospitality at Ashfield
House. Many period features
remain inside the house,
including window seats and
fireplaces. There are two cozy
lounges, and local produce is
used extensively in meals served
in the dining room. Bedrooms
are individual in design and well-
equipped.

🛏 7   Closed Jan. & early Feb.
🅿 💳 💳

SOUTHAMPTON D1
Brockenhurst

Thatched Cottage Hotel & Restaurant $$
16 Brookley Road, SO42 7RR, Hampshire
☎ 01590 623090
▤ 01590 623479
www.thatchedcottage.co.uk
🅴 thatchedcottagehotel@email.msn.com
This 17th-century thatched cottage has been converted into a delightful small hotel. Bedrooms vary in size, but the lack of space in some is compensated for in the quality of the appointments and the useful extras. The stylish restaurant with its open kitchen offers interesting and well-prepared dishes.

🛏 5 Closed Jan. 4-31

🅿 💳 VISA

The Cottage Hotel $$
SO42 7SH, Hampshire
☎ 01590 622296
▤ 01590 623014
www.cottage-hotel-new-forest.co.uk
🅴 terry_eisner@compuserve.com
This extended cottage retains many of its original features, highlighted by the occasional period furniture and memorabilia within the public areas. Bedrooms have individual furniture and decor schemes plus lots of homey extras to enhance guest comfort.

🛏 7
Closed Dec-Jan

🅿 💳 VISA

Fordingbridge

Alderholt Mill $
Sandleheath Road, SP6 1PU, Hampshire
☎ 01425 653130
▤ 01425 652868
www.smoothhound.co.uk/hotels/alder.html.
🅴 alderholtmill@zetnet.co.uk
One pleasure of staying here is home-baked bread, made from flour freshly ground in the working mill. The machinery is intact, and guests can enjoy milling demonstrations. Bedrooms are individually decorated and well furnished; there also is a comfortable lounge. The dining room is decorated in lovely bold colors and a super breakfast is served around the large table. Dinner is available by prior arrangement.

🛏 4
🅿 💳 VISA

Lymington
The Old Barn $
Christchurch Road, Downton, Hampshire, SO41 0LA
☎ 01590 644939
▤ 01590 644939
Julie and Simon Benford warmly welcome guests to their beautiful home, a carefully converted 17th-century barn. The bedrooms are stylishly decorated, thoughtfully appointed and feature spacious bathrooms. Breakfast is served around the farmhouse table, and a choice of a full cooked English breakfast or a lighter Continental alternative is offered. This is a no-smoking establishment.

🛏 2

Efford Cottage $
Everton, SO41 0JD, Hampshire
☎ 01590 642315
▤ 01590 641030/642315
🅴 effcottage@aol.com
Efford Cottage is a charming property set in attractive gardens. Bedrooms are comfortably furnished, well-equipped and feature a host of thoughtful extras. There is a large, comfortable lounge to relax in. Guests can enjoy a wide choice at breakfast in the smartly appointed dining room.

🛏 3
🅿

SOUTHWOLD F2
Fressingfield

Chippenhall Hall $$
IP21 5TD, Suffolk
☎ 01379 588180
🖹 01379 586272
www.chippenhall.co.uk
e info@chippenhall.co.uk
Mrs. Sargent offers guests a warm welcome to this Tudor manor house. Chippenhall is steeped in history, and dates in part to the 11th century. The building features exposed beams throughout, and has been superbly decorated and furnished in period style. During the winter a roaring log fire burns in the living room. Bedrooms are spacious, sumptuously furnished and retain all of their original character.

🛏 4 🅿 🏊 💳 💳 💳

ST. AUSTELL C1
Fowey

Carnethic House $$
Lambs Barn, PL23 1HQ, Cornwall
☎ 01726 833336
🖹 01726 833296
www.crescom.co.uk/carnethic
e carnethic@btinternet.com
This attractive property is set in award-winning gardens with an outdoor heated swimming pool, putting green and a grass tennis court. Guests are assured of a warm welcome from David and Trish Hogg. Equipped with many thoughtful extras, the bedrooms have attractively co-ordinated furnishings. Dinner is available by prior arrangement.

🛏 8 Closed Dec.-Jan.
🅿 🏊 💳 💳 💳 💳

Trevanion Guest House $
70 Lostwithiel Street, PL23 1BQ, Cornwall
☎ 01726 832602
🖹 01726 832602
www.users.globalnet.co.uk/~trefoy/fowey.htm
e trefoy@globalnet.co.uk
A warm and genuine welcome is assured at this 16th-century merchant's house, conveniently located within easy walking distance of this historic town. The well-equipped, comfortable bedrooms are decorated with pretty co-ordinated fabrics, and the elegant dining room retains many original features. Hearty hot breakfasts and lighter alternatives are offered.

🛏 5 Closed Nov.-Feb. 🅿

STOKE-ON-TRENT D3
Nantwich

The Limes $
5 Park Road, CW5 7AQ, Cheshire
☎ 01270 624081
🖹 01270 624081
In a quiet residential area not far from the town center, this impressive Victorian house is impeccably maintained and has a warm and friendly atmosphere. The spacious bedrooms are well-equipped, and one has a four-poster bed. The lounge is elegantly furnished, and breakfast is served in a delightful dining room. The house is surrounded by pleasant gardens.

🛏 3
Closed Nov.-Jan.
🅿

Oakamoor
Bank House $$
Farley Lane, ST10 3BD, Staffordshire
☎ 01538 702810
🖹 01538 702810
www.dialspace.dial.pipex.com/town/parade/fi88
e john.orme@dial.pipex.com
Originally a small farmhouse, this delightful property has been lovingly restored and extended by owners John and Muriel Orme. Bedrooms, one with a four-poster bed, are spacious and every conceivable luxury is provided. An elegant drawing room also is available and guests dine family-style with Mr. and Mrs. Orme in the dining room. Excellent meals are provided, and the gardens are a joy to behold.

🛏 3 Closed week of Dec. 25
🅿 💳 💳 💳

Key to Symbols: 🖹 Fax e Email 🛏 Rooms 🅿 Parking 🏊 Swimming
💳 American Express 💳 Diners Club 💳 MasterCard 💳 Visa

Whitchurch

Dearnford Hall $$
Tilstock Road, SY13 3JJ,
Shropshire
☎ 01948 662319
🖹 01948 666670
📧 dearnford_hall@yahoo.com
This impressive country house combines modern comforts with 18th-century elegance. It is surrounded by its own farm-land, which includes a spring-fed trout pool and offers many interesting walks. Inside, the beauty of the architecture has been enhanced by Jane Bebbington's stylish selection of antique furniture, rich fabrics and family treasures that adorn the living and dining rooms. The genuine hospitality of the Bebbingtons makes a stay here truly memorable.
🛏 2 Closed Dec. 25 🅿

STRATFORD-UPON-AVON D2

Broadway

Leasow House $
Laverton Meadows,
WR12 7NA, Worcestershire
☎ 01386 584526
🖹 01386 584596
www.leasow.co.uk
📧 leasowe@clara.net
Set in the peaceful Cotswold countryside, this beautiful 16th-century stone farmhouse offers comfortable, well-equipped and tastefully decorated bedrooms, with most retaining original oak beams. Two bedrooms are situated within the converted barn, and one has been adapted for the less able. Delicious breakfasts are taken in the attractive dining room that overlooks the gardens.

The library lounge is comfortable and relaxing.

🛏 7 🅿 💳 💳

Old Rectory $$
Church Street, Willersey,
WR12 7PN, Worcestershire
☎ 01386 853729
🖹 01386 858061
homepages.tesco.net/~j.walker/
📧 beauvoisin@btinternet.com
This mellow Cotswold stone house has been restored to provide guest accommodations. Bedrooms have modern facilities and homey extras. The breakfast room has period furniture and a small living area in front of the log fire. Trees in the walled garden, some centuries old, produce fruit for breakfast.

🛏 8
Closed Dec. 23-27

🅿 💳 💳

Stratford-upon-Avon

Glebe Farm House $
Stratford Road, Loxley,
CV35 9JW, Warwickshire
☎ 01789 842501
🖹 01789 841194
www.glebefarmhouse.com
📧 scorpiolimited@msn.com
Situated in landscaped grounds, this house dates from the 18th century. Bedrooms are spacious and comfortable, with antique furniture. Public areas feature a spacious and very comfortable lounge with an open fire for the cooler months, and a conservatory dining room which is reached via the charming farmhouse kitchen.

🛏 3
🅿 💳 💳

SWINDON D2

Woolstone

The White Horse $$
SN7 7QL, Oxfordshire
☎ 01367 820726
🖹 01367 820566
📧 WHorseUffington@aol.com
Set in the heart of Oxfordshire countryside, Woolstone is a 16th-century village and this inn is no exception. The bar has an Old World ambience, with beams, an open fire and a fine collection of malt whiskies. Smart bedrooms and bathrooms are located in the annex; they are simply decorated, well-maintained and comfortable.

🛏 6
🅿

Key to Symbols: 🖹 Fax 📧 Email 🛏 Rooms 🅿 Parking 🏊 Swimming American Express Diners Club MasterCard Visa

TAMWORTH D2

Tamworth

Oak Tree Farm $$
Hints Road, Hopwas, B78 3AA,
Staffordshire
☎ 01827 56807
🖹 01827 56807

Oak Tree Farm is a beautifully restored farmhouse in rural Staffordshire, overlooking the Tame River and well-kept gardens. Bedrooms are attractively furnished, comfortable and contain many thoughtful extras. Two rooms are located in the main house, while others are in a converted farm building. Additional features include a spacious lounge, a breakfast room and a small swimming pool. Mrs. Purkis is an attentive and caring hostess.

 🛏 7 🅿 🏊

TAUNTON C1

Taunton

Creechbarn Bed & Breakfast $
Vicarage Lane, Creech-St-
Michael, TA3 5PP, Somerset
☎ 01823 443955
🖹 01823 443955
www.somersite.co.uk
🄴 mick@somersite.co.uk

This lovingly converted, stone-built Somerset Longbarn is surrounded by well-tended gardens. Adjacent to the two comfortable bedrooms is a studio living room where books, table tennis and a television are provided. Breakfast is served around one large table; a set dinner is available by prior arrangement.

🛏 3

Closed Dec. 15-Jan. 15

🅿

Heathfield Lodge $
Heathfield, Nr Hillcommon,
TA4 1DN, Somerset
☎ 01823 432286
🖹 01823 432286
🄴 heathfieldlodge@
tinyworld.co.uk

This delightful, fully restored Regency house is the family home of Sue and Phil Thornton. Set in five acres of gardens and grounds, Heathfield Lodge is about a 10-minute drive from the center of Taunton. The individually furnished and decorated bedrooms are equipped with many thoughtful touches. By prior arrangement, imaginative home-cooked dinners are available; vegetarian and special diets catered for.

🛏 3 Closed Dec. 20-Jan. 2

🅿

Meryan House Hotel $
Bishop's Hull, TA1 5EG,
Somerset
☎ 01823 337445
🖹 01823 322355
🄴 anglo@dircon.co.uk

Just over a mile from the center of town, this 17th-century property has a village setting. Each bedroom has its own unique blend of period furniture and modern comforts. Interesting dishes, carefully prepared by Mrs. Clark, are available from a nicely balanced à la carte menu. The public areas include an attractive bar-lounge and a spacious and comfortable living room.

🛏 12

🅿

TORQUAY C1

Bovey Tracey

Front House Lodge $
East Street, TQ13 9EL, Devon
☎ 01626 832202
🖹 01626 832202
🄴 fronthouselodge@
yahoo.co.uk

This charming 16th-century property is decorated in English cottage style. Dried flowers brighten the beamed ceiling of the dining room and other areas. Bedrooms are individually decorated, with many extra touches. Carefully prepared, home-cooked dinners are available by prior arrangement.

🛏 6

🅿

Key to Symbols: 🖹 Fax 🄴 Email 🛏 Rooms 🅿 Parking 🏊 Swimming
American Express Diners Club MasterCard Visa

Dartmouth

Broome Court   **$$**
Broomhill, TQ6 0LD, Devon
☎ 01803 834275
📄 833260
Located in an area of outstanding natural beauty, Broome Court is tucked away at the end of a quiet lane. Modern, individually furnished accommodations have lots of extras. There are two lounges, and the freshly prepared, traditional breakfast is served in the old farmhouse kitchen. The self-catering Granary also is available.

🛏 3   🅿

Ford House   **$$**
44 Victoria Road, TQ6 9DX, Devon
☎ 01803 834047
📄 01803 834047
www.ford-house.co.uk
📧 richard@ford-house.freeserve.co.uk
A Regency house just a short walk from the waterfront and town center. Bedrooms are well-equipped and individually furnished, with many thoughtful extras. Dinner is served around a large mahogany table. The lounge has a vast selection of books and an open fire. It also is possible to book the whole house for private dinner party weekends.

🛏 3   Closed Nov.-Mar.

🅿 ▭ 💳 💳

South Brent

Coombe House   **$**
North Huish, TQ10 9NJ, Devon
☎ 01548 821277
📄 01548 821277
www.coombehouse.uk.com
📧 coombehouse@hotmail.com
Delightfully located, Coombe House is set in four acres of grounds with a large pond and two streams attracting wildlife. Benefiting from the country views, the spacious public areas are very comfortable. The individually furnished and decorated bedrooms are equipped with modern facilities; while self-catering accommodation is available in the adjacent converted barns. Dinner, served by prior arrangement, is prepared using local produce whenever possible.

🛏 4   🅿

Torquay

Norwood Hotel   **$**
60 Belgrave Road, TQ2 5HY, Devon
☎ 1803294236
📄 01803 294236
www.norwood-hotel.co.uk
📧 enquiries@norwood-hotel.co.uk
Located in a popular area of Torquay, this family-run hotel is conveniently located to the town center, promenade and beaches. Bedrooms are comfortable and well-equipped, and good traditional home-cooked meals are served in the attractive dining room.

🛏 11
Closed Dec. 25
🅿
💳 💳

TRURO   **C1**

Falmouth

Prospect House   **$**
1 Church Road, Penryn, TR10 8DA, Cornwall
☎ 01326 373198
📄 01326 373198
www.cornwall-selectively.co.uk
📧 prospecthouse@cornwall-selectively.co.uk
Convenient for touring mid and west Cornwall, this Georgian town house was built for a ship captain around 1820. Situated at the head of the Penryn River, Prospect House is set in a traditional walled plantsmans' garden. Guests are invited to sit in the Victorian conservatory in summer, or the elegant drawing room with log fires in winter.

🛏 4   🅿   💳 💳

St. Austell

The Wheal Lodge $$
91 Sea Road, Carlyon Bay,
PL25 3SH, Cornwall
☎ 01726 815543
🖹 01726 815543
Hospitality is a strength of this charming guest house which stands in its own gardens near Carlyon Bay and the golf club. Most of the spacious bedrooms are on the ground floor and overlook the garden. There also is a resident lounge and a dining room with a bar. Mrs. Martin is an excellent baker and a charming hostess.

🛏 6
Closed Dec. 23-Jan. 2

🅿 💳 VISA

TUNBRIDGE WELLS E1
Royal Tunbridge Wells

Danehurst House $
41 Lower Green Road, Rusthall,
TN4 8TW, Kent
☎ 01892 527739
🖹 01892 514804
🅴 danehurst@zoom.co.uk
Bedrooms at this Victorian house are furnished in period style and are well-equipped with lots of thoughtful extras. There is an elegant living room with a grand piano, self-service bar and library. Breakfasts are served in the charming conservatory dining room.

🛏 4
Closed Dec. 25 and last week in Aug.
🅿
💳 💳 VISA

Uckfield

Hooke Hall $$
250 High Street, TN22 1EN,
East Sussex
☎ 01825 761578
🖹 01825 768025
Lovingly restored by the owners, this classic Queen Anne town house features pleasant public rooms full of antique furniture, fine paintings and ornaments, creating a wonderful country house feel. The bedrooms have been individually decorated in great style. Breakfast (charged as an extra) is served in the elegant restaurant.

🛏 10
Closed Dec. 25-Jan. 1
🅿
💳 VISA

WARWICK D2
Henley-In-Arden

Ashleigh House $$
Whitley Hill, B95 5DL,
Warwickshire
☎ 01564 792315
🖹 01564 794126
Set in two acres of grounds a mile from the village, this impressive Edwardian house offers well-equipped and homey bedrooms. Public areas include a spacious dining room where guests can enjoy comprehensive English breakfasts, or dinners by arrangement. There is a choice of living rooms in addition to a conservatory that overlooks the gardens.

🛏 10 🅿 💳 VISA

Royal Leamington Spa

Comber House $$
2 Union Road, CV32 5LT,
Warwickshire
☎ 01926 421332
🖹 01926 313930
www.comberhouse.
freeserve.co.uk
🅴 b-b@comberhouse.
freeserve.co.uk
This carefully renovated Georgian house stands in a residential area near the town center. Bedrooms are furnished to a high standard, in keeping with the period of the property. Full English breakfasts are served in the dining room overlooking the pretty gardens; there also are a comfortable lounge and snooker room.

🛏 5   Closed mid-Dec. to mid-Jan.
🅿 💳 VISA

Key to Symbols: 🖹 Fax 🅴 Email 🛏 Rooms 🅿 Parking 🏊 Swimming 💳 American Express 💳 Diners Club 💳 MasterCard 💳 Visa

Bekynton House $
7 St Thomas Street, BA5 2UU,
Somerset
☎ 01749 672222
📄 01749 672222
📧 reservations@bekynton.
freeserve.co.uk
Bekynton House offers spacious,
comfortable accommodations
throughout, from the attractively
decorated bedrooms to the

relaxing lounge and well-
furnished dining room, where
enjoyable breakfasts are served at
separate tables. There is a good
choice of restaurants within easy
walking distance for evening
meals.

 4
Closed Dec. 24-26

Double-Gate Farm $
Godney, BA5 1RX, Somerset
☎ 01458 832217
📄 01458 835612
www.somerset-farm-
holiday.co.uk/double_gate_
farm_home_page.htm
📧 hilary@doublegate.
demon.co.uk
Guests receive a warm welcome
from owners Hillary and Terry

Millard. Bedrooms are pleasantly
decorated and have all the
modern creature comforts. There
is an impressive bedroom and
bathroom specifically designed
for the less able.

🛏 8   Closed Jan. 1 and Dec. 25

Southway Farm $
Polsham, BA5 1RW, Somerset
☎ 01749 673396
📄 01749 670373
Southway Farm is ideally
situated between the towns of
Glastonbury and Wells and is
easy to find. Bedrooms are
spacious and well furnished, with
many thoughtful touches. There
is a comfortable lounge in which

to relax after a day exploring the
Somerset region. Breakfast is
served at separate tables in the
tastefully decorated dining room.

🛏 3
Closed Nov.-Feb.

The Old Farmhouse $
62 Chamberlain Street,
BA5 2PT, Somerset
☎ 01749 675058
📄 01749 675058
www.plus44.com/oldfarmhouse
📧 theoldfarmhouse@
talk21.com
The Old Farmhouse is in the
center of Wells, so everything is
within easy walking distance.

Elegant decoration and a
relaxed, friendly atmosphere are
the hallmarks of this charming
17th-century house. The quality
of the furnishings, including the
comfortable beds, is superb.
Dinner, available by prior
arrangement, should not be
missed.

🛏 2

Link Lodge $
3 Pickersleigh Road, WR14
2RP, Worcestershire
☎ 01684 572345
📄 01684 572345
An elegant Queen Anne house
where composer Edward Elgar
once taught music. Set on an
acre of gardens, it has views
across Malvern Link Common.
Two well-equipped, comfortable

bedrooms are supplemented by a
small single room suitable for an
accompanied child. Breakfast is
served in the kitchen at a large
table. The whole house is non-
smoking.

🛏 3

The Dell House $
Green Lane, Malvern
Wells, WR14 4HU,
Worcestershire
☎ 01684 564448
🖹 01684 893974
www.dellhouse.co.uk
🄴 diana@dellhouse.co.uk
Standing on beautiful grounds,
this well-proportioned early
Victorian house retains many
original features. Bedrooms are
spacious and comfortable.
Breakfast is served at one table
in the dining room and a large
living room is available for guest
use.

🛏 3 🅿

WORKINGTON C4
Cockermouth

Toddell Cottage $
Brandlingill, CA13 0RB,
Cumbria
☎ 01900 828696
🖹 01900 828696
www.eden-bandb.co.uk
🄴 toddell@waitrose.com
Standing in peaceful countryside
this charming Cumbrian
longhouse has modern amenities
that blend perfectly with the Old
World charm of the cottage.
Beamed ceilings are a feature of
the bedrooms, which are stylishly
furnished and well-equipped.
Freshly prepared meals
incorporating local produce are
served in the dining room. There
is a guest lounge.

🛏 3   Closed Dec. 25-Jan. 1
🅿

YEOVIL D1
Crewkerne

Manor Farm $
Wayford, TA18 8QL, Somerset
☎ 01460 78865
🖹 01460 78865
www.manorfarm.com
Peacefully located off the beaten
track, this fine Victorian country
house has extensive views over
Clapton towards the Axe Valley.
The comfortably furnished
bedrooms are well-equipped,
with the front-facing rooms
enjoying splendid views.
Breakfast is served at separate
tables in the dining room, and a
spacious lounge also is provided.

🛏 4

🅿

Evershot

Rectory House $$
Fore Street, DT2 0JW, Dorset
☎ 01935 83273
🖹 01935 83273
Rectory House is an 18th-
century listed building situated
at the center of the unspoiled
village of Evershot. Three of the
five bedrooms are situated in a
converted stable block, and have
views over the garden. All rooms
are elegantly furnished and boast
modern comforts. Dinner is
available in an attractive dining
room, and breakfasts offer fresh
fruit and freshly squeezed orange
juice.

🛏 5

🅿 💳 💳

Ilminster

The Old Rectory $$
Cricket Malherbie, TA19 0PW,
Somerset
☎ 01460 54364
🖹 01460 57374
🄴 theoldrectory@malherbie.
freeserve.co.uk
Complete with thatched roof
and Strawberry Hill gothic
windows, this enchanting
building fits in perfectly with its
peaceful surroundings. Michael
and Patricia Fry-Foley offer
unobtrusive hospitality and
service. Bedrooms are furnished
and equipped with comfort in
mind, and provide lovely views
over the garden and countryside
beyond. Patricia uses only the
finest ingredients when
preparing her wonderful
breakfasts and dinners, the latter
available by prior arrangement.

🛏 5 🅿 💳 💳

Key to Symbols: 🖹 Fax 🄴 Email 🛏 Rooms 🅿 Parking 🏊 Swimming
American Express Diners Club MasterCard Visa

Nettlecombe

The Marquis of Lorne $$
DT6 3SY, Dorset
☎ 01308 485236
🖷 01308 485666
www.holidayaccomm.com/marquis-of-lorne.htm
📧 ian_barrett@compuserve.com

In the heart of the Dorset countryside but only a short drive from the seaside town of Bridport, The Marquis of Lorne enjoys a tranquil setting with super views. There are various bars and dining rooms that retain much original character. A good selection of tasty dishes feature the freshest ingredients. Bedrooms are decorated and furnished to a high standard and have modern facilities.

🛏 6   P 💳 💳

Sherborne

The Old Vicarage $-$$
Sherborne Road, Milborne Port, DT9 5AT, Dorset
☎ 01963 251117
🖷 01963 251515
www.milborneport.freeserve.co.uk

This charming, Victorian house is steeped in history and offers high quality accommodations. The guest lounge and conservatory are particularly pleasant and relaxing. Bedrooms in the main house are spacious and styled with considerable flair. Other rooms, in the adjacent coach house, are smaller but very comfortable and stylish.

🛏 7   Closed Jan.
P 💳 💳 💳

Somerton

Lydford House $
Lydford-on-Fosse, TA11 7BU, Somerset
☎ 01963 240217
🖷 01963 240413
www.jamesribbons.demon.co.uk
📧 lynn@jamesribbons.demon.co.uk

Built in 1860 as a gentleman's residence, Lydford House has had a variety of uses including a vicarage and a country club, and is now an elegantly furnished guest house. There also is an antique shop in part of the house. Spacious bedrooms with attractive decor and quality furnishings are well-equipped, and all have modern facilities. The living room and dining area are elegantly furnished, and an English breakfast is served around one large table.

🛏 4   P

Sturminster Newton

Stourcastle Lodge $$
Goughs Close, DT10 1BU, Dorset
☎ 01258 472320
🖷 01258 473381
www.stourcastle-lodge.co.uk
📧 enquiries@stourcastle-lodge.co.uk

A charming 18th-century house with a warm, friendly atmosphere. Bedrooms are spacious, well-presented and comfortably appointed, and all are equipped with modern facilities, including many useful extras. Fine home-cooked meals are provided at dinner and breakfast, served in the attractive dining room.

🛏 5
P 💳 💳

Yeovil

Holywell House $$
Holywell, East Coker, BA22 9NQ, Somerset
☎ 01935 862612
🖷 01935 863035
www.holywellhouse.co.uk
📧 b&b@holywellhouse.freeserve.co.uk

This beautiful house was built in the 18th century from mellow Hamstone and is set in three acres of land. The bedrooms offer individual touches of charm and character. The Masters Suite has fine antique furniture and a Victorian-style paneled bathroom. The award-winning gardens include water and herb gardens, croquet lawns and a tennis court.

🛏 3   Closed Jan. 1 & Dec. 25   P

Key to Symbols: 🖷 Fax   📧 Email   🛏 Rooms   P Parking   ≋ Swimming
💳 American Express   💳 Diners Club   💳 MasterCard   💳 Visa

Acacia Lodge $$
21 Ripon Road, HG1 2JL,
North Yorkshire
☎ 01423 560752
▣ 01423 503725
A delightful Victorian semi-detached house only a short walk from the town center and conference venues. The comfortable, attractively decorated bedrooms are very well appointed, especially a separate two-bedroom family suite. Public areas consist of a guest lounge with an open fire and the charming oak-furnished dining room. Old paintings and antiques characterize the public areas.

 6
P

Britannia Lodge Hotel $$
16 Swan Road, HG1 2SA,
North Yorkshire
☎ 01423 508482
▣ 01423 526840
This town house is just a few minutes' walk from the center. Bedrooms are individually decorated and tastefully furnished. Downstairs, a small bar and comfortable lounge enable guests to relax after a busy day. Hearty English breakfasts are served in the attractive dining room.

 12
P
▣ ▣ ▣ ▣

York

Four Seasons Hotel $$
7 St Peters Grove, Bootham,
YO30 6AQ, North Yorkshire
☎ 01904 622621
▣ 01904 620976
www.fourseasons-hotel.co.uk
🄴 roe@fourseasons.nettineuk.net
This spacious and attractive house stands on a quiet, leafy side road within easy walking distance of the city center. A large, comfortable lounge is provided, and bedrooms are spacious and very well-equipped. Guests can expect attentive service from the hospitable proprietors.

🛏 5
Closed Jan. & Dec. 24-26

P ▣ ▣

Hazelwood $$
24-25 Portland Street, Gillygate,
YO31 7EH, North Yorkshire
☎ 01904 626548
▣ 01904 628032
www.thehazelwoodyork.com
This elegant Victorian town house is quietly situated only 400 yards from York Minster. The breakfast room is graced with smart linen and the walls are hung with an interesting collection of floral prints. The bedrooms are individually styled and have been tastefully decorated using designer fabrics.

🛏 14

P ▣ ▣

Holmwood House Hotel $$
114 Holgate Road, YO24 4BB,
North Yorkshire
☎ 01904 626183
▣ 01904 670899
www.holmwoodhousehotel.co.uk
🄴 holmwood.house@dial.pipex.com
Holmwood House occupies an attractive row of substantial Victorian houses, within easy walking distance of the city center. It has well-equipped, richly decorated and pleasantly furnished bedrooms with many antiques. There is a comfortable lounge, and a substantial breakfast is served in the pleasant dining room.

🛏 14
P ▣ ▣ ▣

ANSTRUTHER   D5
Anstruther

**Beaumont Lodge
Guest House**   **$-$$**
43 Pittenweem Road,
KY10 3DT, Fife
☎ 01333 310315
🖹 01333 310315
e reservations@beau-
lodge.demon.co.uk
Guests are warmly welcomed by
the Anderson family to their
comfortable detached home. The
bedrooms, which vary in size,
have pretty color schemes,
comfortable modern furnishings
and are thoughtfully equipped.
One room offers the luxury of a
four-poster bed. Quality local
ingredients are used in the
preparation of the enjoyable
homemade fare. This is a non-
smoking house.

🛏 5 P 💳 VISA

The Spindrift   **$$**
Pittenweem Road, KY10 3DT,
Fife
☎ 01333 310573
🖹 01333 310573
www.thespindrift.co.uk
e info@thespindrift.co.uk
Many guests return again and
again to this delightful Victorian
house. The McFarlane family
spare no effort in ensuring that
their guests are properly cared
for. Bedrooms are comfortable
and individually furnished. There
is a comfortable lounge with a
self-service bar, while hearty
breakfasts and, by prior
arrangement, homemade dinner
is served in the smart dining
room. This is a non-smoking
house.

🛏 8 Closed Nov. 17-Dec. 10 & Dec. 25

P 💳 VISA

AYR   C4
Dalbeattie

Auchenskeoch Lodge   **$$**
DG5 4PG, Dumfries &
Galloway
☎ 01387 780277
🖹 01387 780277
This fine Victorian shooting
lodge is surrounded by 20 acres
of grounds, including a vegetable
garden, croquet lawn, small
fishing loch and a maze. The
house is full of charm, graced
with antique and period
furniture. Two of the bedrooms
have a lounge area and one can
be adapted as an extra, single
bedroom.

🛏 3
Closed Nov.-Mar.
P
💳 VISA

Darvel
Scoretulloch House   **$$$**
KA17 0LR, East Ayrshire
☎ 01560 323331
🖹 01560 323441
www.btinternet.com/~
scoretulloch
e mail@scoretulloch.com
Donald and Annie Smith have
restored this property into a
dream house. Set high on a
hillside it enjoys fine views. The
original walls date back 500
years, otherwise all is new. Enjoy
first class cooking in the dining
room, or simpler food, served all
day, in Oscar's brasserie. A cozy
library-bar has many wildlife
books – Donald is a naturalist,
author and photographer.

🛏 4 P 💳 VISA

BIGGAR   C4
Biggar

**Toftcombs Country House &
Restaurant**   **$$**
Peebles Road, ML12 6QX,
South Lanarkshire
☎ 01899 220142
🖹 01899 221771
e toftcombs@aol.com
Situated on the outskirts of
town, this turreted red sandstone
mansion offers both the comfort
and relaxation of a country house
and the convivial atmosphere of
a restaurant with rooms. There
are two lounges, one with a bar,
and also a restaurant. The well-
appointed bedrooms come in a
variety of sizes.

🛏 4
P
💳

Key to Symbols: 🖹 Fax   e Email   🛏 Rooms   P Parking   🏊 Swimming
💳 American Express   💳 Diners Club   💳 MasterCard   VISA Visa

BRORA C6
Brora

Glenaveron $
Golf Road, KW9 6QS,
Highland
☎ 01408 621601
▤ 01408 621601
✉ glenaveron@hotmail.com
Glenaveron stands in well-tended grounds a short distance from the beach and the town center. Bedrooms are spacious, well equipped and comfortable,

and offer all expected amenities. A specially equipped ground-floor room is suitable for guests with limited mobility. An attractive lounge, where a fire burns on colder evenings, is ideal for relaxation. Breakfast is served in the elegant and charming dining room.

🛏 3 P 💳 💳

DUMFRIES C4
Kirkcudbright

Baytree House $$
110 High Street, DG6 4JQ,
Dumfries & Galloway
☎ 01557 330824
▤ 01557 330824
✉ baytree@currantbun.com
This delightful Georgian town house has been beautifully restored to offer a high standard

of accommodation. Bedrooms are attractively furnished and feature many thoughtful touches. Public rooms are equally impressive, including a luxurious living room and attractively appointed dining room which overlooks the pretty gardens. Guests can enjoy a high standard of cooking at dinner, and breakfast also is of excellent

quality. This is a strictly non-smoking establishment.

🛏 3 P

DUNFERMLINE C5
Dunfermline

Pitreavie Guest House $
3 Aberdour Road, KY11 4PB,
Fife
☎ 01383 724244
▤ 01383 724244
members.aol.com/pitreavieg/pit
reavie/pitreavie
✉ pitreavieg@aol.com
Anne Walker looks forward to

welcoming you to her comfortable home, a semi-detached house at the junction of Aberdour Road and A823. Bedrooms with pleasing color schemes are comfortably furnished in pine and offer a good range of amenities, including VCRs. Hearty breakfasts and, by arrangement, evening meals are served in the

combined lounge/dining room. This is a non-smoking house.

🛏 5 P 💳 💳

EDINBURGH C5
Edinburgh

Dunstane House Hotel $$-$$$
4 West Coates, Haymarket,
EH12 5JQ, City of Edinburgh
☎ 0131337 6169
▤ 0131 337 6169
www.dunstanehousehotel.co.uk
✉ reservations@dunstanehouse
hotel.co.uk
Mr. and Mrs. Mowat are the friendly owners of this delightful period property, conveniently

located to the city center, and they have upgraded the house to the highest standards. Bedrooms are generously proportioned and offer high levels of comfort and quality. Public areas include a relaxing lounge with bar and an elegant dining room where breakfast and dinner is served.

🛏 15 P 💳 💳 💳 💳

Inveresk House $$
3 Inveresk Village,
Musselburgh, EH21 7UA,
City of Edinburgh
☎ 0131 6655855
▤ 0131 6650578
www.btinternet.com/~chute.inv
eresk
✉ chute.inveresk@btinternet.
com
Set in large gardens, this

mansion house – once used as a base by Oliver Cromwell – is steeped in history. As a family home, it has a friendly, relaxed atmosphere. The public rooms are massive and graced with interesting heirlooms. Bedrooms are well proportioned and furnished with a glorious jumble of antiques and period pieces.

🛏 3 Closed Dec. 22-27 P 💳 💳

Kew House $$
1 Kew Terrace, Murrayfield,
EH12 5JE, City of Edinburgh
☎ 0131 313 0700
🖹 0131 313 0747
www.kewhouse.co.uk
🅴 kewhouse@worldsites.net
This charming establishment forms part of a Victorian terrace. The attractive bedrooms come in a variety of sizes, but all have been thoughtfully equipped for the comfort of both the leisure and business traveler. Full Scottish breakfasts are served in the dining room, and there is a guest lounge offering a supper and snack menu. The house has a private, secure parking lot.

🛏 6

The International Guest House $-$$
37 Mayfield Gardens,
EH9 2BX, City of Edinburgh
☎ 0131667 2511
🖹 0131 667 1112
www.s-h-systems.co.uk/hotels/
internat. html
🅴 intergh@easynet.co.uk
You'll receive a delightfully warm welcome and enthusiastic service from Mr. and Mrs. Niven at their attractive Victorian terraced house, situated just south of the city center. The smartly presented bedrooms are thoughtfully decorated and comfortably furnished. A hearty Scottish breakfast is served in the traditionally styled dining room, which boasts a beautiful ornate ceiling.

🛏 9

The Lodge Hotel $$
6 Hampton Terrace, West
Coates, EH12 5JD, City of
Edinburgh
☎ 0131337 3682
🖹 0131 313 1700
www.thelodgehotel.co.uk
🅴 thelodgehotel@btconnect.com
Situated within easy walking distance of the city center, The Lodge is an elegant Georgian home. Bedrooms are beautifully decorated and presented. A comfortable lounge and atmospheric bar are available for guests' use, and delicious evening meals and hearty breakfasts are served at individual tables in the bright dining room.

🛏 10   Closed Dec. 24-25

The Stuarts $$
17 Glengyle Terrace, EH3 9LN,
City of Edinburgh
☎ 0131229 9559
🖹 0131 229 2226
www.the-stuarts.com
🅴 gloria@the-stuarts.com
Spacious, comfortable bedrooms have luxury en suite bathrooms, easy chairs and extras such as a stereo and VCR (CDs and videos are available), refrigerator with wine, pants press and ironing center. The dining room is available during the day, and breakfast is served here around one table.

🛏 3
Closed Dec. 25

Faussetthill House $-$$
20 Main Street, EH31 2DR,
East Lothian
☎ 01620 842396
🖹 01620 842396
This delightful Edwardian house is set in well-tended gardens and is easily accessible to Edinburgh. The house is both comfortable and inviting. The tastefully decorated bedrooms are well proportioned and equipped. There is an attractive lounge on the second floor. Breakfast is served at two tables in the elegant dining room.

🛏 3
Closed Jan.-Feb.
🅿

Key to Symbols: 🖹 Fax 🅴 Email 🛏 Rooms 🅿 Parking 🏊 Swimming
American Express 🆔 Diners Club 💳 MasterCard 💳 Visa

EYEMOUTH D5

Eyemouth

Dunlaverock Country House $$$
TD14 5PA, Scottish Borders
☎ 018907 71450
🖨 018907 71450
📧 dunlaverock@lineone.net
Fine views across the bay are just one of the features of this clifftop house, where owners Mari and Ronnie Brown enjoy welcoming guests to their home. Bedrooms, including one on the ground floor, are furnished with many antiques and original oil paintings. A carefully prepared evening meal, using the best of local ingredients, is served around one table, before guests retire to the comfortable lounge, warmed by a roaring fire during the colder months.

🛏 6 Closed Dec.-Jan.
🅿 💳 💳

FORT WILLIAM C5

Fort William

Ashburn House $$
8 Achintore Road, PH33 6RQ, Highland
☎ 01397 706000
🖨 01397 702024
www.scotland2000.com/ashburn
📧 ashburn.house@tinyworld.co.uk
This elegant Victorian home overlooking Loch Linnhe has been lovingly restored. The charming bedrooms are spacious, individually decorated and offer a wide range of amenities. There is a sunny conservatory lounge, and the attractive dining room is an appropriate setting for Sandra's noteworthy breakfasts.

🛏 7
Closed Dec.-Jan.
🅿 💳 💳 💳

Mansefield House $
Corpach, PH33 7LT, Highland
☎ 01397 772262
🖨 01397 772262
📧 mansefield@aol.com
The friendly proprietors welcome guests to this former Victorian manse. The comfortable lounge has been carefully refurbished to reflect its Victorian character, with a roaring fire on colder evenings. The attractive dining room, with individual tables, is the setting for delicious homemade dinners and breakfasts.

🛏 6
Closed Dec. 24-28
🅿
💳 💳

The Grange $$
Grange Road, PH33 6JF, Highland
☎ 01397 705516
🖨 01397 701595
📧 jcampbell@grangefortwilliam.com
This lovely Victorian villa has attractive decor, and pretty fabrics have been used to good effect in the charming bedrooms, two of which enjoy beautiful views over Loch Linnhe. There are books and fresh flowers in the comfortable lounge, and the dining room is a lovely setting for a hearty breakfast.

🛏 4
Closed Nov.-Mar.
🅿

GALASHIELS D4

Galashiels

Maplehurst Guest House $-$$
42 Abbotsford Road, TD1 3HP, Scottish Borders
☎ 01896 754700
🖨 01896 754700
Set in wooded gardens on the south side of the town, this magnificent house was built for a wealthy mill owner in 1907. Original features have been lovingly retained, including fine art deco stained glass, splendid wood paneling and a recessed dresser in the dining room. The bedrooms are on the first floor and are individual in character. The turret suite has a cast iron bathtub, from which views of the surrounding Border hills can be enjoyed. Janice Richardson's home cooking is well worth sampling but dinner must be requested in advance.

🛏 3 Closed Dec. 25 & Jan. 1
🅿 💳 💳

GLASGOW C5

Cardross

Kirkton House $$
Darleith Road,
G82 5EZ, Argyll & Bute
☎ 01389 841951
🗎 01389 841868
www.kirktonhouse.co.uk
🇪 info@kirktonhouse.co.uk
This delightful 18th-century
converted farmstead enjoys
lovely views of the Clyde River.
Inviting public areas have a
comfortable traditional feel, with
a welcoming open fire in the
relaxing lounge. Bedrooms are
individual in style, with lots of
extra amenities provided. Home-
cooked meals are served in the
rustic dining room.

🛏 6   Closed Dec.-Jan.

P ■ 🔘 💳 💳

Carradale

Dunvalanree Guest House $-$$
Port Righ Bay, PA28 6SE,
Argyll & Bute
☎ 01583 431226
🗎 01583 431339
www.milstead.demon.co.uk
🇪 house@milstead.demon.co.uk
Alyson and Alan Milstead
delight in welcoming guests to
their charming home, which
enjoys splendid views across
Kilbrannan Sound to the hills of
Arran beyond. Bedrooms, one of
which is suitable for disabled
visitors, are attractively decorated
and comfortably furnished.
Relaxing public areas include an
inviting lounge. Enjoyable
home-cooked food based on
fresh local ingredients is the
order of the day in the adjacent
dining room which is also open
to the public.

🛏 7 P 💳 💳

Helensburgh

Lethamhill $-$$
West Dhuhill Drive, G84 9AW,
Argyll & Bute
☎ 01436 676016
🗎 01436 676016
From the red telephone box in
the garden to old typewriters and
slot machines inside, Douglas
and Jane Johnston's fine house is
an Aladdin's cave of collectibles
and memorabilia. Beyond this
insight into British heritage is a
house offering spacious,
comfortable bedrooms with
superb bathrooms. Jane's home-
cooked meals draw praise.
Breakfast and, by prior
arrangement, freshly prepared
evening meals are served in the
elegant dining room. This is a
non-smoking house.

🛏 3 P

INVERNESS C6

Inverness

Ballifeary House Hotel $$
10 Ballifeary Road, IV3 5PJ,
Highland
☎ 01463 235572
🗎 01463 717583
www.ballifearyhousehotel.co.uk
🇪 ballifhotel@btinternet.com
Situated in a quiet residential
area close to the Eden Court
Theatre, this delightful detached
house provides pretty bedrooms
with many thoughtful touches.
There is an elegant lounge and
an attractive dining room where
breakfast is served at individual
tables.

🛏 5

Closed mid-Oct.-Easter

P

💳 💳

Moyness House $$
6 Bruce Gardens, IV3 5EN,
Highland
☎ 01463 233836
🗎 01463 233836
www.moyness.co.uk
🇪 stay@moyness.co.uk
This elegant Victorian villa is in
a quiet residential area just
minutes from the town center. It
features beautifully decorated
bedrooms and well-equipped
bathrooms. Inviting public
rooms overlook the garden to the
front. Guests are welcome to use
the secluded and well-
maintained back garden.

🛏 7
P
💳 💳

MOFFAT   C4

Moffat

Hartfell House   **$**
Hartfell Crescent, DG10 9AL,
Dumfries & Galloway
☎ 01683 220153
www.freespace.virgin.net/robert.
white
✉ robert.white@virgin.net
Enjoying lovely country views,
this fine Victorian house sits high
above the town yet is within
walking distance of the center.
Beautifully maintained and
retaining all its original character,
the house boasts well-
proportioned bedrooms offering a
high degree of quality and
comfort plus a host of thoughtful
touches. There is an inviting
guest lounge on the first floor,
and guests can enjoy delicious
home-cooked meals and choose
from a well-chosen wine list in
the elegant dining room.

🛏 8   🅿

OBAN   C5

Connel

Ards House   **$$$**
PA37 1PT, Argyll & Bute
☎ 01631 710255
www.ardshouse.demon.co.uk
✉ jb@ardshouse.demon.co.uk
Jean and John Bowman delight
in welcoming guests old and new
to their charming home and its
views over Loch Etive to the
Morvern Hills beyond.
Bedrooms are attractively
decorated and comfortable.
Guests can relax with an aperitif
in the sitting room, before
moving on to the dining room,
where John's set menu continues
to attract much praise. This is a
non-smoking house.

🛏 7

Closed Dec.-Jan.

🅿   💳   💳

Oban

Glenburnie Private Hotel **$-$$**
The Esplanade, PA34 5AQ,
Argyll & Bute
☎ 01631 562089
🖨 01631 562089
www.argyllinternet.co.uk/
glenburnie
✉ graeme.strachan@btinternet.
com
This elegant Victorian house,
situated on the oceanfront with
stunning views over the bay to
the Isle of Mull, has been
lovingly restored by dedicated
owners. The bedrooms (which
include a four-poster room and
a mini suite) are beautifully
decorated and comfortably
furnished.

🛏 14   Closed Nov.-Mar.

🅿   💳   💳

PITLOCHRY   C5

Boat Of Garten

Glenavon House   **$$**
Kinchurdy Road, PH24 3BP,
Highland
☎ 01479 831213
🖨 01479 831213
✉ glenavonhouse@aol.com
This charming, detached
Edwardian home stands in
carefully tended gardens on the
western edge of the village. The
spacious bedrooms are
comfortable and modern in style,
offering a good range of
amenities. Public areas include a
relaxing lounge on the first floor.
Fresh breakfasts are served at
individual tables in the elegant
dining room.

🛏 5

🅿   💳   💳

Grantown-On-Spey

Ardconnel House   **$-$$**
Woodlands Terrace, PH26 3JU,
Highland
☎ 01479 872104
🖨 01479 872104
freespace.virgin.net/ardconnel.g
rantown/index.html
✉ ardconnel.grantown@virgin.
net
This delightful Victorian house
stands in a landscaped garden on
the south side of town. The
charming bedrooms, one with a
four-poster bed, are furnished to
a high standard and offer a range
of thoughtful accessories. Public
areas include an inviting living
room and a tastefully appointed
dining room. This is a non-
smoking house.

🛏 6   Closed Nov. 1-Easter

🅿   💳   💳

Key to Symbols: 🖨 Fax   ✉ Email   🛏 Rooms   🅿 Parking   🏊 Swimming
💳 American Express   💳 Diners Club   💳 MasterCard   💳 Visa

The Pines $-$$
Woodside Avenue, PH26 3JR,
Highland
☎ 01479 872092
🖹 01479 872092
www.pinesgrantown.freeserve.
co.uk
e enquiry@pinesgrantown.free
serve.co.uk
This large Victorian house has
been sympathetically restored

over the past two years and offers
comfortable and practical
bedrooms. The lounges,
including a small library, feature
some fine period pieces and
artwork. The substantial
breakfast includes an interesting
choice of dishes; dinner also
receives a great deal of care.

🛏 8   Closed Nov.-Feb.

🅿 💳 VISA

Kingussie

Avondale House $
Newtonmore Road, PH21 1HF,
Highland
☎ 01540 661731
🖹 01540 661731
e walsh.lorraine@talk21.com
Guests are made welcome in this
delightful Edwardian house,
which stands in its own gardens
south of the village. Bedrooms,
which include two ground-floor

rooms, are tastefully decorated
and comfortably furnished. The
lounge invites relaxation, and
enjoyable, traditional Scottish
meals are served in the attractive
dining room.

🛏 7
🅿

☎ 01540 661402
🖹 01540 661652
www.columba-hotel.co.uk
e reservations@columba-
hotel.co.uk
Myra Shearer delights in
welcoming guests old and new to
her comfortable small hotel on
the northern edge of town.
Bedrooms, which include two
four-poster rooms and a family

**Columba House Hotel &
Restaurant** $$
Manse Road, PH21 1JF,
Highland

suite, are comfortably furnished
and offer a good range of
amenities and thoughtful
personal touches. The lounge,
with its welcoming open fire,
invites relaxation. Enjoyable
home-cooked food is served in
the attractive dining room
overlooking the garden.

🛏 8 🅿

ST ANDREWS   D5
St Andrews

**Fossil House Bed &
Breakfast** $-$$
12-14 Main Street,
Strathkinness, KY16 9RU, Fife
☎ 01334 850639
🖹 01334 850639
www.fossil-guest-house.co.uk
e the.fossil@virgin.net
Wonderful hospitality, high

standards of guest care and
memorable breakfasts are the
hallmarks of any visit to Kornelia
and Alistair Inverarity's
charming home. Bedrooms are
attractive, two in the house and
two in an adjacent cottage. The
family room has a sun lounge
extension featuring lots of
thoughtful extras for children.
Kornelia's delicious breakfasts

attract much praise.

🛏 4 🅿 💳 VISA

Glenderran $$
9 Murray Park, KY16 9AW, Fife
☎ 01334 477951
🖹 01334 477908
e glenderran@telinco.co.uk
Glenderran is a smartly
presented house located just a
short stroll from the Old Course
and seafront. Attractive public
areas are enhanced by fresh
flowers. Bedrooms come in a

variety of sizes, from cozy singles
to a large mini suite suitable for
families. All are beautifully
decorated. Breakfasts are
enjoyable and make use of fresh
local produce.

🛏 5
💳 VISA

Key to Symbols: 🖹 Fax e Email 🛏 Rooms 🅿 Parking 🏊 Swimming
💳 American Express 🔘 Diners Club 💳 MasterCard 💳 Visa

STIRLING C5
Callander

Arden House $$
Bracklinn Road, FK17 8EQ,
Stirling
☎ 01877 330235
🖷 01877 330235
www.smoothhound.co.uk./
hotels/arden.html
This large Victorian house in a quiet part of the village, just a short walk from the main street, and enjoys fine views over the area. Comfortable, recently refurbished bedrooms are complemented by a stylish lounge, and a hearty Scottish breakfast is served in the airy dining room.

🛏 6   Closed Nov. 1-Mar. 30
P 💳 💳

Brook Linn Country House $
Leny Feus, FK17 8AU, Stirling
☎ 01877 330103
🖷 01877 330103
www.brooklinn-scotland.co.uk
🇪 derek@blinn.freeserve.co.uk
Enthusiastic owners Fiona and Derek House look forward to welcoming you to their delightful Victorian home, which stands on two acres of grounds above town. Bedrooms are attractively decorated and have a traditional feel. Public areas include a lounge and separate dining room where breakfast is served. This is a non-smoking house.

🛏 7
Closed Nov. 1-Easter
P 💳 💳

Dunblane

Rokeby House $$
Doune Road, FK15 9AT,
Stirling
☎ 01786 824447
🖷 01786 821399
home.btconnect.com/
rokeby.house/
🇪 rokeby.house@btconnect.com
This charming, detached Edwardian home stands in carefully tended gardens on the western edge of the village. The spacious bedrooms are comfortable and modern in style, offering a good range of amenities. Public areas include a relaxing lounge on the first floor. Fresh breakfasts are served at individual tables in the elegant dining room.

🛏 3 P 💳 💳

TAIN C6
Tain

Aldie House $
IV19 1LZ, Highland
☎ 01862 893787
🖷 01862 893787
Set in four acres of well-tended, secluded grounds full of rare and exotic plants, this traditional country residence has been lovingly restored by Chris and Charles De Decker, complete with antiques from their home in Belgium. Guests can make use of a spacious and comfortable lounge, dining room and sun lounge overlooking the gardens. Large bedrooms are individually furnished and decorated.

🛏 3

P 💳 💳

Golf View House $
13 Knockbreck Road,
IV19 1BN, Highland
☎ 01862 892856
🖷 01862 892172
🇪 golfview@btinternet.com
Formerly a manse, set in two acres of secluded gardens, Golf View House offers splendid views from the front lawn, across the nearby golf course to Dornoch Firth. Bedrooms are attractively decorated and comfortably appointed in both modern and traditional styles. There is a lounge for guests, and the dining room, with individual beech tables, is the setting for traditional breakfasts.

🛏 5   Closed Dec.-Jan.

P 💳 💳

Key to Symbols: 🖷 Fax 🇪 Email 🛏 Rooms P Parking 🏊 Swimming
💳 American Express 💳 Diners Club 💳 MasterCard 💳 Visa

WALES

ABERGAVENNY C2
Abergavenny

Dyffryn Farmhouse $-$$
Dyffryn, Aberhafesp, SY16 3JD, Powys
☎ 01686 688817
🖹 01686 688324
www.daveandsue.clara.net
e daveandsue@clara.net
Dave and Sue Jones have lovingly restored this 17th-

Llanwenarth House $$
Govilon, NP7 9SF, Monmouthshire
☎ 01873 830289
🖹 01873 832199
Built by the ancestors of Sir Henry Morgan, the infamous privateer who eventually became lieutenant governor of Jamaica, this beautifully preserved manor house provides charmingly

appointed bedrooms, one on the ground floor. There is an elegant drawing room and an attractive dining room. Brecon Beacons National Park is on the doorstep.

🛏 5
P

ABERYSTWYTH C2
Newtown

century, half-timbered barn over the last few years. Part of a fully working farm, it is surrounded by pretty gardens and a rushing mountain stream. Children are especially welcome. There is a play area and many country walks can be taken on the surrounding farmland. Guests have use of a comfortable living room and dining is family style.

🛏 2 P

BRECON C2
Crickhowell

Glangrwyney Court $-$$
NP8 1ES, Powys
☎ 01873 811288
🖹 01873 810317
e glangrwyne@aol.com
The highest standards of quality await guests at this country house set in its own grounds. Bedrooms are particularly

spacious and well furnished, while the dining room and lounge combine elegance, and comfort.

🛏 5
P

Hay-on-Wye

York House Guest House $-$$
Hardwick Road, Cusop, HR3 5QX, Powys
☎ 01497 820705
www.hay-on-wye.co.uk/yorkhouse/welcome.htm
This fine Victorian house lies in its own extensive gardens, just half a mile from Hay town center. Olwen and Peter Roberts

offer a friendly welcome to their guests. Bedrooms are attractively decorated and well-equipped with modern facilities. Some rooms are also suitable for families. There is also a comfortable lounge for residents.

🛏 4

P

Llandrindod Wells

Guidfa House $
Crossgates, LD1 6RF, Powys
☎ 01597 851241
🖹 01597 851875
www.guidfa-house.co.uk
e guidfa@globalnet.co.uk
This established country guest house is home to Anne and Tony Millan. Bedrooms are individually decorated and

equipped with modern facilities and extras. A comfortable lounge is available, with log fire. Small business meetings can be catered to. Anne is a qualified chef and offers imaginative dishes using fresh local produce whenever possible.

🛏 6

P

Key to Symbols: 🖹 Fax e Email 🛏 Rooms P Parking 🏊 Swimming
American Express Diners Club MasterCard Visa

CAERNARFON C3
Caernarfon

Hafoty $
Rhostryfan, LL54 7PH, Gwynedd
☎ 01286 830144
🖹 01286 830441

Hafoty has been created over several years from converted farm buildings and provides well-equipped, modern accommodations, with spacious bedrooms. The main house has comfortably furnished, attractively decorated public areas with open fireplaces. One bedroom is in a nearby coverted farm building, and self-catering cottages also are available.

🛏 4
Closed Dec.-Feb.
P ● VISA

Pengwern Farm $
Saron, LL54 5UH, Gwynedd
☎ 01286 831500
🖹 01286 831500
✉ jhjgr@enterprise.net

This delightful farmhouse is surrounded by 130 acres of farmland running down to Foryd Bay, which is noted for its birdlife. Bedrooms are generally spacious, and all are well-equipped with modern facilities. A comfortable lounge is provided, and good home cooking is served.

🛏 3
Closed Dec. & Jan.
P
◉ ● VISA

CARMARTHEN C2
Carmarthen

Cwmtwrch, Four Seasons Restaurant with Rooms $$
Nantgaredig, SA32 7NY, Carmarthenshire
☎ 01267 290238
🖹 01267 290808
www.geocities.com/thetropics/cove/3380
✉ jen4seasons@aol.com

This delightful, family-run small hotel has been developed around the nucleus of a fine old farmhouse. Also on the extensive grounds is the Four Seasons Restaurant, which has a deserved reputation for good food. Bedrooms are tastefully furnished and three are on the ground floor. There is a charming breakfast room and a comfortable lounge.

🛏 6 Closed 12/23-28
P 🏊 ● VISA

CONWY C3
Betws-y-Coed

Aberconwy House $
Lon Muriau, LL24 0HD, Conwy
☎ 01690 710202
🖹 01690 710800
www.betws-y-coed.co.uk/aberconwy/
✉ aberconwy@betws-y-coed.co.uk

This large Victorian house has splendid views over the Llugwy and Conwy valleys from many rooms. Bedrooms are attractively decorated and comfortably furnished. Pants presses and ironing facilities are provided, as are thoughtful touches such as fresh fruit and electric blankets. Two family rooms have been added, and there is a lounge and separate breakfast room.

🛏 8 P ● VISA

Conwy

Gwern Borter Country Manor $-$$
Barkers Lane, LL32 8YL, Conwy
☎ 01492 650360
🖹 01492 650360
www.snowdoniaholidays.co.uk
✉ gwern@borter.freeserve.co.uk

A delightful creeper-clad mansion in several acres of lawns and gardens. Children are very welcome, there is a rustic play area, games room and many farmyard pets. Bedrooms are furnished with period or antique pieces and equipped with modern facilities, one has an Edwardian four-poster bed. There is an elegant lounge and Victorian-style dining room. Freshly cooked hearty breakfasts are served.

🛏 3 P ● VISA

Llandudno

Abbey Lodge $
14 Abbey Road, LL30 2EA,
Conwy
☎ 01492 878042
🖷 01492 878042
A former gentleman's residence
close to the town center and
beaches. Rooms are attractively
decorated and equipped with
such extras as mineral water and
bathrobes. Guests have the

choice of two lounges and the
use of the patio and delightful
garden in summer months.

🛏 4
Closed Jan. 1 & Dec. 25
P

Bryn Derwen Hotel $$
34 Abbey Road, LL30 2EE,
Conwy
☎ 01492 876804
🖷 01492 876804
www.bryn-derwen-hotel.co.uk
e brynderwen@msn.com
The hotel was built as a
gentleman's residence in 1878
and has been converted with
impeccable taste by Stuart and

Valerie Langfield. Stuart's
intuitive cooking has gained a
fine reputation. Bedrooms are
individually designed, and
imaginative use is made of rich
colors and matching fabrics.
Public rooms are elegantly
furnished; a beauty salon and a
sauna also are available.

🛏 10   Closed Nov.-Feb.

P 💳 💳

Bryn-y-Bia $$
Craigside, LL30 3AS, Conwy
☎ 01492 549644
🖷 01492 549644
www.brynybia.demon.co.uk
e carol@brynybia.demon.co.uk
The house is set in well-tended
grounds. Public rooms include a
beautifully furnished lounge and
spacious restaurant. Dinner (by
arrangement) is well prepared,

with good use of fresh local
produce. Bedrooms are
traditionally furnished.

🛏 12
P
💳 💳

**Cranberry House
Guest House** $
12 Abbey Road, LL30 2EA,
Conwy
☎ 01492 879760
🖷 01492 879760
www.accomodata.co.uk/201097.
htm
An impeccably maintained,
welcoming Victorian guest house
in a quiet residential area, with

pretty lawns and gardens.
Llandudno's main shopping
center and seafront are a short
walk away. Pretty bedrooms are
equipped with fine period
furnishings and modern
amenities. A comfortable living
room is available.

🛏 5   Closed Dec.-Jan.

P 💳 💳 💳

The Lighthouse $$$
Marine Drive, Great Ormes
Head, LL30 2XD, Conwy
☎ 01492 876819
🖷 01492 876668
www.lighthouse-
llandudno.co.uk
e enquiries@lighthouse-
llandudno.co.uk
Built in the style of a small
fortress in 1862 and fully

operational until 1985, The
Lighthouse has comfortable
bedrooms furnished with quality
pieces. Two have lounge areas,
one being the glazed dome itself.
Bedrooms enjoy views of the
Irish Sea and are equipped with
binoculars. A spacious,
comfortable guest lounge has a
solid fuel stove. Sumptuous
breakfasts are served.

🛏 3 P 💳 💳

Key to Symbols: 🖷 Fax e Email 🛏 Rooms P Parking 🏊 Swimming
💳 American Express 💳 Diners Club 💳 MasterCard 💳 Visa

Ruthin

Eyarth Station $
Llanfair Dyffryn Clwyd,
LL15 2EE, Denbighshire
☎ 01824 703643
🖷 01824 707464
www.smoothhound.co.uk/
hotels/eyarth.html
Until 1964 this was a sleepy
country railroad station. A
comfortable lounge and outdoor
swimming pool occupy the space
once taken up by the railroad
and platforms. Bedrooms are
tastefully decorated and full of
thoughtful extras. Family rooms
are available, and two rooms are
in the old station master's house
adjoining the main building.

🛏 7
P 🏊 🌑 🌑

DOLGELLAU C2

Bontddu

Borthwnog Hall Hotel $$-$$$
LL40 2TT, Gwynedd
☎ 01341 430271
🖷 01341 430682
homepages.enterprise.net/borth
wnoghall
e borthwnoghall@enterprise.
net
This 17th-century country house
on the edge of the Mawddach
Estuary has views towards Cader
Idris and the Arran mountains.
An elegant sitting room with a
fire opens onto the gardens.
Bedrooms are spacious and
comfortable; one has a private
living room. The Library Art
Gallery has original water-colors
and oils. The Garth Gell nature
reserve adjoins the property.

🛏 3 Closed Nov. 12-27
P 🌑 🌑 🌑

Llanfachreth

Ty Isaf Farmhouse $$
LL40 2EA, Gwynedd
☎ 01341 423261
e raygear@tyisaf78.freeserve.
co.uk
This delightful 16th-century
long house was a working farm
until recently, but chickens still
provide fresh eggs each morning.
Bedrooms are fitted with
stripped pine furniture and
comfortable beds. There is a
television lounge and separate
reading room for guests. The
pretty grounds are home to pet
llamas.

🛏 3
Closed Jan. 1 & Dec. 25

P

Llansilin

The Old Vicarage $
Llansilin, SY10 7PX, Powys
☎ 01691 791345
🖷 01691 791345
users.breathemail.net/
rbjohnson/
e oldvicarage@breathemail.net
This delightful former vicarage
dates from 1792 and is
surrounded by large gardens. It is
in a peaceful little village near
Oswestry and offers attractively
decorated accommodations.
Evening meals are available at
the village pub. Good breakfasts
are provided by friendly owners
Pam and Rick Johnson.

🛏 3
Closed Dec. 25
P

Machynlleth

Yr Hen Felin (The Old Mill) $
Abercegir, SY20 8NR, Powys
☎ 01650 511868
This lovely house started life as a
water mill and is on the banks of
the Gwydol River. Two
bedrooms overlook the stream,
where trout and herons often can
be seen. The mill has been
restored, but exposed beams and
timbers remain. There is a very
comfortable lounge. Bedrooms,
although not particularly large,
are attractively furnished and
decorated.

🛏 3
Closed Jan. 1 & Dec. 25
P

Key to Symbols: 🖷 Fax e Email 🛏 Rooms P Parking 🏊 Swimming
🌑 American Express 🌑 Diners Club 🌑 MasterCard 🌑 Visa

Tal-y-Llyn

Dolffanog Fawr $-$$
LL36 9AJ, Gwynedd
☎ 01654 761247
This delightful small guest house is a beautifully restored 17th-century farmhouse at the foot of Cader Idris. There are superb views toward the mountain and across Tal-y-Llyn lake. Bedrooms are attractively decorated and furnished, and the

comfortable lounge has patio doors leading out to the garden. Dinner is served in convivial house-party style.

 4
P

Fishguard

Erw-Lon Farm $
Pontfaen, SA65 9TS,
Pembrokeshire
☎ 01348 881297
Traditional Welsh hospitality is offered by the very friendly McAllister family to guests visiting their home. A beef farm, it lies above the lovely Gwaun

Valley and there are superb rural views to be enjoyed. Bedrooms are comfortably furnished and well-equipped, and there is a relaxing lounge for residents. Maintenance standards are high throughout and a homey atmosphere prevails. Mrs. McAllister serves up some of the finest examples of traditional farmhouse cooking, where the

size of the portions matches the warmth of the hospitality.

🛏 3 P

Harlech

Gwrach Ynys Country Guest House $-$$
Ynys, Talsarnau, LL47 6TS,
Gwynedd
☎ 01766 780742
🗎 01766 781199
www.gwrachynys.co.uk
e gwynfor@talk21.com
This well-maintained Edwardian

house is set amid pretty lawns and gardens, and the family's pet ponies graze in the adjoining paddock. Bedrooms have pretty wallpaper and modern facilities; some are suitable for families, and children are especially welcome. Two comfortably furnished lounges are provided. Hospitality is warm and welcoming, with hearty breakfasts and dinners.

🛏 7   Closed Nov.-Feb. P

Cemaes Bay

Hafod Country House $
LL67 0DS, Isle of Anglesey
☎ 01407 710500
🗎 01407 710055
e hirst.hafod@tesco.net
This fine Edwardian house is set on the edge of a pretty fishing village and lies in an acre of attractive lawns and gardens with a wildlife pond. The three smart, modern bedrooms are

attractively decorated and well-equipped. A spacious drawing room is provided and breakfast, including home-made preserves and fresh juices when in season, is served in a separate dining room. Evening meals can be obtained at a pub a short stroll away.

🛏 3   Closed Oct.-Feb. P

Holyhead

Yr Hendre $
Porth-y-Felin Road,
LL65 1AH, Isle of Anglesey

☎ 01407 762929
🗎 01407 762929
e rita@yr-hendre.freeserve.co.uk
This delightful house was once the local manse. Owned and run by Rita Lipman for more than 15 years, it is a short walk from the town promenade and is convenient for travelers on the nearby Irish ferries. Bedrooms

are attractively decorated with rich fabrics and wallpaper, and all are equipped with pants presses and other thoughtful extras. Rita is an accomplished cook, and she provides wholesome meals with a distinctly Welsh flavor.

🛏 3 P

NEATH C2
Neath

Green Lanterns Guest House $
Hawdref Ganol Farm, Cimla,
SA12 9SL, Neath Port Talbot
☎ 01639 631884
e stuart.brown7@virgin.net
This 18th-century farmhouse is
part of a 46-acre equestrian and
horseback riding center and has
superb views over the area.

Bedrooms are spacious and
equipped with modern facilities.
An impressive guest lounge
features an enormous inglenook
fireplace. Meals are served family
style in the attractive dining
room.

🛏 4 P

NEWPORT D2
Tintern

Highfield House $-$$
Chapel Hill, NP16 6TF,
Monmouthshire
☎ 01291 689286
🖷 01291 689890
www.highfieldhouse.com
e highfieldhouse@
callnetuk.com
Perched on a hillside above
Tintern, this stylish stone-built
house offers wonderful views.

The building was once just a tiny
cottage, but has been expanded.
Both bedrooms and public areas
are decorated with imagination.
Dinner is lovingly prepared by
the proprietor, Mr. Caffery. The
six acres of land around the
house include woodland areas
offering lovely walks.

🛏 4 P

PEMBROKE C2
Pembroke

Poyerston Farm $-$$
Cosheston, SA72 4SJ,
Pembrokeshire
☎ 01646 651347
🖷 01646 651347
hhtp:/home.btclick.com/
poyerston
e poyerston@btclick.com
Situated on a 300-acre working

dairy farm that includes private
nature trails, this extended
Victorian house offers
comfortable accommodations
close to Pembroke and its many
attractions. Bedrooms are
tastefully decorated and
furnished, and include modern
en suite facilities. Two bedrooms,
located in the former adjoining
dairy, are ideal for families

🛏 5 Closed Dec. 20-27 P

ST DAVID'S B2
St David's

Y-Gorlan Guest House $-$$
77 Nun Street, SA62 6NU,
Pembrokeshire
☎ 01437 720837
🖷 01437 721148
This charming guest house is
just a short walk from the city
center and cathedral. Bedrooms
are attractively appointed, well

equipped and modern, with
some enjoying lovely rural views
towards Whitesands Bay.
Separate tables are provided in
the cottage-style dining room,
which also contains a small bar.
Dinner is available on request.

🛏 5

P 💳 💳

SWANSEA C2
Oxwich

Woodside Guest House $-$$
SA3 1LS, Swansea
☎ 01792 390791
This charming old cottage and
adjoining former barn have been
cleverly converted to provide
well-equipped accommodations.
Separate tables are provided in
the conservatory dining room,
which also contains a lounge
area. During cold weather,

welcoming fires burn in the
quaint bar.

🛏 5
Closed Dec.-Jan.
P

Denmark

The smallest of the four Scandinavian nations, a mosaic of peninsulas and islands just over 200 miles long, Denmark had a far-reaching influence in the days of Viking seafarers. Today it is one of the most progressive countries in the world. Strung across the entrance to the Baltic Sea at Europe's maritime heart, Denmark is made up of three main land masses: the Jutland peninsula, only 75 miles wide; the largest island, Zealand (Sjælland), home to the charming capital, Copenhagen (København), and the second-largest, Funen (Fyn), separated from Jutland by only a sliver of water.

The Jutland Peninsula

In the west and the north, Jutland has a bracing coast of sandy beaches, dunes and moors, and in Lindholm Høje, near the city of Aalborg, the nation's Viking past has left its mark in a burial ground of nearly 700 graves, many with stones resembling long ships. In the east, Jutland's landscapes change their character, as the western heathlands give way to undulating agricultural land, dotted with pretty towns and villages. Denmark's second city, Århus, with its mighty cathedral and restored, timber-framed Old Town, sits on the east coast; to the south is a swath of woodland, to the southwest the ever-popular Legoland.

The Islands

More than 400 islands are scattered around the Danish coast and across the Kattegat and the Baltic Sea, only about a quarter of them inhabited. Funen is lush and rural, with pleasant beaches on Langeland island, off its southeastern coast. A remarkable 11-mile-long rail and road bridge, the Great Belt, connects Funen with Zealand via the island of Sprogø. Zealand's main destination is Copenhagen, but beyond that wonderful city there is a wealth of historic buildings, such as magnificent Frederiksborg Castle and Elsinore Castle, setting for Shakespeare's "Hamlet". West of Copenhagen, the medieval capital of Roskilde has a splendid cathedral, resting place of no fewer than 37 monarchs; and on the west coast you can find the remains of Denmark's finest Viking fort.

Danish Style

Swedish furnishing design has long been prized in other European countries, but Denmark has its own distinctive style known as "Danish Modern," combining - in true Scandinavian form - practicality and function with attractive, clean lines. Another specialty in the Danish design world is amber, made into fine jewelry and sold throughout the country.

Visitors enjoy a trip around Svaneke on Bornholm

Denmark

Accommodations

A variety of accommodations are available in Denmark, from luxury city hotels to the smaller inns and pensions of the coastal resorts. Standards of service and comfort are uniformly high, but in common with neighboring Sweden, Denmark's overnight accommodations are an expensive commodity.

A range of room types is usually available in Danish hotels, with double rooms having two single beds as standard. The majority of good hotels now offer private bathrooms containing either a bath or a shower, but in older hotels these will often be quite small. Often a bathroom will have been added after the building's original construction. It's a good idea to pack a nice thick towel, as hotel towels are often very thin.

It is unusual for breakfast to be included in the cost of a room in Denmark, so be careful to request this when making a reservation. A typical hotel breakfast will be served buffet-style, with a large array of breads, cheeses, cooked meats and fish to choose from.

Food and Drink

The *morgenmad*, or "morning meal," refers to breakfast as we know it; *frohkost*, though literally translating as "breakfast," is usually lunch. Danes love the mixes of open sandwiches, meats and seafood known here as smørrebrød and popular throughout Scandinavia. It's a favorite meal at lunchtime, along with other options such as *frikadeller*, fried meat or fish patties with salad and potatoes; or the heavier buffet-style selection called *koldt bord*. For fuller meals try *kogt torsk* (poached cod in mustard sauce) or good, old-fashioned Danish stew, *hvid labskovs*. Every town and sizable village has a bakery selling delicious Danish pastries, called *wienerbrød* and available in a confusion of different sizes, shapes and flavors.

Smørrebrød, one of the country's specialties, can be enjoyed as lunch or dinner. These open sandwiches can range from a simple slice of bread with a single filling to a multi-layered mixture of cooked meats and salad. In the evening, you'll find that most Danish dishes are based around either fish or meat served with potatoes. Salmon and lamb are particularly popular.

Danish breweries – especially Carlsberg and Tuborg – produce some of the world's most popular beers, and as you might expect the beer in Denmark is excellent. The environment-conscious Danes have banned soft drinks in ring-pull cans because of their potentially damaging effect on the surroundings and wildlife when discarded. Bottled drinks are common, but carry a hefty deposit; this is refunded when the empty bottles are taken back to the place of purchase.

Danes dress fashionably to eat out in restaurants, especially during the summer months.

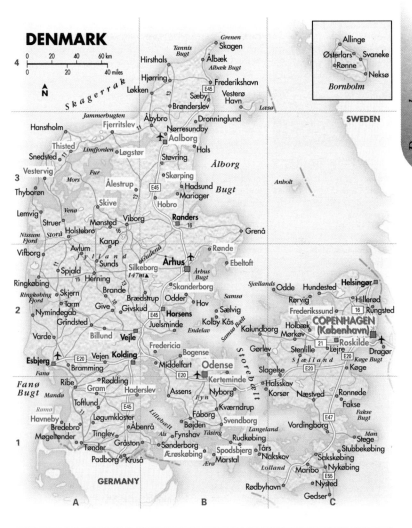

DENMARK

0   20   40   60 km
0   20   40 miles

Skagerrak

Grenen
Skagen
Tannis Bugt
Hirtshals
Hjørring
Løkken
Frederikshavn
Vesterø Havn
Sæby
Brønderslev
Albæk
Albæk Bugt
Læsø
E45

Jammerbugten
Hanstholm
Fjerritslev
Åbybro
Dronninglund
Nørresundby
Aalborg

SWEDEN

Thisted
Limfjorden
Løgstør
Hals
Snedsted
Støvring
Ålborg
Vestervig
Fur
Mors
Skørping
Ålestrup
Hadsund
Bugt
Thyborøn
Skive
Mariager
Anholt
Lemvig
Venø
Hobro
Struer
Monsted
Viborg
Holstebro
Randers
Nissum Fjord
Storå
Karup
Grenå
Vinderup
Avlum
Jutland
Rønde
Spjald
Sunds
Silkeborg
Århus
Ebeltoft
Ringkøbing
Skjern
Herning
147m ▲
Århus Bugt
Sjællands Odde
Hundested
Helsingør
Ringkøbing Fjord
Brande
Bræedstrup
Odder
Samsø
Rørvig
Hillerød
Tarm
Give
Givskud
Hov
Sælvig
Frederikssund
Rungsted
Nymindegab
Horsens
Kolby Kås
Holbæk
COPENHAGEN
Grindsted
Juelsminde
Endelav
Kalundborg
Mørkøv
(København)
Varde
Billund
Vejle
Fredericia
Bogense
Gørlev
Stenlille
Lejre
Roskilde
Dragør
Esbjerg
Vejen
Kolding
Middelfart
Odense
Sjælland
Køge Bugt
Fanø
Bramming
E20
Kerteminde
Slagelse
Køge
Fanø Bugt
Ribe
Rødding
Assens
Nyborg
Halsskov
Korsør
Næstved
Ronnede
Gram
Haderslev
Fyn
Kværndrup
Fakse
Mandø
Toftlund
Lillebælt
Fåborg
Svendborg
Vordingborg
Fakse Bugt
Rømø
Havneby
Løgumkloster
Åbenrå
Bøjden
Langeland
Stege
Bredebro
Tingløv
Als
Fynshav
Tåsing
Rudkøbing
Møn
Møgeltønder
Gråsten
Sønderborg
Spodsbjerg
Tårs
Stubbekøbing
Tønder
Kruså
Ærøskøbing
Marstal
Nakskov
Sakskøbing
Nykøbing
Padborg
Ærø
Lolland
Maribo
E55
Nysted

GERMANY
Rødbyhavn
Gedser

A   B   C

Allinge
Østerlars
Svaneke
Rønne
Neksø
Bornholm

Denmark

Getting Around

The construction of the Great Belt – and the subsequent work on a similar bridge joining Zealand and Sweden – illustrates the efficiency and high standards that mark the transportation and road network of this country. Although Copenhagen's busy center can be daunting for drivers, beyond the capital exploring by car is easy and enjoyable. Ask at a tourist office for information about the Marguerite Route, a series of linked routes along quiet country roads, identified by a daisy motif on a brown background. Public transportation is almost as convenient, thanks to the fast, comfortable trains that can whisk you from Zealand to Funen and on to Jutland in a matter of hours. Buses are a less expensive but slower way of seeing the countryside.

DENMARK

AALBORG   B3
Mou

Mou Hotel $$
Gl. Egensevej 8, Mou DK-9280 Storvorde
☎ 098 31 17 00
📄 098 31 02 22
Mou Hotel is in the village of Mou in the lovely East Himmerland district - close to Lim Fiord and the Kattegat coast and only about a 15-minute drive from the city of

Aalborg. This is an elegant, well-maintained hotel with attractive rooms, first-class cuisine, and an enticing and varied menu.

🛏 15
Closed Dec. 24-25

ÆRØSKOBING   B1
Ærøskobing

Hotel "Ærøhus" $$
Vestergade 38 DK-5970 Ærøskøbing
☎ 062 52 10 03
📄 062 52 21 23
www.aerohus-hotel.dk
📧 mail@aerohus.dk
A romantic family hotel that occupies peaceful surroundings

in this old merchant town. It has an excellent restaurant and a fine garden, with service available on the large terrace. Rooms are attractive, and there is a popular conference center. Tennis courts, indoor swimming pool and weekend dancing are offered.

🛏 20   Closed Dec. 24-Jan. 24
🏊

ALESTRUP   A3
Aars

Aars Hotel $$
Himmerlandsgade 111, DK-9600 Aars
☎ 098 62 16 00
📄 098 62 11 87
www.aarshotel.dk
📧 aars@aarshotel.dk
In-town hotel with an indoor swimming pool and sauna. All rooms are equipped with satellite TV, and an enjoyable à la carte

menu is offered. There are five golf courses close by, and many places of interest in the area.

🛏 27
Closed Dec. 23-25 and Dec. 31-Jan. 2
🏊

Aars

St. Binderup Kro $$
Hovedvej 13 DK-9600 Aars
☎ 098 65 83 33
📄 098 65 83 50
Family-run roadside inn, with a royal charter from 1749, centrally situated between Viborg and Ålborg in beautiful surroundings with woods and rivers. It provides attractive rooms in a large garden setting. The cozy

restaurant serves high-quality cuisine, including many special dishes. There is a lounge with billiards, table tennis, darts and TV.

🛏 23
Closed Dec. 23-Jan. 8

BILLUND   A2
Billund

Billund Kro $$
Buen 6 DK-7190 Billund
☎ 075 33 26 33
📄 075 35 31 91
Cozy inn situated in the center of the town of Billund, a perfect base for tours to Legoland, Givskud Safari Park and walks in magnificent countryside. It is

close to public baths, a trotting racetrack and Billund Airport, and good fishing is available. The restaurant serves Danish inn food and a wide selection of international dishes.

🛏 30
Closed Dec. 25-27
Jan. 1 by arrangement

Key to Symbols: 📄 Fax   Email   🛏 Rooms   🅿 Parking   🏊 Swimming

BOGENSE — B2
Bogense

Bogense Hotel $$
Adelgade 56 DK-5400 Bogense
☎ 064 81 11 08
🖹 064 81 36 04
Charming hotel in the center of this 700-year-old market town, one of the most picturesque in Denmark with its many half-timbered houses. The hotel has Bogense's best restaurant, with a comprehensive and varied menu, and is within walking distance from a sandy beach, large marina and fishing lake.

🛏 36
Closed Dec. 24-26

COPENHAGEN — C2
Herlev
Herlev Kro Hotel $$
Herlev Torv 9-11 DK-2730 Herlev
☎ 044 94 00 03
🖹 044 53 00 22
www.herlev-kro.dk
e hotel.herlev@email.dk
This inn re-opened in May 2000 with 56 new rooms. All rooms are furnished in accordance with the old inn's coziness and atmosphere, but offer modern facilities. Rooms for the disabled, allergy-free and no-smoking rooms are all available. The inn is peacefully situated 20 minutes from the center of Copenhagen, near public transportation and with good parking facilities.

🛏 56   Closed Dec. 21-Jan. 8

EBELTOFT — B2
Ebeltoft

Hotel Vægtergården $$
Hovedgaden 31A, Femmøller Strand DK-8400 Ebeltoft
☎ 086 36 22 11
🖹 086 36 22 21
www.vaegtergaarde.dk
e vaegtergaarde@vaegtergaarde.dk
This establishment is well known for its French/Danish kitchen and high-class gourmet menus. It has newly renovated rooms and a terrace with magnificent views over Ebeltoft Vig. It is located in quiet surroundings with an excellent beach, just a five-minute drive from Ebeltoft town and golf courses.

🛏 33

FJERRITSLEV — A3
Fjerritslev
Fjerritslev Kro $$
Østergarde 2 DK-9690 Fjerritslev
☎ 098 21 11 16
🖹 098 21 37 72
Lovely old roadside inn with delightful modernized rooms. The surrounding countryside is magnificent, close to sand dunes, woodlands and an attractive beach. Fjerritslev is the main town in the Hanherred district.

🛏 14
Closed Dec. 22-Jan. 4 and Sun., Sept. 15-May 1

FREDERICIA — B2
Fredericia
Hotel Hybylund $$
Fælledvej 58 DK-7000 Fredericia
☎ 075 92 98 00
🖹 075 91 15 81
www.sima.dk/hybylud
e hybylud@post3.tele.dk
Centrally located accommodation in Fredericia, close to a good bathing beach and convenient for excursions to Legoland, Lion Park and Hans Christian Andersen's House in Odense. It provides cozy lounges with a personal atmosphere, first-class cuisine and friendly, attentive service. A special golf package is available.

🛏 12
Closed Dec. 23-27 and Dec. 31-Jan. 2

Key to Symbols: 🖹 Fax   e Email   🛏 Rooms   P Parking   ⛵ Swimming

FREDERIKSSUND   C2
Skuldelev
Hotel Skuldelev Kro $$
Østergarde 2A-D, Skuldelev
DK-4050 Skibby
☎ 07 52 03 08
📄 047 52 08 93
This inn is situated in the idyllic
Hornsherred district, only a few
miles from the city's castles and
fiord. It offers attractively

furnished new rooms, an atrium
garden, a lounge with an open
fireplace, a restaurant well known
for its excellent cuisine, a
swimming pool and a sauna.
There also is a new conference
wing and club room.

🛏 30   Closed Dec. 23-Jan. 4
🏊

GRAM   A1
Gram
Den Gamle Kro $$
Slotsvej 47 DK-6510 Gram
☎ 074 82 16 20
📄 074 82 34 95
In the castle town of Gram in
central South Jutland, only 30
miles from the Danish-German
border, you will find The Old
Inn. All rooms have telephones

and TVs, and there is an indoor
swimming pool, spa bath and
sauna. A large, varied menu is
offered.

🛏 18
Closed last 2 weeks of Dec.
🏊

HADERSLEV   A1
Christiansfeld

Tyrstrup Kro $$
Tyrstrup Vestervej 6 DK-6070
Christiansfeld
☎ 074 56 12 42
📄 074 56 19 70
Idyllically situated in the
beautiful countryside around
Christiansfeld, this 350-year-old
inn has been completely restored
to reflect its original style. The
inn's new hotel building, opened

in 1998, offers 12 cozy rooms
and four luxury suites - all with
bath and toilet, and whirlpools in
the suites. All rooms have
modern equipment, including
TV, telephone, fax and modem
facilities.

🛏 16
Closed Dec. 22-Jan. 4

HOBRO   B3
Fårup
Purhus Kro $$
Præstevejen 6 Purhus DK-8990
Fårup
☎ 086 45 28 55
📄 086 45 22 08
Purhus Kro is a typical Danish
roadside inn offering first-class
cuisine. The inn has a large
garden with a children's

playground, and is only half an
hour from the Djurs
Sommerland amusement park.

🛏 19
Closed Dec. 23-Jan. 4

KERTEMINDE   B2
Munkebo

Munkebo Kro $$
Fjordvej 56-58 DK-5330
Munkebo
☎ 065 97 40 30
📄 065 97 55 64
Old roadside inn with a royal
charter, set beside the main road
between Kerteminde and
Odense and overlooking the sea.
The inn, which has been
carefully renovated, is a lovely

example of the traditional Funen
building style, and has a large,
well-established garden.

🛏 20
Closed Dec. 23-27 and Dec. 31-Jan. 3
🏊

Key to Symbols: 📄 Fax   🅔 Email   🛏 Rooms   🅟 Parking   🏊 Swimming

LØGSTØR A3
Løgstør

Hotel du Nord **$$**
Havnevej 38 DK-9670 Løgstør
☎ 098 67 21 00
🖹 098 67 12 99
www.hotel-duord.dk
🅴 hotel-duord@hotel-duord.dk
This newly modernized family hotel, where all rooms have TV and telephone, is just one mile from a nature conservancy area, attractive marina and beach.

Local attractions include the automobile-free island of Livø, the remains of a Viking stronghold, Aqualand, Vitskøl Cloister and Frederik VII Canal. The hotel has agreements with two golf courses.

🛏 17
Closed Dec. 22-Jan. 15

ODENSE B2
Broby
Brobyværk Kro **$$**
Marsk-Billesvej 15, Brobyværk
DK-5672 Broby
☎ 062 63 11 22
🖹 062 63 21 22
www.brobyvaerk-kro.dk
🅴 brobyvaerk.kro@post5.tele.dk
Centrally situated on the island of Funen, this inn resides in

beautiful countryside beside the Odense River. It provides attractively decorated accommodations, including four rooms for non-smokers, and is well known for its excellent cuisine.

🛏 19
Closed Dec. 22-Jan. 5

RØMØ A1
Havenby

Hotel Færgegaarden **$$**
Vestergade 1 Havneby DK-6792
Rømø
☎ 074 75 54 32
🖹 074 75 58 59
Unique and carefully restored captain's residence dating from 1813, situated in beautiful surroundings close to Rømø's most southerly point. It is full of interesting antiques from south

Jutland, and all the rooms are equipped with shower/toilet, color TV and radio. The hotel has an indoor swimming pool and whirlpool.

🛏 34
🏊

RONDE B2
Hornslet
Den Gamle Kro **$$**
Rosenholmsvej 3 DK-8543
Hornslet
☎ 086 99 40 07
🖹 086 99 63 13
Situated in beautiful countryside, this carefully restored inn dates from 1864. It is widely recognized for its cuisine, and all

the rooms are equipped with telephones, TVs, radios and minibars. Ideal base for excursions to Aarhus, Randers, Ebeltoft, Rosenholm Castle, Clausholm Castle, Djurs Sommerland amusement park, Kattegat Aqua Center and the frigate *Jylland*.

🛏 19 Closed Dec. 22-Jan. 2

ROSKILDE C2
Jyllinge
Hotel Søfryd **$$**
Søfrydvej 8 DK-4040 Jyllinge
☎ 046 78 80 11
🖹 046 78 80 91
Hotel Søfryd is situated in one of the most attractive districts in Denmark, with wonderful views of the Roskilde Fjord. The restaurant serves both

international cuisine and local specialties. All rooms have a shower/toilet, clock radio, color TV and telephone. There also is a clubroom with billiards and table tennis.

🛏 26
Closed 12/23-1/3

Key to Symbols: 🖹 Fax 🅴 Email 🛏 Rooms 🅿 Parking 🏊 Swimming

SILKEBORG   B2
Ans By

Kogensbro Kro $$
Gl. Kongevej 70, Kongensbro
8643 Ans By
☎ 086 87 01 77
▤ 086 87 92 17
www.kogesbro-kro.dk
With five golf courses within 25
miles offering special greens fee
arrangements, this old inn, rich
in tradition, is your ideal base.
Situated in beautiful surroundings on the banks of the
Gudenå River, it is well known
for its delicious food, cozy
atmosphere and professional
service.

🛏 14
Closed Dec. 23-25 and Dec. 30-Jan. 5

Låsby
Låsby Kro $$
Hovedgaden 49 DK-8670
Låsby/Ry
☎ 086 95 17 66
▤ 086 95 10 92
www.laasby-kro.dk
🅔 ifo@laasby-kro.dk
Låsby Kro has offered quality
through three generations. Its
lounges and rooms still have the
atmosphere of a bygone era.
Facilities include a playground,
table tennis, sauna, solarium,
tennis, outdoor swimming pool
and jogging path, plus six
neighborhood golf courses.

🛏 35 🏊

Ry

Gammel Rye Kro $$
Ryesgade 8 DK-8680 Ry
☎ 086 89 80 42
▤ 086 89 85 46
This attractive inn is situated in
beautiful surroundings by the
lakes of Silkeborg. Modern
rooms with color TVs and
telephones are located in a newer
guest wing, along with a heated
indoor swimming pool and
solarium. Cozy village
environment with an
opportunity for fishing.

🛏 20
Closed Dec. 24-25 and 31
🏊

SKANDERBORG   B2
Nørre Vissing

Nørre Vissing Kro $$
Låsbyvej 122, Nørre Vissing
DK-8660 Skanderborg
☎ 086 94 37 16
▤ 086 94 37 57
www.r-vissig-kro.dk
This inn has held its royal
charter since 1801, and is
situated near woods, lakes and
hills in beautiful countryside.
Here brothers Morten and Mads
Mygind take pride in creating a
pleasant atmosphere for their
guests. They unite imagination
and tradition in cozy
surroundings and serve exquisite
gourmet meals.

🛏 14
Closed Dec. 22-Jan. 11

SKIVE   A3
Roslev
Roslev Kro $$
Jernbanegade 11 DK-7870
Roslev
☎ 097 57 17 55
▤ 097 57 20 04
This inn has a cozy family
atmosphere and is situated close
to a golf course, Aqualand, the
beach and woods. It's an ideal
base for excursions to Jesperhus
Floral Park. The high-class
kitchen offers exclusive cuisine
with many specialties.

🛏 12
Closed Dec. 23-Jan. 1 and
Sun. Sept. 1-May 1

Key to Symbols: ▤ Fax 🅔 Email 🛏 Rooms 🅿 Parking 🏊 Swimming

SKØRPING B3

Arden

Rold Gammel Kro $$
Hobrovej 11, Rold DK-9510
Arden
☎ 098 56 17 00
🖹 098 56 25 11
www.roldkro.dk
✉ rold-gl-kro@ethotel.dk
Set on the fringe of Rold skov
(forest) in tranquil surroundings,
the building has a new wing with
a sauna and solarium. Traditional
Danish inn cuisine is served, as
well as a five-course gourmet
menu. There are good hunting
and golfing opportunities nearby,
and sights include chalk mines,
Cirkusmuseum and the
Willestrup Barok Garden.

🛏 26

SPODSBJERG B1

Humble

Humble Kro $$
Ristingevej 2 DK-5932 Humble
☎ 062 57 11 34
🖹 062 57 11 24
www.lagelad.com/Humblekro
✉ Humble-kro@get2et.dk
Humble Kro provides
comfortable accommodations
and good food from a traditional
kitchen. Situated in the southern
part of Funen, it is a good
starting point for visiting a
splendid nature site, wonderful
beaches and area museums, as
well as engaging in windsurfing,
fishing and golf. The rooms are
located in an annex, all with
shower, television and minibar.

🛏 4

SVENDBORG B1

Tåsinge
Hotel Troense $$
Strandgade 5-7, Tåsinge DK-
5700 Svendborg
☎ 062 22 54 12
🖹 062 22 78 12
www.sima.dk/Hotel-troese
✉ Hotel-troese@ethotel1.dk
The hotel is situated in an idyllic
little town with well-preserved
half-timbered houses and easy
access to historical sights.
Weekend guests are entertained
with music and dance from mid-
August to mid-June. Parking is
provided.

🛏 27
Closed Dec. 23-24 and Dec. 30-Jan. 5

THISTED A3

Thisted
Hotel Thisted $$
Frederiksgade 16 DK-7700
Thisted
☎ 097 92 52 00
🖹 097 92 61 23
This newly restored, traditional
family hotel is in the center of
town. A varied choice of dishes
is offered from the regular and
daily menus. Easy access is
afforded to historic attractions in
the area and to Nordvestjysk
Golf Course.

🛏 12
Closed Dec. 22-Jan. 2

VESTERVIG A3

Hvidbjerg -Thyholm

Tambohus Kro $$
Tambohuse DK-7790 Hvidbjerg
- Thyholm
☎ 097 87 53 00
🖹 097 87 51 55
www.tambohus.dk
✉ tambohus@tambohus.tele.dk
This old ferry inn, given a royal
charter by the king of Denmark
in 1850, is set in its own natural
paradise beside Lim Fjord. An
authentic atmosphere remains,
despite recent modernization,
and fried eel is a specialty of the
house. This is a good base for
exploring northwest Jutland; row
boats and bicycles can be rented.
Facilities for the disabled are
available.

🛏 29
Closed Dec. 18-Jan. 7

Key to Symbols: Fax Email Rooms Parking Swimming

France

La Belle France – beautiful France – is western Europe's largest country. Its six natural boundaries are themselves part of its beauty: the Atlantic pounding rocky cliffs and the English Channel lapping against long beaches on the western coasts; the dramatic Pyrenees and Alps to the southwest and southeast; the sparkling Mediterranean along the sunny southern shore, and the mighty Rhine River dividing France from Germany in the northeast. Within these borders is a stunning diversity of landscape, taking in wide arable flatlands and forested hills, vineyards, lush river valleys and daunting mountain *massifs*, not to speak of the 2,000-mile coastline. The architecture is as varied as the natural scenery, from hilltop villages and narrow, shaded streets in the rural south to steep-roofed wooden chalets in the mountain areas. Noble châteaux stand as reminders of the aristocratic power and wealth of the past, and the growing prosperity of the 17th and 18th centuries has left its legacy of churches and civic buildings, spacious squares and well-planned streets. And the preservation of past monuments hasn't prevented a program of modern building that's produced imaginative architecture in every major city.

The French Way of Life

Apart from a couple of brief periods, France has been a republic almost as long as the United States. Their Revolution gave the French a tremendous sense of patriotism, which still exists, but there also are very distinct and proudly maintained regional traditions, and even languages – such as Breton – that refuse to be swamped by a homogenous French identity. Paris, of course, is a law unto itself, as is any busy, popular, modern city, and there can be a tendency to brusqueness. But even in the capital, there's a profound appreciation of leisure time. After a hard day's work, people will readily sit for hours at a time discussing politics, the arts, economics and other issues over a lengthy meal. And even in the most offhand Parisian exchange, you'll find that formal courtesies play their part: always preface any inquiry with "*bonjour*," and end with "*merci*."

Most visitors are seduced by the innate French sense of style, which can present itself in the artfully stacked produce of market stalls or the sensible layout of an airport. Shopping is something of an art form in the country that makes champagne, world-famous perfumes, and some of the world's most desirable clothes and accessories. And French food still enjoys its long-established high reputation, from the simplest snack to the richest gourmet meal. Even the smallest village in the remotest corner of France will have a *boulangerie* (bakery) or *pâtisserie* (cake shop) full of mouthwatering, freshly baked goodies whose aroma fills the street. There's immense pleasure to be had window-shopping at the *boucheries* (butchers), *traiteurs* (delicatessens) and *épiceries* (grocers), whose displays are often works of art in themselves. Unbelievably fresh seafood, served in massive portions, is naturally a specialty in coastal areas; and the whole of France benefits from its agricultural wealth, with delicious dairy products, fruit and vegetables in plentiful supply.

A view past an equestrian statue towards Paris's most famous landmark, the Eiffel Tower

Accommodations

France has an enormous range of hotels, and accommodations are generally an excellent value when compared to other northern European countries. Double rooms usually contain two single beds, although there are double and single bedded rooms, too. Private bathrooms are always available, but you'll pay more for a bath than for a shower. Baths usually have a hand-held shower, too, but no shower curtain.

Breakfast is not normally included in the price of a room but traditionally consists of tea, coffee or hot chocolate, with bread, perhaps a croissant and jam. It can be more interesting to have breakfast at a local *café bar*, which is often bustling from early in the day. Rates for dinner, bed and breakfast (*demi pension*) are usually an excellent value. Many establishments, especially those in rural areas, also have "gîtes" available in addition to the main guest rooms. These are self-catering accommodations, often cottages or converted farm buildings with kitchens, enabling guests to cook for themselves.

Food and Drink

Classic French cooking means quality ingredients, subtle sauces, tender meat and ripe cheeses. Lyon is generally acknowledged as France's gastronomic center. Here, the specialty is *boudin blanc*, veal sausage, or *quenelles*, lightly poached fish dumplings, served with the local crayfish-based sauce Nantua. Pommes Lyonnais (potatoes fried with onions) and *gratin dauphinois* (potatoes baked in cream and cheese) are now enjoyed all over the world.

In France you will generally be served with French wine. It can be pricey, but restaurants all serve house wine in carafes, which is often a good value. Restaurants must, by law, serve faucet water if you ask for it. French coffee is very strong: a *café americain* is the weaker version. Unless you ask for a *café crème*, your coffee will be served black.

If you don't want to eat in a formal restaurant, try a brasserie, which serves simple cooked meals, drinks and snacks all day; or a bistro, more modest – though not necessarily cheaper – than French restaurants. If planning a picnic, visit the *boulangerie* (bakery), *pâtisserie* (cake shop) and local market.

FRANCE

ABBEVILLE   C5
Melleville
La Marette $
rte de la Marette,
Seine-Maritime
☎ 235508165
🖹 325508165
This house was built at the turn
of the last century, and it set in
rural surroundings within easy
driving distance of the coast.

Bedrooms are comfortable with
modern facilities and the living
room overlooks the garden.
Continental breakfast includes
delicious home-made jams, and
there is a kitchen in the annex
where guests can prepare their
own meals.

🛏 5

St Riquier
Hôtel Jean de Bruges $$
18 place de l'Église, BP 4, 80135,
Somme
☎ 322283030
🖹 322280069
e jeandebruges@minitel.net
Modern art and surprisingly
comfortable Lloyd loom
furniture harmonize easily
within the solid stone walls of

this ancient building. Guests can
eat in the glass-roofed dining
room with its summerhouse
design before retiring to the
classical white bedrooms, three
of which are family size. There is
a covered terrace and a lounge
for afternoon tea. English,
Dutch and German spoken.

🛏 9   Closed Jan.

AGEN   C2
Montaigu-De-Quercy

Les Chênes de Sainte Croix $
82150, Tarn-Et-Garonne
☎ 563953078
🖹 563953078
e adhunt@gofornet.com
The house dates back at least as
far as 1750 and the present
owners, Arthur and Deborah
Hunt (both architects), have
converted it with care, retaining
the oak beams and exposed stone

walls. Facilities include a floodlit
swimming pool, boules,
badminton and table tennis.
Dinner is served at the family
table, or outside whenever
possible.

🛏 6

AIX-LES-BAINS   E3
St Felix

Les Bruyeres $$
Mercy, 74540, Haute-Savoie
☎ 450609653
🖹 450609465
The foot of the Alps is the
stunning setting for this
rambling old farm building,
which provides comfortable
accommodations. The garden is
ablaze with flowers for much of
the year, and guests may play

tennis and croquet. Tea is served
on the terrace, and breakfast
includes a variety of regional
dishes. A fixed-price evening
meal also can be provided.
English is spoken.

🛏 3

ALBI   C2
Cordes
Les Tuileries $
81170, Tarn
☎ 563560593
🖹 563560593
There are exceptional views of
the old walled town of Cathares
from this 200-year-old property.
Guests are invited to enjoy the
garden, and when the weather is

fine meals are served in the
shade of the chestnut trees.
There is a swimming pool on the
grounds, and table tennis and
boules are available. English is
spoken.

🛏 5   🏊

Key to Symbols: 🖹 Fax   e Email   🛏 Rooms   P Parking   🏊 Swimming

ALENCON   B4

Champfleur
Garencière $
Sarthe
☎ 33317584
Stone-built 18th-century farmhouse looking out over open fields. The comfortable bedrooms have been individually designed and furnished; all have private bathroom facilities.

Meals prepared from the best local farm produce are served at the hosts' table. There is a heated indoor swimming pool, and a pretty garden with boules outside. English is spoken.

 5

Monhoudou
Château de Monhoudou $$
Sarthe
☎ 243974005
🖹 243331158
Built between the 16th and 18th centuries, this château still belongs to the Viscount de Mouhoudou, who offers a warm welcome to his ancestral home. It is an attractive white stone building with turrets and a lake in front. It is fully restored and combines period furnishings with modern comfort. Candlelit dinners are served on request. English is spoken.

 4

AMBOISE   C3

Amboise

Le Fleuray $$
Indre-et-Loire
☎ 247560925
🖹 247569397
e lefleurayhotel@wandoo.fr
Englishman Peter Newington welcomes guests to his beautiful manor house in the heart of the Loire Valley. Service is friendly and attentive, and the excellent cuisine incorporates local fruit, vegetables and cheese. Bedrooms are decorated in a delightful rustic style. In summer guests can relax in the pretty garden, and in winter enjoy the log fire in the sitting room.

 11
Closed one week around All Saints Day (Nov. 1), two weeks at Christmas

Château des Ormeaux $$
Nazelles, Indre-et-Loire
☎ 247232651
🖹 247231931
The château is set on a hillside, so that from its tall windows or the Italian terrace and swimming pool below, you can look across the grounds to the majestic elm trees after which it is named. The owner is an antiques dealer - there is an antiques store on the grounds - and the château is furnished with expert care.

 6

Chancay
Ferme de Launay $
Indre-et-Loire
☎ 247522821
🖹 247522821
This attractive farmhouse has been renovated to provide luxurious accommodations. Guests can make use of the lounge, with its wooden beams and big fireplace. A Continental or English breakfast is served, and evening meals are available by prior arrangement, featuring regional specialties and local wines. Guests must stay for a minimum of two nights May-September. English, German and Italian are spoken.

3

Francueil

Le Moulin Neuf   **$$**
28 rue du Moulin Neuf,
Indre-et-Loire
☎ 247239344
🗎 247239467

Surrounded by leafy woodland and set beside a river, this beautiful old water mill makes a perfect rural idyll. Fully renovated by its Franco-British owners to include modern comforts, it still retains its character and many original features. The four guest rooms are decorated with colorful fabrics and stencil designs. Smoking is not permitted.

🛏 5

AMIENS   C5

Albert

Hotel de la Basilique   **$**
3-5 rue Gambetta, 80300,
Somme
☎ 322750471
🗎 322751047

The hotel is located in the middle of town, and its hospitable owners speak English. The restaurant is renowned for its high-quality food, and the chef has won awards for his house specialties and regional cuisine. There also is a bar where guests can enjoy an aperitif or coffee. The 10 spacious guest rooms are well equipped, and three have balconies.

🛏 10
Closed Aug. 13-Sep. 3 and Dec. 23-Jan. 7

ANGERS   B4

Champigne

Château des Briottières   **$$$**
Maine-et-Loire
☎ 241420002
🗎 241420155
📧 briottieres@wanadoo.fr

The price of staying in this magnificent Anjou château reflects the level of luxury awaiting its privileged guests. Bedrooms are beautifully furnished, and most have superb views. Evening meals feature traditional family recipes. Facilities include a heated swimming pool, bicycles, billiards, table tennis, badminton, archery and a playground. Hot air balloon rides also are available. English and Spanish spoken.

🛏 14

Charce-St-Ellier-Sur-Aubance

La Pichonnière   **$**
Maine-et-Loire
☎ 241912937
🗎 241912937

Two brothers and their families share this small agricultural business, owned by the family for over 50 years. Here flowers are grown for their seed, and rooms are rented during the tourist season. The pretty horseshoe-shaped building offers simple bed-and-breakfast accommodations. Bicycles are available, and there is a garden for strolling. Credit cards are not taken; English is spoken.

🛏 3

Montreuil-Sur-Loir

Château de Montreuil   **$**
Maine-et-Loire
☎ 241762103

The château was constructed in 1840 in the "Troubadour" style, with neo-Gothic arched windows, turrets and spires. It owes much to its location on the banks of the River Loire, and has a terrace perched right above the water. One floor of the château is exclusively for guests. A lounge is provided, and dinner is available by appointment.

🛏 5
Closed Nov. 16-Mar. 14

Key to Symbols: 🗎 Fax   📧 Email   🛏 Rooms   🅿 Parking   🏊 Swimming

St Georges-Sur-Loire

Prieure de L'Épinay $
Maine-et-Loire
☎ 241391444
🖻 241391444
📧 bgaultier@compuserve.com
There is an abundance of character at this former priory, now converted to provide comfortable guest house accommodations. The spacious bedrooms all have televisions and en suite facilities. In the gardens there is a swimming pool and fishing, and bicycles can be rented. A fixed-price evening meal can be provided by the hosts, and English is spoken.

🛏 3
Closed Nov.-Mar.

St Martin-Du-Bois

La Pigeonnerie $
18 rye du Prieure,
Maine-et-Loire
☎ 241613352
Guest rooms are all en suite and individually decorated in this comfortable home. It offers good value for the money, both for accommodation, which is priced per room rather than per person, and for the optional evening meals, which use fresh produce from the garden. A spacious living room leads out to the terrace and gardens. English is spoken; no credit cards.

🛏 4
Closed Nov.-Mar.

St Mathurin-Sur-Loire

La Bouquetterie $
118 rue du Roi René,
Maine-et-Loire
☎ 241570200
🖻 241573190
A 19th-century house with views of the Loire, where the communal rooms are bright and comfortable and all the bedrooms have en suite facilities. Two rooms with kitchenette and independent entrance have been created from converted outbuildings, and the delightful gardens include a summerhouse and games for children. The owner speaks English.

🛏 6

ANGOULEME B3
Roullet-St-Estephe

Logis de Romainville $
Romainville, 16440, Charente
☎ 545663256
🖻 545663256
The rooms in this well-proportioned house are all en suite and steam-heated. In addition, there are two self-catering studios, perfect for two or three people. A flower-decked terrace decorated with a pretty wrought-iron pergola is ideal for barbecues. Outside there is a swimming pool, and bicycles can be rented. English and Italian are spoken.

🛏 5

St Paul-Lizonne

La Vieille Maison $
St Paul-Lizonne, 24320,
Dordogne
☎ 553916131
🖻 553916131
This typical Perigordian building has original features such as fine oak beams and stone fireplaces, which are still used in colder months. After a day's sightseeing or lying by the pool, guests can dine in the hotel's renowned restaurant, where a delicious combination of international dishes and local specialties is served either in the dining room or on the leafy terrace.

🛏 12
Closed Nov. 1-Easter

Key to Symbols: 🖻 Fax 📧 Email 🛏 Rooms 🅿 Parking 🏊 Swimming

ANNECY   E3
Talissieu

Domaine de Château Froid   **$**
01510, Ain
☎ 479873999
🖹 479874569
🅔 chateau.froid@wanadoo.fr

This château was built in 1625 by Carthusian monks, and despite its name (Cold Castle), the building has full steam heating. Bedrooms, some in the round turrets, are luxuriously spacious. A huge mirror and magnificent chandeliers are features of the public rooms, and regional specialties are served at dinner. English is spoken, and facilities include a heated outdoor pool, tennis courts and bicycles.

🛏 10

ARGENTON-SUR-CREUSE   C3
Angles-Sur-L'Anglin
Le Relais du Lyon d'Or   **$**
4 rue d'Enfer, 86260, Vienne
☎ 549483253
🖹 549840228
🅔 thorea@lyondor.com

Tastefully decorated accommodations are offered here, with each room in its own period style and up-to-the-minute conveniences provided. The restaurant only uses local produce and provides local wines. Pamper yourself in the relaxation center with steam baths, massage, shiatsu and beauty treatments – your own personal program will be devised by the resident specialist. English is spoken.

🛏 10   Closed Jan. 3-Feb. 28

Journet
La Boulinière   **$**
86290, Vienne
☎ 549915588
🖹 549915588

A charming house set in extensive grounds, where only the sounds of birds will disturb your peace. There is an outdoor swimming pool, and Futuroscope is only 40 minutes away. Bedrooms are stylishly furnished and each has a private bathroom. An optional fixed-price dinner is served in the evenings, and vegetarian dishes can be provided. English and Italian are spoken.

🛏 6

Rivarennes
Château de la Tour   **$$**
Indre
☎ 254470612
🖹 254470608

The Château de la Tour nestles romantically into the scenery of the Indre Valley, with its turrets reflected in the River Creuse. It is an elegant and comfortably furnished hotel with many original features. Breakfast can be taken in the dining room or on the covered terrace. There are 10 spacious en suite rooms, including three suitable for families.

🛏 10

ARLES   D1
Alzon

Château du Mazel   **$$**
rte du Villaret, 30770, Gard
☎ 467820633
🖹 467820637

The former residence of the Bishops of Nîmes, this château is a haven of peace with colorful gardens bordered by grand old trees. The bedrooms are spacious, each decorated in an individual style, with a pleasing blend of period and modern furniture. The restaurant, which also brings in non-guests, serves lunch and a table d'hôte menu at dinner. English is spoken.

🛏 6
Closed mid-Nov. to Palm Sunday

ARRAS C5
Duisans

Le Clos Grincourt $
18 rue du Château, 62161,
Pas-de-Calais
☎ 321486833
▤ 321486833
This charming manor house is
surrounded by a private park.
Elegantly decorated and
furnished in 19th-century style,
it has a comfortable family
atmosphere. There is an en suite
double bedroom and a suite with
a double room, a twin room and
a bathroom. Breakfast is served
in the guests' salon, which has a
television and library. Smoking is
not permitted.

🛏 3

Grand-Rullecourt

**Château de Grand-
Rullecourt** $
62810, Pas-de-Calais
☎ 321580637
▤ 141279730
Magnificent château occupying
its own parkland among the
gentle hills of Artois. It has an
aristocratic history that can be
traced back to the passage of
Joan of Arc when she was a
prisoner of the English. The
refined accommodations
comprise spacious en suite
rooms, some with four-poster
beds. Living rooms and a library
also are available for guests' use.

🛏 6

Saulty

Bed & Breakfast $
82 rue de la Gare, 62158,
Pas-de-Calais
☎ 321482476
▤ 321481832
Despite its imposing appearance,
there is a convivial atmosphere at
this grand 18th-century château.
The hospitable English-speaking
owners invite guests to make use
of the library and to wander in
the quiet gardens. Indoors there
is a comfortable living room in
which to relax, and the bedrooms
all have full en suite facilities.
There are several restaurants in
the area.

🛏 5
Closed Jan.

AUCH C1
Mielan
La Tannerie $
32170, Gers
☎ 562676262
▤ 562676262
English owners offer a warm
welcome to this attractive 19th-
century house. A refrigerator and
tea and coffee-making facilities
are provided for guests'
convenience in the sitting room.
The spacious bedrooms look out
over the gardens to a beautiful
view of the Pyrenees. In summer
breakfast is served on the elegant
terrace, which is bordered by a
carved stone balustrade.

🛏 4
Closed Nov.-Feb.

AUXERRE D4
Chevannes

Château de Ribourdin $
Yonne
☎ 386412316
▤ 386412316
This elegant Burgundy château
makes an ideal base for visiting
the local vineyards and historic
monuments. Converted
outbuildings house the guest
rooms, which are individually
furnished with antiques. One
room is suitable for guests with
disabilities. The well-kept
grounds include an outdoor
swimming pool, and bicycle
rental is available. Dinner is
served in the château, and
English is spoken.

🛏 5

St Aubin-Chateau-Neuf

La Posterle $
2 pl Aristide Briand, Yonne
☎ 386736409
▤ 386736409
Proprietors Daniel and Jeannette Chaumet offer individually decorated and furnished bedrooms at La Posterle. All have en suite facilities and steam heating, and two have televisions. Meals, available by reservation, are eaten around the family table from 6 p.m. There is supervised parking space, both open and covered.

🛏 4

AVALLON   D4

La Motte-Ternant
Le Presbytère $
Côte-d'Or
☎ 380843485
▤ 380843532
🄴 Le Presbytere@aol.com
Standing tall at the highest point of the village, the 16th-century Presbytère has wonderful views across a rural landscape. The interior has been tastefully decorated with white-painted walls in the beamed bedrooms. The same eye for detail is evident in the pretty garden. Dinner with vegetarian options is served, and private fishing and bicycle rental are available. English is spoken.

🛏 3

Semur-en-Auxois
Château de Flée $$$
Côte-d'Or
☎ 380971707
▤ 380973432
Guests are offered an unforgettable stay at this former home of the treasurer to King Louis XV. In the gardens there is a swimming pool and boule; private fishing and bicycle rental are available, and special arrangements have been made for guests at the Château de Chailly golf course. A fixed-price dinner is served, and the hosts speak English and German.

🛏 2
Closed Nov. 15-Feb. 28

AVIGNON   D2

Apt

Auberge du Presbytère $
pl de la Fontaine, 84400, Vaucluse
☎ 490741150
▤ 490046851
🄴 auberge.presbtere@ provence-luberon.com
The Presbytere has been created by integrating three medieval stone buildings overlooking the picturesque village square. The interior is charming, and the individually decorated bedrooms include two with their own balconies affording views across the Apt plain. The restaurant is renowned for its traditional Provençal cuisine, and the hospitable family who run the inn speak English.

🛏 10

Moulin de Lavon $
84400, Vaucluse
☎ 490743454
▤ 490742013
Mireille and Yves Nief welcome guests to their family home, which is surrounded by the vines and cherry trees they cultivate. En suite accommodations in the farmhouse can sleep 11 people, while a gîte (self-catering cottage) offers beds for an additional 12. Typical Provençal dinners are served, except on Sunday. Facilities include a swimming pool, table tennis, boules, a piano and a TV room.

🛏 10

Key to Symbols: ▤ Fax 🄴 Email 🛏 Rooms 🅿 Parking 🏊 Swimming

Crillon-Le-Brave

Domaine la Condamine $
84410, Vaucluse
☎ 490624728
🖹 490624728

La Condamine is surrounded by vineyards that produce award-winning wines. The attractive accommodations include an apartment for four people, and all decorated in typical Provençal style. Breakfast can be had by the side of the swimming pool or in the superb garden amid the lavender and lush shrubs. English, Italian and Spanish are spoken.

🛏 4

L'Isle-Sur-La-Sorgue

Domaine de la Fontaine $$
920 chemin du Bosquet, 84800, Vaucluse
☎ 490380144
🖹 490385342

This charming old manor house lies on the outskirts of the village, surrounded by lush gardens complete with a swimming pool. Evenings can be spent playing boule or enjoying a romantic dinner on the terrace under the plane trees. The guest rooms are pleasantly furnished; one has a balcony and two are suitable for families. The hospitable owners speak English.

🛏 5
Closed Jan. 16-Feb. 28

AVRANCHES   B4
Bacilly

Le Grand Moulin Le Comte $
Manche
☎ 233709208

This rambling 18th-century Normandy farmhouse offers comfortable accommodations. The original granite fireplace graces the large dining room, and there is a pleasant lounge with a television receiving English and French channels. Two ground-floor bedrooms have private entrances, and one of these has a kitchenette. The English hosts speak an impressive number of languages, including Welsh, French and German.

🛏 5

Le Mesnil-Gilbert
La Motte $
Manche
☎ 233598309
🖹 233694546
e lemarchant@wanadoo.fr

At this granite and shale farmhouse you can meet the animals, ramble through fields or fish in the river. You also can play boules, table tennis or a local game, "galoche." There is a guest room with its own kitchen, and good home cooking is served – outside in fine weather. La Motte sells its own Calvados, cider, honey and jams.

🛏 5

St Senier-Sous-Avranches
Château du Champ du Genêt $
rte de Mortain, Manche
☎ 233605267
🖹 233605267
e cheval-plaisir@wanadoo.fr

The château is fairly compact as châteaux go, but perfectly formed. It is built of chunky stone, with a round turret and white shutters at the long windows. The bedrooms are furnished in traditional style, all with en suite facilities. This is the perfect place for a riding vacation, since there are riding stables within the grounds. English is spoken.

🛏 4

Key to Symbols: 🖹 Fax   e Email   🛏 Rooms   P Parking   ⛱ Swimming

Vergoncey
Château de Boucéel $$
Manche
☎ 233483461
🗎 233483461
This historic monument, built in 1763, was the site of a bloody battle during the French Revolution. It is surrounded by a large estate, with romantic gardens, lakes, an island, ancient trees and a chapel. The interior boasts superb carvings, parquet floors, period antiques and family portraits throughout, combined with modern comforts and stylish en suite bathrooms.

🛏 4

Bayeux

River Cottage $
3 Impasse Moulin de la Rivière, Calvados
☎ 231923123
🗎 231923123
Not surprisingly, given its name, the owner of this pretty house speaks English. An English influence also is evident in the bedroom décor. Guests are encouraged to enjoy the garden, which extends as far as the river, where fishing is an option. A fixed-price evening meal is available on request, including regional specialties. This is a non-smoking house.

🛏 3

St Pee-Sur-Nivelle
Bidachuna $$
rte Oihan Bidea, 64310, Pyrénées-Atlantiques
☎ 559545622
🗎 559473100
This pretty house with shuttered windows is in a quiet location looking out across undulating countryside toward the Pyrenees. The interior has plain white walls and beamed ceilings, and there are some beautiful antique pieces. The comfortable bedrooms have views of the mountains, and an ample breakfast is served in the living room or on the sunny terrace. English and Spanish are spoken.

🛏 3

Bayac

Relais de Lavergne
La Vergne, 24150, Dordogne
☎ 553578316
🗎 553578316
This 17th-century house has been tastefully restored to provide a high standard of comfort. The steam-heated bedrooms include a ground-floor suite suitable for disabled visitors. Guests have the use of the dining room, living room and library, and evening meals can be ordered in advance. There also is a swimming pool and barbecue. English is spoken; credit cards are not accepted.

Razac-D'Eymet
La Petite Auberge
24500, Dordogne
☎ 553246927
🗎 553610263
The grounds of this converted 17th-century Perigordine farmhouse include a swimming pool, sun terraces, giant chess, boules and badminton. One of the comfortable bedrooms is suitable for disabled guests. There is a large lounge, bar and library of English books. Regional specialities and vegetarian dishes are served in the small restaurant. English is spoken, and two self-catering gîtes are also are available.

🛏 7

Closed Nov.-Mar.

Key to Symbols: 🗎 Fax 📧 Email 🛏 Rooms 🅿 Parking 🌊 Swimming

Ste Alvere
Le Moulin Neuf $
Paunat, 24510, Dordogne
☎ 553633018
🖹 553733391
The English owners offer a warm welcome to this lovely old water mill. The comfortable guest rooms include a private sitting room and are in a building that is separate from the proprietors' house. Breakfast, which is included in the room price, is served on a vine-covered terrace in summer. Credit cards are not accepted.

🛏 6

Pesmes
La Maison Royale $
70140, Haute-Saône
☎ 384312323
The 14th-century buildings of this medieval fort took several years to renovate, and are now considered a tourist attraction in their own right. The traditional is blended with the modern in the striking interior decorations, and there is nothing old-fashioned about the facilities. Private fishing, bicycle rental and billiards are available, and the hosts speak English, German, Spanish and Italian.

🛏 12

Auchy-Au-Bois

Les Cohettes $
28 rue de Pernes, 62190, Pas-de-Calais
☎ 321020947
🖹 321028168
📧 temps-libre-evasion@wanadoo.fr
Guests stay here to visit the battlefields of the Somme, the cemeteries and memorials, but also to enjoy the present-day tranquility and glorious sandy beaches. The farmhouse is delightful, with whitewashed walls, wooden shutters and colorful window boxes. The spacious en suite guest rooms have a country flavor, decorated in yellow and blue. English is spoken.

🛏 5

Roquebrun

Les Mimosas $
av des Orangers, 34460, Herault
☎ 467896136
🖹 467896136
📧 la-touche.les-mimosas@wanadoo.fr
This charming 19th-century mansion has been transformed into an elegant country guest house by Sarah and Denis La Touche, a New Zealander and an Englishman with a French name. A sumptuous breakfast and evening meals featuring regional specialties are served. Sarah runs a cookery course at Les Mimosas, concentrating on French country cooking for the family.

🛏 5

Villeneuve-Les-Beziers

Bed & Breakfast $
7 rue de la Fontaine, 34420, Herault
☎ 467398715
🖹 467398715
Down a quiet road in the center of the village of Villeneuve-Lès-Béziers can be found the lovingly restored home of Andrew and Jennifer Viner. Dating from the 15th century, the building has many authentic period features, including murals, frescos and a staircase in the tower dating from the Middle Ages. Evening meals reflect Jennifer's Australian background, English experience and local influences.

🛏 4

Key to Symbols: Fax Email Rooms Parking Swimming

BLOIS · C4
Cheverny

Ferme des Saules $
Loir-et-Cher
☎ 254792695
🗎 254799754
📧 merlin.cheverny@infonie.fr
This converted farmhouse is in the center of the Loire, surrounded by its most spectacular châteaux. Owner Didier Merlin is a professional chef who serves up regional specialties using local produce (reservations are a must). Spacious guest rooms are simply but stylishly decorated with tiled floors, white walls and rustic furniture. The farmhouse has a peaceful garden with a pool and sun terrace.

🛏 5
Closed Jan.

Cour-Cheverny

Le Beguinage $
Loir-et-Cher
☎ 254792992
🗎 254799459
This charmingly decorated house is set in its own beautiful parkland with a river running through. It is located close to Château de Cheverny, one of the most elegant of the Loire castles. Six en suite guest rooms are provided, and a fixed-price dinner is available in the restaurant. The staff speaks English, and fishing in the river is permitted year-round.

🛏 6

BORDEAUX · B2
Bourg-Sur-Gironde
Château de la Grave $
33710, Gironde
☎ 557684149
🗎 557684926
Dating from 1740, this charming château was later rebuilt in its present Louis XIII style. Inside it has a warm, rustic look and is furnished with antiques. Spacious and elegant guest rooms enjoy views over the surrounding vines and woods. There is a terrace where breakfast is served and a glass of the château's wine can be enjoyed. Tasting sessions also are available.

 3

Closed mid-Aug. to Aug. 31

Cissac-Medoc
Le Luc
6 rte de Larrivaux, 33250, Gironde
☎ 556595290
🗎 556591184
This charming guest house in the Médoc region, renowned for its rich red wines, is comfortable, attractively decorated and steam-heated. The owners are hospitable, speak English and can arrange tours and wine-tastings at the many stunning wine-growing châteaux nearby. There is a garden with tables and chairs and an adjoining one-bedroom gîte with kitchen and living room.

🛏 4

BOURGES · C3
Foecy

Le Petit Prieure $
7 rue l'Église, Cher
☎ 248510176
The colorful display of flowers at this old priory has won a national award for the owners, Chantal and Claude Alard. Claude is a sculptor, and some of his work can be seen in the garden. Bedrooms take their names from Greek legend, and guests have independent access to the property. An information pack on places to visit is provided.

🛏 3

BREST   A4
Guisseny

Kéraloret $
Finistère
☎ 298256037
▤ 298256988
The Auberge de Kéraloret is a traditional granite farmhouse offering comfortable bedrooms with tasteful antique furnishings. The delightful day rooms include three dining areas. There is plenty to keep younger visitors amused, including a well-equipped gameroom and a volleyball net. You can try many Breton specialties at dinner. English, German and Spanish are spoken.

🛏 6

BRIVE-LA-GALLIARDE   C2
Beaulieu-Sur-Dordogne

Chateau d'Arnac $$
Nonards, 19120, Corrèze
☎ 555915413
▤ 555915262
This romantic 12th-century turreted château is surrounded by a large private park – with fishing in the lake or trout stream, an outdoor swimming pool and a tennis court. The château is charming and full of character, with log fires in all the rooms in colder weather. There is a dining room where a Continental breakfast is served, and an open terrace.

🛏 4

Montignac

La Licorne $
Valojoulx, 24290, Dordogne
☎ 553507777
▤ 553507777
La Licorne is an ensemble of three buildings, dating from the 13th, 17th and 18th centuries, in the center of the tiny village of Le Bourg. Evening meals featuring home-grown seasonal produce are served in an attractive dining room, while breakfast can be eaten in the garden arbor. Credit cards are not accepted. English and Italian are spoken.

🛏 4
Closed Oct. 15-Apr. 15

CAEN   B4
Bretteville-Sur-Laize
Château des Riffets $$
Calvados
☎ 231235321
▤ 231237514
Elegant château set in wooded parkland offering spacious en suite bedrooms. The park borders the region known as "Norman Switzerland," and here you can go horseback riding, canoeing, rock climbing, mountain biking or hang gliding. Alternatively, you could just relax by the pool before enjoying one of the delicious table d'hôte dinners. English and German are spoken.

🛏 4

Crepon
Le Haras de Crépon $
Calvados
☎ 231213737
▤ 231211212
Beautiful manor house, combining original features with modern amenities, located within easy walking distance of the historic beaches. It is just outside the village, surrounded by a racehorse breeding estate. The hosts are welcoming, speak English, and serve a full breakfast in the dining room.

🛏 5

Key to Symbols: ▤ Fax   Email   🛏 Rooms   Parking   Swimming

Manoir de Crépon $
rte d'Arromanches, Calvados
☎ 231222127
🖹 231228880
With sandy beaches within walking distance, this traditional Normandy manor house makes an ideal location for a shore vacation. Bright and spacious guest rooms on the first floor overlook the garden and park.

They are furnished with antiques, and some have stone fireplaces. Continental breakfast is served in the dining room.

 5

Monts-En-Bessin

La Varinière $
La Vallée, Calvados
☎ 231774473
🖹 23771172
An attractive bourgeois house, built of mellow Caen stone and set in a picturesque valley in the Pré-Bocage area of Calvados. There are four comfortable bedrooms and one suite, and guests have the use of a living room and large garden. A refrigerator and freezer are available for keeping picnic food fresh, and the proprietor is happy to recommend local restaurants.

 5

CAHORS   C2

Albas
La Méline $
rte de Sauzet D37, 46140, Lot
☎ 565369725
🖹 565369725
La Méline is situated on a hillside in the Lot Valley, with beautiful views over forests and the Cahors vineyards. It offers well-equipped accommodations and good-value meals. Cycling and walking tours as well as visits to nearby farms and vineyards are added attractions, and within the grounds guests can play boules. English, Dutch and German are spoken.

🛏 3
Closed Oct.-Mar.

Florimont-Gaumier
La Daille
24250, Dordogne
☎ 553284071
The beautiful old main building of this guest house was formerly a farmhouse, and its secluded location offers total peace and relaxation. Guests enjoy the colorful gardens, lawns, shady trees and terraces. Rooms are bright, spacious and comfortable. The owners speak English, offer a warm welcome and serve a fine breakfast, either in your room or on the main terrace.

Mercues
Le Maz Azemar $
46090
☎ 565309685
🖹 565305382
This attractive 18th-century manor house is located in the Cahors vineyard and furnished to a high standard. Meals may be taken with your hosts, who speak English, and only regional produce is used. The bedrooms are all well equipped, and a heated outdoor swimming pool is an added attraction. The house is not suitable for small children.

 6

Key to Symbols: Fax   e Email   Rooms   P Parking   Swimming

St Antonin-Noble-Val
La Residence $
rue Droite, 82140,
Tarn-Et-Garonne
☎ 563682160
🖹 563682160
Lovingly restored house set in the breathtaking Aveyron Gorge, with some stunning views of the Roc d'Anglars. The owners have created an atmosphere of luxury and style, providing spacious bedrooms, one with its own secluded terrace. Guests may choose from the table d'hôte menu, or sample local specialties in the many nearby restaurants. English is spoken.

🛏 5

CARCASSONNE C1
Bouisse

Domaine des Goudis $
11190, Aude
☎ 468700276
🖹 468700074
✉ delattre-goudis@mnet.fr
The Pyrenees Mountains extend for 120 mile beyond the hill on which this renovated house stands. There is a heated outdoor swimming pool as well as table tennis and plenty of good walking. A table d'hôte dinner menu of wholesome regional cuisine is served, and vegetarian dishes can be prepared. English and German are spoken. Young children cannot be accommodated.

🛏 6
Closed Nov. 15-Mar. 28

Fanjeaux
Relais de Saint Dominique $
11270, Aude
☎ 468246817
🖹 468246818
Located at the foot of Prouilhe's monastery in the heart of Cathar country, this establishment offers en suite accommodations and a garden with a swimming pool for guests' use. Each room has its own color scheme and character, and a buffet breakfast is served on a beamed, covered terrace as soon as the sunny days begin.

🛏 6

Garrevaques

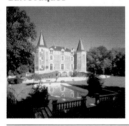

Château de Garrevaques $$
81700, Tarn
☎ 563750454
🖹 563702644
✉ m.c.combes@wanadoc.fr.garr
evaques.htm
This 15th-century château was renovated in the 19th century after some fire damage during the Revolution. The interior is full of period treasures: sketches by Zuber, ancestral paintings and marble fireplaces. Within the extensive grounds there is a swimming pool, tennis court, table tennis, petanque, swings and a children's playground. The château runs courses in cooking, language, painting, music and yoga.

🛏 10

Pepieux
Carrefour $
1 rue de l'Étang, 11700, Aude
☎ 468916929
🖹 468916929
This rambling 17th-century house is situated in the Languedoc region, which produces over 80 percent of French wine. It has long shuttered windows and is furnished with a pleasing mixture of antique and contemporary pieces. Bedrooms are large, and two are suitable for family occupation. Three-course dinners and picnic lunches are available on request. English is spoken.

🛏 4

Puicheric
Château de St-Aunay $
11700, Aude
☎ 468437220
🖹 468437672
Large, early 19th-century house in the heart of a Minervois vineyard. A shady park surrounds the house, and you can relax by the swimming pool under the pines. An American billiard table graces the grand entrance hall of this traditionally furnished house. The attractive dining room overlooks the large terrace, and meals are served by prior arrangement. English is spoken.

🛏 10

Closed Oct. 5-Mar. 31

CASTRES C1
Cambounet-Sur-Le-Sor

Château de la Serre $$
81580, Tarn
☎ 563717573
🖹 563717606
A 16th-century nobleman's castle, this château was fully restored in the 19th century and is set in private parkland at the foot of the Black Mountains. Bedrooms are romantically decorated in classical style, with period furniture and modern comforts. Beautiful trees border the secluded swimming pool, and guests can play boules on the grounds. English and Spanish are spoken.

🛏 3

Closed Nov. 2-Apr. 30

CHALONS-SUR-MARNE D4
Matougues
La Grosse Haie $
chemin de St-Pierre, 51510, Marne
☎ 326709712
🖹 326701242
Some beautiful specimen trees and shrubs grow around this attractive whitewashed building, which is located in a rural setting with a vineyard on one side. The bedrooms all have en suite facilities, and a fixed-price meal is available in the evening. There is also an extensive garden. Bicycles can be rented from the hospitable owners, who speak both English and German.

🛏 3

CHARTRES C4
St-Lucien

Les Quatre Oiseaux $
Seine-Maritime
☎ 235905195
This cottage is set in grounds dotted with cider apple trees. There are some farm animals and an enclosed garden. Bedrooms with hefty timber beams and sloping attic ceilings are individual in style and simply furnished. Breakfast and evening meals are served in the owners' dining room, and a sitting room with TV, games and books is provided.

🛏 4

CHATEAUBRIANT B4
Chaze-Sur-Argos

La Chaufournaie $
Maine-et-Loire
☎ 241614905
🖹 241614905
This 19th-century farmhouse is owned by Susan and Peter Scarboro. It is set in extensive grounds where you can play giant checkers or petanque. The lounge offers books, board games, a full-size snooker table and "Pete's Bar." Continental breakfast, or a hot alternative, is eaten around the kitchen table or in the garden. An evening meal is available by arrangement.

🛏 5

Key to Symbols: 🖹 Fax 🄴 Email 🛏 Rooms 🄿 Parking ⛱ Swimming

Renaze
Le Petit Bois Gleu $
Mayenne
☎ 243068386
🖹 243068386

English owners, the Goodmans, welcome guests to their farmhouse – a paradise for ramblers, birdwatchers and painters. Sue Goodman is an artist and runs painting classes here. The restaurant (also open to non-guests) serves lunch and dinner, with vegetarian options. All the bedrooms have en suite facilities; four are suitable for disabled guests, and one for families.

🛏 5

CHATEAUROUX   C3
Buzancais

Château de Boisrenault $
Indre
☎ 254840301
🖹 254841057
📧 yves.dummanoir@wanadoo.fr

Grand 19th-century château, elegantly decorated and furnished with antiques. It is set in private woods and gardens with an outdoor heated pool and table tennis. Guests can enjoy drinks on the terrace or make use of the library or television in the guests' salon. The guest rooms are all en suite, and the hospitable owners speak English.

🛏 7
Closed Dec. 16-Feb. 1

Tendu

La Chasse $
Prunget, Indre
☎ 254240776

This traditional farmhouse, built about 100 years ago, has been sympathetically renovated by its English owners. An ample and varied breakfast is served, and home-cooked evening meals using local produce are available by prior arrangement. The beamed bedrooms are spacious and have pleasant views over the farm. Smoking is not permitted.

🛏 4

CHATELLERAULT   C3
Dange-St-Romain
La Grenouillère $
17 rue de la Grenouillère, 86220, Vienne
☎ 549864868
🖹 549864656

Converted farm buildings in a delightful setting on the Vienne River, within reach of the Loire Valley and the ancient region of Poitou. The rooms are named after flowers, and one is wheelchair accessible. The lady of the house likes to know by 9 a.m. if you would like dinner. English and Spanish are spoken. Smoking is not permitted.

🛏 5

Monts-Sur-Guesnes
Relais de Bourg-Ville $
Vienne
☎ 549228158
🖹 549228989

This ancient fortified farm became the property of the secretary to King Louis XVI in 1791. He was guillotined in 1794, but his family still owns the farm. The rooms are snug, with beamed ceilings and antique furniture. You can dine with your hosts, by candlelight, or on the patio in good weather. Organic food is used, and vegetarian options are possible. English is spoken.

🛏 5

Key to Symbols: 🖹 Fax 📧 Email 🛏 Rooms 🅿 Parking 🏊 Swimming

CHERBOURG B5

Acqueville
La Belangerie $
Manche
☎ 233945949
Some rare features distinguish
this 16th-century manor house.
An unusual chimneybreast in the
dining area, for example, has
been recognized as exceptional
by the Department of Fine Arts.

The bedrooms are situated on
the first floor, and all of them
have beamed ceilings. There is a
TV room, and a fixed-price
evening meal is available on
request. English is spoken.

 3

Catteville
Le Haul $
Manche
☎ 233416469
🖹 233416469
Horses are bred here, and other
farm animals can be seen on the
extensive grounds. The reserve of
marshland bordering the farm is
used for hunting October-
January, and fishing is available.

There is plenty for breakfast, and
guests are invited to dine with
the owners. The communal day
room has a refrigerator and
microwave, and the sitting room
a TV, stereo and piano.

 5

**St Germain-De-
Tournebut**
Château de la Brisette $
Manche
☎ 233411178
🖹 233412232
A long driveway leads through
the grounds and into the
courtyard of this imposing
château. To the rear, its glory is
reflected in the lake below, with

the original chapel close by. The
bedroom styles embrace Empire,
Gothic and Louis XVI, all with
modern comforts. Public rooms
include a grand salon and a
dining room where Continental
breakfast is served.

 3
Closed Nov.-Apr.

Tamerville

Manoir de Belaunay $
Manche
☎ 233401062
This manor house was built
between the 15th and 16th
centuries on the ruins of a
monastery, and makes a
charming base from which to
explore the Cotentin peninsula.
The owners are hospitable, speak
English and serve a French

breakfast. The spacious en suite
guest rooms are furnished with
Normandy antiques and
overlook the surrounding park.

 3
Closed Nov. 15-Mar. 15

CHINON B3

Continvoir
La Butte de l'Epine $
Indre-et-Loire
☎ 247966225
🖹 247960736
This attractive farmhouse has
been renovated to provide
luxurious accommodations. It is
an unusual house, built in a
17th-century style using

traditional materials, and has low
walls and a delightful long
sloping roof. Guests have
independent access to the
comfortable bedrooms on the
first floor. Breakfast is served in
the large dining room, and there
is a choice of restaurants nearby
for evening meals.

 3

Key to Symbols: 🖹 Fax   Email   Rooms   Parking   Swimming

Ingrandes-de-Touraine

Le Clos Saint André $
Indre-et-Loire
☎ 247969081
🗎 247969081

In the heart of the châteaux region, surrounded by the Bourgueil vineyards, Le Clos Saint André is itself a wine estate, and you can try its wine with your dinner. The bedrooms are located in a stately building, added in the 18th century to the 16th-century farmhouse. A traditional evening meal is available on request, and English is spoken.

🛏 6

Closed Nov. 16–Mar. 14

Richelieu

La Maison $
6 rue Henri Proust, 37120, Indre-et-Loire
☎ 247582940
🗎 247582940

En route to the châteaux of the Loire, the town of Richelieu is a fine example of 17th-century town planning. La Maison enchants guests with its grace and sobriety, and provides a town center base from which to explore. There are two reception rooms, one with a log fire, and a shady garden where guests can relax. English and Italian are spoken.

🛏 4
Closed Oct.–Apr.

La Varenne $$
Chaveignes, Indre-et-Loire
☎ 247582631
🗎 247582747
📧 dru_sauer@wanadoo.fr

This beautiful 17th-century manor is set in a sunny garden with wide lawns, an outdoor pool and bicycles free for guests' use. Inside it is fully renovated, harmoniously blending original features and antiques with modern comforts such as steam heating. The three guest rooms are spacious and peaceful, and a television is available on request.

🛏 3

Les Religieuses $
24 place de Religueuses/1 rue Jarry, Indre-et-Loire
☎ 247581042
🗎 247581042

This mansion, set in the center of this 17th-century town, is a study in French charm and elegance. Madame offers a warm welcome and serves up a hearty breakfast. The en suite guest rooms are smallish in size, but are comfortable and exquisitely decorated. Situated in the Loire Valley, it is an ideal base for sightseeing.

🛏 4
Closed Jan.

CLERMONT FERRAND D3

Beauregard-Vendon

Bed & Breakfast $
Chaptes, Puy-de-Dôme
☎ 473633562

Elisabeth Beaujeard welcomes guests to her elegantly appointed home in Chaptes, furnished with antiques, pictures and ornaments. By the side of the house the roof of a huge barn provides cover for an area with seats and tables where guests can relax and enjoy the peace of the garden. English is spoken.

🛏 3

Key to Symbols: Fax Email Rooms Parking Swimming

CLUNY   D3

Tournus

Le Domaine de Tremont   **$$**
rte de Plottes, Saône-et-Loire
☎ 385510010
📄 385321228
This pretty pink stone building, covered in wisteria and green vines, offers en suite bedrooms that combine traditional furnishings and modern comforts. Honest cooking is served in the informal restaurant, and afterward you can relax in the reading room with its ancient books, harpsichord and card table, or on the terrace overlooking the garden. English is spoken.

 6

COGNAC   B3

Brives-Sur-Charente

Logis de Louzignac   **$$**
2 r des Verdiers, 17800, Charente-Maritime
☎ 546964572
📄 546961609
This peaceful country residence is on the banks of the Charente River, surrounded by a large walled garden with an outdoor swimming pool and terrace. The house is furnished with a stylish combination of 18th-century furniture, Oriental porcelain and modern art. The lounge has a library and music corner. Accommodations comprise two large guest rooms, a family room and another room with its own kitchenette.

🛏 2

Cherves-Richemont

Logis de Boussac   **$**
16730, Charente
☎ 545831301
📄 545832121
Jacques Perrin de Boussac made his fortune in the 17th century by distilling brandy from the wine produced from the vineyards that still surround this house. His magnificent country home is of such historical interest that it is open for guided tours on weekends. It is furnished with authentic period furniture and canopied four-poster beds, and guests can join the owners for dinner by candlelight.

🛏 3

Mainxe

La Cour des Cloches   **$**
Chez Juillier, Charente
☎ 545808686
📄 545320438
📧 cloche7172@aol.com
Once producing grapes for the major cognac houses, La Cour des Cloches still has its own wine press and copper still. The house, which dates from 1812, has been restored by English owners, who have made the most of its historical features. Bedrooms offer a simple taste of luxury, and there is a swimming pool in the garden.

🛏 9

COLLEVILLE-SUR-MER   B4

Ecrammeville

Ferme de l'Abbaye   **$**
Calvados
☎ 231225232
📄 231224725
This solid Norman building looks out onto the floodlit abbey church, close to the World War II landing beaches. The house has a fine stone staircase and columns, a large fireplace and exposed beams. It is part of a farm that breeds trotting horses and cattle and produces its own cider. Evening meals are available by arrangement at a fixed price.

 5

Longueville
Le Roulage $
Calvados
☎ 231220349
🖹 231220349
This charming 18th-century manor house makes a peaceful base from which to explore the Normandy beaches, castles and medieval towns. Though recently renovated, the interior retains its rustic style. A hearty breakfast is served in the dining room, including homemade jams. Spacious guest rooms are simply furnished with wooden floors, white cotton bedspreads and carved antique wardrobes. English is spoken.

Picauville
Château de l'Isle-Marie $$
Manche
☎ 233213725
🖹 233214222
Standing high on the site of a Viking fortress, this beautiful castle has wonderful country views. It is elegantly decorated with fine carvings, parquet flooring, period furniture and a wealth of family portraits. The addition of modern conveniences makes it a luxurious base from which to explore the nearby coast. Three apartments are available in the adjacent 17th-century manor house.

🛏 5
Closed Oct. 1-Easter

Trevieres
Château de Colombieres $$$
Calvados
☎ 231225165
🖹 231922492
Set amid its own landscaped park and surrounded by a moat, this elegant château is an ideal place for a romantic break. It dates from the 14th to the 18th centuries and is full of character and original features. Guests are free to enjoy the beautiful grounds, complete with tennis court, fishing in the river and bicycles for rent. Smoking is not permitted.

🛏 3
Closed Oct.-Apr.

COLMAR E4
Dieffenbach-Au-Val

La Romance $
17 rue de Neuve-Eglise, 67220, Bas-Rhin
☎ 388856709
🖹 388576158
This idyllic timbered house is situated in the picturesque foothills of the wooded Vosges mountains. The sumptuous bedrooms are traditionally decorated and well equipped, with e-mail access available. Designer towels and quality linens are a feature. One suite has its own living room in a timbered turret. There are many restaurants nearby; your English and German-speaking hosts will be happy to advise.

🛏 4

Les Trois-Epis

Villa Rosa $
68410, Haut-Rhin
☎ 389498119
🖹 389789045
Pretty Alsatian house located near the Rhine. Soft colors and flowers have inspired the rustic décor in the restaurant and the peaceful en suite bedrooms. There is a garden of old roses and a heated outdoor swimming pool. The proprietor offers a one-day cooking course for two students at a time, which includes an overnight stay in the hotel. English and German spoken.

🛏 10
Closed Feb. 12-Apr. 1

Key to Symbols: 🖹 Fax 📧 Email 🛏 Rooms 🅿 Parking 🏊 Swimming

DIEPPE C5
Eu

Manoir de Beaumont $
Seine-Maritime
☎ 235509191
✉ cd@fnac.net
This old Normandy manor house has huge arched windows and doors set into stone walls. The property occupies parkland on a hilltop with wonderful views. The three bedrooms, all with en suite shower and toilet, are furnished with antiques like the rest of this elegant house. Bicycles may be rented on the premises, and English is spoken by the hosts.

🛏 3

Les Landes-Vieilles-Et-Neuves

Château des Landes $
Seine-Maritime
☎ 235940379
🖷 235940379
This château is built of brick and is set on a wooded estate. The bedrooms are large, individually designed and furnished with family heirlooms. In summer Continental breakfast is taken on the veranda, and dinner is available by arrangement. Children are welcome, with a discount for those under three years of age. English is spoken.

🛏 5

DIJON D3
Epernay-sous-Gevrey
La Vieille Auberge $
2 pl des Tilleuls, Côte-d'Or
☎ 380366176
🖷 380366468
This former farmhouse has long been used as a local inn. It has recently been renovated by a young English couple, who have combined modern comforts with original charm in the six attractive guest rooms. The inn is family-friendly and there is a play area with swings in the garden. No smoking is permitted.

🛏 6

Closed Dec. 16-31

Vosne-Romanee
La Closerie des Ormes $$
21 rue de la Grand-Velle, Côte-d'Or
☎ 380623519
🖷 380623519
You will love your stay at this charming ivy-covered house, surrounded by the Vosne-Romanée vineyard in the heart of the ancient kingdom of Burgundy. The local map reads like a wine list, and local events include many based around the excellence of the local wines. The comfortable bedrooms are decorated in English style, and both English and German are spoken.

🛏 5

DINAN B4
Dinan

Moulin de la Fontaine des Eaux
Vallée de la Fontaine des Eaux, Côtes-d'Armor $
☎ 296879209
🖷 296879209
This 18th-century water mill makes an ideal base for a vacation exploring the many attractions of Brittany. The British owners, Marjorie and Harry Garside and their two young children, welcome couples and families alike. The garden has a lake and a sun deck where you can relax in the peace of the Breton countryside. Dinner is often available by prior arrangement.

🛏 5
Phone for schedule Oct.-Mar.

St Pierre-De-Plesguen
Le Petit Moulin du Rouvre $
Ille-et-Vilane
☎ 299738584
🖹 299737106
Named after a species of oak tree that grows locally, this 17th-century mill has used much of the wood in its attractive refurbishment. There's fishing in the millpond, and bicycles can be rented. A swimming pool with Jacuzzi is currently under construction. Bedrooms are steam heated, and all are en suite; one has a balcony. Evening meals are available and English is spoken.

 4

DINARD   B4
Frehel

Le Relais de Fréhel $
Plevenon, Côtes-d'Armor
☎ 296414302
🖹 296413009
The long, ivy-clad building of this old coaching inn features gabled windows on the first floor jutting out of the tiled roof, some opening from ceiling to floor. Outside are lawns, conifer trees, shrubs and flowers, including colorful hydrangeas. Guests are free to use the garden, where there are tennis courts and table tennis. English is spoken.

🛏 5
Closed Nov.-Mar.

Plouer-Sur-Rance

La Renardais $
Le Repos, Côtes-d'Armor
☎ 296868981
🖹 296869922
e Suzanne.Robinson@wanadoo.fr
Restored with great care by proprietors John and Suzanne Robinson, this 19th-century stone-built house stands in a large garden close to the River Rance. The lounge has an open fire, and original watercolors hang on the dining room walls. The spacious bedrooms are reached by the original chestnut staircase, and additional beds can be installed to accommodate family groups.
🛏 4
Closed Feb.

DISNEYLAND   C4
Neufmoutiers-en-Brie
Bellevue $
Seine-et-Marne
☎ 164071105
🖹 164071927
Isabelle and Patrick Galpin offer a warm welcome to their charming farmhouse in Neufmoutiers-en-Brie, which is only 10 minutes away from the Disneyland entertainment park. The bedrooms are all en suite and large enough to accommodate families, five in the farmhouse and one in a lodge in the garden. Evening meals are available by prior arrangement. English is spoken.

🛏 6

Pommeuse
Le Moulin de Pommeuse $
32 avenue du General Huerne, Seine-et-Marne
☎ 164200098
🖹 164200098
Charming water mill, set in lovely gardens beside a stream, only an hour's journey from the heart of Paris and even closer to Euro Disney. English owners have lovingly restored the mill in authentic local style to provide comfortable accommodations. It is family-friendly, and two of the en suite guest rooms have an extra bed. Smoking is not permitted.

🛏 6

DOUARNEZ A4

Pouldergat

Hotel le Cadran $
5 rue de l'Eglise, Finistère
☎ 298746120
🗎 298746120

Le Cadran takes its name from the sundial, which adorns the wall of this town center hotel. It offers comfortable bedrooms furnished in contemporary style, three suitable for families. The dining room has a display of hunting memorabilia, including old firearms and stuffed animals. The daily menu features local produce and fish dishes. A garden is available for guests' use.

 8

ETRETAT C5

Rouville

Ferme du Château $
Seine-Maritime
☎ 235311398
🗎 235390077

This attractive redbrick and gray stonework house has great character. All the bedrooms have been prettily decorated and equipped with TV. The open fireplace in the dining room is a welcome feature on cooler days. Dinner is served at a fixed price, and vegetarian dishes are available. The garden, with its terrace and brightly colored flowerbeds, is a particular attraction.

 3

EVREUX C4

Bemecourt

Le Vieux Château $
Eure
☎ 232299047

Built on the site of a fortified castle, this château is flanked by two 15th-century towers and encircled by a medieval moat. Private fishing, horseback riding, boule and bicycle rentals are available. The hearty breakfast is more like a brunch, and includes homemade jams and bread. There are no en suite facilities in the bedrooms. English and German are spoken.

🛏 3
Closed Dec. 16-31

FIGEAC C2

Figeac

Liffernet Grange $
46100, Lot
☎ 565346976
🗎 565500624

Local delicacies are a feature of dinner at Liffernet Grange, along with a large range of French wines. In fact, there are wine-tastings and a special "Stock a Cellar" wine week. Facilities include an outdoor swimming pool, private fishing, riding stables, boules, bicycle rental and tennis courts. English, German and Spanish are spoken.

🛏 6
Closed Oct.-Apr.

FOIX C1

Serres-Sur-Arget

Le Poulsieu $
09000, Ariege
☎ 561027772
🗎 561027772

Beautifully renovated farmhouse, up in the hills among woods and meadows, offering simply furnished rooms. At 8 p.m. a table d'hôte dinner is served around the family table. Guest facilities include a refrigerator, washing machine, barbecue and swimming pool. There are lots of animals - horses, a donkey and Newfoundland dogs, which the owners breed. English, Dutch and German are spoken.

🛏 5
Closed Oct. 1-Apr. 1

Key to Symbols: 🗎 Fax **e** Email 🛏 Rooms **P** Parking 🏊 Swimming

FONTAINBLEAU C4
Treuzy-Levelay

Bed & Breakfast $
3 rue Creuse, Seine-et-Marne
☎ 164290747
🖷 164290521
📧 gillescaupin@compuserve.com

This old stone barn with long windows and white wooden shutters is located in the heart of the village. The barn stands independent of the main house, and has been refurbished to provide well-equipped bedrooms. Beds can be provided for adjoining rooms to make family suites. Sample the delicious local produce for breakfast, either in your room or at the family table.

🛏 4

GIEN C4
Briare
Domaine de la Thiau $
Loiret
☎ 238382092
🖷 238674050

This family-owned estate, set in extensive grounds beside the Loire, makes an ideal base for visiting the famous châteaux. Guest rooms are located separately from the family living quarters. There is a tennis court on the estate and a swimming pool within walking distance. Guests also can enjoy a drink before dinner on the open terrace.

🛏 4

Nevoy
Domaine de Sainte-Barbe $
route de Lorris, Loiret
☎ 238675953
🖷 238672896

This charming cottage is tucked away in countryside near the Forest of Orléans. The spacious bedrooms, with period furniture and wooden floors, look out across the gardens. In the morning a generous breakfast is served in the dining room, or on the terrace in summer. There is tennis and an open-air swimming pool within the grounds, as well as a self-catering cottage.

🛏 3

Souvigny-en-Sologne
Auberge de la Croix Blanche $
1 rue des Etangs, Loir-et-Cher
☎ 254884008
🖷 254889106

Welcoming inn in the center of a typical Sologne village. There are en suite rooms in the main half-timbered and brick-built house, and more in the annex. Though small, they are all cozy and comfortable. A Continental breakfast is served in the restaurant, where you also can enjoy a feast of local and seasonal specialties at lunch or dinner.

🛏 8

Closed mid-Jan. to Feb. 28

GIVERNY C4
Fourges

Bed & Breakfast $
24 rue du Moulin, Eure
☎ 232521251
🖷 232521312

Only a short distance from the Monet Museum at Giverny, this 17th-century farmhouse boasts its own flower-filled garden, complete with lily pond. It is beautifully restored and furnished with antiques. A generous breakfast is served in the guest salon, which retains its old bread oven and an open fire. The guest rooms open directly onto the terrace or garden.

🛏 3

Key to Symbols: 🖷 Fax 📧 Email 🛏 Rooms 🅿 Parking ≋ Swimming

GRENOBLE D2
Bouvante
Auberge du Pionnier $
26190, Drôme
☎ 475485712
🖹 475485826
This inn is located in Vercors National Park, and a specialist guide can take you on walks to observe the wildlife. Local dishes are cooked on a wood-burning stove, and dinner is served until 8 p.m. The comfortable chalet-style rooms and natural wood décor of the dining room lend a restful atmosphere. English and Italian are spoken.

🛏 9
Closed Oct. 20-Dec. 20

Villard-Reculas

La Source
38114, Isère
☎ 476803032
🖹 476803032
This stone-built grange, overlooking spectacular mountain scenery, has been carefully renovated to retain its old world charm. The living and dining room has a fine vaulted ceiling, a wood-burning stove and comfortable seating. Dinner is served in the evening, and the proprietor speaks English. On reserving, ski insurance must be taken out.

🛏 5

GUERET C3
St Silvain-Montaigut

Le Pont du Cher $
Le Pont du Cher, 23320, Creuse
☎ 555819517
🖹 555819517
Guests are assured of a warm welcome at this country house, set in extensive grounds yet only 10 minutes from shops and local amenities. Guests can come and go as they please through their own private entrance, and the beamed bedrooms have personally controlled heating. Continental breakfast is served around the family table, and five-course evening meals are available by arrangement.

🛏 4

HONFLEUR C4
Genneville
La Bourrelerie $
Le Bourg, Calvados
☎ 231987563
La Bourrelerie is named after the saddlery it once was, and you can imagine where the stables used to be around the yard. The house, which dates from the 18th and 19th centuries, has been beautifully converted to provide comfortable bedrooms. Breakfast is served in the attractive dining room, and garden furniture is set out on the lawn. Gîte accommodation is available within the grounds.

🛏 5

Pont L'Eveque
Manoir du Poirier Chio $
40 av Libération, Calvados
☎ 231641178
🖹 231641178
📧 inormandy@online.fr
This delightful 17th-century timbered manor house is surrounded by a large garden with pretty rose bushes. It offers four fully en suite rooms, including two suitable for families, and a separate apartment accommodating up to five. The English-speaking proprietor serves delicious table d'hôte meals in the evening (don't miss her specialty, country pâté with onion jam).

🛏 4

Key to Symbols: Fax   📧 Email   🛏 Rooms   🅿 Parking   🏊 Swimming

HUELGOAT · A4

Brasparts
Garz ar Bikln $
Finistère
☎ 298814714
🗎 298814799

This traditional Breton farmhouse is set in a region rich in Celtic mythology, between hills and sea. Excellent table d'hôte meals, prepared from home-grown vegetables and local produce, are served in front of an open fire in winter or a magnificent sunset in summer. Guests have independent access to the four steam-heated rooms. English is spoken.

 4

JUMIEGES · C5

Appeville-Annebault

Les Aubepines $
aux Chauffourniers, Eure
☎ 232561425
🗎 232561425

Delightful cottage surrounded by pretty gardens in the peaceful Normandy countryside. Its comfortable bedrooms are full of character, but have many modern facilities. The galleried reception rooms are especially charming.

By prior arrangement, you can eat delicious table d'hôte dinners with the proprietors, who are happy to serve a vegetarian alternative if required. English and Spanish are spoken.

🛏 4
Closed Oct.-Mar.

LA FLECHE · B4

Durtal
Château de la Motte $
Baracé, Maine-et-Loire
☎ 241769375

All the bedrooms at this romantic château are south facing, with views over the park. The park is a haven for wildlife and you can fish or boat on its two lakes, or go for a bicycle ride through the woods. Enjoy a complimentary aperitif before sitting down to an excellent dinner (vegetarian dishes by arrangement). English and Spanish are spoken.

🛏 5

LA ROCHELLE · B3

Marans

Barbecane $
rive droite de la Sevre, 17230,
Charente-Maritime
☎ 546017959
🗎 546017959

This guest house makes an excellent base for a varied family vacation, with sandy beaches within easy reach and canal trips, fishing and cycling inland. Facilities include an outdoor swimming pool, boules, table tennis and a leafy terrace where guests can use the barbecue. Rooms are comfortable and attractively decorated. No smoking is permitted in the house.

🛏 4

Moreilles

Le Château $$
Vendée
☎ 251561756
🗎 251563030

Cardinal Richelieu was once abbot of this former priory. Today, the château offers luxurious accommodations and paneled reception rooms with elegant furniture and open fires. There are eight rooms in the main building, two in the annex, and all have en suite facilities. Generous helpings of local produce are served at the candlelit dinners, and the château has its own swimming pool.

🛏 8

Key to Symbols: Fax Email Rooms Parking ⛱ Swimming

Puyravault

Le Clos de la Garenne $
9 rue de la Garenne, 17700, Charente-Maritime
☎ 546354771
🖷 546354791
📧 bpaml.francois@wanadoo.fr
This mid 17th-century property is part of an extensive walled estate that encompasses oak woods and an outdoor play area. Rooms are bright and spacious,

and there is a family suite in a separate cottage, also suitable for disabled guests. Public areas comprise a reception room, bar, play area, kitchen corner, billiard room, living room with library, and dining room where breakfast and dinner are served.

🛏 3

LA ROCHE-SUR-YON B3

L'Oie
La Gauvrière $
Vendée
☎ 251661305
🖷 251661305
This delightful 250-year-old Vendée farmhouse has a large garden, ideal for children. There are tennis rackets and boules to keep them and their parents

amused. The old part of the house contains the kitchen and the dining/living room, which has big oak beams and an open wood fire. The newer wing houses the spacious, country-style bedrooms. English, Chinese and Spanish are spoken.

🛏 6
Closed Nov. 1-week before Easter

St Denis-La-Chevasse
Château du Breuil $
Vendée
☎ 251414014
The Vendée forest is a popular spot for hunting and fishing. These pursuits can be enjoyed while staying in this attractive château. Guests also can make use of the pool, stables or bicycles. Inside, there is a salon

with a library and piano and a paneled dining room. The spacious bedrooms are stylishly furnished with wooden floors, coordinating fabrics and elegant antiques.

🛏 11
Closed Nov. 1-Easter

LANGON B2
Naujan-Et-Postiac

Les Ormeaux $
1 Chassereau, 33420, Gironde
☎ 557846908
🖷 557846908
There are plenty of opportunities for wine tasting in the vicinity of this early 18th-century house, now owned by an Anglo-French couple. Guests have their own entrance to the accommodation, and use of part of the garden,

where breakfast can be served under a beautiful maple tree. Evening meal available by prior arrangement. English and German are spoken.

🛏 3
Closed Jan. 1-14 and Dec. 16-31

LANGRES D4
Langres
Auberge des Voiliers $
1 rue des Voiliers, Lac de La Liez, 52200, Haute-Marne
☎ 325870574
🖷 325872422
Visitors to the Lac de la Liez can enjoy the beach, water sports on the lake, and stunning views of the fortified city of Langres. The

hotel offers en suite bedrooms, all with satellite TV and direct dial telephones. The restaurant serves a wide range of local specialties and regional dishes, including vegetarian food. English is spoken.

🛏 8
Closed Jan. 31-Mar. 14

LAON · D5

Ste Croix
La Besace
21 rue Haute, 02820, Aisne
☎ 323224874
🖹 323224874
This old farmhouse has stone walls and a red-tiled roof. It has a wide terrace at the front and a long garden where breakfast is served in summer. Guests can play volleyball, boules or table tennis, and ride bicycles. There are five en suite guest rooms, all elegantly furnished. Dinner is available by request, and vegetarian options are available.

 5

LAVAL · B4

Château-Gontier

Château de Mirvault-Azé $
Mayenne
☎ 243071082
🖹 243071082
This castle has belonged to the same family since 1573 and was restored in the 19th century. You can relax on the riverside terrace, or take a small boat across the river to dine at the restaurant on the opposite bank. The rooms are a picture of elegance, with period furniture, parquet floors and long windows with river views.

 5

Hostellerie de Mirwault $
rue du Val de la Mayenne,
Mayenne
☎ 243071317
🖹 243076690
Family-run hotel on a peaceful stretch of river just outside Château-Gontier. It has 11 en suite bedrooms, three with a balcony, and two family rooms. The attractive restaurant, which caters to vegetarians, will set you up to tour the nearby Loire Valley. Special fishing, boating or cycling breaks also are offered, and English, Spanish and German are spoken.

 11
Closed Dec. 23-Jan. 14

La Jaille-Yvon
Château du Plessis-Anjou $$
Maine-et-Loire
☎ 241951275
🖹 241951441
This château is set in extensive parkland and offers a taste of stylish country house life. It was built between the 16th and 18th centuries and combines the charm of original features such as wood paneling, exposed beams and parquet floors with full modern comforts. A candlelit, haute-cuisine dinner is served in the intimate dining room.

 8
Closed Nov.-Mar.

La Roe

Château Le Boulay $
Mayenne
☎ 243065104
🖹 243065104
Le Boulay is a 19th-century château set in grassy grounds sheltered by mature trees. Some of the bedrooms have en suite showers, and all have lovely views. Those at the back look across open countryside. First-floor bedrooms are classical in style with marble fireplaces, while those on the second floor are more rustic, with exposed beams.

 5

Key to Symbols: Fax Email Rooms Parking Swimming

Laval

Le Bas du Gast   **$$**
6 rue de la Halle aux Toiles, Mayenne
☎ 243492279
🗎 243564471

This fine example of a town mansion from the reign of Louis XIV was the home of the "salt tax" inspector for this region. Public rooms have been carefully preserved, with delicately carved paneling, crested marble fireplaces and period furniture. The en suite bedrooms are decorated in elegant 18th-century style. Transportation is available to nearby restaurants.

🛏 5
Closed Dec-Jan

LE MANS   B4
Dissay-Sous-Courcillon

La Chataigneraie   **$**
Sarthe
☎ 243794530

Often described as a "fairy-tale cottage," this ivy-clad guest house is built of mellow stone with white shutters. The bedrooms have views over the large garden or onto fields of sunflowers. Meals can be served in the house by prior arrangement. The owners speak English and are happy to share their knowledge of local places of interest.

🛏 3

Lavenay

Les Patis du Vergas   **$**
Sarthe
☎ 243352818
🗎 243353818

With its own pond and another lake and river nearby, this is an ideal spot for a fishing vacation. You need not leave the grounds to enjoy various other sports, including volleyball, table tennis and croquet, followed perhaps by a sauna. The hotel is attractively furnished and comfortable, with central heating throughout. There is a restaurant, and English is spoken.

🛏 5
Closed Nov. 4-Feb. 28

LE PUY   D2
Jullianges

Domaine de la Valette   **$**
Haute-Loire
☎ 471032335
🗎 471032335

Breathtaking scenery surrounds this charming manor house in the Auvergne forest, with its deep gorges, winding rivers, waterfalls and mountainous slopes. Rooms are beautifully decorated and furnished with antiques, and guests can enjoy table tennis or croquet in the lovely garden. A kitchen is available for guests' use, and a local grocer can deliver prepared meals. No smoking is permitted.

🛏 5

LISEUX   C4
Orbec

Manoir de l'Engagiste   **$**
14 rue de Géolé, Calvados
☎ 231325722
🗎 231325558

This recently restored house is sheltered by high walls covered in rambling roses and clematis. The garden of lawns and apple trees reflects the attributes of the Normandy countryside. The peaceful surroundings, warm welcome and comfortable accommodations will ensure a memorable stay. Breakfast is served in a gallery lined with paintings. English and Spanish are spoken.

🛏 5

Key to Symbols: 🗎 Fax   **e** Email   🛏 Rooms   **P** Parking   ≋ Swimming

Montviette
Le Manoir d'Annique $
La Gravelle, Calvados
☎ 231202098
🖹 231207436
English hosts Anni and Nick
Wiltshire have restored this
16th-century manor house with
tremendous sensitivity, and the
bedrooms are decorated in
traditional country style.

Breakfast is served at the
family table, and a four-course
evening meal is available by
arrangement. A range of
weekend breaks is offered, called
"Tastes of Normandy," covering
topics such as photography,
cookery, French conversation and
golf.

🛏 7

LOCHES   C3
Ligueil

Moulin de la Touche $
Indre-et-Loire
☎ 247920684
🖹 247599638
This former mill, set in 30 acres
of land with private fishing,
offers comfortable
accommodations in a pretty
English style. A set four-course
menu is available, incorporating
produce grown on the grounds

or locally. In summer, dinner is
served in the large timber-
framed conservatory, and there is
a fabulous swimming pool with
terrace and sun loungers. English
is spoken.

🛏 5
🏊
Closed Dec. 25

Loches
Le Moulin $
St-Jean St-Germain,
Indre-et-Loire
☎ 247947012
🖹 247947798
A private island in the middle of
the Indre River is the idyllic
setting for this old water mill.
Lawned gardens run down to the
water's edge and a small sandy

beach. Two rowboats are
available for guests' use, and
anglers can enjoy private fishing.
All of the rooms are well
furnished, and the English
owners serve meals prepared
from local produce.

🛏 6
Closed Dec.-Feb.

St Branchs

La Paqueraie $
Indre-et-Loire
☎ 247263151
🖹 247263915
An ivy-clad cottage offering
neatly decorated bedrooms and a
cozy living room with a fire. A
delicious dinner of traditional
Touraine cuisine and local wines
is served, and vegetarians are
accommodated. The garden has

some 100-year-old oaks and
exquisite flowers, as well as a
swimming pool, private fishing
and boules. English and Spanish
are spoken.

🛏 4
🏊

Verneuil-sur-Indre
La Capitainerie $
Indre-et-Loire
☎ 247948815
🖹 247947075
📧 captain@creaweb.fr
This pretty house and garden
offers an intimate atmosphere
with all en suite rooms, one with
a balcony. The three acres of
grounds are ideal for strolling,

and there is an outdoor
swimming pool. In the evening
the proprietor, Mme. Masselot,
takes pride in introducing her
guests to the gourmet pleasures
of authentic Touraine cooking,
subject to reservation.

🛏 4   🏊

Key to Symbols: 🖹 Fax 📧 Email 🛏 Rooms 🅿 Parking 🏊 Swimming

LONS-LE-SAUNIER

Poligny
Domaine V~ ~~adoo.fr
rte d~ ~g hills painted in
~~t hues of mauve is this
beautiful 18th-century mill. It
has been carefully converted to

~nic views from
~ tne three terraces.
Creative cuisine, served in the
beamed dining room, combines
delicious local produce with
home-grown herbs. English,
German and Spanish are spoken.

📠 9

Hostellerie des Monts
de Vaux **$$**
Monts de Vaux, 39800, Jura
☎ 384371250
📄 384370907
e mtsvaux@hostellerie.com
At the very edge of the ancient
Jura mountains, perched on a
spectacular cliff, is this beautiful
inn. The 10 en suite bedrooms
are comfortably furnished, and

there is a cozy sitting room with
a fireplace and beautiful wood
paneling. Tennis courts are
available for guests' exclusive use.
The cuisine is traditional and
simple, and English, German
and Italian are spoken.

🛏 10
Closed Oct. 31-Dec. 29

LORIENT A4

Ile-De-Groix
La Grek **$**
3 pl du Leurhé, Morbihan
☎ 297868985
📄 297865828
Regular ferries from Lorient
bring you to the island of Groix.
It is a perfect size to explore by
foot, and the whole coast is easily
accessible from this typical

Breton house. It provides
comfortable en suite
accommodations, fully restored,
steam-heated and furnished with
antiques. The owners are
hospitable, family-friendly and
speak English. Smoking is not
permitted.

🛏 4

Inzinzac-Lochrist

Tymat-Penquesten **$**
Morbihan
☎ 297368926
📄 297368926
In the heart of the Blavet Valley
between Vannes and Quimper,
Catherine and Mathieu Spence
offer rooms and breakfast in
their charming squire's house, set
in grounds bordering the local
forest. The steam-heated rooms

are all en suite, spacious,
carefully decorated and furnished
with antiques. The generous
breakfast is served in the family
dining room. English is spoken.

🛏 4

Moelan-Sur-Mer

Trénogoat **$**
Finistère
☎ 298396282
📄 298397809
This long stone-built farmhouse,
run by English owners, is just
two minutes from the sea, with
sandy beaches nearby. The
grounds include an orchard, a
children's play area, boules,
barbecue and a farmyard of small

animals. Breakfast, served at
separate tables, uses fresh local
produce, and there is a large,
comfortable living room and
indoor gameroom. Babysitting
service is available.

🛏 6
Closed mid Oct.-Easter

Key to Symbols: 📄 Fax e Email 🛏 Rooms P Parking 🏊 Swimming

MANOSQUE E2
Cucuron
L'Arbre de Mai $
rue de l'Église, 84160, Vaucluse
☎ 490772510
📄 490772510

Traditional May tree celebrations have given their name to this 18th-century house. The furnishings are tasteful and comfortable, and the top-floor room has its own balcony overlooking the town. In the attractive restaurant, local produce is prepared according to local recipes, and the results can be enjoyed with local wines. English, Spanish and Italian are spoken.

 6

Closed Nov.-Feb.

MEAUX C4
Armentieres-en-Brie

Bed & Breakfast $
44 r du Chef de Ville, Seine-et-Marne
☎ 164355122
📄 164354295

A striking stone building with shuttered windows and balconies, offering all en suite accommodations. Although relatively close to Paris, the house has attractive gardens, an open terrace and country views. A large Continental breakfast is served, including homemade jams. Guests benefit from special arrangements at the Meaux Boutigny golf course. English is spoken.

 4

Closed Nov.-Feb.

MEGEVE E3
Crest-Voland

Le Saphir $
Le Saphir, Paravy, 73590, Savoie
☎ 479316958
📄 479316958

This chalet is up in the Alps at an altitude of 4,100 feet, close to the ski lift. All of the bedrooms are en suite, and two are suitable for families. Lunch and evening meals are available, served in the living room with the hosts and the other guests. English is spoken.

🛏 3

MENTON E2
Sospel
Domaine du Paraïs $
Chemin du Paradis, La Vasta, 06380, Alpes-Maritimes
☎ 493041578

This 19th-century, Italian-style villa looks across to an ancient monastery and the mountains that tower along the horizon. At the gateway to Mercantour National Park, it is an ideal place for walking and birdwatching. The house has tiled floors, white walls and simple wooden furniture. Bedrooms are very comfortable, and there is a homey dining room.

🛏 4

MONTARGIS C4
St Fargeau

Château de Dannery $
Yonne
☎ 386740901

Charming château in a pretty village setting, close to numerous abbeys, castles and renowned local vineyards. It has been beautifully refurbished and combines original features with modern comforts. The three spacious guest rooms are attractively decorated and have en suite bathrooms. One also has a television. The owners are hospitable and speak English.

🛏 3

Key to Symbols: 📄 Fax 📧 Email 🛏 Rooms 🅿 Parking 🏊 Swimming

MONTAUBAN   C2

Beaumont-de-Lomagne
L'Arbre d'Or $
16 rue Déspéyrous, 82500,
Tarn-Et-Garonne
☎ 563653234
🖺 563652985
English hosts greet guests at this former gentleman's residence in the center of the ancient walled town of Beaumont-de-

Lomagne. Behind the house is a tree-shaded garden where meals are eaten in summer. Dinner can be eaten with the family by prior agreement. Special arrangements have been made for guests to use the golf course at Sielh, and bicycles can be rented.

🛏 6

MONT-DE-MARSAN   B2

Garein

Moulin Vieux $
40420, Landes
☎ 558516143
🖺 558516143
This country mansion in the heart of the Landes Forest overlooks a lake where you can swim, fish or take out a boat. It is a center for many activities, and dormitory rooms and studios are provided for yoga and art groups.

Bedrooms generally feature wooden beams and beautiful antique furniture. You can have dinner with the family for a reasonable price. English and German are spoken.

🛏 7

MORLAIX   A4

St Thegonnec
Ar Presbital Koz $
18 rue Lividic, Finistère
☎ 298794562
🖺 298794847
The bedrooms are well decorated, spacious and comfortable at this attractive establishment. The rooms have en suite facilities, with bath or

shower, and full steam heating. Breakfast features a range of jams and marmalades made on the premises by Mme. Prigent, the proprietor. Parking is available, and English is spoken.

🛏 6

MOULINS   D3

St Aubin-sur-Loire

Les Lambeys $
Saône-et-Loire
☎ 385539276
Everything about Les Lambeys has an understated style and quality, yet prices for rooms and evening meals are reasonable. Guests are assured of a peaceful stay in elegant surroundings with exceptional cuisine. The proprietors' vineyard produces

Pinot Noir red and Macon St. Véran white wines. Breakfasts feature homemade bread and pastries. A billiard room and swimming pool are available. English is spoken.

🛏 5
Closed Jan. 2-Mar. 31

MURET   C1

St Ybars

Château de Soulès $
09210 Ariege
☎ 561692012
🖺 561692168
Majestic château, extensively renovated and surrounded by woodland and gardens, providing spacious en suite rooms. Four-course dinners also are available to guests at a reasonable price. There is a large heated

swimming pool, shaded terrace and plenty of lounging space in the surrounding orchard. English, German and Spanish are spoken. No babies or credit cards.

🛏 4

Key to Symbols: 🖺 Fax 🄴 Email 🛏 Rooms 🅿 Parking 🏊 Swimming

NANTES · B3
St Etienne-De-Montluc

Château de Saint Thomas **$$**
Loire-Atlantique
☎ 240869060
📄 240869762

This is one of the last châteaux along the Loire just before the estuary runs into the Atlantic. Its garden is a veritable botanic experience, and a private lake for fishing is available. The en suite rooms are steam-heated, and there is a separate apartment with kitchenette suitable for families. The château is open May-September. Evening meals must be eaten at the hotel.

🛏 5
Closed Oct.-Apr.

NEVERS · D3
Alluy
Bouteville **$**
Nièvre
☎ 386840665
📄 386840341

A collection of old stone farm buildings has been converted to create this attractive house, surrounded by a lovely garden where guests can enjoy superb views of the countryside. The bedrooms, including a family suite, are comfortable and well equipped. A dining room and small kitchen are provided for guests' use. There is no smoking inside.

🛏 4

St Reverien
La Villa des Prés **$**
Nièvre
☎ 386290457
📄 386296522

A free dinner on the evening of arrival is offered to guests who stay for a week at this establishment. Breakfasts are a highlight, featuring homemade organic breads and jams, eggs from the proprietors' free-range hens, honey from their hives, and butter and cheese from a neighboring farm. English, German and Dutch are spoken; credit cards are not accepted.

🛏 6
Closed Nov.-Mar.

NIMES · D2
Aramon

Le Rocher Pointu **$**
Plan de Dève, 30390, Gard
☎ 466574187
📄 466570177
📧 amk@imaginet.fr

Attractively renovated farmhouse, where the spacious rooms have been furnished in a simple country style. In addition to the four bedrooms in the main farmhouse, there are two studio flats and two apartments in an annex. After a swim in the hotel pool, you can enjoy a generous breakfast on the terrace. Smoking is not permitted on the premises. English is spoken.

🛏 4
Closed Nov.-Mar.

NIORT · B3
Arcais

Du Canal **$**
rue de l'Ouché, 79210, Deux-Sevres
☎ 549354259

This guest house is right on the banks of a canal, and there are canoes, punts and bicycles available so that guests can start their exploration of the region at the front door. There are four guest rooms, one of which has disabled access. Other facilities include a heated indoor swimming pool and a small kitchen. No smoking is permitted.

🛏 4

Vallans

Le Logis d'Antan $
140 rue St-Louis, 79270,
Deux-Sevres
☎ 549049150
🖷 549048675
ⓔ lelogisdantan@wanadoo.fr
This welcoming old house of
honey-colored stone has its own
private entrance to the Parc du
Marais Poitevin. The
accommodation has been
restored and modernized, and
the same light stonework has
been left exposed in the
impressive bedrooms and public
rooms. In the evenings guests
may dine with the family by
reservation. Boats are available to
rent nearby.

🛏 6

ORANGE   D2

Barjac

Le Mas Escombelle $
route de Vallon Pont-d'Arc,
La Villette, 30430, Gard
☎ 466245477
🖷 466245477
This authentic 18th-century
farmhouse is set in lush gardens
complete with a swimming pool.
Guests have independent access
to the stylishly decorated
bedrooms, which successfully
combine traditional and modern
furnishings with original
features. Delicious homemade
jams are served at breakfast,
which is served in the dining
room or on the covered terrace in
summer. Meals featuring
regional dishes can be provided
by arrangement.

🛏 4

Laudun

Château de Lascours $
30290, Gard
☎ 466503961
🖷 466503008
Magnificent 16th-century
château, the interior of which
has been beautifully preserved,
retaining original wooden
ceilings, paneling and stone
fireplaces. It is decorated
throughout in Renaissance style,
with fine period furniture,
paintings and chandeliers, and
some of the elegant guest rooms
have four-poster beds. There is a
swimming pool by the lawn, and
guests can fish in the moat.

🛏 6

Loriol-Du-Comtat

Château Talaud $$$
84870, Vaucluse
☎ 490657100
🖷 490657793
ⓔ chateautalaud@interlog.fr
The villa is shaded by plane
trees, decorative motifs and faces
are carved into the geometrical
stone façade, and a stone
staircase sweeps up to the first
floor. Dutch owners Conny and
Hein Deiters-Kommer provide a
warm welcome, and the large
bedrooms are designed around a
single color. There is a charming
breakfast room and a cozy living
room.

🛏 6
Closed Feb.

Piolenc

Auberge de L'Orangerie $
4 rue de l'Ormeau, 84420,
Vaucluse
☎ 490295988
🖷 490296774
ⓔ orangerie@wanadoo.fr
This traditional farmhouse has
been tastefully upgraded to
provide comfortable
accommodations. Gérard and
Micky Delarocque have designed
the rooms carefully so that each
one has an individual and
interesting character. A pool is
provided for guests, and the
restaurant serves both lunch and
dinner. English, German and
Spanish are spoken.

🛏 6
Closed 2 weeks in Nov.

Key to Symbols: Fax   Email   Rooms   Parking   Swimming

Vaison-La-Romaine

L'Evêché $
Ville Medievale, 84110, Vaucluse
☎ 490361346
▤ 490363243
🅴 eveche@aol,com
In the midst of this medieval town, with its stone villas, paved alleys, small squares and fountains, is the Bishop's Palace, built in the 17th century. Here guests are welcomed by hosts who are happy to share some delicious wine. Breakfast can be served on the fabulous walled terrace, with stunning views over the town.

🛏 5

ORLEANS C4
Tavers

Le Clos de Pont-Pierre $
115 rue des Eaux Bleues, Loiret
☎ 238445685
▤ 238445894
This beautifully renovated 18th-century farmhouse is set amid a private park with gardens and woods. There is a conservatory-style sitting room overlooking the gardens, or guests can sit on the terrace or swim in the outdoor pool. Local specialties are served in the dining room, and the guest rooms, each with their own separate entrance, have wonderful views over the park.

🛏 4
Closed Dec.-Feb.

Vannes-sur-Cosson

Bed & Breakfast $
6 rue de la Croix Ste Madelein, Loiret
☎ 238581543
The woodlands, rivers and lakes surrounding the village are renowned as excellent hunting and fishing grounds. Visitors at this pleasant, family-owned establishment can enjoy these traditional pursuits, with rights to fish in the nearby river. Alternatively, guests can play a game of tennis, boules or mini-golf on the grounds. The hospitable hosts speak English.

🛏 4

PARIS C4
1st arrondissement
Hotel Louvre Saint Romain $$$
5 rue St-Roch, Paris
☎ 142603170
▤ 142601069
Recently refurbished hotel on the Right Bank, close to elegant Rue de Rivoli and the Louvre. The staff speaks English, and service is available from the 24-hour concierge. The spacious guest rooms are well equipped, fully soundproofed and air-conditioned, and all have en suite marble bathrooms. An American buffet breakfast is served in a stone-vaulted cellar, or a Continental breakfast in the room.

🛏 34

Relais du Louvre $$$
19 rue des Pretres St Germain, l'Auxerrois, Paris
☎ 140419642
▤ 140419644
🅴 au-relais-du-louvre@dial.oleane.com
This 18th-century building with classical décor and period furniture is located near the Seine and the famous Pont Neuf. The spacious guest rooms are furnished with antiques and have all modern conveniences. Front-facing rooms have a good view of the Louvre, while the rooms at the back are very peaceful. There are a couple of suites, and a large, one-bedroom apartment.

🛏 21

Key to Symbols: ▤ Fax 🅴 Email 🛏 Rooms 🅿 Parking 🏊 Swimming

2nd arrondissement
Grand Hôtel de Besançon $$
56 rue Montorgueil, Paris
☎ 142364108
📄 145080879
A pleasant spot from which to explore the city, the hotel has a relaxed elegance and is tastefully decorated in a classical style. An elevator takes you to the spacious guest rooms. These are furnished in 18th-century style but are fully soundproofed and air-conditioned and equipped with direct dial phone, satellite television, radio, mini-bar and safe. English is spoken.

🛏 26

Hôtel des Boulevards $
10 r de la Ville-Neuve, Paris
☎ 142360229
📄 142361539
For such a central spot, ideal for business and leisure, this clean and comfortable hotel is a very good value. It is in a traditional 19th-century Parisian block with tall windows and wrought-iron balustrades. Reception rooms, where breakfast is served, are bright and welcoming, and the spacious guest rooms are simply but elegantly furnished.

🛏 18

4th arrondissement

Hotel Sansonnet $
48 rue de la Verrerie, Paris
☎ 147879614
📄 148873046
This quiet hotel is in one of the city's most seductive quarters – the Marais. It is housed in an elegant honey-sandstone block with wrought-iron balustrades and shutters. The dining room is furnished in art deco style, as are the guest rooms. These are all en suite, with direct dial phones and satellite television, and three have a balcony. English is spoken.

🛏 25

Lutèce
65 rue St-Louis-en-l'Ile, Paris
☎ 143262352
📄 143296025
Delightfully located on one of the narrow streets of the Île St. Louis, this hotel is housed in the tall, elegant buildings typical of medieval Paris. It retains original features such as oak beams, tiled floors and carved stone fireplaces, and is furnished with antiques. There is an elevator to the guest rooms, which offer modern comforts. English is spoken.

🛏 23

6th arrondissement
Aramis Saint-Germain $$
124 rue de Rennes, Paris
☎ 145480375
📄 145449929
This stylish, modern hotel is surrounded by the Left Bank's famous cafés and bars. It has a large sitting room and private bar in art deco style. The classically furnished guest rooms are spacious and well equipped. Most are air-conditioned; nine have Jacuzzis and four balconies. Meeting rooms are available, and the helpful staff speak English.

🛏 42

Key to Symbols: 📄 Fax Email 🛏 Rooms 🅿 Parking 🏊 Swimming

Grand Hotel Littré $$$
9 rue Littré, Paris
☎ 145443868
🖷 145448813
Stylish hotel on a quiet street in the midst of the lively Left Bank. It is decorated in the Empire style throughout, with a sophisticated yet comfortable atmosphere. The dining room is very grand, with beautifully set tables and heavy linen tablecloths at breakfast. There is a cozy private bar, and meeting rooms are available on request.

🛏 91

Hotel Left Bank St-Germain $$$
9 rue de l'Ancienne-Comédie, Paris
☎ 143540170
🖷 143261714
Fully renovated 17th-century building with exposed stone walls, tiled floors and oak beams. It is furnished with antiques and Aubusson tapestries, and features interior gardens. Rooms are large, well equipped and traditionally decorated, with carved oak furniture and marble bathrooms, but all modern conveniences are provided. St.-Germain is one the most dynamic parts of the city.

🛏 31

Le Saint-Beuve $$$
9 rue St-Beuvé, Paris
☎ 145482007
🖷 145486752
Beautiful 19th-century hotel, superbly renovated to offer both comfort and style. The reception sets the tone, offering a warm welcome (English is spoken) amid graceful Ionic columns and tasteful modern art. The lounge is a perfect place to relax, with comfortable seating in front of an open fire. Guest rooms are decorated in classical style and furnished with fine antiques and paintings.

🛏 23

Lutetia $$$
45 bd Raspail, Paris
☎ 149544646
🖷 149544600
🇪 lutetia-paris@lutetia-paris.com
Beautifully renovated hotel in the original art deco style, with a popular brasserie and the renowned Paris restaurant serving outstanding cuisine. There also is a piano bar, which hosts live jazz evenings. Stylish guest rooms maintain the 1920s color scheme to match the period furniture. Many have balconies, some with views of the Eiffel Tower.

🛏 250

Relais Médicis $$$
23 rue Racine, Paris
☎ 143260060
🖷 140468339
Beautifully renovated hotel just off the Odéon, with exposed polished beams, carved woodwork, antique furniture and vintage photographs throughout. The guest rooms, also decorated in a rustic style, are set around a leafy courtyard with a fountain. Despite the timeless atmosphere, full modern amenities are provided, including marble en suite bathrooms. English is spoken.

🛏 16

Relais Saint-Germain $$$
9 Carrefour de l'Odéon, Paris
☎ 143291205
▤ 146334530
The Odéon, where this handsome 17th-century hotel is situated, lies right in the center of Boulevard Saint-Germain, where some of the most elegant designer boutiques and famous cafés and restaurants can be found. The hotel itself is charming, decorated in a classic style with spacious guest rooms and en suite marble bathrooms. English is spoken.

🛏 22

Royal Saint-Germain $$
159 rue de Rennes, Paris
☎ 144392626
▤ 145490923
Impressive hotel standing on a grand 19th-century boulevard between Montparnasse and Saint-Germain. Recently renovated, the reception rooms, including a breakfast room and lounge, are richly decorated with marble tiles, tapestry-style curtains, Turkish rugs and antique furniture. The guest rooms have a simple, modern elegance. Some offer balconies and others have lovely views toward the Eiffel Tower. English is spoken.

🛏 43

7th arrondissement

Hotel de l'Academie $$$
32 rue des St-Pères, Paris
☎ 145498000
▤ 145498010
e aaacademie@aol.com
Fine 18th-century building at the heart of the Saint-Germain quarter, with exposed stonework and oak beams inside. Facilities include a restaurant, private bar, conference room and lounge. The latter is richly furnished with crimson sofas, antique furniture, Turkish carpets and green silk curtains. Guest rooms are fully sound insulated and air-conditioned. Suites also are available, with marble bathrooms complete with Jacuzzis.

🛏 33

8th arrondissement
Beau Manoir Best Western $$$
6 rue de l'Arcade, Paris
☎ 142660307
▤ 142680300
e beau.manoir@wanadoo.fr
The hotel, like its prestigious location, is discreetly luxurious with its oak beams, tiled floors, paneled walls, antique furniture and tapestries. The guest rooms are similarly decorated, but include modern conveniences such as air conditioning, satellite television, radio and mini-bar, and all of them have en suite marble bathrooms. The buffet breakfast is served in a stone-vaulted cellar. English is spoken.

🛏 32

Hôtel Cordélia $$
11 rue de Greffulhe, Paris
☎ 142654240
▤ 142651181
This hotel owes its name to the celebrated Duchess of Guermantes, who held glittering soirées in the Paris of her day. Her passion for receiving guests is emulated today by Mme. Marche, the hotel's proprietor. You can sit by the fireside, browse in the library or relax with a drink from the bar. Languages spoken are English, German and Spanish.

🛏 30

Key to Symbols: Fax Email Rooms Parking Swimming

Hotel Lido Best Western **$$$**
4 passage de la Madeleine, Paris
☎ 142662737
▤ 142666123
With exposed oak beams, stone walls and antique furnishings, this hotel retains the atmosphere of another era. The elegant hall is beautifully appointed with oak-carved furniture and tapestries. In the bedrooms the traditional style is combined with full modern conveniences. Guests also have use of the stone-vaulted breakfast room and tranquil garden filled with flowers. English is spoken.

🛏 32

Royal Hotel **$$$**
33 av Friedland, Paris
☎ 143590814
▤ 145636992
This 19th-century building offers the same luxurious grandeur as the street upon which it stands. Two faun statues welcome you to the reception, beneath a sweeping 1920s staircase, and the lounge bar is decorated in the same period style. The large bedrooms combine rustic charm with modern conveniences, and a buffet is served in the elegant breakfast room.

🛏 58

9th arrondissement

Brebant **$$**
32 bd Poissonnière, Paris
☎ 147702555
▤ 142466570
The belle époque reception rooms at this elegant hotel really live up to their name, with their period-style furnishings and chandeliers. The restaurant, where breakfast is served, has original art nouveau features, a mural of the French countryside and a bright conservatory. Guest rooms are simply furnished with antiques, and a fully equipped conference room is available. English is spoken.

🛏 122

10th arrondissement

Français **$**
13 rue du 8 Mai 1945, Paris
☎ 140359414
▤ 140355540
Over the years this establishment has built up a faithful following of international guests. The well-equipped bedrooms are soundproofed and partially air-conditioned, and 20 of them have balconies. An excellent breakfast buffet is served in the spacious dining room and its modern furnishings, and guests can relax in the bar-lounge. English, German, Italian and Spanish are spoken.

🛏 71

11th arrondissement

Hotel de Méricourt **$$**
50 rue de la Folie-Méricourt, Paris
☎ 143387363
▤ 143386613
Recently renovated hotel with a contemporary look and a sophisticated atmosphere. Furnishings throughout have clean, simple lines, and modern paintings add a touch of color. Breakfast is served in the elegant reception room, and a curving staircase (or elevator) takes you up to the guest rooms, where tall windows overlook a peaceful side street.

🛏 28

12th arrondissement
Le Pavillon Bastille $$
65 rue de Lyon, Paris
☎ 143436565
🖷 143439652
📧 hotel-pavillon@alzamail.com
The innovative interior design of this contemporary hotel has been awarded a prize for excellence by "Hotel and Restaurant Design International." Reception areas are full of character, with modern furniture and lighting. There is a bar and dining room, although in good weather the buffet breakfast is served on the terrace. The air-conditioned, en suite bedrooms provide satellite television and mini-bars.

🛏 25

14th arrondissement

Hotel Istria $$
29 r Campagne-Première, Paris
☎ 143209182
🖷 143224845
This hotel is very much part of the artistic heritage of the district. Man Ray and Marcel Duchamp brought their mistresses here, and other famous guests have included Francis Picabia, Eric Satie, Josephine Baker and Mayakovski. Louis Aragon even wrote a poem about it. The sitting room retains the stylish elegance of the 1930s, as do the guest rooms, enhanced now with modern conveniences. English is spoken.

🛏 26

15th arrondissement
Hotel Montcalm Best Western $$
50 av Félix Faure, Paris
☎ 145549727
🖷 145541505
http://bestwestern.com/bedt.html
Conveniently located hotel, opposite a metro station and just 10 minutes' walk from the International Exhibition Center. The reception rooms are simply decorated in warm natural tones, and there is a big sunny conservatory overlooking the beautiful garden. Guest rooms are bright and spacious, with modern wooden furniture and stylish fabrics.

🛏 41

Hotel Tour Eiffel Dupleix $$
11 rue Juge, Paris
☎ 145782929
🖷 145786000
📧 dupleix@club-internet.fr
An ideal base for tourists and business people, close to the main ministries, UNESCO and the International Exhibition Center. It has a conference room and private parking nearby. The reception area is open 24 hours a day and has a safe, fax, photocopier and laundry service. There is a bright buffet breakfast room, and the elegantly decorated guest rooms have pale-wood furniture.

🛏 40

16th arrondissement

Hotel Etoile-Maillot $$
10 rue du Bois de Boulogne, Paris
☎ 145004260
🖷 145005589
Tucked between the business district around the new arch at La Défense and the Champs-Elysées, the Beaux Quartier neighborhood makes an attractive base for tourists and business people alike. This traditional hotel is elegantly appointed with antique furniture and paintings. Spacious guest rooms offer en suite marble bathrooms, and 10 of the rooms have balconies. English is spoken.

🛏 28

Key to Symbols: 🖷 Fax 📧 Email 🛏 Rooms 🅿 Parking 🏊 Swimming

Hôtel St-James Paris $$$
43 av Bugeaud, Paris
☎ 144058181
🖹 144058182

This hotel was built in 1892 to accommodate students at the Paris universities. Its conversion provides bright, spacious and individually decorated bedrooms. Third-floor rooms open on to the winter garden, and each has a private terrace. Facilities include a gourmet restaurant (closed on weekends) and a fully equipped gym. English, German, Spanish and Italian are spoken.

🛏 48

Kleber $$
7 rue de Belloy, Paris
☎ 147238022
🖹 149520720

Despite being in the heart of a business quarter, the Kleber's location is quiet, and guests will appreciate the hotel's collection of fine furniture and paintings. An annex, offering a combination of en suite and family rooms, augments the main hotel building. There is a bar where drinks and light meals are served. English, Arabic, Hebrew, Japanese and Spanish are spoken.

🛏 22

17th arrondissement
Hôtel Champerret-Elysées $$
129 av de Villiers, Paris
☎ 147644400
🖹 147631058
📧 75162.750@compuserve.com

With its elegant lounge and welcoming private bar, the Champerret-Elysées is the perfect hotel to return to after a hard day's sightseeing. For guests who cannot survive without e-mail, the hotel offers a full range of high-tech facilities, including electronic games. A first-class breakfast is served in a pleasant dining room decorated with flowers. English, German and Italian are spoken.

🛏 45

18th arrondissement

Eden Hotel $
90 rue Ordener, Paris
☎ 142646163
🖹 142641143

You are assured of a warm welcome by the husband and wife proprietors of this intimate hotel, which nestles at the foot of Montmartre, just a few minutes' walk from the Sacré Coeur Cathedral. The rooms are all en suite with bath or shower and toilet, and have direct dial telephone and satellite TV. English and German are spoken.

🛏 35

PARTHENAY   B3
St Loup-Lamaire
Château de Saint-Loup $$
79600, Deux-Sèvres
☎ 549648173
🖹 549648206

Rebuilt at the beginning of the 17th century, the château, still with its medieval moat, is a gem of French classical architecture. The current owner has meticulously restored the gardens, and the bedrooms are no less authentic. The house and gardens are open to the public, along with a garden shop, and teas are served in summer. Meals are available on request.

🛏 14

Key to Symbols: 🖹 Fax 📧 Email 🛏 Rooms 🅿 Parking 🏊 Swimming

PAU   B1

Gan

Le Clos Gourmand $
40 av Henri IV, 64290,
Pyrénées-Atlantiques
☎ 559215043
🗎 559215663
🇪 clos.gourmand@wanadoo.fr

The hotel is a typically Béarnaise building, with a half-timbered upper half and a steep roof, set in a beautiful garden. The restaurant serves delicious French cuisine, and guests have the choice of staying under bed-and-breakfast, half-board or gastronomique terms. The hospitable owners also can arrange visits and wine tastings at nearby Jurançon vineyards. The spacious guest rooms are simply but comfortably furnished.

🛏 8

Lay Lamidou

Bed & Breakfast $
64190, Pyrénées-Atlantiques
☎ 559660044

Set in a small village in the beautiful Gave d'Oloron Valley at the foot of the Pyrenees, this 18th-century house is a perfect base for exploring the mountains by foot, by bicycle or by rafting through the gorges. Guest rooms are spacious, comfortable and attractively decorated with fine antique furniture. No smoking is permitted on the premises.

🛏 2

PERIGUEUX   C2

Brantome

Maison Fleurie $
54 rue Gambetta, 24310,
Dordogne
☎ 553351704
🗎 553051658

In the center of Brantôme, a medieval market town on an island in the middle of the Dronne, stands this grand "maison bourgeoise" owned and run by a British family. In summer, a copious Continental breakfast is served in the sunlit courtyard, and there is a swimming pool surrounded by reclining chairs. The accommodation is particularly elegant.

🛏 5
Closed Feb. 1-21

Hautefort

Hotel L'Enclos $$
Pragelier Tourtoirac, 24390,
Dordogne
☎ 553511140
🗎 553503721
🇪 rormsteers@yahoo.com

Beautifully restored 18th-century cottage set on a historic country estate. It forms part of a complex that is virtually a village in itself, with a bakery and chapel all surrounded by lovely terraced gardens. The hosts speak English, Italian and Spanish. Boules can be played, and there is horseback riding and bicycle rental nearby.

🛏 8
Closed early Oct.-Apr. 30

PERPIGNAN   C1

Alenya

Domaine du Mas Bazan $
66200, Pyrénées-Orientales
☎ 468229826
🗎 468229737

This 19th-century villa is shaded by two ancient plane trees. Four of the spacious first-floor bedrooms have balconies, and a separate suite is ideal for family groups. The large heated outdoor swimming pool is a popular attraction, as is the sun terrace beneath the palm trees. Delicious home cooking is prepared from the farm's own produce. English and Spanish are spoken.

🛏 10
🏊

Key to Symbols: 🗎 Fax   🇪 Email   🛏 Rooms   🅿 Parking   🏊 Swimming

Caixas
Mas Saint Jacques $
66300, Pyrénées-Orientales
☎ 468388783
🖹 468388783
English owners have fully
renovated this former farmhouse
to provide stylish and relaxing
accommodations. There are five
comfortable guest rooms, four of
which have balconies with lovely views, and there is a swimming
pool in the well-kept garden.
This is an area popular with
artists; the nearby port of
Collioure was Matisse's summer
home.

 5

POITIERS C3
Chauvigny

La Veaudepierre $
8 rue du Berry, 86300, Vienne
☎ 549463081
🖹 549476412
Situated in the middle of
Chauvigny at the foot of the
beautiful medieval Old Town,
this 18th-century house offers
superb views of the ruined
fortress. It is stylishly decorated
and furnished throughout with antiques. There are five guest
rooms, one suitable for families
and another with disabled access.
The owners are warmly
welcoming, speak English and
are delighted to recommend
places to visit.

 5
Closed Nov. 1-Easter (except holidays
& advance bookings)

Poitiers
Château de Vaumoret $
rue du Breuil Mingot, Vienne
☎ 549613211
🖹 549010454
Dating back to the 17th century,
this château is a fitting place to
stay while exploring the historic
delights of the surrounding
region. For a complete change,
Futuroscope Park also is close by. The château, set in extensive
parkland, is charmingly
furnished, and the welcoming
owners speak English. Bicycles
can be rented, and there are
stables and tennis courts nearby.

🛏 3
Closed Nov. 15-Jan. 15 (except school
holidays)

QUIMPER A4
Plomeur

La Chaumière de Keraluic $
Finistère
☎ 298821022
🖹 298821022
Farm buildings have been
tastefully renovated to provide
six independent rooms (one with
its own kitchenette). Breakfast
and evening meals are served in a
family atmosphere by the fire.
The sea is within easy reach, and the local Celtic culture can be
explored in organized excursions,
or through the on-site videos
and library. English and Spanish
are spoken.

 5

REIMS D4
Brouillet
Ariston Fils $
4 & 8 Grande Rue, 51170,
Marne
☎ 326974346
🖹 326974934
📧 champagne.ariston-
fils@wanadoo.fr
Bed-and-breakfast
accommodations in spacious en suite rooms is provided at this
solid 18th-century house, where
the family's business of
champagne production has been
handed down for five
generations. Guests can sample
the wines and visit the cellars,
and there is a collection of
ancient equipment including an
old press and grape basket.
English is spoken.

🛏 3 Closed 2 weeks in Aug.

Key to Symbols: 🖹 Fax 📧 Email 🛏 Rooms 🅿 Parking 🏊 Swimming

FRANCE

Passy-Grigny
Le Temple $
51700, Marne
☎ 326529001
🗎 326521886
A working farm situated close to the Champagne region of northern France. The farmhouse offers a good choice of accommodations, with some en suite rooms. Guests are encouraged to stroll in the gardens, and non-French speakers can communicate with their hosts in English. A fixed-price meal of traditional French cooking is available in the evenings.

🛏 9

RENNES B4
Pace

Manoir de Méhault $
Ille-et-Vilane
☎ 299606288
Built in the 17th century, this manor house has been fully restored to a high degree of comfort and has full steam heating. There are five en suite guest rooms, elegantly furnished, two of which are suitable for families. Guests may enjoy a barbecue on the leafy grounds, where parking also is available. English is spoken.

🛏 5
Closed Nov.-Mar.

ROCAMADOUR C2
Le Vigan

Manoir La Barrière $
46300
☎ 565414073
🗎 565414020
📧 mamanoir@aol.com
With its tall stone tower, this 13th-century manor house stands as dignified as a church. Bedrooms have period furniture, and each has its own external entrance. Dinner, by arrangement, features delicious regional dishes. In the magnificent garden there is a river and a lake; cross over the wooden footbridge and you reach the swimming pool, with a trickling waterfall and terrace beside it.

🛏 5
Closed Nov. 1-Easter

ROUEN C4
Bourgtheroulde
Château de Boscherville $
Eure
☎ 235876212
🗎 235876212
Madame Henry du Plouy welcomes you to her attractive country château set in extensive grounds. There are five comfortable en suite bedrooms, one suitable for families. A traditional French breakfast is served, and you can sample Norman specialties direct from the farm. A card-operated telephone and a fax machine are available, and English is spoken.

🛏 5

ROYE C5
Peronne
Château d'Omiécourt $
rte de Chaulnes, 80320, Somme
☎ 322830175
🗎 322832183
📧 thezy@terre-net.fr
This château is set in landscaped grounds, with sweeping lawns and a covered courtyard terrace. Bedrooms have oak parquet floors and marble fireplaces, but each one is individually decorated. There is a small kitchen for guests' use, and breakfast is served in the magnificent dining room. For some really special French cuisine, reserve for a gourmet weekend.

🛏 3 Closed Dec. 24-Jan. 1

Key to Symbols: 🗎 Fax 📧 Email 🛏 Rooms P Parking ⛱ Swimming

SARLAT-LA-CANEDA C2

Domme
Le Jaonnet $$
Liaubou-Bas, Nabirat, 24250, Dordogne
☎ 553295929
🖹 553295929

A rugged stone-built house in a country location, just a walk away from a sandy lakeside beach. Continental breakfast and five-course table d'hôte dinners are served either in the living room, which has a log fire and an oak gallery, or in the courtyard in summer. The proprietor is a professional chef, trained in his native Austria. English, German and Italian are spoken.

🛏 5
Closed Nov.-Feb.

Sergeac
Auberge de Castel-Merle $$
24290, Dordogne
☎ 553507008
🖹 553507625

This ancient inn is idyllically located on a clifftop looking down the beautiful Vézère Valley. The original stone walls and oak beams are left exposed, and the inn is furnished with antiques throughout. The comfortable, steam-heated rooms are individually decorated, and traditional food is served, such as wild boar stew and truffle omelette. English is spoken.

🛏 4
Closed Sep. 23-30 and Nov. 2-Feb. 28

SAUMUR B3

Saumur

La Bouère Salée $
rue Grange Couronne, St-Lambert des Levées, Maine-et-Loire
☎ 241673885
🖹 241511252

Sympathetically restored over the last 15 years by the Bastid family, this early 19th-century house, set in a shady park, retains much of its original charm. The en suite bedrooms include one suite, and one of the rooms has a balcony. There also is a gîte (self-catering accommodations) on the grounds. Breakfast is a real highlight, prepared from organic produce. English is spoken.

🛏 4

Les Rosiers-Sur-Loire

Auberge Jeanne de Laval $
54 rue Nationale, Maine-et-Loire
☎ 241518017
🖹 241380418

This is a beautiful example of the small châteaux owned by many old families throughout France. The spacious bedrooms, divided between the house and annex, are tastefully furnished and equipped with all modern comforts. Traditional local dishes are served in the restaurant, especially fish from the Loire, all enhanced by the best of wines, both local and national.

🛏 10
Closed late Nov.-Dec. 31

SOISSONS D4

Vic-Sur-Aisne
Domaine des Jeanne $
rue Dubarle, 02290, Aisne
☎ 323555733
🖹 323555733

This grand house has been overlooking the waters of the Aisne for nearly 400 years, and was once the property of Napoleon's finance minister. It has extensive grounds, and can be reached by road, river or helicopter. Inside, there are some impressive marble fireplaces, and all the en suite bedrooms face south. An outdoor swimming pool and tennis court are available.

🛏 5

Key to Symbols: 🖹 Fax 🅴 Email 🛏 Rooms 🅿 Parking 🏊 Swimming

Le Charmel

Bed & Breakfast $
6 rue du Moulin, 02850, Aisne
☎ 323703127
🖹 323701508
This modern home has
traditional country farmhouse
features, such as stone walls and
shutters at some of the windows.
The large garden is full of trees
and bright flowers, and there are
pretty window boxes. You can eat

on the terrace in good weather,
or in the dining room otherwise.
All the bedrooms have en suite
bathrooms, and one has a
balcony.

🛏 4

ST BRIEUC   A4
Erquy

Les Ruaux Les Bruyeres $
Côtes-d'Armor
☎ 296723159
🖹 296720468
The port and beaches are both
within walking distance of this
typical Breton home, which is
furnished simply but comfortably
in the local style. Breakfast is
served in the living room, and
there is a conservatory

overlooking the well-kept
garden. Guests are welcome to
use the kitchen and dining room,
although the harbor offers plenty
of restaurants where local
seafood can be enjoyed.

🛏 6

ST DIE   E4
Gerbepal
Bed & Breakfast $
17 rte de Gérardmer, 88430,
Vosges
☎ 329507385
The French and Swedish
proprietors provide comfortable
en suite accommodations at this
former postal relay station. The
room price includes breakfast,

which makes this establishment
ideal for budget-conscious
visitors. Evening meals are
available during the summer
season, featuring Vosgean and
Swedish specialties incorporating
local produce. Outside there is a
terrace and garden. English and
Swedish are spoken.

🛏 4

ST FLOUR   C2
Collanges
Château de Collanges $
Puy-de-Dome
☎ 473964730
🖹 473965872
This 15th-century château is
located in France's famous
volcanic region. Charming
period furniture is a feature of
the bedrooms, and the open fire

in the dining room lends it a
relaxed and intimate atmosphere.
Evening meals are available by
reservation. Facilities at the
château include a games area,
French billiards and a piano.
English is spoken.

🛏 6

St Alban-Sur-Limagnole

Relais Saint Roch $$
Château de la Chastre, 48120,
Lozère
☎ 466315548
🖹 466315326
📧 rsr@relais-saint-roch.fr
This beautiful château, built of
pink granite, is the perfect place
for a peaceful stay, attentive
service and good food. Much use
of natural wood is made

throughout the hotel, notably in
the restaurant, La Petite Maison.
Discerning drinkers will
appreciate the list of over 130
wines and the choice of 230
whiskies. English, German and
Spanish are spoken.

🛏 9
Closed Nov.-Mar.

Key to Symbols: 🖹 Fax 📧 Email 🛏 Rooms 🅿 Parking 🏊 Swimming

ST LO — B4
Caumont-L'Evente

Bed & Breakfast $
19 rue Thiers, Calvados
☎ 231774785
🖹 231775927
📧 lerelais19@aol.com
A warm welcome awaits visitors to this rambling, creeper-clad residence, where English-speaking owners Andrew and Elizabeth Bamford offer comfortable en suite accommodations. Close to the house is a good-sized pool, and guests can play snooker, tennis, mini-golf, boule and table tennis or rent bicycles. Dinner is available by reservation.

🛏 5

Percy

Le Cottage de la Voisinnière $
Manche
☎ 233611847
🖹 233614347
Attractively furnished cottage with a beautifully kept garden. The five guest rooms all have en suite bathrooms, and two are suitable for families. It is an idyllic spot, perfect for relaxing and enjoying the lovely countryside, historic sites and fine sandy beaches. The hosts are English speakers and are able to recommend places to eat and places to visit.

🛏 5

ST MALO — B4
Bazouges-La-Perouse
Château de la Ballue $$
Ille-et-Vilane
☎ 299974786
🖹 299974770
Period style has been carefully re-created in this commodious 17th-century property. The individually designed bedrooms are spacious, and each one features a magnificent canopied bed. A fixed-price evening meal can be prepared by the owners, who speak English and Italian. Fishing, riding and tennis are available, and special arrangements have been made for golfers at Les Orme at Epiniac.

🛏 5 Closed Jan. 6-Feb. 14

St Jouan-Des-Guerets
La Malouiniere des Longchamps $$
Les Longchamps, Ille-et-Vilane
☎ 299827400
🖹 299827414
Fully renovated manor house, minutes from the sea, with a heated pool, tennis, mini-golf, boule, and bicycles for rent on the grounds. In colder weather a fire burns in the beamed dining room. There also is a cozy sitting room with a fireplace, antique furniture and pool table. Guest rooms are spacious and comfortably furnished, and two-bedroom gîtes (self-catering accommodations) are available on site.

🛏 9
Closed Nov. 15-Apr. 1

ST NAZAIRE — B3
Herbignac

Château de Coëtcaret $$
Loire-Atlantique
☎ 240914120
🖹 240913746
This charming château occupies extensive grounds and has its own stables so that guests can explore the grounds on horseback. There also is table tennis, billiards and boules. The owners are hospitable, speak English and are delighted to host candlelit dinners on request. The en suite guest rooms are comfortable, and include two family rooms.
No smoking is permitted.

🛏 4

Key to Symbols: 🖹 Fax 📧 Email 🛏 Rooms 🅿 Parking 🏊 Swimming

ST OMER C5
St Omer

Au Vivier $
22 rue Louis Martel, 62500, Pas-de-Calais
☎ 321957600
📄 321954220

Despite its location in the busy center of Saint Omer, this hotel offers peaceful accommodations. All the rooms have beautifully appointed en suite facilities, as well as TV, satellite, minibar and direct dial telephone. The intimate restaurant benefits from air-conditioning and, in addition to Continental breakfast, offers a varied menu featuring fresh local fish, oysters and seafood. Vegetarians also are taken care of.

🛏 7

ST-JEAN-DE-LUZ B1
Ciboure
Villa Erresinolettean $
4 rue de la Tour Bordagain, 64500, Pyrénées-Atlantiques
☎ 559478788
📄 559472741

Within walking distance of the beaches and close to the spectacular countryside and hilltop villages of the Pyrenees, this is a tranquil place to unwind, swim in the private pool or relax on the terrace overlooking St.-Jean-de-Luz Bay. The three guest rooms, two of which are suitable for families, are fully steam heated and well equipped. One has a balcony with wonderful views.

🛏 3

ST-LAURENT-MEDOC CB2
Vertheuil-Medoc

Cantemerle $
9 rue des Châtaigniers, 33180, Gironde
☎ 556419624
📄 556419624

The white exterior of the house, with large arched windows and little balconies, stands out against the lush green of the lawns and trees. It evokes the Moorish architecture of Spain, which is not that far away. Inside the décor is outstanding, as one might expect, since the owners are artists. You can have dinner with your hosts (English and Spanish are spoken).

🛏 3

TARBES B1
Marciac
Setzères $$
32230, Gers
☎ 562082145
📄 562082145

An 18th-century former farmhouse, now fully restored to make a delightful family home. The flower-filled garden has a saltwater swimming pool, sun terrace and arched veranda. The English owners offer a warm welcome and cook traditional Gascon dinners made from local produce. The house is decorated in traditional style and furnished with elegant 18th-century antiques throughout.

🛏 3
Closed Jan. 1 and Dec. 25

TOURS C3
Hommes

Relais du Vieux Château d'Hommes $$
Indre-et-Loire
☎ 247249513
📄 247246867

Fully restored 15th-century château in the Loire Valley, combining original features with full modern conveniences. The Knight's Hall now serves as a restaurant, and a tithe barn has been converted to provide guest accommodations. There is a swimming pool, and guests can fish in, or cycle around, the extensive, well-kept grounds. English is spoken.

🛏 5

Key to Symbols: 📄 Fax 📧 Email 🛏 Rooms 🅿 Parking Swimming

Montlouis-sur-Loire

Château de la Bourdaisière $$
25 rue de la Bourdaisiere,
Indre-et-Loire
☎ 247451631
🖹 247490911
Beautiful château set in extensive parkland with formal French gardens. The luxurious interior has been carefully restored and is furnished throughout with antiques. There are 11 en suite guest rooms and three apartments in the château, as well as six rooms in the Choiseuil pavilion. All the rooms are bright, spacious and exquisitely decorated with rich silk fabrics.

🛏 20

Rochecorbon

Les Hautes Gatinières $
7 chemin de Bois Soleil,
Indre-et-Loire
☎ 247528808
🖹 247528590
English-speaking Jacqueline Gay extends a warm welcome to guests at her home, situated in peaceful surroundings above the village center and troglodyte caves. Guests have independent access to the house, and all bedrooms feature antique furniture, color TV and en suite bathrooms. A hearty breakfast of croissants, cereals, marmalade, honey, juices, yogurt, eggs and more is served at individual tables.

🛏 4

St Christophe-sur-le-Nais

Les Glycines $
5 pl Johan d'Alluyé,
Indre-et-Loire
☎ 247293750
🖹 247293754
Situated in the center of town, Les Glycines is an attractive, fully renovated property providing modern amenities and a high level of comfort. Regional specialties are served in the restaurant, prepared from local produce. The quality of service is high, and English is spoken.

🛏 7

St Michel-sur-Loire

Château de Montbrun $$
Indre-et-Loire
☎ 47965713
🖹 47965713
With its corner turrets and ivy-clad stone facade, this is truly a fairy-tale castle, set in dreamy gardens surrounded by ancient trees. In summer the restaurant's traditional cuisine is served on the terrace. In winter, guests can relax in front of an open fire in the salon. Guest rooms are elegantly furnished with antiques, and some have four-poster beds.

🛏 5
Closed Feb

TROYES D4

Estissac
Moulin d'Eguebaude $
10190, Aube
☎ 325404218
🖹 325404092
This superbly renovated mill dates from 1255. The grounds include a play area and small animal park. Trout and salmon are farmed, and fishing is available. All the rooms have en suite facilities and TV, and the restaurant serves country cuisine. Guests can relax in the living room, sauna or out on the terrace. English, German and French are spoken.

🛏 5

Key to Symbols: 🖹 Fax   Email 🛏 Rooms   Parking   Swimming

VENDOME　　　C4

Danze
La Borde　　　$
Loir-et-Cher
☎ 254806842
🖹 254806368
This manor is now a family-run
guest house with suites and
double rooms, two with
balconies and all with pleasant
views over the grounds. The
estate is scattered with many
beautiful old trees, and there is a
large indoor swimming pool that
can be opened up in fine
weather. English and Spanish are
spoken.

 5

Troo
Château de la Voûte　$$
Loir-et-Cher
☎ 254725252
🖹 254725252
Impressive 18th-century château
with two medieval towers, set in
parkland with breathtaking views
of the Loire Valley. Spacious en
suite guest rooms have been
tastefully decorated and
individually furnished with
antiques, including four-poster
beds and tapestry fabrics.
Delicious breakfasts can be
served in the rooms or on the
terrace. English and Spanish are
spoken.

 5

VERDUN　　　D4

Ancemont

Château de Labessière　$$
55320, Meuse
☎ 329857021
🖹 329876160
e rene.eichenauer@wanadoo.fr
Delightful château, beautifully
renovated and furnished
throughout in the original 18th-
century style. Bedrooms are all
en suite, and the large living
room has an impressive fireplace,
paneled walls, tiled floor and
Louis XV furniture. The dining
room, where breakfast is served
and a four-course dinner is
available, is similarly elegant.
Outside, the attractive garden
has a sun terrace and an open-air
swimming pool.

 4

VESOUL　　　E4

Pressigny
Maison Perrette　$
24 rue Augustin Massin, 52500,
Haute-Marne
☎ 325888050
🖹 325888049
Maison Perrette is an elegant
19th-century house surrounded
by private gardens and terraces.
There is a living room with a
library and a dining room where
traditional French food is served
(children's menu available). The
spacious guest rooms are
comfortable, charmingly
decorated and all have en suite
facilities. There is a garage, and
bicycles are available free of
charge.

🛏 4

VIERZON　　　C3

Chabris

Les Bizeaux　$
Indre
☎ 254401451
The Loire Valley is the
stunningly scenic setting for this
welcoming farmhouse, set in the
countryside beside the River
Cher. All bedrooms (one suitable
for families) have lovely views. In
fine weather breakfast is served
on the terrace, and the garden
may be enjoyed at any time.
English is spoken by the hosts.

 3

Key to Symbols: 🖹 Fax　e Email　🛏 Rooms　P Parking　🏊 Swimming

VILLEFRANCHE-SUR-SAONE   D3

Arnas

Château de Longsard $$
69400, Rhône
☎ 474655512
🗐 474650317
✉ longsard@wanadoo.fr

This beautiful château in the foothills of the Beaujolais offers exquisitely furnished bedrooms, all with views of the park. Dinner can be reserved in advance, the price including all drinks. Wine appreciation courses in English and tours of the 18th-century winery and vineyard are available. Horseback riding, boules, table tennis and bicycles are available. English, Spanish and Portuguese spoken.

 5

Lancie

Les Pasquiers $
69220, Rhône
☎ 474698633
🗐 474698657

This large family home presides over the surrounding vineyards. All bedrooms have en suite facilities, one is suitable for families, and there are facilities for those with mobility difficulties. The beautiful grounds feature an outdoor swimming pool and a covered terrace; guests also can play tennis or enjoy a game of boules. Delicious evening meals are available.

 4

VILLENEUVE-SUR-LOT   C2

Cancon

Chanteclair $
47290, Lot-Et-Garonne
☎ 553016334
🗐 553411344

Spacious accommodations are offered at this friendly house, and one of the rooms is equipped for families. Television is provided in a separate communal sitting room. Guests are invited to join their hosts for dinner, where a fixed-price meal is served. Other amenities include an outdoor swimming pool, boule, a pool table and bicycle rental. English is spoken.

 4

Clairac

Château le Caussinat $
47320, Lot-et-Garonne
☎ 553842211
🗐 553842211

Aimé and Gisèle Massias take great pleasure in welcoming guests to their home, an imposing, brown-shuttered building at the end of a flower-bordered driveway. Good-value table d'hôte meals can be eaten with the family around a communal table. The grounds include a swimming pool, barbecue, *petanque*, table tennis and children's games. A self-catering inn also is available.

 5

Closed Nov.-Feb.

Laussou

Manoir du Soubeyrac $$
47150, Lot-Et-Garonne
☎ 553365134
🗐 553363520

This charming 18th-century manor house has a romantic courtyard, imposing stone portals, idyllic park, colorful flower gardens and outdoor pool. The elegant bedrooms combine period furniture with modern facilities, including luxurious bathrooms featuring Jacuzzis. The cuisine is of a high standard – a real symphony of local flavors. English is spoken.

5

Key to Symbols: 🗐 Fax   ✉ Email   🛏 Rooms   🅿 Parking   🏊 Swimming

Luxembourg

The Grand Duchy of Luxembourg is a miniscule country – only 50 miles from north to south and 35 from east to west – which sits at Europe's heart and is its political and financial center. And yet it has a remarkably varied rural landscape, taking in part of the hilly Ardennes region, which lies across the country's northern third and extends into Belgium. This distinctive area of forested plateaus split by deep valleys and beautiful rivers is guarded by fairy-tale medieval castles.

Accommodations

This small duchy has a surprisingly wide choice of hotels, including a small number of luxury establishments equal to any found around the world. Hotel-keeping seems to go hand-in-hand with restaurant ownership, and many comfortable hotels are set above popular cafés and restaurants.

Hotel bedrooms are similar in style to those of neighboring Belgium and France and, helpfully for the traveler, Luxembourg's star-rating system is the same as that used in Belgium and the Netherlands. Rooms with two single beds are most common, although rooms with one single or double bed also are available in most hotels. Outside of the major international chains, many hotels in Luxembourg still do not offer private bathroom facilities as standard. This situation is changing, however, and in hotels of three stars or above, you should have no problem securing a room with a private bathroom. Nevertheless, check to see if your room has a private bathroom when you make the reservation.

Telephone contacts/websites

To phone from the United States or Canada prefix the number with country code 011 352. To phone the United States or Canada, prefix the area code with 001.

The national tourist office website is: **www.visitluxembourg.com**

Food and Drink

Bordered by Belgium to the north and west, France to the south and Germany to the east, Luxembourg has an appropriately mixed tradition of cooking style and tastes. The German influence is evident in dishes of smoked pork

Travel Tips

Both Belgian and Luxembourg francs are legal tender in Luxembourg, but it's wise to exchange larger amounts of Luxembourg francs for Belgian francs if you intend to cross the border and visit Belgium.

The Grand Duchy enjoys a temperate climate, without any dramatic extremes. The sea is generally a moderating influence, and sea winds from the southwest and northwest shed a great part of their moisture before reaching the Luxembourg frontiers.

May to mid-October is a particularly good time to visit: July and August are warm but can be wet; May and June are the sunniest months, and September and October often enjoy a late burst of Indian summer.

A stroll in the forest of the Ardennes

(*judd mat gaardebounen*), and French flair emerges in the wonderful *pâtisserie* – the pastries and fruit tarts served for dessert. Popular lunchtime dishes include Oesling ham from the Ardennes; selections of cold meats and sausages with salad; and in rural areas, *friture* – tasty fried river fish.

The Moselle region produces Luxembourg's dry white and sparkling vintages, such as the subtle Rivaner; Pinot Blanc (perfect with fish dishes) or the much stronger Pinot Gris, an ideal accompaniment for smoked pork.

Getting Around

Luxembourg has an excellent road system, and as distances between towns and villages are short, independent travel is an easy option. The train and bus network in the Grand Duchy covers more than 870 miles; practically every locality has a bus connection. Timetables (for both buses and trains) are on sale at the stations and at some bookstores, and departure and arrival hours are listed at bus stops and railroad stations. A road map of Luxembourg, showing the main roads and tourist attractions, is available free of charge at the Luxembourg national tourist office.

Germany

The name "Germany" covers a confusing range of territories, cultures and landscapes. Before 1871 there was no single country by that name: This was an area of loosely allied states, whose identities continue to take precedence in many Germans' minds. Between the end of World War II and 1990, Germany was a nation split between West and East, two very different worlds which are still coming to terms with each other, with varying degrees of success.

Towns and Landscapes

In the north, Germany has a maritime feel, its shoreline running from the fjords of the Baltic to the windy North Sea beaches. The northern cities such as Hamburg, Lübeck and Bremen, which as the Hanseatic League once dominated world politics and trade, have emerged from the destruction of World War II with traces of this proud past either intact or restored.

From the Swiss Alps in the south, the Rhine River flows through the west and the industrial Ruhr country toward Rotterdam, passing the vineyards of its own and its tributaries' valleys, as well as picture-book castles with Gothic towers, built on the profits of river traffic tolls.

Since the integration of West and East, visitors have crossed the erstwhile borders in droves. Those from the west have rediscovered the delights of cities such as Dresden, which recreated itself after its devastation in 1945, restoring fine 18th-century buildings on the bank of the Elbe that house a marvelous collection of museums in the baroque Zwinger pavilions. In Weimar, you can retrace the steps of such worthies as Goethe, Liszt, Richard Strauss and Nietzsche, as well as enjoying historic buildings, parks and boulevards.

In southern Germany, the Black Forest (Schwarzwald) is a magnet for walkers and hikers, with its 3,900-foot highlands, pretty villages, meadows, orchards and dense woods. To the east, on the Swabian Jura's limestone cliffs, fortresses overlook the Danube River, and the Neckar flows past romantic Heidelberg. In Munich (München), the capital of Bavaria, the beer garden comes into its own; beyond the city lie wooded hills, lakes, picturesque villages and, eventually, magnificent Alpine peaks. The Alpine Road takes full advantage of this wonderful scenery; this and the Romantic Road, running 217 miles to the Alps from ancient Würzburg, are two of the most popular routes in the country.

The Spa

Germans love sports and are heavily preoccupied with health and fitness. Employees are given six weeks off a year, in addition to their statutory annual vacations, to enjoy the faciliites of the spa towns that exist all over the country. This involves taking the waters, believed to prevent all kinds of ills, and indulging in mud baths, saunas and steam treatments. In the graceful, 19th-century town of Baden-Baden, therapies include a little relaxation in Germany's oldest casino. Other interesting spa towns are Kaiser Wilhelm's favorite, Bad Ems, in the Rhineland; and Bad Kissingen, Bavaria's most popular spa, on the banks of the Saale River.

Germany

GERMANY

0   50   100   150 km
0   50   100 miles

5

NORTH
SEA

DENMARK

Westerland
Nord-
friesische
Inseln   Sylt
Flensburg
Schleswig   Kieler
Bucht   Puttgarden
Kiel
Fehmarn
Mecklenburger
Bucht
Rostock
Bad
Doberan
Greifsw
Deutsche
Bucht
Heide   Neumünster
A23   Itzehoe
Wismar   A19   Teter
Ostfriesische
Inseln
Cuxhaven   Brunsbüttel   A7   Lübeck   Güstrow   E55   Neubran
A1   Schwerin   Waren   Ne
Wilhelmshaven   Bremerhaven   Stade   E45   E22   Mecklenbur   gische S
Emden   Hamburg   A24   E26   Parchim   Müritz
See
Oldenburg   Bremen   Lüneburg   Ludwigslust   Ne
E22   A7   Elbe   Wittenberge   Havel   A24
Soltau   Uelzen
Aller   E45   Salzwedel   Stendal   BER
Cloppenburg   Nienburg   Celle   Posta
A1   Weser   Wolfsburg
Lingen   E37   Wolfsburg   A9
NETHERLANDS   Osnabrück   Minden   A2   Braunschweig   Magdeburg   Brander
Gronau   Rheine   E30   A30   Hannover   Braunschweig
Bocholt   Münster   Bielefeld   Herford   Hildesheim   Wolfenbüttel   Treuenbrietzen
Wesel   A43   Lemgo   Detmold   Saltgitter-Bad   Goslar   Brocken   Halberstadt   E51
A57   A2   Gütersloh   Northeim   1142m   Quedlinburg   Dessau   Luth
Oberhausen   Gelsenkirchen   E34   Paderborn   Harz   Halle   Wit
Moers   Bochum   Lippstadt   Scherfede   Göttingen   Nordhausen   Leipz
Duisburg   Essen   Dortmund   A44   Kassel   Naumburg   A4
Düsseldorf   Wuppertal   Ruhr   Waldeck   Mühlhausen   Buchenwald   Weimar   E40
Mönchengladbach   Solingen   Eder   Schmallenberg   Werra   A4   Gotha   Erfurt   Jena   A4   Ch
Cologne   Leverkusen   Siegen   Marburg   Eisenach   Gera   Zwickau   Pobers
(Köln)   Siegburg   A45   Fulda   Thüringer   Wald   Arnstadt
Aachen   Bonn   E41   Alsfeld   Bad   Saale   Plauen   Erzg
A1   Westerwald   Giessen   Hersfeld   Rhön   A72   Hof
Euskirchen   Remagen   Lahn   Wetzlar   Bad Neustadt   A9
BELGIUM   Koblenz   Bad   Limburg   Fulda   E51
Cochem   Ems   Taunus   Bad Nauheim   Bad   Coburg   Hof
Eifel   E35   Bad Homburg   Kissingen
Bitburg   Mosel   Rüchtal   Wiesbaden   Frankfurt am Main   Schweinfurt   A70
LUXEMBOURG   A61   Rüdesheim   Offenbach   Main   Bamberg   Bayreuth
A1/   Aschaffenburg   A3   E45   Erlangen   Weiden
Trier   A48   Mainz   Main   Würzburg   Fürth   Bambergische Alb   Amberg
A1   Bad Kreuznach   E31   Worms   Darmstadt   Michelstadt   Wertheim   Rothenburg ob   Nürnberg   Naab   Böh
Idar-Oberstein   A5   Odenwald   der Tauber   A3
Kaiserslautern   A6   Mannheim   Bad   Ansbach   A9   A56   A93
Homburg   Ludwigshafen   Heidelberg   Bad   Mergentheim   Bad Wimpfen   A6   Donau
Saarlouis   Neustadt-an-der-   Neckar   Dinkelsbühl   Regensburg
Saarbrücken   Pirmasens   Weinstrasse   Öhringen   Eichstätt   Deggen
Landau   Heilbronn   Schwäbisch   A92   Is
Karlsruhe   Maulbronn   Hall   Nördlingen   Ingolstadt
Rastatt   Pforzheim   A7   Landshu
Baden-Baden   Stuttgart   E43   Inn
Offenburg   Tübingen   Reutlingen   Donau   A8   Dachau   Amper   Freising
A81   Schwäbische Alb   Augsburg   Rosenheim
Freudenstadt   Ulm   Lech   Munich   A8
FRANCE   Hechingen   Sigmaringen   (München)   Burghausen
A5   Triberg   Ravensburg   A96   Chi
E35   Villingen   Ottobeuren   Tegernsee   Berck
Freiburg   Donaueschingen   Überlingen   Kempten   Oberammergau
Titisee   Meersburg   Friedrichshafen   Füssen   Garmisch-   271
Lorrach   Konstanz   Lindau   Allgäuer   Partenkirchen
SWITZERLAND   Bodensee   Alpen   2962m   Mittenwald
Oberstdorf   Zugspitze

4

3

2

1

A   B   C

BALTIC
SEA

dom

am

zlau

POLAND

erswalde

Frankfurt
(Oder)

E30

•Guben

pree ▫Cottbus

ammer

Neisse

en Bautzen

sische
chweiz Görlitz

Zittau

CH
BLIC

STRIA

Germany

Accommodations

In the West a vast range of options is available, from small bed and breakfast guest houses to prestigious country retreats. The complex range of hotel classifications and grading is singularly user-unfriendly, but standards of cleanliness, comfort and facilities are good. Private bathrooms are all but standard and bedrooms are usually of a good size , with two single beds along with a television and telephone.

In the former East Germany, hotel choice is more limited, particularly away from the cities. Many still provide only basic accommodations, and bathrooms are often shared. Breakfast is usually included in the price of your room and typically consists of a choice of grain breads, cheese, cold garlic sausage or smoked ham, jam and honey. Coffee is the usual drink, but tea is becoming more widely available.

Food and Drink

Meals are hearty and tasty; specialties include *Sauerkraut* (pickled cabbage), *Wurst* (sausage), dumplings, and pork and potatoes. Desserts, if not subtle, can be irresistible – such as the famous Schwarzwälder Kirschtorte, or Black Forest Cake. Snack stands, known as *Imbiss*, sell hamburgers, meatballs, sausages and the like.

German wine is mainly white and, at its best, is superb. Some of the best grapes are *Riesling*, fruity *Müller–Thurgau* and spicy *Gewürztraminer*. The national drink is beer: hundreds of local brewers operate all over the country, and varieties range from strong *Bock* (popular in Bavaria) to pale *Weisse* or unfermented black malt beer, *Malz*. Beer and wine are celebrated in festivals such as Munich's Oktoberfest and Weinfeste, the harvest festival in the Rhine-Mosel area.

GERMANY

AACHEN   A3
Würselen
Alte Mühle $
52146, Alte Mühle 1-8
☎ (0 24 05) 8 00 90
🖷 (0 24 05) 80 09 10
In the heart of the Wurmtal
Nature Reserve – close to
Aachen on the old road between
Kohlscheid and Bardenberg –
this hotel, first documented in
1568, offers comfortable rooms,
excellent conference facilities, a
stylish restaurant and a leisure
suite. Visit the idyllic garden and
attractive café terrace.

 20

AMBERG   C2
Wernberg-Köblitz
Burg Wernberg $$
92533, Schlossberg 10
☎ (0 96 04) 93 90
🖷 (0 96 04) 93 91 39
The Wernberg castle, at the edge
of the Upper Palatinate Forest,
has been extensively restored and
converted into an exclusive hotel.
The rooms are individually
furnished, elegant and decorated
in warm colors. The conference
center, a distinctive wood and
glass building set in an orchard,
is linked to the medieval
complex by a winding path.

25

ANKLAM   D5
Usedom

Oasis $$
17424, Puschkinstrasse 10
☎ (03 83 78) 26 50
🖷 (03 83 78) 2 65 99
Art Nouveau villa built in 1896,
on the promenade between the
Ahlbeck Bridge and the
Heringsdorf Bridge. Set in a
secluded location, the hotel
grounds are reached by a long
drive. Additional rooms are
provided in the
"Jagdschlösschen"; a parking
garage also is available. For meals
choose between the Poseidon
restaurant, the café, the bright
modern bistro or the attractive
garden terrace.

13

Ostende $$
17419, Dünenstrasse 24
☎ (03 83 78) 5 10
🖷 (03 83 78) 5 14 03
Splendid house built in 1919,
not far from where the Aalbeck
flows into the Baltic. Typical of
the region, with balcony
ornaments and dormer windows,
it retains features of the early Art
Nouveau period. It is extensively
restored and is furnished with a
timeless elegance in nautical
colors.

21

Strandhotel Atlantic $$
17429, Strandpromenade 18
☎ (03 83 78) 6 05
🖷 (03 83 78) 6 06 00
www.seetel.de/neu
A comfortable haven on the
promenade with uninterrupted
views of the Baltic. In addition
to its splendid location, the hotel
offers comfortable and spacious
rooms (marble baths with floor
heating) and excellent facilities
for celebrations and conferences.

25

ANSBACH C2
Ansbach

Buchenmühle $

Bürger-Palais $$
91522, Neustadt 48
☎ (09 81) 9 51 31
🖨 (09 81) 9 56 00
A historic baroque building located in the pedestrian section of the city. The converted hotel has exclusive rooms and offers Franconian specialties in its country-style restaurant as well as homemade cakes in the Rose Garden or Rosé Café.

🛏 9
🅿

ASCHAFFENBURG B2
Lohr
Buchenmühle $
97816 , Buchentalstrasse
☎ (0 93 52) 8 79 90
🖨 (0 93 52) 87 99 87
The Buchenmühle was originally an 18th-century hunting lodge used by the prince-bishops of Würzburg. Later it provided accommodation to pilgrims on their way to the abbey church of Maria Buchen. The tradition of hospitality continues today, in a hotel offering comfortable modern rooms, cozy restaurants, an old sandstone cellar, quiet lounge and an attractive terrace.

🛏 16
🅿 🇪

AUGSBURG C1
Augsburg
Altstadthotel Ulrich $-$$
86150, Kapuzinergasse 6
☎ (08 21) 3 46 10
🖨 (08 21) 3 46 13 46
www.hotel-ulrich.de
This property is located in a tastefully restored 16th-century palace formerly owned by a leading Augsburg family, on a picturesque quiet side street off Maximilianstrasse. Entering the hotel through the old wooden doorway, you are confronted with a splendid foyer with vaulted ceiling. Rooms are modern and individually designed. Enjoy a fine breakfast in the light and elegant breakfast room.

🛏 31 🅿

BAD DOBERAN C5
Kühlungsborn

Strandhotel Sonnenburg $-$$
18225, Ostseeallee 15
☎ (03 82 93) 83 90
🖨 (03 82 93) 8 39 13
The Strandhotel Sonnenburg, on the promenade just a few yards from the sea, is built in the maritime style and offers distinctive rooms and suites. The Melange café-restaurant serves international specialties, and coffee and cakes in the afternoon. Relax in the sauna or on the terrace. The same management also runs the Sonnenburg vacation apartments, also on the promenade.

🛏 25
🅿

Verdi $
18225, Ostseeallee 26
☎ (03 82 93) 85 70
🖨 (03 82 93)8 57 11
The Verdi Hotel in Kühlungsborn, one of the Baltic's most famous seaside resorts, is just a few yards from the beach and backs onto municipal woodland.

🛏 20
🅿

Key to Symbols: 🖨 Fax 🇪 Email 🛏 Rooms 🅿 Parking 🏊 Swimming
American Express 💳 Diners Club 🇪 Eurocard 💳 Visa

BAD EMS   A3
Oberwesel

Burg Hotel Auf Schönburg   **$$-$$$**
55430, Auf Schönburg
☎ (0 67 44) 9 39 30
🗎 (0 67 44) 16 13
www.hotel-schoenburg.com
Experience pure romance in this 1,000-year-old castle, with stylish lobbies, reading rooms, comfortable bedrooms, splendid four-poster beds and excellent conference facilities. Eat breakfast on the terrace overlooking the Rhine.

🛏 20
P

BAD HOMBURG   B2
Königstein (Taunus)

Sonnenhof   **$$**
61462, Falkensteiner Strasse 9
☎ (0 61 74) 2 90 80
🗎 (0 61 74) 29 08 75
Formerly the palace of the Barons von Rothschild, dating from 1900, the hotel enjoys a tranquil setting in the midst of a nature reserve. Behind the romantic half-timbered facade, guests will find elegant rooms (some with balconies), prestigious conference suites and excellent leisure facilities. Relax in the cozy foyer bar or on the attractive terrace.

🛏 41
P 🏊

BAD KISSINGEN   C2
Bad Kissingen

Laudensacks Parkhotel   **$$**
97688, Kurhausstrasse 28
☎ (09 71) 7 22 40
🗎 (09 71) 72 24 44
Spa hotel, health farm and gourmet restaurant - a successful concept developed by owner Hermann Laudensack. It is an attractive building, used by members of the Bavarian royal family, offering quality accommodations overlooking Luitpold Park. Excellent leisure facilities are provided, and guests can relax on the terrace, in the winter garden or in the bar.

🛏 20
P

Wartmannsroth

Neumühle   **$$-$$$**
97797, Neumühle 54
☎ (0 97 32) 80 30
🗎 (0 97 32) 8 03 79
www.hotel-neumuehle.de
On the banks of the Franconian Saale, this splendid building's history can be traced back to 1520. Today it houses a fine hotel with a harmonious mix of old exterior and modern interior. It offers distinctive, elegant rooms and first-class conference facilities.

🛏 20
P 🏊

BAD MERGENTHEIM   B2
Mulfingen

Altes Amtshaus   **single $**
74673, Kirchberg Weg 3
☎ (0 79 37) 97 00
🗎 (0 79 37) 9 70 30
A fine old house with thick walls, situated near the village square and fountain, which until 1784 was the official residence of the Teutonic Knights. It has been extensively restored and now offers exquisite rooms, some with facilities for cooking.

🛏 7
P

Key to Symbols: 🗎 Fax   🇪 Email   🛏 Rooms   P Parking   🏊 Swimming
   American Express   ⑩ Diners Club   🇪 Eurocard   VISA Visa

Landgasthof Jagstmühle $
74673, Jagstmühlenweg
☎ (0 79 38) 9 03 00
🖹 (0 79 38) 75 69
A rural inn nestling in the romantic Jagst Valley, offering comfortable and distinctive rooms. The Mühlenscheune (Mill barn) is the ideal venue for parties, or you could celebrate on Jagst Island.

BAD NAUHEIM B3
Bad Nauheim

Herrenhaus von Löw $$
61231, Steinfurther Hauptstrasse 36
☎ (0 60 32) 9 69 50
🖹 (0 60 32) 96 95 50
Behind historic walls dating back to AD 914 you will find elegant rooms furnished in a man-about-town style. Excellent conference facilities are available, as well as a leisure complex with a steam

bath, solarium, sauna and fitness room.

BAD NEUSTADT C3
Bad Neustadt (Saale)

Kur- & Schlosshotel $$
97616, Kurhausstrasse 37
☎ (0 97 71) 6 16 10
🖹 (0 97 71) 25 33
A baroque castle about half a mile from the Old Town, set on parkland with ancient trees and a stream. Behind the historic facade is a small, exclusive hotel

offering exquisite rooms and suites with fine furnishings and parquet flooring. Prestigious conference facilities are available, and the adjacent spa center is open to hotel guests.

Meiningen

Sächsischer Hof $$
98617, Georgstrasse 1
☎ (0 36 93) 45 70
🖹 (0 36 93) 45 74 01
www.romantikhotels.com/meiningen
Built 1798-1802, the Sächsischer Hof was a coaching inn before assuming its present form at the end of the 19th century. It is a "Romantic Hotel" with spacious

rooms, furnished with fine antiques and decorated with costume drawings and theatrical sets designed by Duke Georg II. There are excellent conference facilities, and an extensive menu in the restaurant.

Schloss Landsberg $-$$
98617, Landsberger Strasse 150
☎ (0 36 93) 4 40 90
🖹 (0 36 93) 44 09 44
A neo-Gothic castle on the northwest outskirts of town, now converted into a romantic hotel with valuable sculptures, stuccoed ceilings and old paintings. The rooms have modern conveniences, and there

is an attractive terrace where guests can relax, perhaps after a day in one of the excellent conference rooms. There also is an elegant restaurant and a choice of bars.

Key to Symbols: 🖹 Fax 🇪 Email 🛏 Rooms 🅿 Parking 🏊 Swimming
🔲 American Express 🔘 Diners Club 🇪 Eurocard 🔲 Visa

BAD WIMPFEN　B2
Neckarzimmern

Burg Hornberg　$$
74865
☎ (0 62 61) 9 24 60
🖹 (0 62 61)92 46 44
Once the home of the legendary
knight Götz von Berlichingen,
the hotel now offers
accommodation for the
discerning guest. The 11th-
century castle, surrounded by
vineyards, has been in the von

Gemmingen family since 1612
and offers stylish rooms, a
restaurant with panoramic views,
attractive lounges, a shady castle
yard and a woodland chapel.

🛏 22

BADEN-BADEN　B2
Bad Herrenalb
Mönch's Posthotel　$$
76332, Dobler Strasse 2
☎ (0 70 83) 74 40
🖹 (0 70 83) 74 41 22
📧 moenchsposthotel@
t-online.de
The history of the Post Hotel
dates back to 1148. Built on the
foundations of a Cistercian

monastery, it was a coaching inn
for the Württemberg royal mail
service. Not surprisingly, it still
serves beer brewed in the
traditional way, and the facilities
are all of excellent quality. Guests
can relax in the park, indoor pool
or beauty parlor.

🛏 18

Baden-Baden
Bad-Hotel zum Hirsch　$$
76530, Hirschstrasse 1
☎ (0 72 21) 93 90
🖹 (0 72 21) 3 81 48
A historic building in the
pedestrian area of the old spa
town. The hotel has its own
thermal baths, thalassotherapy
(sea water therapy) and laser
center. Exquisitely decorated

rooms have spring water piped
into most of the bathrooms.
There is an attractive stuccoed
ballroom and superb banqueting
facilities. The idyllic terrace in
the garden of this former spa
house is one of the "must-see"
attractions in Baden-Baden.

🛏 58

BAMBERG　C2
Bamberg

Weinhaus Messerschmitt　$$
96047, Lange Strasse 41
☎ (09 51) 2 78 66
🖹 (09 51) 2 61 41
www.hotel-messerschmitt.de
Located in a building dating
back to 1422, this is now a
"Romantic Hotel" offering
guests comfortable rooms,
conference facilities and an
extensive menu. In the summer

relax in the romantic
Brunnenhof garden.

🛏 17

Wiesenttal

Feiler　$$
91346, Oberer Markt 4
☎ (0 91 96) 9 29 50
🖹 (0 91 96) 3 62
www.hotel-feiler.de
The Feiler has a romantic half-
timbered exterior and, behind
the attractive facade, rooms
furnished with great attention to
detail and fine spacious baths.
Excellent conference facilities; in

summer relax on the splendid
courtyard terrace, or in the
evening in the bar.

🛏 10
🅿

BAUTZEN — D3
Kirschau

Zum Weber $-$$
2681, Bautzener Strasse 20
☎ (0 35 92) 52 00
📠 (0 35 92) 52 05 99
www.zum-weber.de
A historic "Romantic Hotel" with a family atmosphere, charming rooms and first-class conference facilities. Also provided are a beauty salon, sauna, grotto steam bath, solarium, massage, hairdressing salon and florist. Diners have their choice of a gourmet restaurant, the typical Upper Lusatian Weberstube or the intimate Al Forno Italian restaurant.

🛏 31
🅿
AMEX ⬤ E VISA

Wilthen

Erbgericht Tautewalde $
2681, Nr. 61
☎ (0 35 92) 3 83 00
📠 (0 35 92) 38 32 99
www.tautewalde.de
This attractive building on the outskirts of Wilthen has a history dating back 150 years. It offers guests individually furnished, comfortable rooms and suites, superb conference facilities (the old barn is just wonderful) and for relaxation a sauna, steam bath, solarium and tennis. In summer sit in the attractive beer garden or on the splendid terrace.

🛏 30
🅿
AMEX ⬤ E VISA

BAYREUTH — C2
Bayreuth
Jagdschloss Thiergarten $$
95448, Oberthiergärtner Strasse 36
☎ (0 92 09) 98 40
📠 (0 92 09) 9 84 29
www.schlosshotel-bayreuth.com
A former hunting lodge built for the Margraves of Brandenburg-Bayreuth, this small hotel with elegant rooms (Laura Ashley style) also has a restaurant, library, small shop, a baroque room and splendid grounds complete with sauna and lawns.

🛏 8
🅿 🏊
AMEX ⬤ E VISA

Baden-Baden

Key to Symbols: 📠 Fax 🄴 Email 🛏 Rooms 🅿 Parking 🏊 Swimming AMEX American Express ⬤ Diners Club E Eurocard VISA Visa

BERGEN C5
Rügen

Panorama Lohme $-$$
18551, Dorfstrasse 35
☎ (03 83 02) 92 21
🖹 (03 83 02) 92 34
www.lohme.com
One of Rügen's most famous destinations, this villa overlooking the sea enjoys unrivaled views. The rooms are spacious, charming and comfortable. The terrace has a view of the headland at Arkona. There is an elegant restaurant (international specialties with a regional touch), and last but not least wonderful scenery (Jasmund National Park).

🛏 38
🅿

Villa Aegir $-$$
18546, Mittelstrasse 5
☎ (03 83 92) 30 20
🖹 (03 83 92) 3 30 46
www.ringhotels.de
Built in 1896, this villa has comfortable rooms and modern conference facilities, a splendid terrace with sea views, and an intimate restaurant.

🛏 34
🅿

Villa Neander $-$$
18609, Hauptstrasse 16
☎ (03 83 93) 52 90
🖹 (03 83 93) 5 29 99
This attractive villa has a splendid roof with decorated red tiles and Art Nouveau features adorning the windows and balconies, and offers comfortable rooms and apartments. The sauna and solarium in the nearby Getreuer Eckart apartment hotel are available to hotel residents.

🛏 12
🅿

Villa Salve $-$$
18609, Strandpromenade 41
☎ (03 83 93) 22 23
🖹 (03 83 93) 1 36 29
www.ruegen-schewe.de
Attractive Art Nouveau palace on a promenade overlooking the Baltic with comfortable rooms, excellent conference rooms, a French brasserie-style restaurant (with terrace) and a local bar.

🛏 7
🅿

Sassnitz

Villa Seestern $
18546, Mühlenstrasse 5
☎ (03 83 92) 3 32 57
🖹 (03 83 92) 3 67 65
Writer Theodor Fontane was an early admirer of the beauty of Sassnitz and immortalized it in his novel *Effi Briest*. This impressive seaside resort has an historic Old Town, harbor and steep chalk cliffs. The nautical-style hotel building offers guests spacious rooms with sea views. The restaurant, with its fabulous view of the sea, serves an extensive menu.

🛏 11
🅿 🅴

Key to Symbols: 🖹 Fax 🅴 Email 🛏 Rooms 🅿 Parking 🏊 Swimming 🖼 American Express 🅳 Diners Club 🅴 Eurocard 🖼 Visa

BIELEFELD   B4

Bielefeld

Wintersmühle $
33689 , Sender Str. 6
☎ (0 52 05) 8 82 50
🖹 (0 52 05) 98 25 33
www.wintermuehle.de
This former water mill on the
southern outskirts of Bielefeld
has been converted into a
modern hotel. Comfortable

rooms are equipped with all-
modern conveniences. Enjoy a
visit to the sauna or solarium, or
relax on the attractive terrace or
the extensive lawns. The
restaurant offers guests an
extensive menu of fine food,
including traditional
Westphalian dishes and
international specialties.

🛏 15

🅿

BITBURG   A2

Daun

**Schloss-Hotel Kufürstliches
Amthaus** $$-$$$
54550 · Dauner Burg
☎ (0 65 92) 92 50
🖹 (0 65 92) 92 52 55
This castle and hotel complex
rises impressively over the Eifel
village of Daun. The building
exudes style, with old furniture,
carpets and clocks. Bedrooms
feature antique beds. A particular

attraction is the indoor pool
chiseled into lava rock, complete
with sauna, steamroom and
solarium. After a fine dinner in
the restaurant enjoy a drink in
the rustic Knight's Bar.

🛏 24

🅿

Dudeldorf

Zum alten Brauhaus $-$$
54647, Herrengasse 2/An der
Kirche
☎ (0 65 65) 9 27 50
🖹 (0 65 65) 92 75 55
www.romantikhotels.com/
dudeldorf
The "Alte Brauhaus" is almost
the first thing you see as you
enter the idyllic town of
Dudeldorf, a "Romantic Hotel"

that has been offering hospitality
for more than 200 years. It offers
comfortable rooms, an elegant
restaurant and a splendid
sandstone terrace.

🛏 15

🅿

Eisenschmitt

Molitors Mühle $-$$
54533, Eichelhütte 15
☎ (0 65 67) 96 60
🖹 (0 65 67) 96 61 00
www.molitor.com
Molitors Mühle, an extremely
attractive country inn in the
Rhineland Palatinate, originally
was a rolling mill and later a
grain mill. Today it offers idyllic,
romantic and elegant rooms plus

excellent conference facilities.
After work, unwind in the sauna,
solarium, indoor pool or beauty
salon, or play tennis.

🛏 23
🅿

BONN   A3

Bonn

Am Hohenzollernplatz $$-$$
53173, Plittersdorfer Strasse 56
☎ (02 28) 95 75 90
🖹 (02 28) 9 57 59 29
🄴 www.akzent.de/hotels
This hotel is in the heart of the
Bad Godesberg villa quarter near
museums, congress centers and
the Rhine. It is housed in two

interconnected Art Nouveau
buildings dating from 1904, both
classified as historic monuments.
It offers comfortable rooms, each
individually designed.

🛏 18

🅿

BREMEN · B4
Bremen

Landhaus Höpkens Ruh $$
28355, Oberneulander
Landstr. 69
☎ (04 21) 20 58 53

The name, redolent with associations, harks back to one of Bremen's elder statesmen, Johann Höpken, who bequeathed the villa in Oberneuland Park to his home town in 1877. Today it offers comfortable rooms, individually furnished in elegant country-house style, superb conference facilities and fine food in the Rauchfang restaurant, or in the summer months on the splendid terrace.

 8

P

Osterholz-Scharmbeck

Tietjens Hütte $$
27711, An der Hamme 1
☎ (0 47 91) 9 22 00
📄 (0 47 91) 92 20 36

This thatched, half-timbered hotel is in the Hammeniederung nature reserve on the edge of Devil's Moor. The comfortable rooms are decorated in the local Worpswede style, and there is a small room, the Moordiele, available for parties or conferences. The restaurant, with its carved doorway, lead glazing and nostalgic lamps, offers local specialties, and coffee and homemade cakes are served on the attractive terrace.

 9

P

Worpswede

Eichenhof $$
27726, Ostendorfer Strasse 13
☎ (0 47 92) 26 76
📄 (0 47 92) 44 27

Approached along a splendid drive between an avenue of oak trees, the hotel offers an attractive older exterior and modern interior. The colors used in the rooms give them a pleasant feeling of warmth. A large park with mature trees, flowers and lawns surrounds the four buildings that make up the hotel.

 17

P

BREMERHAVEN · B5
Bad Bederkeesa

Waldschlösschen Bösehof $$
27624, Hauptmann-Böse-Strasse 19
☎ (0 47 45) 94 80
📄 (0 47 45) 94 82 00
www.boesehof.de

This half-timbered house built in 1826 is now a "Romantic Hotel" with comfortable rooms, modern conference facilities and a superb leisure complex (pool, sauna, whirlpool, solarium and bowling).

38

P ≋

BURGHAUSEN · D1
Burghausen

Reisingers Bayerische Alm $-$$
84489, Robert-Koch-Strasse 211
☎ (0 86 77) 98 20
📄 (0 86 77) 98 22 00
www.bayerischealm.de

Enjoy the rural elegance of rooms set in a quiet countryside location. It has been in the ownership of the same family since 1878. There are some ancient trees in the Almwirtsgarten, if you can take your eyes off Germany's longest castle complex - the view of the castle is particularly fine from the Mediterranean terrace restaurant.

23 P

Key to Symbols: 📄 Fax 📧 Email 🛏 Rooms 🅿 Parking ≋ Swimming
American Express Diners Club Eurocard Visa

CHEMNITZ C3

Chemnitz

Hohenstein-Ernstthal

Drei Schwanen $
9337, Altmarkt 19
☎ (0 37 23) 65 90
🖹 (0 37 23) 65 94 59
Following a fire in 1881 this
18th-century building was
rebuilt in its current classical
style. Now tastefully restored, it
offers spacious and comfortable
rooms, excellent banqueting and

Olbernhau

Saigerhütte $
9526, In der Hütte
☎ (03 73 60) 78 70
🖹 (03 73 60)7 87 50
The Saigerhütte, with its huge
copper hammer, was first
established in 1537 when its role
was to remove silver from crude
copper. Today the site houses an
open-air museum and a

COCHEM B2

Bad Bertrich

Cochem

Schlosshotel Klaffenbach $-$$
9123, Wasserschlossweg 6
☎ (03 71) 2 61 10
🖹 (03 71) 2 61 11 00
www.schlosshotel-
klaffenbach.de
This impressive hotel in part of a
splendid Renaissance castle in
the Würschnitzaue Valley has
rooms overlooking the idyllic
inner courtyard. It offers

conference facilities, and an
elegant restaurant.

 32

comfortable hotel with stylish
rooms and suites. It provides a
copious breakfast buffet and
regional specialties in the
restaurant. Other features
include a sauna and conference
facilities.

 27
P

Bertricher Hof $
56864, Am Schwanenteich 7
☎ (0 26 74) 9 36 20
🖹 (0 26 74) 93 62 62
Bad Bertrich is known for its salt
springs, so it is no wonder that
owners Sabine and Bernhard
Pellio decided to offer health
breaks and other specialist health
and dietary weeks. The
comfortable rooms have splendid

Alte Thorschenke $-$$
56812, Brückenstrasse 3
☎ (0 26 71) 70 59
🖹 (0 26 71) 42 02
www.castle-thorschenke.com
The Thorschenke, dating from
1332, is one of Germany's oldest
wine-growing estates. It also is a
charming hotel with stylish
rooms, a comfortable restaurant,
a conference room, an attractive

honeymoon suites, a stylish
restaurant with an extensive
menu (including regional
specialties), café and an
impressive Saxon vehicle
museum.

 51
P

views from the terrace or
restaurant over the lake and
woodland.

 16
P

terrace and a wine bar.

35

Traben-Trarbach

Jugendstilhotel Bellevue **$$**
56841, Am Moselufer
☎ (0 65 41) 70 30
🖹 (0 65 41) 70 34 00
📧 bellevue@net-art.de
This art nouveau building was
built in 1903 by Richard Feist.
It still exudes the vibrant
atmosphere of the time,
combining it with modern
comforts. The rooms are

distinctive and tastefully
decorated, and an attractive
terrace overlooking the Moselle
is open in summer.

🛏 36
P ☑
☐ ◐ Ⓔ ☑

Zell

Schloss Zell **$**
56856, Schlossstrasse 8
☎ (0 65 42) 9 88 60
🖹 (0 65 42) 98 86 90
Kaiser Maximilian stayed here in
1521, and in 1847 the castle
accommodated Prussian king
Friedrich Wilhelm IV. Today it
is an attractive hotel offering
regal accommodation in bright,
elegant and historic rooms.

It also offers superb conference
facilities, an elegant restaurant
with an extensive menu and a
splendid terrace.

🛏 7
P
☐ ◐ Ⓔ ☑

DEGGENDORF   D2

Moos

Gottfried **$-$$**
78345, Böhringer Strasse 1
☎ (0 77 32) 9 24 20 + 41 61
🖹 (0 77 32) 5 25 02
www.bodenseehotels.com
The hotel offers comfortable,
modern rooms and a splendid
terrace. For relaxation there is
tennis, a fitness room, swimming

pool and sauna.

🛏 11
P ☑
☐ ◐ Ⓔ ☑

St. Englmar

Gut Schmelmerhof **$-$$**
94379, Rettenbach 24
☎ (0 99 65) 18 9
🖹 (0 99 65) 18 91 40
The Schmelmerhof, a "Romantic
Hotel" with a long tradition of
hospitality set in an idyllic rural
location, provides both rest and
comfort. Feel at home
immediately in its spacious

interior. For health it offers an
indoor pool, sauna, steambath
and solarium, and for relaxation
the café terrace or the bar.

🛏 25
P ☑
☐ Ⓔ ☑

DETMOLD   B3

Detmold

Detmolder Hof **$-$$**
32756, Lange Strasse 19
☎ (0 52 31) 9 91 20
🖹 (0 52 31) 99 12 99
www.ringhotels.de
This "Ring Hotel" is a gem from
the Weser Renaissance (c 1560),
classified a historic monument
and furnished with antiques.
Individually designed rooms all
have modern conveniences, and

the same applies to the
conference facilities.

🛏 38
☐ ◐ Ⓔ ☑

Key to Symbols: 🖹 Fax 📧 Email 🛏 Rooms P Parking ☑ Swimming
☐ American Express ◐ Diners Club Ⓔ Eurocard ☑ Visa

DINKELSBUHL · B2
Rosenberg

Landgasthof Adler $-$$
73494, Ellwanger Strasse 15
☎ (0 79 67) 5 13
📄 (0 79 67)71 03 00

The facade of the 14th-century Adler has been restored to more than its former glory. The rooms have exposed timber beams and are furnished in a comfortable country style with attractive parquet floors. Enjoy the breakfast buffet which your host, Hildegard Brenner, regularly replenishes with fresh delicacies (e.g. homemade yogurt and cheese).

🛏 12

Feuchtwangen

Greifen-Post $$
91555, Marktplatz 8
☎ (0 98 52) 68 00
📄 (0 98 52) 6 80 68

Two historic houses, the Post (whose origins date back to 1369) and the Greifen (dating to 1450) now combined to form a "Romantic Hotel". Individually designed rooms range from Laura Ashley to Biedermeier. There are superb conference facilities, a pool complex with sauna and a solarium.

🛏 38

DORTMUND · A3
Herdecke
Landhotel Bonsmanns Hof $-$$
58313, Wittbräucker Strasse 38
☎ (0 23 30) 8 00 20
📄 (0 23 30) 7 15 62

This tastefully decorated country hotel, with an attractive half-timbered facade, has been family-owned since 1750. The comfortable restaurant offers an extensive menu and a fine selection of wines.

🛏 15

Dortmund
Lennhof $$
44227, Menglinghauser Strasse 20
☎ (02 31) 7 57 26
📄 (02 31) 75 93 61
www.romantikhotels.com/dortmund

Pure romance prevails from the moment you approach the splendid half-timbered facade of this architectural gem on the edge of the city. Inside you will find comfortable rooms, a cozy country-style restaurant, and two conference rooms, both with modern equipment. Unwind in the indoor pool, sauna or solarium or play tennis, then relax on the garden terrace.

🛏 33

Iserlohn
Korth $$
58636, In der Calle 4-7
☎ (0 23 71) 9 78 70
📄 (0 23 71) 97 87 67
www.s-auer-land.com

A long-established hotel in an idyllic setting surrounded by mature trees. It has a genuine half-timbered facade and exudes a cozy rural charm. The rooms offer all-modern conveniences, and fully equipped conference facilities also are available. Unwind in the indoor pool, sauna or solarium, or relax on the attractive garden terrace.

🛏 36

Key to Symbols: 📄 Fax 🅴 Email 🛏 Rooms 🅿 Parking 🏊 Swimming · American Express 🅓 Diners Club 🅴 Eurocard · Visa

Iserlohn

Dresden

Pattis   **$$-$$$**
1157, Merbitzer Strasse 53
☎ (03 51) 4 25 50
▤ (03 51) 4 25 52 55
www.romantikhotels.com/
dresden
Set in large landscaped gardens,
this former mill is now a unique
"Romantic Hotel". It has

Villa Emma   **$$**
1324, Stechgrundstrasse 2
☎ (03 51) 26 48 10
▤ (03 51) 2 64 81 18
This fantastic Art Nouveau villa
dating from 1914, lovingly
restored with filigree Art
Nouveau windows, is now an
elegant hotel with individually
designed rooms (including
superb baths). The charming

Moritzburg

Churfürstliche Waldschänke
    $-$$
1468, Grosse Fasanenstrasse
☎ (03 52 07) 86 00
▤ (03 52 07) 8 60 93
In the 17th century August the
Strong invited guests to the
Churfürstliche Waldschänke.
Today you can stay in the
splendid rooms and see for

Langenfeld

Gravenberg   **$$**
40764, OT Wiescheid,
Elberfeld. Str. 45
☎ (0 21 73) 9 22 00
▤ (02173) 2 27 77
www.romantikhotels.com/
solingen
Guests are assured of hospitality
at this "Romantic Hotel," which

Neuhaus   **$**
58644, Parkingösseler Strasse
149
☎ (0 23 74) 9 78 00
▤ (0 23 74) 76 64
www.hotel-neuhaus.de
A splendid half-timbered house
on the outskirts of town
overlooking open countryside.
The accommodation comprises
an attractive gallery and foyer,

exquisitely decorated rooms,
conference facilities, a library and
lobby, bright breakfast room and
a terrace. Fitness and beauty
facilities include a Stendhal
cosmetics studio, massage,
Turkish baths, sauna, solarium,
whirlpool, herb grotto and
fitness room.

terrace, with its airy
Mediterranean-like feel, is a
popular meeting place. Relax in
the sauna or play golf on the
nearby course just a 5-minute
walk from the hotel (reduced
green fees for hotel guests).

yourself why he was so
enthusiastic. "Prince's Room" has
leather wall coverings and an old
tiled stove. The spacious
maisonette rooms are worthy of
particular recommendation. On
warm days enjoy the terrace,
inner courtyard and garden.

has been in the family since
1774. It features a winter garden,
comfortable public areas and
large rooms. A new extension
provides additional
accommodation. Conference and
leisure facilities are offered, and
the restaurant has an ambitious
menu.

---

comfortable rooms and suites,
and first-class conference
facilities. For relaxation there is a
sauna, solarium, fitness room,
bowls, practice putting green,
terrace and garden. The
farmhouse offers creative courses
and is equipped with a studio
and puppet workshop.
🛏 14

🛏 41 🅿

🛏 45
🅿 ⊠

Key to Symbols: ▤ Fax   🅴 Email   🛏 Rooms   🅿 Parking   ⊠ Swimming
   ▦ American Express   ⓓ Diners Club   🅴 Eurocard   ▦ Visa

EICHSTÄTT   C2
Eichstätt

Schiessstätte $
85072, Schiessstättberg 8
☎ (0 84 21) 9 82 00
 (0 84 21) 98 20 80
This hotel is a short 7-minute walk from the heart of town. Behind its historic facade you will find charming, modern rooms. Stock up for the day from the copious buffet served in the stylish breakfast room. After that relax on the attractive garden terrace.

🛏 26
🅿
🔘 🇪 💳

EISENACH   C3
Eisenach
Hotel auf der Wartburg $$-$$$
99817, Auf der Wartburg
☎ (0 36 91) 79 70
 (0 36 91) 79 71 00
www.wartburghotel.de
Stone walls serve to emphasize the castle-like character of this house. It offers charming rooms, conference facilities, a lounge and library and an attractive room with an open fireplace. The hotel is an ideal setting for festivities and business functions. Other attractions include the terrace, a romantic inner courtyard and a restaurant.

🛏 35
🅿

Schlosshotel Eisenach $
99817, Markt 10
☎ (0 36 91) 21 42 60
 (0 36 91) 21 42 59
Former Franciscan monastery dating from 1280, located between Market Square and Luther's House. In its time it has been both a monastery brewery and a restaurant. In 1994 it was extensively restored to become a modern hotel and conference center (some of the old vaulting is still visible).

🛏 40
🅿

The architecture of Eisenach

EMDEN A4

Emden

Alte Posthalterei $

Hesel

Alte Posthalterei $
26835, Leeraner Strasse 4
☎ (0 49 50) 22 15
🖹 (0 49 50) 35 12
www.alte-posthalterei.de
The Alte Posthalterei, where travelers took refreshment while coachmen changed the horses, has been a meeting place for 150 years. Relax in the indoor pool,

Alt-Emder Bürgerhaus $
26725, Friedrich-Ebert-Strasse 33
☎ (0 49 21) 97 61 00
🖹 (0 49 21) 2 42 49
This traditional hotel is close to the town center and the "Wall," Emden's famous park. The family-run hotel attaches particular importance to service. The cozy restaurant serves

international and regional cuisine specializing in fish dishes. Relax in the sauna. Rooms are provided with every comfort.

🛏 11

sauna or solarium and then dine in the cozy restaurant offering East Friesian specialties.

🛏 19

Norderney

Kurhotel Norderney $$-$$$
26548, Weststrandstrasse 4
☎ (0 49 32) 88 30 00
🖹 (0 49 32) 88 33 33
The Kurhotel was built between 1837 and 1838 as a residence for the Crown Prince of Hanover, later King Georg V. The historic core of the building may be one of the oldest in the area, sympathetically converted to

create a modern hotel. It has an elegant restaurant with an extensive menu featuring fish specialties.

🛏 10

Aurich

Piqueurhof $-$$
26603, Burgstrasse
☎ (0 49 41) 9 55 20
🖹 (0 49 41) 6 68 21
The hotel, with its particularly attractive and inviting foyer, dates back to the 17th century. It offers comfortable rooms with fully equipped, modern conference facilities. The

Panorama pool complex offers a sauna, solarium, and fitness and beauty center. Dine in the relaxing surroundings of the restaurant or beer cellar, choosing from international cuisine or regional specialties.

🛏 38

ESSEN A3

Essen

Résidence $$
45219, Auf der Forst 1
☎ (0 20 54) 9 55 90
🖹 (0 20 54) 8 25 01
www.hotel-residence.de
The hotel, run by Uta and Berthold Bühler, was created from a splendid Art Nouveau villa high on a hill overlooking Kettwig. Great attention has been given to architectural detail

– the reception area is chic, the restaurant elegant, the rooms and suites stylish and individual. Excellent service combines charm and professional expertise.

🛏 16

Key to Symbols: 🖹 Fax 🄴 Email 🛏 Rooms 🅿 Parking 🏊 Swimming ▭ American Express ▭ Diners Club 🄴 Eurocard ▭ Visa

Sengelmannshof $$
45219, Sengelmannsweg 35
☎ (0 20 54) 9 59 70
🖹 (0 20 54) 8 32 00
This attractive half-timbered house was formerly part of a feudal estate and has been in family ownership since 1817. Today it houses an attractive hotel with comfortable rooms and modern conference facilities.

The restaurant offers an extensive menu specializing in local dishes.

 26

FLENSBURG   B5
Oeversee

Historischer Krug $-$$
24988, An der Bundesstrasse 76, Nr. 4
☎ (0 46 30) 94 00
🖹 (0 46 30) 7 80
www.historischer-krug.de
The Krug, dating from 1519, may be the oldest hotel in Schleswig-Holstein and the longest in the ownership of one family. It also is the only establishment on German soil favored by the Danish court since 1624. A "Romantic Hotel," it offers spacious rooms in the country house style with top-quality conference facilities, a health suite and beauty salon.

 27

FRANKFURT   B2
Hofheim am Taunus

Burkartsmühle $$
65719, Kurhausstrasse 71
☎ (0 61 92) 96 80
🖹 (0 61 92) 96 82 61
This historic mill, in a quiet location overlooking Hofheim municipal park, has been converted into an exquisite country house hotel, where some of the comfortable rooms have exposed beams. Enjoy the sauna, solarium, swimming pool and tennis court, and relax in the bar or inner courtyard.

25

FREIBERG   C3
Freiberg (Sachsen)
Silberhof $-$$
9599, Silberhofstrasse 1
☎ (0 37 31) 2 68 80
🖹 (0 37 31) 26 88 78
www.silberhof.de
This Art Nouveau building in the heart of the town center dates from 1906 but is completely renovated and decorated throughout in warm pastel colors and furnished with high-quality furniture. It offers comfortable rooms and suites, first-rate conference room and an attractive terrace.

27

Münstertal
Spielweg $$-$$$
79244, Hauptstrasse 61
☎ (0 76 36) 70 90
🖹 (0 76 36) 7 09 66
A "Romantic Hotel" offering comfortable rooms, a superb conference room and excellent health facilities. A passageway connects the main building to the annexes.

 36

FREIBURG   A1
Badenweiler

Zur Sonne $-$$
79410, Moltkestrasse 4
☎ (0 76 32) 7 50 80
📄 (0 76 32) 75 08 65
www.zur-sonne.de
A traditional "Romantic Hotel" with an impressive half-timbered facade, offering tastefully designed rooms. Relax on the terrace, enjoy the country-style wine bar or dine in the comfortable restaurant with its extensive menu.

 35
P

Emmendingen
Parkhotel Krone Maleck $
79312, Brandelweg 1
☎ (0 76 41) 9 30 96 90
📄 (0 76 41) 5 25 76
www.krone-maleck.de
The "Krone," located in the heart of a charming park with a pond and flamingos, offers well-equipped conference facilities and comfortable, individually designed rooms. In fine weather relax in the garden or on the attractive terrace.

27
P

Freiburg

Markgräfler Hof $$
79098, Gerberau 22
☎ (07 61) 38 64 90
📄 (07 61) 3 86 49 44
www.t-com-hotels.com/hotels/markgraefler-hof
This hotel offers excellent accommodations in a quiet and central location in the Old Town. The building dates to 1406, but rooms are decorated in modern country-house style. Relax in the sauna and solarium in the nearby Minerva Hotel.

17

Heitersheim
Ochsen $
79423, Am Ochsenplatz 10
☎ (0 76 34) 22 18
📄 (0 76 34) 30 25
📧 ochsen-heitersheim@t-online.de
Heitersheim is closely associated with the Knights of Malta and has a splendid castle. The Ochsen, an imposing building dating from 1864, is now a hotel offering comfortable rooms/apartments and excellent cuisine from a choice of restaurants – the country-style Maltese Room or the attractive Zunftstube. For relaxation there is tennis and golf nearby.

28

P

FREUDENSTADT   B1
Baiersbronn

Ailwaldhof $$
72270, Ailwald 3
☎ (0 74 42) 83 60
📄 (0 74 42) 83 62 00
This modern hotel is located on a hill overlooking town and occupies grounds of mixed pasture and woodland. The rooms make ample use of pine and bright materials. The pool area offers a massage pool, sauna and solarium. Relax on the splendid terrace or lawn, and before you leave choose from the many culinary delicacies on sale in the shop.

8
P

Pfalzgrafenweiler

Waldsägmühle $-$$
72285, Waldsägmühle 1
☎ (0 74 45) 8 51 50
🖹 (0 74 45) 67 50
www.waldsaegmuehle.de
Over the years this old sawmill and simple inn has been transformed into an imposing "Silence Hotel," now among the most famous in the Black Forest.

It is set in splendid woodland and offers rest and relaxation in comfortable rooms, most of which have balconies. Excellent conference and leisure facilities are provided, including a sauna, solarium and indoor pool.

🛏 38
P 🏊 🇪 VISA

FULDA B3
Fulda

Goldener Karpfen $$-$$$
36037, Simpliziusbrunnen 1
☎ (06 61) 8 68 00
🖹 (06 61) 8 68 01 00
www.hotel-goldener-karpfen.com
This well-run hotel has an attractive facade and individually designed rooms in styles ranging from Art Deco to Californian and from Bauhaus to Florentine,

making it a fun place to stay. Cozy bar.

🛏 50
P
AMEX 🇩 🇪 VISA

FÜSSEN C1
Pfronten

Berghotel Schlossanger Alp $$
87459, Am Schlossanger 1
☎ (0 83 63) 91 45 50
🖹 (0 83 63) 91 45 55 55
www.schlossanger.de
Situated at the foot of the Falkenstein, Germany's highest castle ruin, is this imposing mountain hotel created from a simple hut dating from 1913. Escape the rush of everyday life

and enjoy the atmosphere of the comfortable rooms, suites and lounges, decorated in the local style. The hotel offers excellent health facilities and a prestigious conference room.

🛏 25
P 🏊
AMEX 🇩 🇪 VISA

Füssen
OT Bad Faulenbach $
87629, Alatseestrasse 28
☎ (0 83 62) 40 17
🖹 (0 83 62) 3 89 47
Located in the spa area of Füssen and nestling at the edge of woodland the hotel, with its pretty towers, has the air of a small castle. The rooms are light and decorated in warm colors.

Relax on the terrace or on the lawn.

🛏 10
P
🇪 VISA

Pfronten
Alpenhotel Krone $$
87459, Tiroler Strasse 29
☎ (0 83 63) 6 90 50
🖹 (0 83 63) 6 90 55 55
www.alpenhotel-krone.de
Originally home to a religious order and later a tavern, this hotel has a long tradition of hospitality. It has an impressive exterior with bright blue shutters

and steep gables. Guests enter the marble hall and take the glass elevator to beautiful rooms with old balconies and designer furniture. Excellent conference facilities are available, plus a pavilion and terrace for relaxation.

🛏 30
P AMEX 🇩 🇪 VISA

Key to Symbols: 🖹 Fax 🇪 Email 🛏 Rooms P Parking 🏊 Swimming
AMEX American Express 🇩 Diners Club 🇪 Eurocard VISA Visa

GARMISCH-PARTENKIRCHEN C1

Garmisch-Partenkirchen

Staudacherhof **$$**
82467, Höllentalstrasse 48
☎ (0 88 21) 92 90
🖹 (0 88 21) 92 93 33
www.staudacherhof.de
A pleasant hotel built in the alpine style, in a quiet location 5 minutes' walk from the town center. It has an attractive foyer with an open fireplace and bar, and a terrace serving coffee and cakes in the afternoon. The rooms are comfortable and exude country-style elegance with an abundant use of wood. Relax in the health suite, sauna, solarium or on the lawn. In the evening the restaurant offers Bavarian specialties.

🛏 35 P ☰ E VISA

GERA C3

Grossebersdorf

Adler **$**
7589, Hauptstrasse 22
☎ (03 66 07) 50 00
🖹 (03 66 07) 5 01 00
Located just outside Gera in an attractive setting, the Adler's rooms are decorated in either a contemporary or farmhouse style. It has well-equipped conference facilities, a sauna and a comfortable restaurant offering an extensive menu. Enjoy the garden terrace in good weather.

🛏 40
P
☰ ⓓ E VISA

GIESSEN B3

Lich

Alte Klostermühle **$-$$**
35423, Kloster Arnsburg
☎ (0 64 04) 9 19 00
🖹 (0 64 04) 91 90 91
Impressive Cistercian monastery founded in 1174 with splendid baroque additions. Overnight accommodations are provided in the former hostel building, which has been converted into a stylish hotel with comfortable rooms. The restaurant, located in the former mill, offers an extensive menu. Excellent conference facilities also are available.

🛏 26
P ☰ ⓓ E VISA

GOSLAR C4

Clausthal-Zellerfeld

Goldene Krone **$-$$**
38678, Am Kronenplatz 3
☎ (0 53 23) 93 00
🖹 (0 53 23) 01 00
www.gastrogehrke.de
Contemporary furniture provides a pleasant contrast to a traditional building dating from 1845. It offers first-class conference facilities, and elegant restaurant and a bar.

🛏 21
P
☰ E VISA

GOTHA C3

Friedrichroda

Kavaliershaus **$-$$**
99894, Am Schloss Reinhardsbrunn
☎ (0 36 23) 30 42 53
🖹 (0 36 23) 30 42 51
www.tc-hotels.de
The Rehihardsbrunn Castle was built on the foundations of an 11th-century monastery, and within the same parkland is the equally historic and attractive Kavaliershaus – an ideal center from which to discover Thuringia. The rooms are stylish and the restaurant menu extensive.

🛏 11
P
☰ ⓓ E VISA

Key to Symbols: 🖹 Fax e Email 🛏 Rooms P Parking ☰ Swimming American Express ⓓ Diners Club E Eurocard VISA Visa

GÖTTINGEN B3

Duderstadt

Zum Löwen $$
37115, Marktstrasse 30
☎ (0 55 27) 30 72
📄 (0 55 27) 7 26 30
www.hotelzum loewen.de

The Zum Löwen hotel, situated in the heart of the Old Town, has an attractive classical facade with a projecting terrace. The entrance foyer is light and elegant, the rooms welcoming and decorated in warm colors. Relax in the leisure suite with its sauna and solarium, with tennis and squash close by. The restaurant offers an extensive menu, or you can relax in the comfortable bar and enjoy draft Pils.

🛏 41
P 🏊

⬛ ⓓ Ⓔ ▥▥

HALBERSTADT C4

Halberstadt

Parkhotel Unter den Linden $$
38820, Klamrothstrasse 2
☎ (0 39 41) 60 00 77
📄 (0 39 41) 60 00 78
www.parkhotel-halberstadt.de

The Parkhotel was built as a private villa in 1910-11 by Hermann Muthesius. The rooms in the main house, with their rounded arches, wall closets, balconies and bay windows, have a particular charm. The restaurant has a splendid stucco ceiling.

🛏 45
P ⬛ ⓓ Ⓔ ▥▥

Ilsenburg

Landhaus Zu den Rothen Forellen $$-$$$
38871, Marktplatz 2
☎ (03 94 52) 93 93
📄 (03 94 52) 93 99

Built for an aristocrat in 1752, the property is set at the foot of the Brocken mountain overlooking a trout lake. It has been extensively restored and converted into an exclusive hotel with all-modern conveniences. Popular meeting places are the terrace, the winter garden and the bar. Well-equipped conference rooms and excellent leisure facilities are available.

🛏 51
P 🏊
⬛ ⓓ Ⓔ ▥▥

Schlosshotel Ilsenburg $
38871, Schlossstrasse 26
☎ (03 94 52) 9 70
📄 (03 94 52) 9 72 13

Built in the 11th century as a Benedictine monastery, the property was later converted into a castle and more recently into a hotel. It is situated at the foot of the Brocken mountain, and is renowned for its homemade cakes and extensive restaurant menu.

🛏 38
P ⬛ ▥▥

HAMBURG B5

Aumühle

Waldesruh am See $-$$
21521, Am Mühlenteich 2
☎ (0 41 04) 30 46 + 31 39
📄 (0 41 04) 20 73

In an idyllic location on the edge of the Forest of Saxony, this half-timbered building was constructed in 1750 as a hunting lodge and is now owned by the Bismarck family. The hotel displays tasteful country-style elegance throughout (including genuine antiques). An extensive menu is available in the Jagdrestaurant, the Orangery or the splendid terrace overlooking the lake.

🛏 15
P
⬛ ⓓ Ⓔ ▥▥

Key to Symbols: 📄 Fax Ⓔ Email 🛏 Rooms P Parking 🏊 Swimming
⬛ American Express ⓓ Diners Club Ⓔ Eurocard ▥▥ Visa

Hamburg

Landhaus Flottbek   **$$**
22607, Baron-Voght-
Strasse 179
☎ (0 40) 8 22 74 10
▤ (0 40) 82 27 41 51
www.landhaus-flottbek.de
This country house has origins
dating back to the 18th century.
It offers stylish, spacious and
charming rooms, each

individually designed. The
restaurant and garden room are
also available for events,
celebrations and conferences.

🛏 24
🅿
▨ ⓪ 🇪 📧

Strandhotel Blankenese   **$$**
22587, OT Blankenese,
Strandweg 13
☎ (0 40) 86 13 44
▤ (0 40) 86 49 36
The Strandhotel Blankenese, a
unique combination of style and
comfort, is located in a bright
white villa built in 1902,
overlooking the Elbe. It offers
individually designed and

extremely elegant rooms, and a
superb breakfast buffet.

🛏 15
⓪ 🇪 📧

Quickborn

Jagdhaus Waldfrieden   **$$**
25451, Kieler Strasse (B 4)
☎ (0 41 06) 6 10 20
▤ (0 41 06) 6 91 96
The romantic Jagdhaus, built in
1902 as the private residence for
a ship owner, has a charm that
none can resist. Enjoy the
enormous park, the lake, the
stylish rooms and the elegant
winter garden. Tennis courts are

available nearby.

🛏 24
🅿
▨ ⓪ 🇪 📧

Herrenhausen Gardens, Hannover

Key to Symbols: ▤ Fax   🇪 Email   🛏 Rooms   🅿 Parking   🏊 Swimming
▨ American Express   ⓪ Diners Club   🇪 Eurocard   📧 Visa

HAMELN B4
Springe

Schäfers' Hotel & Restaurant $
31832, Pfarrstrasse 9
☎ (0 50 44) 9 51 50
🖹 (0 50 44) 95 15 15
A unique mix of hospitality, tasteful décor and charm prevails in this idyllic half-timbered building dating back 200 years. Distinctive rooms and suites each have an individual touch. The first-class conference and function rooms, impressive old fireplace, picturesque courtyard and stylish restaurant are other reasons for visiting the property.

 27
🅿️
🖭 🄴 🖾

HANNOVER B4
Bad Nenndorf
Die Villa $$-$$$
31542, Kramerstrasse 4
☎ (0 57 23) 94 61 70
🖹 (0 57 23)94 61 88
www.villa-badnenndorf.de
This villa dates from the 19th century and is protected by law from extensive change. It has an old facade with pretty neo-Gothic turrets and bay windows. The light, elegant rooms are individually decorated in warm colors. Well-equipped function rooms are available, and there is a splendid terrace and restaurant serving sophisticated gourmet food.

 13
🅿️ 🄴 🖾

Burgwedel
Menge's Hof $$
30938, Isernhägener Strasse 3
☎ (0 51 39) 80 30
🖹 (0 51 39) 8 73 55
Two splendid half-timbered houses combine to form this property; the older one dates from 1556. In the cellar of the main house guests can enjoy a bathing paradise with whirlpool, massage showers, steambath, Finnish sauna, bio-sauna, adventure pool and bar. The restaurant evokes the atmosphere of a 16th-century estate. The rooms are designed in elegant country-house style with heavy whitewashed wooden furniture.

 42
🅿️ 🏊 🖭 🄾 🄴 🖾

HECHINGEN B1
Haigerloch

Schloss Haigerloch $$
72401, Schloss
☎ (0 74 74) 69 30
🖹 (0 74 74) 6 93 82
Haigerloch Castle, formerly the governor's residence and built between 1577 and 1595, has been converted into a stylish hotel offering light, welcoming rooms with all-modern conveniences. There is an attractive terrace, bar and a restaurant serving seasonal specialties.

 30
🅿️
🖭 🄾 🄴 🖾

HEIDE B5
Friedrichstadt
Historic Hotel Holländische Stube $
25840, Am Mittelburgwall 22-26
☎ (0 48 81) 9 39 00
🖹 (0 48 81) 93 90 22
One of the oldest merchant houses in Friedrichstadt, built between 1621 and 1625. In 1796 it was home to the future French King Louis Philippe, and today the antiques evoke the atmosphere of that era. There are modern, comfortable rooms in the adjacent Art Nouveau building, and a superb conference room.

 10
🅿️
🖭 🄾 🄴 🖾

Key to Symbols: 🖹 Fax 🄴 Email 🛏 Rooms 🅿️ Parking 🏊 Swimming
🖭 American Express 🄾 Diners Club 🄴 Eurocard 🖾 Visa

Karolinenkoog
Landhaus Pfahlershof $
25776, Koogstrasse 15-17
☎ (0 48 82) 6 50 00
🖹 (0 48 82) 65 00 60
The Pfahlershof is synonymous with relaxation, offering comfortable rooms and a wide range of leisure facilities. It is situated between the Karolinenkoog dykes and only a few minutes from Tönning harbor.

🛏 49
🅿 ≋
▭ 🔘 🄴 VISA

HEIDELBERG B2
Eberbach

Altes Badhaus $$
69412, Am Lindenplatz 1
☎ (0 62 71) 9 23 00
🖹 (0 62 71) 92 30 40
The medieval Alte Badhaus in the heart of Eberbach, a classified historic monument, was formerly the municipal baths. Behind the picturesque half-timbered facade are stylish rooms, which combine historic atmosphere with modern comfort. The restaurant, with its Gothic vaulting, now offers tempting delicacies from Swabia and Baden, which in summer also can be enjoyed on the attractive terrace.

🛏 7
▭ 🄴 VISA

Heidelberg

Landhaus Grenzhof $$
69123, OT Grenzhof, Grenzhof 9
☎ (0 62 02) 94 30
🖹 (0 62 02) 94 31 00
www.landhaus-grenzhof.de
The first documented evidence of the Grenzhof dates from AD 771. The hotel and its historic walls is set in attractive grounds and offers elegant rooms (including maisonettes) with a pleasantly rustic charm. Relax in the beer garden under the chestnut trees or in the winter garden pavilion. A superb conference room also is available.

🛏 27
🅿 ▭ 🄴 VISA

Leimen

Zum Bären $-$$
69181, Rathausstrasse 20
☎ (0 62 24) 98 10
🖹 (0 62 24) 98 12 22
The Leimen Bären offers a winning combination of traditional hospitality and modern comfort. It has been owned by the same family since 1666, and great importance is attached to tradition. Guests will find stylish rooms, a restaurant, a relaxing bar and a beer garden. Excellent conference facilities also are provided.

🛏 26
🅿 🄴 VISA

Schwetzingen
Zum Erbprinzen $-$$
68723, Karlsruher Strasse 1
☎ (0 62 02) 9 32 70
🖹 (0 62 02) 93 27 93
Historic, restored house opposite the castle of the Electoral Princes. This is a popular summer destination, not the least because of its splendid terrace. It offers comfortable rooms and a first-class conference room, in addition to the intimate restaurant and café.

🛏 25
▭ 🄴 VISA

Neckarwestheim

Bad Friedrichshall
Schloss Lehen $-$$
74177, Hauptstrasse 2
☎ (0 71 36) 9 89 70
🖹 (0 71 36) 98 97 20
Schloß Lehen, built on the banks of the Kocher, dates from the 12th century, and was converted in 1553 into a Renaissance castle. It is now a hotel and restaurant under the

🛏 26
🅿
[AmEx] [E] [Visa]

Ludwigsdorf

Schwaigern
Zum Alten Rentamt $-$$
74193, Schlossstrasse 6-8
☎ (0 71 38) 54 06
🖹 (0 71 38) 13 25
The historic Rentamt, with its old walls and attractive half-timbered facade, now has all the features you would expect from a first-class establishment: distinctive rooms (such as the

Horbruch

Liebenstein $$
74382, Liebenstein 1
☎ (0 71 33) 9 89 90
🖹 (0 71 33) 60 45
The Schloßhotel Liebenstein, with the second-oldest Renaissance gables in Württemberg, feels like an ancient manor house but much more comfortable. It offers attractive rooms and an extensive

menu – regional delicacies in the Kurfürst restaurant and cakes on the terrace. Ideal for weddings (it has its own chapel) and for dances, banquets and conferences.

🛏 23
🅿

expert guidance of Friedheinz Eggensberger. Individually designed rooms range from ancient to modern.

🛏 26
🅿
[AmEx] [E] [Visa]

Gutshof Hedicke $
2829, Dorfstrasse 114
☎ (0 35 81) 3 80 00
🖹 (0 35 81) 38 00 20
This three-sided building, a former farm, has a splendid inner courtyard and terrace. It has been converted into a small hotel providing comfortable accommodations. A converted barn is used for concerts and

conferences and has a bar and bistro.

🛏 14
🅿
[AmEx] [E] [Visa]

stylish Spitzweg-Zimmerle), a romantic garden and terrace for relaxation, and excellent conference facilities in the Marshal Room, which has old cross vaulting.

🛏 13
🅿
[E] [Visa]

Historic Schlossmühle $$ 🛏 17
55483, An der L 190
☎ (0 65 43) 40 41
🖹 (0 65 43)31 78
www.schlossmuehle.com
The Schlossmühle, dating from the 17th century, exudes romance. It offers comfortable rooms and superb conference facilities. In summer guests can relax on the splendid terrace.

Page 196

GERMANY

ITZEHOE B5
Hennstedt (near Itzehoe)

Landhotel Seelust No $
25581, OT Seelust, Seelust 6
☎ (0 48 77) 6 77
🖹 (0 48 77) 7 66
This hotel is situated among rolling hills in the heart of Aukrug National Park. It is a charming building, dating from the end of the 19th century and offering comfortable rooms, an attractive lakeside terrace and a

restaurant with an extensive menu. There also is a lounge room with an open fireplace.

 14

KAISERSLAUTERN A2
Föckelberg
Turmhotel $
66887, Auf dem Potzberg 3
☎ (0 63 85) 7 20
🖹 (0 63 85) 7 21 56
Built on the Potzberg mountain, this property evokes the atmosphere of the Middle Ages. Bedrooms are comfortable. There is falconry in the deer

park, and country-style restaurants are available.

 46

KARLSRUHE B2
Ettlingen
Erbprinz $$-$$$
76275, Rheinstrasse 1
☎ (0 72 43) 32 20
🖹 (0 72 43) 1 64 71
www.hotel-erbprinz.de
The Erbprinz offers a sophisticated atmosphere and a superb interior, is close to the picturesque Alb Valley and has

been dispensing hospitality for more than 200 years. Enjoy the tasteful and stylish rooms and excellent conference facilities. In summer relax on the attractive terrace or treat yourself to coffee and cakes.

 44

KASSEL B3
Hann. Münden

Berghotel Eberburg $
34346, Tillyschanzenweg 14
☎ (0 55 41) 50 88 + 50 89
🖹 (0 55 41) 46 85
This hotel is located in the former summer residence of Professor Eberlein, the famous sculptor. It offers nine rooms in the main house and 17 in the annex, all both elegant and comfortable. There also are

splendid views of the town and the Fulda Valley.

 26

Spangenberg

Schloss Spangenberg $-$$
34286, Schlossberg
☎ (0 56 63) 8 66
🖹 (0 56 63) 75 67
Behind the historic walls of this former hunting castle is a comfortable hotel with stylish rooms, first-class conference facilities, an intimate vaulted cellar (wine tasting is available) and a splendid terrace.

 23

Key to Symbols: 🖹 Fax 🄴 Email 🛏 Rooms 🅿 Parking 🏊 Swimming
American Express 🔘 Diners Club 🄴 Eurocard 💳 Visa

Trendelburg

Burg Hotel Trendelburg **$$**
34388, Steinweg 1
☎ (0 56 75) 90 90
🖹 (0 56 75) 93 62
The first documented evidence of the "Burg Trendelburg" dates back to the early 14th century, when half the castle was mortgaged to Heinrich 1st, the Landgrave of Hesse. Repeatedly conquered, damaged and rebuilt over the centuries, it opened as a hotel and restaurant after World War II. All rooms and suites are individually designed and furnished with antiques and period furniture, giving it a unique atmosphere.

🛏 20
American Express · Diners Club · Eurocard · Visa

KIEL B5

Bosau

Strauers Hotel am See **$$**
23715, Gerold Damm 2-4
☎ (0 45 27) 99 40
🖹 (0 45 27) 99 41 11
www.strauer.de
Quiet hotel on the eastern bank of Greater Lake Plön in the heart of the delightful landscape of Holstein Switzerland. Rooms are spacious and individually furnished. Business travelers benefit from modern conference facilities and after work can unwind in the indoor pool, outdoor pool sauna, solarium or beauty salon. Relax on the lawns, on the splendid terrace or visit the medicinal baths.

🛏 35 | P | Swimming | Eurocard

Schönberg

Stadt Kiel **$**
24217, Markt 8
☎ (0 43 44) 13 54
🖹 (0 43 44) 30 51 51
Attractive, comfortable, stylish and friendly hotel close to Kiel. All rooms have radio, color television, telephone, minibar and safe. Feel at home immediately in this modern but elegant environment. Function and conference rooms are available, and there are health facilities (fitness center, sauna and solarium), a beer garden and a terrace.

🛏 15
P | Swimming
American Express · Diners Club · Eurocard · Visa

KOBLENZ A3

Braubach

Zum Weissen Schwanen **$**
56338, Brunnenstrasse 4
☎ (0 26 27) 98 20
🖹 (0 26 27) 88 02
This splendid half-timbered house has been giving sustenance to travelers since 1693, and even now guests can enjoy the romance of the mill – some of the 17th-century mill equipment and the large mill wheel have been retained (plus a small rural museum). Enjoy the comfort of the rooms over the winepress in the adjacent 13th-century town mill.

🛏 16
P
Eurocard · Visa

KÖLN (COLOGNE) A3

Köln

Brenner'scher Hof **$$-$$$**
50858, Wilh.-v.-Capitaine-Str.15-17
☎ (02 21) 9 48 60 00
🖹 (02 21) 94 86 00 10
www.brennerscher-hof.de
Built as a country house in 1754, the hotel is now in a quiet suburb of Cologne. Most bathrooms in the exclusive rooms and suites have wall paintings, and apartments are available on a monthly basis. Conference rooms are light and airy, and guests can relax in the inner courtyard or on the terrace. The three restaurants include Greek and Italian options.

🛏 28
American Express · Diners Club · Eurocard · Visa

Key to Symbols: 🖹 Fax Email 🛏 Rooms P Parking ≋ Swimming · American Express · Diners Club · E Eurocard · Visa

Viktoria **$$-$$$**
50668, Worringer Strasse 23
☎ (02 21) 9 73 17 20
🖷 (02 21) 72 70 67
www.hotelviktoria.com
Art Nouveau-style property built
in 1905 as the Museum of the
History of Music, now converted
into a character hotel. It has an
attractive façade with apse,
carved relief and external
staircase. Inside are distinctive
rooms and apartments, a stylish
foyer, gallery bar and elegant
atrium breakfast room.

 43
P

KONSTANZ B1
Reichenau
Seehotel Seeschau **$$-$$$**
78479, An der Schiffslände 8
☎ (0 75 34) 2 57
🖷 (0 75 34) 72 64
www.seeschau.mdo.de
Art Nouveau building in a
splendid quiet location on the
southern shore of Reichenau
island. It offers rest and
recuperation in bright, spacious
and carefully furnished rooms.
Relax in the sauna or on the
terrace.

 22
P

LANDSHUT C1
Landshut

Fürstenhof **$-$$**
84034, Stethaimer Strasse 3
☎ (08 71) 9 25 50
🖷 (08 71) 92 55 44
www.romantikhotels.com/
Landshut
Built in 1906, this Art Nouveau
hotel has a bright yellow facade.
It is now an attractive "Romantic
Hotel" offering friendly rooms,
the cheerful Pavilion bistro café
and, for relaxation, a sauna and
solarium.

🛏 21
P

LIMBURG B3
Holzappel
Altes Herrenhaus zum Bären **$**
56379, Hauptstrasse 15
☎ (0 64 39) 9 14 50
🖷 (0 64 39) 91 45 11
The Herrenhaus, overlooking
Market Square, dates from 1705,
and Goethe stayed here in 1815.
Attractive rooms with quality
bathrooms are provided for
today's discerning guest, and the
Melander restaurant offers
excellent wines.

🛏 10
P

LINDAU B1
Lindau

Lindenhof **$$**
88131, Dennenmoos 3
☎ (0 83 82) 9 31 90
🖷 (0 83 82) 93 19 31
The Lindenhof enjoys a splendid
location overlooking Lake
Constance between Lindau's Old
Town and the spa town of
Wasserburg. The hotel offers
comfortable rooms, a restaurant
and a large garden with lawns.
Leisure facilities include an
indoor pool, sauna and solarium.

 17
P ≋

Key to Symbols: 🖷 Fax 🄴 Email 🛏 Rooms 🄿 Parking 🏊 Swimming
American Express 🄾 Diners Club 🄴 Eurocard 🆅 Visa

Schachen Schlössle $
88131, Enzisweilerstrasse 1-7
☎ (0 83 82) 50 69
🗎 (0 83 82) 39 56
Originally a knight's residence, the Schachen Schlößle dates from the 15th century. It now offers modern comforts in distinctive rooms, all with radio and TV. Apartments also benefit from a balcony. In the morning,

enjoy a copious breakfast buffet in the winter garden. An indoor pool, sauna and solarium are available in an adjacent building.

LIPPSTADT   B3
Möhnesee
Haus Delecke $$
59519, Linkstrasse 10-14
☎ (0 29 24) 80 90
🗎 (0 29 24) 80 91 67
www.haus-delecke.de
Idyllic location in the midst of splendid parkland overlooking Lake Möhne, with superbly furnished rooms and conference

facilities including the latest technical equipment. There are excellent sports amenities, including water sports on the lake and bicycles for rent. An extensive menu is served in the restaurant and there is a terrace, bar and garden bar.

🛏 21

Sassendorf
Hof Hueck $-$$
59505, Im Kurpark
☎ (0 29 21) 9 61 30
🗎 (0 29 21) 96 13 50
This half-timbered farmhouse, originally located in Unna-Niedermassen, dates back to the 14th century. It is now an attractive hotel with elegant rooms and a conference room.

The restaurant, housed in a former barn, offers a sophisticated menu. There is a splendid terrace for the summer, a comfortable reading room and a therapy center.

🛏 53

Lindau Harbor

Key to Symbols: 🗎 Fax e Email 🛏 Rooms P Parking ⚄ Swimming
American Express D Diners Club E Eurocard Visa

LÜBBEN   D4

Lübbenau

Schloss Lübbenau $$
3222, Schlossbezirk 6
☎ (0 35 42) 87 30
🖹 (0 35 42) 87 36 66
www.schloss-luebbenau.de
This castle was built in 1820 and is set in parkland within the Forest of Spree. It has fine rooms and excellent health facilities, including massage, whirlpool, sauna, solarium and fitness room.

🛏 40
🅿 ▦ 🅴 📶

LÜBECK   C5

Dassow

Schloss Lütgenhof $$-$$$
23942, Ulmenweg 10
☎ (03 88 26) 82 50
🖹 (03 88 26) 8 25 22
This splendid castle hotel (built in 1839) is framed by chestnut trees and reed grass and surrounded by a park with mature trees. It has elegant rooms as well as a restaurant, bar, café-bistro and terrace.

🛏 34
🅿
▦ 🅓 🅴 📶

Ratzeburg

Farchauer Mühle $-$$
23909, Farchauer Mühle 6
☎ (0 45 41) 8 60 00
🖹 (0 45 41) 86 00 86
The Farchauer Mühle, dating from 1377, is an attractive former water mill in a quiet location on Lake Ratzeburg. It now offers rooms with modern comforts. Rates include breakfast from the copious buffet, served in the room on request. The restaurant, with its rustic exposed beams, offers an extensive menu including regional specialties.

🛏 19
🅿
▦ 🅓 🅴 📶

Telgte

Heidehotel Waldhütte $$
48291, Im Klatenberg 19
☎ (0 25 04) 92 00
🖹 (0 25 04) 92 01 40
🅴 heidehotel-waldhuette@t-online.de
Attractive half-timbered building on the outskirts of town, offering guests comfortable rooms with a charming rustic touch, plus excellent conference and leisure facilities. Enjoy the cozy, country-style restaurant, and in summer the splendid café terrace and large garden.

🛏 31
🅿
▦ 🅓 🅴 📶

Timmendorfer Strand

Gorch Fock $-$$
23669, Strandallee 152
☎ (0 45 03) 89 90
🖹 (0 45 03) 89 91 11
www.timmendorf.sh/gorch-fock/
Behind the bright façade of this historic building you will find modern, comfortable rooms and suites (many with an uninterrupted view of the beach and the Baltic) as well as an ideal conference venue. Spoil yourself in the restaurant or in summer in the café garden.

🛏 38
🅿 🅴

Key to Symbols: 🖹 Fax 🅴 Email 🛏 Rooms 🅿 Parking ☄ Swimming
▦ American Express 🅓 Diners Club 🅴 Eurocard 📶 Visa

LUDWIGSLUST C4

Ludwigslust

Mecklenburger Hof $-$$
19288, Lindenstrasse 40-44
☎ (0 38 74) 41 00
🖹 (0 38 74) 41 01 00
e mecklenburger-hof@
t-online.de

Traditional house dating from 1796 in the baroque town of Ludwigslust, situated in the southern part of the historic center near the castle complex. Spacious rooms offer all-modern conveniences, and excellent conference facilities are provided. In spring and fall the hotel hosts the popular Operetta Balls; it also is a regular venue for baroque music and coffee concerts.

 37

LÜNEBERG C4

Lauenburg

Lauenburger Mühle $-$$
21481, Bergstrasse 17
☎ (0 41 53) 25 21
🖹 (0 41 53) 5 55 55

A country-house hotel has been added to the original mill building (now a museum) built in 1871. The rooms, which have fax and PC connections, are decorated with great attention to detail. An extensive menu is offered in the cozy country-style restaurant, and other facilities include a winter garden and a room with a stage.

🛏 34
P
🔲 🔲 🔲

MAGDEBURG C4

Barleben

Mariannenhof $$
39179, Hansenstrasse 40
☎ (03 92 03) 6 09 44/45
🖹 (03 92 03) 6 13 34

The Mariannenhof – in a rural location and yet convenient to Magdeburg – offers spacious and individually designed rooms. There is excellent walking and cycling on Colbitz-Letzling Heath (bicycles can be rented) and the largest lime woodland in Europe. Lakes and outdoor swimming pools are nearby. A well-equipped room is suitable for conferences, seminars and parties.

🛏 18
P
🔲 🔲 🔲

MEERSBURG B1

Meersburg

Löwen $-$$
88709, Marktplatz 2
☎ (0 75 32) 4 30 40
🖹 (0 75 32) 43 04 10
www.hotel-loewen-
meersburg.de

The Löwen in the old town of Meersburg is 400 years old and now offers guests tasteful accommodations. For 50 years it was the bastion of the legendary mayor Simon Winzürn and the main outlet for Meersburg's state-owned vineyard. Enjoy good wine in the wood-paneled lounge, and excellent cuisine – try fish from Lake Constance wrapped in puff pastry.

🛏 21

MINDEN B4

Bückeburg

Altes Forsthaus $$
31675, Harrl 2
☎ (0 57 22) 2 80 40
🖹 (0 57 22) 28 04 44
www.altes-forsthaus.de

Rich in tradition, Bückeburg has been renovated and improved to satisfy modern requirements. It offers comfortable rooms, conference facilities fitted with audiovisual equipment (including the splendid historic banqueting hall), an elegant and stylish restaurant, and the cozy atmosphere of the Forstschenke and Grotto bars.

🛏 38
 P

MÖNCHEN-GLADBACH   A3

Viersen

Kaisermühle $$
41747, An der Kaisermühle 20
☎ (0 21 62) 2 49 02 40
▤ (0 21 62) 24 90 24 24
e kaisermuehle@online-club.de

Dating back to the 13th century, this building has been extensively restored and offers attractive, comfortable rooms and a tastefully furnished restaurant serving international specialties and local delicacies. In the summer relax on the terrace.

 11
P

Wegberg

Burg Wegberg $$
41844, Burgstrasse 8
☎ (0 24 34) 9 82 20
▤ (0 24 34) 9 82 22 22

The old tower of this imposing building dates from 1343 and was originally erected by the knight Johann von Berck. The hotel is a harmonious mix of modern comfort and historic atmosphere, with the "pièce de résistance" undoubtedly the exclusive bridal suite (not just for honeymooners). The restaurant is well known for its extensive menu.

 19
P

MUNICH   C1

Aying

Brauerei-Gasthof Aying $$
85653, Zornedinger Strasse 2
☎ (0 80 95) 9 06 50
▤ (0 80 95) 90 65 66

Traditional, romantic brewery inn offering all-modern comforts in individually designed rooms. Rooms have cozy tiled stoves and wonderful four-poster beds. In the summer relax in the beer garden under old chestnut trees and enjoy locally brewed beer.

 28

Holzkirchen

Alte Post $$
83607 , Marktplatz 10
☎ (0 80 24) 3 00 50
▤ (0 80 24) 3 00 55 55

The Alte Post has a long history and was at one time the stable block for the royal Bavarian mail. A tasteful modern extension has been added, and it now offers distinctive accommodations. It also is renowned for the regional delicacies served in the wood-paneled restaurant.

44
P

MÜNSTER   A4

Münster

Landhaus Eggert $$
48157, Zur Haskenau 81
☎ (02 51) 32 80 40
▤ (02 51) 3 28 04 59
www.landhaus-eggert.de

This splendid Münster estate dates from 1030 and has managed to retain its historic character. It is a "Ring Hotel," set in parkland, and provides an ideal base from which to visit the neighboring water castles. The charming rooms are decorated country-house style, and an imaginative menu is offered in the restaurant. Well-equipped conference facilities are available.

35

P

Warendorf

Im Engel $
48231, Brünebrede 35-37
☎ (0 25 81) 9 30 20
🖹 (0 25 81) 6 27 26
In family ownership since 1692
the Warendorf Engel is located
in the heart of Westphalia. The
attractive hotel has spacious
rooms and a rustic wine bar with
an extensive wine list – the
establishment runs its own wine
shop as well. Breakfast buffet
served in the morning.

🛏 21
P
🕮 🅾 🄴 📧

NEUSTADT-AN-DER-WEINSTRASSE B2

Deidesheim
Deidesheimer Hof $$
67146, Marktplatz
☎ (0 63 26) 9 68 70
🖹 (0 63 26) 76 85
www.deidesheimerhof.de
This building on the Markplatz
was first constructed in 1781. The
hotel, a member of the "Relais &
Châteaux" group, offers
exquisitely decorated rooms. The
excellent suites are extremely
popular. In the morning guests
can enjoy the extensive breakfast
buffet. The bread and sausage
specialties are famous and make
excellent souvenirs. The
Deidesheimer Hof offers
excellent facilities for parties and
conferences.

🛏 18 P 🕮 🅾 🄴 📧

Hassaloch
Sägmühle $
67454, Sägmühlweg 140
☎ (0 63 24) 9 29 10
🖹 (0 63 24) 92 91 60
This former sawmill is located at
the edge of woods overlooking
pastureland. Enjoy the country-
style elegance of the rooms, the
stylish restaurant with its
extensive menu, and the splendid
terrace in the inner courtyard
draped with vines.

🛏 27
P
🕮 🅾 🄴 📧

Hinterzarten
Reppert $$-$$$
79856, Adlerweg 21-23
☎ (0 76 52) 1 20 80
🖹 (0 76 52)12 08 11
www.reppert.de
This hotel is situated in the
health resort of Hinterzarten
high up in the Black Forest, and
its Center for Body and Soul
offers a range of specialist
baths.The excellent rooms and
suites are named after local
places. Public rooms comprise a
spacious foyer, the Harlequin
cocktail bar, and a restaurant
featuring wonderful views and an
extensive menu.

🛏 38
P 🏊
🕮 🅾 🄴 📧

Speyer

Domhof $$
67346, Bauhof 3
☎ (0 62 32) 1 32 90
🖹 (0 62 32) 13 29 90
www.domhof.de
The traditional and impressive
Domhof is not only a brewery
but also a comfortable hotel. The
restaurant offers an extensive
menu with international and
regional cuisine as well as good
homemade food. Guests can use
the terrace.

🛏 49
P
🕮 🅾 🄴 📧

St. Martin
St. Martiner Castell $
67487, Maikammerer Strasse 2
☎ (0 63 23) 95 10
🖹 (0 63 23) 20 98
The St. Martiner Castell offers guests elegant, country-style rooms, a cozy wine bar, the Martinsstube room for parties and two conference rooms. Relax in the sauna, solarium

or on the terrace.

🛏 26

P

NORDHAUSEN　C3
Benneckenstein

Harzhaus $
38877, Heringsbrunnen 1
☎ (03 94 57) 9 40
🖹 (03 94 57) 9 44 99
A hotel in the Harz Mountains suitable throughout the year for conferences, short breaks or vacations. It has a quiet location with comfortable rooms and a wide range of leisure facilities – sauna, solarium, library, table

tennis, tennis, billiards and bowling. There is an extensive menu in the Harzstube restaurant.

🛏 36

P

NORTHEIM　B3
Nörten-Hardenberg
Burghotel Hardenberg $$
37176, Im Hinterhaus 11
☎ (0 55 03) 98 10
🖹 (0 55 03) 98 16 66
Nestling below castle ruins, this hotel is located in a group of romantic buildings that include a splendid half-timbered structure and a former mill. It offers

exquisite rooms and prestigious modern conference facilities. Relax in the reception lobby, one of the three terraces or the excellent health suite with its sauna, solarium, whirlpool and fitness room. There also is a winter garden.

🛏 43

P

Uslar
Menzhausen $$
37170, Lange Strasse 12
☎ (0 55 71) 9 22 30
🖹 (0 55 71) 92 23 30
The stunning half-timbered facade of the main house, with its woodcarvings and foundation stone laid in 1565, is a magnificent example of Weser Renaissance architecture. This

building houses some of the bedrooms, while a bridge leads to the new extension, the Mauerschlößchen. With its gables, bay windows and roof dormers, it is a harmonious addition to the original building.

🛏 36

P 🏊

NÜRNBERG　C2
Nürnberg

Rottner $$
90451,
Winterstrasse 17
☎ (09 11) 65 84 80
🖹 (09 11) 65 84 82 03
www.jve.net
The Rottner, a country hotel, offers exclusive rooms and suites with circular baths and modern conference facilities. Relax in the bar or the attractive garden

restaurant with its mature lime trees.

🛏 33

P

OBERSTDORF · B1
Oberstdorf

Exquisit $$-$$$
87561, Prinzenstrasse 17
☎ (0 83 22) 9 63 30
🖺 (0 83 22) 96 33 60
www.hotel-exquisit.de
This attractive hotel with its own health facilities is set amid extensive grounds on the southern edge of Oberstdorf, a five-minute walk from the lively resort. Rooms are carefully furnished, and balconies provide wonderful mountain views. In addition to the indoor pool, sauna, solarium and beauty salon, there is a putting green for golfers and a winter training course for cross-county skiers.

🛏 34

Kleinwalsertal

Almhof Rupp $$
87567, Walserstrasse 83
☎ (0 83 29) 50 04
🖺 (0 83 29) 32 73
www.almhof-rupp.de
Alpine-style building with a splendid exterior. The suites, which form the heart of the building, are light, airy and extremely elegant. Excellent leisure and health facilities are provided, and you can ski almost to the hotel door. Food ranges from a buffet with local specialties to homemade cakes served on the terrace in summer to gourmet dinners.

🛏 9

OFFENBURG · A1
Oberkirch

Oberen Linde $$
77704, Hauptstrasse 25-27
☎ (0 78 02) 80 20
🖺 (0 78 02) 30 30
www.romantikhotels.com/oberkirch
This hotel, a member of the "Romantic" group, was formed from several half-timbered buildings situated near the Upper Gate. It has been superbly restored and offers distinctive, modern rooms, most of which have balconies overlooking the garden. Dine in the restaurant or the cozy wine bar, the latter serving substantial local specialties. Excellent conference facilities are provided.

🛏 36

Oppenau

Schwarzwaldhotel Erdrichshof $
77728, Schwarzwaldstrasse 57
☎ (0 78 04) 9 79 80
🖺 (0 78 04) 97 98 98
A traditional building located amid the splendid scenery of the Upper Rench Valley, now converted into a hotel offering comfortable rooms, a conference room and, for the more energetic, an indoor pool, sauna, solarium and fitness room.

🛏 15

Gengenbach

Pfeffermühle $
77723, Victor-Kretz-Strasse 17
☎ (0 78 03) 9 33 50
🖺 (0 78 03) 66 28
Two splendid half-timbered houses have been combined to form the Pfeffermühle Hotel, which is located in the heart of the picturesque old town of Gengenbach. It offers comfortable rooms with all-modern conveniences. The conference room offers excellent multimedia facilities. Choose from the extensive menu in the cozy restaurant, and in summer relax on the terrace.

🛏 21

Seelbach

Löwen/Geroldseck $-$$
77960, Ludwigstrasse 1
☎ (0 78 23) 20 44
📄 (0 78 23) 55 00

This is said to be the oldest inn in Germany. The comfortable rooms and apartments, modern conference facilities, and indoor pool, sauna and solarium all make the hotel a popular destination. The restaurant facilities are excellent.

🛏 27
🅿 🏊
💳 💳 💳 💳

OLDENBURG B4

Ganderkesee

Hof Hoyerswege $
27777, Wildehauser
Landstr. 66
☎ (0 42 22) 9 31 00
📄 (0 42 22) 93 10 55

The family at Hof Hoyerswege has been dispensing hospitality for almost 150 years. Guests can enjoy the lawns and garden shaded by trees, plus bowling and a shooting range. Bicycle rental as well as golf and tennis are nearby.

🛏 20
🅿
💳 💳 💳 💳

OSNABRÜCK B4

Ankum

Schmidt $
49577, Hauptstrasse 35
☎ (0 54 62) 88 90
📄 (0 54 62) 8 89 88

The Hotel Schmidt, opposite the cathedral, has been known for its hospitality since 1722. It offers the visitor tasteful rooms, excellent conference facilities, a cozy foyer, the Dom-Stübchen restaurant and the rural charm of the bar. After a hearty breakfast rent a bike and discover the delights of the area. Follow this with bowling or a sauna.

🛏 19
🅿
💳 💳 💳 💳

OTTOBEUREN C1

Mindelheim

Alte Post $
87719, Maximilianstrasse 39
☎ (0 82 61) 76 07 60
📄 (0 82 61) 7 60 76 76

Kaiser Franz I was a visitor here, welcomed by then-owner Cäcilie von Dreer, whose intervention had saved the town from pillage in the revolutionary turmoil of 1796. Now an elegant haven for the discerning guest, the hotel offers a sauna, solarium, library and conference room, plus an extensive menu in the restaurant, wine bar or terrace.

🛏 22

🅿 💳 💳 💳 💳

PADERBORN B3

Dellbrück

Landgasthaus Waldkrug $-$$
33129, Graf-Sporck-Strasse 34
☎ (0 52 50) 9 88 80
📄 (0 52 50) 98 88 77

In a quiet location on the edge of the pleasant town of Delbrück, the Landgasthaus Waldkrug offers tastefully furnished, spacious and comfortable rooms, superb conference facilities, a comfortable restaurant together with a café terrace, a beer cellar and an impressive range of leisure facilities.

🛏 35
🅿 🏊
💳 💳 💳 💳

Bad Birnbach

Sammareier Gutshof $-$$
84364, Pfarrkirchner
Strasse 20 + 22
☎ (0 85 63) 29 70
▤ (0 85 63) 2 97 13
With its splendid combination
of Rottal manorial architecture
and nostalgic Art Nouveau, this
hotel is only a few minutes' walk
from the spa gardens.
Comfortable rooms and suites –

many with balcony or terrace –
are individually designed, with
abundant use of wood giving a
feeling of warmth. Superb pool
and physical therapy facilities.
Dine in one of the cozy,
country-style restaurants, or relax
in the wine bar and sun lounge.

Hohenau

Die Bierhütte $-$$
94545, Bierhütte 10
☎ (0 85 58) 9 61 20
▤ (0 85 58) 96 12 70
www.romantikhotels.com
A "Romantic Hotel" created
from a woodland glassworks
(1512) and a brewery, Die
Bierhütte offers a quiet location,
tasteful interior and friendly
atmosphere. The comfortable

rooms, in the main house and
annexes, are furnished in
country-house style. There are
excellent conference and leisure
facilities, including a sauna and
solarium. Other features are the
chapel and attractive terrace.

Passau

Passauer Wolf $$
94032, Rindermarkt 6-8
☎ (08 51) 9 31 51 10
▤ (08 51)9 31 51 50
A traditional house on the banks
of the Danube, with the river on
one side and a pedestrian area on
the other. It offers superior
rooms and excellent conference
facilities. The Paulus-Stube, with
its splendid vaulting dating from

1503, is ideal for parties.

Teinach-Zavelstein, Bad
Bad Hotel Bad Teinach $$
75385, Otto-Neidhart-Allee 5
☎ (0 70 53) 2 90
▤ (0 70 53) 2 91 77
www.bad-hotel.de
Dating from 1835, this hotel has
a harmonious mix of classic and
modern architecture, and
impressive rooms with Ionic

columns. However, its tradition
of hospitality dates back even
further – to 1472, when it was
already dispensing its famous
healing waters.

Pobershau
Schwarzbeerschänke $
9496, Hinterer Grund 2
☎ (0 37 35) 9 19 10
▤ (0 37 35) 91 91 99
Stay in the Schwarzbeerschänke
and enjoy the charm of the
Schwarzwassertal nature reserve.
The hotel offers modern rooms,
excellent conference facilities and

the friendly atmosphere for
which the region is famous.
Relax in the swimming pool,
sauna or solarium, in front of an
open fire or out on the terrace.

Key to Symbols: ▤ Fax ◳ Email ▦ Rooms ◰ Parking ⌇ Swimming American Express ◑ Diners Club ◳ Eurocard ▦ Visa

QUEDLINBURG C3

Quedlinburg

Theophano $-$$
6484, Markt 13-14
☎ (0 39 46) 9 63 00
🖹 (0 39 46) 96 30 36
www.hoteltheophano.de
A half-timbered building on the Market Square, Theophano has been extensively restored and converted into an exquisite "Romantic Hotel." It offers distinctive, modern rooms decorated in warm colors, with parquet floors and quality furnishings. The hotel is an ideal base from which to explore the interesting town, including the wonderful Ottonian cathedral.

 22

REGENSBURG C2

Bad Abbach

Gut Deutenhof $-$$
93077,
Deutenhof 2
☎ (0 94 05) 95 32 30
🖹 (0 94 05) 95 32 39
www.gut-deutenhof.de
Stylish rural inn overlooking a golf course and furnished in the manner of an English country house. Spacious, uncluttered rooms are decorated in warm colors. Excellent conference facilities.

 13

REMAGEN A3

Bad Neuenahr-Ahrweiler

Burg Adenbach $$
53474 , Adenbachhutstrasse 1
☎ (0 26 41) 3 89 20
🖹 (0 26 41) 3 17 14
This impressive medieval castle has changed hands several times over the centuries and was held by France in the Napoleonic era. It is now a stylish hotel with comfortable rooms and a rustic wine cellar serving excellent Ahr wines and regional delicacies. Events include romantic knights' banquets, wine tastings and guided tours of the adjacent vineyard.

 7

Fürstenberg $
53474 ,Mittelstrasse 4-6
☎ (0 26 41) 9 40 70
🖹 (0 26 41) 94 07 11
The Metzler family traces its roots to Vienna, and something of the charm of the Austrian capital has found its way into the hotel. Some rooms are in the Beethoven House, where the composer spent several summers. Start the day with a copious breakfast from the buffet and dine in the elegant Habsburg restaurant, which serves regional cuisine and fine Ahr wines.

 20

ROSENHEIM C1

Bad Aibling

Lindner $$
83043, Marienplatz 5
☎ (0 80 61) 9 06 30
🖹 (0 80 61) 3 05 35
www.romantikhotels.com/bad-aibling
The former Prantshausen Castle, dating back more than 1,000 years, has been transformed into a fine "Romantic Hotel" with attractive rooms and public areas. The ancestral portraits and antiques evoke memories of its former life. Dine in the Johannesstube restaurant or the elegant country-style Ratholdusstube. Relax in the attractive garden.

 15

Key to Symbols: 🖹 Fax 🇪 Email 🛏 Rooms 🅿 Parking 🏊 Swimming
American Express 🅳 Diners Club 🅴 Eurocard 🆅 Visa

Frasdorf

Landgasthof Karner **$-$$**
83112, Nussbaumstrasse 6
☎ (0 80 52) 40 71
🖹 (0 80 52) 47 11
www.landgasthof-karner.de
This rural inn is a designated historic building. Behind its attractive facade you will find elegant, country-style rooms and modern, well-equipped conference facilities. For health

and fitness there is a sauna and swimming pool.

🛏 25
P 🏊
⬛ ⓞ Ⓔ ▭

ROSTOCK **C5**

Dierhagen
Blinkfüer **$-$$**
18347, Schwedenschanze 20
☎ (03 82 26) 8 03 84/86
🖹 (03 82 26) 8 03 92
www.all-in-all.com/1262.htm
The "Blinkfüer" is a haven for guests seeking relaxation. With its designation as a national park-friendly house you will find

miles of long white beaches, genuine marshland and secluded woodland almost at your doorstep. Comfortable rooms and suites await you on your return, as well as excellent leisure facilities such as a fitness suite, sauna, solarium and whirlpool. There also is a cozy bar and excellent conference facilities.

🛏 23
P Ⓔ ▭

Rostock
KurParkHotel **$$-$$$**
18119, Kurhausstrasse 4
☎ (03 81) 51 98 90
🖹 (03 81) 5 19 89 38
This exclusive hotel is just a stone's throw from the beach and offers comfortable and tastefully decorated rooms and suites. The spacious health facilities and elegant restaurant, coupled with

a wide range of available water sports, makes a stay at this seaside resort a pleasant experience.

🛏 14
P ⬛ ⓞ Ⓔ ▭

A beer stand in Rostock

Key to Symbols: 🖹 Fax 🄴 Email 🛏 Rooms P Parking 🏊 Swimming
⬛ American Express ⓞ Diners Club Ⓔ Eurocard ▭ Visa

ROTHENBURG OB DER TAUBER   B2

Rothenburg ob der Tauber

Bären   **$$-$$$**
91541, Hofbronnengasse 9
☎ (0 98 61) 9 44 10
🖹 (0 98 61) 94 41 60
This hotel has been offering
hospitality since the 11th
century, making it one of the

oldest inns in Germany. Now
carefully restored, it features fine
antiques, which lend a stylish
atmosphere to the hotel. Your
host, Olaf Kappelt, will arrange
historic banquets on request.

 31

Mittermeier   **$-$$**
91541, Vorm Würzburger Tor 9
☎ (0 98 61) 9 45 40
🖹 (0 98 61) 94 54 94
www.mittermeier.rothenburg.de
A modern hotel just outside the
town wall of this city, elegantly
furnished in bright country-
house style. Relax in the indoor
pool, sauna and solarium or on
the terrace.

🛏 16

RÜDESHEIM   A2

Bacharach

Rhein-Hotel   **$**
55422, Auf der Stadtmauer
☎ (0 67 43) 12 43
🖹 (0 67 43) 14 13
The Rhein-Hotel is a historic
half-timbered building forming
part of the 1,000-year-old town
wall. The rooms, all named after
vineyards, are comfortably
furnished and decorated with
modern art. A restaurant and

terrace overlooks the Rhine.

🛏 12

Bingen

Mühle   **$-$$**
79589, Mühlenstrasse 26
☎ (0 76 21) 9 40 84 90
🖹 (0 76 21) 6 58 08
www.muehle-binzen.de
e hotel-muehle.binzen@
t.online.de
A tasteful hotel and restaurant
only five minutes from the free-
way. The aim of your hosts, Gill
and Hansjörg Hechler, is to offer

"fine aristocratic hospitality." The
rooms, either in the main house
or annex, evoke a rural elegance
with their warm, welcoming
colors. Dine in the comfortable
restaurant. For the business
traveler the Mühle, dating back
to 1603, offers excellent
conference facilities.

🛏 20

Rüdesheim

**Breuer's Rüdesheimer
Schloss**   **$$**
65385, Steingasse 10
☎ (0 67 22) 9 05 00
🖹 (0 67 22) 4 79 60
www.ruedesheimer-schloss.com
This hotel is a harmonious mix
of historic building (dating from
1729) and modern design, with
an emphasis on wine and art.
Enjoy the wonderful castle

garden or the wine-tasting
sessions offered by the Georg
Breuer vineyard.

🛏 18

Jagdschloss Niederwald $$
65385, Auf dem Niederwald 1
☎ (0 67 22) 10 04
🗎 (0 67 22) 4 79 70
Dating from 1726, this property stands high above Rüdesheim on the Niederwald. It offers guests splendid accommodation in elegant rooms and suites, plus prestigious conference rooms and first-class leisure facilities like a sauna, solarium, indoor pool and tennis court. In summer relax on the splendid garden terrace.

SCHMALLENBERG B3
Winterberg
Berghotel Astenkrone $$
59955, Astenstrasse 24
☎ (0 29 81) 80 90
🗎 (0 29 81) 80 91 98
This hotel has a long tradition of hospitality, having provided accommodations since the 18th century. Behind the attractive slate walls is an exclusive hotel with comfortable rooms and elegant suites. For the business traveler it offers modern conference facilities.

SCHWÄBISCH-HALL B2
Schwäbisch-Hall

Goldener Adler $-$$
74523, Am Markt 11
☎ (07 91) 61 68
🗎 (07 91) 73 15
The Gothic-style Adler was built around 1500 for a local patrician. Records show that it was already an inn in the 14th century, when it was frequented by the higher echelons of society. It now offers comfortable, romantic rooms and, from the attractive terrace, a wonderful view of the splendid buildings of this city.

SCHWERIN C5
Banzkow
Lewitz Mühle 1 $-$$
9079, An der Lewitz Mühle 40
☎ (0 38 61) 50 50
🗎 (0 38 61) 50 54 44
Set in one of Mecklenburg's largest nature reserves, this is a former Dutch gallery mill built in 1874. Until 1958 it ground grain for the entire region, but it now contains stylish rooms and apartments and a restaurant serving sophisticated cuisine. In the summer it offers a beer garden with adjacent children's play area. There also is a therapy pool, diving pool, sauna, whirlpool and solarium.

Schwerin
Niederländischer Hof $$
19055, Karl-Marx-Strasse 12-13
☎ (03 85) 59 11 00
🗎 (03 85) 59 11 09 99
A traditional Schwerin hotel, established in 1901 and owing its name to the marriage between the Duke of Mecklenburg and Queen Wilhelmina of the Netherlands. Central location (not far from the castle, the Old Town, the cathedral and station). The splendid interior has wood paneling dating from 1881. The hotel offers spacious, tastefully decorated rooms.

Key to Symbols: 🗎 Fax 🄴 Email 🛏 Rooms 🄿 Parking 🏊 Swimming 🔲 American Express 🔘 Diners Club 🄴 Eurocard 🔲 Visa

SIEGEN   B3

Burbach

Hilchenbach

SOLTAU   B4

Fassberg

Niemeyer's Posthotel   **$-$$**
29328, Hauptstrasse 7
☎ (0 50 53) 9 89 00
🖹 (0 50 53) 98 90 64
e www.posthotels.de/fassberg
Hermann Löns, the poet of the heath, wrote passionately about his visits to the Posthotel. Behind its attractive half-

Schneverdingen

STADE   B5

Buxtehude

Seeburg   **$**
21614, Cuxhavener Strasse 145
☎ (0 41 61) 7 41 00
🖹 (0 41 61) 74 10 74
www.seeburg.de
The history of the building dates back to the 17th century. Today it offers comfortable rooms in a separate annex. Eat in the

Fiester Hannes   **$$**
57299, Flammersbacher Strasse 7
☎ (0 27 36) 2 95 90
🖹 (0 27 36) 29 59 20
Fiester Hannes, an architectural gem, is one of several half-timbered buildings in town. Next to the restaurant is a charming cottage in which the

Wolf family offers tasteful accommodation.

🛏 6
🅿

Landhotel Siebelnhof   **$**
57271, OT Vormwald, Siebelnhofstr. 49
☎ (0 27 33) 8 94 30
🖹 (0 27 33) 70 06
The Siebelnhof, located at the foot of Rothaar mountain, has a history going back more than 400 years. Guests now enjoy its warm hospitality and comfort. The owner, Erich W. Steuber,

has considerably improved the facilities, and the property offers all modern conveniences. Unwind in the pool, sauna or solarium and then relax on the courtyard terrace.

🛏 10
🅿 ☒

timbered façade you will find modern comfort (stylish rooms/suites, perfect conference facilities and a fitness area).

🛏 26
🅿

Hof Tütsberg   **$-$$**
29640, Im Naturschutzpark
☎ (0 51 99) 9 00
🖹 (0 51 99) 90 50
www.tuetsberg.de
This former estate dates from 1592 and is in the heart of Lüneburg Heath Nature Reserve. This "Romantic Hotel" offers distinctive rooms and excellent conference facilities.

Relax in the whirlpool, sauna or solarium. Dine in the restaurant, the garden bar or the Hofschänke, with its open fireplace.

🛏 18
🅿

"Amtskrug," the "Bauernstube" or the Viennese tea room. Splendid terrace and in winter ice discos on the lake.

🛏 14

Jork

Zum Schützenhof $
21635, Schützenhofstrasse 16
☎ (0 41 62) 9 14 60
🖹 (0 41 62) 91 46 91
www.schuetzenhof-jork.de
This hotel epitomizes the old and new in harmony; the new wing, with its light and airy rooms, is particularly inviting to guests. There is an excellent function room, a comfortable

beer garden, a beer cellar and a restaurant. Relax with a game of bowls or tennis.

🛏 14
🅿
🟦 🅾 🇪 🟦

Rottach-Egern
Walter's Hof $$
83700, Seestrasse 77
☎ (0 80 22) 27 70
🖹 (0 80 22) 27 71 54
This property is situated on an attractive inlet in Tegernsee, known locally as the "artists' corner." Comfortable rooms and spacious apartments carefully

furnished with rustic antiques provide all you need for a relaxing stay. The country restaurant, with its open fireplace, offers Bavarian and international specialties. Relax on the splendid terrace.

🛏 17
🅿
🟦 🅾 🇪 🟦

Tegernsee
Bayern $$
83684, Neureuthstrasse 23
☎ (0 80 22) 18 20
🖹 (0 80 22) 37 75
www.hotel-bayern.de
Situated high above this spa town, with a wonderful view of a lake, the Wallberg and the Tegernsee Alps. This spacious hotel consists of four inter-

connected houses forming a harmonious whole. The oldest part is the splendid Art Nouveau Sengerschloß, with bright rooms and high ceilings.

🛏 83
🅿 ≊
🟦 🇪 🟦

Bülow

Schloss Schorssow $$-$$$
17166, Am Haussee 5
☎ (03 99 33) 7 90
🖹 (03 99 33) 7 91 00
www.schlosshotel-mv.de
This classically designed castle (erected 1808-12) is set in the midst of lakes and an English landscape garden, and offers elegant accommodations. The health facilities are superb.

🛏 32
🅿 ≊
🟦 🅾 🇪 🟦

Bonndorf

Gasthof Sommerau $
79848, Sommerau 5/Im Steinatal
☎ (0 77 03) 6 70
🖹 (0 77 03) 15 41
This Black Forest inn is built of wood and has an imposing full-hipped roof. It is a member of the "In search of nature" group of properties, with comfortable rooms – some with enclosed

glazed balconies and panoramic views – and a cozy lounge with a large tiled stove.

🛏 12
🅿

Breitnau

Kaiser's Tanne-Wirtshus **$$**
79874, Am Wirbstein 27
☎ (0 76 52) 1 20 10
🖹 (0 76 52) 15 07
The Kaiser's Tanne-Wirtshus, a holiday hotel of particular charm, exudes typical Bavarian comfort, and the abundant use of wood, particularly in the entrance foyer, gives it warmth. It offers three room categories,

each reflecting a feature of the landscape. Superb breakfasts can be enjoyed on the garden terrace. Relax in the indoor pool, sauna, solarium or fitness center.

 31

P 🏊

Titisee-Neustadt

Adler Post **$$**
79822, Hauptstrasse 16
☎ (0 76 51) 50 66
🖹 (0 76 51) 37 29
This "Romantic Hotel" was formerly a staging post dating back to 1516, and continuing that long tradition it offers comfortable rooms, excellent conference facilities, extensive menus, and for leisure a sauna,

solarium and massage suite.

 22

Todtmoos

Rössle **$-$$**
79682, Kapellenweg 2
☎ (0 76 74) 9 06 60
🖹 (0 76 74) 88 38
www.hotel-roessle.de
Built in 1670 as a staging post and coaching inn on the old road to the Hochkopf Pass, this pleasant family hotel offers superb conference facilities, sophisticated cuisine and such

leisure facilities as a sauna (including a roof terrace) and a solarium.

 24

P

E 💳

TREUENBRIETZEN **D4**

Luckenwalde

Vierseithof **$$-$$$**
14943, Haag 20
☎ (0 33 71) 6 26 80
🖹 (0 33 71) 62 68 68
www.vierseithof.com
A top-quality hotel in a building dating from 1782, with a romantic inner courtyard and spacious terrace. Neighboring

factory buildings, converted to provide function rooms, give the whole complex a particular charm. The guest rooms are attractive, decorated in warm colors with abundant use of wood. There are excellent health facilities, including a sauna, solarium and indoor pool.

🛏 39 P 🏊

TRIER **A2**

Brauneberg

Brauneberger Hof **$**
54472, Moselweinstrasse 136
☎ (0 65 34) 14 00
🖹 (0 65 34) 14 01
www.mittelmosel.de/
brauneberger-hof
The history of this attractive half-timbered building dates back to 1750. In addition to its

restaurant and vaulted cellar, it offers comfortable rooms in either a traditional or modern design.

🛏 14

P

E 💳

Trier

Überlingen

Klosterschenke $-$$
54293 , Klosterstrasse 10
☎ (06 51) 96 84 40
🖹 (06 51) 9 68 44 30
An old building in a historic part of town. The former monastic buildings were first used as an inn in 1824. They offer stylish, distinctive rooms (with comfortable old-style balconies and attractive baths), prestigious

🛏 11
P
▦ 🇪 💳

UBERLINGEN B1
Überlingen
Johanniter-Kreuz $$
88662 , Johanniterweg 11
☎ (0 75 51) 6 10 91
🖹 (0 75 51) 6 73 36
www.romantikhotels.com/ueberlingen
The main house was originally a farm, which for several centuries was run by the Knights of St.

John of Jerusalem. Now it provides a refuge for those seeking relaxation and excellent conference facilities. The rooms are light, with abundant use of natural materials. Relax in the sauna, solarium, fitness room or on the wonderful terrace.

🛏 33
P

function and conference facilities, a spacious garden terrace overlooking the Moselle and a restaurant with excellent menus.

▦ 🇩 🇪 💳

UELZEN C4
Uelzen

Stadt Hamburg $-$$
29525, Lüneburger Strasse 4
☎ (05 81) 9 08 10
🖹 (05 81) 9 08 11 88
Located in the heart of the old quarter of Uelzen; behind the wonderfully restored façade is a comfortable hotel with modern, prestigious facilities for conferences and celebrations.

🛏 34
▦ 🇪 💳

Titisee

ULM `B1`

Niederstotzingen
Schlosshotel Oberstotzingen $$
89168, Stettener Strasse 35-37
☎ (0 73 25) 10 30
🖹 (0 73 25) 1 03 70
www.vilavitaschlosshotel.de
Renaissance water castle, dating from 1608, overlooking the Danube marshlands in the heart of Oberstotzing Park. The hotel offers distinctive rooms and top-quality conference rooms and leisure facilities. Relax on the terrace or in the Schenkengarten.

14
P

Biberach an der Riss
Eberbacher Hof $-$$
88400, Schulstrasse 11
☎ (0 73 51) 1 59 70
🖹 (0 73 51) 15 97 97
Built in 1519 as a house for the needy of the parish, this is one of the oldest buildings in the lively capital of Upper Swabia. It is now a tasteful "Flair Hotel," with light and elegant rooms and a superb conference room. The restaurant is elegant and comfortable and offers an extensive menu. In summer relax on the attractive terrace or under the arbor.

25
P

Erolzheim
Schloss Erolzheim $
88453, Schlossstrasse 6
☎ (0 73 54) 9 30 50
🖹 (0 73 54)93 05 40
This was originally the fortified castle of a medieval knight but developed at the end of the 16th century into a castle residence, the external facade of which has been retained. It offers individually designed rooms and suites, a conference room and restaurant in the vaulted cellar.

8
P
E

WALDECK `B3`
Waldeck

Schloss Waldeck $$
34513
☎ (0 56 23) 58 90
🖹 (0 56 23) 58 92 89
www.schloss-waldeck.de
This splendid castle, high above Lake Eder, offers elegant suites and comfortable rooms, excellent conference facilities, a restaurant serving fine food, and for relaxation a pool, sauna, solarium, lawn, bar and terrace.

36
P 🏊

WAREN `C5`
Grossplasten

Schloss Gross Plasten $-$$
17192,
Dorfstrasse 43
☎ (03 99 34) 80 20
🖹 (03 99 34) 8 02 99
Fantastic neo-baroque castle dating in part from 1751 and set in a spacious landscaped park. It offers elegant rooms, superb facilities for conferences and entertaining, a stylish restaurant and bar, and excellent leisure facilities.

19
P 🏊

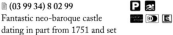

Weimar

Dorotheenhof
99427, Dorotheenhof 1
☎ (0 36 43) 45 90
🖹 (0 36 43) 45 92 00
Hidden behind mature trees is the former residence of the cavalry captain Carl von Kalckkreuth, now a hotel with comfortable rooms, a library, a sauna and a solarium. Other attractive rooms include the Rittmeisterstube, which has an open fireplace.

🛏 58
🅿

Isselburg

Anholt $$
46419,
Klever Strasse
☎ (0 28 74) 45 90
🖹 (0 28 74) 40 35
www.burg-hotel-anholt.com
This hotel, with its splendid parkland, has a hint of Versailles about it. Expect elegant rooms and suites, superb conference facilities, a fine terrace and an extensive menu served in three restaurants.

🛏 26
🅿

Hamminkeln

Haus Elmer $$
46499, An der Klosterkirche 12
☎ (0 28 56) 91 10
🖹 (0 28 56) 9 11 70
A "Romantic Hotel" in Marienthal surrounded by rhododendron bushes, oak trees and an avenue of limes. It offers distinctive rooms and suites in a modern or country style, first-class conference facilities and a sauna. The hotel also can organize visits to the nearby distillery, or you can explore the surrounding area by bicycle or hot-air balloon.

🛏 25
🅿

Braunfels

Altes Amtsgericht $$
35619, Gerichtsstrasse 2
☎ (0 64 42) 9 34 80
🖹 (0 64 42)93 48 11
www.braunfels.de/hotels/altes-amtsgericht
The experience starts in the foyer with its exquisite elegance, a splendid mix of old structure and modern design. Stylish rooms and modern conference facilities are augmented by a sauna, solarium and tennis facilities.

🛏 21
🅿

Herborn

Zum Löwen $
35745, Turmstrasse 2
☎ (0 27 72) 9 27 00
🖹 (0 27 72) 92 70 25
The Zum Löwen has a long tradition of hospitality dating from 1577, when it was called the Roter Löwe. The half-timbered building, quietly situated in the heart of the Old Town, is a comfortable hotel. Its romantic atmosphere stems partly from the warmth of the interior décor. Enjoy live music in Leo's bar, with its splendid stone vaulting.

🛏 12
🅿

Eltville

Kronenschlösschen $$
65347, Rheinallee (B 42)
☎ (0 67 23) 6 40
🖹 (0 67 23) 76 63
www.kronenschloesschen.de
This historic small castle dates from 1894 and has been converted into an enchanting hotel with stylish rooms and suites and superb, fully-equipped conference facilities. Dine in the

Wiesbaden
Landhaus Diedert $$
65195,
Am Kloster Klarenthal 9
☎ (06 11) 1 84 66 00
🖹 (06 11) 1 84 66 03
The journey from Wiesbaden to this former monastery (with small bell tower) is an easy 2 miles. The rooms are individually furnished and comfortable, with

Wiesmoor

Gästehaus Kloster Eberbach $
65346, Kloster Eberbach
☎ (0 67 23) 99 30
🖹 (0 67 23) 99 31 00
In terms of historic atmosphere few places can rival the former Cistercian monastery of Eberbach, famous also as a movie location. Situated in the former working quarters of the monastery, the hotel offers

restaurant, bistro or wine bar and finish off the evening in style in the bar. The property is surrounded by splendid parkland and has a garden terrace.

🛏 8
P

Zum Krug $$
65347, Hauptstr. 34
☎ (0 67 23) 9 96 80
🖹 (0 67 23) 99 68 25
www.rheingau.de
Built as a farmhouse in 1720 and converted into the "Krug" in the 1920s. Behind the attractive half-timbered facade, it now offers comfortable rooms. Ample opportunities to sample the

views of the garden and its plane trees.

🛏 12
P

Blauer Fasan $
26639, Fliederstr. 1
☎ (0 49 44) 9 27 00
🖹 (0 49 44) 92 70 70
e blauer-fasan@planet-interkom.a
A friendly hotel with an attractive thatched roof and traditional East Friesian decor. It has comfortable rooms and lounges (all with open fireplace)

comfortable, individually decorated rooms. Fine wines are served in the Klosterschenke.

🛏 30
P

house wine.

🛏 10
P

and a splendid garden terrace with carved figures. In summer enjoy a traditional Friesian tea ceremony on the terrace; in winter tea is served in front of an open fire.

🛏 26
P

WORMS B2

Neuleiningen

Alte Pfarrey $$
67271, Untergasse 54
☎ (0 63 59) 8 60 66
🖹 (0 63 59) 8 60 60

The charm of this old half-timbered building is apparent as soon as you descend toward the hotel and stride through the sandstone gateway. In summer enjoy the idyllic garden or the terrace. The stylish interior is adorned with precious antiques and paintings. Distinctive rooms offer modern conveniences; the most stunning is the bridal suite.

🛏 9
P 🆔 🆔 VISA

Alzey

Am Schloss $
55232, Amtgasse 39
☎ (0 67 31) 9 42 24
🖹 (0 67 31) 94 22 55
www.hotel-am-schloss.com

Guests staying at this enchanting hotel can enjoy comfortable rooms, excellent conference rooms all with modern equipment. Enjoy the convivial atmosphere of the wine bar and beer cellar, the comfortable restaurant offering excellent food and in summer relax on the garden terrace.

🛏 24
P
🆔 🆔 🆔 VISA

WÜRZBURG B2

Marktbreit

Löwen $
97340 , Marktstrasse 8
☎ (0 93 32) 5 05 40
🖹 (0 93 32) 94 38

The history of the Löwen, an imposing half-timbered house, dates back to 1450; later King Ludwig I was a guest here. Today it offers comfortable rooms; the restaurants serve fine food accompanied by Franconian wine or beer.

🛏 30
P
🆔 🆔 VISA

Dettelbach

Akzent Hotel Franziskaner $
97337, Wallfahrtsweg 14
☎ (0 93 24) 97 30 30
🖹 (0 93 24) 97 30 59

The hotel is in a parklike setting adjacent to the Maria in the Sand pilgrimage church. It offers comfortable rooms; well-equipped, modern conference facilities; and a cozy restaurant serving regional and international specialties, along with a wine bar in the historic vaulted cellar.

🛏 14
P
🆔 🆔 VISA

Marktheidenfeld

Anker $-$$
97828, Obertorstrasse 6
☎ (0 93 91) 6 00 40
🖹 (0 93 91) 60 04 77
www.hotel-anker.de

The motto of owners the Deppish family, "Fränkisch voller Leben," refers to the love of life that is typical of the region and that is an apt description of the hotel. It combines tradition and innovation, offering comfortable rooms, excellent conference facilities (including one room with exposed roof timbers).

🛏 35
P
🆔 🆔 VISA

Key to Symbols: 🖹 Fax 🅴 Email 🛏 Rooms 🅿 Parking 🏊 Swimming
American Express 🆔 Diners Club 🅴 Eurocard 💳 Visa

Volkach
Zur Schwane $-$$
97332, Hauptstrasse 12
☎ (0 93 81) 8 06 60
▤ (0 93 81) 80 66 66
www.romantikhotels.com/
volkach/
The Zur Schwane, both a vineyard and a "Romantic Hotel," has a reputation far beyond the borders of Franconia and offers comfortable rooms named after the classic wine varieties of the region. There also is a prestigious conference room.

🛏 22
🅿

Würzburg
Mühlenhof Daxbaude $
97078, Frankenstrasse 205
☎ (09 31) 25 04 70
▤ (09 31) 25 04 72 50
This 16th-century mill about five minutes from the city has been converted into a pleasant hotel with comfortable rooms. The barn, with its old roof timbers, is ideal for celebrations and conferences (the other conference room has a fine vaulted ceiling). The restaurant offers excellent regional cuisine.

🛏 32
🅿

ZWICKAU   C3
Hartenstein

Schloss Wolfsbrunn $$
8118, Stein 8
☎ (03 76 05) 7 60
▤ (03 76 05) 7 62 99
www.leo-info.de/hotel
This architectural gem in the Art Nouveau style, built by Emanuel von Seidl, is surrounded by acres of parkland. It makes an idyllic hotel with elegant rooms and luxury suites. Portraits of notable Germans hang in the Senator Lounge, and the Blue Room features a painted Art Nouveau ceiling; both rooms are fully equipped for conferences.

🛏 21
🅿 🏊

Eibenstock

Ratskeller $
8309, Schönheider Strasse 9
☎ (03 77 52) 6 78 90
▤ (03 77 52) 67 89 50
The Ratskeller offers tastefully decorated rooms and a restaurant built in 1852. The honeymoon suite has its own whirlpool, and one room has its own water bed.

🛏 22
🅿

Meerane

Parkhotel Meerane $
8393, Martinstrasse 54
☎ (0 37 64) 4 72 77
▤ (0 37 64) 4 72 78
In a romantic setting overlooking a splendid park, the hotel offers comfortable rooms, excellent business facilities and an extensive menu. Relax in the sauna, solarium, whirlpool or fitness room.

🛏 41
🅿

Key to Symbols: ▤ Fax 🅔 Email 🛏 Rooms 🅿 Parking 🏊 Swimming American Express Diners Club Eurocard Visa

Scheibenberg
Sächsischer Hof $
9481, Markt 6
☎ (03 73 49) 7 90 46
🖹 (03 73 49) 7 90 48

A splendid building from the 16th century, offering distinctive rooms with under-floor heating and marble baths. The materials used include basalt, wood and exposed stonework. There are two popular restaurants and a bar with organ pipes.

🛏 23
🅿
American Express / Diners Club / Eurocard / Visa

Schneeberg
Büttner No $
8289, Markt 3
☎ (0 37 72) 35 30
🖹 (0 37 72) 35 32 00
www.schneeberg.de/buettner

A stylish hotel has been created from the former Café Büttner. With its 400-year-old vaulting reminiscent of a silver mine, the hotel is a harmonious mix of old and new. You will immediately feel at home in the charming rooms.

🛏 11
🅿
Eurocard / Visa

Würzburg

Key to Symbols: 🖹 Fax 🅔 Email 🛏 Rooms 🅿 Parking 🏊 Swimming
American Express 🅓 Diners Club 🅔 Eurocard Visa

Ireland

Ireland

There are few who fail to fall under the spell of the "land of saints and scholars." Ireland's romantic reputation goes before it, in the creativity, wit, charm and musicality of its people; and the country itself exceeds all expectations in its physical beauty. The Celtic influence lives on, linking ancient past with present, in songs, stories, the evocative Gaelic language and thousands of haunting prehistoric sites, such as the extraordinary Newgrange burial complex in County Meath, north of Dublin.

with its lunar rock formations, stone burial chambers and hill forts, and the huge Cliffs of Moher. The Aran Islands – Inishmor, Inishmaan and Inisheer – lie offshore.

In Galway city's vigorous student population you'll see the contemporary manifestation of Gaelic culture. Here, you're on the threshold of the Gaeltacht – the heart of Gaelic-speaking Ireland. Here the country is wilder, and more dramatic, with the Connemara mountains and the Corrib and Mask loughs lying inland from a rocky coastline.

The South and West

Dublin, capital of Eire (southern Ireland), is an essential part of the Irish experience. This is a truly European center, with a buzzing cultural life and a bright, friendly, easygoing atmosphere. Here theaters and museums, stores and restaurants sum up the vibrancy of modern Ireland. To the south, right on the city's doorstep, are the lovely Wicklow Mountains, with popular Glendalough at their heart – half religious site and wholly spectacular from a scenic point of view. Farther south is the Viking town of Wexford. From here, the countless bays, peninsulas and islands of the coast extend toward the west. Following a route through the west you can visit the charming, historic city of Kilkenny, kiss the Blarney Stone at Cork, the Republic's second-largest city, and head for the mountains and lakes of beautiful County Kerry.

Beyond Kerry is the unbelievably lovely Dingle peninsula. Heading north from here, you enter an entirely different landscape in County Clare,

To the North

There's yet more spectacular beauty to be found in the remote county of Mayo, where pilgrims clamber for hours up the holy mountain of Croagh Patrick. Golden beaches and crashing surf mark the shores of Sligo and Donegal, before the coast turns toward Londonderry, a handsome historic town scarred by political and religious divide and forming the gateway to Northern Ireland and the six counties of Ulster.

The bitter divisions of this British-ruled area have left their mark, and in places the graffiti, barbed wire and sectarian posters are intimidating. But this troubled part of the country is astonishingly beautiful. The Giant's Causeway, on County Antrim's north coast, is a strange and popular landscape of perfectly shaped hexagonal rocks. Beyond the seaside town of Ballycastle are the towering cliffs of Fair Head and the greenery of the Antrim Glens. South of Antrim is Belfast, capital of Ulster, which despite many years of violence and conflict has survived as a robust, lively and attractive city.

Allihies on the west coast of Co. Cork

Accommodations

Ireland boasts an excellent range of hotels, from traditional wayside inns to impressive country houses set in their own grounds. Standards of accommodation are usually excellent, with even guest houses offering facilities and comfort usually associated with hotels.

Most rooms have two single beds, but many hotels also provide single and double bedded rooms. Bedding tends to consist of sheets and blankets, but quilted covers also are common. Rooms are more likely to be carpeted than tiled, and will usually have attractive furnishings and pictures on the walls. You may find a small tray of items for tea- and coffee-making. Private bathroom facilities are standard, with small packets of soap and shampoo often provided. There will generally be a television in the room – although there also may be a communal TV lounge elsewhere in the hotel.

Breakfast tends to be included in the price of the room. A full Irish breakfast is likely to be a plate of cooked sausage, egg and bacon, with perhaps mushrooms, baked beans or tomatoes. Irish soda bread (made from flour and buttermilk) also is served, along with toast, jam and honey. Hotels and most guest houses provide evening meals.

Food and Drink

Irish food is typically simple but hearty, with an emphasis on meat stews served with potatoes and cooked vegetables – the perfect accompaniment to a glass of the famous Irish stout (whose best-known brand is, of course, Guinness). In towns and cities there's a selection of restaurants with menus featuring a wide range of international cuisines.

In rural Ireland, the pub is much more than a place to have a drink. It's an essential part of social and cultural life, where there are regular, spontaneous performances of heart-stopping, foot-tapping Irish music and song to accompany the lively conversation and laughter. One of the best parts of Ireland to find pub life at its most energetic is County Clare. In towns such as Ennis you can hear the greatest Irish music of all, and enjoy a glass or three of stout into the bargain.

Getting Around

Ireland's road system is being modernized at a rapid pace, but there are still some very poor public roads, especially in rural areas. But Ireland also has the least congested roads in Europe, and traveling by car through deserted, stunning countryside can be a very special experience.

In counties Cork, Kerry and Wicklow you can rent horse-drawn caravans and take your touring at a relaxed, Irish pace. Be prepared to put in some work, though, and to travel with patience. You're unlikely to cover more than 10 miles a day, and your horse needs to be fed, groomed and harnessed – a time-consuming affair. Caravans generally cater to four people and come with a gas stove and utensils, but do not have toilet facilities.

Cabin cruisers can be rented for leisurely trips along the River Shannon and on the Grand Canal. The boats range in size from two to ten berths; all have refrigerators, gas stoves, safety equipment, dinghies and navigation charts, and most have heating, hot water and showers. Experience in handling boats is an advantage, but training can be provided.

The People

The Irish are known for their hospitality and friendliness although it can be a bit overwhelming. You're quite likely to be taken to your destination rather than being burdened with directions, or to be bought a drink or invited to a meal on the strength of a few minutes' cordial conversation. The Irish are unfailingly curious and will take a genuine interest in you, your life and your opinions. However, this is a country that has endured an often bleak and unforgiving past, and is still wrestling with a complex and sensitive peace process. It may be best not to get involved in too much political discussion, particularly in Northern Ireland. The Republic of Ireland is entirely separate from the United Kingdom – refer to Ulster as Ulster or Northern Ireland.

Ireland

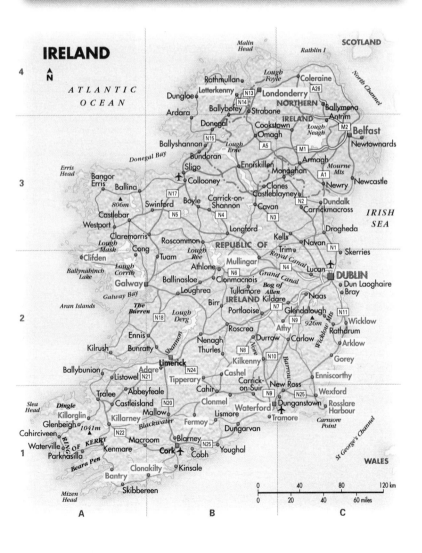

IRELAND

ADARE   B2
Ardagh

ARKLOW   C2
Avoca
Sheepwalk House & Cottages $
Beech Rd, Co. Wicklow
☎ 40235189
🖷 0402 35789
www.sheepwalk.com
e sheepwalk@tinet.ie
This 18th-century Georgian house is 2 miles (3 kilometers)

ATHY   C2
Athy

BANTRY   A1
Goleen
The Heron's Cove $
The Harbour, Co. Cork
☎ 028 35225
🖷 028 35422
www.heronscove.com
e suehill@tinet.ie
This big white house lies in a sheltered cove on Ireland's most southwesterly point, near Mizen

BELFAST   C3
Holywood

Reens House $
Co. Limerick
☎ 069 64276
🖷 069 64276
www.esatclear.ie/~joanandliam/reenshouse
e reenshouse@esatclear.ie
A 400-year-old Jacobean property, Reens House is located on a dairy and livestock farm. The bedrooms are individually

from Avoca, with lovely views across Arklow Bay. The cozy, comfortably furnished bedrooms are equipped with every thoughtful extra, and guests can breakfast in the informal sun lounge while enjoying sea views. Owner Jim McCabe is a mine of information on golfing, shooting and fishing vacations.

 6   Closed Dec.-Jan.

Coursetown Country House $
Stradbally Road, Co. Kildare
☎ 50731101
🖷 0507 32740
This charming Victorian country house is set on a 250-acre tillage farm and bird sanctuary. It has recently been extensively refurbished, and all bedrooms are furnished to the highest standards. Convalescent or

Head. There is a wine bar in the lounge, where glowing fires at either end create a warm, friendly atmosphere. The restaurant is run by award-winning chef/owner Sue Hill. Bedrooms are comfortable, some with balconies overlooking the harbor.

 5   Closed Dec. 25

Rayanne Country House & Restaurant $$
60 Desmesne Road, BT18 9EX, Co. Down
☎ 028 90425859
🖷 028 90423364
Genuine Irish hospitality and excellent food are part of the appeal at this Victorian house in Holywood. There are two charming lounges, but the focal

---

decorated and furnished with period pieces. Guest areas are elegantly furnished, and breakfast is served around a large mahogany table where guests can enjoy home-baked breads.

 4
P

disabled guests are especially welcome, and Iris and Jim Fox are happy to share their knowledge of the Irish countryside and wildlife.

🛏 5
P

point is the elegant restaurant and its award-winning breakfasts. Bedrooms are quite individual in style and have a wide range of extras.

 9
Closed Dec. 24-Jan. 3

Key to Symbols: 🖷 Fax   e Email   🛏 Rooms   P Parking   🏊 Swimming
American Express   Diners Club   MasterCard   Visa

CASHEL   B2
Cashel

Ashmore House $
John Street, Co. Tipperary
☎ 062 61286
🖷 062 62789
Ashmore House is set in a pretty walled garden in the town center and has its own enclosed parking lot. Guests have use of a large living and dining room, and bedrooms come in a variety of sizes from big family rooms to a compact double.

🛏 5
Closed Dec. 25
P
▬ 💳 💳

CLIFDEN   A2
Clifden
Mal Dua House $$
Galway Road, Co. Galway
☎ 095 21171
🖷 095 21739
www.maldua.com
📧 info@maldua.com
Occupying its own grounds in the heart of Connemara, Mal Dua House offers luxury, hospitality and enjoyable food in a peaceful atmosphere. Bedrooms are spacious, and facilities include a lobby, a relaxing living room and an attractive breakfast room. Ample parking is available.

🛏 14   P ▬ 💳 💳

CLONAKILTY   B1
Clonakilty
Duvane Farm $
Ballyduvane, Co. Cork
☎ 023 33129
A cheerfully decorated house, comfortable throughout, where guests have their own sitting room. The dining room serves a wide choice at breakfast; dinner is available by arrangement. One bedroom has a four-poster bed, and two are on the ground floor and share a bathroom, ideal for family groups or those who don't like stairs. Local amenities include beaches, riding and golf.

🛏 4
Closed Nov.-Mar.
P

CLONMEL   B1
Ballymacarbry

Glasha Farmhouse $$
Glasha, Co. Waterford
☎ 052 36108
🖷 052 36108
homepage.eircom.net/~glasha
📧 glasha@eircom.net
Excellent accommodation and a warm welcome are assured at this comfortable country house. Two of the bedrooms are on the ground floor, and all rooms are individually styled with tasteful furnishings and lots of personal touches. Home cooking is a specialty, and trout fishing is available on the river that runs through the grounds.

🛏 8
Closed Dec. 1-27
P 💳

COLERAINE   C4
Coleraine

Greenhill House $
24 Greenhill Road, Aghadowey, BT51 4EU, Co. Londonderry
☎ 028 70868241
🖷 028 70868365
www.btinternet.com/~greenhill.house
📧 greenhill.house@btinternet.com
Situated in the Bann Valley overlooking the Antrim Hills, this lovely Georgian house stands in well-tended gardens. Rooms for guests are traditional in style, and include a lounge and tastefully appointed dining room where home cooking is offered. The bedrooms are well equipped.

🛏 6
Closed Nov.-Feb.
P 💳 💳

Key to Symbols: 🖷 Fax   📧 Email   🛏 Rooms   P Parking   🏊 Swimming
▬ American Express   💳 Diners Club   💳 MasterCard   💳 Visa

DUBLIN C2
Dublin

Beaufort Town House **$$**
25 Pembroke Park, Ballsbridge,
Co. Dublin
☎ 16689080
🖹 01 6609963
www.beauforthousedublin.com
🅴 rosemary@beauforthouse
dublin.com
Hospitality and personal

attention are priorities here, where comfortable, well-equipped bedrooms are attractively decorated. Breakfast is served in the conservatory, and a wide range of dishes is offered. There is some off-street parking available, as well as on-street parking with a permit.

🛏 7 🅿 ▬ ⓓ ● ▬

Cedar Lodge **$$**
98 Merrion Road, Ballsbridge,
Co. Dublin
☎ 16684410
🖹 01 6684533
🅴 info@cedarlodge.ie
A lovely old house with a modern extension, Cedar Lodge is set back from Dunlaoghaire Road opposite the new British Embassy. It offers comfortable,

fully equipped bedrooms and ample parking, with a secure area to the rear and full access for the disabled.

🛏 15 🅿
▬ ● ▬

DUNDALK C3
Carlingford

Beaufort House **$**
Ghan Road, Co. Louth
☎ 042 9373878/9
🖹 042 9373878
Newly built house on the coast road offering spacious, well-equipped bedrooms that have views of the lough (lake). There are two guest lounges, and an interesting breakfast menu that includes fresh fish and

traditional fare is served in the dining room. Dinner is available for large parties with prior notice.

🛏 5 🅿 ● ▬

ENNISCORTHY C2
Enniscorthy

Ballinkeele House **$$$**
Ballymurn, Co. Wexford
☎ 053 38105
🖹 053 38468
www.ballinkeele.com
🅴 info@ballinkeele.com
Set amid farmland, this classical house - built in 1840 by Daniel Robertson - has retained its original features while incorporating modern comforts.

Its fine portico leads to the entrance hall, where a welcoming fire blazes. A decanter of sherry awaits guests in the bedrooms, and dinner is served in the elegant dining room. Facilities include a billiard room and tennis court.

🛏 6 🅿 ● ▬

FERMOY B1
Fermoy

Ballyvolane House **$$**
Castlelyons, Co. Cork
☎ 025 36349
🖹 025 36781
www.iol.ie/ballyvolane/
🅴 ballyvol@iol.ie
Italianate country house in a magnificent setting of woods and gardens, which are open to the

public in May. The comfortable bedrooms all have en suite bathrooms. Public rooms, filled with antiques, include a pillared reception hall with a baby grand piano and an elegant dining room serving dinner at a fine table. Croquet and private fishing are available.

🛏 6

🅿 ▬ ⓓ ● ▬

GALWAY · A2
Galway

Killeen House $$
Killeen, Bushypark, Co. Galway
☎ 091 524179
📠 091 528065
This charming 19th-century house stands in extensive grounds stretching down to the shores of the loch. The interior is beautifully appointed with antique furnishings, hand-woven carpets, fine linen and exquisite crystal. The well-equipped bedrooms reflect the character of the house, and guests have the use of two reception rooms and a breakfast room overlooking the garden.

🛏 5
Closed Dec. 23-28

GOREY · C2
Gorey
Woodlands House $
Killinierin, Co. Wexford
☎ 40237125
📠 0402 37133
📧 woodlnds@iol.ie
This Georgian-style residence is tucked back from the main road in a wooded area of farmland. Bedrooms are well appointed, and three have balconies. A garden patio stands between the guest lounge and the dining room, which serves a good set dinner. Leisure facilities include a tennis court and a games room. Smoking is only allowed in the living room.

🛏 6

KILKENNY · B2
Kilkenny

Butler House $$$
Patrick Street, Co. Kilkenny
☎ 056 65707
📠 056 65626
www.butler.ie
📧 res@butler.ie
Once the dower house of Kilkenny Castle, this fine Georgian building fronts onto Main Street, with secluded gardens to the rear. Built in 1770, many of the original features remain, including ornate plasterwork and marble fireplaces. The bedrooms feature contemporary decor, and there are spacious suites overlooking the gardens and castle. Public areas include a foyer lounge and a rustic breakfast room.

🛏 13   Closed Dec. 24-29

KILLARNEY · A1
Killarney

Old Weir Lodge $
Muckross Road, Co. Kerry
☎ 064 35593
📠 064 35583
www.oldweirlodge.com
📧 oldweirlodge@eircom.net
This Tudor-style lodge is set in attractive gardens within walking distance of the town center. Home baking is a feature at breakfast, and evening meals are available by arrangement. The comfortable bedrooms are equipped to a high standard, and the delightful living room overlooks the gardens. There is ample off-street parking.

🛏 30
Closed Dec. 23-26

KILORGLIN · A1
Dingle
Heatons Guest House $$
The Wood, Co. Kerry
☎ 066 9152288
📠 066 9152324
www.euroka.com/dingle/heatons
📧 heatons@iol.ie
A family-run guest house located on the waterfront and near town. Most bedrooms have views of Dingle Bay, and are very comfortable and well appointed. Guests also can enjoy the views and relax in the spacious foyer lounge. The breakfast room is brightly decorated and offers an impressive range of choices.

🛏 12

LETTERKENNY   B4
Letterkenny

Castle Grove Country House & Restaurant   **$$**
Castle Grove, Ballymaleel,
Co. Donegal
☎ 074 51118
▤ 074 51384

Magnificent 17th-century country house located at the end of a long drive and surrounded by lovely grounds. A major extension has enhanced facilities without loss of atmosphere or charm. The house is luxuriously furnished throughout with fine antiques, public rooms have blazing log fires in winter, and a notable restaurant offers tempting menus.

🛏 8
Closed Jan. 8-30

Dunfanaghy

Sandhill House   **$**
Port-na-Blagh, Co. Donegal
☎ 074 36602
▤ 074 36603

Distinctive cream-painted, detached house in a prominent position close to the golf club and sandy beach. Appealing color schemes and high-quality furnishings characterize the ground-floor lounges. Bedrooms are full of charm and have all-modern facilities. One room on the ground floor, with a shower room, is adapted for use by those with disabilities.

🛏 7
Closed Dec.-Jan.

LONDONDERRY   B4
Carrigans
Mount Royd Country Home   **$**
Co. Donegal
☎ 074 40163
▤ 074 40400

Mount Royd is an attractive creeper-clad house set in mature gardens, with the Foyle River running behind. The friendly Martins have brought hospitality to new heights – nothing is too much trouble for them. Breakfast is a feast of choices, including an eye-catching display of fresh fruits. Bedrooms are very comfortable with lots of personal touches.

🛏 4

MULLINGAR   B2
Mullingar
Crookedwood House   **$$**
Crookedwood, Co. Westmeath
☎ 044 72165
▤ 044 72166
www.iol.ie/~cwoodhse
🅴 cwoodhse@iol.ie

As charming as its name, this beautifully restored old rectory overlooks Lake Derravaragh and offers exceptionally comfortable bedrooms. There also is an inviting lounge where tea is served, and a bar for drinks before dinner. The evening meals are the highlight of a stay here, and have earned great praise for chef/patron Niall Kenny.

🛏 8
Closed 2 wks. in Jan.

ROSSLARE HARBOUR   C1
Rosslare Harbour

Churchtown House   **$$**
Tagoat, Co. Wexford
☎ 053 32555
▤ 053 32577
churchtown-rosslare.com
🅴 churchtown.rosslare@indigo.ie

Charming period house, set in mature grounds on a link road between Rosslare Harbour and Rosslare Strand. Bedrooms are varied, attractive and comfortable, and the reception rooms are spacious and elegant. There is a living room, a dining room and a breakfast room adjoining the conservatory. Visits to the Viking town of Wexford, the local wildlife preserve and golf courses are recommended.

🛏 12   Closed Nov.-Mar.

Key to Symbols: ▤ Fax   🅴 Email   🛏 Rooms   🅿 Parking   🏊 Swimming
     American Express   Diners Club   MasterCard   Visa

TIPPERARY B2
Kilmallock

Flemingstown House $
Co. Limerick
☎ 063 98093
🖹 063 98546
www.ils.ie/flemingstown
✉ keltec@iol.ie
A lovely 18th-century farmhouse, modernized to provide stylish en suite facilities throughout. Rooms for guests include a comfortably furnished lobby with antiques and a dining room with beautiful stained glass windows. Imelda Sheedy-King produces an award-winning breakfast, and much of the produce comes from her own farm. She will provide dinner for her guests by arrangement.

🛏 5

TRAMORE B1
Annestown
Annestown House $$
Co. Waterford
☎ 051 396160
🖹 051 396474
homepage.eircom.net/~annestown
✉ annestownhouse@eircom.net
This period house stands in an elevated position overlooking a sandy cove, with private access to the beach. The well-equipped bedrooms successfully combine period furnishings and contemporary bathrooms. Guest areas comprise a spacious sitting room, a library, a billiards room and a dining room serving dinner by arrangement only.

🛏 5 Closed Dec. 1-Mar. 1

WATERFORD B1
Waterford

The Coach House $$
Butlerstown Castle,
Butlerstown, Cork Road,
Co. Waterford
☎ 051 384656
🖹 051 384751
homepages.iol.ie/~coachhse
✉ coachhse@iol.ie
Built in 1870 as the coach house to Butlerstown Castle, this comfortable establishment has been skilfully refurbished. There is a fine lounge, and the bedrooms are well equipped and furnished in traditional pine. A sauna also is available.

🛏 7
Closed Dec. 20-Feb. 1

WEXFORD C1
Wexford
Ard Ruadh Manor $
Spawell Road, Co. Wexford
☎ 053 23194
🖹 053 23194
A former vicarage, this magnificent house on the edge of Wexford has rooftop views to Slaney Estuary. The bedrooms and public rooms are spacious and luxurious, and the Cahill family takes a particular pride in looking after their guests.

🛏 6
Closed Dec. 24-29

WICKLOW C2
Wicklow

**The Old Rectory Country
House & Restaurant** $$
Co. Wicklow
☎ 40467048
🖹 0404 69181
www.wicklow.ie/hotels/h-oldrec.htm
✉ mail@oldrectory.ie
A charming Victorian residence on the edge of Wicklow town, beautifully restored by Linda and Paul Saunders, the friendly owners. Sample some of Linda's expert cuisine, which makes good use of organic vegetables and fresh local produce (vegetarians are welcome here). A peaceful atmosphere prevails throughout the guest areas and the pretty bedrooms.

🛏 8 Closed Jan.-Feb.

Key to Symbols: 🖹 Fax ✉ Email 🛏 Rooms 🅿 Parking 🏊 Swimming
 American Express   Diners Club 💳 MasterCard 💳 Visa

Italy

*I*taly is blessed with some of the world's most beguiling landscapes – from the Alps in the north, through the fertile heartlands, to the stark beauty of the south. In the north, Tuscany's rolling hills are terraced with cypresses, olive trees and vineyards; the Dolomites (Dolomiti) provide drama with their rugged peaks and forested cliffs dropping toward turquoise seas. In the south, the long summers bring a fierce beauty to the bleached, ocher mountains and azure waters. This is a mountainous country: the Apennines run almost from top to bottom and extend virtually from coast to coast. In Tuscany and Umbria in central Italy, the lush hills are fertile; in Basilicata and Calabria in the south, they are arid and suffer climatic extremes.

Who are the Italians?

Italian loyalties lie locally and regionally rather than nationally. An Italian is first and foremost from Tuscany, or Rome, or Naples, and will characterize other Italians in the same way. Each region has its stereotypes: the fiery Sicilians; the urbane and efficient Milanese; the cool, rational Tuscans; the abrasive Romans. Modern Italian is largely based on medieval Tuscan, but there are 1,500 dialects spoken around the country, only recently succumbing to the homogenizing power of the mass media. Regionalism also is apparent in the cultural and economic divide between the fertile, progressive north and the impoverished south.

Cities, towns and villages are crammed with fine buildings, churches and artworks, all reminders of the days before the unification of Italy in 1870, when each district had its own rich history and culture. Urban areas have been developed since World War II, however, with industrial sprawls and soulless apartment buildings on their fringes. But town dwellers still benefit from central piazzas, each surrounded by grand civic buildings and a church.

In rural areas, large numbers of *contadini*, peasant farmers and small shareholders, still work the land according to age-old traditions, despite the development since the 1960s of an affluent middle class and the growth of employment in high-tech industries.

Traveling through Italy

An excellent road network makes driving a pleasure. There are toll roads and highways, and Italians generally drive safely, though fast and sometimes with aggression. Minor roads in rural areas are often unsurfaced. Trains are cheap and run on time and the inter-city services are fast, but country lines have slow, complicated timetables. The bus network serves even the smallest villages.

Accommodations

Italy has an enormous range of hotels, and the national system of regulation works well. Bedrooms typically have two single beds, but double beds are quite common. Rooms in hotels of three Italian stars or more invariably have a television and telephone, and a private bath, toilet and washbasin. Rooms with showers can be cheaper, but they frequently dribble when turned on (water is precious in many parts of the country), and many don't have curtains. Air-conditioning is becoming more widespread, but is not universal, and buildings can be stifling in summer. By law, heating in public places is not

Italy

turned on until November 1. "Agritourism" is a term used to describe accommodations available on working farms. "Stube" or Tyrolean stove rooms can be found in hotels mainly in mountain regions and are cosy, communal rooms where food and drinks may be served.

Food and Drink

Italian cooking is simple, fresh and dictated by the seasons. Although lunch is the main meal by tradition, dinner is now becoming more important and often consists of *antipasto* (appetizers); a first course (*primo*) of pasta, soup or rice; a second course (*secondo*) of meat or fish with *contorni*, vegetables, or *insalata*, salad; and finally *formaggio* (cheese), *dolce* (dessert) or *frutta* (fruit). Wine is always taken with meals, but drunkenness is regarded with deep disapproval.

The terms *ristorante*, *osteria* and *trattoria* are fairly interchangeable, but *tavola calda* and *pizzeria* suggest a more modest establishment. It's unusual to eat dinner before 7:30 or 8, and lunch is served from around 12:30 to 2:30, while museums, churches, galleries and stores shut down for the daily siesta. Bars open from dawn until midnight or later, serving coffee and tea, soda, snacks and pastries, as well as alcohol. Italian coffee is very strong: a *caffe americano* is weaker. Children are almost always welcomed in restaurants – even in the most upscale places.

AGRIGENTO   C1
Agrigento

Villa Athena $$$
via Panoramica dei Templi 33, 92100, Sicily
☎ 0922 596288
🖹 0922 402180
Gracious 18th-century villa located in the magical Valley of the Temples, 45 yards from the Concordia Temple. Rooms are tastefully furnished, with some painted decorations in the traditional Sicilian style. There is a wonderful terrace with a panoramic view of the temples, and a swimming pool set in the greenery of the garden.

🛏 40

ALBA   A4
Alba

La Meridiana $$
Altavilla 9, 12051, Piedmont
☎ 0173 440112
🖹 0173 440112
The main family house is an elegant villa in Art Nouveau style. Attached is the rustic, creeper-covered annex given over to accommodations. Views from the rooms are of the Alps, the towers of Alba and the ancient city. A reading room, breakfast room, gym and billiards room are available to guests, with table tennis, bocce (bowls) and archery in the lovely garden.

🛏 6

Cortemilia

San Carlo $$
corso Divisioni Alpine 41, 12074, Piedmont
☎ 0173 81435
🖹 0173 8125
📧 sancarlo@langhe.monferrato.roero.it
Modern villa providing carefully appointed bedrooms with modern furnishings and equipment. It is located in upper Langa in a region noted for its gastronomy and fine wines. The restaurant serves typically Piedmontese dishes, and more than 600 vintage wines from all over the world are kept in the stone cellar. The hotel organizes courses on cooking and Piedmontese wines.

🛏 19

Dogliani

Foresteria Poderi Einaudi $$ - $$$
borgata Gombe 31, 12063, Piedmont
☎ 0173 70414
🖹 0173 742017
Charming 18th-century residence set in the middle of vineyards on the Einaudi estates. The main house was used as the winter residence of Luigi Einaudi, the first president of the Italian republic. The large, airy rooms are furnished entirely in early 20th-century style. The bathrooms are simple but comfortable and spacious. Breakfast is served in the parlor next to the small kitchen.

🛏 4

Trezzo Tinella

Antico borgo del Riondino $$
via dei Fiori 13, 12050, Piedmont
☎ 0173 630313
🖹 0173 630313
This elegant hotel overlooks the little streets of the medieval village and the countryside beyond. The pleasantly welcoming interior has been renovated using traditional materials, and the stone walls and beamed ceilings have been combined with modern furniture to good effect. The bedrooms have been created from former agricultural buildings: the olive press, the drying room and the apple storeroom.

🛏 8

ALESSANDRIA B4
Montegrosso D'Asti
Locanda del Boscogrande $$
via Boscogrande 47, 14048,
Piedmont
☎ 0141 956390
🖨 0141 956800

A late 19th-century farmhouse
in the hills of upper Monferrato
was renovated to create this inn,
just a 10-minute drive from Asti
in an area of great wines and
gastronomic tradition. It offers
airy, well-furnished rooms with
parquet floors, and an elegant
restaurant. The large garden
includes terraces for relaxing and
enjoying the view and an open-
air swimming pool.

🛏 8

Vignale Monferrato
Dré Castè $ - $$
via Piave 2, 15049, Piedmont
☎ 0142 933442
🖨 0142 933442
📧 mongetto@italnet.it

Dré Castè means "behind the
castle," although this grand guest
house belonging to the Mongetto
farm is actually underneath what
was once Cardinal Callori's
castle, looking out over the hills
of Montferrato Casalese. The
lovely rooms have painted
ceilings and antique furnishings,
and are named after the farm's
vineyards. Meals are served in
two attractive rooms with
fireplaces and comfortable sofas.

🛏 5

ALGHERO A2
Alghero

Villa Las Tronas $$$
lungomare Valencia 1, 07041,
Sardinia
☎ 079 981818
🖨 079 981044

In the 1940s this villa was the
vacation residence of the Italian
royal family. It is built on a
private promontory facing a
rocky coast. The bedrooms vary
in form and style, but all are well
equipped. Elegant parlors feature
antique furniture, and the dining
rooms offer enchanting views.
Facilities include bicycles, a gym,
fishing rods and a seawater
swimming pool.

🛏 28

AMALFI D2
Furore
Hostaria di Bacco $
via G.B. Lama 9, 84010,
Campania
☎ 089 830360
🖨 089 830352

The hotel is 1,500 feet above sea
level, with the gulf of Salerno
below. Originally it was a
trattoria, serving those going up
to the Agerola Pass; nowadays it
is a complex of little
Mediterranean-style buildings.
The large bedrooms all have
terraces, and the communal
rooms are simple but attractive.
A buffet breakfast includes local
breads, and the restaurant serves
honest cooking.

🛏 19

ANCONA C4
Falconara Marittima

Villa Amalia $$
via degli Spagnoli 4, 60015,
Marche
☎ 071 9160550
🖨 071 912045
📧 villa.amalia@fastnet.it

A charming villa dating from the
early 20th century, surrounded
by a lovely garden. Guests are
received in three little rooms on
the ground floor or, during the
summer, on the delightful
veranda. Bedrooms are
comfortably sized and have the
warmth and simplicity of
wooden furniture. Food is rooted
in the local tradition, but with a
touch of innovation.

🛏 7

Key to Symbols: 🖨 Fax 📧 Email 🛏 Rooms 🅿 Parking 🏊 Swimming
American Express Diners Club MasterCard Visa

Serra de' Conti

De' Conti   **$ - $$**
via S. Lucia 58, 60030, Marche
☎ 0731 879913
📄 0731 879913
Modern hotel beautifully situated amid the Verdicchio hills. The graceful lines of the exterior are replicated inside, where the communal rooms are comfortably furnished in an understated style and the spacious bedrooms have designer details. There is a terrace, with bar and breakfast service, overlooking the gentle hills of the Marches. The restaurant serves traditional dishes.

🛏 14   💳 🅾 💳

Sirolo

Conchiglia Verde   **$$**
via Giovanni XXIII 14, 60020, Marche
☎ 071 9330018
📄 071 9330019
This modern building has many terraces adorned by plants and flowers. Bedrooms feature wrought-iron beds, and there are stylish furnishings and signed paintings in the communal rooms. The restaurant, specializing in fish, has a floor of hand-decorated tiles. The swimming pool walls imitate rocks, and the heated hydromassage area has stalactites, stalagmites and waterfalls. Conference facilities are available.

🛏 26   💳 🅾 💳

AOSTA   A5

Antey St. André

Des Roses   **$**
Poutaz 5, 11020, Valle d'Aosta
☎ 0166 548527
📄 0166 548248
Pretty hotel in the classic chalet style set amid green fields. The neat bedrooms are furnished with pine and all have satellite television, while the pleasant bar and dining room are appointed in the typical Valle d'Aosta way. The lobby leads out to the hotel's delightful garden, where an area for bocce (a kind of bowls) adds to the attractions.

🛏 21
🅾 💳

Aosta

Milleluci   **$$**
Porossan-Rooppoz 15, 11100, Valle d'Aosta
☎ 0165 235278
📄 0165 235284
📧 hotel.milleluci@galactica.it
Old wood and stone-built farmhouse, completely renovated to provide traditional, rural-style accommodation with modern comforts. It stands out on a hill with wonderful views of the collegiate church of Sant'Orso, close to historic Aosta. All the bedrooms are romantic in style, and they include 10 non-smoking rooms, attic rooms with sloping ceilings and two suites with additional facilities.

🛏 33
💳 💳

Cogne

La Barme   **$**
Valnontey, 11012, Valle d'Aosta
☎ 0165 749177
📄 0165 749213
📧 labarme@netvallee.it
A recently renovated alpine hut in the heart of Gran Paradiso National Park, the hotel is a refuge for those who love the natural world, walking and skiing. It has comfortable rooms (all non-smoking) with satellite television. The restaurant serves fine food, including regional dishes. Also available are a ski-waxing room, sauna, children's playroom, garden, solarium and bicycles for rent.

🛏 15
💳 🅾 💳

Key to Symbols: 📄 Fax   📧 Email   🛏 Rooms   🅿 Parking   🏊 Swimming
💳 American Express   🅾 Diners Club   💳 MasterCard   💳 Visa

Cogne

Notre Maison $$
Cretaz 8, 11012, Valle d'Aosta
☎ 0165 74104
🖹 0165 749186
📧 notremaison@netvallee.it
A typical mountain chalet built of stone and wood with a tiled roof. It is set in the middle of a well-tended garden at the edge of the wooded slopes. The restaurant, open to non-guests, serves specialty dishes from the Cogne region. Facilities include a swimming pool, hydro-massage, sauna, Turkish bath and fitness center, plus a garage and ski storage facilities.

🛏 23

Gignod

La Clusaz $$
La Clusaz 1, 11010,
Valle d'Aosta
☎ 0165 56075
🖹 0165 54426
This delightful hotel is located in the valley leading up toward Gran San Bernardo Pass. It offers a high standard of cooking, prepared from ingredients cultivated by the family business. Dishes are regional in style, and there is an extensive wine list. The interior decoration is in the style of the valley, with pretty rooms and pleasing color schemes.

🛏 14

Prè-Saint-Didier

Beau Séjour $
Au Dent du Géant 18,
Pallesieux, 11010, Valle d'Aosta
☎ 0165 87801
🖹 0165 87961
Peacefully located hotel offering spacious rooms, nearly all with a balcony and well-equipped bathrooms. The welcoming lounge has an open fire, and the large dining room offers homemade dishes. Guests can use the bar, cellar bar, table tennis room and children's playroom. There also is a veranda with views of the Mont Blanc range.

🛏 33

AREZZO C4
Sansepolcro

Podere Violino $$
Gricignano 99, Gricignano,
52037, Tuscany
☎ 0575 720174
🖹 0575 720174
📧 violino@technet.it
Podere Violino has a lovely farmhouse at its center, with arches and loggias opening on to the garden. The building has been carefully refurbished and features 19th-century furniture. Facilities include an open-air swimming pool, outdoor and indoor playgrounds, bicycles and a horseback riding center on the estate. During the winter a stay of three nights includes one free night.

🛏 8

ÁSCOLI PICENO C3
Amandola

Le Piane $$
villa Piane 21, fraz. Taccarelli,
63021, Marche
☎ 0736 847641
🖹 0736 848557
📧 marcosel@tin.it
This large estate offers agritourism accommodations within Monte Sibillini National Park. The 18th-century village has recently been restored, and a number of dwellings – some very large – have been created within it. Each apartment has a kitchen area, private garden, heating and parking. There is a swimming pool, and guests may rent bicycles.

🛏 7

Montelparo

La Ginestra $ - $$
63020, Marche
☎ 0734 780449
🖹 0734 780706
📧 info@laginestra.it

An old farmhouse and its outbuildings make up this hotel, which offers both bedrooms and apartments with rustic furniture and some majolica floors. The firelight in the dining room is reflected in the copper pots hung on the walls, and the bar extends onto a veranda, where breakfast is served. Swimming, tennis, riding and many other activities are available.

🛏 13

ASSISI   C4

Assisi

Malvarina $$
via Malvarina 32, Viole, 06081, Umbria
☎ 075 8064280
🖹 075 8064280
📧 malvarina@umbria.net

Pleasantly rustic stone farmhouse with a welcoming family atmosphere. Agritourism accommodations are provided in various buildings, where antique furniture is blended with more sober modern pieces. Terra-cotta floors and fresh white walls dominate, and in the restaurant and the communal areas there are little dressers and late 19th-century prints. A swimming pool is available in the garden.

🛏 7

ASTI   A4

Canelli

La Casa in Collina $$
Sant'Antonio 30, 14053, Piedmont
☎ 0141 822827
🖹 0141 823543
📧 g.amerio@areacom.it

Elegantly reconstructed Piedmontese farmhouse standing on the side of a hill. The simple yet beautiful materials used in rebuilding – stone, brick, terra-cotta, wrought iron – are complemented by the interior of the house with its antique furniture. In the bedrooms there are light canopies trimmed in white, and on the ground floor there is a lounge and airy breakfast room.

🛏 6

La Luna e i Falò $$
regione Aie 37, 14053, Piedmont
☎ 0141 831643
🖹 0143 831643

This hotel is rustic in style, with broad arches and panoramic views. Below is the town of Canelli, around are hills criss-crossed with vine trellises, and on top is this charming building, rebuilt by its wine-producing owners. Inside, the period furniture and other family heirlooms contribute to the welcoming atmosphere.

🛏 9

AVEZZANO   C3

Pescasseroli

Paradiso $$
via Fonte Fracassi 4, 67032, Abruzzo
☎ 0863 910422
🖹 0863 910498
📧 a.paradiso@ermes.it

Friendly, family-run hotel in typical mountain style. It has recently been refurbished, and all the rooms have white walls and terra-cotta floors, with some antique Abruzzi furniture. The bedrooms are warmly welcoming, with checked duvets, wooden furniture, iron beds and lace curtains at the windows. Some rooms also have a balcony. Outside there is a lovely garden and terrace.

🛏 20

Key to Symbols: 🖹 Fax   📧 Email   🛏 Rooms   🅿 Parking   🏊 Swimming
American Express   Diners Club   MasterCard   Visa

BARI — D3
Polignano a Mare

Grotta Palazzese **$$**
via Narciso 59, 70044, Apulia
☎ 080 4240677
🖹 080 4240767
Modern hotel in the historic center of the town, standing directly above the sea and providing breathtaking views. Antique furniture and modern paintings are featured, and the bedrooms are delightfully furnished in Mediterranean style. Small suites are located in converted buildings with terra-cotta floors and stone walls. The summer restaurant has been created within a large and very beautiful natural grotto formed by the sea.

🛏 19

BAVENO — B5
Cannero Riviera

La Rondinella **$ - $$**
via Sacchetti 50, 28821, Piedmont
☎ 0323 788098
🖹 0323 788365
e hrondine@tin.it
At sunset Lake Maggiore's own particular light reflects on the facade of this Art Nouveau villa. The colors are astonishing, and the effect is very atmospheric. The morning light, on the other hand, can be enjoyed at breakfast on the veranda or under the trees. The rooms have wrought-iron bedsteads and large windows and are decorated in period style.

🛏 13

BELLAGIO — B5
Bellagio

Florence **$$ - $$$**
piazza Mazzini 46, 22010, Lombardy
☎ 031 950342
🖹 031 951722
e hotflore@tin.it
This delightful old lakeside house has been a hotel for more than 150 years, during which time Mark Twain, Puccini, Toscanini, Sartre and Simone de Beauvoir stayed here. The large rooms are handsomely appointed with antique furniture and parquet flooring. Communal rooms have great character, and the informal restaurant-bar is reached through the hotel's lakeside porticoes.

🛏 32

Chiavenna

Crimea **$**
viale Pratogiano 116, 23022, Lombardy
☎ 0343 34343
🖹 0343 35935
Chiavenna is an ancient Roman town, full of history and tradition, with palaces and notable works of art. Furthermore, the city is in the San Giacomo valley, surrounded by mountains in a wonderful position of natural beauty. This elegant hotel offers attractive bedrooms with wooden paneling and ceilings. The restaurant serves local and international specialties.

🛏 36

Varenna

Du Lac **$$ - $$$**
via del Prestino 4, 23829, Lombardy
☎ 0341 830238
🖹 0341 821081
This romantic villa preserves the architectural form of medieval Varenna, although the house was built in 1823 on old foundations. There is a choice of drawing rooms, and the large bedrooms open out onto the lake with terraces and balconies. The restaurant has a private dock, and in summer meals are served on the terrace facing the lake.

🛏 18

BELLUNO C5

Puos D'Alpago

Locanda San Lorenzo $ - $$
via IV Novembre 79, 32015,
Veneto
☎ 0437 454048
🖨 0437 454049
📧 loslor@tin.it

This little inn was the work of paternal grandparents, who built it as a simple tavern. The next generation added accommodations and a restaurant, and the place has been improved still further by the third generation. The cooking is among the best in the area. Charming bedrooms offer new bathrooms with hydromassage.

🛏 12

BERGAMO B5

Castione della Presolana

Aurora $$
via Sant'Antonio 19, 24020,
Lombardy
☎ 0346 60004
🖨 0346 60246
📧 hotel.aurora@cooraltur.it

A modern building along traditional lines, with pretty little bedrooms furnished in a country style. Communal rooms are more contemporary, and a fireplace makes the television room cozy. There is a well-appointed terrace, tennis, bocce (bowls) and table tennis in the garden. The home cooking is typical of the region, and breakfast includes pastries made on the premises.

🛏 28

Trescore Balneario

Della Torre $$
piazza Cabour 26-28, 24069,
Lombardy
☎ 035 941365
🖨 036 941365
📧 info@albergotorre.it

This hotel leans against a 14th-century tower made of rough stone - one of the most important monuments of Trescore. It is an attractive, elegantly furnished building, with large windows and balconies. Bedrooms are comfortable and modern in style, and there is a drawing room with an open fire. The restaurant offers local gastronomic specialties combined with some international touches.

🛏 29

BOLZANO C5

Vigo di Fassa

Ai Pini $ - $$
via Nuova 19, 38039,
Trentino-Alto Adige
☎ 0462 764501
🖨 0462 764109
📧 aipini@tin.it

A graceful chalet with carved balustrades located near the funicular. The bedrooms have all been refurbished, and most have balconies. There is a choice of sitting rooms, and big windows in the dining and breakfast rooms offer fine views. Additional attractions include a pizzeria, games room, French billiards, and a health center with sauna, Turkish bath, hydromassage and a gym.

🛏 30

BOLOGNA B4

Bologna

Al Cappello Rosso $$$
via De' Fusari 9, 40123,
Emilia-Romagna
☎ 051 261891
🖨 051 227179

This building has had a rich and varied history since 1375, when it provided accommodation for architects and artists working on the nearby basilica of San Petronio. Following careful restoration, it was reborn as a sophisticated hotel. Bedrooms are endowed with every comfort, and the meeting rooms, lounges, bar and breakfast room are elegantly furnished and welcoming in every respect.

🛏 35

Key to Symbols: 🖨 Fax 📧 Email 🛏 Rooms 🅿 Parking 🏊 Swimming
American Express 🔘 Diners Club MasterCard Visa

Bologna

Dei Commercianti $$$
via de' Pignattari 11, 40124,
Emilia-Romagna
☎ 051 233052
🖹 051 224733
📧 hotcom@tin.it
The hotel has been intelligently restored to preserve character while offering modern comforts. Antique forms are set against vivid colors to achieve an elegant

effect. Many of the bedrooms have a terrace overlooking the wonderful stained-glass windows of the Duomo (cathedral). The buffet breakfast is especially well prepared.

🛏 34

Orologio $$$
via IV Novembre 10, 40123,
Emilia-Romagna
☎ 051 231253
🖹 051 260552
📧 hotoro@tin.it
Delightful small hotel in the heart of Bologna. Bedrooms are attractive, and some of them overlook the splendid piazza Maggiore and the Asinelli tower.

The lounge and breakfast room are on the first floor, and a good buffet breakfast includes both savory and sweet dishes. On special holidays or feast days, typical sweets also are offered.

🛏 35

San Vitale $$
via San Vitale 94, 40125,
Emilia-Romagna
☎ 051 225966
🖹 051 239396
This hotel is near the university, one of the oldest in Italy, and beneath the porticoes that are another famous feature of the city. The bedrooms vary in size and design, and all have modern

furniture. There is a delightful internal garden that provides guests with a quiet corner in spring and summer. The family management is both willing and friendly.

🛏 17

Touring $$ - $$$
via de' Mattuiani 1/2, 40124,
Emilia-Romagna
☎ 051 584305
🖹 051 334763
📧 hoteltouring@hoteltouring.it
Situated in the historic center of Bologna, the hotel offers comfortable rooms with well-chosen fabrics and modern furniture. Light stuccowork

forms a background to the recently renovated furnishings. A terrace roof garden overlooks a charming view of rooftops and churches as far as the Bolognese hills. The hotel also has a private garage.

🛏 38

Pieve di Cento

Le Quattro Piume $ - $$
via XXV Aprile 15, 40066,
Emilia-Romagna
☎ 051 6861500
🖹 051 974191
The unusual name kindles memories of dueling musketeers, although it is actually very quiet here. The hotel is in a little white house with dark shutters, offering spacious bedrooms on

two floors with minibars, color televisions, ceiling fans, simple modern furniture in light wood, white bedcovers and spotless curtains on the windows.

🛏 16

Locanda Calori $$ - $$$
piazza Calori 16, 40018,
Emilia-Romagna
☎ 051 811111
🖩 051 818818
The inn is housed in a period
building, sympathetically
refurbished and situated in the
historic center. While the rooms
retain their original character
and wooden beams, the

furnishings are attractively
modern. The restaurant is a focal
point, renowned for its good
food, especially the pasta, of
which there must be a thousand
and one forms in every shape
and color.

🛏 11

BOLZANO   C5

Badia

Gran Ander $ - $$$
via Runcac 29, Pedraces, 39036,
Trentino-Alto Adige
☎ 0471 839741
🖩 0471 839741
📧 granander@altabadia.it
Large, modern, recently
refurbished chalet with plenty of
wood in evidence. Bedrooms are

spacious and bright, and the
lounges open onto a well-
equipped terrace where breakfast
is served and big barbecues are
prepared. The Tyrolean stube
(stove) room is characteristically
welcoming and serves typical
dishes of the region. Table tennis
and bicycles are available.

🛏 29

Campo di Trens

**Romantik Hotel
Stafler** $$ - $$$
Mules 10, Mules, 39040,
Trentino-Alto Adige
☎ 0472 771136
🖩 0472 771094
📧 stafler@acs.it
This hotel has been providing
hospitality since around 1270,
first as a post house, then an inn.
Standards of accommodation

and comfort have changed, but
the rustic beauty of the
architecture has been retained.
The attractive rooms are adorned
with antique Tyrolean furniture,
lovely chests and painted 19th-
century cabinets. Particularly
charming is the cozy stube (stove
room).

🛏 38

Castelrotto

Cavallino d'Oro $ - $$$
piazza Kraus 1, 39040,
Trentino-Alto Adige
☎ 0471 706337
🖩 0471 707172
📧 cavallino@cavallino.it
Ancient inn restored with care
and enriched by Tyrolean
ornaments and antique pieces. It
offers romantic bedrooms with

canopied beds and pretty painted
furniture. The à la carte
restaurant and two intimate
stube (stove rooms) add the
finishing touches. Additional
attractions are the Finnish sauna,
Turkish bath and solarium. The
hotel also has its own ski school.

🛏 20

Renon

Lichtenstern $ - $$$
Lichtestern 8, Soprabolzano,
39059, Trentino-Alto Adige
☎ 0471 345147
🖩 0471 345635
📧 hotel_lichtenstern@dnet.it
This hotel is located on the high
plateau of Renon in the heart of
Alro Adige, overlooking the
Dolomites. It is a typical alpine-
style building, with wooden

balconies, little parlors and the
more elegant dining room. The
kitchen produces homemade ice
cream and local specialties for
breakfast and lunch. There also is
a Turkish bath and an open-air
swimming pool.

🛏 27

Key to Symbols: 🖩 Fax 📧 Email 🛏 Rooms 🅿 Parking 🏊 Swimming
🔲 American Express 🔘 Diners Club 💳 MasterCard 💳 Visa

BORDIGHERA A4

Dolceacqua

Altavia $
strada militare la Colla Gouta, 18035, Liguria
☎ 0184 206754

This mountain retreat is reached along an old military road. It is built of stone and has characteristically charming architecture with thick walls, windows framed in light stone and a little iron stairway with a gallery on the upper floors. Bedrooms are simple and welcoming, and the sitting rooms feature wood, stone and terra-cotta together with rustic furniture and Provencal stoves.

🛏 4

Ventimiglia

Baja Benjamin $$$
corso Europa 63, Grimaldi Inferiore, 18036, Liguria
☎ 0184 38002
🖷 0184 38027

The hotel stands on the gentle slopes of a hill leading down to the sea and its own private beach. The modern building blends well with the surrounding countryside and has a restaurant renowned for its cooking and refined service. The recently renovated bedrooms are elegantly decorated and have period-style furniture. Guests can enjoy the panoramic view from little terraces.

🛏 5 ⬛ ⬛ ⬛

BRÉSCIA B5

Adro

Cornaleto $ - $$
via Cornaletto 2, 25030, Lombardy
☎ 030 7450554/030 7450507
🖷 030 7450552

A modern building in the traditional style, set high up among the vineyards and affording good views of its surroundings. Well-furnished rooms and apartments have rustic details such as terra-cotta floors and ceilings decorated with wood. The restaurant is modern and serves dishes that complement the farm's wine cellar. A small conference room is available, and there are bicycles for rent.

🛏 7

⬛ ⬛

Capriolo

Ricci Curbastro & Figli $ - $$
via Adro 37, 25031, Lombardy
☎ 030 736094
🖷 030 74600558
📧 agrit.riccicur@imp.it

A number of late 19th-century rural buildings have been converted to provide guest house accommodations on the edge of the village, stretching between the Oglio River and Monte Alto. These apartments, with names like "butterfly" or "cherry," are individually designed, comfortable and practical. Visits can be made to the farm's wine cellar and the agricultural museum.

🛏 7

⬛ ⬛

Gargnano

Du Lac $$
via Colletta 21, Villa, 25084, Lombardy
☎ 0365 71107
🖷 0365 71055
📧 info@hotel-dulac.it

This early 20th-century mansion is perfectly located at the foot of the mountain, right by a lake in a charming little village. It makes a stylish hotel, filled with antique furniture, paintings and prints, and six of the bedrooms overlook the lake with balconies or terraces. There is a little parlor with a piano and a pretty dining room extending onto a balcony.

🛏 11

⬛

Key to Symbols: 🖷 Fax 📧 Email 🛏 Rooms 🅿 Parking 🏊 Swimming
⬛ American Express ⬛ Diners Club ⬛ MasterCard ⬛ Visa

Manerba del Garda

Pian Camuno

Sale Marasino

Sirmione

Villa Schindler **$$**
via Bresciani 68, 25080,
Lombardy
☎ 0365 554877
▤ 0365 554877
🄴 villaschindler@tin.it
An old villa set amid beautiful
countryside looking out over the
gulf of Manerba. Recent
restoration work has enriched
the building with many works of
art: sundials and sculptures
outside, valuable frescoes inside.
The attractive bedrooms all have
parquet flooring and dark wood
furniture. A splendid terrace
overlooks the lake and
mountains, and the restaurant
serves local and classic dishes.

🛏 8

Stube **$ - $$**
via Fane 12, 25050, Lombardy
☎ 036 4590100
A typical mountain chalet
covered with finely worked
wood. There is plenty of wood in
the interior decoration too, and
the bedrooms are charmingly
simple. On the ground floor the
restaurant is both heated and
adorned by a big majolica stove:
the cooking is regional, featuring
mushrooms, game and
homemade pasta.

🛏 9

Villa Kinzika **$$**
via Provinciale 1, 25057,
Lombardy
☎ 030 9820975
▤ 030 9820990
🄴 snerett@tin.it
Surrounded by the luxuriant
green of a large garden full of
olive trees, the hotel is situated in
a quiet spot by the lake. The
drawing room and reading room
are both tastefully decorated,
with elegant furniture, paintings
and valuable carpets. The
breakfast room and the
American bar are both attractive
and welcoming places for
lingering and relaxing.

🛏 18

Dogana **$$**
via Verona 149, Lugana, 25019,
Lombardy
☎ 030 919026
▤ 030 9196066
🄴 dogana@gardanet.it
Recent renovation has enhanced
the elegant harmony of this early
18th-century building. It is
family-run, tried and tested by
30 years of experience, and the
atmosphere is friendly and
informal. Nearly all the
bedrooms look out onto the lake,
and the restaurant serves
carefully prepared dishes typical
of the Lombardy/Veneto region.

🛏 29

BRINDISI **E3**
Ostuni
Il Frantoio **$$ - $$$**
72017, Apulia
☎ 0831 330276
▤ 0831 330276
🄴 ilfrantoio@pugliaonline.it
Beautiful fortified farmstead
constructed between the 16th
and 19th centuries and
surrounded by an ancient olive
grove. The bedrooms are all
charming, with antique furniture
and many embellishments.
Communal areas include
drawing rooms and parlors, a
library, a dolls' room, children's
playroom, ever-open bar and a
kitchen where guests may
prepare themselves snacks at any
time of day.

🛏 8

Key to Symbols: ▤ Fax 🄴 Email 🛏 Rooms 🅿 Parking 🏊 Swimming
▦ American Express ◉ Diners Club 💳 MasterCard 💳 Visa

Ostuni
Lo Spagnulo $ - $$
contrada Spagnulo, 72017,
Apulia
☎ 0831 350209
🖹 0831 333756

Beautiful 17th-century farmhouse, built for defense, work and habitation, and set amid ancient olive trees. It has been restructured to provide accommodation in bedrooms and little apartments with simple, rustic furniture. The farm business provides the restaurant with produce for its regional dishes. There's a private beach, a riding school, tennis court and bicycles for guests' use.

🛏 36 ▪▪ ⓪ 💳

CÁGLIARI B2
Pula

Nora Club $$ - $$$
viale Nora, 09010, Sardinia
☎ 070 924422
🖹 070 9209129

It is called a club but seems more like a little village, with houses grouped around a big garden within walking distance of the sea. The interior is spacious, light and varied with arches and bright ceramic panels, furnished with lovely handmade Sardinian pieces in carved wood. There is a swimming pool and bar service in the garden.

🛏 25

CAMPOBASSO D3
Sepino

La Taverna $
contrada Piana d'Olmo 6,
86017, Molise
☎ 0874 79626
🖹 0874 790118

The massive front door of this old inn opens onto a lovely interior. A steep stone staircase leads up to pretty bedrooms furnished with late 19th-century and period-style furniture. The stone walls, low arches and vaults contain rustic tables for hungry wayfarers, as they would have done centuries before. Outside there is a garden and pergola.

🛏 14

CASTELLABATE D2
Agropoli

La Colombaia $
via Piano delle pere, 84043,
Campania
☎ 0974 821800
🖹 0974 823478

This old villa is surrounded by a big olive grove and enjoys a magnificent view over the Gulf of Salerno and Capri. The bedrooms are bright and well furnished, with air-conditioning and televisions. Communal rooms are charmingly furnished with antiques, and the dining room is cozy and welcoming. Outside there is a big garden and open-air swimming pool with solarium.

🛏 7 ▪▪ 💳

Castellabate

La Mola $$
via A. Cilento 2, 84048,
Campania
☎ 0974 967053
🖹 0974 967714
📧 lamola@mediatek.it.com

Skillful restoration has created rooms out of the interior of this 12th-century palace, and all have views of the sea. They are comfortable and full of atmosphere, with stylish furniture, safes, televisions and minibars. The communal rooms feature exposed stone walls, and the garden has charming terraces. The restaurant, open in the evening, specializes in fish dishes.

🛏 5 💳

CASTROVILLARI   D2
Altomonte

Barbieri   **$ - $$**
via San Nicola 30, 87042, Calabria
☎ 0981 948072
🖷 0981 948073
📧 barbieri@mail.telso.it

Altomonte is a pretty little town that stands high on a mountain. The hotel offers well-equipped bedrooms with functional modern furnishings, and large communal rooms where functions and conferences can be accommodated. The restaurant is among the best in the region, and in summer meals can be served in the garden. Guided art and nature tours are organized in the vicinity.

🛏 24

Francavilla Marittima

La Mandria   **$**
contrada Sferracavallo 89, 87072, Calabria
☎ 0981 992576
🖷 0981 992576

Farm complex in Pollino National Park, where an old herdsman's house has been converted for communal use. The restaurant serves traditional food using produce from the farm. A modern building houses the bedrooms and four little apartments. There is a swimming pool on the terrace, and mountain bicycles are available. Courses on cooking and crocheting are organized. Minimum stay three nights.

🛏 8

Morano Calabro

La Locanda del Parco   **$**
contrada Mazzicanino, 87016, Calabria
☎ 0981 31304
🖷 0981 31304

A fine modern building, set in Pollino National Park and inspired by traditional mountain architecture. Accommodation is offered in attractive bedrooms with central heating. The charming restaurant, heated by a large fireplace, serves food prepared from fresh farm produce. The establishment organizes cookery courses, animal observation and exploration of the neighborhood. Guests may rent bicycles from the farm.

🛏 6

CATÁNIA   D1
Giarre

Codavolpe   **$**
strada 87 n. 35, Trepunti, 95010, Sicily
☎ 095 939802
🖷 095 939802
📧 codavolpe@dns.omnia.it

Late 19th-century villa set in a defensive position on the slopes of Mount Etna. It is surrounded by citrus trees, and a vegetable garden ensures a supply of fresh produce. In front of the villa is a pergola, and there are flowers everywhere. The rooms and apartments blend rustic and modern styles, featuring wooden tables and floors, exposed stone and wrought iron.

🛏 6

CATANZARO   D2
Sellia Marina

Contrada Guido   **$ - $$**
88050, Calabria
☎ 0961 961495
🖷 0961 961495

Agritourism operation set in a shady garden on a farm facing the sea. A pine wood separates the property from the private beach. There are pretty guest rooms with stylish furniture and modern bathrooms. The cooking is inspired by Calabrian and Mediterranean specialties and uses farm produce. There is a soccer field, tennis, riding and golf in the immediate vicinity.

 🛏 10

CEFALÚ C1

Tusa

Atelier sul mare $ - $$
via Cesare Battisti 4, Castel di
Tusa, 98070, Sicily
☎ 0921 334295
▤ 0921 334283
e apresti@eniware.it
The rooms at this unique hotel
have been designed by major
contemporary artists to stunning

effect. It stands by a beautiful
bay in a park within the Nebrodi
Mountains. Other works are
strewn across the valley and
include a wall of ceramics made
by 40 artists. A studio on site
runs courses on ceramic art.
There also is a wide range of
sporting activities, and the hotel
has a private beach.

🛏 40 ▦ ▦

CHIETÍ C3

Guardiagrele

Villa Maiella $$
via Sette Dolori 30, 66016,
Abruzzo
☎ 0871 809319
▤ 0871 809362
e info@villamaiella.it
Modern, functional building
standing at the entrance to
Guardiagrele, at the foot of the
Maiella Park. The bedrooms are
equipped with air-conditioning,

minibars and satellite televisions,
and furnished with care to create
a welcoming atmosphere. The
restaurant serves typical food
from the Abruzzi region,
imaginatively adapted traditional
fare, seasonal dishes and seafood
specialties. There also is a good
wine cellar.

🛏 14

COMO B5

Cantello

Madonnina $$
largo Lanfranco 1, 21050,
Lombardy
☎ 0332 417731
▤ 0332 418403
The facade of this beautifully
designed 18th-century building
is a fitting introduction to the
gracious interior and its period

furniture and beautiful objects,
which have the charm and patina
of age. The bedrooms are
classically pretty, each with its
own personality. The standard of
cooking in the restaurant is
renowned in the area.

🛏 15

Lurago d'Erba

La Corte $$
via Mazzini 20, 22040,
Lombardy
☎ 031 699690
▤ 031 982069-9755990
Converted 18th-century
farmhouse with an enclosed
courtyard typical of the Brianza
region. It is set on a hill with
views over the peaks surrounding

Erba and Lecco. Inside, the hotel
is elegantly rustic with
comfortable bedrooms. The
restaurant serves a wide variety
of dishes of the Como region,
accompanied by a vast selection
of vintage wines from the
attached cellar.

🛏 8

CORTINA D'AMPEZZO C5

Rasun Anterselva

Bagni di Salomone $
Anterselva di Sotto, 39030,
Trentino-Alto Adige
☎ 0474 492199
▤ 0474 492378
e bagnidisalomone@dnet.it
Charming hotel with Tyrolean
architecture and exterior wall
paintings. Inside there are
antique furnishings, rustic
fabrics, wooden floors and rooms

opening onto the garden. The
elegant dining room serves
traditional fare, with
consideration given to modern
dietary requirements. The winter
garden, covered and heated
veranda and terraces provide the
finishing touches. It also has its
own fishing reserve.

🛏 24

CORTONA   C4
Castiglione del Lago

Casal de' Cucchi   **$$ - $$$**
Petrignano del Lago, 06060,
Umbria
☎ 075 9528116
🖹 075 5171244
📧 dinfani@tin.it
A stone-built house and a
number of converted agricultural
buildings provide
accommodations deep in restful
countryside with beautiful views.

The restaurant serves
traditionally based dishes using
products from the farm and the
surrounding area, and there also
is a wine canteen. Facilities
include a children's playground,
open-air swimming pool, table
tennis and bicycles for rent.

🛏 4

Miralago   **$$**
piazza Mazzini 6, 06061,
Umbria
☎ 075 951157
🖹 075 951924
📧 miralago@ftbcc
Delightful little mansion dating
from the end of the 19th century.
The recently refurbished interior
is in Art Nouveau style with
marble and floral-patterned

carpets in the pretty hall, and
spacious bedrooms all facing the
historic square or beautiful Lake
Trasimeno. An ample buffet
breakfast is the prelude to the
good food served in the
restaurant.

🛏 19

💳 ⑩ 💳

Cortona

Podere La Vecchia Fornace   **££**
San Lorenzo 257, San Lorenzo,
52042, Tuscany
☎ 0575 692245/ 0368 3039300
🖹 0575 692245
📧 vecchiafornace@technet.it
Agritourism accommodations
provided in an old stone
farmhouse and converted
outbuildings in a beautiful hilly
location. The comfortable

apartments retain their original
charm, with period furnishings
and lovely stone fireplaces in
addition to central heating. The
separate entrances open directly
onto the garden, with its
children's playground, swimming
pool and various sporting
facilities.

🛏 4

Cortona Church, St. Margherita

Key to Symbols: 🖹 Fax   📧 Email   🛏 Rooms   🅿 Parking   🏊 Swimming
💳 American Express   ⑩ Diners Club   💳 MasterCard   💳 Visa

COSENZA D2
Amantea
Mediterraneo $ - $$
via Dogana 54, 87032, Calabria
☎ 0982 426364
🖹 0982 426247
📧 mediterraneo1@libero.it
This hotel has been created from a mid 19th-century palace in the center of Amantea. The public rooms are lit by big windows opening onto a shady garden, and Mediterranean arches give character to the communal rooms. Bedrooms are comfortably furnished and well equipped. A beach is reserved for guests, with facilities for windsurfing and scuba diving. Bicycles are available for rent.

🛏 31 📺 💿 💳

Spezzano della Sila
Camigliatello $$
via Federici, Camigliatello Silano, 87052, Calabria
☎ 0984 578496
🖹 0984 578628
Graceful, modern building set deep in the countryside, with lovely views down toward the valley. It is just a short distance from the center of the village and about a mile from the ski lifts. The hotel has spacious bedrooms, many opening onto large balconies. Comfortable public areas include lounges, a delightful bar and a dining room overlooking the pine wood.

🛏 29
📺 💿 💳

CUNEO A4
Costigliole Saluzzo

Castello Rosso $$$
via Ammiraglio Reynaudi 5, 12024, Piedmont
☎ 0175 230030
🖹 0175 239315
Castello Rosso offers individually styled rooms combining modern comfort with period furnishings. There are many valuable pieces, particularly in the Contessa Constantia living room, and during restoration work frescoes by Maestro d'Elva came to light. A buffet breakfast is served, and in the evening the restaurant provides local dishes. Guests have use of the health center on the lower floor.

🛏 16
📺 💿 💳

ERICE C1
Erice
Elimo $$ - $$$
via Vittorio Emanuele 75, 91016, Sicily
☎ 0923 869377
🖹 0923 869252
📧 elimoh@comeg.it
This little hotel has been created from a 17th-century house in the historic center of this lovely little town. The modern bedrooms are tastefully furnished with elegant upholstery. Restoration has preserved the charm of the communal areas, which have an exotic Oriental atmosphere. Guests will also enjoy the courtyard, panoramic terrace, pretty garden and solarium.

🛏 21 📺 💿 💳

FAENZA C4
Castel Guelfo

Locanda Solarola $$$
via Santa Croce 5, 40023, Emilia-Romagna
☎ 0542 670222
🖹 0542 670222
📧 solarola@imola.queen.it
A little gravel road framed by neat lines of trees leads to the hotel, a pretty, early 20th-century-style building.. The romantic interior is full of charming objects and furnished with the family's period pieces. There is a lovely restaurant serving high-quality meals, as well as a lounge and billiards room.

🛏 15
📺 💳

Dozza

Monte del Re $$ - $$$
via Monte del Re 43, 40050,
Emilia-Romagna
☎ 0542 678400
🖹 0542 678444
📧 montedelre@mail.asianet.it
This former religious house,
built in the 13th century, is now
an enchanting hotel. Bedrooms
are large and comfortable and
the reception rooms gracious,
with spaces for reading and
meetings. Conference facilities
are in the former cloisters and
refectory. Other attractions are
the bar, restaurant, winter garden
and inner courtyard, and outside
a soccer field and tennis court.

🛏 38
🔲 ⓪ 💳

FERRARA   C4
Codigoro

Locanda del Passo Pomposa $$
via Provinciale per Volano 13,
44020, Emilia-Romagna
☎ 0533 719131
This hotel rises up against the
water on the left bank of the Po
River at Volano, in the national
park of the Po delta, and it has
private mooring for boats. The
bedrooms are very new and
attractive, with tasteful
furnishings to blend with the
rustic architecture of the house.
Some have a private terrace, and
the bathrooms all have
hydromassage.

🛏 26
🔲 ⓪ 💳

Ferrara

Annunziata $$ - $$$
piazza Repubblica 5, 44100,
Emilia-Romagna
☎ 0532 201111
🖹 0532 203233
📧 annunzia@tin.it
Charming hotel closely
connected to the artistic life of
the city, and a treasure house in
its own right. Paintings, signed
ceramics, books and art catalogs
enrich the interior. The
bedrooms and suites, with views
of Estense Castle or the
Duchesse Garden, are endowed
with every comfort. Guests have
free use of bicycles, and Internet
access is available.

🛏 22
🔲 ⓪ 💳

Duchessa Isabella $$$
via Palestro 70, 44100,
Emilia-Romagna
☎ 0532 2202121
🖹 0532 202638
📧 isabelld@tin.it
The Renaissance facade,
unadorned bricks and pilaster
strips of this property are all
simple and perfectly
proportioned. Inside there are
painted ceilings, grand fireplaces
and a sumptuous stairway
leading up to the reception
rooms on the upper floor. The
restaurant is exquisitely
appointed, and the bedrooms
equally elegant, with romantic
floral themes prevalent. A lovely
garden completes the picture.

🛏 28   🔲 ⓪ 💳

Locanda Borgonuovo $$
via Cairoli 29, 44100,
Emilia-Romagna
☎ 0532 211100
🖹 0532 248000
This inn, distinguished only by a
little door, is situated in a
wonderful architectural group
that in 1600 was the religious
house and theological school of
the Teatini Fathers. There are
single and double rooms
furnished with period pieces, all
with private bathrooms and air
conditioning. An abundant
breakfast may be taken in the
pretty garden.

🛏 4
🔲 💳

Key to Symbols: 🖹 Fax 📧 Email 🛏 Rooms 🅿 Parking 🏊 Swimming
🔲 American Express ⓪ Diners Club 💳 MasterCard 💳 Visa

Ferrara

Ripagrande $$$
via Ripagrande 1, 44100,
Emilia-Romagna
☎ 0532 765250
🖹 0532 764377
The old mansion that houses this hotel stands in the historic center, close to the city's major cultural and artistic attractions. The bedrooms, which are really suites, are all elegant and welcoming. The entrance hall has fragments of frescoes and wooden beams, and there is an inner courtyard with Renaissance architecture. The high-class restaurant serves good regional dishes.

🛏 20

Ostellato

Villa Belfiore $$ - $$$
via Pioppa 27, 44020,
Emilia-Romagna
☎ 0533 681164
🖹 0533 681172
This family villa is close to where the valley loops in one of the region's most beautiful areas, surrounded by a great park. Inside, the hotel is furnished in classic style with antique and rustic furniture. The restaurant serves food prepared by the same agriturismo business that runs the hotel: vegetables from the organically cultivated land and vegetarian dishes along with traditional Emilian recipes.

🛏 10

FLORENCE (FIRENZE) B4
Barberino Val d'Elsa

Il Paretaio $
strada delle Ginestre 12, 50021,
Tuscany
☎ 055 8059218
🖹 055 8059231
📧 ilparetaio@tin.it
There are wonderful views from this isolated 18th-century farmhouse. Attractive bedrooms are provided, and good Tuscan cooking is served at the large larch table in the old dining room. The owners' main business is their riding school, which has 25 horses and offers courses at every level from beginner to expert. A swimming pool and children's playground are also available.

🛏 6

Florence

Cimabue $$
via Bonifacio Lupi 7, 50129,
Tuscany
☎ 055 471989
🖹 055 475601
This family-run hotel takes great care in service and welcoming details: The result is a charming establishment with the right balance in the quality/price ratio. It is situated in a 19th-century mansion, recently refurbished, in the historic center of Florence. Communal rooms have a pleasing atmosphere and the attractive bedrooms are furnished in period style, some with frescoed ceilings.

🛏 16

Il Guelfo Bianco $$$
via Cavour 29, 50129, Tuscany
☎ 055 288330
🖹 055 295203
Centrally located hotel converted from a 16th-century palace, a short distance from the Duomo (cathedral), St. Mark's Square, the Accademia museum and Medici chapels. Bedrooms in the old building are pretty and full of character, furnished in period style with plenty of modern equipment. The breakfast room, with its vaulted ceiling and paneled walls, faces a little courtyard.

🛏 29

Mario's   **$$$**
via Faenza 89, 50123, Tuscany
☎ 055 216901
🖹 055 212039
e hotel.marios@webitaly.com
An old palace is the setting for this pretty hotel. Guests go up to the first floor and are welcomed into a large salon furnished in the Florentine style with high paneled ceilings, Persian carpets, paintings and diffused lighting. Bedrooms are furnished in traditional Tuscan style, and there is a secluded, country-style breakfast room as well as a bar/reading room.

🛏 16

Mornadi alla Crocetta   **$$**
via Laura 50, 50121, Tuscany
☎ 055 2344747
🖹 055 2480954
e welcome@hotelmorandi.it
The hotel, a former religious house, is situated in the heart of the historic center, five minutes from the Duomo (cathedral). The bedrooms, which vary in size and style, have parquet flooring, individually controlled air-conditioning and safes. Most also have period furniture. High ceilings and wooden beams give the communal rooms a special charm.

🛏 10

Villa Le Rondini   **$$$**
via Bolognese Vecchia 224, Trespiano, 50139, Tuscany
☎ 055 400081
🖹 055 268212
e mailbox@villalerondini.it
This villa stands within a park that is part cultivated with vineyards and part wooded. Bedrooms vary in size and have antique and period-style furniture. Large communal rooms include a dining room facing the garden, and breakfast is served in the loggia looking over the garden. There are tennis and horseback riding facilities, a swimming pool, a heliport and meeting rooms.

🛏 43

Castello di Lamole   **$$**
via di Lamole 82, Lamole, 50022, Tuscany
☎ 055 630498
🖹 055 630611
e castellodilamole@arscanora.it
Since 1200 Lamole Castle has dominated the Chianti hills, defending Florentine borders in time of war with Siena. The apartments have been created out of castle rooms, with antique furniture, terra-cotta floors and beamed ceilings. Pretty windows open onto country views, and a lovely open-air swimming pool has been introduced within the old structure. Evenings of traditional music and Tuscan folklore are organized.

🛏 8

Villa Calcinaia   **$$**
via di Citille 84, Greti, 50022, Tuscany
☎ 055 854008
🖹 055 854008
e capponis@ftbcc.it
In 1524 the family of the Capponi counts bought Villa Calcinaia, and they are still its proprietors. It is surrounded by olive groves, vines and woods in the heart of the Chianti area, convenient to Florence and Siena. Two apartments have been created out of the 13th-century presbytery, and another apartment was originally a farmhouse. An open-air swimming pool is available for guests.

🛏 3

Greve in Chianti

Villa San Michele $ - $$
Monte San Michele, 50020, Tuscany
☎ 055 851034
🖹 055 851034

On the highest hill of Florentine Chianti stands the 10th-century former convent of San Michele and a chapel with some precious frescoes. Today the old group of buildings is a villa-farm in the middle of a public park, with a hostel offering simple accommodations. Facilities include a billiards room, soccer field, children's playroom and bicycle rental. Food is typically Tuscan.

🛏 6

Montelupo Fiorentino

Fattoria de Petrognano $$
via Bottianccio 116, 50056, Tuscany
☎ 0571 913795
🖹 0571 913796

Within this lovely property two 18th-century farmhouses have been transformed, after careful restructuring, into cozily furnished apartments equipped with every comfort. Facilities include an open-air swimming pool, hydromassage, tennis, bocce (bowls), table tennis and mountain bikes. The old barn with its lovely portico is used as a meeting room. Courses are organized on decorating ceramics, watercolors, art history and bonsai.

🛏 2

Teunta San Vito in Fior di Selva $$
via San Vito 32, San Vito, 50056, Tuscany
☎ 0571 51411
🖹 0571 51405
📧 sanvito@san-vito.com

Three farmhouses have been refurbished to provide character accommodations in the form of apartments created from old farm buildings. They feature terra-cotta floors and rustic but modern furniture. The farm business has used organic methods since 1982, and the buildings are scattered among neat vineyards, woods and olive groves. Amenities include a restaurant, mountain bike rental, swimming pool, and courses in cookery, ceramics and painting.

🛏 14

Palazzuolo sul Senio

Locanda Senio $$
borgo dell'Ore 1, 50035, Tuscany
☎ 055 8046019
🖹 055 8046485
📧 locanda.senio@newnet.it

Lovely stone-built inn standing at the entrance to this medieval village, facing the Capitano del Popolo mansion. It is rustic in style, with welcoming bedrooms furnished in early 20th-century style. During winter months meals are served in the little restaurant, and in summer out on the veranda. Much care is taken in the preparation of the regional and seasonal dishes.

🛏 6

Reggello

Il Crocicchio $$
via San Siro 133, 50066, Tuscany
☎ 055 8667262
🖹 055 869102
📧 info@crocicchio.com

This former farmhouse is set amid a woven fabric of olive groves and vineyards in beautiful countryside. Accommodations are in little apartments and well-furnished bedrooms that preserve the rustic character of the original building, and the same is true of the communal rooms. There is a swimming pool and children's playground in the garden, and horseback riding lessons are available.

🛏 2

Vicchio di Mugello

Villa Campestri $$$
via di Campestri 19, Campestri, 50039, Tuscany
☎ 055 8490107
🖹 055 8490108
📧 villa.campestri@villacampestri.it
This 12th-century villa is set in a large park on a hill. The spacious bedrooms are divided between the main house and converted outbuildings and are furnished with antique or period pieces. The main salon can accommodate small conventions. Beautifully furnished communal rooms face the big terrace, and the restaurant serves Tuscan dishes. There is a lovely outdoor swimming pool.

🛏 21   💳 💳

GARDA   B5
Torri del Benaco
Gardesana $$ - $$$
piazza Calderini, 37010, Veneto
☎ 045 7225411
🖹 045 7225771
📧 gardesana@easynet.it
This 15th-century palace was transformed into a hotel 110 years ago, and immediately attracted a clientele from the world of art and culture. It is an elegant building offering recently refurbished rooms with 19th-century Venetian furniture. The lounges are delightful, and the restaurant is in a former council room. Summer meals are served on the romantic terrace overlooking the lake.

🛏 34   💳 💳 💳

GÉNOVA   B4
Stazzano

La Traversina $$
cascina Traversina 109, 15060, Piedmont
☎ 0143 61377
🖹 0143 61377
A pretty house covered with creepers and surrounded by a wonderful garden with more than 400 roses. It is on a farm that specializes in the cultivation of perennial herbaceous plants. Guests are welcomed like friends, and the attractive rooms recall the history and interests of the owning family. Other attractions are the indoor swimming pool and bocce (bowls).

🛏 3

GROSSETO   B3
Isola del Giglio
Pardini's Hermitage $ - $$
Cala degli Alberi, 58013, Tuscany
☎ 0564 809034
🖹 0564 809177
📧 hermit@ats.it
Wonderfully located villa reached by boat from Giglio Porto. (The alternative is an hour and a half walk.) A wide range of activities includes excursions by donkey, bocce (bowls), table tennis, archery, windsurfing, rowboats, motorboats, an astronomical observatory, gymnastics, and courses on watercolors and ceramics. Guests are asked to stay for at least two nights.

🛏 12   💳

GÚBBIO   C4
Gubbio

La Locanda del Gallo $
Santa Cristina, 06020, Umbria
☎ 075 9229912
🖹 075 9229912
📧 locanda.del.gallo@infoservice.it
This inn started as a noble residence and dates from the 17th century. It stands in a panoramic position surrounded by green hills dotted with stone farmhouses. Under the high-beamed ceilings, antique and Oriental furniture alternate, set against terra-cotta floors and pastel walls. The food includes vegetarian dishes and draws its inspiration from the tradition and products of the area.

🛏 10   💳

Oderisi e Balestrieri $
via Mazzatinti 2-12, 06024,
Umbria
☎ 075 9220662
🖹 075 9220663
This establishment consists of
two separate buildings with a
common reception area, set in
the medieval heart of town.
Recent refurbishment has
brightened the rooms with
graceful modernity. The
bedrooms are furnished in
various styles, all with restraint
and warm simplicity. Breakfast is
served in a delightful little room
which also is a bar.

🛏 35

Villa Montegranelli $$
Montelviano, 06024, Umbria
☎ 075 9220185
🖹 075 9273372
e montegra@tin.it
This beautiful villa dates back to
the 13th or 14th century, and
retains the atmosphere of the
past. The severe facade is
softened by an avenue of old
Cypress trees that leads up to the
entrance. The rooms have high
ceilings adorned with stucco,
antique furnishings and prints,
and marble pillars framing the
doors and walls. The spacious
bedrooms have a simple
elegance.

🛏 21

Pietralunga

La Cerqua $$
case San Salvatore 27, 06026,
Umbria
☎ 075 9460283
🖹 075 9460283
e lacerqua@krenet.it
In the 14th century this big
stone farmhouse was the
monastery of San Salvatore. It
stands on a hill in a panoramic
position and is part of an organic
farm business. Bedrooms are
large and stylishly furnished, and
reading, music and television
rooms are provided. Outside
there is a swimming pool,
playground, archery, bicycles and
a family restaurant serving
organic food.

🛏 8

IMPERIA A4
Laigueglia

Splendid $ - $$$
piazza Badaro 3, 17053, Liguria
☎ 0182 690325
🖹 0182 690894
e splendid@ags.sv.it
A former monastery, constructed
1300-1400 and retaining
charming original features. Some
of the bedrooms have terraces
overlooking the sea. Communal
rooms – the bar, sitting rooms,
restaurant and television lounge
with vaulted ceiling – are
reached by means of a lovely old
black and white tiled stairway.
There also is a garden,
swimming pool and private
beach.

🛏 48

ISERNIA C3
Venafro
**Dimora del Prete di
Bel Monte** $$
via Cristo 49, 86079, Molise
☎ 0865 900159
🖹 0865 900159
This old mansion, restructured
in 1860, stands in the heart of
Venafro's historic center. Beyond
the large and distinguished
entrance door are wide corridors,
columns and cross-vaulted
ceilings. Each of the four guest
bedrooms is different, but all
have period furniture. The
frescoed rooms, big terraces and
the garden recall memories and
traditions of times past.

🛏 4

Agnone

Antica Masseria Mastronardi dei Maranconi **$$$**
Maranconi, 86081, Molise
☎ 0865 770002
🖹 0865 770086
e maranconi@tin.it
After World War II emigration depopulated this area of the upper Molise. Today, brought to new life, these old stables have been transformed into a welcoming tavern, while the barns and part of the old farmhouse contain the bedrooms of this agritourism operation. The lovely facade has been preserved, as have the mostly stone-walled rooms and the vaulted or wooden ceilings.

 3

ISOLA DE PANTELLERIA C1

Isola di Pantelleria

Papuscia **$ - $$**
contrada Sopra Portella 28, Tracino, 91010, Sicily
☎ 0923 915463
🖹 0923 915463
This 18th-century building reflects typical island style interpreted from Arabian architecture and is just a few hundred yards from one of the most beautiful coves in Pantelleria. Bedrooms are simple and modern in design, located in the three low buildings that make up the hotel. They enclose a lovely courtyard where guests may have breakfast or rest after swimming in the sea.

🛏 11

ISOLA DI CAPRI C2

Capri

Villa Sarah **$$ - $$$**
via Tiberio 3/A, 80073, Campania
☎ 081 8377817
🖹 081 8377215
e info@villasarah.it
A little hotel surrounded by a large area cultivated with an orchard and vineyard. The building, in the style of Capri, has broad arches opening onto the garden. The bedrooms are simple with rustic furniture, and some have terraces with sea views. A copious breakfast is served in the garden or in guests' rooms on their private terraces.

🛏 20

ISOLE EOLIE D1

Isole Eolie

Locanda del Barbablù **$$ - $$$**
via Vittorio Emanuele 17-19, 98059 Stromboli, Sicily
☎ 090 986118
🖹 090 986323
This pretty inn offers six charming bedrooms on the top floor of what used to be a sailors' hostel. Some face the sea and the islet of Stombolicchio, and others overlook Stromboli's volcano. All of them have restored antique floors and period furniture. Food is skillfully prepared by the lady of the house, and in fine weather meals are served on the terrace.

🛏 6

Augustus **$ - $$$**
vico Ausonia 16, 98055 Lipari, Sicily
☎ 090 9811232
🖹 090 9812233
e villaaugustus@tin.it
This hotel is close to the sea, its privacy protected by a lovely enclosing wall. A big portal leads into a patio garden that looks almost Arabic, and a gazebo is used for bar service outside. Facing the garden is the entrance to the villa and its reception rooms, breakfast room and parlor. Little avenues and courtyards lead to the simply furnished bedrooms.

🛏 34

Key to Symbols: 🖹 Fax e Email 🛏 Rooms P Parking 🏊 Swimming
American Express Diners Club MasterCard Visa

IVRÉA A5

Chiaverano

Castella San Giuseppe **$$ - $$$**
Castello San Giuseppe, 10010,
Piedmont
☎ 0125 424370
🖷 0125 641278

High up on a hillside and
surrounded by parkland, this
17th-century building was
originally a monastery, then a
military fortress, and now a
romantic hotel with period-style
rooms. At the beginning of the
20th century notable artists and
writers congregated here. A
conference room is provided in
the former chapel, and the
restaurant is dedicated to the
wife of Napoleon Bonaparte.

 16

LA SPEZIA B4

Ameglia

**Locanda Delle
Tamerici** **$$ - $$$**
via Litoranea 106, Fiumoretta,
19031, Liguria
☎ 0187 64262
🖷 0187 64627

Converted farmhouse by the sea
with a private beach and bathing
facilities, where in summer there
is bar service and a restaurant.
Bedrooms are furnished with
charming old pieces and
coordinated fabrics. Outside
there is a garden with a pergola
for aperitifs, and breakfast as
soon as the weather permits.

 7

Arcola

Villa Ducci **$$**
via Nosedro 2, Monti, 19021,
Liguria
☎ 0187 982918
🖷 0187 982918
✉ villaducci@yahoo.it

The building is white, with gray
stone details, inspired by the
architecture of neighboring
Tuscany. The charming
bedrooms have frescoes on the
walls, light stuccowork in pastel
colors, and period furniture.
Communal rooms retain the
atmosphere of a large and well-
furnished family house. The big
garden is shaded and romantic.

 3

Levanto

Stella Maris **$$ - $$$**
via Marconi 4, 19015, Liguria
☎ 0187 808258
🖷 0187 807351
✉ renza@hotelstellamaris.it

The two women who inherited
this property were unable to
overcome their rivalry, and so it
was divided, with one part
forming this charming hotel.
A late 19th-century atmosphere
pervades throughout, and there
are ceiling frescoes, stuccowork
and antique furniture. The hotel
also has an annex with more
modern comforts just a stone's
throw from the sea.

 15

Pontremoli

Villa Emilia **$ - $$**
via Versola 4, Versola, 54027,
Tuscany
☎ 0187 836455
🖷 0187 836455
✉ info@villaemilia.com

Refined 1920s villa surrounded
by a large garden and located a
short distance from Pontremoli.
Refurbishment has brought out
many pretty details, and the
bedrooms have period and
period-style furniture. On the
ground floor there are sitting and
reading rooms and an attractive
kitchen. A minimum stay of two
nights is requested.

2

Key to Symbols: 🖷 Fax ✉ Email Rooms P Parking Swimming
American Express Diners Club MasterCard Visa

LAGONEGRO `D2`

Chiaromonte

Ricciardi Chiaromonte $
via Calvario 27, 85032,
Basilicata
☎ 0973 571031
🖹 0973 571031
The hotel is located high above sea level on a natural terrace that dominates the Sinni Valley. It is in the heart of Pollino National Park, an area of great natural beauty where wolves, otters, woodpeckers and wild boar live. The building is modern, linear and simply furnished. From the sunny terrace there is access to the large communal rooms.

🛏 36

Lagonegro

Midi Hotel $ - $$
viale Colombo 76, 85042,
Basilicata
☎ 0973 41188
🖹 0973 41186
Hotel located on the edge of Pollino National Park, at the foot of Sirono-Papa Massif and near the ski station of Laudemio. Guests are accommodated in a modern structure with a large hall on the ground floor, and there are rooms for meetings and banquets. A children's playground, illuminated tennis court and bocce (bowls) are available in the garden.

🛏 36 🔳 🄾 🔲

Maratea

Villa Cheta Elite $$
via Timpone 24, Acquafredda,
85041, Basilicata
☎ 0973 878134
🖹 0973 878135
Art Nouveau-style building overlooking a sheltered inlet, a few hundred yards from one of the Mediterranean's most charming beaches. The early 20th-century villa has an old rose-colored facade decorated with white floral designs and surrounded by a Mediterranean garden. Period furniture is a feature, and bedrooms have lovely views. In summer meals are served on the flower-filled terrace.

🛏 20 🔳 🄾 🔲

MACERTA `C4`

Treia

Il Vecchio Granaio $$
contrada Chiaravalle 49, 62010,
Marche
☎ 0733 8434488
🖹 0733 541312
The complex, surrounded by a large old park, arose out of the refurbishment of farmhouses, a granary, wine store, stables and other 18th-century farm outbuildings. These have lovely walls made from terra-cotta and river stone. The comfortable apartments offer large rooms with simple period furniture. There is a delightful veranda, and a restaurant in the 16th-century main house.

🛏 19
🔳 🄾 🔲

Macerta

Arena $
via Sferisterio 16, 62100,
Marche
☎ 0733 230931
🖹 0733 236059
The hotel, situated in the historic center of the city, offers attractive bedrooms, some recently refurbished. Nearly all have safes and air conditioning. The bathrooms are fairly practical, with hair dryers and towel heaters. Altogether this is a simple, friendly place where nothing is overlooked.

🛏 22
🔳 🄾 🔲

MANCIANO　　　　C3
Manciano

Da Caino　　　　$$$
via Chiesa 4, Poderi di
Montemerano, 58050, Tuscany
☎ 0564 602817
🖹 0564 602807
e caino@ftbcc.it
The attention to detail that has
made this hotel's food famous is
also found in the care given the accommodations. The bedrooms
are very pretty, warm and
welcoming, with antique
furniture, beamed ceilings and
light wooden floorboards. In the
restaurant there is clever contrast
between the rustic building and
the elegant crystal and
silverware.

🛏 3　　

Le Pisanelle　　　　$$
S.P. 32 al km 3,8, Le Pisanelle,
58014, Tuscany
☎ 0564 628286
🖹 0564 625840
e lepisanelle@
laltramaremma.it
This old farmhouse, dating from
1786, has been transformed into
an attractive and hospitable
residence. The comfortable bedrooms have 19th-century
furniture, and the communal
rooms have the warmth of a
private home with fires burning
in the hearths, books and corners
for reading. The garden is full of
ornamental plants and flowers,
fruit and olive trees, and vines.

🛏 5

MANTOVA　　　　B5
Pomponesco

Il Leone　　　　$$
piazza IV Martiri 2, 46030,
Lombardy
☎ 0375 86077/ 0375 86145
🖹 0375 86770
Lovely 16th-century building
situated close to the Po River
and historic Pomponesco. The
focus is the dining room, with its
wonderful paneled ceiling and
precious frescoes, where 19th- century recipes reproduce the
traditional cooking of the Po
region. The comfortable
bedrooms are both stylish and
practical. Outside there is a large
walled courtyard with herb
gardens and a swimming pool.

🛏 8

MARSALA　　　　C1
Marsala

Villa Favorita　　　　$$
via Favorita 27, 91025, Sicily
☎ 0923 989100
🖹 0923 980264
This old "baglio" building, where
wine was produced, dates from
the early 19th century and
immediately became a meeting
place for Sicilian intellectuals.
It has been restored, and some
bungalows have been created in a large park. The villa provides
communal rooms and an elegant
restaurant. A tennis court, soccer
field, children's playground and
swimming pool are available in
the garden.

🛏 29

MASSA　　　　B4
Montignoso

Eden　　　　$$ - $$$
via A. Gramsci 26, Cinquale,
54030, Tuscany
☎ 0585 807676
🖹 0585 807594
e eden@bicnet.it
Recently refurbished, modern
building surrounded by a large
garden under shady pine trees.
The hotel has spacious, well-
equipped bedrooms, many with terraces. Communal rooms are
light, with big windows opening
onto the surrounding greenery.
The hotel has a mini club for
children, candlelit evenings for
tasting local dishes, and bicycles
that may be rented by guests.

🛏 27

Key to Symbols: 🖹 Fax　e Email　🛏 Rooms　P Parking　🏊 Swimming
▆▆▆ American Express　◑ Diners Club　● MasterCard　▆▆▆ Visa

MATERA   D2
Matera

Del Campo   **$$ - $$$**
via Lucrezio, 75100, Basilicata
☎ 0835 388844
📄 0835 388757
📧 hdc@hsh.it

Modern-looking hotel created from an 18th-century residence that was owned by Senator Domenico Ridola, founder of the national museum bearing his name. It is located in the vicinity of the train station, not far from the town center. It has well-equipped bedrooms with avant-garde design and furnishings. Local and Mediterranean food is served in the restaurant overlooking the garden.

🛏 16
▨ ⓓ ▨

MELFI   D3
Rionero in Vulture

Villa Maria   **$**
Laghi di Monticchio, 85020, Basilicata
☎ 0972 731025
📄 0972 721355

The hotel has sloping roofs inspired by rustic architecture and practical for winter snow. It provides large communal rooms, a meeting room, two apartments and spacious bedrooms with modern furniture. There is a swimming pool for adults, another for children, and a tennis court in the surrounding park. Regional food is prepared from local produce.

🛏 31
▨ ⓓ ▨

MERANO-MERAN   B5
Lagundo

Der Punthof   **$$ - $$$**
via Steinach 25, 39022, Trentino-Alto Adige
☎ 0473 448553
📄 0473 449919

This farmstead dates back to medieval times, and the facade is still decorated with paintings. Inside there is a Tyrolean stube (stove room) and an elegant restaurant with antique furniture, parquet flooring, family photographs and hunting trophies. Bedrooms are spacious, and four apartments are available for family use. The garden has an open-air swimming pool, tennis court and sauna.

🛏 14   ▨ ⓓ ▨

Merano

Castel Fragsburg   **$$ - $$$**
via Fragsburg 3, Labers, 39012, Trentino-Alto Adige
☎ 0473 244071
📄 0473 244493
📧 info@fragsburg.com

This little chalet was built according to Tyrolean tradition with a steep roof and fretwork balconies. The bedrooms have wooden floors and furniture, and the style is similar in the dining room, the living room and the pretty stube (stove room). In front of the hotel is a lovely lawn with a swimming pool and terrace for sunbathing.

🛏 18

MILAN (MILANO)   B5
Besate

Cascina Caremma   **$**
via Cascina Caremma, 20080, Lombardy
☎ 02 9050020
📄 02 9050020
📧 caremma@demosdata.it

This very old farmhouse, with its rectangular courtyard, has been transformed into an agritourism guest house. The farm is run on modern organic principles, ideal for those interested in environmental issues. The spacious rooms are rustic in style and give the impression of being full of human warmth. All the rooms have air conditioning.

🛏 10

Key to Symbols: 📄 Fax   📧 Email   🛏 Rooms   🅿 Parking   🏊 Swimming
▨ American Express   ⓓ Diners Club   ▨ MasterCard   ▨ Visa

MODENA B4

Zocca

Cà Monduzzi Zocca $ - $$
via Vignolese 1130 D, 41100,
Emilia-Romagna
☎ 059 986206
This 17th-century farmhouse
was completely restructured in
1990 to create three one-
bedroom and four two-bedroom
apartments in an attractive rustic
style. Views from the hillside
location are over the upper valley
of the Panaro River, with oak
trees and chestnuts as far as the
eye can see. It is open July-
August, and weekends only the
rest of the year.

 7

MOLVENO B5

Andalo

Serena $
via Crosare 15, 38010,
Trentino-Alto Adige
☎ 0461 585727
🖷 0461 585702
📧 hotel.serena@interline.it
Modern building in a traditional
style, close to ski lifts and the
center of Andalo. It offers rustic
bedrooms with practical
bathrooms, airy lounges and a
dining room heated by a large
majolica stove. There is a
spacious children's play area with
lots of games, and the garden
and solarium terrace complete
the picture.

 39
⬛ 🔵 ⬛

MONFALCONE C5

Aquileia

Patriarchi $ - $$
via Giulia Augusta 12, 33051,
Friuli-Venezia Giulia
☎ 0431 919595
🖷 0431 919596
📧 patriarchi@hotelpatriarchi.it
This hotel is very close to
Aquileia's famous basilica, and
has large bedrooms with modern
furniture, air conditioning,
television and minibar. Wood
paneling gives the communal
rooms a welcoming but simple
appearance, and the restaurant
serves fine food. Guests are
provided with a large umbrella to
take to the beach.

⬛ 23
⬛ 🔵 ⬛

Milan, La Scala

Key to Symbols: 🖷 Fax 📧 Email ⬛ Rooms 🅿 Parking 🏊 Swimming
⬛ American Express 🔵 Diners Club 🔴 MasterCard ⬛ Visa

MONÓPOLI   E3

Alberobello

Abbondanza $$
contrada Lama Colonna 5,
70011, Apulia
☎ 080 4325762
🖹 080 4325762
📧 abbond@tin.it

This property, part of a farm business, is situated in the heart of the Barsento reserve, high above sea level and the valley below. A recently built addition enlarges the round stone "trulli" buildings that date back to the 17th century. The interior is rustic, with exposed stone walls and simple wooden furniture. Guests are served local dishes and wines.

🛏 3

Castellana Grotte

Relais Le Jardin $$
contrada Scamardella 59, 70013,
Apulia
☎ 080 4966300
🖹 080 4865520
📧 lejardin@mail.media.it

Romantic building in the Mediterranean style, standing in open countryside surrounded by a garden. The light, bright bedrooms are furnished in rustic fashion and open onto flower-filled terraces. Communal rooms are equally welcoming. The restaurant is in a glazed veranda, and in summer meals are served outside under the gazebos. Food is carefully prepared and presented.

🛏 10   ▦ ⓪ ▦

Fasano

Masseria Salamina $$
Pezze di Greco, 72010, Apulia
☎ 080 4897307
🖹 080 4898582

This fortified farmhouse, the nucleus of which dates from the 17th century, was an Allied headquarters during World War II. Nowadays there are seven guest rooms and eight apartments with spacious rooms. Another beautifully proportioned room houses the restaurant. Features include a garden with bocce (bowls), a children's playground, archery and bicycles for rent.

🛏 7   ▦

NAPLES (NAPOLI)   C3

Napoli

Villa Medici $$
via Nuova Bagnoli 550, 80124,
Campania
☎ 081 7623949/ 081 7623040
🖹 081 7623949/ 081 7623040
📧 info@sea-hotels.com

Early 20th-century villa in the Fuorigrotta district, offering hotel accommodations or residence in apartments for a minimum period of a week. The bedrooms have practical furniture, and all the apartments have kitchen areas. Guests can be served meals ordered in a nearby trattoria. There is a delightful garden and an open-air swimming pool with hydromassage.

🛏 15   ▦ ⓪ ▦

NUORO   B2

Dorgali

Il Querceto $ - $$
via Lamarmora 4, 08022,
Sardinia
☎ 0784 96509
🖹 0784 95254

This hotel is set in a park of oak trees, the peaceful green contrasting with the bright sea. The large bedrooms are simply furnished in rustic style, and there are sculptures by Pisano in some of the communal rooms. Dishes with authentic regional flavors are offered in the restaurant. Outside there is a tennis court, children's playground and a patio.

🛏 22
▦ ⓪ ▦

Dorgali

L'Oasi   **$ - $$**
via Garcia Lorca 13, Cala
Gonone, 08020, Sardinia
☎ 0784 93111
🖹 0784 93444
The hotel stands in the middle
of a Mediterranean garden
overlooking one of the most
beautiful gulfs in Sardinia. The
bedrooms are arranged in separate buildings, and all of
them have balconies and simple,
modern furnishings. There also
are five one-room apartments
accommodating two people
each. Bicycle rental, tennis courts
and rock climbing are all
available in the vicinity.

 30

Monteviore   **$ - $$**
Monteviore, 08022, Sardinia
☎ 0784 96293
🖹 0784 96293
This hotel has been created from
an old farmhouse situated in a
cultivated basin dominated by
the Supramonte Massif, within
Gennargentu Park. The building
extends onto a panoramic terrace
that is, in turn, enclosed by a shady patio. Bedrooms are
simple and bright, some of them
split-level, and there are two
bungalows suitable for families
or groups of friends.

 20

Oliena

Cikappa   **$$ - $$$**
corso M.L. King 2/4, 08025,
Sardinia
☎ 0784 288024/ 0784 288733
Cikappa (CK) is the name of the
hotel in which the "C" stands for
Cenceddu and the "K" for
Killeddu – the nicknames of the
two proprietors. It is a small pink
building with lots of arches
adding interest to the facade. The bedrooms are attractive and
comfortable. Homey food is
served in the restaurant, and
there also is a renowned pizzeria.

 7

OLBIA   B3
Arzachena

Cà la Somara   **$ - $$**
Sarra Balestra, 07021, Sardinia
☎ 0789 98969
🖹 0789 98969
This organic agritourism
business breeds endangered
Sardinian donkeys. Guest
accommodations are provided in
carefully converted stables with
rustic furniture, all strictly non-
smoking. Guests may use the communal kitchen to cook
meals, or else may sample the
vegetarian dishes offered.
Bicycles are available. The farm
also is the center of an
organization running energy-
giving and relaxation courses.

 9

Le Querce   **$ - $$**
via Vaddi di latta, Baia Sardinia,
07020, Sardinia
☎ 0789 99248
🖹 0789 99248
📧 lequerce@esweb.it
A group of "stazzi" (shepherds'
houses) on the slopes of Mount
Moro have been transformed
into apartments, each with its
own private garden. The rooms are cleverly rustic in style, and
the bathrooms are decorated
with antique majolica tiles.
Facilities are available for
massage, aromatherapy, yoga,
stretching and postural
relaxation.

 5

Key to Symbols: 🖹 Fax 📧 Email 🛏 Rooms 🅿 Parking ≋ Swimming
▦ American Express ⑩ Diners Club ● MasterCard ▥ Visa

Golfo Aranci

Margherita   **$$ - $$$**
via Libertà 91, 07020, Sardinia
☎ 0789 46906
🖹 0789 46851
📧 hotelmargherita@tiscalinet.it
A modern building in the center
of the village but close to the sea.
The reception hall also serves as
a sitting room, with a large
veranda overlooking the garden
and the swimming pool with its
hydromassage and solarium.
The comfortable bedrooms are
classically furnished and face
the sea or pool. The carefully
prepared breakfast is served
as a buffet.

🛏 26

ORISTANO   **A2**
Arbus

Le Dune   **$$ - $$$**
via Bau 1, Piscina di Ingurtosu,
09030, Sardinia
☎ 070 977130
🖹 070 977230
This hotel is a piece of industrial
reclamation, created from an old
storehouse for mineral materials,
and the complex has been
declared a national monument
for its historical interest and
artistic value. It is set against a
dramatic landscape of sand
dunes. Three buildings are linked
by an internal courtyard and a
small square opening onto the
sea.

🛏 25

ORVIETO   **C3**
Bolsena

La Riserva Montebello   **$ - $$**
Montebello, 01023, Lazio
☎ 0761 798965
🖹 0761 799492
Accommodation is provided in
the old farmhouses of a farm
business in a panoramic location.
The refurbished buildings offer
pretty bedrooms furnished with
antique farm and wicker
furniture. A number of sporting
and cultural opportunities are
available, including swimming
and archery courses, sailing on
the nearby lake, mountain biking
and horseback riding.

🛏 12

Orvieto
Valentino   **$$**
via Angelo da Orvieto 30,
05018, Umbria
☎ 0763 342464
🖹 0763 342464
This Renaissance palace is a few
steps from the Duomo
(cathedral) on a medieval street.
The bedrooms vary in size and
shape, following the lines of the
old building. All of them have
parquet flooring and pleasant
modern furniture. Communal
rooms are small but full of
character, and marble
predominates in the reception
hall. A buffet breakfast is served.

🛏 19

San Casciano dei Bagni
7 Querce   **$$ - $$$**
viale Manciati 215, 53040,
Tuscany
☎ 0578 58174
🖹 0578 58172
📧 settequerce@krenet.it
This hotel stands right at the
entrance to the village amid
ancient oak woods. Originally an
inn, it has been restored to
provide modern comforts while
retaining its original character.
Bedrooms are well equipped, and
the bathrooms modern and
practical. Furnishings are in the
Tuscan tradition, with canopied
beds and bright upholstery set
against stone walls, vaulted
ceilings and large fireplaces.

🛏 9

Key to Symbols: 🖹 Fax   📧 Email   🛏 Rooms   🅿 Parking   🏊 Swimming
American Express   Diners Club   MasterCard   Visa

La Torre $$
piazza Capitello 27, 35038,
Veneto
☎ 049 9930111
🖹 049 9930033

Since 1993 this hotel, which dates from the late 19th century, has been protected as a building of cultural and historical interest, and it was recently carefully restored. The bedrooms have elegant period furnishings, and the communal rooms are attractive and welcoming. Regional cooking is served in three little dining rooms; the wine cellar has over 200 labels.

 13

Il Poggio degli Olivi $$
frazione Passaggio di Bettona,
Montebalacca, 06084, Umbria
☎ 075 9869023
🖹 075 9869023
🄴 poggiodeglioli@edisons.it

Elegant rural complex, dating from the 17th century, surrounded by olive trees and vines. The bedrooms are warm and comfortable, furnished in the mountain style, with balconies and big windows. A lovely fireplace warms the communal rooms, and the restaurant overlooks the Umbrian valley. In the garden there is a tennis court and swimming pool.

6

Il Poggio dei Pettirossi $$
vocabolo Pilone 301, 06031,
Umbria
☎ 0742 361744
🖹 0742 360379
🄴 albergo@
ilpoggiodeipettirossi.com

This complex is made up of restored old buildings and new ones built along traditional lines. It has well-tended fields, gravel paths, a lovely swimming pool and a summerhouse. The comfortable bedrooms combine rustic furnishings with practical modern touches, and the suites on two levels have little cooking areas. The restaurant serves authentic dishes incorporating produce from the farm.

 24

Locanda Enoteca Piazza Onofri $$
piazza onofri 2, 06031, Umbria
☎ 0742 321290
🖹 0742 321290

Located in an austere stone palace, this *enoteca-locanda* (wine shop/ inn) is inspired by the warm hospitality of Italian taverns. It has a big fireplace, lovely brick vaults and simple rustic furnishings, and the canteen offers a list of 400 wines. The simply furnished little apartments have thick walls, beamed ceilings and arches framing the windows.

13

La Mondorla $$
via Venturi, San Mariano,
06073, Umbria
☎ 075 5140643
🖹 075 5140643

This lovely gray stone building dominates a hill and looks down on the Umbrian valley. The garden enclosing the house includes a big swimming pool surrounded by luxuriant greenery, from which the peace of the neighborhood can be enjoyed. The interior is typically rustic in character, with mini-apartments arranged in a number of buildings. Bedrooms are large, welcoming and comfortable.

8

Passignano sul
Trasimeno

Perugia

Il Covone **$ - $$**
strada Fratticiola 2, Ponte
Pattoli, 06085, Umbria
☎ 075 694140
🖷 075 694503
e covone@mercurio.it
Villa dating back to medieval
times with a watchtower at its
center, set in a big park sloping
down to the Tevere river. Large

Spello

Torgiano

I Mori Gelsi **$ - $$$**
via Entrata 37, 06089, Umbria
☎ 075 982192
🖷 075 982192
e fspinola@host.dex.net.com
This group of old farm buildings
is located in the center of a
quality wine-producing farm in
the Tevere Valley. The main
farmhouse and an annex have

PÉSARO   **C4**
Pesaro

Poggio del Belveduto **$$**
via San Donato 65, 06065,
Umbria
☎ 075 829076
🖷 075 8478014
This agritourism establishment
is situated in peaceful
countryside overlooking Lake
Trasimeno and offers facilities for
horseback riding enthusiasts.
Various apartments are available,

communal rooms have interior
loggias and balconies that look
onto the salon. Period
furnishings and big fireplaces
give them a particular character.
Bedrooms are located in a nearby
farmhouse. A minimum stay of
two days is requested.

Le due Torri **$$**
via Torre Quadrano 1, Limiti di
Spello, 06038 Spello, Umbria
☎ 0742 651249
🖷 0742 352933
Two stone farmhouses provide
hospitality in this agritourism
establishment. Skillful
restoration has retained the
wooden beams, paneled ceilings
and floors of brick and

been transformed into two
apartments accommodating
between six and eight people.
They are surrounded by a garden
with a swimming pool and fruit
trees. A big organic vegetable
plot is free for guests' use.

Villa Torraccia **$$**
strada Torraccia 3, 61100,
Marche
☎ 0721 21852
🖷 0721 21852
This 15th-century villa was
constructed around a 13th-
century watchtower. All
restoration work since has been
committed to the faithful
preservation of the architectural

---

pleasantly furnished in rustic
style. Other activities include
swimming, archery, practice golf,
beach volleyball and mountain
bike rentals. There are many
suggested tours to satisfy those
interested in sport, art and
gastronomy.

🛏 14 ▪▪▪

🛏 10 ▪▪▪ ⓪ ▪▪▪

limestone. Accommodations are
in two-room apartments and
bedrooms, carefully furnished
with late 17th- and 19th-century
furniture. A rustic restaurant is
reserved for guests, and outside
there is a lovely swimming pool
and a children's playground.

🛏 4
⓪ ▪▪▪

🛏 3

features. The villa's *frontale*
(front) has a monumental
entrance, and the interior is
charming, with attractive rooms
and suites. Each room is unique,
a little haven with antique
furniture and terra-cotta
flooring.

🛏 5
▪▪▪ ▪▪▪

San Lorenzo in Campo

Giardino $$
via Mattei 4, 61047, Marche
☎ 0721 776803
🖹 0721 735323
📧 massimo@netforce.it

This modern family-run hotel offers beautifully furnished accommodations with lovely views of the surrounding hills. Facilities include a large bar, a good restaurant and a delightful swimming pool (open in summer only) in the little garden. Of particular note is the cooking: the carefully prepared dishes are served on elegantly laid tables. An ample wine cellar completes the picture.

 20

Serrungarina

Casa Oliva $
via Castello 19, 61030, Marche
☎ 0721 891500
🖹 0721 891500

The windows of this noble old palace overlook the square of the medieval village and on out to the hills and sea. Bedrooms, divided between the main building and outbuildings, offer modern equipment, terra-cotta floors, "tassello" furniture, and communal areas are elegantly furnished. The restaurant, serving regional specialties, is located in another of the village houses.

16

PESCARA C3
Pianella

Le Georgiche Country House $$
contrada Santa Maria, 65019, Abruzzo
☎ 085 412500
🖹 085 299216
📧 tcolavi@tin.it

An old mill, dating from the 19th century, completely restructured to form the center of a farm business. The bedrooms and suites are prettily furnished with period pieces. Fireplaces warm the communal areas, and guests meet around rustic tables for breakfast and other meals. Recreational facilities include tennis, bocce (bowls) and swimming. There also is a health farm, herbalist and cookery courses.

1

PIAZZA ARMERINA D1
San Michele di Ganzaria

Pomara $$
via Vittorio Veneto 84, 95040, Sicily
☎ 0933 978143
🖹 0933 977090

This is a newer building with modern architecture in a panoramic location. Bedrooms are of a comfortable size and the contemporary furniture is made of warm, cherry-colored wood. Sitting rooms also are bright and attractive in a similarly modern style. The restaurant, a short distance away, is well known in the area for its good food.

39

PISA B4
Palaia

La Cerbana $$
via delle Colline per Legoli 35, 56036, Tuscany
☎ 0587 632058
🖹 0587 632058

Agritourism accommodations are provided here, in estate houses dating back to the early years of the 20th century. Guests have use of a large swimming pool and a rustic restaurant serving wholesome food. Hunting also is permitted, following the rules of the reserve, which breeds deer, pheasants, hares, wild boars, mountain sheep and aquatic fauna.

12

Key to Symbols: 🖹 Fax 📧 Email 🛏 Rooms 🅿 Parking 🏊 Swimming
American Express 🔟 Diners Club 💳 MasterCard 💳 Visa

San Giuliano Terme

Villa Anna Maria $$
S.S. 12 dell'Abetone, Molina di Quosa 146, 56010, Tuscany
☎ 050 850139
🗎 050 850139

An 18th-century country villa on three floors, surrounded by a botanical park. The frescos adorning the interior have been restored, and the rooms are furnished with antiques.

Accommodation is provided in well-equipped bedrooms and suites, and there are three two-roomed apartments with washing machines, dishwashers and refrigerators. A swimming pool is being built and bicycles are available for rent.

🛏 5

POMPEII   D2
Pompeii

Forum $$
via Roma 99, 80045, Campania
☎ 081 8501170
🗎 081 8506132

This hotel is in the nerve center of the city, but in a peaceful bend sheltered from intense traffic. The building is recent, providing large well-equipped bedrooms with modern furniture. Public rooms include a small sitting room incorporating the reception area. The dining room looks onto the garden and terrace, and there is a roof garden equipped with a solarium.

🛏 24
🔲 ⓓ 💳

PORDENONE   C5
Fiume Veneto

L'ultimo Mulino $$
Molino 45, Bannia, 33080, Friuli-Venezia Giulia
☎ 0434 957911
🗎 0434 958483
🅔 filonder@tin.it

This working 17th-century mill – one of the last in the Friuli region – is situated by the clear waters of the Sile River in a large park with a private lake. Eight bedrooms have been constructed inside, welcoming guests into a romantic atmosphere with paneled ceilings and period furniture. Other facilities include a bar, sitting room and restaurant.

🛏 8   🔲 ⓓ 💳

Motta di Livenza

La Casa Di Bacco $ - $$
via Callalta 52, 31045, Veneto
☎ 0422 768488
🗎 0422 765091
🅔 contact@casadibacco.it

A very pretty early 19th-century farmhouse, carefully restored to offer air-conditioned accommodations. The communal rooms, which include a wine-tasting cellar, library and bar, have a welcoming atmosphere with lots of wood decoration, stone floors, open fires and shining copper pans. Outside there is a play area for children and bicycles for rent.

🛏 11   💳

POTENZA   D2
Terranova di Pollino

Picchio Nero $$
85030, Basilicata
☎ 0973 93170/ 0973 93181
🗎 0973 93170/ 0973 93181

A modern building inspired by traditional mountain architecture, with a rustic style and wooden furniture in the bedrooms. The lounges combine traditional and functional modern furnishings, and the restaurant has all the warmth of a kitchen offering authentic local dishes. There is a little garden for guests' use.

🛏 23
🔲 ⓓ 💳

RAGUSA D1
Ragusa

Eremo dell Giubiliana **$$ - $$$**
97100, Sicily
☎ 0932 669119
🖹 0932 669119

In the 1400s this building was a hermitage and religious house, then became a fortified building in the 18th century – the property of a noble Sicilian family. Descendants of that family have converted it to provide charming accommodations and a restaurant also open to non-guests. Special features include shuttle service to the beach and a nearby airport and riding school. Archery is offered.

🛏 9 ▦ ⑩ ▦

Santa Croce Camerina

Capo Scalambri **$**
via Cagliari 42, Punta Secca, 97010, Sicily
☎ 0932 239938
🖹 0932 915600

The buildings of this agriturismo establishment stand practically on the sea at Punta Secca. They are white, modern and small, surrounded by a green pine wood separating them from the very long, almost empty golden beach. Accommodations are in small stone houses and apartments, and a few pre-fabricated bungalows. Leisure facilities for guests include bocce (bowls), soccer and a children's playground.

🛏 7

RAVELLO D2
Ravello

Villa San Michele **$$**
via Carusiello 2, Castiglione, 84010, Campania
☎ 089 872237
🖹 089 872237
🄴 smichele@starnet.it

A typical Mediterranean-style villa constructed on the edge of cliffs with a sheer drop to the sea. Each bedroom is different, but all have sea views, including some with a little terrace. There is a pretty restaurant, but breakfast also may be eaten on the terrace. A large garden slopes down to the sea, and a jetty has been dug out between the rocks.

🛏 12 ▦ ⑩ ▦

RAVENNA C4
Ravenna

Cappello **$$ - $$$**
via IV Novembre 41, 48100, Emilia-Romagna
☎ 0544 219813
🖹 0544 219814

A 16th-century mansion set in a pedestrian zone in the historic center of Ravenna. The beautiful bedrooms feature paneled ceilings, papered walls, parquet flooring, period furniture and sumptuous marble bathrooms. A gallery often displays paintings or modern sculpture. The cozy restaurant is open to non-guests.

🛏 9
▦ ⑩ ▦

REGGIO NELL'EMILI B4
Quattro Castella

Casa Matilde **$$$**
via Ada Negri 11, Puianello, 42030, Emilia-Romagna
☎ 0522 889006
🖹 0522 889006

This graceful villa is set amid a beautiful park. Solemn sitting rooms are softened by flower arrangements, cretonne curtains and large fireplaces. The big bedrooms have warm parquet flooring, antique furnishings and high beds made of brass or wrought iron. Local dishes are the inspiration for the cooking, and for relaxation there is the garden lounge and large terrace.

🛏 4 ▦ ⑩ ▦

Key to Symbols: 🖹 Fax 🄴 Email 🛏 Rooms 🅿 Parking ≋ Swimming
▦ American Express ⑩ Diners Club ▦ MasterCard ▦ Visa

RIETI   C3

Fara in Sabina

RIMINI   C4

Gatteo a Mare

Imperiale   **$ - $$**
viale G. Cesare 82, 47043,
Emilia-Romagna
☎ 0547 86875
🖹 0547 86875
📧 hotelimperiale@icot.it
Pink-painted building with
Oriental-style details facing the
sea. Graceful restructuring has

Poggio Berni

I Tre Re   **$$**
via F.lli Cervi 1, 47824,
Emilia-Romagna
☎ 0541 629760
🖹 0541 629368
This hotel, parts of which date
from the 14th century, stands in
a rural area less than half a mile
from the sea. The rustic stone
building retains many original

ROME (ROMA)   C3

Rome

Ille Roif   **$$**
Coltodino, 02030, Lazio
☎ 0765 386749/ 0765 386783
🖹 0765 386783
The Fiorelli family is responsible
for this charming establishment
(read the name backwards to
reveal the mystery). Each of the
rooms has its own personality,
and all are furnished creatively
with unerring taste. The sinks

transformed it into a bright
hotel. The bedrooms all have a
terrace and simple but attractive
furnishings. Communal rooms
retain some Art Nouveau-style
details. Bicycles are available to
guests, together with a children's
game room, a garage and an
American bar.

🛏 37   ▨ ▨ ▨

features, such as wooden beams
and fireplaces. There is a
restaurant with summer service
on the patio under a big canopy,
and a wine canteen with old oak
casks and selected wines.

🛏 13
▨ ▨ ▨

Augustea   **$$**
via Nazionale 251, 00184, Lazio
☎ 06 4883589
🖹 06 4814872
Noise from the via Nazionale rail
station does not disturb the quiet
of this little hotel, which is
located on the second and third
floors of a late 19th-century
palace. It has recently been
attractively refurbished, with

Casa in Trastevere   **$$$**
via della Penitenza 19, 00165,
Lazio
☎ 0335 6205768
🖹 06 69924722
This is a convenient first-floor
apartment in the Trastavere
quarter, carefully restored to
retain original features, such as
vaulted ceilings and octagonal-
tiled floors in red and gray

---

are hand-made and beautifully
sculpted. The bedrooms are
large, and those on the ground
floor are partially made from
rock to add to the fantasy.

🛏 12
▨ ▨ ▨

stylish furniture in pastel colors
in the large bedrooms. The
communal rooms are simple but
not without adornment.

🛏 20
▨ ▨ ▨

marble. It provides bed-and-
breakfast accommodations for up
to six people and has a living
room with a kitchen area, two
bedrooms and two bathrooms.
A minimum stay of three nights
is requested.

🛏 3

Key to Symbols: 🖹 Fax   📧 Email   🛏 Rooms   🅿 Parking   🏊 Swimming
▨ American Express   ▨ Diners Club   ▨ MasterCard   ▨ Visa

Domus Aventina $$$
via di Santa Prisca 11/B, 00153, Lazio
☎ 06 5746135
🖹 06 57300044
📧 domus.aventina@flashnet.it
This hotel has an 18th-century facade and a lovely terrace with a view over the center of ancient Rome. It offers spacious and tastefully furnished bedrooms, many with balconies from which to enjoy the lovely view. Modern equipment includes minibars, satellite television and pc access. The communal areas are agreeably furnished and embellished with *trompe l'oeil*.

🛏 26
▬ ⓓ 💳

Gregoriana $$$
via Gregoriana 18, 00187 Roma, Lazio
☎ 06 6794269
🖹 06 6784258
The hotel stands on the site of an old religious house, and is small but notably quiet despite its central location. The bedrooms are furnished in a simple but elegant style. In summer breakfast is served on the lovely terrace, but at other times it is brought to guests' bedrooms.

🛏 19

Montreal $$$
via Carlo Alberto 4, 00185, Lazio
☎ 06 4457797/ 06 4460514/ 06 4464701
🖹 06 4465522
📧 info@hotelmontrealroma.com
This attractive hotel is located in an elegant mansion, dating from the beginning of the 19th century, which also contains some private homes. The reception hall is small but recently refurbished, and the communal rooms are simply presented. Bedroom are stylishly furnished and decorated in cheerful pastel colors. The practical bathrooms are equipped with showers, and five have baths.

🛏 22 ▬ ⓓ 💳

Parlamento $$
via delle Convertite 5, 00187, Lazio
☎ 06 69921000
🖹 06 69921000
This hotel is situated on the third and fourth floors of a lovely 17th-century mansion. The furniture is stylish, and the entrance is embellished with an airy *trompe l'oeil* reproducing the roofs and domes of Rome. Bedrooms are practical and well equipped, and breakfast is served on the delightful terrace. It is in a restricted-traffic zone, but convenient parking is provided a few yards away.

🛏 23
▬ ⓓ 💳

Villa Borghese $$$
via Pinciana 31, 00198, Lazio
☎ 06 8549648
🖹 06 8414100
📧 hotel.villaborghese@quipo.it
A pretty little villa, the former home of Alberto Moravia, this property is a few steps from the Villa Borghese art galley. The communal rooms retain many features in the Art Nouveau style, and the large bedrooms are tastefully furnished and well equipped. There is a pleasant garden, with bar and breakfast service under the pergola. A small meeting room and a convenient garage are available.

🛏 31 ▬ ⓓ 💳

Key to Symbols: 🖹 Fax 📧 Email 🛏 Rooms 🅿 Parking 🏊 Swimming
▬ American Express ⓓ Diners Club 💳 MasterCard 💳 Visa

Cozzo di Simari $ - $$
via Cozzo di Simari 8, contrada
Crocicchia, 87068, Calabria
☎ 0983 520896
🖹 0983 520896
📧 sere_flower@hotmail.com
Old whitewashed house with
flower-filled terraces, located on
a hillside with the perfect blue
sea on the horizon. It offers large
bedrooms furnished with period pieces. The owner is a
Commandeur des Cordons-
Bleus and personally oversees the
cooking. Cookery courses are
offered, and other amenities
include an open-air swimming
pool, small gym, sauna and table
tennis.

🛏 12

**Masseria Torre di
Albidona** $ - $$
contrada Piana della Torre,
87075, Calabria
☎ 0981 507944
🖹 0981 507944
This farmstead stands high on a
little plateau with wonderful
views over the Gulf of Sibari.
Old stone-built farm workers'
houses have been transformed into separate apartments
accommodating from two to
eight people. Breakfast and
dinner prepared from farm
produce is served at a communal
table. There also is a restaurant
serving local dishes, a swimming
pool, tennis and beach access.

🛏 10

La Favorita $
strada San Pietro 1, 18030,
Liguria
☎ 0184 208186
🖹 0184 208247
La Favorita was built in 1972 in
the rustic style with a sloping
tiled roof. Accommodations are
in simple bedrooms that are neat and restful. On the ground floor
is the restaurant, where delicious
local and regional cooking is
served. At the heart of the room
is the large grill that heats the
interior and tempts the appetites
of diners.

🛏 7

Hieracon $ - $$
corso Cavour 62, 09014,
Sardinia
☎ 0781 854028
🖹 0781 854893
This little mansion is surrounded
by a large garden, where guests
can relax and cool off at the end
of a long day by the sea. The
large, light-filled bedrooms are
furnished with antiques and retain their graceful Art
Nouveau style. There also are
attractive one- and two-room
apartments. An interesting menu
in the restaurant offers local,
Arabic and Ligurian food.

🛏 16

Paola $ - $$
Tacca Rossa, 09014, Sardinia
☎ 0781 850098
🖹 0781 850104
This hotel is situated on the little
island of San Pietro, off the
southwest coast of Sardinia.
Bedrooms are divided between
the main building and an annex
in the Mediterranean garden.
The furnishings are simple but full of character, and there is a
lovely lounge arranged around a
big fireplace. The restaurant
serves local dishes on a terrace
overlooking the sea.

🛏 24

Sant'Antioco

Moderno $ - $$
via Nazionale 82, 09017,
Sardinia
☎ 0781 83105
🖺 0781 840252
🅔 albergomoderno@yahoo.it
This small hotel has been taken
over by the second generation of
the Pinna family, who opened it
in 1955. It has recently been
refurbished, and the bright
bedrooms are decorated in pale
colors with great simplicity and
elegant details. The restaurant is
open only from June to
September and serves delicious
seafood on a comfortable
terrace/garden.

🛏 10

SAVONA A4
Finale Ligure

Arabesque $$ - $$$
piazza Cappello da Prete,
Varigotti, 17024, Liguria
☎ 019 698262, 019 698263
This typical little village of
sailors' houses on the beach is
quite Oriental in style. The hotel
has shaded patios, courtyards
with luxuriant palm trees, rooms
where archways are ornately
curved, and arabesque shapes
decorating the pale blue and
white bedrooms. In the bright
and relaxing communal rooms
the furniture is wicker and
bamboo.

🛏 32

SIENA B4
Buonconvento

La Ripolina $ - $$
Pieve di Piana, 53022, Tuscany
☎ 0577 282280
🖺 0577 282280
Accommodations at this
agritourism complex are
provided in a 19th-century
parish church or in 16th- and
19th-century Tuscan farmsteads,
and comprise bedrooms and
apartments sleeping four to 10
people. The buildings are of
warm-colored stone and have
beamed ceilings and period
furniture. Laundry facilities, a
barbecue, children's playground,
bicycles, table tennis and two
artificial lakes for fishing are
available.

🛏 6

Castellina in Chianti

Belvedere de San Leonino $$
San Leonino, 53011, Tuscany
☎ 0577 740887
🖺 0577 740924
🅔 info@hotelsanleonino.com
The hotel buildings date back to
the 15th century and have
maintained their character and
original atmosphere. Communal
areas are attractive and
welcoming, and the large
bedrooms have terra-cotta floors,
beamed ceilings and period
furniture. The complex is
surrounded by a lovely garden,
and there are panoramic views
from the open-air swimming
pool.

🛏 28

Salivolpi $$
via Fiorentina 89, 53011,
Tuscany
☎ 0577 740484
🖺 0577 740998
🅔 info@hotelsalivolpi.com
This old country house has been
sympathetically converted to
retain its original character. It is
situated on a hill with views over
the Elsa Valley and the towers of
San Gimignano. The bedrooms
are furnished in period style,
with wrought iron and wooden
beds, and the lounges are large
and welcoming. Outside there
are pleasant terraces and a large
swimming pool.

🛏 19

Castiglione d'Orcia

Casa Ranieri $ - $$
podere la Martina, Campiglia
d'Orcia, 53020, Tuscany
☎ 0577 872639
▤ 0577 872639
✉ naranier@tin.it
Old farm holding converted to
provide agriturismo accommodations in three rustic buildings.
During their stay, guests may take
part in activities at the riding
school, including excursions on
horseback with expert guides.
Courses are offered on horse
behavior, the environment, bridge,
ceramics, gardening, cooking and
fungi. There also is a swimming
pool, bocce (bowls), table tennis
and a children's playground.

🛏 7

Colle di Val d'Elsa

La Vecchia Cartiera $$
via Oberdan 5/7/9, 53034,
Tuscany
☎ 0577 921107
▤ 0577 923688
✉ cartiera@chiantiturismo.it
This hotel is in an 18th-century
building that used to be a paper
mill. With complete restoration,
attractive modern extensions
have been added to the original
structure. Several bedrooms have
been created, all with modern
furnishings. Communal rooms
retain their original proportions
and also have contemporary
appointments. Conference
facilities are available, as well as a
garage.

🛏 38

Relais della Rovere $$$
La Badia, 53034, Tuscany
☎ 0577 924696
▤ 0577 924489
✉ dellarovere@chaintiturismo.it
This 16th-century building
started out as an abbey, became
the home of Cardinal Giuliano
della Rovere, and then
functioned as an inn. Noble in
appearance, it has many graceful
details, including molded stone
and bricks shaped into vaults.
Bedrooms are rich in atmosphere
and furnished in period style.
The restaurant serves dishes
based on local ingredients along
with quality Tuscan wines.

🛏 30

Monteriggioni

Castel Bigozzi $$
Bigozzi - Strove, 53035, Tuscany
☎ 0577 300000
▤ 0577 300001
The Bigozzi Castle is a medieval
fortress that after skillful
restoration has been transformed
into a hotel. There are various
apartments accommodating
between two and four people,
well furnished and equipped
with the most modern comforts.
In addition, there is a swimming
pool and a solarium in the
garden. The hotel has a elevator,
and a meeting room for around
50 people.

🛏 16

Monteroni d'Arbia

Tenuta della Selva $ - $$
La selva 34, Ville di Corsano,
53010, Tuscany
☎ 0577 377063
▤ 0577 377063
✉ fabioin@tin.it
This stone-built house has been
perfectly renovated to provide
accommodations with antique
furniture and modern comforts.
Apartments vary in style and can
sleep from two to 10 people. On
the surrounding estate there is an
open-air swimming pool, three
lakes for fishing and a center
where quarter horses are bred
and trained. Nature walks and
horseback riding are offered.

🛏 5

Key to Symbols: ▤ Fax ✉ Email 🛏 Rooms 🅿 Parking 🏊 Swimming
American Express ⓓ Diners Club 💳 MasterCard 💳 Visa

Radda in Chianti

Radicondoli

Siena

Castelvecchi   **$**
Castelvecchi 17, 53017, Tuscany
☎ 0577 738050
🖹 0577 738608
Castelvecchi takes the form of splendid farmhouses grouped together like a little village around a lovely main house. Accommodations are provided in little rustic village-style apartments and bedrooms, with

Fattoria Solaio   **$$**
Solaio, 53030, Tuscany
☎ 0577 791029
🖹 0577 791015
There is a wonderful vista over the Cecina valleys and over the upper part of Pomarance from where this 16th-century villa is located. Some attractive old farmhouses have been renovated to provide three apartments.

Santa Caterina   **$$$**
via E. S. Piccolomini 7, 53100, Tuscany
☎ 0577 221105
🖹 0577 271087
e hsc@sienanet.it
This 18th-century residence is close to the Porta Romana, the old entrance to the city of Siena. The bedrooms are carefully furnished in period style; some

more elegant rooms available in the 18th-century villa. In the large park there are two swimming pools, tennis courts, table tennis and riding schools.

🛏 7

There is a large garden with an open-air swimming pool and tennis court. The length of the minimum stay requested varies according to the season.

🛏 6
▦ ⑩ VISA

have paneled ceilings. A lovely stairway leads up from the pretty reception area, and the communal rooms are small but attractive. The large garden overlooks Siena countryside, with a veranda where a buffet breakfast is served.

🛏 19
▦ ⑩ VISA

SORRENTO   D2

Massa Lubrense

Taverna del Capitano   **$$**
piazza delle Sirene 10, Marina del Cantone, 80061, Campania
☎ 081 8081028
🖹 081 8081892
The foundations of this little building sink almost into the sea. The rooms, although very simple, are welcoming and

attractive, nearly all with a superb view over the bay. Food is prepared with skill and imagination, and the dishes are inspired by tradition and local produce. Homemade jams are served for breakfast, along with homemade cakes and brioche.

🛏 15   ▦ ⑩ VISA

Sorrento

La Minervetta   **$$**
via Capo 25, 80067, Campania
☎ 081 8073069
🖹 081 8773033
Stunningly located, La Minervetta overlooks a giddy drop down to the village and the little fishing port below. The bedrooms are spacious, with very modern furnishings. There is a

large restaurant, but in summer meals are served outside on the lovely terrace. The traditional cooking is delicious and homey. Parking is on the hotel roof – at road level.

🛏 12
▦ ⑩ VISA

SPOLETO — C3
Spoleto
Charleston $
piazza Collicola 10, 06049, Umbria
☎ 0743 220052
🖹 0743 221244
📧 hotelcharleston@krenet.it
This 17th-century palace in Spoleto's historic center has recently been refurbished and equipped with many comforts. The bedrooms are large, all with beamed ceilings, modern furnishings and signed paintings. Attractive communal areas are simply furnished and arranged over several rooms. A buffet breakfast is served outside in summer. The hotel has a private garage, sauna, gym and conference room.

🛏 18

STRESA — B5
Azzate

Locanda dei Mai Intees $$$
via Nobile Claudio Riva 2, 21022, Lombardy
☎ 0332 457223
🖹 0332 459339
📧 maintees@tin.it
A handful of houses make up the ancient center of the village of Azzate. However, these are no ordinary houses, but mansions and castles of considerable architectural interest. This romantic inn is situated in an aristocratic 16th-century residence and is delightfully furnished with period pieces. The owner takes care of every detail of the accommodation and the restaurant as if it were her own house.

🛏 6

Lesa

Villa Lidia $$
via Giuseppe Ferrari 9, 28040, Piedmont
☎ 0322 7095/02 58103076
🖹 02 34973214
📧 lanfranconiconsulta@interbusiness.it
Bed-and-breakfast accommodations are provided at this villa, built in the typical Lake Maggiore style of the 1930s, with original period furnishings. Recently renovated, it has large welcoming rooms, each with a bathroom, and a terrace looking out over the park. Breakfast is served in the ground-floor dining room with its garden views. The minimum stay is two nights.

🛏 3

Piode

Giardini $
via Umberto I 9, 13020, Piedmont
☎ 0163 71135
🖹 0163 71988
Charming early 19th-century building in the center of Piode village, facing the Sesia River. Accommodations are in neat single and double apartments, available for a week or a weekend. Some have terraces with views over the valley, and all of them have satellite television, linen and crockery. The bar and restaurant are particularly welcoming, and diners may use the well-appointed solarium terrace.

🛏 17

TAORMINA — D1
Taormina
Villa Sirina $$ - $$$
contrada Sirina, 98039, Sicily
☎ 0942 51776
🖹 0942 51671
An old villa at the foot of Taormina, 1,350 feet above sea level. All the bedrooms have balconies or terraces and are furnished with 19th-century pieces. Lovely antique furniture in the spacious sitting rooms tells the history of the house. The rustic restaurant serves traditional regional dishes. There is a private beach and a swimming pool on the terrace.

🛏 15

Avetrana

Martina Franca

Pulsano

Civitella del Tronto

Zunica $$
piazza Filippi Pepe 14, 64010,
Abruzzo
☎ 0861 91319
🖹 0861 918150
Little 17th-century mansion on
Civitella's central square, in the
shadow of the Bourbon Fortress.
The elegant furnishings are early

Sant'Omero

La Meridiana $$
Santa Maria a Vico, 64027,
Abruzzo
☎ 0861 736336
🖹 0861 786336
This old farmhouse, surrounded
by a large garden, provides
agritourism accommodations
and reflects the natural customs
and traditions of the Abruzzi

Bosco di Mudonato $ - $$
via per Salice Salentino, km 3,
74020, Apulia
☎ 099 9704597
🖹 099 9704597
A large estate of olive groves,
orchards and vineyards surrounds
this old fortified farmhouse. The
guest quarters, set in a wood of
oak trees and Mediterranean
vegetation, are in period

Il Vignaletto $$
via Mindo di Tata 1, 74015,
Apulia
☎ 080 4490354
🖹 080 4490387
e vignaletto@peg.it
The valley of the "trulli"
dwellings is a magical place, and
this old farmstead on a hillside is
in the center of the valley,
offering guest rooms and well-

Tenuta del Barco $ - $$$
Strada provinciale 123, contrada
Porvica, 74026, Apulia
☎ 059 5333051
🖹 059 5333051
e tenuta@iname.com
These old buildings were
designed for defense and hard
work, but today provide
accommodations with gracious
style and lots of character.

20th century, and bedrooms
overlook the lanes of the
medieval village. In the attached
restaurant there is a rustic grotto
with a cross-vaulted ceiling.
Here you can enjoy high-quality
cooking employing the classic
flavors of the area.

region. The bedrooms look out
onto cultivated land, and the
small apartments are equipped
with everything necessary to
prepare delicious meals with
ingredients from the local area.
There also is a garden with a
vegetable plot and orchard.

---

buildings with rustic furnishings.
The four two-room apartments
are equipped with a range of
comforts. Guests can sample the
flavors of the region in the
restaurant.

🛏 10

furnished little apartments. The
buildings are white, and an
open-air swimming pool has
been created between their
shining reflections. Diversions
include bike rides, riding with
"murgesi" horses, table tennis or
walks in the woods.

🛏 7 VISA

Former storehouses and stables
have been restructured to create
seven apartments. The courtyard
is the heart of the farmstead, and
from it there is access to the
restaurant, which serves typical
Apulian dishes. The farm has
private access to the public
beach.

🛏 7 VISA

🛏 21 Diners Club VISA

🛏 13

Acquasparta

Castello di Casigliano $$
piazza Corsini 1, 05021, Umbria
☎ 0744 943428
🖹 0744 944056
🄴 casigliano@mail.
caribusiness.it

This big 17th-century palace stands on a hill overshadowing an old village of low stone houses, and an attractive inn has been created in the castle's old wine stores. The rustic atmosphere is warmed by a large fireplace, and by traditional cooking using fresh herbs, precious truffles and game. Houses in the village have been converted to provide attractive little apartments.

🛏 6   🄳 🄼

Amelia

Carleni $$
via Pellegrino Carleni 21, 05022, Umbria
☎ 0744 983925
🖹 0744 978143
🄴 carleni@tin.it

Hotel created from an old palace dating from the 18th century, in the heart of Amelia's historic center. It is surrounded by a luxuriant garden and encircled by lovely stone walls. Beautiful rustic-style furniture and big fireplaces warm the communal areas. The restaurant serves refined cooking alternating between traditional Umbrian flavors and French cuisine.

🛏 7   🄰 🄳 🄼

Montecchio

Le Casette $$
Le Casette, 05020, Umbria
☎ 0744 957645
🖹 0744 950500

This farm stands at the foot of Croce di Serra Mountain looking across the Tevere Valley. Old farmhouses and agricultural buildings on the estate have been transformed into little apartments. Each has a complete kitchen and a bathroom with shower. The restaurant, in the main house, is rustic and welcoming, and there is a big swimming pool surrounded by terraces.

🛏 16   🄼

San Gemini

La locanda di Carsulae $$
via Tiberina 2, 05029, Umbria
☎ 0744 630163
🖹 0744 333068
🄴 ascassi@tin.it

Completely refurbished inn surrounded by a pleasant garden with a large terrace. It offers nine big bedrooms attractively decorated with simple furniture, terra-cotta floors and ceramics from nearby Deruta. There is a rustic restaurant and a little bar with a veranda, but no sitting rooms. The restaurant serves homey cooking utilizing truffles, porcini mushrooms and homemade bread.

🛏 9   🄰 🄳 🄼

Stroncone

La Porta del Tempo $$
via del Sacramento 2, 05039, Umbria
☎ 0744 608190
🖹 0744 430210
🄴 info@portadeltempo.com

This castle village on a hill was built in the 10th century, and reconstructed in 1215. The hotel is in a 16th-century palace, recently refurbished with great care and attention. It has eight stylishly furnished bedrooms, all with satellite television and minibar. The communal rooms also are charming.

🛏 8   🄰 🄳 🄼

TODI   C3

Todi

Tenuta di Canonica $ - $$$
Canonica 75, 06059, Umbria
☎ 075 8947545
🖹 075 8947581
📧 tenutadicononica@tin.it
http:www.tenutadicanonica.com
Former defensive structures,
including a castle with ramparts
and a medieval tower, have been
transformed to provide excellent
guest accommodation. The big
rooms have vaulted ceilings,
wooden beams, antique fireplaces
and period furniture. A modern
swimming pool also is provided.

🛏 11

TURIN (TORINO)   A5

Turin

Liberty $$
via Pietro Micca 15, 10121,
Piedmont
☎ 011 5628801
🖹 011 5628163
This famous hotel, located on
the third floor of a residential
villa, has always accommodated
noted members of the
aristocracy. The drawing rooms
are very elegant, and there is
antique furniture in nearly all of
the very large guest rooms. The
buffet breakfast includes hot
dishes, and the restaurant offers
homey regional cooking. Twenty
four-hour bar service is available.

🛏 35
💳 ◑ VISA

TRÁPANI   C1

Valderice

Baglio Santacroce $$
S.S. 187 al kn 12,300, 91019,
Sicily
☎ 0923 891111
🖹 0923 891192
This 17th-century "baglio," or
wine-producing house, is on the
slopes of Mount Erice
overlooking the Gulf of Comino.
The interior courtyard leads into
the reception rooms, all
furnished in an elegantly rustic
style. Bedrooms, with beams and
terra-cotta floors, feature
wrought-iron beds and olive
wood chairs. The restaurant
serves regional specialties, and
there is a swimming pool on the
terrace.

🛏 25   ◑ VISA

TRENTO   B5

Caldonazzo

Due Spade $
piazza Municipio 2, 38052,
Trentino-Alto Adige
☎ 0461 723113
🖹 0461 723113
Small and simple building with a
long tradition of hospitality. It
offers bedrooms that vary in style
from rustic to modern. Period
furnishings, pastel decor and
flower arrangements create a
welcoming atmosphere in the
lounges, bar, restaurant and
breakfast room. The little
reception hall opens onto a well-
equipped veranda, garden and
swimming pool.

🛏 24   VISA

Pinzolo

Chalet dei Pini $$ - $$$
via Campanile Basco 24,
Madonna di Campiglio, 38084,
Trentino-Alto Adige
☎ 0465 441489
🖹 0465 441658
📧 jalla@tin.it
A little chalet set amid pine trees
but close to the town center and
ski lifts. More like a private
home than a hotel, it has few
rooms and is looked after by the
exceptionally kind lady of the
house. The rooms are furnished
in wood and are simple and
welcoming. The period stube
(stove room) has a really cozy
atmosphere.

🛏 11   VISA

Key to Symbols: 🖹 Fax 📧 Email 🛏 Rooms 🅿 Parking 🏊 Swimming
💳 American Express ◑ Diners Club ● MasterCard 💳 Visa

Follina

Villa Abbazia $$ - $$$
piazza IV Novembre, 31051,
Veneto
☎ 0438 971277
🖹 0438 970001
🆔 info@hotelabbazia.it
A 17th-century palace with an
Art Nouveau annex, where the
ambience is very refined: dim
lighting, the glow of candles,
tables with beautiful cloths and
antique furniture. Bedrooms are
lovely, and the sitting rooms a
delight for relaxation. Leisure
facilities include an open-air
swimming pool, reduced fees at
the nearby Asolo golf course, and
bicycle rental at the hotel.

🛏 24

Gorgo al Monticano

Villa Revedin $$ - $$$
via Palazzi 4, 31040, Veneto
☎ 0422 800033
🖹 0422 800272
🆔 info@villarevedin.it
A noble Venetian family built
this villa and barns from 1400 to
1500. Today it provides modern
comforts in a historic
atmosphere, with well-equipped
bedrooms and suites with
hydromassage or Turkish baths.
The large, decorative drawing
rooms are well suited to
conferences or ceremonies. Food
is prepared with great care, and
fish is a specialty.

🛏 32

Pieve di Soligo

Da Lino $$
via Brandolini 31, Solighetto,
31050, Veneto
☎ 0438 82150 3261
🖹 0438 980577 3265
🆔 dalino@tmn.it
This inn is situated on the
Prosecco road in a carefully
refurbished old farmhouse. A
collection of more than 2,000
copper pans and cauldrons
adorns the ceilings and walls.
Paintings and flowers give a
particular character to the
restaurant. Bedrooms, too, are
simple, charming and carefully
prepared. During the summer,
restaurant service is transferred
to the garden under a lovely
pergola.

🛏 17

Cividale del Friuli
Locanda al Castello $$
via del Castello 20, 33043,
Friuli-Venezia Giulia
☎ 0432 733242
🖹 0432 700901
🆔 castello@ud.nettuno.it
Hotel housed in a 19th-century
castle on a hill near the historic
center. It offers large bedrooms,
period-style furniture and
panoramic views. There are two
dining rooms, one more intimate
and a pillared room for banquets.
The kitchen prepares typical
Friuli dishes, served on the
terrace in summer. The hotel has
a sitting room, bar, solarium and
garden.

🛏 17

Locanda al Pomo d'Oro $
piazza San Giovanni 20, 33043,
Friuli-Venezia Giulia
☎ 0432 731489
🖹 0431 731489
This pretty little hotel, painted
pink, looks over a square in the
historic center of Cividale. It has
been carefully restored and has
practical rooms with simple
modern furnishings. Some
overlook the old city walls. Stone
walls, wooden beams and brick
arches dating back to 1300 are
characteristic of the communal
rooms. The rustic restaurant
serves dishes representative of
the Friuli area.

🛏 17

Manzano

Il Borgo Soleschiano $
via Principale 24, 33044,
Friuli-Venezia Giulia
☎ 0432 754119
🗎 0432 755417
An old country house
surrounded by a large garden,
where bedrooms are
appropriately appointed with
wooden floors and period
furnishings. Guests should note
that the stairway is rather steep
and no elevator is provided.
There is an attractive restaurant,
a welcoming sitting room and a
little bar. Guests may eat
breakfast under a lovely pergola
outside.

🛏 10

Ravascletto

Valcalda $ - $$
via Edelweiss 8/10, 33020,
Friuli-Venezia Giulia
☎ 0433 66120
🗎 0433 66420
🅴 hotelvalcalda@ud.nettuno.it
This hotel is in a pretty, modern
building using wood in a way
that recalls traditional mountain
houses. It has spacious
communal rooms and light, airy
bedrooms with lovely views over
the valley. The attractive
restaurant offers local and
regional dishes with a seasonal
flavor. A free garage is available.

🛏 13

Sauris

Riglarhaus $ - $$
Lateis 3, 33020, Friuli-Venezia
Giulia
☎ 0433 86013
🗎 0433 86049
This building is typical of the
Sauris area and has recently been
refurbished. The base is in stone;
a wooden gallery surrounds the
space once occupied by barns.
There are 14 bedrooms with
terraces (six for non-smokers),
furnished in a simple,
comfortable style. The kitchen
serves dishes from the Carnic
region, based on local
ingredients.

🛏 14

URBINO C4

Cagli

Casale Torre del Sasso $$ - $$$
61043, Marche
☎ 0721 782655
🗎 0721 701336
🅴 torresasso@info-net.it
This farmhouse was developed
around a sentry post and a tower
with a pigeon coop, which were
part of a 15th-century defense
system throughout the territory
of Cagli. Accommodations are
provided in well-equipped
apartments sleeping from two to
ten people and equipped with
antique and rustic furniture.
Within the grounds guests can
enjoy a swimming pool, archery,
birdwatching and jogging.

🛏 4

Urbino

Raffaello $$
via Santa Margherita 38, 61029,
Marche
☎ 0722 4784
🗎 0722 328540
This palace is in the pedestrian
zone of the historic center of
Urbino. It is a hospitable hotel
blending modern furnishings
with the ancient fabric of the
building. Lovely marble and
carpets furnish the reception
halls, and the bedrooms are
equipped with every comfort.
There is a convenient shuttle
service for guests to the main
parking lots and the bus station.

🛏 14

Key to Symbols: 🗎 Fax 🅴 Email 🛏 Rooms 🅿 Parking 🏊 Swimming
American Express 🅓 Diners Club 💳 MasterCard 💳 Visa

VENICE (VENEZIA) C5

Dolo

Villa Ducale $$ - $$$
riviera Martiri della Libertà 75,
Cesare Musatti, 30031, Veneto
☎ 041 5608020
🖹 041 5608004
e info@viladucale.it
This villa in the Palladian style is
surrounded by an age-old park.
Recent refurbishment has

bought it up to modern
standards of accommodation and
comfort. Features include a
lovely facade with arches, period
frescoes, antique furniture,
stuccowork, marble fireplaces
and original Venetian floors. The
restaurant overlooks the garden,
where it is possible to rent
bicycles.

🛏 11

Venice

American $$ - $$$
San Vio 628, 30123, Veneto
☎ 041 5204733
🖹 041 5204048
e hotameri@tin.it
Pretty building in a central
location, offering bedrooms with
Venetian-inspired furnishings.
Restoration work has preserved
original features, which add
charm to the interior.

Communal rooms are furnished
in period style, and there is a
terrace covered with a pergola
where breakfast is served during
the spring and summer. A
private dock is available for
gondolas and motor launches.

🛏 28

Firenze $$ - $$$
San Marco - San Moisé 1490,
30124, Veneto
☎ 041 5222858
🖹 041 5252668
e hotel.firenze@flashnet.it
This hotel, literally a few steps
from St. Mark's Square, has
maintained a facade with the
detail, marble decoration and
wrought-iron workmanship of

the Art Nouveau style.
Bedrooms are furnished in a
classically elegant style, and there
is a pretty room for breakfast.
The terrace on the top floor has
bar service, and breakfast is
served here in summer.

🛏 25

Iris $$ - $$$
San Polo 2910/A, 30125, Veneto
☎ 041 5222882
🖹 041 5222882
e htliris@tin.it
Most of the furniture in this
hotel is modern, but some rooms
retain the decorated ceilings. The
lovely bedrooms are furnished in
period style. The little breakfast
room still has beamed ceilings,

but the furniture is modern.
There is no restaurant, but the
nearby Giardinetto is under the
same ownership and specializes
in fish.

🛏 30

Pausania $ - $$$
Dorsoduro 2824, 30123, Veneto
☎ 041 5222083
🖹 041 5222083
This ancient palace in Venetian
Gothic style stands in the
Dorsoduro quarter. Architectural
details include a little courtyard
with a 14th-century wellhead
and a marble stairway with
graceful pillars. Bedrooms have

modern facilities but are
furnished in period style.
Breakfast is served in a room
that opens onto the garden.

🛏 26

Key to Symbols: 🖹 Fax e Email 🛏 Rooms P Parking 🏊 Swimming
🔲 American Express ⊙ Diners Club 💳 MasterCard 🔲 Visa

Santo Stefano $$$
Campo Santo Stefano, San
Marco 2957, 30124, Veneto
☎ 041 5200166
🖹 041 5224460
Housed in the 14th-century
watchtower of the adjacent
religious house, the hotel is a
Gothic-style building a few steps
from St. Mark's square. The little
entrance hall, recently renovated,
retains its period ceiling
decorated with panels. The
pretty bedrooms have Venetian-
style furniture and Murano
lamps. The breakfast room is
small and carefully furnished.

🛏 11

Wildner $$$
riva degli Schiavoni 4161,
30122, Veneto
☎ 041 5227463
🖹 041 5265615
🄴 wildner@veneziahotels.com
The Schiavoni bank is a wide
promenade built during the 19th
century. Along it is this hotel
that offers elegant bedrooms
furnished in period style. They
also have air conditioning and
satellite television, and some
look over the lagoon. On the top
floor there is a lovely terrace-
veranda, which acts as a
restaurant and bar and has
breathtaking views of the basin
of St. Mark's.

🛏 16

VERONA C5
Lazise

Casa Mia $$
Risare 1, 37017, Veneto
☎ 045 6470244
🖹 045 7580554
🄴 casamia@lazise.com
This modern building in the
traditional style has recently
refurbished bedrooms. Living
areas are spacious, and there are
attractive terraces with a bar and
breakfast service. In the garden a
little bridge leads to a pavilion on
a small island. Other amenities
include a swimming pool, tennis,
table tennis, bicycle rental and a
restaurant noted for the quality
of its cooking.

🛏 39

VIARÉGGIO B4
Camaiore

Locanda Le Monache $ - $$
piazza XXIX Maggio 36, 55041,
Tuscany
☎ 0584 989258
🖹 0584 984011
🄴 lemonache@caen.it
This simple hotel faces the main
street in the historic center of
Camaiore. Recently refurbished,
it offers attractive bedrooms
furnished along modern lines,
and practical bathrooms with
showers and hair dryers. The
busy restaurant is run by the
owners, and since 1923 has
served regional cooking. Guests
are required to stay for a
minimum of three days,
including meals.

🛏 13

VICENZA C5
Altavilla Vicentina

Genziana $$
via Mazzini 75/77, 36077,
Veneto
☎ 0444 572398
🖹 0444 574310
This rustic Tyrolean-style hotel
is situated at the foot of the
Berici hills. Elegant furnishings
and carefully chosen decorations
are complemented by original
paintings adorning the walls.
There is a welcoming
atmosphere in the little stube
(stove room) that can
accommodate only 20 people.
Other facilities are a tennis court
and an open-air swimming pool.

🛏 27

Key to Symbols: 🖹 Fax 🄴 Email 🛏 Rooms 🅿 Parking 🏊 Swimming
American Express Diners Club MasterCard Visa

Bolzano Vicentino

Locanda Greco   **$ - $$**
via Roma 24, 36050, Veneto
☎ 0444 350588
🖹 0444 350695
e grego@mail.protec.it

This classic inn has been in the same family for four generations. The restaurant is noted for its refined cooking, a mixture of traditional and original dishes using local ingredients in season.

The bedrooms are comfortable and welcoming. The inn, which is located in the center of town, has special arrangements with the neighboring sports centers.

🛏 19

Longare

Le Vescovane   **$$**
via San Rocco 19, San Rocco, 36023, Veneto
☎ 0444 273570
🖹 0444 273265

This farmhouse complex dates from the 15th century and has been extended over the years. Recently restored, it has a lovely architectural style with stone walls, arches and beamed ceilings enhanced by period furniture. The spacious bedrooms are equipped with baths, air conditioning and satellite television. A solarium and a summerhouse are provided in the large garden.

🛏 9

San Vito di Leguzzano

Locanda Due Mori   **$**
via Rigobello 39, 36030, Veneto
☎ 0445 671635
🖹 0445 511611

An 18th-century mansion with wooden shutters and flowers in the windows. Everything is very refined, from the real lace curtains and fresh flowers to the genuine courtesy. The bedrooms are simple but neat and friendly, and the communal rooms have a period feel with rustic wooden furniture. The restaurant serves local dishes, and a fire burns in the big hearth.

🛏 10

VITERBO   C3
Caprarola

Tenuta La Vita   **$$**
La Vita, Valle di Vico, 01032, Lazio
☎ 0761 612077
🖹 0761 612077

This estate stands within the nature reserve of Lake Vico, and the old farmhouse has been completely refurbished to offer five well-equipped and elegantly furnished bedrooms. The same family has worked on the estate for three generations, and they have great enthusiasm for open-air life and authentic food. Fresh ingredients are provided each day from the farm, together with local wine and olive oil.

🛏 5

Civita Castellana

Casa Ciotti   **$**
via Terni 14, 01033, Lazio
☎ 0761 513090
🖹 0761 599120
e agriciot@tin.it

This 17th-century coaching inn has been skillfully refurbished to maintain its original character. It comprises several buildings set in the middle of a large and well-tended park, which includes a swimming pool.
Accommodations are provided in large one- and two-room apartments with beamed ceilings and terra-cotta floors. The two three-room apartments enjoy a lovely portico that leads directly to the garden.

🛏 11

Key to Symbols: 🖹 Fax e Email 🛏 Rooms P Parking 🏊 Swimming
American Express Diners Club MasterCard Visa

Monterosi

Axel   **$ - $$**
Macchia del Cardinale, 01030,
Lazio
☎ 0761 699535
🖹 0761 699535

Elegant agrotourism operation in a modern building, all on one level and facing Lake Vico. It has six bedrooms (two non-smoking) and an apartment that can accommodate up to six people.

Other facilities include an attractive restaurant and television room. Outside there is a large garden with an open-air swimming pool and solarium. Bicycles can be rented, and there also is a riding school.

🛏 6

Orte

La Chiocciola   **$$**
Seripola, 01028, Lazio
☎ 0761 402734
🖹 0761 490254

Agrotourism operation based around a 15th-century farmhouse and an old farm worker's cottage, set within a large estate. Both have been carefully restored to retain their original character, and period

furniture features in the individually designed bedrooms. Breakfast is taken on the veranda, while lunch and dinner are served in the rustic restaurant. A swimming pool and mountain bicycles are available.

🛏 8 🖭

Tuscania

Locanda della Mirandolina **$$**
via del Pozzo Bianco 40/42,
01017, Lazio
☎ 0761 436595
🖹 0761 436595
📧 info@mirandolina.it

On the ground floor of this pretty hotel guests are welcomed into a tiny restaurant with five tables that operates during the winter. On the floor above the

bedrooms are simply furnished, each in a different color. During the summer meals are served outside, next to the ancient walls of the city. The seasonal dishes are Mediterranean with a touch of Sicilian inspiration.

🛏 5 🖭

Piazza dei Signori, Vicenza

Netherlands

*L*and is a valuable resource in the Netherlands. Amsterdam, the lively capital, lies 10 feet below sea level. Its landward neighbors are Germany, to the east, and Belgium, once part of the United Provinces of the Netherlands, to the south. The North Sea borders the Netherlands to the north and west, and the Dutch have a unique relationship with this most unpredictable neighbor.

The Water Lands

Head north to Noord Holland and Friesland, or south to Zeeland, and you will appreciate the achievements of Dutch engineers and laborers in their struggle with the sea. The Zuiderzee Museum in Enkhuizen tells the story of land reclamation. For a direct look at the significance of water here, travel across the Afsluitdijk, the 20-mile dam sealing the inland lake of Ijsselmeer and connecting Noord Holland with Friesland. In Zeeland, the Delta Expo Museum explains the Delta Plan, a system of dams and barriers erected after the sea breached the old dykes in 1953, killing more than 1,800 people.

The western provinces, Noord and Zuid Holland, contain the main towns: Amsterdam, with its charismatic air of freedom and a touch of wickedness; Rotterdam; and The Hague, dignified and historic seat of political power. These three are known collectively as Randstad, the "Ring Town." Beyond the urban centers is a very different Netherlands.

Inland

The image of the Netherlands as a flat land, criss-crossed by canals and dotted with windmills, does nothing to convey the variety and complexity of the country's landscapes and communities. In the south, the area of Limburg is the nation's hill country; the De Kempen region, in the province of Noord Brabant, is a swath of sandy heaths and woods. There are the meadows and orchards of Gelderland, the pretty villages and waterways of Overijssel, and the moors and flower-filled bogs of Drenthe. Go north, to Groningen, to find the famous windmills, along with clogs and green, flat expanses of land. But neighboring Friesland seems like another country altogether, with its own language and cultural heritage.

The Dutch

The Dutch have a long history of toleration of others, blended with a powerful sense of mutual respect. Their history of struggling for independence, and for survival in the face of natural and human aggression, has given them a quiet self-confidence; the strong Protestant tradition carries with it a sense of modesty and restraint. It takes a while to break the ice, but once it's broken, the Dutch are enthusiastic and friendly companions.

Getting Around

Public transportation is inexpensive and efficient, and most places are within a three-hour train ride from Amsterdam. Good bus services run between the cities and link provincial towns and villages. Driving in rural areas is straightforward, but in towns it can be a stressful experience. There are regulated routes in large cities for pedestrians, trams and cyclists.

Colorful cafés in Amsterdam's Leidseplein

Accommodations

Good-quality hotels abound in the Netherlands, in the cities, along the coast and in the smaller inland towns. National legislation lays down standards of safety and hygiene for accommodations, and this is augmented by a voluntary system of star ratings. Between one and five stars are awarded on the basis of comfort and facilities; the criteria used is the same as in neighboring Belgium and Luxembourg.

Bedroom accommodations will typically comprise two single beds, although most hotels will also have a number of double and single bedded rooms available. Private bathrooms, usually with a shower, are fast becoming standard, but shared facilities are still common in many mid-priced hotels. You're likely to find a TV and telephone in your room, which will usually have good drawer and hanging space for clothes.

Breakfast will commonly be included in the cost of a room. This will usually include cold ham, Dutch cheeses, jam, honey and bread rolls. Tea or coffee is always available. Most hotels have plentiful buffet breakfasts, including smoked meats, pickled herring and a variety of cheeses. In the evening the most economical meals are usually to be found in local restaurants and cafés.

Amsterdam's replica Magere Brug (Skinny Bridge)

well, serving recipes from countries such as China and Surinam. These are often a good value.

Traditional Dutch lunch menus might include *erwtensoep*, a satisfying soup of peas and pork, or *uitsmijter*, an open sandwich of meat or ham with cheese and topped with a fried egg. There's a wide range of popular snacks, such as *patat* (French fries) with mayonnaise or spicy sauce dips; *kroketten*, small rolls of meat filling covered in bread crumbs and fried; *broodjes*, baguettes filled with smoked sausage, spicy meat or cheeses, and pickled herring or smoked eel. To sample raw herring, follow the local

Food and Drink

Dutch food has suffered from a dull reputation, but modern trends are fast reversing that view. Fish dishes in particular are being produced in fresh and innovative ways. In the larger cities, especially Amsterdam, the country's colonial past has left a legacy of fine Indonesian cooking. Specialties include *rijsttafel* ("rice table"), a mix of several dozen spiced, sauced, tangy titbits. The large immigrant city populations have introduced other ethnic restaurants as

Shopping

The real shopping experience in the Netherlands is for antiques and crafts, and particularly specialties such as jewelry and porcelain, which are on sale throughout the provinces. Delftware porcelain is a popular but much imitated choice. Make sure your item is the genuine article by checking that the trade name has a D, and by shopping only at reputable outlets.

custom and dip it in a bowl of diced onions, holding it by the tail, before tipping your head back and savoring. Dinner Dutch-style might be *hutspot*, a stew of vegetables, smoked bacon and other meat, or *stampotten*, mashed potatoes and vegetables with smoked sausage or bacon.

Sweet favorites include *pannekoek*, pancakes covered in *stroop* (molasses) or *poedersuiker* (powdered sugar). Street stalls often serve a smaller type of pancake, known as *poffertjes*.

Beer is the national drink here – generally light, but substantial in the traditional bars, or "brown cafes". Grolsch is an excellent light beer, often drunk with meals in preference to wine. Heavier brews include *jenever*, a grain spirit (*oude jenever* being the sweetest version), and *jonge*, for strong palates. Beer, vintage gins and liqueurs can be enjoyed in a *proeflokalen*, or "tasting house."

NETHERLANDS

Bergen

Parkhotel $
Breelaan 19, 1861 GC Bergen, Noord-Holland
☎ 072 589 78 67
🖹 072 589 74 35

The village of Bergen is a much-visited artists' colony with many galleries and museums. People spend their time drinking on the cozy terraces during balmy summer evenings. One of those places is the Parkhotel, in the heart of the village. There is a cozy lounge with a roaring fire on cold days, and attractive, comfortable bedrooms. A generous breakfast buffet is served in the morning, and there is a stylish restaurant on the first floor.

🛏 26

Schoorl

Merlet $
Duinweg 15, 1871 AC Schoorl, Noord-Holland
☎ 072 509 36 44
🖹 072 509 14 06
📧 merlet@worldonline.nl

The Bourgogne family has created a truly homey atmosphere in the restaurant-hotel Merlet. Many objets d'art and contemporary statues adorn the interior, but the real attraction of this place is the famous restaurant. From the Provencal-style dining room you can look into the open kitchen, where the chefs are busy with fresh produce and herbs from the kitchen garden. The rooms are attractive and comfortable. Guests can use the sauna and swimming pool in the basement.

🛏 18

Amsterdam

Canal House $$
Keizersgracht 148, 1015 CX Amsterdam, Noord-Holland
☎ 020 622 51 82
🖹 020 624 13 17
www.canalhousehotel.nl
📧 info@canalhousehotel.nl

The Canal House is especially popular with American visitors. The owners of this 17th-century building have kept the interior very much in style with the architecture. The bedrooms vary in size and decor, but the furnishings and beds are antique. Breakfast is served in the lounge, which has a view of the quiet inner garden.

🛏 26

Otterlo

Carnegie's Cottage $
Toplangs 35, 6731 BK Otterlo, Gelderland
☎ 0318 59 12 20

Carnegie's Cottage can be found at the very end of a country lane and offers its guests a stay in peaceful surroundings. The country-style bedrooms offer comfortable accommodation, but the pick of the crop is the "lovers' cottage" - a blue thatched cottage with a beautiful view over the woods and fields. The attractive restaurant serves a range of refined dishes from the hands of the owner.

🛏 12

Delft

De Plataan $
Doelenplein 10261,1 BP Delft, Zuid-Holland
☎ 015 212 60 46
🖹 015 215 73 27
www.hoteldeplataan.nl
📧 hoteldp@casema.net

The Hotel De Plataan is located at de Doelenplein, in the heart of Delft. Downstairs is a contemporary grand café, and an animated atmosphere permeates throughout the building. The bedrooms come in various looks, sizes and prices. There are 2 themed fairy-tale rooms and a "desert island" room, as well as many others. Breakfast is served in the café, and for dinner, guests can choose between the many restaurants and eating places Delft has to offer.

🛏 30

Key to Symbols: 🖹 Fax   📧 Email   🛏 Rooms   🅿 Parking   🏊 Swimming

DELFZIJL · C4
Delfzijl

Eemshotel $
Zeebadweg 2, 9933 AV Delfzijl,
Groningen
☎ 0596 61 26 36
🖹 0596 61 96 54
www.eemshotel.nl
🅴 info@eemshotel.nl
The Eemshotel is built on stilts above the mouth of the Eems River. It can be reached from the dike via a footbridge. In clear weather there is a wonderful view from the hotel over the harbor and sea, with the German coastline in the distance. During the summer guests can enjoy the beach near the hotel. There are fitness facilities with sauna and a Turkish bath. The cozy café and restaurant are decorated in appropriate maritime style. The excellent cuisine is known for its fish specialties.
🛏 20

EDAM · B3
Edam
De Fortuna $
Spuistraat 3, 1135 AV Edam,
Noord-Holland
☎ 0299 37 16 71
🖹 0299 37 14 69
www.fortuna-edam.nl
🅴 fortuna@fortuna-edam.nl
The attractive hotel-restaurant De Fortuna consists of five renovated 17th-century houses and some small wooden dwellings built later. It is situated right in the center of Edam on the edge of the water. The bedrooms are located in different buildings and are stylishly furnished with wooden furniture and handmade quilts. The restaurant and cozy bar give off a nostalgic old Dutch atmosphere, with painted beams and copper chandeliers. The restaurant is known for its original and innovative dishes.

🛏 23

GIETHOORN · C3
Blokzijl

Kaatje bij de Sluis $$$
Zuiderstraat 1, 8356 DZ
Blokzijl, Overijessel
☎ 0527 29 18 33
🖹 0527 29 18 36
www.kaatje.nl
🅴 kaatje.bij@wxs.nl
On both sides of the drawbridge in the small harbor town of Blokzijl lies the legendary restaurant-hotel Kaatje bij de Sluis. Guests can dine in the tastefully decorated restaurant on one side of the bridge and have a comfortable night on the other side of the lock. In the morning there is a choice between a traditional Dutch breakfast or the famous "Dégustation du Matin," which consists of seven courses.
🛏 8

GOOR · C2
Holten
Hoog Holten $$
Forthaarsweg 7, 7451 JS Holten,
Overijessel
☎ 0548 36 13 06
🖹 0548 36 30 75
🅴 hoogholten@a1.nl
The hotel-restaurant Hoog Holten is situated in the middle of the woods at the Sallanse Heuvelrug nature reserve. This former hunting lodge dates back to 1919 and has an intimate interior scattered with beautiful flower arrangements. The bedrooms are comfortable, and the restaurant serves a range of seasonal dishes prepared with local produce and herbs from the kitchen garden. There is a private tennis court, and guests can explore the surrounding woods and heaths.

🛏 21

GRONINGEN · C4
Groningen
Corps de Garde $
Oude Boteringestraat 72-74,
9712 GN Groningen
☎ 050 314 54 37
🖹 050 313 63 20
www.corpsdegarde.nl
🅴 info@corpsdegarde.nl
The Auberge Corps de Garde was established in 1991 in two old houses within the canal circle of Groningen. The corner house was where guards, in the old days, watched the bridge during the night. Nowadays it is an informal hotel with an intimate restaurant. Antique features have been preserved and go hand in hand with the modern furnishings. The bedrooms are all different in style and color. The cozy canal-side restaurant serves excellent French-influenced cuisine.

🛏 24

Key to Symbols: 🖹 Fax 🅴 Email 🛏 Rooms 🅿 Parking 🏊 Swimming

HEUSDEN   B2
Heusden

In den Verdwaalde Koogel $
Vismarkt 1, 5256 BC Heusden,
Noord-Brabant
☎ 0416 66 19 33
▤ 0416 66 12 95
This hotel is housed in an
historic building dating back to
1620. It is named after the bullet
lodged in the stepped gable
during one of the sieges this
little fortress town has endured.

The rustic restaurant, with its
old beams and fireplace, is well
known for excellent French
cuisine. The comfortable rooms
are surprisingly modern, with
stylish furniture.

🛏 13

HILVERSUM   B2
Baarn
La Promenade $
Amalialaan 1, 3743 KE Baarn,
Utrecht
☎ 035 541 29 13
▤ 035 541 57 75
www.lapromenade.nl
✉ promenade@wxs.nl
The historic 1875 building La
Promenade is on the edge of

Baarn's town center. This hotel-
restaurant has a country
atmosphere in a contemporary
setting. The hotel serves a
wonderful English-style tea with
hot pastries and scones. The cozy
restaurant offers predominantly
French and Mediterranean
dishes. The classic-style
bedrooms have modern
amenities and offer comfortable

accommodations.

🛏 21

Lage Vuursche
De Kastanjehof $$
Kloosterlaan 1, 3749 AJ Lage
Vuursche, Utrecht
☎ 035 666 82 48
▤ 035 666 84 44
www.dekastanjehof.nl
✉ kastanj@worldonline.nl
On the edge of the busy village
of Lage Vuursche is de
Kastanjehof – an oasis of peace

and quiet. It is a small hotel,
surrounded by woods, with a
country-like coziness
accentuated by the many antique
pieces scattered around the place.
The restaurant offers French-
Italian cuisine which also is
served – weather permitting –
on the attractive terrace. The
cozy bedrooms and idyllic
garden at the back complete

this romantic package.

🛏 10

HOLWERD   B4
Dokkum

De Abdij van Dockum $
Markt 30-32, 9101 LS Dokkum,
Friesland
☎ 0519 22 04 22
▤ 0519 22 04 14
www.abdijvandockum.nl
✉ abdij.dockum@wxs.nl
The Abdij van Dockum was
formerly part of an old abbey,
but its present neoclassic form
dates back to 1854. It has been

completely renovated and
changed into a luxury hotel, with
rooms housed in the former
cloisters. There are two cozy
dining rooms where guests can
enjoy excellent dishes prepared
by Ilonca van der Werf, "Lady
Chef of the Year 1999."

🛏 16

KAATSHEUVEL   B2
Drunen
De Duinrand $$
Steegerf 2, 5151 RB Drunen,
Noord-Brabant
☎ 0416 37 24 98
▤ 0416 37 49 19
This hotel is an oasis of peace,
situated on the edge of the
dunes. The beautiful interior of
the villa-style establishment

consists of contemporary
furniture, bronze statues and
paintings. The comfortable
bedrooms are very luxurious,
furnished with a Jacuzzi and
private terrace. The restaurant
serves a choice of international
dishes accompanied by excellent
wines from the large wine cellar.

🛏 15

Key to Symbols: ▤ Fax   ✉ Email   🛏 Rooms   🅿 Parking   🏊 Swimming

LEIDEN B2
Noordwijk

De Edelman $
Emmaweg 25, 2202 CP
Noordwijk, Zuid-Holland
☎ 071 361 73 00
🖨 071 361 73 01
📧 info@marierosehotel.nl
Located directly on the North
Sea beach, the hotel De
Edelman is housed in a beautiful
early 20th-century building. A
stylish interior and a relaxed

atmosphere are prevalent
throughout. There is a cozy bar,
terrace and conservatory with a
view of the sea. The bedrooms
are comfortable, with individual
furnishings. The restaurant
serves a choice of excellent
dishes under head chef Teun
Bakker.

🛏 32

LEMMER B3
Rijs
Jans $
Mientwei 1, 8572 WB Rijs,
Friesland
☎ 0514 58 12 50
🖨 0514 58 16 41
www.hoteljans.nl
📧 info@hoteljans.nl
This 100-year-old establishment
is well-known for its à la carte

restaurant which attracts many
local visitors as well as those
from outside the region. The
menu offers a choice of refined
dishes prepared with regional
produce and herbs from the
kitchen garden. The hotel has
comfortable bedrooms as well as
Swedish chalet-style apartments
in a separate building. The
garden has a sauna to accentuate

this Swedish atmosphere.

🛏 21

MAASTRICHT B1
Berg en Terblijt
Kasteel Geulzicht $$
Vogelzangweg 2, 6325 PN Berg
en Terblijt, Limburg
☎ 043 604 04 32
🖨 043 604 20 11
www.kasteelgeulzicht.nl
📧 mail@kasteelgeulzicht.nl
Geulzicht, located on the edge of
a nature reserve, belongs to the

last generation of castles designed
at the end of the 19th century.
The architecture is English neo-
gothic. On the ground floor is a
large lobby with an exuberantly
painted ceiling, a small bar and a
stylish restaurant. The bedrooms
are individually furnished, some
with sunken Roman baths made
of marble. The rooms on the top
floor have a roof terrace with a

wonderful view.

🛏 9

MEPPEL C3
De Schiphorst

De Havixhorst $$
Schiphorsterweg 34-36, 7966
AC De Schiphorst, Drente
☎ 0522 44 14 87
🖨 0522 44 14 89
📧 havixhorst@hospitality.nl
Situated on the banks of a small
river, this building dates back to
1753 and was renovated in the
1980s into a majestic
château/hotel and restaurant.

There is a cozy lounge with a
beautiful old wine cellar, and an
airy, sunny restaurant. Weather
permitting, guests can dine on
the small square in front of the
castle. The Havixhorst has eight
exclusive bedrooms decorated in
individual style, plus a romantic
bridal suite.

🛏 8

ORVELTE C3
Westerbork
Ruyghe Venne $
Beilerstraat 24a, 9431 TA
Westerbork, Drente
☎ 0593 33 14 44
🖨 0593 33 28 88
The Ruyghe Venne is a modern
hotel located right in the middle
of the woods. Behind the
contemporary front is a classic

interior with an attractive
restaurant serving fish specialties
and regional dishes. The
bedrooms vary in size, and some
have their own terrace or
balcony. There are marked hiking
routes from the hotel into the
woods or onto the heath.

🛏 14

ROERMOND   C1

Herkenbosch

Kasteel Daelenbroeck   **$$**
Kasteellaan 2, 6075 EZ
Herkenbosch, Limburg
☎ 0475 53 24 65
▤ 0475 53 603 0
www.daelenbroeck.nl
🅴 info@daelenbroeck.nl
The history of the estate of
Kasteel Daelenbroek goes back
to the 14th century. The main
building was destroyed during
the Eighty-Year War, but the
16th-century front building
continued to be occupied. A
1993 renovation turned it into a
hotel. The restaurant serves
delicious French specialties; in
the summer, meals also are eaten
on the floating terrace. The
rooms, in two buildings, have
romantic themes

🛏 17

SNEEK   B3

Bolsward

Hid Hero Hiem   **$$**
Kerkstraat 51, 8701 HR
Bolsward, Friesland
☎ 0515 57 52 99
▤ 0515 57 30 52
www.tip.nl/users/hidherohiem
🅴 hidherohiem@tip.nl
Established in 1995 in a former
orphanage, Hid Hero Hiem is
situated in the heart of Bolsward,
close to the old Martini church.
The 14 stylish apartments, with
separate bedrooms and
bathrooms (some with a terrace)
offer very comfortable
accommodations. A
cafe/restaurant serves both
traditional and contemporary
cuisine. The hotel also has a
lovely terraced courtyard and an
orchard.

🛏 14

TERNEUZEN   A1

Schoondijke

De Zwaan   **$**
Prinses Beatrixstraat 1,
4507 AH Schoondijke, Zeeland
☎ 0117 40 20 02
▤ 0117 40 12 12
🅴 ulijn@zeelandnet.nl
The hotel De Zwaan is a very
successful enterprise managed by
enthusiastic proprietors Hans
and Nicole Ulijn. The spacious
bedrooms have every modern
amenity and offer comfortable
accommodations. There is a large
sun terrace at the front with a
cozy lounge and conservatory.
The à la carte restaurant is
welcoming, with beautiful flower
arrangements and cuisine that
features fish specialties and fresh
produce.

🛏 12

VALKENBURG   B1

Valkenburg

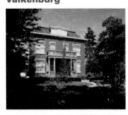

Prinses Juliana   **$$**
Broekhem 11, 6301 HD
Valkenburg, Limburg
☎ 043 601 22 44
▤ 043 601 44 05
🅴 info@juliana.nl
The hotel Prinses Juliana has
been in the hands of the Stevens
family for three generations.
There is a spacious lounge and a
stylish restaurant decorated in
warm yellow and orange, with
classic-style furniture. The dishes
are definitely "haute cuisine";
weather permitting, meals are
served in the idyllic garden-hall
or on the terrace in the peaceful
garden. The bedrooms are
modern and equipped with every
amenity.

🛏 25

Epen

Creusen   **$**
Wilhelminastraat 50, 6285 AW
Epen, Limburg
☎ 043 455 12 15
▤ 043 455 21 01
www.heuvelland.com/creusen
🅴 creusen@heuvelland.com
At the edge of the village of
Epen is the hotel Creusen where
visitors can enjoy a relaxing stay
in South Limburg. At the back is
a beautiful garden that extends
to the rolling fields of the Geul
Valley. The comfortable
bedrooms have up-to-date
amenities and classic-style
furniture, and those at the back
have a balcony. A breakfast
buffet is served in the morning
and a delicious 4-course dinner
in the evening.

🛏 19

Key to Symbols: Fax   Email   Rooms   Parking   Swimming

Mechelen

Brull $
Hoofdstraat 26, 6281 BD
Mechelen, Limburg
☎ 043 455 12 63
🖹 043 455 23 00
The Brull is a pleasant family
hotel in Mechelen. Visitors enter
this beautiful 1780 building via a
gateway. The hotel has many
paintings by local artists on the
walls, an old-style lounge and

two sun terraces. The airy,
spacious rooms have individual
colors and furnishings. A
breakfast buffet awaits guests in
the morning, and an innovative
4-course dinner courtesy of host
and head-chef Jo Kockelkoren in
the evening.

🛏 25

VEERE   A2

Veere

De Campveerse Toren $
Kaai 2, 4351 AA Veere, Zeeland
☎ 0118 50 12 91
🖹 0118 50 16 95
🄴 campveer@zeelandnet.nl
The hotel De Campveerse Toren
enjoys an idyllic location. The
original fortress-tower was
turned into an inn around 1500,

one of the oldest in Holland.
Reputedly, it served the wedding
meal in 1574 to William of
Orange; today excellent cuisine is
served in the romantic tower
restaurant. The hotel boasts a
beautiful art collection and many
antique pieces of furniture. Most
bedrooms have a good view over
the yachting harbor.

🛏 12

WINTERSWIJK   C2

Winterswijk

Stad Munster $$
Markt 11, 7101 DA
Winterswijk, Gelderland
☎ 0543 51 21 21
🖹 0543 52 24 15
This authentic 1911 Jugenstil
building is located at the
marketplace of Winterswijk. The
name of the hotel derives from

the peace treaty of Munster in
1648, the same year that the inn
was founded, making it one of
the oldest inns in Holland. The
bedrooms are comfortable and
have modern amenities, but the
reason why people come to the
hotel is the restaurant, which is
famous for its game specialties.
Weather permitting, dinner also
is served in the beautiful

English-style garden at the back.

🛏 20

ZUTPHEN   C2

Bronkhorst

De Gouden Leeuw $
Bovenstraat 2 , 7226 LM
Bronkhorst, Gelderland
☎ 0575 45 12 31
🖹 0575 45 25 66
🄴 oechies@worldonline.nl
Right in the heart of the smallest
historic town in the Netherlands
sits this renovated inn, the perfect
spot for hot chocolate and a piece
of the famous local cake. The

cozy lounge with fireplace has a
17th-century atmosphere. The
restaurant serves a choice of
excellent dishes. Six of the bed-
rooms are furnished in English
country style, and those in the
annex have views of the Ijssel
River.

🛏 11

Hummelo

De Gouden Karper $
Dorpsstraat 9, 6999 AA
Hummelo, Gelderland
☎ 0314 38 12 14
🖹 0314 38 22 38
The De Gouden Karper is
housed in a building that dates
back to 1642 and is one of the
best-known eating establish-
ments in the region. It has been
in the capable hands of the same

family for generations. The
spacious dining room serves
large helpings of various game
specialties. The hotel has an old-
fashioned bar and a large garden
with chestnut trees. The
comfortable bedrooms are
located mostly in the annex.

🛏 15

Key to Symbols: Fax   Email   Rooms   Parking   Swimming

Portugal

*P*ortugal is small, diverse and beautiful. Lying on the western edge of the European continent, it squeezes an astonishing variety of landscapes into its 350-mile length, including mountains (the highest being 6,500-foot Torre), plateaus, river valleys, flat dry plains, rolling forested hills and a beautiful coastline. Weather conditions range from the hot sun of southern Portugal to the notably mild, very damp conditions of the north. The Algarve, a vacation area on the southern coast, has a micro-climate all its own: backed by two mountain ranges, it enjoys a Mediterranean climate and has subtropical vegetation. The country is divided roughly in half by the River Tejo (Tagus).

Changing Fortunes

Portugal's fortunes have seen many ups and downs. The Portuguese empire once stretched from South America to Africa, India and the Far East, as Portuguese explorers pushed far into the unknown, rounding the Cape of Good Hope in 1487. However, the Golden Age, when spices, slaves and gold made Portugal hugely rich, barely lasted a hundred years or so, and for a long time this was one of the poorer European nations. Now its fortunes are on the rise again, but Portugal remains an intriguing mix of the old and new, the progressive and the undeveloped.

The People

The Portuguese are conservative people who are generally courteous and respectful. Northerners tend to be more devoutly religious than southerners, although the Catholic church holds sway everywhere. Most of the population still lives in rural areas, even though there was a large urban increase in the 1970s.

The Portuguese tend to be welcoming and unhurried. Many men, especailly in rural areas, have old-fashioned ideas and attitudes toward women. It's considered disrespectful to wear skimpy clothing, and is expected that you will speak formally and politely until you get to know people.

The Language

Despite, or because of, the proximity to Spain, the Portuguese do not take kindly to being addressed in Spanish. However, if you can read Spanish, you'll have no problems reading Portuguese. English is generally spoken in major tourist areas, although rarely in the

Shopping tips

The area known as the Chiado in downtown Lisbon is the fashionable shopping district, with streets lined with classy clothing, shoe and jewelry boutiques. The wonderful carpets from Arraiolos are a superb buy, as is the exquisite porcelain manufactured by Vista Alegre. Linen and cotton tablecloths and sheets are another Portuguese specialty. You can even have the lovely glazed tiles, *azulejos*, made to order, or track down something made from cork, one of Portugal's biggest exports.

National Palace, Sintra

deep countryside. Do try and tackle one or two words; your efforts will be appreciated

Accommodations

Hotels in Portugal offer some of the best values in Europe. Although true bargains are now harder to find, a reasonable budget will still secure relatively high standards of service and comfortable accommodations. Apart from the usual range of international hotels and small, family-run pensions, a particular feature of Portugal is its network of *pousadas*. Similar in concept to the *paradores* of Spain, *pousadas* are restored and converted former castles, palaces and monasteries offering quality accommodations with an authentic Portuguese flavor.

Typically, hotel bedrooms are simply furnished but often with traditionally styled furniture and decoration. Rooms with single or double beds are often available, but rooms with two single beds are most common, especially in cities and the larger coastal resort towns. Private bathrooms, usually with a shower rather than a bath, are common. Outside the summer months, it may be worth confirming that your bedroom will have heating; if the establishment caters mainly to the tourist trade, this may well be an optional feature.

Amarante

Breakfast is often not included in the price of your room, but Portuguese law dictates that all hotels must clearly display a list of meal charges at the reception desk. Breakfast is usually standard Continental fare such as breads, cold meats, cheese, and honey, with larger hotels offering this as a buffet with additional options of cooked eggs, cereals and perhaps yogurts.

Food and Drink

Lisbon has a wide range of restaurants at every price level, with the emphasis on traditional Portuguese cooking, although fast-food outlets are very much part of the scene. Breakfast is small and sweet, with hotels usually geared to foreign tastes, and lunch is more substantial than in most capitals. Whether you choose to stay in a *pousada* or not, they are always a good choice for an evening meal.

International dishes are invariably available, but pride is taken in serving regional dishes and specialties. Portions in all restaurants are usually generous. Dishes to look out for in particular include vegetable soups, grilled sole or sardines, smoked ham and pork stews. Heavy soups are popular, salads are surprisingly hard to find year-round, and fresh fruit juice is virtually non-existent. Lisbon inhabitants eat a lot of fish and seafood, and the warming winter stews can be good. Chicken, usually served roasted or barbecued, is delicious, although the variety of accompanying vegetables is limited. In Lisbon it's also relatively easy to take a break from Portuguese food if you've seen enough cabbage soup and salted cod. You may be surprised at the number of pastry and cake shops around: the Portuguese are notoriously sweet-toothed, and Lisbon has many old-fashioned shops selling traditional products.

Portugal makes good red and white wine, national and foreign beers are

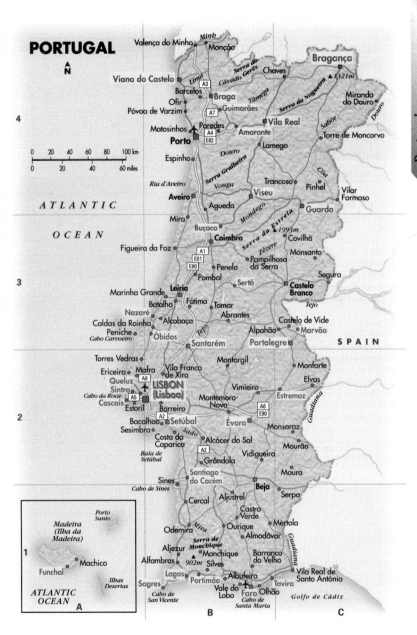

everywhere, and all the usual selections of spirits and aperitifs are available. Generally, when you order house wine in restaurants you'll get something highly acceptable, even if it appears in an earthenware jug. Tea (*chá*) is widely drunk, as is coffee. Water everywhere is safe to drink, although sometimes less than delicious. Avoid tap water in the Algarve in the height of summer; drink bottled water to be on the safe side.

PORTUGAL

AMARANTE   B4
Amarante

Pousada de São Gonçalo $
4600-Amarante, Porto
☎ (055) 46 11 23
🖹 (055) 46 13 53
Dating from 1942, Portugal's second-oldest *pousada* is set in a wooded mountain landscape. Staircases at the front and back lead to the rather small but brightly decorated bedrooms. This is a peaceful place to stay

for a day or two of complete relaxation.

🛏 15

BRAGA   B4
Braga
Castelo do Bom Jesus $
Monte do Bom Jesus, 4710-Braga
☎ (053) 67 65 66
🖹 (053) 67 76 91
Built on the ruins of a medieval castle, this 18th-century manor house enjoys a spectacular location on a hill high above the

city in a delightful garden with peacocks and exotic trees. Surrounding the house is a series of murals in traditional Portuguese blue ceramic tiles showing the most significant castles in the country's history.

🛏 10

Gandarela de Basto
Solar do Souto $
São Clemente de Basto, 4890-Gandarela de Basto, Braga
☎ (053) 65 51 42
An impressive staircase and corridor adorned with portraits of 19th-century nobility are guests' first introduction to this 18th-century mansion. The dining room, gallery and lounge

in the bell tower all have a pleasantly cloistered atmosphere. Bedrooms in the main house have typical Portuguese scrolled bedposts, while the rest are in a separate building with delightful garden views.

🛏 5

BRAGANÇA   C4
Macedo de Cavaleiros

Estalagem do Caçador $
Largo Manuel Pinto de Azevedo, 5340-Macedo de Cavaleiros, Bragança
☎ (078) 42 63 56
🖹 (078) 42 63 81
Trophies brought from Africa by Dr. Chaves de Lemos can now be admired by visitors to his former home, converted into a hotel by the growers of the

prestigious Quinta de Valpedrinhos wines. Some of the late explorer's mementos can be seen in a display cabinet in the elegant main lounge, and more still in the bar and the dining room.

🛏 24

BUCACO   B3
Luso

Vila Duparchy $
José Duarte Figueiredo, s/n, 3050-Luso, Aveiro
☎ (058) 74 16 72
🖹 (058) 74 14 44
French engineer Jean Alexis Duparchy was made a baron by King Carlos of Portugal for his contribution to the development of the nation's railroads. In the late 19th century, Duparchy built

himself this fine country house. The bedrooms upstairs are prettily decorated, and some are furnished with somber antiques. The house is surrounded by a large garden with a swimming pool.

🛏 6   ≈

Key to Symbols: 🖹 Fax   🇪 Email   🛏 Rooms   🅿 Parking   ≈ Swimming
   American Express   Diners Club   MasterCard   Visa

CASCAIS A2

Cascais

Albatroz $$-$$$
Frederico Arouca, 100, 2750-
Cascais, Lisboa
☎ (01) 483 28 21
📄 (01) 484 48 27
This villa, built in 1873 as a summer residence for the Portuguese royal family, is now a luxury hotel. It attracts a famous clientele whose every wish is instantly fulfilled. Below the terrace is a small, secluded cove, perfect for swimming, or you can opt for the hotel's own saltwater pool. The best of the bedrooms have balconies overlooking the sea.

🛏 37 🏊

◼ ⑩ 💳 ▨

Casa da Pérgola $
Avenida Valbom, 13, 2750-
Cascais, Lisboa
☎ (01) 484 00 40
📄 (01) 483 47 91
This charming 19th-century house takes its name from a pergola built at the end of the garden by an Englishman in love with the Lisbon coast. The facade, with its bright ceramic tiles, attracts many a passing photographer. The interior is a blend of domestic museum and stately home. Bedrooms differ in size and atmosphere, but all are perfectly preserved.

🛏 11

Hotel do Guincho $$
Praia do Guincho, 2751-
Cascais, Lisboa
☎ (01) 487 04 91
📄 (01) 487 04 31
Standing on a cliff battered by Atlantic gales, this 17th-century fort is rather alarming at first sight. However, inside the massive walls this grim-looking military installation has been transformed into a luxury hotel. The lounges arranged around the inner courtyard have magnificent ocean views. Bedrooms, overlooking the sea, are elegantly furnished and the bathrooms make sensible use of limited space.

🛏 28

◼ ⑩ 💳 ▨

ESTREMOZ C2

Vila Viçosa

Casa de Peixinhos $
Casa de Peixinhos, 7160-Vila
Viçosa, Évora
☎ (068) 984 72
📄 (068) 88 13 48
Once part of a working farm, this stately 17th-century manor house, built in the traditional style of the region, is surrounded by orange groves in the middle of the Alentejo plains. The accommodation centers on a handsome, white-painted front patio. The en suite bathrooms have marble floors, huge showers and a quality selection of complimentary toiletries.

🛏 7

ÉVORA B2

Évora

Estalagem Monte das Flores $
Monte das Flores, 7000-Évora
☎ (066) 254 90
📄 (066) 275 64
Antique furniture, red terrazzo floors, gilded lamps and traditional local pottery – all the characteristics of a typical old farmhouse. It is set in the middle of an estate that produces wine, olives and wheat, and rears sheep. The pink bedrooms – pink-painted furniture, pink prints, pink bathrooms – may not be to everyone's taste.

🛏 18

◼ ⑩ 💳 ▨

Key to Symbols: 📄 Fax e Email 🛏 Rooms P Parking 🏊 Swimming
◼ American Express ⑩ Diners Club 💳 MasterCard ▨ Visa

Solar Monfalim $
Largo da Misericordia, 1, 7000-Évora
☎ (066) 214 27
🖹 (066) 74 23 67

This 19th-century house with its white walls and graceful loggia has to be one of Portugal's most charming hotels. The public rooms are filled with delightfully quirky details, like an ancient wooden telephone switchboard, old motor horns, family photographs, antiquated furniture and belle époque bureaus. Bedrooms are equally appealing, with bronze canopies and a fabric screen to conceal the TV set.

🛏 27

FARO   B1
Vilamoura

Estalagem da Cegonha $
8125-Vilamoura, Faro
☎ (089) 30 25 77
🖹 (089) 32 26 75

The name of this small hotel, a stately 18th-century home, comes from the large number of storks nesting nearby. The atmosphere recalls the house's noble ancestry. The old stables provide horseback riding for guests, and there is a small racetrack where occasional meets are held. Comfortable bedrooms lead off a courtyard entered from the street through an eye-catching arch.

🛏 9

FUNCHAL   A1
Funchal

Quinta Perestrello $
Dr. Pita, 3, 9000-Funchal, Ilha de Madeira
☎ (091) 76 37 20
🖹 (091) 76 37 77

The 150-year-old Perestrello still retains the flavor of Madeira's quintas, or manor houses, before increasing tourism and the expansion of the city engulfed them. Bedrooms are simple but comfortable. Particularly charming are the later additions, which have more modern facilities and terraces leading to the swimming pool.

🛏 30 🏊

GUARDA   C4
Faia

Quinta da Ponte $
Quinta da Ponte, 6300-Faia, Guarda
☎ (071) 96 126
🖹 (071) 96 126

The focal point of a stay at this stately 17th-century home is the French-style garden, designed in 1740. It would be tempting to spend the whole time relaxing on its lawns, or lazing in a deckchair beside the swimming pool, enjoying views of surrounding Serra de Estrela National Park.

🛏 2 🏊

GUIMARÃES   B4
Guimarães

Paço de São Cipriano $
Tabuadelo, 4800-Guimarães, Braga
☎ (058) 74 16 72
🖹 (058) 74 14 44

The entrance hall of this 15th-century manor house resembles a folk museum with its array of old furniture, and the old oven in what is now the breakfast room is still used to make bread and preserves. The most striking bedroom has parrot wallpaper and a wooden ceiling, but the green-painted tower room with its canopied bed also is a favorite.

🛏 5

Key to Symbols: 🖹 Fax   📧 Email   🛏 Rooms   🅿 Parking   🏊 Swimming
    American Express   Diners Club   MasterCard   Visa

LAGOS B1
Lagos

LISBON (LISBOA) A2
Lisbon

As Janelas Verdes **$$**
Janelas Verdes, 47, 1200-Lisboa
☎ (01) 396 81 43
🖹 (01) 396 81 44
Elegant townhouse named "Green Windows" after the street in which it is situated. The most popular rooms overlook the Tagus estuary; others have views

MARVÃO C3
Marvão

Pousada de Santa Maria **$-$$**
Rua 24 de Janeiro, 7, 7330-Marvão, Portalegre
☎ (045) 932 01
🖹 (045) 934 40
Marvão is a typical medieval village perched on a rocky slope overlooking the plain of Alentejo. One of its finest

NAZARÉ B3
Nazaré

ÓBIDOS B3
Óbidos

Pousada do Castelo **$$**
Paço Real, 2510-Óbidos, Leiria
☎ (062) 95 91 05
🖹 (062) 95 91 48
Contrary to what one might expect from a castle, the rooms here are neither large nor opulent, but they do feel authentic. Apart from stunning

Vivienda Miranda **$$-$$$**
Porto de Mós, 8600-Lagos, Faro
☎ (082) 76 32 22
🖹 (082) 76 03 42
Swiss owner Urs Wild set out to turn this former family home into a thoroughly professional hotel. It is approached through a charming garden with a swimming pool, and offers attractive rooms and suites with

of the city. The coziest room in the house is the little lounge next to the reception area, with its self-service bar. In summer, breakfast is served on the small terrace behind the hotel.

🛏 17
🔲 🔲 🔲

houses, built in the 17th century, became a *pousada* more than 50 years ago. Dinner in the dining room is an unforgettable experience, with dramatic views of the mountains. The bedrooms are furnished in late 19th-century style.

🛏 28
🔲 🔲 🔲

Quinta do Campo **$**
Valado dos Frades, 2450-Nazaré, Leiria
☎ (062) 57 71 35
🖹 (062) 57 75 55
The last surviving farm linked with the Cistercian monastery of Alcobaça, founded in the 12th century, has been transformed into an elegant tourist accommodation.

views, the dining room features an impressively large fireplace and a display of sepia-colored ceramic tiles.
The hotel closes at night, so there is no one available to admit latecomers.

🛏 9

hand-painted furniture, judicious lighting and excellent views of the coast.

🛏 7
🔲 🔲 🔲

The house offers a cozy wood-paneled lounge and a library with 12,000 books. The former wine cellar in a neighboring building has been converted into a large conference room, and there are two independent apartments designed for family vacations.

🛏 8
🔲 🔲 🔲

PORTALEGRE · C3

Crato

Pousada Flor da Rosa $$
7430-Crato, Portalegre
☎ (045) 99 72 10
🖹 (045) 99 72 12

Founded in the 13th century by the Knights of Malta, this castle has a new wing housing a *pousada* unlike any other. With its Bauhaus inspiration, it is surprising, colorful and daring. But somehow the public rooms

and guest accommodations manage to harmonize with their medieval surroundings and achieve a high standard of comfort.

🛏 24
⬛ ⑩ 💳 💳

Portalegre

Quinta da Saude $
Serra de Portalegre, 7300-Portalegre
☎ (045) 223 24
🖹 (045) 272 34

Built by refugees from the Spanish Civil War, this was until quite recently a hospital for tuberculosis patients who benefited from the mountain air of the Serra de São Mamede.

The main attraction is the restaurant, using local products to produce regional specialties. The bedrooms are located in two separate buildings a few yards up the hill from the main house.

🛏 18
⬛ 💳 💳

PORTIMÃO · B1

Portimão

Bela Vista $-$$
Av. Tomás Cabreira, 8500-Portimão, Faro
☎ (082) 240 55
🖹 (082) 41 53 69

High on the cliffs above Praia da Rocha, the palatial silhouette of this 19th-century mansion provides a pleasing contrast to

the lackluster developments along the coast. Inside there are impressive murals of 18th-century tiles depicting Portuguese exploits in South America, a staircase of Brazilian wood, the coffered ceiling in the bar and two lounges with a collection of 19th-century pianos.

🛏 14   ⬛ ⑩ 💳 💳

Vila Lido $
Praia da Rocha, 8500-Portimão, Faro
☎ (082) 241 27
🖹 (082) 242 46

A loyal clientele returns to this modest family hotel to be pampered by the friendly and obliging owners. It is set in a quirky little garden next to the 17th-century fortress of Santa

Catalina. The breakfast room, with its fireplace and hand-painted tiles, has sea views, as do the bedrooms on the floor above.

 🛏 10
💳

QUELUZ · A2

Queluz

Pousada de Dona Maria I $$
2745-Queluz, Lisboa
☎ (01) 435 61 58
🖹 (01) 435 61 89

The Clock Tower, once the servants' quarters of this neo-classical palace, has been converted to become one of Portugal's most refined *pousadas*. Public rooms are positively palatial, with exquisite stucco,

regal chandeliers and opulent curtains. By contrast, the bedrooms comply with the austere standards set by the national *pousada* network. Guests can stroll in the palace gardens, reminiscent of Versailles.

🛏 24
⬛ ⑩ 💳 💳

Key to Symbols: 🖹 Fax 🅴 Email 🛏 Rooms 🅿 Parking 🏊 Swimming
  ⬛ American Express ⑩ Diners Club 💳 MasterCard 💳 Visa

SAGRES   B1
Sagres

Fortaleza do Beliche $
Estrada do Cabo São Vicente,
km5, 8650-Sagres, Faro
☎ (082) 641 24
▤ (082) 642 25
This 15th-century fort is a
reminder of the great era of
Portuguese exploration. The
small hotel within its walls – an
annex to the nearby *pousada* – is
a rather gloomy place, with an
odd memorial chapel, a lounge
overlooking the sea and four
bedrooms arranged in a row. In
summer – wind permitting –
breakfast can be taken on the
terrace.

🛏 4
▨ ⓓ 💳 VISA

Pousada do Infante $$
8650-Sagres, Faro
☎ (082) 642 22
▤ (082) 642 25
Standing on a headland with
views along the length of the
western coast of the Algarve, this
pousada pays homage to Henry
the Navigator. Although built in
the 1960s, it has a distinctly
monumental feel. Public rooms
are elegant, and the bedrooms
bright and thoughtfully
appointed. They all overlook the
ocean, and sometimes the wind
whistles eerily through the
arcade on the terrace.

🛏 39
▨ ⓓ 💳 VISA

SANTARÉM   B3
Rio Maior

Quinta da Ferraria $
suite 15.700 $
Ribeira de Sao João, Estrada N-
114, 2040-Rio Maior, Santarém
☎ (043) 950 01
▤ (043) 956 96
Converted farmhouse featuring
its own small museum of country
life. There are well-appointed
double rooms in the main house,
and the owners also have
provided a lounge with an open
hearth and a billiard room,
containing the remains of an old
flour mill. Local specialties are
served in the dining room
overlooking the woods.

🛏 13
💳 VISA

SANTIAGO
DO CACÉM   B2
Santiago do Cacém

Pousada de São Tiago $
Estrada de Lisboa, 7540-
Santiago do Cacém, Setúbal
☎ (069) 224 59
▤ (069) 224 59
This stylish house, dating from
1947, is the most architecturally
pleasing of Santiago's two
pousadas. Designed to
harmonize with its surroundings,
it came to set the standard for
custom-built *pousadas* around
the country. The rooms are
somewhat spartan and newly
arrived guests may often find the
reception desk unattended or
manned by hotel school trainees.

🛏 8   ▨ ⓓ 💳 VISA

Pousada Quinta da Ortiga $
7540-Santiago do Cacém, Beja
☎ (069) 228 71
▤ (069) 220 73
The swimming pool, sheltered
by an arcade of ceramic tiles, is
much more romantic than the
main house of this *pousada*. But
the bedrooms are comfortable,
pleasantly decorated and well
appointed. Guests can explore
the surrounding countryside on
horseback or bicycle. Watch out
for the unguarded level crossing
on the railroad track in the
middle of the woods as you
approach the house.

🛏 8   🏊
▨ ⓓ 💳 VISA

Key to Symbols: ▤ Fax 🅔 Email 🛏 Rooms 🅿 Parking 🏊 Swimming
▨ American Express ⓓ Diners Club 💳 MasterCard VISA Visa

SERTA   B3
Cernache do Bonjardim

Estalagem Vale de Ursa   **$**
6100-Cernache do Bonjardim,
Castelo Branco,
☎ (074) 909 81
▤ (074) 909 82
This hotel stands alone in
unspoiled countryside on the
banks of Portugal's largest
artificial reservoir. The rooms are
spacious, spotless and sweet
smelling, with views of the

unpolluted Zézere River. Apart
from walking through the
neighboring hills, the more
active guest can take advantage
of the swimming pool and tennis
court, or engage in water sports
on the reservoir.

 12 

SETÚBAL   B2
Setúbal
Pousada de São Filipe   **$$**
Castelo de São Filipe, 2900-
Setúbal
☎ (065) 52 38 44
▤ (065) 53 25 38
Built in 1590, this fortress was
clearly designed for military
purposes rather than hospitality.
This is no place for those

unwilling or unable to walk, as
the elevators do not always work,
but one can always take a
breather in the 18th-century
chapel halfway up the stairs. The
glorious views from the ramparts
are the *pousada's* main attraction.

🛏 13

Vila Fresca d'Azeitão
Club d'Azeitão   **$$**
Estrada N-10, 2925-Vila Fresca
d'Azeitão, Setúbal
☎ (01) 218 22 67
▤ (01) 219 16 29
This house has connections with
the Almada family (leading
figures in Portugal's colonial and
diplomatic history). The 17th-
century diplomat Rui Fernandes

de Almada amassed a priceless
collection of Flemish art, some
of which is preserved here. The
main building was reconstructed
as a hotel in the 19th century
after the original was destroyed
by fire.

🛏 10

SINTRA   A2
Sintra

Palacio de Seteáis   **$$$**
Barbosa do Bocage, 8, 2710-
Sintra, Lisboa
☎ (01) 923 32 00
▤ (01) 923 42 77
A glorious palace in the Garden
of Eden is the only way to
describe this national
monument, completed at the
beginning of the 19th century.
All the magnificence was

retained when the palace was
converted into a hotel, with a
succession of stately rooms
decorated in rococo style, with
18th-century furniture and
murals, statuary and chandeliers
all creating a regal atmosphere.

🛏 28

Quinta da Capela   **$$**
Estrada de Monserrate, 2710-
Sintra, Lisboa
☎ (01) 929 01 70
▤ (01) 929 34 25
🄴 The sights that inspired the
poet Lord Byron can be enjoyed
from this beautiful 16th-century
manor house, which was
completely reconstructed after
the devastating earthquake of

1755. Countless antiques and
works of art adorn the interiors,
and each of the rooms and suites
is individually styled with
canopied beds and oil paintings
by one of the owners.

🛏 7

TAVIRA B1

Tavira

Qinta do Caracol $
Bairro de São Pedro, 8800-Tavira, Faro
☎ (081) 224 75
🖹 (081) 231 75

Regular guests at this 17th-century estate, now a sophisticated vacation village, particularly appreciate its southern ambience – whitewashed walls, pots of geraniums, a well at the entrance and the undulating Moorish roof tiles. The cottages, some with sea or mountain views, are deliberately rustic and delightfully homey. The shady garden has a swimming pool and is patrolled by two friendly peacocks.

 7

VIANA DO CASTELO B4

Ponte de Lima

Paço da Gloria $
Jolda, 4970-Ponte de Lima, Viana do Castelo
☎ (058) 94 71 77
🖹 (058) 94 74 97

In converting this fine 17th-century house into a hotel, the owner wisely left its massive towers largely untouched. Instead, eight of the 10 rooms are in a recently built annex. The real glory of the mansion is the gallery extending from end to end, lined with busts of kings copied from those in the Louvre.

 10

Vila Nova de Cerveira

Estalagem da Boega $
Quinta do Outeiral, 4920-Vila Nova de Cerveira, Viana do Castelo
☎ (051) 79 52 31
🖹 (051) 79 60 71

This 16th-century Augustinian convent stands in an idyllic setting among vineyards and woodland. Suites, arranged around the ancient cloister, feature coffered wooden ceilings and bedcovers of Portuguese lace. Don't miss the chapel – its walls lined with a dazzling display of traditional ceramic tiles – and try to catch one of the occasional theatrical performances staged in these delightful surroundings.

 28

VILA REAL B4

Caldas de Moledo

Casa das Torres de Oliveira $
Oliveira, Mesão Frio, 5050-Caldas de Moledo, Vila Real
☎ (054) 2 37 43
🖹 (01) 387 95 49

Fine guest rooms are offered at this 18th-century manor house – bright, spacious and elegantly furnished. The house, with its massive towers standing high above the Douro Valley, is part of a large port-producing estate. Inside, the stately simplicity of bare stone walls, coffered ceilings and wooden floors will delight those visitors fortunate enough to find this charming country hotel open.

 5

VISEU B4

Mangualde

Casa d'Azurara $
Nova, 78, 3530-Mangualde, Viseu
☎ (032) 61 20 10
🖹 (032) 62 25 75

An excellent example of how to preserve the nation's heritage, this delightful country house, built in the late 18th century for the Counts of Mangualde, was converted by their latest descendent into a hotel in the 1990s. The dining room has an agreeably rustic ambience, with an open hearth and a veranda leading to the garden.

 15

Spain

Spain is a land of contrasts. It has many landscapes, peoples, climates and cultures. In the most mountainous nation in Europe, tourists flock to lie on Mediterranean beaches; in a largely rural, traditional country, the cities are stylish, dynamic and forward-looking. Since the end of Spain's long isolation under General Franco's dictatorship, the monarchy has been restored as a symbol of unity, while acknowledging the differences of regions such as Catalonia and Galicia by granting them autonomy, and maintaining an uneasy relationship with the Basques, who continue to call for separate powers. Spain is fascinating and beautiful, and never ceases to surprise.

Mountains and Beaches

The Pyrenees mountain chain divides Spain and the Iberian Peninsula from the rest of Europe. From the Sierra Nevada in the south to the Cordillera Cantábrica in the north, the land is dominated by the Meseta, a huge plateau surrounded by mountain ranges with an average altitude of 2,100 feet. On the northern coast, the dramatic Asturian peaks are a match for the mighty Pyrenees.

Unlike the mild, moist Atlantic Costa Verde in the north, the southern Mediterranean coast stretches in a series of sun-baked beaches to the shore of the Straits of Gibraltar, only 9 miles from Africa. Here the summers are hot and dry, and winters mild and wet. But inland, winters can be very cold. The Spanish island groups of the Balearics and Canaries have weather characteristics all their own.

Cities and Castles

Barcelona is the most cosmopolitan and economically active Spanish city, a center of Modernist architecture and especially of the works of Antoni Gaudí. Madrid, the capital since 1562, sits at the heart of the Iberian Peninsula. Its fine medieval center dates back to the Habsburg Empire's 16th-century golden age. Seville is a focus of Andalusian culture, where flamenco and bullfighting still inspire passion, and the elegant Moorish architecture stands as a monument to 800 years of occupation. Córdoba is another Andalusian treasure, where the most famous of many monuments is the Mezquita, or Moorish mosque. Granada, the long-established capital of Moorish Andalusia, is home of the world-famous Alhambra.

Keeping your Cool

The Spanish have a lifestyle that makes the most of the cool mornings and evenings, and keeps out of the hot summer sun. Most rise very early and work until about 1 p.m. From then until 5 p.m., Spain takes its siesta. Stores, offices, churches and museums close; everyone goes home for a late lunch and to sleep through the worst heat of the day. Spaniards are now ready for a late night. In the fresh evening air you can shop, or sit until the early hours in a café or restaurant. Whole families, including small children, eat out at 9 or 10 p.m., when entertainment usually begins; clubs aren't likely to get going until after midnight.

A street in Estepona

Spain

Accommodations

Away from the cities and popular beach resorts of the south and east, Spain's accommodations have traditionally been dominated by small pensions and guest houses. However, today the country boasts a range of attractive and good-quality hotels, led by the network of *paradores*. Created within converted buildings, such as fortresses and monasteries, these state-run hotels mix heritage and style with excellent levels of comfort and service. Even if they're beyond your budget, you're usually welcome to look around and have a drink at the bar or terrace.

Hotel rooms in Spain are usually attractively decorated, often with

traditional furnishings, and contain two single beds as standard. Telephones and televisions are common, as is air conditioning, in hotels of three Spanish stars or more. Rooms are generally of good size, and storage space for clothes is often plentiful. Private bathrooms are common, often containing a bathtub rather than a shower.

Breakfast can vary from a simple meal of hot coffee or chocolate and doughnut-style *churros* to more sumptuous buffet spreads, typically offered by four-star hotels. In addition to the usual Continental fare, these will offer boiled eggs, sausages, toast, fresh fruit and cereals.

"Agritourism" is a term used to describe accommodations available on working farms. "Green" or "rural" tourism are terms used to describe accommodations located in the countryside, by the sea or in the mountains.

Spain

Food and Drink

Eating out is a real pleasure in Spain, and there's much to choose from. Fresh fish and seafood are always worth trying, and appetizers often include a selection of shellfish, tiny grilled sardines or giant prawns. In Barcelona, local main seafood dishes are often a type of *sarsuela*, fish stew, or *suquet de peix*, a soupy fish and potato casserole.

In Catalonia, *mar i muntanya* (sea and mountain) cooking uses local ingredients to create combination dishes featuring rabbit, shrimp, prawns, chicken and meat.

Main dishes are usually accompanied by flavored vegetables, a saffron sauce, a garlic mayonnaise or a crisp salad. *Tapas* bars specialize in delicious selections of hot or cold savory mouthfuls served with drinks. The dozens available will include fish, smoked ham, stewed peppers, salads, local almonds and olives. Cured ham, spicy sausages and garlic snails are often part of a *tapas* lunch in Barcelona.

Tea, coffee, soda and fruit juice are served in bars, along with alcohol. Local red, white and rosé wines come from the Penedés area; Torres and Masia Bach are reliable labels. Cava, a great aperitif, is a light, sparkling wine, made the same way as champagne.

A POBRA DE TRIVES A4

A Pobra de Trives

Casa Grande de Trives   **$**
Marqués de Trives, 17, 32780,
Ourense
☎ 988332066
🖹 988332066
📧 casagtrives@tpi.informail.es

Inspired by the bed and breakfast establishments of neighboring Portugal, Adelaida and her sons offer the same services in this 17th-century manor house set in a tranquil garden shaded by chestnut trees. Here, a chapel dedicated to Our Lady of the Sea houses a magnificent 18th-century altarpiece. Of the seven rooms, the two on the ground floor most deserve the label "charming."

🛏 7   🅿

Pazo Paradela   **$**
Ctra. de Barrio, km 2, 32780,
Ourense
☎ 988330714
🖹 988330714

Like so many generations of Gallegos, Manuel Rodríguez emigrated far afield to seek his fortune. After years in New York, homesickness drove him to exchange the Big Apple for the smaller ones he now cultivates on the 120-acre estate surrounding his country home. The 17th-century manor house has five rooms, and is an excellent center for cycling around the surrounding hills. You may be lucky enough to be there on an evening when Manuel organizes a *queimada*, an authentically Galician party centering around the preparation and drinking of hot and very potent punch.

🛏 7   Closed Dec. 23-Feb. 1   🅿

ABEJAR C4

Herreros

Casa del Cura   **$**
Estación, s/n, 42145, Soria
☎ 975270464
🖹 975270465

High praise goes to José Luis Gómez for the enormous effort he has put into the meticulous restoration of a former priest's house in this remote corner of the province of Soria. Refurbished with local stone, the house in its woodland setting has become a cozy weekend retreat for city dwellers in search of clean country air. The rooms are decorated with antiques rescued from old houses in the surrounding countryside, and dinner consists of hearty local dishes. In the fall, the surrounding woods are full of edible mushrooms.

🛏 12   🅿

Molinos de Duero

Real Posada de la Mesta   **$-$$**
Plaza Cañerías, s/n, 42156,
Soria
☎ 975378531
🖹 975231539
📧 posadamesta.3017@cajarural.com

Built in 1729, this stately mansion at the foot of the Picos de Urbión beside the beautiful Laguna Negra combines period charm with modern features, such as a billiard room, a children's playroom supervised by video cameras and a dining room with huge windows looking out onto the garden. The bedrooms, arranged around a courtyard, are decorated with examples of local craftsmanship enhanced by clever lighting.

🛏 13   Closed Jan. 10-31   🅿

AGUILAR DE CAMPOO C4

Aguilar de Campoo

Posada de Santa María la Real $
Avda. Cervera, s/n, 34800,
Palencia
☎ 979122000
🖹 979125680

The northern part of Palencia province offers a veritable feast for lovers of Romanesque architecture with a vast number of hermitages, churches and monasteries now in the process of restoration. Among them is the ninth-century Cistercian monastery of Santa María la Real, one wing of which has been converted to provide tourist accommodations. Bedrooms are arranged as duplexes, with beds on the upper level and baths below.

🛏 22   Closed Dec. 23-25   🅿

Key to Symbols: 🖹 Fax   📧 Email   🛏 Rooms   🅿 Parking   🏊 Swimming

Santa María de Mave

El Convento   **$**
Monasterio de Santa María de Mave, 34492, Palencia
☎ 979123611
🖹 979125492
📧 convento@arrakis.es

More and more former church properties are now catering to the needs of travelers in Spain, especially in the relatively unexplored mountains of Palencia. One such example is the ancient priory of Santa María de Mave, set among trees on the banks of the Pisuerga River, and owned by the Moral family. The intricate winding passageways between the tranquil rooms come straight out of *The Name of the Rose*.

🛏 25 🅿

ALBARRACÍN   D3

Albarracín

Casa de Santiago   **$**
Subida a las Torres, 11, 44100, Teruel
☎ 978700316

This charming little hotel created in former headquarters of the Knights of the Order of Santiago harmonizes to perfection with its medieval surroundings. Its greatest charm is undoubtedly the tastefully chosen and skilfully executed interior decor drawing on traditional rural craftsmanship. There is not even a TV in the rooms to spoil the atmosphere. From both the lounge and some of the bedrooms, notably #1 and #2, there are views across the historic town.

🛏 8   Closed Feb.

ALCALÁ DE HENARES   C3

Pastrana

Hospedería Real de Pastrana   **$**
Convento del Carmen (Ctra. C-200 Pastrana-Zorita), 19100, Guadalajara
☎ 949371060
🖹 949371060

St. Teresa of Avila founded this former Carmelite convent, and the great Spanish mystic St. John of the Cross was its first prior. The cell in which he prayed is still preserved. Vaulted corridors lead to the austere bedrooms, overlooking the Sierra de Altomira and the rooftops of Pastrana.

🛏 25
🅿

ALCAÑIZ   D3

Alcañiz

Parador de Alcañiz   **$-$$**
Castillo de los Calatravos, s/n, 44600, Teruel
☎ 978830400
🖹 978830366

From its hilltop position above the town of Alcañiz, this 12th-century castle-monastery, once the seat of the Order of Calatrava, dominates the surrounding country. Despite the formidable size of the building, the parador only provides 12 bedrooms, although these are complemented by spacious lounges, two dining rooms and an interior courtyard below the medieval tower. The furniture in the public rooms is designed to recapture a feudal atmosphere, or at least the Hollywood version of the Middle Ages.

🛏 12   Closed Dec. 18-Feb. 2   🅿

ALCOLEA DEL PINAR   C3

Sigüenza

Molino de Alcuneza   **$**
Ctra. de Alboreca, km 0,500, 19250, Guadalajara
☎ 949391501
🖹 949391508
📧 molinoal@teleline.es

This 500-year-old flour mill is turning once again as the centerpiece of one of the most delightful hotels in the vicinity of Madrid. The bedrooms are individually decorated, with charming rural touches such as the farming implements that adorn the walls. In winter the house is kept cozy and warm, and there is a welcoming open fire.

🛏 11
Closed Jan. 15-Feb. 15
🅿 🏊

Key to Symbols: 🖹 Fax   📧 Email   🛏 Rooms   🅿 Parking   🏊 Swimming

ALCOY D2
Penàguila

Mas de Pau **$**
Ctra. Alcoi-Penáguila, km 9,
3815, Alacant/Alicante
☎ 965513111
🖹 965513109
This 19th-century farmhouse is perched on a hillside and built in the traditional east coast style. The similarly rustic Mas del Jove on one side of the building hosts wedding receptions and business seminars. The proximity of the Mediterranean and views from the terrace, with the Sena tower in the foreground, inspire business visitors and vacationers alike. Rooms and shower facilities are small.

🛏 18

ALGAIDA E1
Algaida
Possessió Binicomprat **$$**
Finca de Binicomprat, s/n, 7210,
Baleares/Mallorca
☎ 971125028
🖹 971125028
This 370-acre estate on the island of Majorca dates from 1229 and has been in the owners' family since the 15th century. The main house contains three bedrooms, the cellar, the former chapel and the kitchen, now a delightful breakfast room. Enormous rooms with canopied beds are faithful to the island tradition, austere but beautiful. Former stables house four apartments and two double rooms.

🛏 8

Pina
Son Xotano **$$-$$$**
Ctra. de Pina a Sencelles, km
1,500, 7220, Baleares/Mallorca
☎ 971872500
🖹 971872501
Stone-built 16th-century Italianate house set at the end of a driveway amid 250 acres of open fields given over to breeding horses. A handsome wrought-iron staircase leads to the bedrooms, situated off the first-floor lounge. In addition to peace, good food and a swimming pool, the hotel offers riding lessons and excursions into the surrounding countryside.

🛏 8

Randa
Es Recó de Randa **$$**
Font, 21, 7629,
Baleares/Mallorca
☎ 971660997
🖹 971662558
🇪 esreco@fehm.es
At the foot of Puig de Randa, 19 miles from Palma, this little hotel has been fashioned from a village house. It is justly renowned for its cooking, based on local produce. Visitors tend to be those who have given up on the coast and its summer crowds, in favor of the Provencal-style rooms overlooking the village rooftops.

🛏 10

ALICANTE D2
Tabarca

Casa del Gobernador **$**
Arzola, s/n, 3138,
Alacant/Alicante
☎ 965114260
🖹 965114260
When the summer crowds have gone the island of Tabarca is virtually deserted, with nothing left but four fishermen's houses, a Civil Guard blockhouse and this little hotel created from the 18th-century former governor's residence. Now that electricity is supplied from the mainland, the hotel will soon be equipped with year-round air conditioning, much appreciated on sultry summer nights.

🛏 14
Closed Jan. 15-Feb. 15

ALMERÍA C1

San José

San José **$$**
Correo, s/n, 4118, Almería
☎ 950380116
🖹 950380002

Eduardo Zárate's waterfront hotel is an imitation of a Basque country house, once used as an esparto grass warehouse. The simple conversion is entertaining and tasteful in a modern way. Bedrooms are spacious, and the air conditioning is a colonial-style ceiling fan. Mealtimes are a bit restricted, and a credit card guarantee is required for telephone reservations.

🛏 8 Closed Nov. 1-Mar. 1   🅿

ALZIRA D2

Xàtiva/Játiva

Hostería de Mont Sant **$$**
Subida al Castillo, s/n, 46800, Valencia
☎ 962275081
🖹 962281905
📧 montsant@servitex.com

Surrounded by acres of lovingly tended gardens full of fragrant Mediterranean vegetation, the hotel was created from an old manor house built on the ruins of a medieval monastery, which in turn stood on the site of a Moorish palace. Silence and tranquility are the watchwords here. The bedrooms are individually styled, and the restaurant serving regional dishes is a definite plus. Departing guests are presented with a gift of oranges grown on the estate.

🛏 6 🅿

ANDORRA LA VELLA E4

Bolvir de Cerdanya

Chalet del Golf **$-$$**
La Devesa del Golf, 17520, Girona
☎ 972880950
🖹 972880966

There is a distinctly British feel to the clubhouse of the Real Club de Golf de la Cerdanya. Although designed to provide accommodation for members, non-members are made to feel just as welcome. Set against the dazzling green of the course, with bungalows overlooking the 18th green, the house stands in the valley below La Molina and enjoys views of the snow-capped mountains.

🛏 5

🅿

Torre del Remei **$$$**
Camí Reial, s/n, 17463, Girona
☎ 972140182
🖹 972140449
📧 t.remei@gro.servicom.es

This belle époque gem standing in huge grounds has been restored to create a small, super-luxury hotel. With Greek marble, Italian furniture, Tibetan rugs and Bang and Olufsen TV and video, no expense has been spared in the 11 bedrooms, each with its own gleaming bathroom equipped with king-size bath and Jacuzzi. The elegant accommodations are complemented by Josep María Boix's imaginative cuisine.

🛏 11

🅿

La Seu d'Urgell

El Castell **$$**
Ctra. N-620 km, 224, 25700, Lleida
☎ 973350704
🖹 973351574
📧 elcastell@relaischateaux.fr

Jaume Tàpies fell in love with the region while doing his military service, and he and his family eventually built one of the most delightful hotels in the Spanish Pyrenees. It has all the qualifications for membership in the prestigious Relais & Châteaux organization: character, courtesy, calm, cuisine and charm. The auditorium hosts year-round concerts, and each of the elegant rooms has a balcony with mountain views.

🛏 32 🅿

Meranges

Can Borrell $
Retorn, 3, 17539, Girona
☎ 972880033
🖹 972880144
e info@canborrell.com
Hidden away in a remote corner of the most prosperous area of the Spanish Pyrenees, this pleasant little hotel is within easy reach of 22 ski resorts. Hewn from the slate and granite of the surrounding mountains, it has wood-paneled walls, exposed beams and rustic furniture. The dining room serves traditional local dishes.

🛏 8
Open Sat.-Sun. only, Jan. 7-Apr. 30
🅿

ANTEQUERA B1
Villanueva de la Concepción
La Posada del Torcal $$
Ctra. de la Joya, 29230, Málaga
☎ 952031177
🖹 952031000
e laposada@mercuryin.es
Beneath the dramatic rock formations of El Torcal National Park stands this charming country house hotel, run with taste and panache by its Finnish owners, Jan and Karen Rautavuori. Its terrace, protected by an awning from the fierce Andalusian sun, has stunning views of the valley below. The individually styled rooms have balconies; others feature semicircular baths, and most have their own fireplaces.

🛏 9 Closed Nov. 14-Feb. 1
🅿 ≋

ARACENA B2
Aracena
Finca Valbono $
Ctra. a Carboneras, km 1, 21200, Huelva
☎ 959127711
🖹 959127679
Adults and children alike will find plenty to do at this estate in Sierra de Aracena National Park. Sports facilities include football, tennis, volleyball and basketball, and stables where a team of professionals are ready to instruct novice riders. Guests are accommodated in a selection of cottages, farmhouses and a new building in traditional Andalusian style.

🛏 26
🅿 ≋

Los Marines
Finca Buenvino $
Ctra. Sevilla-Portugal, km 92 a 1km al oeste de Los Marines, 21293, Huelva
☎ 959124034
🖹 959501029
e sam@fincabuenvino.com
A British couple run this small hotel in a remote corner of Andalusia, tucked away in Los Marines National Park. The red ochre facade is characteristic of 19th-century Andalusian houses, but the atmosphere inside is more reminiscent of an English country house. All the guests eat together, on the terrace in summer and in the dining room in winter.

🛏 4 Closed Aug. & Dec. 15-Jan. 15
🅿

ARANDA DE DUERO C3
Hontoria de Valdearados

La Posada de Salaverri $
Ctra. Peñaranda-Caleruega, km 10, 9400, Burgos
☎ 947561031
For centuries this was a flour mill and bakery until the García Figuero brothers converted the family heirloom into a rustic inn for visitors touring Old Castile. It offers five comfortable rooms with hand-carved wooden furniture and lace curtains reminiscent of grandmother's house. A specialty of the house, provided by the friendly owners, is a delicious lamb stew.

🛏 5
🅿

ARANJUEZ — C3
Chinchón

Parador de Chinchón **$$**
Regimiento de León, 1, 28370,
Madrid
☎ 918940836
🖹 918940908
 caceres@parador.es

A 17th-century Augustinian
convent now converted into a
parador. Tall cypresses and a
mass of rose bushes surround the
fountain in the interior garden,
while the cloister, with its
striking mosaic, provides a
contrast to the severity of the
rest of the building. The
bedrooms have recently been
redecorated in a lively style quite
unlike the usual sobriety of so
many paradors.

🛏 36
🅿 ≋

ARCOS DE LA FRONTERA — B1
Arcos de la Frontera

Cortijo Faín **$**
Ctra. Arcos-Algar, km 3, 11630,
Cádiz
☎ 956231396
🖹 956231396

Once the home of the father of
Andalusian independence, Blas
Infante, this 17th-century
country estate, surrounded by
olive groves, captures all the
charm of traditional Andalusian
architecture. There are 10
bedrooms and suites of varying
sizes, and a library with more
than 10,000 volumes. The
garden provides ample shade and
the swimming pool is just a few
steps away.

🛏 7   🅿 ≋

Hacienda El Santiscal **$**
Avda. del Santiscal, 129, 11630,
Cádiz
☎ 956708313
🖹 956708268
 santiscal@gadesinfo.com

As a reward to Juan de Armario
for his heroism during the siege
of Ronda in 1485, he and his
heirs were given rights to the
Santiscal Mountains, where they
built this ancestral home. Islamic
culture has left its mark in the
interiors; the communal rooms
are pleasing, and the best of the
elegant bedrooms have balconies
overlooking the reservoir.

🛏 11
Closed Jan. 10-20

🅿 ≋

Cortijo Barranco **$$**
Ctra. de Arcos a El Bosque A-
372, km 5,700, 11630, Cádiz
☎ 956231402
🖹 956231402

The former oil mill of this 18th-
century manor house, only
accessible via a twisting, unpaved
road, now provides 8 small and
tranquil rooms for country-
loving visitors. The place would
look more like a working farm
were it not for the gardens and
swimming pool. The owners
offer gracious Andalusian
hospitality and the sort of rustic
detail in which guests delight.

🛏 8
Closed Dec. 20-Jan. 15

🅿 ≋

ARRECIFE — CANARY ISLANDS
San Bartolomé

Finca de la Florida **$-$$**
El Islote, 90, 35550,
Canarias/Lanzarote
☎ 928521136
🖹 928520311
 florida@interlan-stc.es

Willkommen! is the first word
visitors hear on arrival. Since
most guests are German, theirs
has become the official language
here, although non-German
speakers are equally welcome.
The hotel, with its stunning
green veranda, is set in the
island's peaceful interior. It's
located a few miles from San
Bartolomé in the direction of
Uga, and can be a little difficult
to find.

🛏 16
🅿 ≋

ARTÁ MAJORCA   E1
Son Servera

ASTORGA   B4
Castrillo de los
Polvazares
Cuca la Vaina $
Jardín, s/n, 24718, León
☎ 987691078
▯ 987691078
The management of this
pleasant hotel believes that
stressed-out travelers are likely to
find relief by gazing at its serene,

Santiago Millas
Guts Muths $
Matanza, s/n, 24732, León
☎ 987691123
▯ 987691123
🅔 rusticae@edigital.es
Sjoerd Hers came from Holland
to settle in this picturesque
village, where he and his wife
have created a hotel from a
typical muleteer's house. Guests

ÁVILA   B3
Solosancho

AVILES   B4
Cudillero
Casona de la Paca $
El Pito, 33150, Asturias
☎ 985591303
▯ 985590995
🅔 casona@astures.com
Montse Abad's large house on a
hill known as El Pito was once
owned by indianos, Spaniards
who returned home rich from

Petit Hotel Cases de Pula $$$
Crta. Son Servera-Cap de Pera,
km 3, 7550, Baleares/Mallorca
☎ 971567492
▯ 971567271
Set beside a group of talayots
(megalithic stone structures), this
establishment encapsulates the
spirit of "green tourism" in
Mallorca - character, a warm
welcome and good local fare.

 10
🅿 🏊

Part of a complex with a range of
sports facilities including an 18-
hole golf course, the stone house,
built in 1581, has been converted
into a luxury 60-room hotel with
10 spacious suites.

honey-colored stone walls
adorned with works of art. Even
arrival is trouble-free, as guests
can drive right up to the
entrance in the watchtower next
to the parish church. Bedrooms
are small and very peaceful.

🛏 27
Closed Jan. 7-30

🅿

are greeted with a glass of wine,
and the emphasis is on
friendliness rather than luxury.
With the help of a group of art
students, all the bedrooms have
recently been imaginatively
redecorated.

🛏 8

🅿

Sancho de Estrada $
Castillo de Villaviciosa, s/n,
5130, Ávila
☎ 920291082
▯ 920291082
There has been a castle at
Solosancho since Roman times,
and more recent fortifications
were built to defend Ávila
against the Moors. Everything
about this hotel recalls the

turmoil of the Middle Ages: the
battlements, iron door fittings,
solid walls and ancient coats of
arms. Bedrooms are furnished
with austere Castilian pieces and
have superb views of the Amblés
Valley.

🛏 10
🅿

South America, and the
surrounding garden is stocked
with exotic plants. Guests are
likely to spend much of their stay
by the fire in the main lounge,
since the bedrooms, charming as
they are, are not exactly spacious.

🛏 18
Closed Dec. 12-Jan. 28

🅿 🏊

Key to Symbols: ▯ Fax 🅔 Email 🛏 Rooms 🅿 Parking 🏊 Swimming

Pravia

Casa del Busto $
Rey Don Silo, 1, 33120, Asturias
☎ 985822771
🖹 985822772
📧 casadelbusto@estanciases.es
The house built for the noble Don Álvaro del Busto in the 16th century has become a small hotel where the accent is on history and culture. A door leading off the tiled, whitewashed entrance hall provides access to the bedrooms and the courtyard. Whichever room you choose, you are assured of a comfortable bed.

 26
🅿

BADAJOZ   B2
Barcarrota
Monasterio de Rocamador $$
Ctra. Badajoz-Huelva, km 41,100, 6160, Badajoz
☎ 924489000
🖹 924489001
📧 mail@rocamador.com
Dissident Franciscan friars came here in 1512 to build this remote monastery high on the rocks overlooking the Sierra de Salvatierra. The present owners have restored and converted the monastery with respect for the architectural traditions of Extremadura. The rooms are both rustic and elegant, and drawing water straight from the sierra, the bathrooms provide Spain's most invigorating shower.

🛏 26 🅿 ⊠

BAIONA   A4
A Guarda

Convento de San Benito $
Plaza de San Benito, s/n, 36780, Pontevedra
☎ 986611166   🖹 986611517
Flanked by beautifully carved doorposts, the porch of this convent, founded in 1561, conceals the reception desk. Here, too, is the revolving "dumb waiter" used by the nuns to sell sweetmeats they made and conduct their business with the outside world without showing their faces. Leading off the cloister with its fountain and palm trees, the former cells have been converted into charmingly tasteful bedrooms. On Sunday mornings, guests may be awakened by the sound of singing in the neighboring church.

🛏 23 🅿

Baiona

Villa Sol $
Palos de la Frontera, 12, 36300, Pontevedra
☎ 986355691   🖹 986356702
The townhouse on the corner of one of Baiona's busiest thoroughfares seems more like a private residence than a hotel. It is worth ringing the doorbell just to get a glimpse of the cool shady garden and the noble interior. In order to preserve the beautiful mahogany and Cordovan leather furniture, as well as the collection of oil paintings and antiquarian books, the owners have opened their home to guests. On the upper floor are six rooms, all spacious, with very high ceilings and a charmingly archaic feel to them.

🛏 6 Closed Nov.-Apr. 🅿

BARLOVENTO
CANARY ISLANDS
Barlovento
La Palma Romántica $$
Las Llanadas, s/n, 38726, Canarias/La Palma
☎ 922186221
🖹 922186400
📧 palmarom@lix.intercom.es
The delightful setting of this romantic hotel makes it worth the effort of traveling to this side of the island. Bedrooms are spacious, and a traditional wooden balcony encircles the building. The seaward side overlooks the town of Barlovento, while to the rear the view is of mountain peaks. From the rooftop observatory, you can scan the night sky.

🛏 33 🅿 ⊠

Key to Symbols: Fax   Email   Rooms   Parking ⊠ Swimming

BENASQUE   D4
Benasque
Ciria $
Avda. de los Tilos, s/n, 22440, Huesca
☎ 974551612
🖹 974551686

This award-winning establishment, presided over by the efficient and quietly amiable Ciria brothers, exemplifies what a mountain hotel should be. The atmosphere is warm and homey, attracting many winter sports enthusiasts. Bedrooms are comfortable and cozy, particularly the attic rooms overlooking the snowy mountaintops. The rustic restaurant provides an agreeable setting for the excellent regional cuisine.

 37 🅿

Llanos del Hospital $
Camino del Hospital, 22440, Huesca
☎ 974552012
🖹 974551052
e hospital@encomix.es

This establishment in the Aragonese Pyrenees dates from the Spanish Civil War and serves as a mountain refuge with 70 beds, and also has 19 hotel rooms with all-modern conveniences. It is managed by Antonio Lafón, who is happy to share his extensive knowledge of the mountains, and makes an ideal base for cross-country skiers.

🛏 19
Closed Nov.
🅿

BENIDORM   D2
Polop de la Marina

Devachan $$
San Francisco, 13, 3520, Alacant/Alicante
☎ 966895640
🖹 966896233
e hoteldevachan@.ctv.es

Devachan is a Hindu word meaning "home of the gods," a fitting description of Pepa and Paco Ortuño's 300-year-old guildhall, sensitively converted into a hotel. There are five bedrooms decorated in coppery tones or pale celestial blue and furnished with antiques. Guests are welcomed with a dish of fruit and a small bunch of daisies.

🛏 5
🅿

BILBAO   C4
Artziniega

Torre de Artziniega $
Cuesta de Luciano, 3, 1474, Araba/Álava
☎ 945396500
🖹 945396565
e hoteltorre@jet.es

This medieval tower, the crowning glory of historic Artziniega, has been transformed into a hotel-restaurant, with windows, floors and beams lovingly restored. The bedrooms, occupying the three upper floors, have been stylishly decorated with neat touches such as cunningly concealed TV sets. The hotel's major attractions are the views, and the attention lavished on guests by the thoughtful hosts.

🛏 8 🅿

Balmaseda

San Roque $
Campo de las Monjas, 1, 48800, Bizkaia/Vizcaya
☎ 946102268
🖹 946102464

Endowed three centuries ago by a rich local merchant who settled in Panama, this historic monastery has been transformed into a charming hotel. Recent restoration has preserved the dressed stone cloister, its original well and an old oak staircase. The bedrooms, although sparsely decorated, are well equipped, and the quieter rooms at the back enjoy wonderful mountain views.

🛏 21   🅿

Key to Symbols: 🖹 Fax e Email 🛏 Rooms 🅿 Parking 🏊 Swimming

Mundaka

Atalaya $
Itxaropen Kalea, 1, 48360,
Bizkaia/Vizcaya
☎ 946177000
🖹 946876899
✉ rusticae@edigital.es

Facing the Mundaka estuary, a surfers' paradise in summer, this peaceful family hotel was created from a house built in the early 20th century. An extension with a spectacular tent-like roof houses the dining room. Although rather small, the bedrooms are supplied with all kinds of thoughtful details. They look out onto a church and the Bay of Biscay beyond.

🛏 16   🅿

BUITRAGO DEL LOZOYA   C3

Patones de Arriba

El Tiempo Perdido $$-$$$
Travesía del Ayuntamiento, 7, 28189, Madrid
☎ 918432152
🖹 918432148
✉ info@estancias.com

French interior decorator and antique collector François Founier has converted this little house in the center of the village into a hotel. Every suite exemplifies Founier's exquisite taste, with beautiful antique furniture, fine carpets and prints. Some have bathrooms reached by a staircase, others a terrace concealed by the slate roof. Prices, however, are somewhat high.

🛏 5
Closed Mon.-Thurs. & Jul. 30-Aug. 31

Uceda

El Saúco $
Norte, s/n, 19187, Guadalajara
☎ 949856270
🖹 949856023

This 18th-century brick and stone building was formerly known as La Cartuja (the Carthusian monastery) because of its connections with the more famous El Paular monastery in the Lozoya Valley. The *tercias reales*, the tithes collected for the upkeep of the churches in the Uceda region, were kept here. Now it has been faithfully restored to create a pleasant rustic hotel offering 18 rooms.

🛏 18
🅿

Villavieja de Lozoya

Hospedería El Arco $
Arco, 6, 28739, Madrid
☎ 918680911
🖹 918681320
✉ info@estancias.com

The 13th-century Mudejar arch in the dining room sets the tone of this small hotel. Created quite recently from a typical village house, most of the original features have been retained in this skillful modernization. Managed by a dynamic young team, it has fast become popular with weekenders from Madrid. Bedrooms, on the upper floor, combine comfort and good taste.

🛏 9
Closed Mon.-Thu. Sep. 15-Jun.15, and Dec. 25
🅿

BURGOS   C4

Burgos

Landa Palace $$
Ctra. Madrid-Irún, km 235, 9001, Burgos
☎ 947206343
🖹 947264676
✉ landapal@teleline.es

This palace is a Gothic fantasy set beside the Madrid highway. Its only truly period feature is the 14th-century tower brought stone by stone from a village nearby. A series of vaults and stone walls lead to the bedrooms - all extremely comfortable and stylish. The swimming pool, partly covered by a Gothic vault, is one of the hotel's main attractions.

🛏 29   🅿

CABEZÓN DE LA SAL   C4

Carrejo

El Jardín de Carrejo $
Carrejon 1 (finca), 39500, Cantabria
☎ 942701516
📄 942701871
 ELJARDIN@ santandersupernet.com

The early 19th-century home of the López family has been restored by architect Carlos López and is now managed by brother Abilio and his wife Chiqui as an elegant small hotel. The interiors are distinctly minimalist, with bedrooms decorated in shades of gray with geometric wooden bedsteads and stylish lamps and door furniture. The spacious suites with their own terraces are outstanding.

🛏 8   🅿

Terán de Cabuérniga

La Casona del Peregrino $
Barrio de Sepoyo, 39511, Cantabria
☎ 942706343
📄 942706344

Lovingly restored baroque house, dating from 1698, built in a style typical of the region. The modernization has included heat and sound insulation, and the individually designed bedrooms are furnished with antiques in Castilian, Spanish and Gothic styles. There is an open fireplace in the lounge and a wood-burning stove in the dining room, where local dishes are served.

🛏 14
Closed Jan. 7-Feb. 7
🅿

CÁCERES   B2

Cáceres

Parador de Cáceres $$
Ancha, 6, 10003, Cáceres
☎ 927211759
📄 927211759
 caceres@parador.es

This parador in the heart of Cáceres, a World Heritage Site, was created from the Torreorgaz Palace, built on the foundations of a Moorish structure in the 14th century. Access to rooms involves negotiating a maze of doors, staircases and courtyards, completely inaccessible to guests with disabilities. Doors, bedsteads, cabinets and writing desks are all of noble lineage.

🛏 30
🅿

CÁDIAR   C1

Busquístar

Alcazaba de Busquístar $
Ctra. de Órgiva a Láujar, km 37, 18416, Granada
☎ 958858687
📄 958858693
 info@alpurraalcazaba.com

Spectacularly set on a pine-clad hillside above the great ravine cut by the River Trevélez, this apartment hotel is built on several levels up the slope in the traditional style of the Alpujarras. Farming implements, Moorish lamps and terra-cotta floors create a rural ambience in the public rooms, although the decoration in the apartments, some of which sleep up to six people, is plainer.

🛏 43   🅿

Cádiar

Alquería de Morayma $
Ctra. C-332 Cádiar-Torvizón, 18440, Granada
☎ 958343221
📄 958343221

This vacation complex, providing agritourist accommodations of the highest standard, comprises five cottages, built and furnished in the traditional style of the region, surrounded by 85 acres of vineyards and olive, almond and fruit trees. Alpujarra artifacts and antique furniture add character to the simple whitewashed rooms, and the restaurant offers an interesting menu of regional specialties.

🛏 9   🅿

CARBONERAS — D1
Agua Amarga

Mikasa   **$-$$**
Ctra. de Carboneras, s/n, 4149, Almería
☎ 950138073
🖹 950138219
ⓔ suite@aranzadi.es

In the minimalist setting of Mikasa's luminous white architecture, guests are treated to the kind of hospitality usually associated with cruise liners. The rooms, with unpolished marble floors and ceiling fans, have romantic names like Key West or Cala Ermita. There are no telephones, but other appliances add to your comfort, such as the open-air Jacuzzi next to the swimming pool.

🛏 16   Closed Jan. 10-Mar. 15
🅿 ☷

Mojácar

Mamabel's   **$**
Embajadores, 5, 4638, Almería
☎ 950472448
🖹 950472448

Painters, singers and musicians from around the world are among the regulars at this tiny but stylish hotel at the upper end of Mojácar. The artistic touch is evident in every chest of drawers, lace curtain and satin cushion. Rooms 1 and 2 are particularly seductive, but the remaining bedrooms and the dining room await renovation.

🛏 9
🅿

CARMONA — B1
Carmona

Casa de Carmona   **$$-$$$**
Plaza de Lasso, 1, 41410, Sevilla
☎ 954191000
🖹 954190189
ⓔ reservations@casadecarmona.com

This magnificent 17th-century palace, once the domain of the aristocratic Lasso de la Vega family, has been restored and turned into a luxury hotel. Situated in the historic heart of Carmona, it epitomizes the finest in Andalusian Mudejar architecture with its three colonnaded courtyards and interior gardens. The suites and bedrooms, which have canopied beds, recapture the elegance of the 18th century.

🛏 30 🅿 ☷

Santa Maria Church, Carmona

CAZALLA DE LA SIERRA   B2

Cazalla de la Sierra

Hospedería de la Cartuja $
A-455, km 2.5, 41370, Sevilla
☎ 954884516
📄 954884707
✉ cartujsv@teleline.es

Carmen Ladrón de Guevara is dedicated to the preservation of her country's heritage, and to encouraging up-and-coming young artists and musicians. She has restored this monastery and turned it into a center for contemporary art and culture. To help finance this project Carmen, winner of international conservation awards, provides stylish guest accommodations.

🛏 10   Closed Dec. 24 

Las Navezuelas $
Ctra. A-432, km 43, 41370, Sevilla
☎ 954884764   📄 954884594
✉ navezuelas@arrakis.es

This is one of the oldest oil mills in Sierra Morena, producing olive oil since the dawn of the 16th century. Run by a young couple, the simple little hotel offers rustic, no-frills accommodation for eco-tourists eager to explore on foot, bike or horseback the surrounding mountains, where Merino sheep and Iberian pigs share the natural habitat with deer and wild boar. While some of the bedrooms have stunning views, the two independent apartments offer more space.

🛏 8   Phone in advance
P ≋

Posada del Moro $
Paseo del Moro, 9-15, 41370, Sevilla
☎ 954884858
📄 954884858

The attractions of "green tourism" in the Sierra Morena have meant that the number of hotels in the region has increased tenfold in the past few years. Little towns like Cazalla, with their narrow streets and cool courtyards, also have a charm of their own. Julia Piñero was sufficiently captivated to open a hotel here. Her artistic touch is evident throughout, from the objects in the hall and dining room to the paintings hanging in the bedrooms and corridors. The Andalusian courtyard, with a swimming pool and barbecue in summer, occasionally hosts flamenco evenings.

🛏 15   P ≋

CIUDAD REAL   C2

Ballesteros de Calatrava

Palacio de la Serna $
Cervantes, 18, 13432, Ciudad Real
☎ 926842208
📄 926842224
✉ palacioserna@paralelo40.org

Known locally as La Casa Grande (the big house), this neoclassic building was once a farmhouse. Artist and designer Eugenio S. Bermejo has taken an avant-garde approach to the decor, and the rooms look like sets from a Pedro Almodóvar film, with details from baroque to Dada providing a stark contrast to the harsh landscape of La Mancha.

🛏 5
P ≋

CIUDAD RODRIGO   B3

La Alberca

Doña Teresa $
Ctra. de Mogarraz, s/n, 37624, Salamanca
☎ 923415308
📄 923415308
✉ hotelteresa@gpm.es

The entire town of La Alberca has been declared a National Monument. This enchanting hotel, built in traditional local style with dressed stone and wooden balconies, is the ideal place in which to relax after a day visiting the village. Judicious exterior lighting means that Doña Teresa looks even better at night. The stone fountain in the foyer provides an instantly warm welcome. In addition to pleasant and well-appointed rooms, the hotel offers a sauna and gym under the sloping ceilings of the top floor.

🛏 37   P ≋

CIUTADELLA MINORCA
Ciutadella
Sant Ignasi $$-$$$
Ctra. a Cala Morell, s/n, 7760,
Baleares/Menorca
☎ 971385575
🖹 971480537
📧 santignasi@santignasi.com
An 18th-century country house
set among olive groves and
surrounded by a garden with
palms and walnut trees. The
bedrooms have pale cream walls,
matching bedspreads and
curtains, and wrought-iron
bedsteads. On Sundays and
Thursdays the dining room is
closed, which means a drive into
Ciutadella for dinner. Don't
forget your front door key, as
there is no night porter.

🛏 16 P

COLUNGA B4
Collía

Posada del Valle $
Collía (Arriondas), 33549,
Asturias
☎ 985841157
🖹 985841559
📧 hotel@posadadelvalle.com
Old stone and wood house near
the town of Arriondas, on a
hillside overlooking the Fito
hills. Ceramics give a bucolic
flavor to the entrance hall, while
the rural theme continues into
the bedrooms with wooden
beams, wrought-iron bedsteads
and floral prints. Two of them
share a balcony overlooking the
valley, while #5 is a duplex
perfect for family groups.

🛏 7
Closed Oct. 16-Mar. 14
P

Colunga
Los Caspios $
La Isla, s/n, 33320, Asturias
☎ 985852098
🖹 985852097
For more than 75 years this
traditional Asturian country
house has stood facing the sea
like a welcoming lighthouse on a
dark night. The house is
approached along a gravel drive
lined with hydrangeas. The bar
in the main lounge has a large
fireplace. As for the bedrooms,
room #1 is particularly notable
for its bronze bedsteads and
sheltered veranda.

🛏 10

P 🏊

Peruyes

Aultre Naray $
Desvío de la N-634, km 335,
33547, Asturias
☎ 985840808
🖹 985840848
📧 aultre@ciberastur.es
"Aultre naray" (I will have no
other) was the promise made by
medieval knights to their ladies
as they left for the wars, and it is
a fitting name for this romantic
19th-century country house in
the shadow of the Picos de
Europa, close to the Sella River
and not too far from the sea.

🛏 10
P

Villamayor
Palacio de Cutre $
Palacio de Cutre, s/n (La
Goleta), 33583, Asturias
☎ 985708072
🖹 985708019
📧 palacio-de-cutre@
hotelesasturianos.com
Situated on a large country estate
close to the woodlands of Sueve
and not far from the sea, this
16th-century mansion provides
elegant accommodations. The
owners, Javier and Sandra, have a
taste for beautiful things. Both
the communal rooms and guest
bedrooms are perfectly attuned
to the delightful surroundings.

🛏 12 Closed Jan. 25-Mar. 15 P

Key to Symbols: 🖹 Fax 📧 Email 🛏 Rooms P Parking 🏊 Swimming

Villaviciosa

La Casona de Amandi $
A 1 km Villaviciosa-Ctra.
Infiesto, 33300, Asturias
☎ 985890130
🖹 985890129
For some time now, this large house on the outskirts of Villaviciosa has provided a country retreat with the perfect ambience for the stressed-out city dweller. Antique household utensils are displayed in the bedrooms, lounge and new dining room, and 19th-century furniture is arranged in a gallery overlooking a garden richly stocked with hydrangeas and magnolias.

🛏 9 🅿

CRUZ DE TEJEDA
CANARY ISLANDS

Cruz de Tejeda

El Refugio $
Cruz de Tejeda, s/n (San Mateo), 35328, Canarias/Gran Canaria
☎ 928666513
🖹 928666520
Set in the shadow of a trio of volcanic rocks described by one eminent Spanish author as "a petrified tempest," this large stone house is a prime example of traditional Canary Island architecture. The hotel projects a homey and environmentally conscious image, from the wood paneling and home-baked bread to the recycled paper in the bedrooms and bathrooms.

🛏 10 🅿 ☲

DEYÁ   MAJORCA

Binissalem

Scott's $$
Plaza de la Iglesia, 12, 7350, Baleares/Mallorca
☎ 971870100
🖹 971870267
🅔 scotts@britel.es
Distinguished British designer Judy Brabner Scott spent 10 years rejuvenating this 19th-century town house right on the village square. It features an indoor heated pool, a Jacuzzi and an outdoor bar and terrace. Most of the furniture comes from her private collection and has been featured in many interior design magazines. Ms. Scott also offers courses in watercolor painting and Mediterranean cuisine.

🛏 14 Closed Dec. 15-Jan. 15
🅿 ☲

Esporles

Posada del Marqués $$$
Finca Es Verger, s/n, 7190, Baleares/Mallorca
☎ 971611230
🖹 971611213
🅔 posada@posadamarques.com
This 16th-century Majorcan manor house, set in the heart of the Sierra de Tramontana, provides 17 bedrooms decorated in keeping with the noble building and its respectful restoration. The dining room - the most dazzling in the hotel - has been installed among the grindstones, pulleys and chains of a former olive mill. Here a Mediterranean menu is served by knowledgeable staff.

🛏 17
🅿

Orient

L'Hermitage $$$
Ctra. de Alaró a Bunyola, km 8, 7349, Baleares/Mallorca
☎ 971180303
🖹 971180411
🅔 info@hermitage-hotel.com
Convent completed in the 17th century by the addition of a majestic tower and the present gardens. The cloister, with its 16 baroque pillars, encircles a group of citrus trees. Four bedrooms are in the old building, and the rest in the annex. There is a choice of lounges, and breakfast is served on the grindstone of an ancient oil mill.

🛏 24
Closed Nov.-Jan.
🅿 ☲

Key to Symbols: 🖹 Fax 🅔 Email 🛏 Rooms 🅿 Parking ☲ Swimming

Sóller

Ca N'Aí $$$
Camí de Son Sales, 50, 7100,
Baleares/Mallorca
☎ 971632494
🖹 971631899
📧 integral@redestb.es
This manor house had been passed down through 14 generations before Domingo Morell turned it over to agrotourism. The house, with its arches and whitewashed walls, is full of Mediterranean color and has a rich array of local artifacts. It is set among orange trees with panoramic views of the Sóller Valley, and the kitchen uses organically grown produce from the estate.

🛏 10   Closed Nov. 1-Feb. 1   P ≋

Valldemossa

Vistamar $$$
Ctra. de Valldemossa a Andraitx, km 2, 7170, Baleares/Mallorca
☎ 971612300
🖹 971612583
📧 info@vistamarhotel.es
This turn-of-the-20th-century villa, built by emigres returning rich from South America, occupies 250 acres of pinewoods running down to the rocky coast. Chopin and George Sand famously spent a winter at the nearby Carthusian monastery, and the hotel maintains the connection with regular classical music concerts. The bedrooms, all in different styles, are large and have sunny terraces.

🛏 19   Closed Nov.-Feb.   P ≋

DENIA   D2

Denia

La Racona $
Ctra. de Les Rotes, 76, 3700, Alacant/Alicante
☎ 965787960
🖹 965787861
📧 fdr@ctv.es
This small hotel is owned by Italian film and TV celebrity Franco da Rosa. When he is not away on business, Franco himself will show new arrivals to one of the apartments around the swimming pool. Pleasant as the rooms are, the main attraction is the wonderful garden. Nearby is Les Rotes beach, probably the loveliest on the Costa Blanca.

🛏 11
P ≋

Xàbia/Jávea

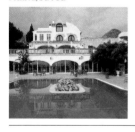

Villa Mediterránea $$$
León, 5 (Crta. Jávea-Jesús Pobre), 3730, Alacant/Alicante
☎ 965795233
🖹 965794581
📧 hotelvillamed@ctv.es
An elegant villa, slightly inland, well away from the noise and confusion of the coast in summer. The interior of the house is delightful, with seven spacious bedrooms that have luxurious bathrooms. New arrivals receive a welcoming bottle of Cava, sweets and a handbook on how to zap among 42 satellite TV channels.

🛏 7
Closed Jan. 9-Feb. 9
P ≋

El Rodat $$
Ctra. Cabo de la Nao, s/n, 3730, Alacant/Alicante
☎ 966470710
🖹 966471550
📧 rodat@mail.todoesp.es
A vacation paradise, El Rodat is a circle of pine trees, under which has grown up a residential complex offering every possible comfort for family vacations. The bungalows are set around a two-level swimming pool and a garden of indigenous plants. Each has at least two bedrooms, a sun terrace and a small garden of its own.

🛏 42   P ≋

Key to Symbols: 🖹 Fax 📧 Email 🛏 Rooms P Parking ≋ Swimming

Hospedería de San Francisco $
Avda. de Pío XII, 35, 14700, Córdoba
☎ 957710183
🖹 957645146
📧 lupi@iberonline.es

Throughout the checkered history of the city this 15th-century monastery has provided hospitality to strangers. The monastery's courtyards, orchards and balconies provide the perfect setting for a quietly contemplative stay. Some of the bedrooms were originally monks' cells. Rather more worldly is the unique culinary style developed by chef Iñaki Martínez, a blend of Basque and Andalusian cuisine.

🛏 22 🅿

La Ventana $$-$$$
Plaza Sa Carrossa, 13, 7800, Baleares/Eivissa
☎ 971390857
🖹 971390145

Hippies from all over Europe once congregated here and, several decades on, the atmosphere of those heady days lives on at this eccentric little hotel. It is aimed at the young and cool in search of a good time. Each bedroom is different and all are very small, with mosquito nets and ceiling fans giving them a distinctly tropical feel.

🅿

La Casa Grande de Gormaz $
Camino de las Fuentes, s/n, 42313, Soria
☎ 975340982

Built by a local emigre returning home after making his fortune in South America, this big house just outside the village was restored and converted into a hotel by María José Marco. Now, with the aid of her mother-in-law, she looks after both the guests and the gardens, with gratifying results in both cases. The bedrooms all have a good view of the magnificent Gormaz castle. The most attractive are #10 and #11 in the tower.

🛏 6 Closed Dec. 24-Jan. 1   🅿

Punta Grande $
Las Puntas, 38911, Canarias/El Hierro
☎ 922559081
🖹 922559081

The "Guinness Book of World Records" lists this as the world's smallest hotel. The former customs post, built in the 19th century on the dock at Las Puntas, is only 25 feet high and has four double rooms. The hotel is decorated with a whole array of maritime memorabilia, and each of the simple bedrooms is unique.

🛏 4
🅿

Los Jándalos $-$$
Amparo Osborne, s/n (Vistahermosa), 11500, Cádiz
☎ 956873411
🖹 956872012
📧 reservas@jandalos.com

It looks like a movie set, with archways, mullioned windows and palm trees. Los Jándalos, in the residential district of Vistahermosa, is a complex of individually styled apartments, well equipped for family vacations, arranged around a garden and swimming pool. If you order breakfast in your apartment, it will arrive in an imaginatively presented picnic basket.

🛏 43
🅿 🏊

ESTELLA C4
Puente la Reina
El Peregrino **$-$$**
Ctra. Pamplona-Logroño, km
19, 31100, Nafarroa/Navarra
☎ 948340075
🖨 948341190

Ángelo Cambero's stone and
wooden country house hotel
stands at a major crossroads
along the road to Santiago,
where two traditional pilgrim
routes once met. Chef Ángelo
and his wife Nina cater to the
comfort of their guests with style
and generosity. The bedrooms
are charmingly decorated, with
the added advantage of
soundproofing.

🛏 13   Closed Dec. 24 and 31
P 🏊

FERROL A4
Neda

Pazo da Merced **$**
Pazo Da Merced, 15510, A
Coruña
☎ 981382900
🖨 981380104
📧 pazomerced@arrakis.es

A house with stout stone walls,
built among ancient oaks at the
end of the El Ferrol estuary. In
the 17th century it was a tannery
for pilgrims on their way to
Santiago de Compostela; today it
is a model hotel combining
respect for historic architecture
with avant-garde use of
materials. All the bathrooms are
strikingly paneled like cabins on
a ship.

🛏 5
P 🏊

FIGUERES E4
Avinyonet de Puigventós

Mas Pau **$**
Ctra. de Figueres a Olot.
Despoblado, s/n, 17742, Girona
☎ 972546154
🖨 972546326
📧 maspau@grn.es

Following their success with the
prestigious El Bulli restaurant in
nearby Roses, Toni Gerez and
Xavier Sagristà have transformed
this 17th-century farmhouse into
a temple of Catalan haute
cuisine. The three
interconnecting dining rooms are
equipped with tables fashioned
from ancient sewing machines.
The bedrooms are housed in a
rustic extension to the main
building. Further major
improvements are planned.

🛏 20   Closed Feb. 8-Mar. 15
P 🏊

FUENTE DÉ B4
Camaleño
El Jisu **$**
Ctra. de Potes-Fuente Dé, km 8,
39587, Cantabria
☎ 942733038
🖨 942733315

In the lounge of this chalet
hotel, on a hillside along the
Liébana Valley, guests can sit
beside an open fire surrounded
by carefully chosen antiques and
enjoy a stunning view of the
south face of the Picos de
Europa. The bedrooms provide
clean, comfortable
accommodations for family
vacations. The south-facing ones
are quieter and have better views.

🛏 8
P

Cosgaya
Hotel del Oso **$**
Ctra. de Potes a Fuente Dé, km
14, 39539, Cantabria
☎ 942733018
🖨 942733036
📧 hoteldeloso@mundivia.es

Set amid a glorious landscape of
snowcapped mountains and lush
orchards, this small hotel beside
the River Deva epitomizes the
finest in rural tourism in the
Picos de Europa. The restaurant
offers a generous selection of
regional specialties, including
river trout and *cocido lebaniego*, a
tasty local meat stew with
chickpeas.

🛏 36
Closed Jan. 7-Feb. 15
P 🏊

Key to Symbols: 🖨 Fax   📧 Email   🛏 Rooms   P Parking   🏊 Swimming

FUENTERRABÍA   **D4**
Fuenterrabía

Pampinot   **$-$$**
Mayor, 5, 20280,
Gipuzkoa/Guipúzcoa
☎ 943640600
▤ 943645128
This little palace in the Calle
Mayor, the historic heart of
town, has been a warehouse,
cider press and stately home.
Princess Maria Theresa spent the
night here on the way to her

Obispo   **$-$$**
Plaza del Obispo, 1, 20280,
Gipuzkoa/Guipúzcoa
☎ 943645400
▤ 943642386
Cristóbal de Rojas y Sandoval,
the Archbishop of Oviedo and
Seville and chaplain to Emperor
Charles V, was born here – hence
the name. He must have enjoyed
gazing upon the Spanish

wedding to Louis XIV.
Converted to a hotel by the
current owners, it retains an
aristocratic atmosphere with its
magnificent staircase, antique
furniture and chandeliers.

Parador de Hondarribia   **$$**
Plaza de Armas, 14, 20280,
Gipuzkoa/Guipúzcoa
☎ 943645500
▤ 943642153
Formerly known as El
Emperador, after Emperor
Charles I, this fortress actually
dates back to the reign of Sancho
Abarca, King of Navarre, in the
10th century. The parador, with

Pyrenees from the balcony, a
pleasure now shared by guests at
this elegant little hotel. Another
striking feature is the centuries-
old Gothic facade. One room is
adapted for use by disabled
visitors.

 15
🅿

 8

its thick stone walls, wrought-
iron staircases, high ceilings,
sober tapestries and sheltered
courtyard, now offers guests
regal and well-heated
accommodations. Rooms look
out onto Mount Jaizkibel or the
Bidasoa River.

 35
🅿

Cafés on the Rambla de la Llibertat, Girona

Key to Symbols: ▤ Fax   🅮 Email   Rooms   🅿 Parking   Swimming

GANDIA D2

Rugat

La Casa Vieja $
Horno, 4, 46842, Valencia
☎ 962814013
🖹 962814013
📧 lacasavieja@xpress.es

No one would ever guess that a small hotel flourishes behind the stout wooden door on a nameless little street in the village of Rugat. You just have to knock, and keep on knocking, even at siesta time. The door will open to reveal an ancient village house charmingly renovated by its British owners. They offer six individually decorated but unpretentious en suite rooms, cozy living and dining rooms, and even a little swimming pool in the back garden to cool off on sultry summer days.

🛏 6 Closed Jan. 7-25 and Sept. 6-30
🅿 🏊

GARACHICO
CANARY ISLANDS

Garachico

San Roque $$-$$$
Esteban de Ponce, 32,
Canarias/Tenerife
☎ 922133435
🖹 922133406
📧 info@hotelsanroque.com

The imaginative conversion of this 17th-century town house richly deserves its membership in Design Hotels International. Both the public spaces and the large bedrooms present a continuous and sometimes daunting display of sumptuous color and designer furniture with interesting interpretations of form and function. The building has an unadorned red facade and centers around a traditional Canary Island patio.

🛏 18 🅿 🏊

El Patio $
El Guincho. Finca Malpaís,
38450, Canarias/Tenerife
☎ 922133280
🖹 922830089

The Ponte family's country house has been designated a protected site for historical, artistic and ecological reasons. Some of the buildings, in the middle of a vast banana plantation, have been converted into a rural hotel. It provides a lounge-dining room and 14 large rooms in the traditional aristocratic style of the island, overlooking a swimming pool and extensive gardens.

🛏 14
Closed Jun. 15-Sep. 15
🅿 🏊

Los Silos

Casa Amarilla $
La Caleta de Iterián, 38470,
Canarias/Tenerife
☎ 922840118
🖹 928682940

A mainly German clientele is attracted to this charming hotel, housed in a yellow colonial-style mansion. Standing in lush subtropical gardens, the house is entered through a peaceful veranda where a staircase leads to the lounge-dining room and the bedrooms. From the solarium there are glorious views across banana plantations to the sea.

🛏 5
Closed Jul.-Aug.
🅿 🏊

GIRONA E4

Corçà

La Mare Michelle $
Major, 8, 17121, Girona
☎ 972630535
🖹 972630535

It is a pity that this charming hotel is only open on weekends and does not accept credit cards. The owner, Michelle Amran, not only provides delicious food, she also has succeeded in creating a delightfully homey and distinctly French atmosphere. The house dates back to 1760, and each of the bedrooms is named after a healing plant.

🛏 4
Phone in advance
🅿

Key to Symbols: Fax   Email   Rooms   Parking   Swimming

Orriols

L'Odissea de L'Empordà **$$$**
Carrer del Castell, 6, 17468,
Girona
☎ 972551718
🖹 972560418
Antonio Ferrer's many years of
experience as a chef in a top-
quality Barcelona restaurant
stood him in good stead when he
created this hotel in the
magnificent Castell Palau
d'Orriols. The rooms are set
around a peaceful courtyard, and
designer furniture and modern
works of art add distinction to
the suites. Paintings by
contemporary artists are hung in
the exquisitely styled lounge.

🛏 10
Closed Jan.
🅿 🏊

Santa Cristina d'Aro

Mas Torrellas **$**
Ctra. Santa Cristina-Platja
d'Aro, km 1,713, 17246, Girona
☎ 972837526
🖹 972837527
The Carrera family has long
been involved in the hospitality
business on the Costa Brava, and
their decision to buy this estate
and devote themselves to rural
tourism has proved to be a wise
one. The 1771 manor house is
instantly recognizable by its
square watchtower. The interiors
have exposed stone walls, and
the dining room has been created
from former stables.

🛏 18
Closed Dec.-Feb.
🅿 🏊

GRANADA C1

Granada

Palacio de Santa Inés **$-$$**
Cuesta de Santa Inés, 9, 18010,
Granada
☎ 958222362
🖹 958222465
📧 sinespal@teleline.es
This little 16th-century palace
boasts a fine Renaissance
courtyard, eight Corinthian
pillars in white marble,
balustraded galleries and
Raphaelesque frescoes. The
Alhambra, Granada's most
famous monument, can be seen
from the windows of the small,
austere rooms. The hotel's
location on a little square in the
historic Albaicín quarter means
having to park elsewhere and
carry luggage by hand.

🛏 13 🅿

Parador de Granada **$$$**
Real de la Alhambra, s/n, 18009,
Granada
☎ 958221440
🖹 958222264
This parador is a former
Franciscan monastery founded in
the 15th century. It stands right
in the gardens of the Alhambra
overlooking the Generalife
gardens, the ancient residential
quarter of Albaicín and the
Sierra Nevada mountains, the
only property in Granada to
enjoy such a privilege. The
dining room is always packed
with busloads of visitors, and you
may have to reserve up to six
months in advance.

🛏 36

🅿

Sierra Nevada

El Lodge **$$-$$$**
Maribel, 8, 18196, Granada
☎ 958480600
🖹 958480506
The regularly varnished trunks
of Finnish pine forming the shell
of this building not only keep it
looking good; they also ensure
warmth and silence. Excellently
equipped for skiers, the hotel
also offers a cozy lounge and bar.
The bedrooms are named after
native mountain flowers, and
there is an open-air Jacuzzi with
views of the snowcapped peaks.

🛏 16
🅿

GUADALUPE B2
Guadalupe

Parador de Guadalupe $
Marqués de la Romana, 10,
10140, Cáceres
☎ 927367075
🖹 927367076
The hospital of St. John the
Baptist provided lodgings for
16th-century pilgrims on their
way to the nearby monastery of
the Virgin of Guadalupe. The
present parador, with its white
walls and red-tiled roofs, has
recently been renovated.
Bedrooms in the old part are
immaculate, while the newer
ones, although spacious and
neat, are somewhat impersonal.
They do offer splendid views of
the monastery and the
mountains.

🛏 41 P ≈

HOYOS DEL ESPINO B3
Hoyos del Espino
El Milano Real $
Toleo, s/n, 5634, Ávila
☎ 920349108
🖹 920349156
e rusticae@edigital.es
Paco and Teresa abandoned city
careers to run this chalet-hotel at
the foot of the Sierra de Gredos.
It is an excellent base for touring
– Paco himself organizes trips.
The library boasts 2,000 books
and a long-range telescope
equipped with software for
scanning the night sky. Four
rooms with sloping ceilings
provide shelter from the cold
night air.

🛏 13
Closed Jan. 10-16 and Nov. 13-30

P

HUELVA A1
El Rocío

**El Cortijo de los
Mimbrales** $-$$
Ctra. A-483 El Rocío-
Matalascañas, km 30, 21750,
Huelva
☎ 959442237
🖹 959442443
e cortijomimbrales@futurnet.es
As well as producing orange
juice, Los Mimbrales is setting
standards for rural and ecological
tourism in the region. The
manor house has been carefully
restored, and former farm
buildings were converted to
create a lounge, dining room and
bar, and a tourist center renting
horses and bicycles. The
bedrooms have tiled floors and
exposed beams, and each is
equipped with a ceiling fan.

🛏 15 P ≈

IBIZA-EIVISSA IBIZA
Sant Rafel
Racó Valensiá $$
San Rafel, detrás del
hipódromo., 7800,
Baleares/Eivissa
☎ 971198340
🖹 971198538
If the beach is not your scene,
head inland to Celia and Paco's
hotel-restaurant, where the rice
dishes are even better than those
found along the Valencian coast,
and can be enjoyed overlooking
the pool. There are nine quiet
and well-equipped bedrooms,
and behind the hotel the San
Rafel racecourse can be seen
between the palms and olive
trees.

🛏 9 Closed Oct. 1 to Easter

P ≈

INCA MAJORCA
Binibona

Ets Albellons $$$
Predio Ets Albellons, s/n, 7314,
Baleares/Mallorca
☎ 971875069
🖹 971875143
e albellons.rese@jet.es
With the interior of the island
becoming increasingly
fashionable, brothers Juan and
Sebastián Vicens set to work to
refurbish their old family home
on the slopes of the Sierra de
Tramuntana, close to the Lluc
Monastery. The brothers provide
relaxed and friendly service in a
homey atmosphere. The
bedrooms upstairs are more
impressive for their equipment
than their decor.

🛏 10
P ≈

Key to Symbols: 🖹 Fax e Email 🛏 Rooms P Parking ≈ Swimming

Campanet

Monnaber Nou   **$$**
Predio Monnaber Nou, 7310,
Baleares/Mallorca
☎ 971877176
📄 971877127
e monnaber@pehm.es
At the foot of the Sierra de
Tramuntana in the northwestern
part of the island stands this
18th-century manor house
surrounded by beautiful
countryside. Next to the parking
area is a clear blue swimming
pool, and there also is a market
garden that supplies the kitchen
with fresh produce. The spartan
bedrooms are decorated with
paintings.

🛏 19
P ≈

Inca

Casa del Virrey   **$$-$$$**
Ctra. Inca-Sencelles, km 2,400
(Son Campaner), 7300,
Baleares/Mallorca
☎ 971881018
📄 971883323
The salmon-pink facade of the
island's only 17th-century
mansion conceals a world of
aristocratic splendor, with
ancient oil paintings, carpets,
writing desks, wooden chests,
four-poster beds and majestic
marble fireplaces. There is a
swimming pool in the extensive
gardens, and shade provided by
palm trees. The Casa del Virrey
also hosts cultural events,
classical music concerts and
Spanish guitar recitals.

🛏 10   P   ≈

JACA   D4

Escarrilla

Mingo   **$**
Ctra. de Francia, s/n, 22660,
Huesca
☎ 974487350
Only recently opened, this little
mountain hotel stands beside the
road leading up to the town of
Formigal, just before the final
tunnel. The conversion of the old
house provides six bedrooms and
bathrooms featuring terra-cotta
tiling. Only breakfast is
provided, but opposite the hotel
the owners have a restaurant
with a good local reputation.

🛏 6   P

Formigal

Villa de Sallent   **$-$$**
Urbanización El Formigal,
22640, Huesca
☎ 974490223
📄 974490150
e hotelvilladesallent@
cempresarial.com
The hotel run by Fidel Tejero
and his family encapsulates the
finest architectural traditions of
Upper Aragon. The same stone,
slate and wood have been used to
create an extension providing
more rooms. The unassuming
accommodations are well
equipped to withstand the winter
cold, as are the hearty dishes
prepared by Fidel.

🛏 41   P

Sallent de Gállego

Almud   **$**
Espadilla, 11, 22640, Huesca
☎ 974488366
📄 974488366
e hotel-almud@ctv.es
Converted from 18th-century
stables and using materials
salvaged from ruined buildings,
this is one of the most charming
hotels in the Aragonese
Pyrenees. To furnish it, the
owners brought together family
heirlooms and scoured local
antique shops to create a
delightful museum of domestic
life. Recent refurbishments have
added three more bedrooms to
the existing eight.

🛏 11   P

Key to Symbols: 📄 Fax   e Email   🛏 Rooms   P Parking   ≈ Swimming

LA GARRIGA E4

Granollers

Fonda Europa $
Anselm Clavé, 1, 8400,
Barcelona
☎ 938700312
📠 938707901

The Parellada family have been innkeepers here since 1714, when travelers to and from France used to stop for a hearty meal and a comfortable bed for the night. There are only seven bedrooms, all on the second floor and decorated in art deco style. The ground-floor dining room is always full, especially on Sundays and Thursdays (market day).

 7

La Garriga

Termes La Garriga $$
Banys, 23, 8530, Barcelona
☎ 938717086
📠 938717887
📧 termes@termes.com

The spa waters and gentle climate have made La Garriga a favorite summer resort with the beautiful people of Barcelona. Its English atmosphere and pastel decor have barely changed since the spa adjoining Montseny Nature Park was inaugurated in 1874. A team of experts offers more than 100 different health and beauty treatments. Visitors can choose between dietetic or local cuisine.

 22

Montseny

Sant Marçal $
Ctra. de Sant Celoni a Sant Marçal, km 28, 8460, Barcelona
☎ 938473043
📠 938473043
📧 tellhoteles@arquired.es

Stressed-out executives from nearby Barcelona find rest, relaxation and good food at this peaceful mountain retreat. The austerity of the stone building recalls its origins as an 11th-century monastery. The interior is all rustic refinement: crisp linen tablecloths in the dining room, a billiard room with a large bowl of candies, and small but comfortable bedrooms named after flowers.

 8

LA LINEA DE LA CONCEPCIÓN B1

Castellar de la Frontera

Casa Convento de la Almoraima $
Ctra. Algeciras-Ronda, s/n, 11350, Cádiz
☎ 956693002
📠 956693214

The ancestral home of the Dukes of Medinaceli is the largest estate in Europe, and the house is now open to visitors. A winding path through woodlands - home to a number of protected bird species - leads to the 17th-century former hunting lodge, where guests can now relax in the aristocratic rooms or play a game in the English-style billiard room.

17

LA OROTAVA CANARY ISLANDS

La Orotava

Parador de Las Cañadas del Teide $$
Las Cañadas del Teide
Apartado de Correos, 15, 38300, Canarias/Tenerife
☎ 922386415
📠 922382352

The parador is located in Las Cañadas del Teide National Park against the backdrop of smoking 10,000-foot Mount Teide, the sulphurous Chachorra crater and the snowcapped Montaña Blanca. Behind the ocher facade, the interiors feature cherry wood paneling and a mighty stone fireplace. Bedrooms are on the small side, but the spectacular mountain views more than compensate.

37

LEÓN   B4

Carrizo de la Ribera

La Posada del Marqués   **$**
Plaza Mayor, 4, 24270, León
☎ 987357171
▤ 987358101
e marques@aletur.es

Part of this Cistercian monastery now provides tourist accommodations. Guests are housed in what was once the ancient pilgrim hospice; the current building dating from the 17th century. Some of the bedrooms feature elaborate canopied beds, and others austere Castilian furniture. A highlight of any visit is hearing the Gregorian chant of the monks in the monastery church.

🛏 11   **P**

León

La Posada Regia   **$**
Regidores, 11, 24003, León
☎ 987213173
▤ 987213031
e regialeon@bornet.es

After 20 years as an award-winning chef, Marcos Vidal of the Bodega Regia has now branched out into the hotel business, converting the floors above the restaurant into guest accommodations. The building rests on the foundations of an ancient Roman wall, and the dignified facade conceals a charming interior with exposed beams and polished wooden floors covered with heavy Astorga rugs.

🛏 27

LLANES   B4

Alevia

Casona d'Alevia   **$**
Alevia, 33579, Asturias
☎ 985414176
▤ 985414426
e alevia@nauta.es

Family-run hotel in the former family home, which stands at the foot of the Picos de Europa, making it a great base for exploring the glories of this natural paradise. The window in room #2, the stone drainage pipe in room #3 and the charming details common to all members of the Rusticae group of hotels add to the homey ambience.

🛏 7
P

Besnes

La Tahona   **$**
Besnes (Alles), 33578, Asturias
☎ 985415749
▤ 985415749
e latahona@ctv.es

This former flour mill and bakery was a pioneer of rural tourism in Asturias. The mountain setting makes it the perfect place to walk in the woods, bicycle, go horseback riding or fish for salmon. Despite improvements to the public areas, the bedrooms still lack finish. The rustic ovens, however, produce excellent fare such as salmon cooked in cider.

🛏 13   **P**

Cuanda

La Montaña Mágica   **$**
El Allende de Viraño, s/n, 33508, Asturias
☎ 985925176
▤ 985925780
e cuanda@helicom.es

Sharing its name with Thomas Mann's famous novel *The Magic Mountain*, about a sanatorium in Davos, this is probably a more sympathetic place to relax in the mountains. It is a small hotel, camouflaged as a village house and managed with quiet skill by Carlos Bueno, himself an author. The spacious bedrooms overlook the Picos de Europa.

🛏 8
P

LLANES B4

Llanes

El Habana $
El Pedroso, s/n (La Pereda),
33509, Asturias
☎ 985402526
🖹 985402075
 elhabana@losintel.net

Adventurer, naturalist and geographer Sirio Sáinz knows his way around 101 countries and has taken part in the Paris-Dakar rally (an auto racing event) eight times. Only the desire to live with his partner at the foot of the mountains of Asturias has made him settle down. The new hotel near Llanes reflects the owners' interests, and none of the rooms are exactly alike.

🛏 10

🅿 ≊

La Posada de Babel $
La Pereda, s/n, 33509, Asturias
☎ 985402525
🖹 985402622

Sometimes rural tourism has an unexpectedly urban face, like this modern country inn set in a meadow five minutes from the beach. The young owners have escaped from Madrid and brought a contemporary touch to this traditional corner of Asturias. An old granary has been converted into a romantic bedroom and the nearby minimalist cube also houses additional rooms.

🛏 10
Closed Jan. 6-Feb. 25
🅿

La Arquera $
La Arquera, s/n, 33500, Asturias
☎ 985402424
🖹 985400175

"The yellow building you can see from the road" is how locals describe La Arquera, a former working farm. The bedrooms each have a glassed-in veranda with views of the steep pastures of the Cuera mountains or the blue horizon of the Bay of Biscay. This is a haven of peace, some distance from the beaches and nightlife of Llanes.

🛏 11
🅿

Pechón

Don Pablo $
El Cruce, s/n, 39594, Cantabria
☎ 942719500
🖹 942719500

The hotel comprises three buildings linked by a long terrace with views of the sea. Nearby, a narrow path leads straight to a delightfully secluded beach. Modestly equipped and prone to fussy decoration, the hotel is nonetheless a favorite with visitors to the region. Breakfast served in the room includes a local specialty, *corbatas de Unquera*, puff pastries shaped like bow ties.

🛏 30

🅿

Tresgrandas de Llanes

El Molino de Tresgrandas $
Tresgrandas, s/n, 33598,
Asturias
☎ 985411191
🖹 985411157
 molino@mail.ddnet.es

Originally a dye works and later a flour mill, this late 18th-century building on the River Cabra has been cleverly converted, and guests can watch the flowing stream through a glass-covered opening in the floor. Bedrooms have just enough space for a bed, a closet and a bathroom, but the old mill's wooded location has made it something of a favorite.

🛏 9
🅿

Key to Symbols: Fax   Email   Rooms   Parking   Swimming

Villanueva de Colombres

La Casona de Villanueva $
Villanueva de Colombres,
33590, Asturias
☎ 985412590
▤ 985412514
🅔 casonavillanueva@
abonados.cplus.es

A simple 18th-century village house encapsulating the spirit of green tourism in Asturias. Traditional techniques and local materials have been used in the restoration, respecting the original structure of stone and wood. Whitewash and pastel shades used for the interior decor create a cool and airy feel.

 8
🅿

LOGROÑO   C4

Arnedillo

Molino del Cidacos $
Ctra de Arnedo, km 14, 26589,
La Rioja
☎ 941394063
▤ 941394200

In its orchard setting, this 17th-century flour mill on the banks of the River Cidacos typifies rural tourism in this part of Spain. As soon as you enter the reception area with its unpretentious bar, you are aware of the good taste and environmental consciousness that have gone into the design. The eight cheerful bedrooms achieve a pleasing harmony with the leafy surroundings.

 8   Closed Jan.

🅿

Laguardia

Castillo El Collado $
Paseo El Collado, 1, 1300,
Araba/Álava
☎ 941121200
▤ 941600878

After many years in the kitchen, chef Javier Arcillona has moved into the hotel business. He now presides over this early 19th-century mansion, which resembles a medieval castle. Each of the bedrooms reflects his flamboyant personality, and the view from any one of them is enough to make guests stay another night to enjoy his company and excellent cuisine.

 7
Closed Dec. 24-Jan. 1 and
Jan. 15-Feb. 15
🅿

Posada Mayor de Migueloa $
Mayor, 20, 1300, Araba/Álava
☎ 941121175
▤ 941121022

A 17th-century mansion with wooden beams, granite walls, earth floors and period furniture, designed to transport guests back to Spain's Golden Age. The owners are wine connoisseurs with special expertise in Rioja, a well-known Spanish wine. Their appreciation of the finer things in life is reflected throughout the hotel. The hotel is in a pedestrianized zone and cars are not permitted on the grounds; call ahead for directions and to make parking arrangements.

 18   Closed Dec. 21-Jan. 21
🅿

Samaniego

Palacio de Samaniego $
Constitución, 12, 1307,
Araba/Álava
☎ 941609151
▤ 941609157
🅔 jonyana@mediaweb.es

Halfway between Haro and Laguardia, on the classic route through Rioja wine country, stands this aristocratic 18th-century house with a stone facade and magnificent coat of arms. The interior is bright and spacious, and the original stone staircase has been preserved. The restaurant takes up most of the ground floor, and the welcoming bedrooms with terra-cotta floors are furnished with antiques.

 12

🅿

LOJA C1
Loja

La Bobadilla $$$
Finca La Bobadilla Ap. 144,
18300, Granada
☎ 958321861
🖹 958321810
📧 info@la-bobadilla.com
Surrounded by olive groves in the heart of Andalusia stands the exquisite combination of arches, fountains, courtyards and gardens that makes up La

Bobadilla, favored by the rich and famous and now part of the Barceló chain of hotels. The foyer resembles a palm grove, and the lush vegetation continues up to the sumptuous bedrooms. The hotel chapel contains a specially built organ with 1,595 pipes.

🛏 51 P 🏊

LUARCA B4
Luarca

Villa La Argentina $
Villar de Luarca, s/n, 33700,
Asturias
☎ 985640102
🖹 985640973
📧 villalaargentina@ctv.es
One of the most spectacular of the opulent houses built by rich *indianos* who returned to

Asturias having made their fortunes in South America, the Pachorro family home dates from 1899 and is located in Barrera park. It has a magnificent facade and gardens, and chandeliers and period furniture characterize the lavish interior.

🛏 12   Schedule varies seasonally; call for details

P 🏊

LUGO A4
Castroverde

Pazo de Vilabade $
Vilabade, 27122, Lugo
☎ 982313000
🖹 982312063
Built in 1650, this great house was once the home of the Viceroy of New Spain, as Mexico was formerly known. There is a colonnaded courtyard and an estate where guests are free to wander. Those who prefer

can head for the library, relax by the open fire or remain in the bedrooms, furnished in sober period style.

🛏 6
Closed Dec. 20-Mar. 3
P

Luarca

Key to Symbols: 🖹 Fax 📧 Email 🛏 Rooms P Parking 🏊 Swimming

MADRID — C3

Madrid

La Residencia de El Viso $$
Nervión, 8, 28002, Madrid
☎ 915640370
🖹 915641965
📧 elviso@estancias.es
Built in the Rationalist style, this 1930s townhouse has been converted into a charming hotel. Only minutes away from the Plaza de los Delfines and the Real Madrid Stadium, it is a favorite with busy executives who like to be pampered. The furniture in the brightly decorated rooms reflects the '30s style of the building.

🛏 12

Orfila $$$
Orfila, 6, 28010, Madrid
☎ 917027770
🖹 917027772
📧 hotelorfila@sei.es
Right in the city center, next to the Palacio de Justicia, this exclusive "boutique" hotel occupies an 1886 townhouse. The owners are great collectors, and works of art and antiques can be found in every corner. Apart from the staircase and the foyer, the building has been refurbished with exquisite attention to detail, providing splendid rooms and suites.

🛏 28   🅿

Santo Mauro $$$
Zurbano, 36, 28010, Madrid
☎ 913196900
🖹 913085477
📧 santomauro@ac.hoteles.es
French architect Louis Legrand was commissioned by the Duke of Santo Mauro to build this mansion in Chamberí. It later became an embassy and is now a luxury hotel. The decor respects the original features and combines them with the latest in contemporary design. In the basement is a swimming pool with vaulted ceilings, and the oak-paneled library now houses the Belagua restaurant.

🛏 37   🅿

MÁLAGA — B1

Rincón de la Victoria

Molino de Santillán $-$$
Ctra. de Macharaviaya, km 3, 29730, Málaga
☎ 952115780
🖹 952400950
📧 msantillan@spa.es
Carlos Marchini came to the Sierra de la Axarquía to set up his country house hotel after the stresses of living in Madrid began to take a toll on his health. He found a much more leisurely pace of life behind the dazzling white facade beside an old ruined mill. The hotel, surrounded by lush subtropical vegetation, comes into view after a long climb up a narrow, dusty road from the coast. Although small, the rooms are attractively decorated and cooled by ceiling fans.

🛏 10   Closed Jan. 11-Feb. 16
🅿

MANACOR — MAJORCA

Manacor

La Reserva Rotana $$$
Camí de Savall, km 3 (Apartado de Correos 69), 7500, Baleares/Mallorca
☎ 971845685
🖹 971555258
This 17th-century manor house, set on a gentle hillside near Manacor, is both a super-luxury hotel and the hub of a working farm. It is surrounded by lawns, pine trees and palms, and has its own nine-hole golf course. Main rooms feature mementos of African safaris, antiques and works of art, while the bedrooms and suites have a traditional Majorcan flavor.

🛏 20
🅿

MARBELLA B1
Denia

Romano **$$**
Avda. del Cid, 3 (subida al
castillo), 3700, Alacant/Alicante
☎ 966421789
🗎 966422958
Hans and Margot Lehmann are
a German couple who fell in love
with Denia. Their hotel, set
beneath a Moorish castle
surrounded by small houses and
Roman ruins, is simple and

discreet. On the roof terrace is a
solarium to catch the
Mediterranean light. The food is
good and the bedrooms large,
five of them with Jacuzzi and
original mosaic tiling.

 7
🅿

Rosa **$**
Congre, 3 - Ctra. las Marinas,
km 1, 3700, Alacant/Alicante
☎ 965781573
🗎 966424774
Michel Kessous came here on
vacation, but stayed to set up a
small hotel on Las Marinas
beach. He is gradually enlarging
the hotel in the Mediterranean
style with Florentine balconies.

This is a place to spend the
summer strolling around in a
bathing suit and enjoying the
laid-back atmosphere. Although
small, the bedrooms are
spotlessly clean and well
equipped.

 35
Closed Jan. 11-Mar. 15
🅿

Monda
El Castillo de Monda **$$**
El Castillo, s/n, 29110, Málaga
☎ 952457142
🗎 952457336
🅴 mondas@spa.es
On the ruins of the ancient
Moorish fortress of La Villeta, at
the exact spot where Julius
Caesar's army defeated the forces
of the brothers Gnaeus and

Sextus Pompey, Briton John
Norris has presided over a
modern reconstruction
incorporating some of the
ancient walls. The public rooms
are on the sixth floor, starting
with a bar full of kitsch detail
and finishing with a swimming
pool overlooking the town of
Monda.

 26 🅿 ≈

Ojén

Refugio de Juanar **$**
Sierra Blanca, s/n, 29610,
Málaga
☎ 952881000
🗎 952881001
🅴 juanar@sopde.es
This former state parador at the
foot of the Serrania de Ronda in
the Juanar nature reserve is run
by a highly effective workers' cooperative. The decor of hunting

trophies reflects the passion of
the original owner, the Marquis
of Larios. Room #3 is where
Gen. Charles de Gaulle stayed
while he finished his memoirs.

 21
🅿

MORELLA D3
Forcall

Palau dels Osset **$**
Plaza Mayor, 16, 12310,
Castelló/Castellón
☎ 964177524
🗎 964177556
A jewel of the Aragonese
Renaissance, the honey-colored
stone exterior of this property is
preserved in its original state.
The interior is elegant
minimalist, especially the Miró

Room on the first floor, whose
three large windows overlook the
town square and whose doors are
masterpieces of 16th-century
woodcarver's art. One room
retains its original late medieval
coffered ceiling, while others are
in the Provencal style.

▭ 20

MOTRIL   C1
Motril

Casa de los Bates   **$-$$**
Ctra. N-340, km 329, 500,
18600, Granada
☎ 958349495
📄 958349122
Set in extensive grounds with
lush vegetation, coral fountains
and flights of marble steps, this
19th-century Italianate palace
has wonderful views of the sea
and the castle of Salobreña.

Inside, 16th-century furniture,
antique clocks, Chinese screens,
old photographs and a grand
piano help preserve the feeling of
an aristocratic family home. The
bedrooms retain their original
high ceilings, and the suites have
coastal views.

 5
🅿 ≋

OURENSE   A4
Barbadás

Palacio Bentraces   **$**
Bentraces, 32890, Ourense
☎ 988383355
📄 988383381
🅔 rusticae@edigital.es
It took three years to restore this
15th-century episcopal palace in
a remote corner of Galicia to its
former glory. Now, entering

through a gate guarded by two
Alsatians whose bark is much
worse than their bite, visitors are
greeted by the colors and scents
of a lovingly tended garden.
Inside, the scene is one of luxury
and splendor. There are only nine
bedrooms, but each is vast and
beautifully appointed with
walnut and chestnut furniture,
Empire-style armchairs, Persian

rugs, porcelain vases and marble
fireplaces.

🛏 9   Closed Dec. 22-Feb. 22
🅿 ≋

O Carballiño

Viña Meín   **$**
Monasterio de San Clodio,
32420, Ourense
☎ 988488400
📄 988488400
In the 10th century, a noble
benefactor presented the monks
of the monastery of San Clodio
with some vines from the Rhine
Valley, so laying the foundation

for the production of Galicia's
own Ribeiro wines. A near
neighbor of the monastery is
Viña Meín, a large country
house that is not only the center
of a thriving vineyard but also a
hotel of special interest to wine
buffs. As well as civilized
accommodations, guests are
offered the chance to savor the
much-praised white Ribeiro

Casal de Meín produced here
and to tour the vineyards with a
knowledgeable guide.

🛏 9 🅿 ≋

PALAFRUGELL   E4
Fonolleres

Mas Crisarán   **$$$**
Fonolleres, 17133, Girona
☎ 972769000
📄 972769219
🅔 agrolodge@ctv.es
This 15th-century house was
formerly owned by a Swiss
painter and sculptor, who
bequeathed some of his works to
the hotel. The current owners'
travels around the world are

reflected in the display of
artifacts from Africa and Asia,
such as teak stools, Massai masks
and shields, and Chinese
lanterns. The doors are always
kept closed and are only opened
to guests who reserve in advance.

🛏 8
Closed Feb.
🅿 ≋

Llafranc

El Far de Sant Sebastiá   **$$**
Playa de Llafrançs, s/n, 17711,
Girona
☎ 972303733
📄 972304328
🅔 hotelfss@intercom.es
The Figueras family, owners of
the nearby Mas de Torrent (see
page 345), were irresistibly
drawn to this rugged stretch of
the Catalan coast. Here the

family has created a hotel
centered on a large courtyard
surrounded by majestic stone
arcades. The hotel interior recalls
the ancient castles and
watchtowers along the coast, and
the bedrooms are arranged
around an elegant lounge with a
vaulted ceiling.

🛏 10 🅿

Key to Symbols: 📄 Fax 🅔 Email 🛏 Rooms 🅿 Parking ≋ Swimming

Llafranc

Peratallada

Castell de Peratallada $
Castillo de Peratallada. Plaza del
Castillo, 1, 17113, Girona
☎ 972634021
▤ 972634011
🅴 casteperat@aplitec.com
A perfect example of how to
survive amid the often unsightly
building development along the
Costa Brava is the venerable

Torrent

Llevant $-$$$
Francesc de Blanes, 5, 17211,
Girona
☎ 972300366
▤ 972300345
🅴 hllevant@arrakis.es
This enchanting little hotel,
created more than half a century
ago from two adjoining houses,
stands half-hidden among pine
trees right on the seafront.

castle of the Marquises of
Torroella. The two most
charming bedrooms, La Luna
(Moon) and Les Estrelles
(Stars), are reached from the
courtyard. There are three more
rooms in an adjoining building.
The main attraction, though, is
the restaurant in the great hall.

🛏 5

Mas de Torrent $$$
Afueras de Torrent, s/n, 17123,
Girona
☎ 972303292
▤ 972303293
🅴 mtorrent@intercom.es
This dazzling 18th-century
farmhouse has spectacular views
of the coast from its balconies.
The simple elegance of the
vaulted reception area is but a

Inside, works of art are displayed
on each floor, while the
bedrooms are adorned with
prints, lithographs and ceramics.
The hotel's biggest attraction is
the dining room, where the
cooking draws gourmets from
miles around.

🛏 24 Closed 15 days in Nov.
🅿

prelude to the delightful rooms,
with their exposed stone walls,
precious woods and antiques. As
well as the suites in the main
building there are 20 bungalows
on the grounds, each with its
own terrace.

🛏 24
🅿 ≋

The coastal path near Palafrugell

Key to Symbols: ▤ Fax 🅴 Email 🛏 Rooms 🅿 Parking ≋ Swimming

PALENCIA   C4

Ampudia

Posada Casa del Abad $
Plaza Francisco Martín
Gormaz, 12, 34160, Palencia
☎ 979768008
📄 979768300
e casadeabad@arquired.es
When the four García Puertas brothers inherited this 17th-century house, which has been in their family for generations, they decided it should be refurbished and converted into a hotel. In addition to preserving many of the original elements, including a spectacular dome, the abbot's chapel and a lounge re-created as a costume museum, the brothers have added state-of-the-art lighting and Internet connections in the bedrooms.

🛏 13   Closed Dec. 20-27   P 🏊

Carrión de los Condes

Real Monasterio de San Zoilo $
Obispo Souto, s/n, 34120,
Palencia
☎ 979880050
📄 979881090
e sanzoilo@logiccontrol.es
This monastery, consecrated in AD 947, was an important staging post on the pilgrim route to Santiago de Compostela, a fact reflected in the cockleshell shape of the key rings. The vast public rooms have been updated with exquisite taste and an eye to practicality, and furnished in traditional Castilian style. The main attraction is the restaurant in the old kitchen, its ceiling supported by 48-foot beams; fruit and vegetables come from the hotel's own orchards and gardens.

🛏 37   P

PALMA   MAJORCA

Puigpunyent

Son Net $$$
Castillo Son Net, 7194,
Baleares/Mallorca
☎ 971147000
📄 971147001
e son.net@jet.es
This 17th-century manor house is set on a hillside above Puigpunyent. No expense has been spared in the refurbishment of the building. The old bakery serves as a restaurant presided over by Thierry Buffeteau (formerly of the Ritz, La Tour d'Argent and Jules Verne in París). The rooms have magnificent views, and the swimming pool overlooks the town's rooftops.

🛏 24
P 🏊

Santa María

Read's $$$
Ctra. vieja Santa María-Alaró,
7320, Baleares/Mallorca
☎ 971140261
📄 971140762
e readshotel@readshotel.com
Far away from the London fog, Vivian and Iris preside over a luxurious country hotel in a converted 18th-century manor house at the foot of the Sierra de Tramuntana. Murals depicting a life of leisure in a typical English country house are a feature, and the bedrooms are furnished with family heirlooms, Oriental carpets and cabinets of Chinese porcelain.

🛏 12   P 🏊

PALMA DE MALLORCA
MAJORCA

Palma de Mallorca

Palacio ca sa Galesa $$$
Miramar, 8, 7001,
Baleares/Mallorca
☎ 971715400
📄 971721579
e reservas@palaciocasagalesa.com
The Pollards, from Wales, have restored this small 17th-century palace overlooking the bay of Palma and the cathedral. Guest facilities comprise a third-floor terrace, a heated swimming pool and the dining room, painted bright yellow and blue and inspired by Monet's house at Giverny in France. Opera music plays in the background, and each of the rooms is named after a composer.

🛏 10   P 🏊

Palma de Mallorca

San Lorenzo $$
San Lorenzo, 14, 7012,
Baleares/Mallorca
☎ 971728200
🖹 971711901
📧 sanlorenzo@fehm.es

In the crowded alleyways of Puig de Sant Pere, next to the fish market, you will come across this luxurious little 17th-century palace. Passing through the original gateway, you will be met by an array of tiles, precious woods, watercolors, paved floors, old-fashioned Majorcan beds and exquisite objets d'art. Parking is at the public lot a short distance away.

🛏 4 🏊

PAMPLONA   D4
Udabe

Venta Udabe $
Basaburua Mayor, 31869,
Nafarroa/Navarra
☎ 948503105

Restored room by room, this inn is an authentic example of traditional regional architecture, with additional modern touches like the swimming pool and the summerhouse.

🛏 9 Closed Dec. 20-Jan. 20
🅿 🏊

PLASENCIA   B3
Losar de la Vera

Hostería Fontivieja $$$
Finca Los Mártires, s/n, 10460,
Cáceres
☎ 927570108
🖹 927570108

Eight suites have been added to this small hotel, which is set in the middle of a vast olive grove. While the bedrooms are a bit small for two people, they are well equipped with pine closets, and a TV suspended from the wall. The main attractions are the swimming pool and horseback riding in the delightful countryside.

🛏 12
🅿 🏊

Malpartida de Plasencia

La Posada de Amonaria $
Nuestra Señora de la Luz, 7,
10680, Cáceres
☎ 927459446
🖹 927459446

Dancing is so important to owners Juan and Cruz that they have created a small dance studio in this 19th-century farmhouse conversion. They have retained the original courtyard, the 100-year-old palm tree, weatherboard roof and wine cellar. The old kitchen has become the dining room and the barn a lounge; the bedrooms are furnished with antiques.

🛏 5
Closed Jul. 1-Aug. 12

PONFERRADA   B4
Molinaseca

La Posada de Muriel $
Pza. del Sto. Cristo, s/n, 24413,
León
☎ 987453201
🖹 987453135
📧 posadamuriel@treway.zzn.com

As a tribute to Molinaseca's historic connections with the Knights Templars, each of this little stone-built hotel's eight rooms is named after a Grand Master of this medieval religious and military order. Although small, they are attractively furnished and full of thoughtful touches. The dining room, closed on Mondays, offers local specialties.

🛏 8 🅿

Key to Symbols: 🖹 Fax 📧 Email 🛏 Rooms 🅿 Parking 🏊 Swimming

PUERTO DE ANDRAITX MAJORCA

Puerto de Andraitx

Villa Italia $$$
Camino de San Carlos, 13,
7157, Baleares/Mallorca
☎ 971674011
🖹 971673350

In the 1920s, an Italian millionaire built this Florentine-style villa overlooking the harbor for his mistress. Stucco ceilings, marble floors, cretonne curtains and Roman columns are typical features, and yachting enthusiasts stop by for a swim and champagne by the pool. Villa Italia also caters to lesser mortals, who can stroll through the sweet-scented gardens pretending to be rich and famous.

🛏 10 🏊

PORT DE POLLENCA MAJORCA

Port de Pollença

Cala Sant Vicenç $$-$$$
Maresers, 2 Cala Sant Vicenç,
7469, Baleares/Mallorca
☎ 971530250
🖹 971532084
📧 h.cala@pobox.com

After years of catering to package vacationers on the northern coast of the island, the Suau family moved upscale to fly the flag of the exclusive Relais & Châteaux chain. The hotel has a garden, and offers piano recitals and lessons on how to prepare paella during the high season.

🛏 21
Closed Dec.-Jan.
🏊

QUINTANAR DE LA ORDEN C2

Belmonte

Palacio Buenavista $
José Antonio González, 2,
16640, Cuenca
☎ 967187580
🖹 967187588

A massive wall encircles the village of Belmonte, birthplace of Spanish humanist Fray Luis de León and home to this 16th-century palace. Perhaps because of the proximity of the collegiate church of San Bartolomé, the hotel has an austere, scholastic air about it. Despite the stark simplicity of the interiors, guests can expect a high standard of comfort.

🛏 18 🅿

RIBADEO B4

Ribadeo

A Cortiña $
Paco Lanza, s/n, 27700, Lugo
☎ 982130187
🖹 982130187

A typical fishing village house, built of dry stone with a slate roof. The old well, the oven and the 18th-century *hórreo* (elevated granary) are still here. The most attractive rooms, with original beams and wrought-iron or wooden headboards salvaged from old beds, are level with the garden, where they can catch the salty smell of the Atlantic.

🛏 9
🅿

Taramundi

La Rectoral $-$$
Cuesta de la Rectoral, s/n,
33775, Asturias
☎ 985646760
🖹 985646777

This 18th-century rectory represents the region's finest architectural, artistic and gastronomic traditions. Particular features are the *hórreo* (elevated granary) at the entrance, the fireplace and the chapel, now an elegant dining room. The extension, housing 18 spacious bedrooms with views across the surrounding countryside, can scarcely be distinguished from the original building. Nine of the rooms have their own terraces.

🛏 18 🅿

Key to Symbols: 🖹 Fax 📧 Email 🛏 Rooms 🅿 Parking 🏊 Swimming

RIPOLL E4

Camprodon

Edelweiss $
Ctra. de Sant Joan, 28, 17867, Girona
☎ 972740614
🖹 972740605

A striking Art Nouveau facade welcomes visitors to the Edelweiss, probably the most attractive small hotel in this popular mountain resort. The interiors also retain period features, with wood-paneled walls and ceilings in the public rooms. Reproduction furniture, heavy floral curtains and Venetian marble in the bathrooms give the guest accommodations a nostalgic late 19th-century ambience.

🛏 21 Closed Dec. 24-26
P

RONDA B1

Benaoján

Molino del Santo $-$$
Barriada Estación, s/n, 29370, Málaga
☎ 952167151
🖹 952167327
📧 molino@logiccontrol.es

Britons Andy Chapell and Pauline Elkin converted this old water mill into a rural hotel. Six of the homey rooms overlook the swimming pool, shaded by trees and heated by solar panels. The original millstones and a charming fireplace are preserved in the lounge. You can rent mountain bikes to explore the surrounding countryside, returning to a dinner of delicious local specialties.

🛏 13 Closed Dec. 11-Feb. 19

P 🏊

El Burgo

Posada del Canónigo $
Mesones, 24, 29420, Málaga
☎ 952160185
🖹 952160185

The first inn was opened here in the 1700s, and the original floors, doors, cupboards and fireplace have been carefully preserved by Loli Cervantes, who inherited the business. The dimly lit lounge and the bedrooms all feature an extraordinary blend of Moorish and classical decor. Loli organizes excursions on horseback into the Sierra de las Nieves.

🛏 16

Gaucín

Cortijo El Puerto del Negro $-$$
Ctra. a El Colmenar, s/n (Aptdo. 25), 29480, Málaga
☎ 952151239
🖹 952151239

On a clear day you can see the Rock of Gibraltar and the coast of North Africa from here. Owners Christine and Anthony Martin provide a cosmopolitan and exotic atmosphere with English-style furniture set beside items from India, Morocco and remote corners of Andalusia.

🛏 6
Closed Nov.-Jan.

P 🏊

SALAMANCA B3

Salamanca

Rector $$
Plaza Rector Esperabé, 10, 37008, Salamanca
☎ 923218482
🖹 923214008
📧 hotelrector@teleline.es

This pink stone building on the site of the former church of Santa María la Blanca is not as old as it seems. It dates from the Franco era of the 1940s and is the work of an architect fond of totalitarian pomp who was also responsible for the city's Palacio de Justicia. The interior design takes its inspiration from the stylized geometry of Art Nouveau, with fine mahogany furniture and eye-catching stained glass in the foyer.

🛏 12 P

Key to Symbols: 🖹 Fax 📧 Email 🛏 Rooms P Parking 🏊 Swimming

SAN LORENZO DE EL ESCORIAL C3

San Lorenzo de El Escorial

El Botánico $-$$
Timoteo Padrós, 16, 28200, Madrid
☎ 918907879
🖹 918908158
Recently opened, this aristocratic little hotel has become a popular destination for city dwellers seeking some fresh mountain air. Magnificent stone steps lead up to a finely carved wooden front door, and the dining room at the rear overlooks the pine woods. The bedrooms are most attractive, and the duplex suite in the tower has views of El Escorial.

 17
P

SAN SEBASTIAN C4

Donamaria

Donamaria'ko Benta $
Barrio Ventas, 4, 31750, Nafarroa/Navarra
☎ 948450708
🖹 948450708
📧 donamaria@jet.es
Tucked away in one of the lesser-known corners of the Navarra Pyrenees, this little hotel has become a favorite destination for lovers of the mountains. In summer and winter alike, they are assured of a warm welcome and friendly service from Imanol and Elixabet. The biggest attraction is the restaurant, run by their daughter Lorea. The two small lounges are enlivened by a host of family heirlooms, including old wooden radio sets, plaster busts and grandma's rocking chair. The bedrooms are housed in a separate building.

🛏 5 P

SANT JOSEP DE SA TALAIA IBIZA

Sant Josep de Sa Talaia

Las Brisas de Ibiza $$-$$$
Porroig, 7830, Baleares/Eivissa
☎ 971802193
🖹 971802328
Emmanuel Gamby, a seasoned traveler, has re-created his personal vision of luxury and good living in indigo, ocher and white, the colors of sky, earth and luminous Mediterranean architecture. The hotel is on the Porroig peninsula looking out onto the pine-clad cliffs of Es Cubells. The bedrooms echo the overall theme, with clever lighting and thoughtful details.

🛏 8
Closed Oct. 30-Apr. 1
P 🏊

SANT MIQUEL DE BALANSAT IBIZA

Sant Miquel de Balansat

Ca's Pla $$
Natalia Sánchez de Fenaroli. Apdo. 777, 7800, Baleares/Eivissa
☎ 971334587
🖹 971334604
Massimo and Natalia's charming country estate lies half-hidden among the pine woods on the prettiest part of the island. The rustic vacation complex comprises several bungalows with colonial-style verandas surrounded by hibiscus, palms and other lush vegetation. The bedrooms are spacious and tastefully decorated with textiles, paintings and ceramics from Níjar in southern Spain.

🛏 3   Closed Dec. 1-Mar. 31
P 🏊

Santa Gertrudis de Fruitera

Cas Gasi $$$
Cami Vell de Sant Halem, s/n, 7814, Baleares/Eivissa
☎ 971197700
🖹 971197899
Typically rustic-style house, built in 1880, with whitewashed facades, stone and mortar walls, shingle and terrazzo floors, cedar beams, and a roof of almond and olive wood. The bedrooms, like the rest of the house, are in authentic Ibicenco style, enhanced by family mementos, antiques, hand-painted tiles and rugs bought in Marrakech, Morocco. Children are made very welcome.

🛏 9
P 🏊

Key to Symbols: 🖹 Fax 📧 Email 🛏 Rooms P Parking 🏊 Swimming

SANTA EULÀRIA DES RIU **IBIZA**
Santa Eulària des Riu

Can Curreu $$
Ctra. Sant Carles, km 12, 7840, Baleares/Eivissa
☎ 971335280
 971335280

A traditional Ibicenco estate transformed into a luxurious hotel. Twelve single-story cottages are linked by paved passageways to the main house. On chilly fall evenings a fire is lighted in each cottage at 6 p.m. The bathrooms feature blue Valencian tiling and indigo-painted ceilings. From the swimming pool there are magnificent views of the surrounding pine woods and Santa Eulària bay.

 8
P 🏊

Les Terrasses $$
Ctra. Ibiza-Santa Eulalia, km 1, 7800, Baleares/Eivissa
☎ 971332643
 971332643
e lesterrasses@interbook.es

The personal touch of owner Françoise Pialoux is obvious in every aspect of this establishment, an austere blue and white country house in the traditional island style. Each of the rooms has its own patio, and no one seems to mind the mild chaos of the charming hotel restaurant.

7
P 🏊

Santa Eulària des Riu

Key to Symbols: 📄 Fax e Email 🛏 Rooms P Parking 🏊 Swimming

SANTANDER   C4

Arnuero

Escalante

San Román de Escalante $-$$
Ctra. de Escalante a Castillo, km
2, 39795, Cantabria
☎ 942677728
▤ 942677643
e sanromanescalante@
mundivia.es
Probably the finest display of
paintings, sculpture and antiques
to grace any hotel in Spain

San Mamés de Meruelo

Casona de Meruelo $
Barrio de la Iglesia, 40, 39142,
Cantabria
☎ 942637092
▤ 942657042
An 18th-century country house
converted into an elegant hotel
furnished with family heirlooms.
It has a cheerful interior with
bright pastel walls and matching

SANTANYI   MAJORCA

Campos

Felanitx

Hostería de Arnuero $
Barrio Palacio, 17, 39194,
Cantabria
☎ 942677121
▤ 942677121
Get away from the traffic jams
heading for the resort of Isla and
stop at this 18th-century house
on the Bay of Biscay. It was just
a restaurant until sisters Noemi
and Margot and their respective

awaits visitors to this restored
17th-century mansion. Close to
Escalante's two convents, there is
an almost reverent silence about
the place in its idyllic woodland
setting not far from the coast.
The restaurant, presided over by
chef David Bosch, is among the
best in the region.

▭ 13   Closed Dec. 20-Jan. 20

fabrics. Surrounded by greenery,
the hotel has a heated open-air
pool and a solarium: guests also
can play skittles, a game similar
to bowling. Only breakfast is
provided, although business
conferences and weddings are
catered to.

▭ 10

Son Bernadinet $$$
Ctra. Campos-Porreras, km 5, 9,
7630, Baleares/Mallorca
☎ 971181650
▤ 971186043
The worldwide travels of
Francisca Bonet and her
daughter Alicia, a pair of truly
elegant and cultured ladies, have
stood them in good stead for
their recent venture into green

Sa Pletassa $$
Camino Viejo S'Horta-Cala
Marcal, 362, 7669,
Baleares/Mallorca
☎ 971837069
▤ 971837320
Bernardo Amengual has created
an impeccable environment for
rest and recuperation at this old
Majorcan manor house.
Accommodations comprise 10

---

partners embarked on a full-scale
restoration program, hired an
expert chef and created a small
rural hotel. Inside, the
atmosphere is bright, relaxing
and rather romantic.

▭ 9
Closed Jan.-Feb.
🅿

🅿

🅿 ≋

tourism. In accordance with the
modern aesthetic, everything is
pared down to the essential.
Tiled floors, exposed roof tiles,
pale walls and big wrought-iron
beds are features.

▭ 10
🅿 ≋

suites arranged around the pool.
From the solarium on top of the
dining room-reception area,
there are views on one side of the
Puig de Sant Salvador and Sa
Roca des Fangar mountains and,
on the other, the greenish-blue
sea.

▭ 10
Closed Dec. 1-15 and Jan. 8-31
🅿 ≋

Key to Symbols: ▤ Fax **e** Email ▭ Rooms 🅿 Parking ≋ Swimming

Felanitx

Sa Posada d'Aumallia $$
Camí de Son Prohens, 1027
(Aumallia), 7200,
Baleares/Mallorca
☎ 971582657
🖹 971583269
María Antonia Martí's majestic estate is on an unspoiled part of the island beneath the Puig de Sant Salvador and Sa Roca des Fangar mountains. Visitor accommodations are provided in a former barn, where the restful rooms are reminiscent of monks' cells with few obvious luxuries. The little garden around the swimming pool is the ideal place for breakfast or lazing in the sun.

🛏 14   Closed Dec.-Jan.

 🅿 🏊

Es Passarell $$
2ª Vuelta nº 117, 7200,
Baleares/Mallorca
☎ 971183091
🖹 971557133
Halfway between the towns of Felanitx and Porreres, Lola Suberviola came across a dilapidated house alone in the countryside. With daring and dedication she has been working on it ever since, adding a little more luxury each year. Lola happily and haphazardly mixes homespun fabrics and designer lamps, clay pots and double-glazing. The walls are hung with paintings of Castilian landscapes.

🛏 7

🅿 🏊

Ses Salines

Es Turó $$
C'as Perets, s/n, 7640,
Baleares/Mallorca
☎ 971649531
🖹 971649548
✉ esturo@globalred.es
This farmhouse is a little museum of Majorcan crafts – traditional textiles, copper pans, ceramic pots and glassware – with apartment-style rooms set around the swimming pool. The place attracts easy-going visitors who demand no more than peace, quiet and hearty home cooking enjoyed by candlelight. Nothing could be further from the crowded beaches!

🛏 10
🅿 🏊

SANTIAGO DE COMPOSTELA A4

Arzúa

Pazo do Sedor $
A Castañeda, 15810, A Coruña
☎ 981193248
🖹 981193248
Galician traditions inspired María Jesús Saavedra in her restoration of this old manor house, which dominates the little village of the same name. With clever lighting, whitewashed or exposed brick walls and paved floors, she has created a truly authentic atmosphere. The best room, with views across the valley, is #1.

🛏 6
🅿 🏊

Calo

Casa Grande de Cornide $
Cornide (Teo), 15886, A Coruña
☎ 981805599
🖹 981805751
This family hotel is the perfect place to relax, with the best of Galicia at your feet. It has a wonderfully nostalgic garden and a gallery of paintings by local artists. Objets d'art, classical and modern but all truly Galician, are scattered about the house. Halogen lights, sloping ceilings and a staircase to the attic all add to the atmosphere.

🛏 7
Closed Dec. 20-Jan. 20
🅿 🏊

Key to Symbols: 🖹 Fax ✉ Email 🛏 Rooms 🅿 Parking 🏊 Swimming

Padrón

Casa Antiga do Monte $
Boca do Monte (Lestrove,
Dodro), 15916, A Coruña
☎ 981812400
▤ 981812401
📧 susavilaocio@nexo.es
Despite its aged appearance, this building was recently constructed of solid stone with a continuous balcony. All doors, including bedrooms, sauna and the garage, are opened by magnetic card. The bedrooms, occupying the two upper floors, are decorated in rustic style, with cane furniture and wrought-iron details.

🛏 10
🅿 ⋙

San Xulián de Sales

Pazo Cibrán $
Lugar de Cibrán, 15885, A
Coruña
☎ 981511515
▤ 981511515
📧 cibran@arrakis.es
Fine 18th-century manor house with stone walls, red tiles and battlements, all restored by Mayka Iglesias. The corridors, staircases and most of the bedrooms provide a dramatic minimalist contrast to the older parts of the building. The best room is the bridal suite, overlooking the vineyards. On winter nights, guests can browse through Mayka's antiquarian library.

🛏 11
🅿

SANTILLANA DEL MAR C4
Oreña

El Sitio del Valle $
Barrio Perelada, 143, 39525,
Cantabria
☎ 942716204
▤ 942716218
This small rural hotel is a simple stone building with rustic furniture, tiled floors and flowers in every corner. It offers four bedrooms, including a charming duplex, and there is not a single TV set in the place. Completing the picture are the dining room serving delicious home cooking, a small garden and an orchard.

🛏 4
Closed Sept. 20-Oct. 6
🅿

Quijas

Posada la Torre de Quijas $
Barrio Vinueva, 76, 39590,
Cantabria
☎ 942820645
▤ 942838255
This stone house with exposed beams, dating from 1872, offers a real home away from home for guests. Ancient farm implements adorn the interior, and toys, storybooks and costume chests are provided in some of the bedrooms to entertain younger visitors. The former stables and hayloft have recently been converted into five bedrooms with direct access to the garden.

🛏 19
Closed Dec. 23-Jan. 7
🅿

Hostería de Quijas $
Barrio Binueva, s/n, 39590,
Cantabria
☎ 942820833
▤ 942838050
Lovingly restored 200-year-old mansion, famous locally for its library and the private chapel of the former owner, Doña Petra González Bustamante. The biggest attraction, however, is the garden with its hydrangeas, trellises and a magnolia tree several centuries old. Inside, Demetrio Castañeda and his wife have created a warm, homey atmosphere, attending to their guests in person.

🛏 13

🅿 ⋙

Santillana del Mar
La Casa de Güela $
Los Hornos, 9, 39330,
Cantabria
☎ 942818250
🖷 942840183
📧 campingsantillan@
ceoecant.es
"Grandma's House" is
everything you might expect
from a village dwelling, with
dried flowers, carved wooden
beams and old-fashioned
household utensils. Although
there is not much communal
space, two of the bedrooms have
balconies with views of the
village. A little fountain in the
garden is all that breaks the
silence. Breakfast includes two
traditional local sweet specialties,
sobaos pasiegos and *quesada*.

🛏 10 🅿

Valle
Torre de Ruesga $
Bárcena, s/n, 39815, Cantabria
☎ 942641060
🖷 942641172
📧 reservas@t-ruesga.com
No expense has been spared in
the conversion of this 18th-
century palace into a hotel. The
facade, with two magnificent
towers housing the bedrooms,
reflects the refined interior.
Upstairs is a regal lounge, a
richly stocked library and a game
room, decorated with an
impressive series of murals by
Catalan artist Ramón Criach.

🛏 6
Closed Jan. 17-31

🅿 ⛱

SANTO DOMINGO DE LA CALZADA — C4
Briñas

Hospedería Señorío de Briñas $
Travesía de la Calle Real, 3,
26290, La Rioja
☎ 941303984
🖷 941304345
📧 hsbrinas@arrakis.es
A comfortable bed, good food
and a warm welcome. In other
words, everything travelers
through the vineyards of the
Rioja could possibly desire is
offered behind the 18th-century
stone facade of this hotel.
Wrought-iron balconies, wooden
floors and ancient radiators
create a charming Old World
atmosphere, in striking contrast
to murals depicting the work of
the region's wine growers by
Polish artist Jull Dziamski.

🛏 14   Closed Dec. 15-Jan. 31   🅿

Ezcaray
Hostería Valle del Oja $
Aldea de Azárrulla, s/n, 26280,
La Rioja
☎ 941427416
🖷 941427432
An abandoned 18th-century
ironworks in the upper Oja
valley was crying out for
restoration, so Emilio Serrano
took up the challenge and set
about converting the various
industrial buildings to create a
hotel with appealing period
features. The well-equipped
bedrooms are in one building,
the dining room in another,
while the old foundry has been
transformed into a magnificent
conference room.

🛏 2

🅿 ⛱

San Millán de la Cogolla

Hostería del Monasterio de S. Millán $
Monasterio de Yuso, s/n, 26226,
La Rioja
☎ 941373277
🖷 941373266
📧 hosteria@sanmillan.com
The Augustinian monastery of
San Millán de la Cogolla,
famous as the cradle of the
Basque and Castilian languages,
has opened its west wing as
tourist accommodations. Of the
bedrooms, only the Royal Suite
in the former abbot's quarters is
truly fit for quiet contemplation,
although the rest are comfortable
and well appointed.

🛏 23
🅿

Key to Symbols: 🖷 Fax 📧 Email 🛏 Rooms 🅿 Parking ⛱ Swimming

SARRIA A4

O Incio

Casa Grande de Romariz $
Romariz, Rendar, 27346, Lugo
☎ 982427234
🗎 982427255
📧 romariz@cempresarial.com
This was mathematician Juan Durán-Loriga's place in the country. He took great care of the house, built between the 16th and 17th centuries, enabling the present owners to convert it into a typically Galician-style hotel. Centered on the courtyard, the dimly lit but cozy rooms are reached through labyrinthine corridors. Ancient oaks and myrtles give a nostalgic feel to the garden.

🛏 10   Closed Jan.   🅿

SEDANO C4

Valdelateja

La Posada del Balneario $
Camino del Balneario, s/n, 9145, Burgos
☎ 947150220
🗎 947150271
📧 valteja@jet.es
This recently restored hotel, dating from 1872, is approached by what was once a goat track along the gorge of the River Rudrón. Guests cannot fail to be impressed by the somber splendor of the lounges and the avant-garde decoration of the foyer. The spacious, rustic bedrooms have pine floorboards, and three duplexes under the sloping roof have pleasant mountain views.

🛏 18   Closed Jan. 10-Feb. 10
🅿 🏊

SEGOVIA C3

Alameda del Valle

La Posada de Alameda $
Grande, 34, 28749, Madrid
☎ 918691337
🗎 918690163
Bauhaus principles were clearly on the minds of the architects when they converted this former dairy in the Lozoya Valley into a hotel. As a result, it has become a popular venue for exhibitions by contemporary Spanish artists. The bedrooms – some with tranquil views across the *alameda*, or poplar grove, with a lake at its center – provide a comfortable weekend refuge.

🛏 19
🅿

Carrascal de la Cuesta

La Abubilla $-$$
Escuelas, 4, 40181, Segovia
☎ 921120236
🗎 916617068
📧 oneto@oneto.com
Mercedes Oneto recently launched her hotel in this typical farmhouse in the foothills of the Guadarrama mountain range. The old hayloft across the courtyard from the main house has been converted into a dining room, lounge and game room. The four suites each have a bedroom, a bathroom and a sitting room with a fireplace.

🛏 4
Reserve in advance

Collado Hermoso

Molino de Río Viejo $
Ctra. N-110, km 172, 40170, Segovia
☎ 921403063
🗎 921403051
Some years ago, Antonio Armero bought this old water mill by the River Viejo as a base for his horseback riding expeditions around the Iberian Peninsula. It is now a hotel with an informal, relaxed atmosphere reminiscent of an English country house, and is a popular stopover for travelers exploring Segovia and the surrounding region. Breakfast is served in the space once occupied by the old grindstone.

🛏 6   🅿

Key to Symbols: Fax   Email   Rooms   Parking   Swimming

La Granja de San Ildefonso

Las Fuentes $
Padre Claret, 6, 40100, Segovia
☎ 921471024
🖹 921471741
In the very spot where Spain's Bourbon kings created the country's finest gardens, the family home of the Counts of Guijasalva, built in 1860, has been converted to allow visitors to enjoy accommodations with a French accent. The modest exterior conceals rooms full of treasures: antique furniture and books, oil paintings and chandeliers.

 9

Rascafría

Santa María de El Paular $$
Ctra. M-604, km 26,500, 28741, Madrid
☎ 918691011
🖹 918691006
✉ javiercortes@ittsheraton.com
The 14th-century former hunting lodge of the Kings of Castile, beside the Benedictine monastery of El Paular and at the foot of the Guadarrama mountains, provides a monastic setting in which a varied clientele of executives and politicians can rest and recuperate. The rooms overlook the mountains, and the restaurant, approached from the courtyard, specializes in Castilian cuisine.

 44   Closed Jan.   ◻P   ≋

Sotosalbos

Hostal de Buen Amor $
Eras, 7, 40170, Segovia
☎ 921403020
🖹 921403022
The name recalls one of the landmarks of medieval Spanish literature, *El Libro de Buen Amor*, whose author, the Archpriest of Hita, spent much time in the region and was as famous for his amorous adventures as his satirical verse. The owners rummaged around in antique shops throughout the area and also commissioned new furniture from the best local craftspeople in order to equip their atmospheric hotel with its spacious and well-appointed rooms, including an attic suite with canopied bed and Jacuzzi.

 11   ◻P

SEVILLE (SEVILLA)   B1

Gerena

Cortijo El Esparragal $$
Ctra. de Mérida, km 795, 41960, Sevilla
☎ 955782702
🖹 955782783
✉ rusticae@edigital.es
This stately house offers a delightfully Andalusian blend of courtyards and elegant lounges, with 18th-century frescoes and furniture of aristocratic severity. All the bedrooms have a pleasant rural feel, with wrought-iron balconies, and traditional walnut cabinets and writing desks. The best have views of the garden and its lush green lawns shaded by huge palm trees.

 9   Closed Aug. 1-15   ◻P   ≋

Guillena

Cortijo Águila Real $-$$
Ctra. Guillena-Burguillos, km 4, 41210, Sevilla
☎ 955785006
🖹 955784330
✉ hotel@aguilareal.com
This country house, surrounded by palms, bougainvilleas and pots of geraniums, has enjoyed many successful years as a hotel after the owners decided that tourism was more profitable than farming. The public spaces are somewhat more stylish than the 11 bedrooms, each named after a flower with the furniture painted accordingly. The old pigeon loft has been converted into a conference room holding up to 300. Flamenco evenings can be organized on request. Be sure to take in a sunset from the minaret.

 11   ◻P   ≋

Key to Symbols: 🖹 Fax   ✉ Email   ◻ Rooms   ◻P Parking   ≋ Swimming

Guillena

Cortijo Torre de la Reina **$$**
Paseo de la Alameda, s/n, 41209, Sevilla
☎ 955780136
🗎 955780122
🅔 torredelareina@saranet.es
At the end of the 13th century, this was the site of a camp for the army of King Ferdinand III attempting to recapture Seville from the Moors. A century later, Queen María de Molina built the present house, which was converted into a luxury hotel by its owner, a descendent of one of Spain's most noble families. The scent of jasmine and the color of the geraniums on the patio are as much a part of the atmosphere as the elegant lounges full of antique furniture and works of art.

🛏 6 🅿 🏊

Sanlúcar la Mayor

Hacienda Benazuza **$$$**
Virgen de las Nieves, s/n, 41800, Sevilla
☎ 955703344
🗎 955703410
🅔 hbenazuza@arrakis.es
The Hacienda Benazuza is steeped in history. It started life as a Moorish estate in the 10th century, later becoming a royal residence, the headquarters of a military and religious order and the seat of a succession of noblemen. Today it is a hotel combining echoes of this checkered past with 21st-century luxury. To enter, you have to pass the fortified medieval bastions that still dominate the facade. Inside courtyards with fountains, arches and coffered ceilings re-create the atmosphere of Andalusia in the days of the Moors.

🛏 26   Closed Aug.   🅿 🏊

Seville

Casa Imperial **$$-$$$**
Imperial, 29, 41003, Sevilla
☎ 954500300
🗎 954500330
🅔 info@casaimperial.com
No better use could possibly be found for this 16th-century palace in the heart of the city, once home of the steward to the noble family in the adjoining Casa de Pilatos, than to transform it into a luxury hotel. Echoing the classic Sevillano style, it boasts three graceful white-painted patios, walls adorned with antique ceramic tiles and richly decorated ceilings. For an early morning treat, climb up to the roof terrace for a panoramic view of the city.

🛏 10 🅿 🏊

Las Casas de la Judería **$-$$**
Callejón Dos Hermanas, 7, 41005, Sevilla
☎ 954415150
🗎 954422170
🅔 judería@zoom.es
The simple elegance of this hotel, created from several houses once owned by the Duke of Béjar, provides a pleasantly stark contrast to the almost excessive romanticism of Santa Cruz, Seville's medieval Jewish quarter, with its patios, fountains, iron-grilled balconies and endless geraniums. Guests cannot fail to be charmed by the austere decor, the discreet floral arrangements, the creaking iron gates and the intense perfume of orange blossoms in the courtyard. All this, plus the courteous service typical of Andalusia.

🛏 104 🅿 🏊

Patio de la Cartuja **$**
Lumbreras, 8 y 10, 41002, Sevilla
☎ 954900200
🗎 954902056
🅔 patiocartuja@estanciases.es
Along with the nearby Patio de la Alameda under the same management, Patio de la Cartuja offers travelers one of the best deals to be had in Seville. This apartment hotel is the pleasing result of the restoration of several old houses in the popular Macarena neighborhood. The well-appointed apartments occupy three floors overlooking a shady central patio. Especially recommended are #201 and #210 on the top floor, with city views from the balconies.

🛏 34 🅿

Key to Symbols: 🗎 Fax   🅔 Email   🛏 Rooms   🅿 Parking   🏊 Swimming

Seville

Taberna del Alabardero $$
Zaragoza, 20, 41001, Sevilla
☎ 954560637
🗎 954563666

Priest and restaurateur Luis de Lezama recently opened this temple of gastronomy. Both a restaurant and an exclusive catering school, the Taberna also offers seven charming guest rooms on the upper floors of the 19th-century house. Decorated in period style with great attention to detail, each one is named after an Andalusian town. The roof terrace overlooks the city's historic center.

🛏 7 Closed Jul. 15-Aug. 15
🅿

SIGUERUELO C3
Cerezo de Arriba

Casón de la Pinilla $
Cerca Merina. Finca La Rinconada, 40592, Segovia
☎ 921557201
🗎 921557209

The nine rooms of Juncal Chaves' little hotel, created from an old dairy in a mountain hamlet 60 miles from Madrid, provides a welcome weekend retreat from the stresses of city life. In winter, the proximity of the ski resort of La Pinilla means that Juncal is kept busy providing food and shelter for large numbers of ski enthusiasts.

🛏 9 🅿

Pedraza

El Hotel de la Villa $$
Calzada, 5, 40172, Segovia
☎ 921508651
🗎 921508653
📧 delavilla@estanciases.es

The Martín Arcones brothers, owners of the Hotel de la Villa, were wise to choose a skilled designer like Paco Muñoz to take responsibility for the interior decor. Each room is papered in appealing colors, perfumed with the scent of wildflowers, decorated with rustic collages and furnished with antiques and designer lamps. The 11 rooms in the attic look out across the rooftops of the village.

🛏 24 🅿

Posada de Don Mariano $
Mayor, 14, 40172, Segovia
☎ 921509886
🗎 921509886

Mariano Pascual was mayor of Pedreza during the dark days of rural decline in Castile, and also the owner of the famous bar on the square. It was in his honor that his children used the savings they had accumulated from helping out behind the bar to build this attractive hotel in keeping with the architectural style of the unspoiled village. Guests will be delighted by the 18 elegantly decorated rooms with their English-style wallpaper and attention to detail.

🛏 18 🅿

Requijada

La Tejera de Fausto $
Ctra. La Salceda a Sepúlveda, km 7, 40173, Segovia
☎ 921127087
🗎 915641520
📧 armero@nauta.es

Converted from an old tile factory, this rustic hotel surrounded by a 12-acre estate is the creation of Jaime Armero, whose uncle Antonio owns the nearby Molino de Río Viejo. Like that old mill, it provides an ideal base for equestrian explorations. One building houses two cozy lounges and a dining room serving hearty local specialties. In the other are the bedrooms, named after animals native to the sierras of Segovia; the most recent additions have their own fireplace.

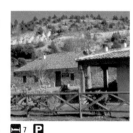

🛏 7 🅿

Key to Symbols: 🗎 Fax 📧 Email 🛏 Rooms 🅿 Parking 🏊 Swimming

Sigueruelo

Posada de Sigueruelo $

L'Espunyola

La Serra del Pla $
La Serra del Pla, s/n, 8619, Barcelona
☎ 937441257
🖹 938220731
e rusticae@edigital.es
As soon as the natural light begins to fade, this former farmhouse is brilliantly

Peramola

Can Boix $
Can Boix, s/n, 25790, Lleida
☎ 973470266
🖹 973470281
e canboixperamola@ empresarial.com
The legendary Can Boix, standing at the foot of the great pinnacles of rock at the source of the Segre River, has been in the

Valdelavilla

Valdelavilla $
San Pedro Manrique, Soria
☎ 975185532
🖹 972300345
e valdelavilla.3017@cajarural. com
Valdelavilla was, until a few years ago, just another village lying abandoned in the sierras of Soria.

Tarifa Alta

Golf Club Bandama $$-$$$
Lugar de Bandama, 14, 35380, Canarias/Gran Canaria
☎ 928353354
🖹 928355220
e hsport@step.es
A distinctly British atmosphere surrounds this golf hotel, with its

Badén, 40, 40590, Segovia
☎ 921508135
🖹 921508135
Only an hour along the highway from Madrid, the village of Sigueruelo still is dependent on cattle farming and is far removed from the Internet, digital TV and other hi-tech gizmos. When they renovated their little hotel, eco-friendly owners Ángel and

Concha refused to let the modern world impose on their rustic idyll. They followed in the local tradition of using only local, natural building materials to create spacious and comfortable accommodations. Activities include organized horesback riding, mountain biking and canoeing expeditions.

🛏 6

illuminated, symbolizing the energy put into the running of the hotel by owners David and Dolors. A display of trophies and photos recalls David's reign as Spanish junior champion in alpine skiing. The decor is a little pallid, but the real attractions here are outdoors.

🛏 4 Closed Nov.

Pallarès family for 10 generations. Accommodations in the original building are very good, but the new rooms in the annex are outstanding for their spaciousness and charming garden views.

🛏 9
Closed Jan. 10-Feb. 10 and 15 days in Nov.

Thanks to the efforts of a local business consortium and many private individuals, it is now a shining example of what thoughtful revitalization can achieve. The cobbled streets are lined with 18th-century stone houses, restored in traditional rustic style but equipped with all-modern conveniences. Visitors can rent anything from a single room

to a whole house for eight people.

🅿

first-class greens expertly created from the island's volcanic soil. Bedrooms overlook the great Bandama crater, with the sea in the background. A continuous balcony, separated by glass screens, runs the entire length of the upper floor, with a swimming pool in the middle.

🛏 33

Key to Symbols: 🖹 Fax e Email 🛏 Rooms 🅿 Parking ☇ Swimming

TARIFA   B1

Tarifa

Dos Mares   **$-$$**
Ctra. N-340, km 79,5, 11380,
Cádiz
☎ 956684035
▤ 956681078
e dosmares@cherrytel.com
Dos Mares, a haven for water
sports enthusiasts, has recently
been refurbished and painted in

vivid Mediterranean colors. Lush
vegetation extends down to the
beach, and the coffee shop has a
jungle feel. The bedrooms, on
three floors, have glorious views,
although the bathrooms are too
stark for comfort. Main
attractions are the gym, tennis
court and swimming pool.

🛏 40

 P ≊

Hurricane   **$-$$**
Ctra. N-340, km 78, 11380,
Cádiz
☎ 956684919
▤ 956680329
e hurricane@redestb.es
Tarifa has to be Europe's liveliest
windsurfing center. After an
English-style breakfast and a
leisurely dip in the pool, the
windsurfers troop off to the

beach, apparently blind to the
hotel's attractive decor and
pleasant atmosphere. The loss is
theirs, for this is a stylish and
exotic place, set in a subtropical
garden of palms, hibiscus and
bougainvilleas.

🛏 28

P ≊

TARRAGONA   E3

Cubelles

Llicorella   **$**
Camino de San Antonio, 101,
8880, Barcelona
☎ 938950044
▤ 938952417
The owner, an architect by
profession, has created
something truly original with
this slate-roofed, two-story villa.
A bizarre group of plaster
sculptures produced by personal

friends echoes the avant-garde
style of the building. The
bedrooms, arranged behind the
house, are named after the artists
who decorated them. The
restaurant is deservedly famous
for its sophisticated cuisine and
excellent cava (champagne-style
sparkling wine).

🛏 12 P ≊

Tarifa

Key to Symbols: ▤ Fax e Email 🛏 Rooms P Parking ≊ Swimming

TOLEDO   C3
Toledo
Pintor El Greco   **$**
Alamillos del Tránsito, 13,
45002, Toledo
☎ 925214250
🖹 925215819
📧 correo@sercotel.es
Skilled architects left the facade of this old bakery virtually intact when they restored the building and converted it into a hotel. Taking its name from the great painter who spent much of his life nearby, the hotel is right in the heart of the city, in the old Jewish quarter. The bedrooms occupy the three upper floors and many have views over the riverside houses immortalized in the master's paintings.

🛏 33   🅿

ÚBEDA   C2
Baeza

Hospedería Fuentenueva   **$**
Paseo Arca del Agua, s/n, 23440, Jaén
☎ 953743100
🖹 953743200
📧 fuentenueva@mx4.redestb.es
Formerly a women's prison and a judge's private residence, this building, with its militaristic facade and neo-Moorish interior, is now operated as a hotel by a hardworking cooperative. A charming room at the rear with a vaulted ceiling and a fountain serves as a lounge.

🛏 12
🅿   🏊

Úbeda

Palacio de la Rambla   **$**
Plaza del Marqués, 1, 23400, Jaén
☎ 953750196
🖹 953750267
📧 rusticae@edigital.es
Cristina Meneses de Orozco and her sister Elena, Marquesa de la Rambla and a Spanish grandee, have opened their family home to visitors who dream of sleeping in beds once occupied by blue-blooded aristocrats. The 16th-century palace boasts one of Andalusia's architectural jewels, a Renaissance courtyard designed by Andrés de Vandelvira.

🛏 8
Closed Jul. 15-Aug. 15
🅿

Parador de Úbeda   **$$**
Plaza Vázquez de Molina, s/n, 23400, Jaén
☎ 953750345
🖹 953751259
This parador began life as a 16th-century mansion, which was completely rebuilt a century later. Carved headboards and hand-painted mirrors are among the features of the bedrooms leading off the corridor overlooking the cobbled courtyard. Bathrooms need updating to match the otherwise high standards.

🛏 34
🅿

VALDERROBRES   D3
Fuentespalda
Torre del Visco   **$$-$$$**
Fuentespalda, 44587, Teruel
☎ 978769015
🖹 978769016
It is well worth driving through Lower Aragon's maze of rough and winding roads to find this splendid 15th-century house. Not only is it the hub of a working farm producing olives, almonds and grain, it also provides rural tourist accommodations of the highest quality. The cuisine draws generously on fresh produce from the property's own kitchen garden. The cork oak woods surrounding the hotel are home to thriving populations of foxes, genets, wild boar and Iberian goats.

🛏 10   Closed Jan. 8-28   🅿

Key to Symbols: 🖹 Fax   📧 Email   🛏 Rooms   🅿 Parking   🏊 Swimming

Ráfales

Moli de l'Hereu $

Rabanella, s/n, 44589, Teruel
☎ 978856266
🖹 978856266
📧 molidelhereu@mixmail.com
Even the mayor took up a pick
and shovel in the effort to ensure
the future of the village and to
preserve the ancient implements
used to produce olive oil. This
18th-century oil mill has now
been lovingly restored and

adapted as a rural hotel providing
simple but comfortable
accommodations and a restaurant
specializing in regional dishes.
The extra virgin olive oil served is
produced by the village
cooperative. The hotel also
houses a little museum containing
all the wheels and pulleys used to
manufacture oil in the old days.

🛏 12   Closed Jan. 11-Feb. 11   🅿

VALDEVERDEJA B3

Valdeverdeja

Casa Bermeja $$
Plaza del Piloncillo, s/n, 45572,
Toledo
☎ 925454586
🖹 925454595
Interior designer Ángela
González remodeled and
decorated her 19th-century
village house in the square next

to the town hall. She installed a
swimming pool in what was once
the courtyard and added nine
studio apartments, furnished to
stunning effect with antiques,
printed fabrics, rustic pottery,
iron lamps and ceiling fans.
In the main house she has
preserved the exposed beams
and fireplaces.

🛏 9   🅿   ⛱

VALENCIA D2

Valencia

Ad Hoc $$
Boix, 4, 46003, Valencia
☎ 963619140
🖹 963913667
📧 adhoc@nexo.net
The spectacular bridge
constructed by the city's favorite
son, architect Santiago
Calatrava, has led to a

renaissance of Valencia's old
quarter. The owner's many years
of experience in the antiques
business has been applied to
good effect in both the decor and
furnishings. The bedrooms are a
pleasing and harmonious blend
of old and new. Service is
efficient and courteous, while the
restaurant offers good value and
Mediterranean specialties.

🛏 28   🅿

VIELHA D4

Arties

Besiberri $
Deth Fort, 4, 25599, Lleida
☎ 973640829
🖹 973640829
This Tyrolean-style hotel with
its flower-laden balconies is a
welcome sight after a hard day
on the slopes. Carmen Lara and
her four sons create the perfect
atmosphere in which exhausted
skiers can relax and settle down

to a hearty dinner. The bedrooms
are warm and cozy; the best
room is the Besiberri suite
looking out toward the
mountains.

🛏 16
Closed May & Nov.
🅿

Tredòs

Hotel de Tredòs $
Ctra. Baqueira-Beret, s/n,
25598, Lleida
☎ 973644014
🖹 973644300
For skiers in winter and
mountaineers in summer, this
little hotel in the Arán Valley, a
few miles from the winter resort
of Baqueira-Beret, is a real find.
Whatever the season, the

amiable Tomo brothers provide
comfortable accommodations
and efficient service. Although
all the rooms are of a similar
standard, guests can ask to be
shown several before making a
final choice.

🛏 37
Closed May, Jun., Oct. & Nov.
🅿

Key to Symbols: 🖹 Fax   📧 Email   🛏 Rooms   🅿 Parking   ⛱ Swimming

Vaqueira-Beret

Chalet Bassibé $$

Urbanización Nin de Beret.
Cota 1700, 25598, Lleida
☎ 973645152
📄 973645032
📧 bassibe@teleline.es

A mountain view is guaranteed at this new chalet hotel. It boasts a heated open-air swimming pool, and the Esquirós chair lift is close by. The bedrooms are larger than winter sports enthusiasts have come to expect, and the dining room and adjacent lounge provide a place to relax after a day on the slopes. In the morning the hotel's own estate car delivers skiers to the ski runs.

🛏 29 Closed Sept. 15-Dec. 1

🅿 🏊

Tryp Royal Tanau $$-$$$

Ctra. de Beret, s/n, 25598, Lleida
☎ 973644446
📄 973644344
📧 tryp.royaltanau@hoteles-tryp.com

Spain's most fashionable winter resort is home to the country's only luxury ski hotel. The 30 sumptuously appointed bedrooms and duplex suites are a perfect combination of form and function. Guests can relax après-ski in one of the English-style lounges. Getting up to the slopes could not be easier, since the ski lift is right beside the hotel.

🛏 25
🅿 🏊

VILADRAU · E4

Viladrau

Hostal de la Glòria $

Torreventosa, 12, 17406, Girona
☎ 938849034
📄 938849465
📧 hostalgloria@informail.lacaixa.es

Simple, welcoming and homey little hotel approached through a restful garden. The tiny room that serves as the reception area is adorned with an abundance of little pictures. Off to one side is the bar, a favorite weekend haunt of elderly locals meeting over a game of cards. The bedrooms are simple, and the dining room serves a hearty four-course menu.

🛏 22
Closed Dec. 20-Jan. 10
🅿 🏊

Xalet La Coromina $

Ctra. de Vic, 4, 17406, Girona
☎ 938849264
📄 938848160
📧 rusticae@edigital.es

This turn-of-the-20th-century chalet, hidden by a neatly trimmed hedge, was once the summer home of a bourgeois family from Barcelona. Behind the creeper-covered facade are four individually decorated bedrooms. Guests can savor a menu based exclusively on seasonal produce in the restaurant, and relax by the original fireplace in the lounge.

🛏 4
Closed Dec. 8-31
🅿 🏊

VILLALBA · A4

Castrocán

Casa de Díaz $

Vilachá, 4, 27260, Lugo
☎ 982187990
📄 982189046

Marked by a shrine at the gate, this former tannery a short distance from the road to Santiago provides bed and breakfast to present-day pilgrims. In the spacious bedrooms guests are welcomed with vases of wildflowers on the bedside tables. For breakfast there is coarse country bread, spicy sausages, pastries and freshly squeezed orange juice.

🛏 10

🅿 🏊

VITORIA-GASTEIZ C4

Axpe

Mendi Goikoa $
Barrio San Juan, 33, 48291,
Bizkaia/Vizcaya
☎ 946820833
🖹 946821136
e mendigoikoa@interbook.net
This hotel, with its stone arch
and green meadow, is famous
throughout Spain as the setting

for a TV commercial for
detergent. Like many other
Basque farmhouse owners, Iñaki
Ibarra has opened his home to
visitors to supplement the family
income. He has sympathetically
converted twin 18th-century
farmhouses to harmonize
perfectly with the lovely
surrounding countryside.

🛏 12 Closed Dec. 15-Jan. 15 **P**

Elosu

Haritz Ondo $
Casa nº 20-22, 1510,
Araba/Álava
☎ 945455270
🖹 945455270
e haritzondo@jet.es
Typically northern country house,
set amid a rich green landscape
close to Monte Gorbea and the
Legutiano reservoir. The interior

boasts oak beams and balustrades.
The former dining room has been
converted to provide nine
bedrooms, bringing the total to
14, one specially adapted for
visitors with disabilities. The
handsome new dining area has
fine mountain views.

🛏 14

P

VIVEIRO A4

Alfoz

Pazo Galea $
Galea, s/n, 27776, Lugo
☎ 982558323
🖹 982558323
From water, stone and light,
garden designer Emilio Méndez
has composed a symphony at his
19th-century house in the idyllic
Ouro Valley. This little paradise
comprises a stone tower where
guests are housed, an adjoining

chapel and an old fulling mill
(where wool was cleansed prior
to weaving) – now a spectacular
fountain. Rooms are modest, so
it is more comfortable to sit in
cozy darkness by the fireside
downstairs.

🛏 5
P

YAIZA
CANARY ISLANDS

Yaiza

Finca Las Salinas $$-$$$

Ctra. Yaiza-Arrecife, 17, La
Cuesta, 35570,
Canarias/Lanzarote
☎ 928830325
🖹 928830329
e fsalina@santandersupernet.
com
This elegant hotel overlooking
Timanfaya National Park was
created from an 18th-century
gentleman's residence. The

arcaded facade evokes all the
mystery of an Arabian palace.
Original stables have been
converted into well-equipped
bedrooms. The gardens
surrounding the swimming pool
have a distinctly Moorish
atmosphere, a reminder that the
island is only 60 miles from the
coast of Africa.

🛏 17 **P**

Sweden

Sweden is a land of wide-open spaces, where even a large city like Stockholm seems to merge with the countryside. Mountains run along its frontier with Norway for more than 1,000 miles. Where Sweden borders Finland, the Arctic Circle sweeps across the Nordic Cap - the farthest reaches of this long, narrow country.

Swedish Scenery

In the south, Sweden is an attractive mix of forest, farmland and lakes – two of which, Vänern and Vättern – dominate the landscape. This is the center of Sweden's industrial base and the location of two major cities of Gothenburg (Göteborg) and Malmö. The relatively short southwestern coastline borders the North Sea, but within the protective shadow of Norway and northern Denmark. Swedes on vacation head for the fine beaches, tranquil waters and warm summer weather of Gotland and Öland, two islands lying off the east coast of Skåne, the rich farming area at Sweden's southernmost point.

The capital, Stockholm, has an enviable east coast setting within a mosaic of inland lakes and offshore islands. Beautiful countryside can be found in the provinces surrounding the city, with magnificent Lake Mälaren a main focus. To the north is the ancient capital, Uppsala, now a lively university town. This region can be explored by ferries and cruise boats navigating a maze of waterways and lakes. East of Sweden, the Gulf of Bothnia gives way to the Baltic Sea.

Norrland, or northern Sweden, is - like neighboring Finland - a land of the midnight sun, where icy mountain streams feed the rivers and vast forests that still cover the area. Lapland, or Sápme, is an immense wilderness of mountains, moors, birch forests and tundra.

The People

Swedes are known for their efficiency and pragmatism. Conservative by nature, they can give an initial impression of seriousness, but once the initial reserve is overcome, you will find the people friendly, helpful and politely curious. Swedes are lively conversationalists, with a great awareness of world affairs. You may mistake Swedish directness for impatience, especially in Stockholm; this is actually just a reflection of the widespread national confidence. Many Swedes are fluent in English, and most people in the cities have some command of the language.

Swedish Weather

Like its Scandinavian neighbors, Sweden has a maritime climate – mild and wet – and you need to be prepared for rain at any time of the year. Generally, though, Sweden has a drier climate than much of Scandinavia, and summer can be as warm and sunny as anywhere else in northern Europe. Along the popular southern coast you may even benefit from a Scandinavian heat wave. July is the favorite time for vacations in Sweden, and city dwellers flock to the countryside and coast.

Grasgard

A Sea God, carved out of smooth black stone

Accommodations

Hotel rates in Sweden are among the highest to be found in Europe. But standards also are very high, which is particularly reassuring as, unlike many European countries, Sweden does not have a national system for grading its hotels (if in doubt, look for the sign of the Swedish Hotel & Restaurant Association – SHR). A number of discount options are available to tourists, but when making a hotel reservation it is always a good idea to ask for their special rates. Many Swedish hotels offer discounts on weekends and during summer months, but these will only be applied if you specifically ask for them.

Bedrooms are usually fresh and light with two single beds. Sheets and blankets are provided rather than quilts, and private bathrooms are the norm, with bathtubs and showers equally common. TVs and telephones are common, and many hotels now also provide a minibar.

A buffet breakfast will be included in the rate for your room and typically consists of hot and cold drinks, bread, cheese, ham, eggs, yogurt, cereals, vegetables and fruit. A number of hotels also offer hot breakfast dishes of scrambled eggs, bacon, sausages and meatballs. Most hotels serve evening meals, but better value can frequently be found in local cafés and restaurants.

Food and Drink

Sweden shares the tradition of open buffets with the rest of Scandinavia. The lunchtime specialty, the *smorgasbord*, is a Swedish institution with a deceptively simple name: *smörgås* means bread, *bord* means table. In fact, a true *smorgasbord* means a lot more than that. It may offer more than 100 different dishes, with items ranging from *gravad lax* (salmon slices in herbs) to *köttbullar* (meatballs), *sillbullar* (herring rissoles) or *kåldolmar* (stuffed cabbage rolls). Steamed, poached or fried fish is the staple ingredient of many other main dishes, with pickled herring a general favorite.

Sweden has the same tight control over alcohol sales as do Norway and

SWEDEN

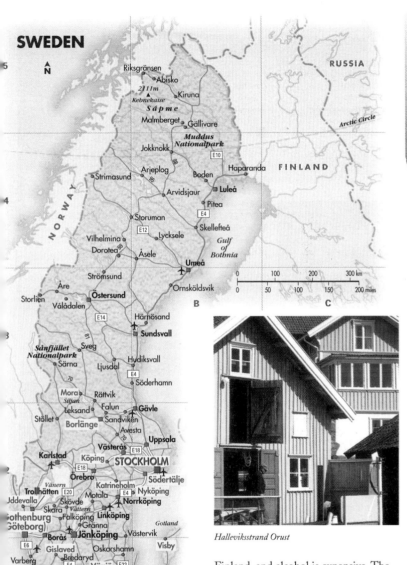

RUSSIA

Riksgränsen
Abisko
2111m
Kebnekaise Kiruna
Sápme
Arctic Circle
Malmberget Gällivare

*Muddus
Nationalpark*
Jokknokk
E10
Arjeplog Boden Haparanda FINLAND
Strimasund Arvidsjaur Luleå
Pitea
Storuman E4
Vilhelmina E12 Lyckele Skellefteå
Dorotea Åsele *Gulf
of
Bothnia*
Strömsund Umeå
Örnsköldsvik
Åre
Storlien Östersund B C
Våladalen
0 100 200 300 km
0 50 100 150 200 miles
E14 Härnösand
*Sånfjället
Nationalpark* Sveg Sundsvall
Särna Hudiksvall
Ljusdal E4
Mora Rättvik Söderhamn
Siljan
Leksand Falun Gävle
Stöllet Borlänge Sandviken
Avesta
Västerås Uppsala
Karlstad Köping E18
Örebro STOCKHOLM
Vänern E18
Trollhättan E20 Katrineholm Södertälje
Uddevalla Skövde Motala E4 Nyköping
Skara Falköping Norrköping
Gothenburg Linköping
Göteborg Gränna *Gotland*
Borås Jönköping Västervik
Gislaved Oskarshamn Visby
Varberg Bredaryd E4
Halmstad Växjö E22 Borgholm
Tylösand Ljungby Kalmar *Öland*
Båstad Älmhult Karlskrona
Helsingborg
Kristianstad
Landskrona *BALTIC
SEA*
Malmö Lund
Falsterbo Ystad
Trelleborg
DENMARK POLAND
A

NORWAY

Halleviksstrand Orust

Finland, and alcohol is expensive. The government-controlled liquor monopoly store, Systembolaget, has branches throughout the country, which are open on weekdays. The main emphasis is on the sale of good wines. For a real taste of Sweden, drink *aquavit* with your meal. This strong drink is distilled from grain or potatoes and is given added taste with spices and herbs. Drink it in small quantities, consumed in one gulp.

BORGHOLM   A1
Borgholm

Halltorps Gästgiveri   **$$**
SE-387 92 Borgholm, Öland
☎ 0485 850 00
▤ 0485 850 01
🄴 halltorps.gastgiveri@
mailbox.calypso.net
This inn is located in the heart of the summer paradise island of Öland, close to Alvaret Nature Reserve. From the terrace and most of the inn itself, there is a wonderful view over Kalmar Sound. Halltorps boasts one of the finest restaurants in Sweden; it also is well known for its cozy atmosphere and warm welcome.

🛏 36

BORLÄNGE   A2
Borlänge

Ulfshyttans Herrgårtd   **$-$$**
SE-781 96 Borlänge, Dalarna
☎ 0243 25 13 00
▤ 0243 25 11 11
🄴 info@ulfshyttan.se
South of Borlänge, in the heart of the iron-producing region of Bergslagen, is this charming manor house. It has a unique turret room with panoramic views in all directions, an art gallery and a library of fascinating old books. The restaurant enjoys a delightful view over Lake Ulfssjön. There are illuminated exercise trails on the promontory, a sauna, and fishing on the lake.

🛏 20

GISLAVED   A1
Hestra

Hestravikens Värdshus   **$$**
SE-330 27 Hestra, Småland
☎ 0370 33 68 00
▤ 0370 33 62 90
🄴 info@hestraviken.se
The inn is known for its beautiful location and good food. It is surrounded by a garden with a swimming pool, and some bedrooms are so close to the river that guests can almost fish from their balconies. Activities in the vicinity include golf on the excellent 36-hole Isaberg course, tennis, canoeing, fishing, windsurfing, rowing and downhill skiing.

🛏 33

GÖTEBORG   A2
Billdal

Johanneshus Hotel and Restaurant
SE-427 36 Billdal, Göteborg
☎ 031 91 01 25
▤ 031 91 31 41
🄴 johanneshus@
beta.telenordia.se
This hotel and restaurant provides a good base for guests to experience all the sights and entertainment of near by Göteborg, as well as the peace and quiet of the locality, with its coastal walks, and ocean swimming. Other activities include golf at the Hovås Golf Club, tennis, croquet, fishing and cycling.

🛏 5

JONKOPING   A2
Kolsva

Kohlswa Herrgård   **$$**
SE-730 30 Kolsva, Västmanland
☎ 0221 509 00
▤ 0221 511 80
🄴 kolsva.herrgard@swipnet.se
History and culture combine with comfort and modernity at Kohlswa, in the beautiful Bergslagen district. There is a sense of timelessness, thanks to the conscientious way in which its historic heritage has been preserved. Events include wine, beer and whiskey tastings, and such activities as sport fishing and Icelandic pony-riding. Indoors, you can enjoy billiards, table tennis, darts or a relaxing sauna.

🛏 45

Key to Symbols: ▤ Fax   🄴 Email   🛏 Rooms   🅿 Parking   🏊 Swimming

KATRINEHOLM A2

Flen

Yxtaholms Slott
SE-642 91 Flen, Södermanland
☎ 0157 122 65
🖹 0157 145 24
📧 info@yxtaholmsslott.se
Guests are treated with utmost
consideration at Yxtaholm
Castle, just outside the town of
Flen. It is in a delightful setting
and offers such activities as
archery, boules (bowls), croquet,
rowing, fishing, cycling, tennis
and horseback riding. During
the summer classical concerts are
held here. The castle also boasts
a collection of vintage Calvados
– there for the tasting!

🛏 30

KRISTIANSTAD A1

Åhus

Åhus Gästgifvaregård
SE-286 30 Åhus, Skåne
☎ 044 28 90 50
🖹 044 28 92 50
📧 info@ahusgastis.com
This establishment is located by
the Helgeå River in old Åhus. It
has a restaurant of the highest
quality and is a popular venue for
weddings, traditional eel parties,
jazz evenings and wine tastings.
It has its own fishing boat, and
local attractions include the
miles of sandy beaches, shooting,
and five golf courses within 15
minutes' reach.

🛏 24

MALMÖ A1

Genarp

Häckeberga Slott
SE-240 13 Genarp, Skåne
☎ 040 48 04 40
🖹 040 48 04 02
📧 wt@hackebergaslott.se
The castle is situated within easy
reach of most of the attractions
and sights of southwest Skåne
and the Österlen district.

🛏 19

MORA A3

Orsa

Fryksås Hotell and Gestgifveri
SE-794 98 Orsa, Dalarna
☎ 0250 460 20
🖹 0250 460 90
📧 fryksas.hotell@
orsa.mail.utfors.se
This hotel is a real gem, set
among old wooden cottages on
the high southern slopes above
Lake Siljan and Orsasjön. It is
within walking distance of the
new Bear Park and Grönklitt Ski
Resort, which has seven ski lifts.
It offers superb food, including
fish and game specialties.
Activities include golf, tennis,
fishing, canoeing, riding,
swimming and skiing (excellent
runs and cross-country trails).

🛏 14

NYKÖPING B2

Jönåker

Wreta Gestgifveri
SE-610 50 Jönåker,
Södermanland
☎ 0155 720 22
🖹 0155 720 32
📧 wreta@swipnet.se
At Wreta, guests are offered the
good things of life. Tradition,
quality and consideration
combine to provide an
experience of total relaxation.
Visit Kolmården Animal Park or
walk a section of the
Sörmlandsleden long-distance
footpath. Enjoy the lovely
countryside on horseback, or try
your hand at hunting or
shooting. Wine tastings and
musical soirèes also are
organized.

🛏 13

Key to Symbols: 🖹 Fax Email Rooms Parking Swimming

SÖDERTÄLJE B2
Gnesta

Södertuna Slott **$**
SE-646 91 Gnesta,
Södermanland
☎ 0158 705 00
🖷 0158 705 10
📧 info@sodertuna.se
From this base guests can visit
Heby Castle, Elghammar Castle,
the Skottvång mine, Engelska
Parken or Södermanland's oldest
oak tree. Leisure facilities on site
include an indoor swimming
pool, sauna and solarium. You
can also try your hand at clay
pigeon shooting, archery, axe-
throwing, wine tasting, tennis,
boules, air-pistol shooting,
Icelandic pony-riding, shooting
and gliding.

 65

STOCKHOLM B2
Stockholm

Lady Hamilton **$$-$$$**
Storkyrkobrinken 5, SE-111 28
Stockholm, Gamla Stan
(Altstadt)
☎ 08 506 401 00
🖷 08 506 401 10
📧 info@lady-hamilton.se
This hotel is located in
Stockholm's Old Town, beside
the Royal Palace and close to all
points of interest. Each of the
rooms is decorated in authentic
country style, and public areas
are furnished with nautical
antiques and Lady Hamilton
memorabilia. Conference
facilities are available in the
medieval vaults. There also is a
sauna and a medieval well for
cooling off.

🛏 34

UDDEVALLA A2
Tanumshede

Tanums Gästgifveri
S-457 31 Tanumshede,
Bohuslän
☎ 0525 290 10
🖷 0525 295 71
📧 info@countrysidehotels.se
No visit to northern Bohuslän
would be complete without a
stop at Tanums Gästgifveri. It
stands in its own grounds in
Tanumshede, 3½ miles from the
most beautiful part of the
Bohuslän archipelago, and offers
exclusive accommodations,
superb cooking and exceptional
service in an elegant setting
dating back to the 17th century.
Activities include golf (delightful
18-hole links course), tennis,
fishing and boating.

🛏 27

VAXJÖ A1
Gemla

Villa Gransholm
SE-360 32 Gemla, Småland
☎ 0470 676 65
🖷 0470 673 37
📧 villa.gransholm@swipnet.se
A small, turn-of-the-20th-
century hotel located in the heart
of the glassworks region, close to
many lakes. Hosts Mr. and Mrs.
Rehnström place great emphasis
on food and create superb local
dishes for their guests. Activities
include billiards, croquet, boules
and cycling. There are three 18-
hole golf courses in the vicinity.

🛏 12

VISBY B1
Visby

Hotell Toftagården **$**
SE-621 98 Visby, Gotland
☎ 0498 29 70 00
🖷 0498 26 56 66
📧 info@toftagarden.se
This hotel is located in parkland
and woods in countryside close
to Tofta Beach. It has one of the
best restaurants on Gotland and
is famous for its Gotland
specialties which feature lamb
and salmon. Local activities
include golf on the 27-hole
Kronholmen golf course, cycling,
tennis, fitness trails, oceanside
walks, swimming in the ocean
and windsurfing.

🛏 25

Key to Symbols: Fax Email Rooms Parking 🏊 Swimming

Karlaby Kro
SE-272 93 Tommarp, Skåne
☎ 0414 203 00
 0414 204 73
 reception@karlabykro.se
This hotel is set in rolling countryside in the heart of Österlen, an area of Skåne rich in myth and legend. Every weekend throughout the year, guests can enjoy gourmet meals and excellent wines in charming surroundings. Facilities include an indoor swimming pool, sauna, gym, boules (bowls), darts and miniature golf. Three of southeastern Skåne's most challenging golf courses are close by.

🛏 21
🏊

Gilded interior of Strangnas Cathedral

Key to Symbols: Fax Email Rooms Parking Swimming

Switzerland

Switzerland's attractions are well-known: stunning Alpine scenery; lush, green meadows; beautiful, sparkling lakes, and picturesque villages, towns and cities. This landlocked nation is a federation of democracies, with a constitution (first drawn up in 1848) modeled on that of the United States. Switzerland maintains neutrality as the cornerstone of its state policy: It makes no alliances, and does not interfere in foreign conflicts.

Swiss financial acumen has made this a wealthy and commercially powerful country, where banking thrives and a superb infrastructure of railroads, tunnels and roads overcomes the mountainous terrain and allows the country to enjoy a trading postion at the center of Europe.

The Swiss Landscape

The central Swiss lowland is sandwiched between two mountain ranges: the Jura to the north, and the mighty Alps, which cover 60 percent of the country, mainly in the south, with their dramatic high glaciers and peaks. Another 25 percent of Switzerland is forested, and the rest is a seductive combination of lakes and meadow pastures, beautiful throughout the year. South of the Alps, Ticino canton basks in a Mediterranean climate, and from the northern Alpine slopes a warm, dry wind known as the *föhn* often blows in. Most of Switzerland, however, has a moderate climate typical of central Europe. Late spring sees the countryside at its best, with carpets of mountain and meadow wildflowers. Fall, when the leaves turn and the first snow whitens the lower peaks, also is

wonderful. Skiing in the mountains is, of course, the main winter attraction, and in summer there's plenty of opportunity for walking, sailing and numerous other outdoor pursuits.

People and Language

Efficiency and formality are characteristics often associated with the Swiss, and as with all generalizations, they carry a grain of truth. This is, on the whole, a very law-abiding country, civic-minded and polite, where punctuality is considered very important. Rules and regulations are followed diligently: You should always cross the street at designated crossings, for instance, and wait for the green man symbol before doing so. Litter must be put in the compartment designated for that particular type of waste; dropping litter on the ground is a finable offense. Manners are formal: hand-shaking and serious toasts mark even the most casual social occasions. It's customary, on public transportation, to give up your seat for the elderly, for pregnant women and for people with disabilities; and in conversation the phrases "*bitte*," "*prego*" and "*je vous en prie*" (you're welcome) are invariably used in return for thanks.

Surrounded by other European nations, the Swiss speak several languages. French, Italian, Romansch (an ancient Latin tongue), Schwyzerdütsch (a Swiss-German dialect) and German are used in everyday life. Many Swiss speak English (especially those connected with tourism), although it's polite not to take this for granted, and to ask whether they speak the language before starting a conversation.

Chateau d'Aigle

Switzerland

Accommodations

Standards of Swiss hotel service and accommodation are among the highest in Europe. Although this equally applies to the price you pay, value for money is usually good and you will certainly be well looked after. Typically, accomodations are sold on a bed and breakfast basis, with rooms containing two single beds as standard. Private bathrooms are common, and lower rates will be charged for rooms with shared facilities. Direct-dial telephones and televisions are usually provided. In Alpine resorts, hotels are often built in traditional chalet style, and many bedrooms have small balconies to give maximum advantage of the spectacular views; many are prettily decorated with geraniums.

Breakfast is usually served buffet-style, and may include a choice of breads, cheeses, cold meats, cereals, fruit juice, tea, coffee, butter, honey and jams. The small plastic tub you'll find on your table is for depositing your empty butterwrappers and cheese rinds – another example of meticulous Swiss efficiency and cleanliness. Most hotels also provide an evening meal, and offer attractive rates for combining dinner, bed and breakfast.

A hotel Garni is an establishment which offers only bed, breakfast and

drinks, but no meals – although it may have a separate licensed restaurant. A hotel U is a hotel and restaurant with a unique style and special features, placing it outside the standard rating system. A country inn is a

Swiss Prices

Switzerland is an expensive country, and you should keep more money available than you think you will need: cash seems to disappear alarmingly quickly here. Credit cards are widely accepted. Travel by public transportation, rather than taking the inordinately expensive taxis. Buses and trains are superbly efficient, and make the whole experience enjoyable and comfortable. There's no state medical health service here, and any treatment has to be paid for on the spot, so valid medical insurance is vital. You can save some money day to day by eating in smaller establishments, away from the upscale areas; and remember that there is no need to tip anywhere – service charges are automatically added to all bills.

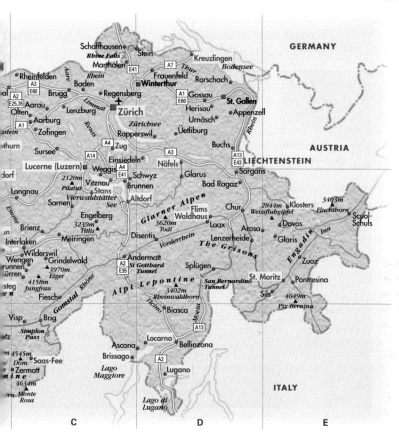

Food and Drink

Ingredients and preparation vary greatly all over the country, but throughout Switzerland you will find a huge selection of bread (white, whole wheat, etc.); dairy products such as milk, yogurt and butter; and, of course, a great variety of world-famous Swiss cheese. Vegetables feature strongly in menus, and sausages and other meat – mainly veal, beef, pork, chicken and turkey – are served in many different ways: grilled, cooked, sliced or cut.

hotel/restaurant typical of a particular area, offering personal service and traditional cooking. You also can find accommodations in Aparthotels – hotels consisting mainly of spacious apartments with cooking facilities.

Popular side dishes include French fries, rice, potatoes and pasta. Local fruits include apples, pears, grapes, blackberries, blueberries, raspberries, red currants and strawberries.

Two favorite traditional Swiss specialties can be found all over the country: *fondu* and *raclette*. *Fondu* consists of a communal dish on a small heater, containing melted, hot cheese and wine, into which everyone dips chunks of bread or meat skewered on a fork. *Raclette* also makes the most of Swiss cheese: a large cheese is rotated on a grill, and the melted cheese poured over small boiled potatoes. Swiss chocolate is another gastronomic treat. The window displays alone, in pretty *chocolatiers*, will make your mouth water.

SWITZERLAND

ALTDORF C2
Altdorf

Der Teufelhof Basel

Goldener Schlüssel $$
6460, Schützengasse 9
☎ (0 41) 8 71 20 02
🖹 (0 41) 8 70 11 67
www.tellweb.ch/schluessel
This hotel, dating from the early 18th century and set among old town houses, has been carefully restored and offers stylish rooms, the Schlüsselstübli and Saal for parties and conferences, a cozy

restaurant and distinctive bar.

 19
🅿

BASEL B3
Basel
Der Teufelhof Basel $$$
4051, Leonhardsgraben 49
☎ (0 61) 2 61 10 10
🖹 (0 61) 2 61 10 04
www.teufelhof.com
Artists were commissioned to design the rooms at the Teufelhof as habitable artworks, and designs are changed every

two to three years. The hotel features exclusive designer furniture; art exhibitions are held in the Weinstube, in the Café & Bar and in the Lower Theater (both the Lower and Upper Theater offer live entertainment). There also is a superb wine and specialty food shop.
29

BERN B2
Bern

Innere Enge $$$
3012, Engestrasse 54
☎ 3 09 61 11
🖹 3 09 61 12
A popular meeting place for the residents of Bern since the early 18th century, the Innere Enge has been converted into a smart hotel with exquisite rooms and suites. Breakfast is served in the historic park pavilion, and the

restaurant serves fine cakes. In the cellar the discerning guest can enjoy Marian's Jazzroom and the Louis Armstrong Bar.

24
🅿

BIEL B3
Ligerz
Kreuz $-$$
2514, Ligerz
☎ (0 32) 3 15 11 15
🖹 (0 32) 3 15 28 14
The Kreuz Hotel is popular with guests enjoying a vacation in Ligerz on Bielersee. It offers comfortable rooms, a sauna, steam bath and a pool garden.

In the restaurant try wine from the hotel's own vineyard (Chasselas/Pinot Noir).

16
🅿 ≋

BRISSAGO C1
Brissago

Villa Caesar $$$
6614, Via Gabietta, Brissago
☎ (0 91) 793 27 66
🖹 (0 91) 793 31 04
e villacaesar@nikko.ch
www.villacaesar.ch
This hotel offers spacious rooms and luxurious suites, all with large balconies and wonderful views of Lake Maggiore. There

is a terrace restaurant and a bar, and service is friendly and accommodating.

 32
🅿 ≋

Key to Symbols: 🖹 Fax e Email 🛏 Rooms 🅿 Parking ≋ Swimming
American Express D Diners Club E Eurocard Visa

BURGDORF B3
Burgdorf
Stadthaus $$-$$$
3402, Burgdorf
☎ (0 34) 4 28 80 00
📄 (0 34) 4 28 80 08
www.slh.com/stadthau/
From 1745 to 1750 the
Stadthaus served as Burgdorf's
town hall. Guests will enjoy its
period decor and the extremely
comfortable and stylish rooms,
including two luxury suites
(prices on request). There also is
a smoking room with an
excellent selection of cigars and
whiskey.

 16
🅿

FLIMS WALDHAUS D2
Flims

Fidazerhof $-$$
7019, Flims
☎ (0 81) 9 11 35 03
📄 (0 81) 9 11 21 75
www.fidazerhof-flims.ch
The house, dating from 1909,
has an attractive exterior and a
bright interior enhanced by light
woods and balconies. Facilities
include a stylish restaurant and
the Prana health suite, with a
sauna, solarium, hairdressing
salon, and cosmetic and massage
departments.

 5
🅿

FRIBOURG B2
Fribourg

De la Rose $$
1702, Rue de Morat 1, Fribourg
☎ (0 26) 3 51 01 01
📄 (0 26) 3 51 01 00
www.mitel.com/hotel
This beautifully restored house,
dating from 1700, is located in
the heart of the Old Town near
St. Niklaus Cathedral. It offers
comfortable rooms and first-class
conference facilities. Guests can
dine in the Chez Dino restaurant
(pizzeria and Grottino grill) or
take an aperitif in the cozy bar.
After dinner enjoy dancing in
the Cave de la Rose.

 35

KANDERSTEG B2
Kandersteg
Waldhotel Doldenhorn $$-$$$
3718, Hauptstrasse, Kandersteg
☎ (0 33) 6 75 81 81
📄 (0 33)6 75 81 85
📧 doldenhorn@compuserve.com
Built in 1911 the Waldhotel
Doldenhorn is set in extensive
parkland surrounded by beautiful
countryside. The individually
furnished rooms come in a range
of styles, and there are
prestigious conference rooms and
leisure facilities. An extensive
menu is served in the Gourmet
Restaurant, the Burestube winter
garden and on the splendid
terrace.

 28
🅿

Adelboden
Bären $-$$$
3715, Dorfstrasse 22
☎ (0 33) 6 73 21 51
📄 (0 33) 6 73 21 90
www.adelboden-a.ch/baeren
The Bären has been providing
hospitality to visitors since 1569,
and it still displays evidence of
this remarkable tradition. It is a
chalet building, decorated with
flowers, offering stylish
restaurants and individually
furnished rooms, most of which
are named after peaks in the
Adelboden range.

 11

KLOSTERS   E2
Klosters

Rätia $-$$
7252, Klosters
☎ (0 81) 4 22 47 47
🖨 (0 81) 4 22 47 49
www.hotelraetia.ch
This hotel is in one of
Graubünden's prettiest valleys.
Enjoy the mild mountain air,
cross-country ski runs almost to
the door, and a wide range of
leisure and sports facilities. The

wood-paneled rooms and rustic
restaurant with its impressive
open fireplace make for a
relaxing ambience. It is family-
friendly, with discounts for
children as well as parkland and
play areas close by.

🛏 32

P
▬ ⓪ 🄴 ▬

KREUZLINGEN   D3
Gottlieben

Krone $$-$$$
8274, Seestrasse 11, Gottlieben
☎ (0 71) 6 66 80 60
🖨 (0 71) 6 66 80 69
www.romantikhotel.ch
The Krone, built in 1698, is now
a "Romantic Hotel" in a quiet
location on the Seerhein river as
it flows toward Lake Constance.

It offers carefully furnished
rooms, superb conference
facilities, a stylish restaurant and
a splendid terrace, all in the heart
of a nature reserve.

🛏 25
P
▬ ⓪ 🄴 ▬

LOCARNO   D1
Orselina

Mirafiori $$
6644, Via al Parco 25, Orselina
☎ (0 91) 7 43 18 77
🖨 (0 91) 7 43 77 39
✉ mirafiori@tinet.ch
Picturesque is the word that
springs to mind when you first
see the Mirafiori. It is a family-
run establishment high above
Lake Maggiore, affording
magnificent views. The

comfortable rooms, each with a
sitting area and balcony, are
decorated in bright colors. Relax
in the swimming pool, whirlpool
or sauna, or out on the shady
garden terrace.

🛏 25
P 🏊
▬ ⓪ 🄴 ▬

LUCERNE   C3
Meggen

Balm $-$$
6045, Balmstrasse 3, Meggen
☎ (0 41) 3 77 11 35
🖨 (0 41) 3 77 23 83
www.balm.ch
Run as a family concern for more
than 150 years, the Balm is a
harmonious mix of rural charm
and modern comfort, and some

of the relaxing bedrooms and
suites are particularly large. The
terrace, popular in summer, has
views of Lake Lucerne and
famous Mount Pilatus. In the
morning, fortify yourself for the
day with the copious Zmorge
buffet.

🛏 16
P ▬ ⓪ 🄴 ▬

LUGANO   D1
Caslano

Albergo Gardenia $$-$$$
6987, Via Valle, Casla
☎ (0 91) 6 06 17 16
🖨 (0 91) 6 06 26 42
This former monastery, set
among palm trees, offers
attractive rooms hung with
original works of art. The elegant
restaurant is widely known for its
fine cuisine, and there is a
swimming pool and a splendid

terrace with views of Malcantone
and Monte Lema. A range of
inclusive packages is available for
golfers, lovers of fine food or
conference delegates.

🛏 26
P 🏊
▬ ⓪ 🄴 ▬

Key to Symbols: 🖨 Fax ✉ Email 🛏 Rooms P Parking 🏊 Swimming
▬ American Express ⓪ Diners Club 🄴 Eurocard ▬ Visa

Magliaso

Villa Magliasina   **$$$**
6983, Via Vedeggi 38, Magliaso
☎ (0 91) 6 11 29 29
🖹 (0 91) 6 11 29 20

A golfing hotel in an idyllic location, suitable for all levels of ability. It offers golfing courses for beginners and for more experienced players, including training with qualified professionals. Additional attractions are a park filled with Mediterranean flora, a heated pool and attractive rooms in a range of categories. Light, full-flavored dishes are the specialty of the chef de cuisine.

 26

MURTEN   B2

Murten

Schiff am See   **$$**
3280, Ryf 53, Murten
☎ (0 26) 6 70 27 01
🖹 (0 26) 6 70 35 31

A long-established hotel that offers attractive rooms with wonderful views of Murtensee. Surrounded by parkland and offering excellent walks, it is an ideal place to relax. Additional features are the splendid lakeside terrace and excellent conference facilities.

🛏 15
🅿

NÄFELS   D3

Amden

Bellevue   **$$**
8873, Amden
☎ (0 55) 6 11 11 57
🖹 (0 55) 6 11 16 12
www.mitel.com

The Bellevue, affording fine views of the Lake of Wallenstadt and the Glarus Alps, offers comfortable rooms and prestigious conference facilities. For relaxation, a terrace, outdoor pool, sauna, solarium and fitness room are provided. An extensive menu is served in the stylish restaurant.

 29

SAAS FEE   C1

Saas Fee

Beau-Site   **$$-$$$**
3906, Saas Fee
☎ (0 27) 9 58 15 60
🖹 (0 27) 9 58 15 65
www.romantikhotels.com/rhsaa

Built in 1893 and now a "Romantic Hotel," the Beau-Site offers exclusive accommodation and superior comforts. Relax in the bar with its open fireplace or in La Ferme restaurant, which has original Saas furnishings and glasswork. Alternatively, try the hotel restaurant, the Philippe pizzeria/steakhouse or the terrace. Pool facilities include a rocky grotto, sauna, aromarium, Roman thermal bath, massage and relaxation zone.

 16

SOLOTHURN   B3

Solothurn

Baseltor   **$$**
4500, Hauptgasse 79, Solothurn
☎ (0 32) 6 22 34 22
🖹 (0 32) 6 22 18 79

The hotel, which dates from the 17th century, is living proof that less can be more. The interior decor is limited to the essentials and makes generous use of white, natural materials and light. The result is a comfortable Mediterranean ambience and an award for the most environmentally friendly urban hotel in Switzerland. The superb rooms are reached via an old stone staircase.

🛏 6

Key to Symbols: 🖹 Fax 🄴 Email 🛏 Rooms 🅿 Parking ⤴ Swimming
American Express 🔘 Diners Club 🄴 Eurocard 💳 Visa

Weissenstein

Weissenstein   **$-$$**
4515, Weissenstein
☎ (0 32) 6 22 02 64
🖹 (0 32)6 23 89 47
The hotel is surrounded by splendid scenery with views of the Mitteland Plateau and the Alps. It offers bright rooms, superb conference facilities and a restaurant decorated in Art Nouveau style.

 24

SPIEZ   B2

Spiez

Strandhotel Belvédère   **$$-$$$**
3700, Schachenstrasse 39, Spiez
☎ (0 33) 6 55 66 66
🖹 (0 33) 6 54 66 33
www.hauensteinhotels.ch
This hotel stands in spacious grounds with splendid views of the Lake of Thun. The stylish rooms have all-modern comforts, and guests can relax in the hotel's own lakeside pool, on the attractive terrace or in the cozy bar. Prestigious function rooms are available, and water skiing, sailing, surfing, rowing or cycling are all within easy reach.

 28

ST. MORITZ   E2

Bever

Chesa Salis   **$$$**
7502, Bügls Suot 2, Bever
☎ (0 81) 8 52 48 38
🖹 (0 81) 8 52 47 06
e chesa.salis@compunet.ch
Chesa Salis, the former home of an aristocrat in the Engadine, dates from 1590 and is now a wonderful hotel with examples of fine craftsmanship and wall paintings. The accommodations include charming, individually furnished rooms, verandas and cozy restaurants.

 17

STANS   C2

Buochs

Rigiblick am See   **$$-$$$**
6374, Am Seeplatz 3, Buochs
☎ (0 41) 6 24 48 50
🖹 (0 41) 6 20 68 74
www.swissdir.ch/rigiblick.html
With Lake Lucerne in the foreground and a backdrop of mountains, this hotel's stunning location is reason enough for a stay. It is ideal for conferences, and the restaurant and Schwarzi Chats bar are both comfortable and elegant.

 14

Hergiswill

Hôtel du Lac   **$-$$$**
6052, Seestrasse 76, Hergiswill
☎ (0 41) 6 30 42 42
🖹 (0 41) 6 30 42 50
The hotel is superbly located on Lake Lucerne with the mountains as a backdrop, and it has a splendid garden terrace surrounded by parkland. The quiet, cozy and comfortable rooms have wonderful views, and in summer guests can enjoy an aperitif overlooking the lake or dine al fresco - a truly magical experience. An extensive menu is served in the elegant French restaurant, the bistro and the du Lac-Stübli.

🛏 17

Stansstad

Winkelried am See **$$-$$$**
6362, Dorfplatz 5, Stansstad
☎ (0 41) 6 10 99 01
🖹 (0 41) 6 10 96 31
www.winkelried.ch
In an idyllic lakeside setting with
its own boat moorings, this hotel
offers attractive rooms and
suites, an elegant foyer and a
splendid lakeside terrace. There
is a wide range of culinary

delicacies. The Hafenrestaurant
serves pizzas from its wood-
burning oven, the elegant
Seeblick classic cuisine, and the
cozy Winkelriedstübli regional
dishes and good home cooking.
Good function and banqueting
facilities are available.

 22

🖼 🔘 🇪 💳

THUN B2
Thun
Krone **$$**
3600, Rathausplatz, Thun
☎ (0 33) 2 27 88 88
🖹 (0 33)2 27 88 90
What would Thun be without
the Krone, a historic but stylish
house in the heart of the city
where the guest is still king? It
offers spacious and elegant

rooms, two restaurants, and a
splendid terrace where in
summer you can enjoy coffee and
a piece of famous (and delicious)
Krone cake. To top it off there's
an extensive breakfast buffet.

 27
🅿

🖼 🔘 🇪 💳

ZUG C3
Risch

Waldheim **$$**
6343, Rischerstrasse 27, Risch
☎ (0 41) 7 99 70 70
🖹 (0 41)7 99 70 79
🇪 hotel.risch@waldheim.ch
Built in 1598 as a residence for
the clergy and converted into a
guest house in 1848, the
Waldheim is situated on a
promontory of the Lake of Zug
with wonderful views of the lake

and mountains. Room types vary
from rustic to an elegant modern
style, and for relaxation there is
the hotel's own lakeside pool or
golf driving range. Stylish
conference facilities are available.

 34
🅿 🏊

🖼 🔘 🇪 💳

ZÜRICH C3
Zürich
Europe **$$$**
8008,Dufourstrasse 8,Zürich
☎ (01) 2 61 10 30
🖹 (01) 2 51 03 67
www.hoteleurope-zuerich.ch
Built in 1905, this stylish hotel is
just behind the opera and a short
distance from the
Bahnhofstrasse, the Shopping

Mile, and the city's wonderful
lakeside promenade. The
bedrooms are all quiet and
individually decorated with
stylish furniture and works of
art. Watch the world go by from
the splendid covered terrace.

 39
🖼 🔘 🇪 💳

Zürichberg **$$-$$$**
8044, Orellistr. 21,Zürich
☎ (01) 2 68 35 35
🖹 (01) 2 68 35 45
Impressive building high above
the city, dating from 1903 and
featuring a tasteful rotunda
extension. The rooms are
charming, and two terraces offer
panoramic views.

 52
🅿

🖼 🔘 🇪 💳

Key to Symbols: 🖹 Fax 🇪 Email 🖼 Rooms 🅿 Parking 🏊 Swimming
🖼 American Express 🔘 Diners Club 🇪 Eurocard 💳 Visa

Norway

Accommodations are usually the most expensive element of any visit to Norway, but standards are reliably high. National legislation demands that all hotels meet minimum requirements, but there is no formal system of stars or grades. In common with other Scandinavian countries, Norway has a range of hotel discount options, and overall prices are generally lower during the summer months.

Bedrooms are typically clean and light, often with a simple decorative style of plain white walls, pine paneling and pine furniture. A twin room will usually contain two single beds, but double and single bedded rooms can also be found. By European standards, rooms are often quite small – particularly single rooms. In guest houses and mountain lodges, bathroom facilities may well be shared, but most hotels now provide private bathrooms, usually with a shower.

Breakfast is one of the treats of a hotel stay in Norway. Usually this is included in the cost of the room, and consists of a large buffet spread. Typical Continental fare is offered, but the range of cheeses and cooked meats will include distinctive Norwegian varieties along with dishes of scrambled eggs and fish. If you decide to reserve for dinner, bed and breakfast, many hotels will also allow you to make up a picnic lunch from the breakfast buffet. All hotels offer a dinner service.

Finland

Most hotels in Finland are custom-built and provide good, comfortable accommodations with a wide range of facilities such as saunas and swimming pools. Standards are generally high and service is friendly, unobtrusive and efficient. But it comes at a price: Hotels here, as in other Scandinavian countries, are very expensive. Cheaper options can be found in the much simpler hostels as well as private rooms. In the summer months (June through August) prices do come down, and you can take advantage of a wide choice of voucher discount options. One such offer, called Finncheque, is administered by the national tourist office.

Hotel bedrooms are usually well furnished and comfortable. You can expect to be provided with television and telephone; minibars and room service are more widespread here than in other European countries. The price includes private bathrooms, generally spotlessly clean and reasonably large. Most bedrooms have two single beds; there are additional charges for single occupancy.

Breakfast is normally included in the cost of the room. A typical breakfast will consist of an extensive buffet of cereals, breads, cheeses, cooked meat, fish (usually herring), honey and jam. Evening meals in hotels and restaurants are also frequently offered buffet-style – an excellent way to sample the various local fish and meat dishes.

Contacts/websites

To phone Norway or Finland from the United States or Canada, omit the first zero from the local number and prefix with the appropriate country code (Finland: 011 358; Norway: 011 47). For example, in Norway the number 011 22 33 44 becomes 011 47 11 22 33 44. The number for the operator in Finland is 115; in Norway it is 117.

To phone the United States or Canada from Europe, prefix the area code with 001.

The national tourism websites are:
Finland: www.mek.fi **Norway:** www.norway.org

Index

The entries in this index are ordered by location name, followed by a country abbreviation.

Beyton, Bri. 48
Beziers Fra. 123
Biberach an der Riss, Ger. 216
Biddenden, Bri. 64
Biel, Swi. 378
Bielefeld, Ger. 179
Biggar, Bri. 86
Bilbao, Spa. 322-3
Billdal, Swe. 370
Billund, Den. 104
Bingen, Ger. 210
Binibona, Majorca, Spa. 335
Binissalem, Majorca, Spa. 328
Bitburg, Ger. 179
Bledlow, Bri. 58
Blockley, Bri. 49
Blois, Fra. 124
Blokzijl, Net. 293
Boat of Garten, Bri. 91
Bogense, Den. 105
Bologna, Ita. 242-4
Bolsena, Ita. 266
Bolsward, Net. 296
Bolvir de Cerdanya, Spa. 317
Bolzano, Ita. 242, 244
Bolzano Vicentino, Ita. 286
Bonn, Ger. 179
Bonndorf, Ger. 213
Bontddu, Bri. 97
Boorgloon, Bel. 34
Bordeaux, Fra. 124
Bordighera, Ita. 245
Borgholm, Swe. 370
Borlänge, Swe. 370
Borrowdale, Bri. 62
Bosau, Ger. 197
Boscastle, Bri. 47
Bosham, Bri. 70
Boston, Bri. 46
Bouisse, Fra. 127
Bourg-sur-Gironde, Fra. 124
Bourges, Fra. 124
Bourgtheroulde, Fra. 158
Bournemouth, Bri. 46
Bouvante, Fra. 138
Bovey Tracey, Bri. 79
Box, Bri. 45
Bradford-on-Avon, Bri. 46
Braga, Port. 302
Bragança, Port. 302
Brantome, Fra. 156
Brasparts, Fra. 139
Bratton Fleming, Bri. 44
Braubach, Ger. 197
Braunau, Aus. 24
Brauneberg, Ger. 214
Braunfels, Ger. 217
Brecon, Bri. 94
Bregenz, Aus. 24

Breitnau, Ger. 214
Bremen, Ger. 180
Bremerhaven, Ger. 180
Bréscia, Ita. 245-6
Brest, Fra. 125
Bretteville-sur-Laize, Fra. 125
Briare, Fra. 137
Bridestowe, Bri. 67
Bridlington, Bri. 47
Brighton, Bri. 47
Briñas, Spa. 355
Brindisi, Ita. 246-7
Brissago, Swi. 378
Bristol, Bri. 47
Brive-la-Galliarde, Fra. 125
Brives-sur-Charente, Fra. 132
Broadway, Bri. 78
Broby, Den. 107
Brockenhurst, Bri. 76
Broechem, Bel. 35
Bronkhorst, Net. 297
Brora, Bri. 87
Brough, Bri. 69
Brouillet, Fra. 157
Bruges, Bel. 35
Brussels, Bel. 36
Bucaco, Port. 302
Bückeburg, Ger. 201
Bude, Bri. 47-8
Buitrago del Lozoya, Spa. 323
Bülow, Ger. 213
Buochs, Swi. 382
Buonconvento, Ita. 275
Burbach, Ger. 212
Burford, Bri. 51
Burgdorf, Swi. 379
Burghausen, Ger. 180
Burgos, Spa. 323
Burgwedel, Ger. 193
Bury St Edmunds, Bri. 48
Busquístar, Spa. 324
Buxtehude, Ger. 212
Buxton, Bri. 49
Buzancais, Fra. 129

C

Cabezón de la Sal, Spa. 324
Cáceres, Spa. 324
Cádiar, Spa. 324
Caen, Fra. 125-6
Caernarfon, Bri. 95
Cagli, Ita. 283
Cágliari, Ita. 247
Cahors, Fra. 126-7
Caixas, Fra. 157
Caldas de Moledo, Port. 309
Caldbeck, Bri. 62
Caldonazzo, Ita. 281

H

M

T

The Automobile Association wishes to thank the following photographers for their help in the preparation of this book.

All photographs listed below are held in the Association's own library (AA PHOTOLIBRARY) and were taken by the following photographers.

ADRIAN BAKER 9, 18, 168, 177, 199, 215, 221; JAMIE BLANDFORD 222; MICHELLE CHAPLOW 325, 332, 345; STEVE DAY 8; J EDMANSON 361; PHILLIP ENTICKNAP 341; J W JORGENSEN 24, 100, 101, ALEX KOUPRIANOFF 30, 385; 102; PAUL KENWARD 110; S & O MATHEWS 40; KIM NAYLOR 366, 369, 373; KEN PATERSON 288, 292; CLIVE SAWYER 10, 232, 251, 263, 287; JAMES TIMS 310, 351; D TRAVERSO 185, 192, 209.